D1431094

Fin-de-Siècle Pressburg

Fin-de-Siècle Pressburg

Conflict & Cultural Coexistence in

Bratislava 1897–1914

Eleonóra Babejová

East European Monographs, Boulder
Distributed by Columbia University Press, New York
2003

EAST EUROPEAN MONOGRAPHS NO. DCXVII

© 2003 by Eleonora Babejova
ISBN 0-88033-515-7
Library of Congress Control Number 2002115752

Printed in the United States of America

CONTENTS

v

Contents

Contents

Contents

Contents

Contents

Contents

TABLES IN THE TEXT

TABLES IN THE APPENDIX

258

FIGURES

Figures

ABBREVIATIONS

ARCHIVES

AMB	Archív Mesta Bratislavy (Archive of the City Bratislava)
SNA	Slovenský Národný Archív (Slovak National Archive)
UMV	Uhorské Ministerstvo Vnútra (Hungarian Ministry of Interior)
i.n.	inventory number
c.	carton
MOL	Magyar Országos Levéltár (Hungarian National Archive)
K 149-1-637	file—section number—number of the document
MTA	Magyar Tudományi Akadémia (Hungarian Academy of Sciences)

POLITICAL ORGANISATIONS

SDPH	Social Democratic Party of Hungary
SEC	Slovak Executive Committee

NEWSPAPERS

CL	*Cirkevné Listy*
KN	*Katolícke Noviny*
ĽN	*Ľudové Noviny*
NN	*Národnie Noviny*
NH	*Nyugatmagyarországi Hiradó*
PL	*Pozsonyvidéki Lapok*
PT	*Pressburger Tagblatt*
PZ	*Pressburger Zeitung*
Mb	*Morgenblatt (PZ)*
Ab	*Abendblatt (PZ)*
RN	*Robotnícke Noviny*
SL	*Slovenské Listy*
ST	*Slovenský Týždenník*
WG	*Westungarischer Grenzbote*
WV	*Westungarische Volksstimme*
WVZ	*Westungarische Volkszeitung*

YEARBOOKS

MSK	*Magyar Statisztikai Közlemények*
PW	*Pressburger Wegweiser*

ACKNOWLEDGMENTS

There are many people to whom I am indebted for their help in researching and writing this book. Firstly, I would like to thank my dear friend and partner Sukumar Periwal for being always available to share ideas about my research, and for his patience, encouragement, support, advice and help in editing my writing. I owe much gratitude to Dr Graham Smith who supervised the doctoral dissertation at the University of Cambridge which forms the basis of this book. He guided me through the first three years of my research and provided valuable suggestions on the structure and focus of my study. After Dr Smith's untimely death, Dr Gerry Kearns kindly agreed to take over my supervision. I am very grateful for all his support, valuable comments and help in the last crucial stages of my work. I would also like to acknowledge the late Professor Ernest Gellner and Professor Jiří Musil for their support at the beginning of this project.

I am grateful to Dr Elena Mannová whose help was crucial in introducing me to archival work and helping to find my way around the sources that were available; for her advice and detailed comments on drafts of parts of this study and for the kindness and generosity with which she always received me. I would like to thank Professor Roman Holec for his thoughtful suggestions and advice on sources and to Dr Ján Buček for his help in orienting me in Slovak literature concerning geographical aspects. I would also like to thank Dr Vojtech Dangl, Dr Vladimír Lehotský, Dr Július Mésároš, Dr Peter Skalník, and Dr Peter Salner for their valuable advice and help in specific areas of the history and ethnography of Bratislava and Habsburg Monarchy. In addition, I would also like to thank my fellow researcher in the Bratislava archives, Christoph Reckhaus, for sharing research ideas on our sometimes overlapping topics. Working in an archive day by day can sometimes be tiring and lonesome and Christoph's enthusiasm and sense of humour helped me to retain a sense of balance. I would like to acknowledge the insights I gained through meeting Frau Katarina Löfflerova, who was born in the period discussed in this book. Further, I would like to express my gratitude to Dr László Szarka for his advice, help and suggestion of interesting archival sources for my research.. Dr Gábor Gyányi shared with me his knowledge on the period and provided me with invaluable insights on the period and comments on pieces of research. I would also like to thank Dr Dorottya Lipták, Dr Éva Ring and Dr András Vári for their help and comments. Professor Jonathan Steinberg offered needed advice, encouragement and detailed comments on pieces of this study. I would like to thank also Professor Rogers Brubaker, Professor John A. Hall and Dr Jenny Robinson for their valuable comments and advice on my work. I am grateful to Owen Tucker for drawing for me the maps in figures 3 and 17 and Niall Johnson for helping me with figures 6-12.

I would like to express my gratitude to the institutions which funded my research: the Central European University, Budapest and the Cambridge Overseas Trust. I would also like to thank the staff of the following archives and libraries: Archive of the City Bratislava, the Regional library, the City Museum of Bratislava, the Slovak National Archive and the University Library in Bratislava; the Library of the Statistical Office in Prague; the Hungarian National Archive, Széchényi Könyvtár and the Library of the Historical Institute of the Hungarian Academy of Sciences, all in Budapest; and the Bibliotheca Hungarica in Šamorín. Their assistance was invaluable during my search for sources.

Finally I would like to express my deepest gratitude to my mother and father and my brother Martin, for their support and encouragement. Martin's help with tables, figures, formatting as well as with any computer problems was absolutely invaluable and saved me much time. I also want to thank all my friends and colleagues who shared this time and their ideas with me.

∽ INTRODUCTION ∾

"B RATISLAVA" DID NOT EXIST UNTIL 1919. A city did exist which was called "Pressburg" in German, "Pozsony" in Hungarian and "Prešporok" in Slovak. Many of the people who lived in this city felt a strong civic identity that resisted the attempts of different nationalists to overwhelm it with their own particular identity. For the sake of convenience, historians and social scientists have generally categorised the residents of multicultural environments in neat ethnic boxes (such as German, Magyar or Slovak) and talk about ethnic groups as if identities were clear-cut and could be tidily defined and divided into differentiated groups. However, attaching such labels is an essentially retrospective exercise in deploying essentialising categories like "ethnic group" and "ethnic identity" and superimposing them onto groups of people that may not have felt much commonality in reality. It is the aim of this study to show how little sense this kind of categorisation makes in Central Europe with its rich history of the intermingling of peoples of different origins.

This book is a study of ethnic coexistence in the Central European city of Pressburg/Pozsony/Prešporok between 1867 and 1914. The study examines the changing relations between the German, Magyar and Slovak ethnic groups in the city against the background of modernisation, industrialisation and urbanisation. I argue that the boundaries between the city's ethnic groups were indistinct in this period and that ethnic affiliations and cultural identities fluctuated in response to the prevailing power relations.[1]

This central argument challenges the conventional division of people into neat groups, especially as done by national historiographies. By focusing on the continuous story of one particular group of people, such histories tend to glorify the inevitable development of their "nation" while neglecting or demonising other people. Furthermore, the economic and social interests of a particular elite may in retrospect be identified as the general interest of the cultural group whom this elite claims to represent.

These cultural traits are then used to legitimise the demands made by an elite. This study aims to point out and avoid these pitfalls of conventional national histories.

This introduction will first briefly outline the structure of this study, summarising the principal arguments of the chapters. I will then review previous descriptions of the city in the period in order to provide historiographical context for this study. The third part situates this work within the relevant theoretical literature on geographies of space, nationalism, and identity. The last part of this introduction considers some methodological issues.

1. OUTLINE

When compared to other Habsburg cities of the period where growing ethnic tensions and the emergence of mass movements led to sharp conflicts, in Bratislava these conflicts were negotiated in more peaceful ways. The fluid cultural identities, multiple loyalties and a specific local identity that were characteristic of Bratislava's population in this period made it possible for the city to more easily resolve or soften ethnic tensions and conflicts.

The first chapter of this study gives a picture of Bratislava around 1867. It describes the ethnic and social structure of the city. I look at the development of industry, crafts and commerce in the city and the modernisation of the city life, examine the languages used in cultural, associational and municipal life of the city, and explain the functioning of municipal politics in the city. This chapter provides the necessary background in order to understand developments in Bratislava described in the next chapters.

The second chapter focuses on the politics of identity in Bratislava, concentrating on changes in the modes of self-identification among the city's inhabitants. This chapter is concerned with the politics of nationalisation of the Hungarian state and its effects in Bratislava. I describe how different ethnic groups reacted to this pressure. Although in 1867 the city appeared predominantly "German," this merely meant that the language used in city politics and culture was predominantly German; it did not, however, express the identification with any one "ethnic group." It was more the sense of belonging to a certain status group which drew borders and decided who was "in" and "out." The existing status quo was challenged after 1867 and the dominant elites had to deal with this challenge. The new Magyar national elite entered into competition for positions in the city life and used nationalism and Hungarian patriotism in their struggle with the traditional elite.

I show the effects of Magyarisation in municipal politics, in social and cultural life as well as in the city's many vibrant associations. The growing pressure to identify with one ethnic group was in contrast to "Pressburger" identity characterised by local patriotism and indistinct "ethnic belonging." Although Bratislava appeared Hungarian towards the end of the period, it was still a multicultural city with multiple loyalties rather than a national Hungarian town.

The third chapter looks at the development of the workers' mass movement as a consequence of growing industrialisation and urbanisation of the city. This mass movement constituted another challenge to the traditional city elite but also to the new Magyar elite. I will consider the workers' activities in Bratislava in the context of the workers' movement in Hungary more generally, paying special attention to questions of ethnicity in the Hungarian workers' movement but especially in Bratislava. In Bratislava, the workers' movement was largely multicultural and it seems that the tension prevalent in the relationships between the Hungarian and non-Magyar social democrats in Hungary did not arise in Bratislava. The refusal of the Hungarian leadership of the social democratic movement to deal with the requests of other nationalities as well as the growing strength of the nationalities' movements in Hungary led to separatism on the part of non-Magyar social democrats, and finally to the splitting up of the "imagined community of class" into "imagined communities of language."

In the fourth chapter I consider politics of identity resulting from the geographic position of Bratislava in the national and imperial landscapes. This chapter explores the place of Bratislava in mythologies of Magyar and Slovak nationalists and its different representations by the nationalists as well as the traditional city elites. I examine the rhetoric of Magyar nationalists when referring to the frontier position of the city but also the ways in which the traditional city elites used the same rhetoric in order to win state support for a university in Bratislava. I also look at two monuments connected with the millennial celebrations of the Hungarian state, one outside the city and another within. While the monument outside Bratislava reconfirmed the borders of the Hungarian state and the Hungarian national identity, the monument inside the city only confirmed the ambiguous position of Bratislava between Budapest and Vienna, and the mixed loyalties of its inhabitants. The national loyalty of the city was also questioned in the parliamentary debate on the construction of an electric railway from Bratislava to Vienna which revealed the anxiety of the Hungarian elites to the prospect of losing Bratislava to the inimical Viennese influence.

The fifth chapter analyses the reactions of the Hungarian state to the workers' and nationalities' movements in Hungary and Bratislava. It is a characteristic of the modern state to collect information about its territory and inhabitants. The state reacted to the emerging workers and nationalities' mass movements with increased surveillance and an effort to control and contain these movements. The flow of information between the central ministries, county authorities and the city authorities was part of competing grids of power and knowledge. Another aspect of surveillance was also the growing "normalising" pressure and the self-disciplining of individuals according to certain socially accepted norms. I examine this self-disciplining aspect as it influenced all social strata in the city.

The next part of this introduction attempts to show why this study is necessary by reviewing the existing literature on Bratislava in this period.

2. HISTORIOGRAPHICAL CONTEXT

> To pass judgement on the practices of the old regime is the constitutive act of the new order.... The present is to be separated from what preceded it by an act of unequivocal demarcation. The trial by fiat of a successful regime is like the construction of the wall, unmistakable and permanent, between the new beginnings and the old tyranny.[2]
> —Paul Connerton

Studies on Bratislava from 1867 to 1914 have tended to focus on history as seen from the viewpoint of one or another ethnic group. There is no study bringing together different viewpoints in order to examine ethnic coexistence without ethnic bias. Perhaps the closest to such a attitude are works from the period, describing Bratislava in terms of its cultural, economic and social development.[3]

From the works written between the two world wars, Emil Portisch's history is the most complex and factually rich.[4] Portisch's work covers many topics in the long-run development of the city of Bratislava. Portisch chronologically lists events in the city but is inconsistent and selective in his choice of significant events and information. Many other works from this period on different aspects of Bratislava's history explicitly assume that the present is better than what came before.[5] The Slovak historian L'ubomír Lipták calls this characteristic a "syndrome of the year zero" and he considers it typical of Slovak historiography and Slovak society in general. After each major social change, the official version of history presents the break from the past as a new beginning. Thus, in the inter-war period, retrospective views of the pre-1918 period were very popular, in which the new elite concentrated on all the negative, conservative, and anti-democratic features of pre-war Hungary, failing to see any positive developments for Slovaks in that earlier period. Slovak historiography defined itself in opposition to the Hungarian "oppressors" of the previous period. A similar development is observable after 1948 when the bright socialist present was compared to the dark capitalist past.[6]

After 1948, a range of articles was written by both historians and ethnographers, dealing with different aspects of Bratislava's history between 1867 and 1914. These studies examined the ethnic composition of the city (albeit with the aim to prove that Slovaks were the autochthonous population in Bratislava),[7] the city administration (considered "bourgeois" and therefore having negative features),[8] the living conditions of workers and workers' housing,[9] and the workers' movement (from the Marxist-Leninist perspective, as described in the later section on methodology).[10] *Dejiny Bratislavy*, the main monograph on the history of Bratislava from this period, over-emphasises the workers' and socialist movement and the Slovakness of the city, presenting the other ethnic groups in the city merely as background.[11] Despite the proclaimed internationalism of the communist elites, Slovak communists were nationalists (as were communists from other socialist countries as well).[12] Much of the socialist historiography, therefore, built on the inter-war perspective on the pre-1918 period, merely adding a strong class perspective to the previously defined Slovak-Hungarian opposition. As Lipták recently pointed out, during the last two hundred years, the Slovak historiography has done most work on the process of "Slovak national emancipation."[13] Consequently, Slovaks were seen mainly as victims of historical circumstances or of oppressive elites, not as active agents who had choices and for whom active resistance was a possibility even in a situation of oppression. Slovak collective memory has been described as based on a "tradition of suffering."[14] Thus Slovak historians portray Slovak masses in the period largely as passive victims of Hungarian oppression and describe the rapid assimilation of Slovaks as a sign of their passivity. However, in the context of Bratislava, the "passivity" of Slovaks as expressed in their lack of interest in nationalist activities and by their rapid assimilation can also be interpreted as an act of choice. By assimilating, Slovaks were actively participating in the creation of that "mélange" of identities typical of Bratislava, a specific "Pressburger" identity.

Slovaks are also presented as victims in much of the historiography of the 1867–1914 period written after 1989. However, several contemporary historians and ethnographers dealing with Bratislava have managed to get beyond the "us" versus "them" mentality and to take more detached stances without a strong bias against the Hungarians. For example, the ethnographer Peter Salner has edited a text on inter-war Bratislava which is also very informative on the pre-1918–period.[15] Similarly, the work of the historian Elena Mannová stresses the multicultural character of the city. Mannová captures the atmosphere of the period and gives an idea of how co-existence and different identities were negotiated in everyday life.[16] Monika Glettler compares Slovaks in Bratislava and Budapest and writes about the ethnic co-existence in these cities. Glettler's analysis, however, relies largely on census information from the period whose reliability has been disputed. Furthermore, while avoiding the nationalist myths or victimisation of Slovaks present in Slovak historiography, Glettler does not have much to say on the every-day negotiation of multiculturality.[17]

The period 1867–1918 still belongs to an area of Slovak-Hungarian misunderstandings and prejudices.[18] Hungarian and Slovak historians primarily differ on the question of assimilation. Assimilation is understood in Hungarian historiography as one aspect of the modernisation processes of the nineteenth century.[19] Historians like Péter Hanák describe assimilation as part of the embourgeoisement process and take large-scale linguistic assimilation in Hungary (based on census data) as proven.[20] This claim is rejected by Slovak demographers and historians,[21] although it is gaining some hearing among some.[22] Slovak historiography associates assimilation with enforced Magyarisation, and considers assimilation in negative terms as the main factor preventing the Slovak nationalist movement from developing into a mass movement.

The Hungarian historian Ferenc Glatz has called for an end to national bias in different historiographies of the nineteenth and twentieth centuries caused by the existence of different national versions of a common history.[23] However, the very concept of a national history makes this a difficult task to accomplish. As Colin H. Williams stresses, in geography (and other social sciences), concepts of nationalism and nation formation are widely used and accepted as unproblematic: "… the traditional liberal emphasis on a common-culture, common-history, common-territory approach to nation formation, so prevalent in our textbooks, does not explain anything about a people or its development. It encourages a tendency to reify group development and promotes one version of history, which almost becomes an examination of the inevitable." There is then a tendency to construct images as "French national development" or "German cultural progress."

Such analytic framework predetermines the outcome, reifies these concepts and is especially difficult to apply in multicultural societies.[24] Rogers Brubaker has also usefully criticised the "substantialist approach" which treats nations as "enduring entities."[25] A good example is Slovak national history which views 1867–1918 as the period of the development of the Slovak national movement and the Slovak nation. Therefore, anything that hampered this process is seen as negative. Furthermore, the "Slovak nation" is taken for granted by Slovak historians as though the existence of this collectivity was a given in the nineteenth century.[26]

Since 1989, there has been much discussion among Slovak historians on the way in which history has been written, criticising previous practices of overemphasising national development and presenting the results of historic processes as inevitable.[27] The Habsburg Monarchy was characterised by ethnic and cultural-linguistic heterogeneity and this pluralism was part of the every-day reality, despite growing assimilation and Magyarisation policies of the state after 1867.[28] However, it is questionable whether it is at all possible within the "national history" paradigm to be able to objectively look at events. Present-day Slovak social scientists (rather than historians) appear more open to considering 'national development and myths' as socially constructed.[29] For example, Miroslav Kusý describes the "Slovak truth" as those myths and legends which were constructed by the Slovak "national intellectuals" and ironically notes that while this national intellectual could be of any political view, religious denomination, or interest group, "mostly his eyes get foggy and sound judgement leaves him as soon as he starts to concern himself with 'Slovak affairs' and especially with Slovak history."[30]

Although there has been an enormous amount of research done in Slovak historiography,[31] most of it is largely descriptive. This has also been the case with histories of Bratislava. With the exception of some recent work, Slovak historical writing has made little use of social theory.[32] More awareness of social theories could bring more sensitivity towards 'other' representations of the same historical period and lead beyond the narrow definitions and blinkers of "national" history. The next part reviews the basic theoretical concepts used in this study.

3. GEOGRAPHIES OF SPACE, NATIONALIM, AND POLITICS OF IDENTITY

This part is a literature review of the principal theoretical fields utilised in this study. I will briefly note relevant theoretical views on nationalism, space, and identity.

3.1. NATIONALISM

The emergence of an independent nation-state is closely connected with the consolidation of a set of nationalist myths and political ideologies. The most important of these is the central nationalist tenet requiring the territorial coincidence of cultural and political boundaries. The newly liberated nation is urged to see itself as an oppressed majority reclaiming an ancestral space which has been theirs from time immemorial, intimately linked with "memories" of past glory and the reversal of more recent oppression. Nationalists emphasise the continuity of a people in time and space. The static simplicity of such nationalist accounts draws sharp distinctions between "us" and "them," between our oppressed nation and those who oppressed us. Nationalist discourses often play down the extent to which identities and inhabitations change, that ethnicity and territory are shaped by complex configurations of culture and power that mutate in time and space. Furthermore, since nationalism emerges from the social, economic, and political transformations involved in the transition to modernity, ironically, nationalism itself emerges from the circumstantial complexities which it denies.

There are different explanations of nationalism and its emergence. The main line is usually drawn between modernist and primordialist explanations.[33] This theoretical divide, however, is to a large extent no more than a convenient fiction, since most significant academic work on nationalism focuses on the aspect of construction and invention.[34] However, it remains important to understand the processes which enable the transformation of pre-modern cultures into modern nations: in particular, the role of national myths, the emergence of a nationalist intelligentsia that 'imagines' a national community, the development of a national 'high' culture, and political opposition to a centralising state.

Continuity in space and time is a crucial component of nationalist ideology, even if demographic continuity was actually interrupted. This is where national mythology comes to the fore, in the reinvention of nations.

Reconstruction of the past or the creation of a "nationalist salvation drama" has some essential characteristics like "naturalism" (when the histories of nations are explained as extension of nature), a sense of growth and development, and a stress on the coherence of the past. Nationalist stories must be rich in events and heroes.[35] Mythologies locate their ethnic communities in homelands which are seen to be "poetic spaces." These mythologies recall golden ages which were 'unnaturally' interrupted. Essential motifs in national mythologies are a myth of origin in time and space; myths of ancestry, migration, and liberation; myths of a golden age, subsequent decline, and finally the myth of rebirth.[36]

Anthony Smith differentiates between the 'eastern' type of nation (so called ethno-nations) which developed into nations through the use of myths and the 'western' type of nation which developed through the evolution of the bureaucratic state. Western Europe "acquired nations almost by accident" whereas outside the West one has "nations created by design."[37] However, this distinction is not very useful, since as historians have shown, even the so-called 'western' nations invented their traditions since cultural homogenisation did not happen until quite late, until around the end of the nineteenth century.[38] Therefore this approach is misleading because it assumes that continuity of a state means automatically also continuity of the nation, whereas there were no homogenised nations within even the 'western' states. Charlotte Tacke also points out the inappropriateness of concepts like "cultural-nation" and "state-nation" as analytical historical categories. She shows that in the nineteenth century both Germany and France used national myths and symbols appealing to the "feelings of community." The opposition between the German cultural-nation and the French state-nation, therefore, merely perpetuates "othering" and national self-perception as it arose in the nineteenth century.[39]

All analysts of classical nationalism agree on the crucial role of the national intelligentsia in the success of national movements. Codifying language and oral tradition, the intelligentsia rewrites history, creating an image of the past in order to influence the future. The work of the intelligentsia is the transformation of folk-culture into 'high' culture. By turning its interest towards masses, through their continuous effort to build up the national consciousness of masses, the intelligentsia sought to mobilise the masses for fight for political power. The intelligentsia was the main social agent of the national movements.[40]

According to Miroslav Hroch, national movements have three phases: phase A in which a small group of intellectuals carries out scholarly research into the history, language, and culture of its ethnic group; phase B in which this scholarly research is used by nationalist activists to gain wider popular support in favour of the national idea; and phase C in which a significant part of the population is responsive to the claims of the nationalist agitation and the national movement turns into a mass movement. In this third phase the nation achieves its full social structure which is necessary for making political demands. Hroch also points out that linguistic demands became centrally important in most national movements which did not have a full social structure in phase B. Hroch divides such linguistic programs into five stages: first, celebration and defence of the language; second, language planning and codification; third, the intellectualisation of the language; fourth, introduction of the language into the schools; and fifth, the achievement of full equality of the minority and state-language.[41]

These linguistic considerations are crucial elements of Benedict Anderson's conception of the nation as an imagined political community.[42] For Anderson, the emergence of print technology makes possible a new sort of community whose members have an altogether different kind of connection with one another than the physical face-to-face contact that takes place in traditional communities. Thus the growth of national awareness depends on the ability of the national leaders to involve increasing numbers of their own ethnic group members in the imagined community of the nation. The most important condition for such an imagined community, then, is the very existence of a common print language, a standardised language shared by a particular ethnic group. As Gellner has pointed out, in an industrial society a homogenous high culture must pervade the whole population. And it is during the transition from the agrarian to industrial society, in the move from an elite high culture to a universal homogeneous high culture, that nationalism occurs. When literacy becomes a "*real entrance-card to full citizenship and human dignity*" but entrance is granted only to those whose mother tongue is identical with that of the state language, then language becomes a central issue.[43]

With romanticism emerges the image of "*the nation as a personalised body*" and the ethnic group becomes an 'us.' This body has one ('our') language and by not using this language the nation as a body is threatened by death. Therefore any attack on the language is seen to represent a murderous attack on the body of the nation and on its very existence. National leaders associate loss of their language to the loss of a loved one. This "sense of being in danger not only characterised national movements during Phase B, but formed one of their key stereotypes, sometimes right up to the present day."[44]

The oppositional and reactive character of nationalism is stressed by John Breuilly, who focuses on the consolidation of the state as the key moment when nations could emerge. For Breuilly, nationalism is best regarded "as a form of politics."[45] A national movement is not merely a fabrication of intellectuals; rather, it reflects the political and social conditions in which it exists. According to Breuilly, the initial nationalism comes from the culturally dominant groups and is expressed in territorial categories while the reaction to this nationalism comes from culturally subordinate groups which express their nationalism in cultural and linguistic terms.[46]

This description accurately describes the relation between Hungarians and Slovaks during the period under consideration. The Hungarian national movement succeeded in reaching an agreement with the imperial government in 1867 and achieved its goal of establishing an autonomous state within the Habsburg Monarchy. The Hungarian government then began the difficult task of creating a high culture and single political nation in what was yet a multinational state. The Hungarian state became a nationalising state i.e. a state "conceived by its elites as a specifically *unfinished* state" as opposed to a "completed" nation-state, as a state "conceived as the state *of* and *for* the core nation."[47] "Magyarisation" produced strong reactions from ethnic minorities that already had by this stage their own codified languages. Ethnic elites in particular reacted sharply to such perceived threats to their status which they regarded as obstacles to advancement. These elites mobilised their ethnic communities to oppose the imposition of an alien language. As Hroch acutely observes, social antagonism was transformed into national antagonism.[48]

This section has briefly reviewed some general theories of nationalism in order to identify the concepts that are most relevant to my research: national myths; the role of the nationalist intelligentsia, the emergence of a national high culture, and political opposition to a centralising state. There is also a growing body of specifically geographical work on nationalism that has informed this study. The next section will briefly look at the connection of nationalism and geography.

3.2. Geography and Nationalism

This section briefly considers in turn the relations between concepts of territoriality and nationalism, memory and the construction of identity, and urban space and the politics of identity.

3.2.1. Territoriality

The rise of nationalism is connected with the rise of the territorial state.[49] Several geographers have explored the role of territoriality in the emergence of nationalism.[50] They stress the importance of territory as a space to which nationalists bind the identity of the group on behalf of which they claim to be speaking. In order to draw mass support, nationalists use distinct geography, history and symbolism to characterise the people whom they claim to represent: "nationalism is a form of social and political movement firmly rooted in territory, in place and space. Nationalist movements do not just operate territorially, they interpret and appropriate space, place and time, upon which they construct alternative geographies and histories."[51] The nation's history is embodied in its territory, in its claimed "homeland." This territory binds it to its ancestors. Territoriality then "involves control over territory—rights to it, access to it, exclusion from it." Territoriality creates "natural borders" and makes them appear "real."[52] If there are different groups of people inhabiting the same territory, there ensues a struggle between different "imaginations of national territory"[53] and between different representations of the past. National narratives need to be set "in allegories of place."[54]

Anthony D. Smith and Colin H. Williams usefully analyse different relationships between the nation and the space it inhabits in their discussion of the "national construction of social space."[55] They depart from the idea that all nationalisms involve struggle for control of land and that a nation is "a mode of constructing and interpreting social space."[56] Nationalism is then "the dominant mode of politicising space by treating it as a distinctive and historic territory." Smith and Williams characterise eight dimensions of national space which are present in "both nationalist ideologies and popular sentiment about the relations between society and its environment": habitat (the notion of the "soil"), folk culture, scale, location, boundary, autarchy, homeland and nation-building.[57] Nationalists "territorialise" the interests of a group and appropriate the moral right to speak in the name of all of this group.[58] Nationalists also invoke a geopolitical dimension in their descriptions of "national" interest, as can be seen in Buček's study of Bratislava analysing the relationships between the city, state and territory.[59]

3.2.2. Nation, Memory, Identity

Territory is the repository of "national memory" and is closely bound to national identity. It is this (frequently falsified) memory which is the main building stone of national identity. This memory is often "framed in terms of resistance and othering."[60] Memory and national identity are constructed and re-constructed, as they are not fixed and discrete entities. When memory enters history, history becomes "the domain of ... disputed memory."[61] National memory is very selective and nations often choose to remember tragedies rather than joy. "Where national memories are concerned, griefs are of more value than triumphs, for they impose duties, and require a common effort."[62]

John R. Gillis differentiates between elite and popular memory as they have evolved historically. While elites were concerned with systematic accounts of past events starting from a point in a linear fashion, popular time was more "episodic," the present including both the past and the future. However, political and economic changes in the late eighteenth century brought about the disappearance of the sense of a living memory and people had to rely on commemoration of the past. "The demand for commemoration was then taken up by the urban middle and working classes, gradually expanding until, today, everyone is obsessed with recording, preserving and remembering." Through commemoration one could trace "the relationship between memory and identity."[63]

In recent years, there has been a growing geographical literature on the construction and representation of identity.[64] In cultural geography there have been studies on the construction of images of landscape.[65] In political geography there are three main approaches to the politics of identity: first, focusing on the boundaries defining identities, second, political-economic approaches stressing "spatial exclusion/inclusion," and, third, post-modern approaches "associating identities with places."[66] However, the concept of 'identity' itself has come under criticism. Richard Handler, for example, draws attention to the problematic nature of the concept of identity, noting that the global diffusion of the discourse of protecting distinct national identities shows how hegemonic ideas about ethnicity have become. Handler believes that the concept of "identity" is unhelpful in scholarly research since its use just seems to confirm the permanent character and fixed nature of given identities whereas it is just a cultural construct. Handler argues that there is no definite way for a social group to define itself at any moment since "'who we are' is a communicative process that includes many voices and varying degrees of understanding and, importantly, misunderstanding."[67] Identity, then, can be seen as an "incomplete process" rather than a fixed state at any point.[68] Soja and Hooper also write about "modernist identity politics" which criticises the "binary ordering of differences" that are constructed by the hegemonic power in order to maintain advantageous positions of dominance through "social and spatial division."[69] It is very important to realise the constructed nature of identity in order to challenge the nationalistic discourses which treat national identity as something unchangeable and forever present.

Brian Graham points out that nationalisms "represent a particular conceptualisation of power, which embodies issues of legitimisation and validation." Identity politics is then tied to the perception of this power by the population as legitimate or illegitimate, "as authority or coercion."[70] Identity politics and its expression in urban space are discussed in the next section.

3.2.3. City, space and the politics of identity

Superficially, cities appear to be "melting pots," locations where traditional markers of ethnic origin are superseded by an enforced assimilation into an economic and social space whose main characteristics is mobility. However, closer examination of the city reveals new divides, often on the basis of class. Social and spatial relations in the city reflect "the interconnections between command of money, space and time as intersecting sources of social power."[71] Various spatial and political discourses underlie the organisation of the city. "The physical form and shape of a city, its official plan and ceremonial places are articulated by political and social configurations that a nation or municipality wants to instil in its public."[72] It is those in power who influence a city's shaping. One discourse involves dividing city space into the 'good city' and the 'bad city.' The effort of the power elites then aims at generating a 'good city', a city that is controllable, has no visual gaps escaping control and thus is rid of vice.[73] The widening control over the city spaces (as well as the space of the state) draws on new technologies of power and surveillance. Julian Thomas talks about "Foucault's panopticon" for which the dissociation of "the see/being seen dyad" is typical. "The hospital, the school, the factory and the social security system are all varieties of panopticon, in which power of the gaze is revealed as more pervasive than domination and repression."[74]

These spatial and political discourses are part of identity politics in the city. There is an uneasy and often contradictory relation between civic culture and nationalism as a popular discourse emanating from mass urbanisation. Mass movements such as the growing workers' movement and the nationalist movement were two competing new popular discourses in Bratislava which challenged previous notions of citizenship and also the traditional usage of space in the city.[75] Those hitherto powerless when joined in mass movements often challenge the dominant use of city spaces.[76]

There have been a number of interesting studies on the transformation of the city landscape through architecture and monuments, and on the city as a spectacle.[77] These studies showed the connection between power elites and the imprint of their values on the landscape[78] and the marking of this landscape by monuments which often became sites of contested representation.[79] In her study of public monuments, Nuala Johnson highlights the importance of these monuments "as a source for understanding the emergence and articulation of a nationalist political discourse."[80] Both the location and iconography of the monuments are suggestive of identity politics, of the construction of differences between different identities, of the messages that the monument is meant to convey (although these messages might be often contradictory and competing).[81] Monuments express the relationship between the ways the past is remembered, public memory and collective identities.

This section has reviewed some of the theoretical concepts used in my analysis in order to show the validity and need of geographical concepts in explaining nationalism, identity construction and the social construction of urban space. The last part of this introduction will look at the methodology and discuss some methodological issues arising in my research.

4. METHODOLOGY

This study draws very largely on extensive archival research. However, archival work is hindered by the destruction and dispersal of considerable amount of primary material since 1918. I concentrated first of all on the sources in the Archive of Bratislava city. This archive has the largest collection of materials on Bratislava between 1869 and 1918, although much of the relevant materials were destroyed during the first Czechoslovak Republic. For example, the records of the meetings of the City Magistracy are missing for most of the period. Also from the materials which were termed collectively "Confidential agenda of the mayor" I received very few for study and had to establish that there is no existing complete file of this name, although listed in the archival guide. I heavily used the materials on city associations, meetings of the municipal assembly and of the municipal theatre committee as well as some private materials of prominent people like Johann Batka. I also read literature published in the period and the daily press. My research was sometimes slowed down by the archival policy of giving out only a certain number of documents and newspapers per day since these were stored in a separate storage place and had to be transported from there, or were stored in the archive but in places with difficult access. Another invaluable source was the Regional library (*Regionálna knižnica*) which has an enormous collection of literature published before 1918 (and also later).

For the materials connected with the developing mass movements (the workers' and nationalities' movements as well as on surveillance of these movements) I used materials in the Slovak National Archive in Bratislava and the Hungarian National Archive in Budapest. Generally in these materials I did not find so much material on the city of Bratislava, but considerably more on Bratislava county. In both cases I also had to adjust my time-table because of the restricted amounts of material handed out each day as a consequence of the archival policy. When working with the workers' movement material in the Slovak National Archive, in many cases I was not able to check originals since only Slovak translations of the original documents were available. For the purposes of the work on surveillance it would have been useful to have used sources in the State Regional Archive in Bratislava (*Štátny oblastný archív*), especially the agenda of both the head of the Bratislava county government as well as his deputy. However, time constraints prevented the use of these materials. A large amount of literature from the period as well as periodical press not found in Bratislava is also available in the Hungarian National Library (*Széchényi könyvtár*).

In addition to primary archival materials, I have also read much of the secondary literature on the period, mostly Slovak and Hungarian. From a methodological point of view, Chapter three was most difficult due to the nature of the sources available on the workers' movement. All the Slovak histories of the workers' movement are heavily influenced by Marxist-Leninist ideology, and the historical events and actions of workers get measured against what Marx or Lenin said. According to such views, the Hungarian or Bratislava social democrats were not real socialists because they refused to embark on a full-scale revolutionary struggle. This bias made it difficult to differentiate between facts and values of historians and the prevailing ideology. This is reflected in problems with language: because of the misuse or overuse of some terms in socialist history, some terms (such as bourgeoisie, proletariat, imperialism, capitalism, class and class struggle) became tantamount to insults and are largely avoided by historians at present.[82] For example, instead of 'class' Slovak historians tend to use 'social stratum.' Socialist historical writing also tended to present the working class as a homogeneous body. Because this writing is hardly informed by social theory, it tends to be very descriptive and lacks the richness and diversity of working class histories as they have been produced in the West.[83] Since working' class history was an obsession of the communist regime, after 1989 historians have tended to concentrate on other, hitherto neglected areas.

Another problem of language is posed by the multi-lingualism of the period, especially with regard to place names. While Hungarian historians use the geographical names employed during the period when writing about the history of Hungary between 1867–1918, Slovak historians use present-day geographical names and refer to what was then "Upper Hungary" (the term used in Hungarian historiography) as "Slovakia" or "Slovak territory."[84] For cities like Vienna, I have retained their standard English names; for other locations I have chosen to use the Hungarian place names. Readers can also find Slovak translations in the appendix. Similarly, I faced problems when translating "Magyar" from Hungarian original documents or often when deciding whether to use the form "Magyar" or "Hungarian" in the text. In German, Slovak as well as English, there is a difference between "Hungarian" which refers to citizenship and "Magyar" which refers to ethnicity. However, in the Hungarian language there is no such distinction. There is only the word "Magyar" which is used both in the ethnic and citizenship senses. Obviously the different understandings between the Magyar and non-Magyar nationalities of what constituted Hungarian state and culture were based already in this linguistic difference. I will describe the basis for the distinction between "Magyar" and "Hungarian" in the relevant parts in the text.

The city that is called Bratislava today had three names that were used throughout the period 1867–1914: Pressburg (German), Pozsony (Hungarian) and Prešporok (Slovak). In this study, my first desire was to use all three names or their combination according to appropriate context. However, since this appeared as rather cumbersome and awkward, I decided to use "Pressburg" as the most commonly used form. I have retained the use of the Hungarian and Slovak names only in quotations. My reason for avoiding the use of "Bratislava" is that when reading Slovak histories of the city, it appears as if the city had always been Slovak in character from their use of Slovakised geographic but also personal names. Such use of names obscures the fact that the name itself is not neutral but carries a meaning as to the national character of the city.[85] Since the present work is about identity politics in Bratislava, sensitivity in this respect seems particularly important.

I would like the reader to keep in mind then that when referring to certain people or groups of people in the study as "German," "Magyar" or "Slovak," this does not mean that these people would define their identity as German, Magyar or Slovak, or that they would define themselves as a part of a cohesive ethnic collective with a consciousness of shared identity, even though the Hungarian authorities in the period might have used the term 'nationality' to categorise them in this manner. Dividing people into neat ethnic groups might well confirm the nationalist argument of the existence of groups of people called nations since the time immorial. Especially in multicultural societies where people use multiple languages, such terminology is difficult and problematic. The relationship between the mother tongue, the language(s) of daily use, and an individual's ethnic identity is not linear. Even being born into an ethnic group does not determine an individual's identity. As Cohen argues, „birth and upbringing do not irrevocably determine an individual's ethnic identity. Individuals may choose to adopt or abandon the distinguishing cultural traits and embrace or renounce the social relationships which unite the group."[86] This understanding of an individual's identity stresses the element of choice rather than a deterministic understanding of one's identity based on biological origin.

Out of the three prevailing 'ethnic groups' in the city, I find it most problematic to use the category 'Slovak' or 'Slovaks.' If one defines an ethnic group as a group of people having a consciousness of shared identity (on the basis of a shared cultural trait) and history,[87] then 'Slovaks' can hardly be grouped together into an ethnic group and certainly not a nation, and the term 'Slovaks' is incorrect. The lack of residential segregation in Bratislava and Budapest as well (see Chapter one, part 2.3.) suggests that there was no generally shared ethnic consciousness among people of Slovak mother tongue.[88] There must have been more important traditional divisions which led Slovak immigrants to behave unlike immigrants of other ethnic groups: not to cluster together with those speaking the same or similar language (or dialect) but to mix with people of different ethnic backgrounds. These divisions could have been caused by both religious affiliation and a strong sense of belonging into a small community since many immigrants came from fairly isolated mountain communities. Immigrants spoke different dialects since the literary Slovak was a privilege of the educated minority.[89] This means that there were no 'Slovaks' in the sense of a clearly defined collective at all. They had to first be made into a nation.

The use of 'German' and 'Magyar' is problematic as well. People with German mother tongue did not always behave like they had a German identity. The use of 'Magyar' seems more appropriate because one could include here individuals who identified themselves with the idea of a homogeneous nation state based on supremacy of the Magyar culture and language. Despite all my reservations noted above, throughout this study I will use terms 'Germans, Magyars, Slovaks' since I am not able to substitute these terms with any satisfactory alternative. Descriptions such as 'persons of Slovak mother tongue' or 'persons of Slovak origin' are too cumbersome and more obscuring than explanatory. While different cultural identities do have to be distinguished, it would be preferable if social scientists were able to develop a different terminology in the discourse about nationalism and ethnicity. Throughout the text (and in footnotes), I will pinpoint places in which the use of established vocabulary about nationalism and ethnicity is especially problematic and explain my understanding and use of these categories.

This study has been unable to explore several important topics in detail because of constraints of space and also time. These include anti-Semitism and its strength in Bratislava.[90] I also could not pay enough attention to urbanisation and all its effects. Also due to the lack of space as well the character of the material examined, I could not examine surveillance as it worked in every-day lives of the people on a popular level. It is my hope to explore these issues in greater detail in future research.

PRESSBURG 1867–1914: OVERVIEW

0. INTRODUCTION

THIS CHAPTER SETS the scene with a sketch of the society and economy of Pressburg between 1867 and 1914. After a brief overview of economic development and modernisation in the city between 1867–1914, successive parts of this chapter will describe the social structure of the German, Hungarian and Slovak ethnic groups in Pressburg as reflected in ethnicity, occupational structure, spatial distribution, language use, and municipal politics.[1]

1. ECONOMIC DEVELOPMENT AND MODERNIZATION, 1867–1914

This section examines Pressburg's position within Hungary and then the ongoing economic developments and the modernisation of the city infrastructure.[2]

1.1. PRESSBURG IN HUNGARY

Pressburg became the capital of Hungary in 1536, after the invading Turks had occupied Buda and a large part of Hungarian territory. After 1848, when finally all important institutions (in 1783 the central administration, in 1848 the Hungarian parliament) had been moved to Buda, Pressburg became a provincial town with a stagnating population.[3] This was caused by the drop of the importance of the city and by a series of epidemics. City life became more dynamic again only after 1867, because of the administrative changes (the Dual Agreement between Austria and Hungary) and processes connected with the modernisation of the country started by the new Hungarian government.[4] Intense industrialisation in Pressburg started in the 1890s. It was during this period that Pressburg was described by contemporaries as the "city of industry and intelligentsia" as a well as a "city of pensioners, due to its pretty location, good air and water, ordered relations in the municipality and its proximity to Vienna."[5] However, Pressburg did not regain its previous position associated with that of a capital city of Hungary until the dissolution of the Habsburg Empire. That dominant role was taken by Budapest, which in 1873 became the capital of Hungary and its administrative, political, economic as well as cultural centre.[6] (For the geographic position of Pressburg within the Habsburg Empire see Figure 1.)

1.2. ECONOMIC DEVELOPMENT

Pressburg became one of the largest industrial centres of Hungary in the second half of the nineteenth century. In 1850, the Trade and Industrial Chamber was founded (*Die Pressburger Handels—und Gewerbekammer*) which administered apart from the city of Pressburg twelve counties in Western and Central Slovakia with a total of 1.5 million inhabitants.[7] However, extensive industrialisation was most marked during and after the 1890s. In 1900, 37.5% of the adult population was employed in industry. There were 51 factories in Pressburg employing 5,790 workers. Their production included brushes, enamel dishes, rubber products, oil-refinery products, explosives, bricks, electrical goods, optical articles, cables, textiles, confectionery and food products. The capital invested in these industries was mostly Austrian, German and Hungarian.[8]

In the second half of the nineteenth century, trade also gained an increasingly important role since many city middle classes channelled their efforts in this direction after the loss of capital city status in 1848. Pressburg became a centre for crafts production and trade. In 1869 there were 150 different kinds of craftsmen in the city, among the best known were tailors and potters. In addition to trade in hand-crafted items such as lace, Pressburg was also a centre for agricultural trade since Pressburg county was an agricultural area.[9] Wine production was of great importance and wines were exported abroad.[10] The development of trade and industry was supported by exhibitions taking place in Pressburg: agricultural exhibitions in 1862, 1877 and 1888, an international exhibition in 1865, the local industrial exhibitions in 1892 and 1899, and then the second Hungarian agricultural exhibition in 1902.[11]

Between 1867 and 1914, Pressburg also became a banking centre. Insufficient capital from the Budapest banks led to the presence of Austrian, German, French and English capital. Slovak capital entered relatively late when a branch of the Slovak bank opened in 1905 while Czech capital came later still with a branch of the Hungarian-Czech industrial bank in 1914.[12]

Growing industrialisation influenced urban development as well. New industrial areas, workers' housing, housing for the poor, apartment buildings, and hospitals were built. The appearance of the city itself was enhanced by new parks, statues and fountains, largely resulting from initiatives undertaken by the *Stadt-verschönerungsverein*.[13] The construction of a steel bridge across the Danube in 1890-1 made feasible the industrialisation of Ligetfalu lying on the right bank of the Danube. The bridge also made it possible for workers from Ligetfalu to commute to other factories. On the right bank of the Danube lay also the favourite relaxation spots of the city inhabitants like the Café named *Au-Café* (*Ligeti kávéház*), and the summer theatre *Arena* (Nyári színház), and it was also the location of the horse races and exhibitions (Figure 4).[14] Urban development was based on the regulation plan worked out in 1849-50 by the engineer Halácsi which was used until 1907. A new plan was created in 1909 by the professor Palóczy at the Budapest University and approved in 1917.[15]

1.3. Infrastructure and Modernisation

The development of industry in the city required construction of transportation and communication infrastructure. The steamship company connecting Vienna with Pressburg and Budapest began to operate in 1830. The horse-railway connecting Pressburg with Nagyszombat was put into use in 1843. In 1872 the steam-railway started operating.[16] The Vienna-Pressburg-Budapest railway line came into operation in 1848-50. Later, Pressburg also became connected by railway to Trencsén (1876), Zsolna (1883), Nagyszombat, Dunaszerdehely (and further to Sopron) and Břeclav in Moravia (Austria) (see Figure 2). A new railway station was built in 1871 by the famous Pressburger architect and construction engineer Ignácz Feigler the younger.[17] Another key transportation project, the construction of the electric train line to Vienna, will be discussed in greater detail in the fourth chapter of this study. In addition to transportation links, Pressburg also received communications connections during this period. The city was connected to the telegraphic network in 1847. In 1884 a telephone network with 50 participants started operating. The Hungarian inter-city telephone network started operation in 1893. By 1916 there were 1,615 telephone network participants in Pressburg.[18]

The beginnings of the modernisation of the city infrastructure are connected with the mayor Heinrich Justi (1867–1875) who was called the "greatest mayor of Pressburg in the nineteenth century."[19] Justi re-built the city administration. All the big works of city modernisation were done during Justi's tenure as a mayor: regulation of the Danube bank, the increase of the nearby Karlsburg (Oroszvár) dam, the creation of the *Tiefweg* (*Mély út*) (the road into the nearby Carpathian mountains), securing the city's right to levy a consumption tax, the creation of the building construction regulations, the purchase of the Ápponyi house (used for the city council), the beginning of the construction of the sewage system, cobblestone-paving of the city, creation of the pension statutes for the city employees, separation of the ownership of the Catholic church and school from the municipal one, and founding of the firemen's association (*Der freiwillige Feuerwehrverein*). Justi was also one of the founders of both the *Stadtverschönerungsverein* and of the City Museum (*Städtisches Museum*).[20]

The modernisation of the city's physical infrastructure proceeded steadily during this period. The gasworks were built in 1856 and in the same year the city had gas lighting of the streets (owned by the city from 1891 onwards). The city waterworks started functioning in 1885. The model of the sewage system was worked out by the Ministry of Interior in Budapest in the years 1897–1904 (the first basics had already been laid down by mayor Justi during his tenure as mayor.) The first tram (in all of Hungary) started operating in Pressburg in 1885. The city electrical works were founded in 1901 and permanent electrical lighting operated from the beginning of 1902.[21] In 1909 the first trolley-bus started operating.[22]

2. ETHNIC COMPOSITION OF THE CITY IN 1867

This part of the chapter describes the ethnic composition of Pressburg in 1867. I will first point out how the geographical location of Pressburg influenced the multi-ethnic character of the city and briefly describe the ethnic structure of the city as reflected in the census. I will then note the effects of migration on the city's ethnic structure. Finally I will consider different sources of possible bias in Hungarian censuses as connected to the processes of 'assimilation' and 'Magyarisation.'

2.1. GEOGRAPHICAL LOCATION AND ETHNIC COMPOSITION

The geographical position of Pressburg had a significant influence on the ethnic composition of the city. Pressburg was characterised by the coexistence of different ethnic groups, although the proportions of the ethnic groups changed through time. The multi-ethnic composition of the city at the turn of the century was the result of previous historical development and was determined by three factors: "the strategic position of the city on an important Central European cross-roads, the very close relationship to Vienna as the capital of the Austro-Hungarian Monarchy, and finally the ethnic structure of the closest surrounding villages."[23]

By the turn of the nineteenth century Pressburg was primarily inhabited by people of three nationalities: Germans, Magyars and Slovaks.[24] The geographer Jan Hromádka described Pressburg as the middle of a German-speaking peninsula which stretched to the east into the Slovak-Magyar language territory. The German belt passed Pressburg from the west where it was connected to a compact German territory in Austria. A small belt of German villages ran from there to the northwest through the southern side of the Small Carpathian mountains and to the western part of the Csallóköz (area below Pressburg between the left bank of the river Danube (*Duna*) and the Small Danube (*Kis-Duna*)). The Slovak belt reached Pressburg from the northwest through Lamacs and from the northeast through Szöllös and Ivánka. From the east Pressburg was reached by the territory inhabited by Magyars who occupied the left bank of the Danube river (Figure 5).[25] In Pressburg there were also present small numbers of Czechs, Poles, Rumanians, Ruthenians, Serbs and a somewhat larger number of Croats.

Germans had been the strongest and most numerous group in the city since the thirteenth century. According to the 1850 census, Pressburg had 42,267 inhabitants, among them 70% Germans, 13% Jews, 10% Slovaks and something above 6% Magyars.[26] The proportions of different ethnic groups in the city changed dramatically after the Dual Agreement of 1867. This change was connected with the effort of the Hungarian state authorities to build one political nation—Hungarian. However, in 1880 Pressburg still had 65.6% Germans, 15.5% Slovaks and 15.7% Magyars (out of a total of 48,006 inhabitants).[27]

In addition to Magyarisation, Pressburg's ethnic structure changed over the period 1867–1914 because of the transition of Hungary from an agrarian to an industrial society. This transition led to other significant changes such as social mobilisation and mass communication that "contributed first of all in cities to the sharpening of the social and national contradictions."[28]

The change of the ethnic and social structure of the Pressburg's population was also brought about by rapid demographic changes which accompanied industrialisation and urbanisation in the city and its immediate environs. The second chapter of this study discusses the changing proportions of the three ethnic groups until 1914 and their assimilation in more detail.

2.2. Importance of Migration

Migration significantly affected Pressburg's ethnic composition since the surrounding villages provided much of the working force for new factories, thus bringing into the city workers of different mother tongues. Research on villages surrounding Pressburg showed that while the villages' population grew steadily until 1890s, on average between 0.5 and 0.75% per annum, in the period 1890–1910 the average annual increase was 1.9%. This accelerated growth was due to the immigration of workers from more distant localities of south-western Slovakia.[29] Pressburg also attracted workers from the areas of the Carpathian mountains and from areas around the river Váh. Most of these migrants spoke two languages: Hungarian and German and German and Slovak.[30] Since living in Pressburg was expensive and also because of the lack of accommodation, many workers from surrounding villages commuted to Pressburg by bicycle and also by train (which would explain why censuses did not reflect increase of Slovaks, although according to historians they provided the bulk of the migrant workers.)[31]

Migration was the most important source of population increase in this period. On the eve of the First World War about one third of the Hungarian population was living away from its birth place.[32] Between 1850 and 1900 Pressburg grew by 19,500 people, while in the first eighteen years of the twentieth century it grew by 21,700 inhabitants.[33] Migration significantly influenced changes in the ethnic structure of the city. I will consider migration into the city and out-migration in more detail in Chapter three.

2.3. Hungarian Censuses

After the Dual Agreement of 1867, successive Hungarian governments saw census data as an important political instrument showing the growth of the Hungarian political nation and the progressing Magyarisation of the non-Magyar nationalities. Slovak historiography (and other non-Magyar nationalities previously in Hungary) consider Hungarian census data to be unreliable and biased. The general assumption is that the Hungarian authorities involved in data collection and processing intentionally falsified the data so as to show off greater numbers of the Magyar ethnic group at the cost of other ethnic groups. There were three possible sources of bias in the census data: the technique of census data collection; different definitions of mother tongue as a criteria for ethnicity; and, finally, the high degree of exogamy in Pressburg.[34]

For census data collection, Pressburg was divided into counting districts with their own agents. There were around fifty agents who collected the completed forms from the house owners. The agents had to fill in these forms only when someone had problems doing it himself.[35] Most probably the quality of data depended on the conscientiousness of each agent, a factor involved in any census.[36] Inhabitants who were interested in more detailed information about the census were encouraged to visit the municipal statistical office. The municipal authorities appealed to the population to be honest when filling in the forms "in the interest of science."[37]

In the censuses in the Hungarian part of the Monarchy the criteria for determining the nationality of people was mother tongue. However, the definition of the mother tongue was not the same in collecting the data for each census.[38] In the first Hungarian census in 1869 nationality and knowledge of foreign languages were not asked at all.[39] The instructions for the 1890 census said: "The mother tongue should be written in the sixth column ... If the child speaks a different language than that of its parents, this language should be inscribed on the child's form."[40] The instructions for the 1900 census (similarly in 1910) said: "As the mother tongue shall be considered that language which the person acknowledges as his/her own and which he/she speaks as the best and which he/she likes most to speak. It should be pointed out that, although in most cases the mother tongue which one learned in childhood, usually from the mother is identical with one's language, however, it can still happen that a child's mother tongue is different than that of its mother, especially if the child, in the kindergarten, in school or as a consequence of other influences, has made another language its own mother language."[41] According to Svetoň, this definition was intended to incorporate the numbers of people won over by assimilation since the language of instruction in schools was Hungarian. In this way statistics could show the growth of the number of Magyars which, however, was not in accordance with reality. Gyányi acknowledges some "conscious distortions of the censuses" especially of the 1910 census. However, he correctly points out that the problem lies in the difficulty of defining "ethnic identity on the exclusive basis of language."[42]

Another important factor which complicates the accurate determination of ethnicity in Pressburg is the existence of mixed marriages. "Demographers estimate that more than one-third of the marriages that took place from 1880–1914 were mixed, and this 'amalgamation of families' influenced the ethnic orientation of much of Pressburg's population as well."[43] One can imagine the difficulty of deciding the mother tongue in a mixed marriage. Personal preferences of the household members could be more complicated to express than in a household where all members were of one mother tongue. One also has to take into consideration the changeable nature of "nationality": "Nationality is not a fixed, given, indelible, objectively ascertainable property; and even subjective, self-identified nationality is variable across time and context of elicitation, and therefore not measurable as if it were an enduring fact that needed only to be registered."[44] Thus census data cannot serve as a sole source of information about ethnic composition and identity also because of the artificiality of the categories constructed for the sake of censuses. In reality, neat ethnic groups as envisioned by statististicians did not exist. On the contrary, one could claim that such groups were created also by the efforts of the authorities to group people together on the basis of their mother tongue.

Different definitions of the mother tongue which did not actually denominate the language of the mother, as well as the different pressures which could result in claiming a native language other than the mother tongue, could be sources of unreliability of the census data.[45] However, one could also argue that this data do reflect real (linguistic) assimilation and that large numbers of non-Magyars were actually being assimilated. For whatever reason the non-Magyars put down Magyar as their mother tongue, this fact showed their political preferences or the will to be assimilated to the ruling nation. Throughout this study, census data will be used for orientation, keeping in mind possible biases as discussed above. I will further discuss assimilation and Magyarisation in Chapter two.

3. OCCUPATIONAL STRUCTURE

In this part of the chapter I will first mention the changing occupational structure of the city between 1890 and 1910. I will then consider participation of three main ethnic groups as well as Jews in the main occupational categories, especially according to the 1910 census. This information provides a clue to the social position of different ethnic groups in the city. Finally I will consider the participation of different ethnic groups in the educational professions because of the great importance of mass literacy for the development of national movements.

3.1. Main Occupational Groups

The main occupational groups as defined by statistical surveys and censuses during the period were agriculture; forestry, fishing and bee-keeping; industry; commerce and credit; transport; mining and metallurgy; state employees and free professions; army; day labourers and servants.[46] If one compares the number of people employed in different categories in years 1890–1910, one can notice a significant growth of the numbers of employed in industry, transport and commerce and credit. This growth was stimulated by the extensive industrialisation and urbanisation of the city at the turn of the century, as described in the first section of this chapter. Most immigrants to the city found jobs in industry, transport and commerce and credit.[47]

3.2. Participation of Members of Different Mother Tongues in the Main Occupational Groups

For the period 1867–1914, there is general information describing typical occupations for different ethnic groups. Detailed statistical evidence, however, is available only for the year 1910. Quantifiable comparison with the earlier period is not possible. However, on the basis of the later developments one can estimate the movements in different occupational groups. Thus it is possible to state that the high proportion of Magyars in the state employee categories as well as free professions (especially in education) in 1910 was a consequence of the nationalising policies of the Hungarian state.[49] Around 1867 and also in 1880 the proportion of people with German mother tongue employed in these categories must have been much higher, especially in education, depending on the rapidity of the change of the language of instruction in the schools in Pressburg.

Germans were traditionally employed in wine growing and wine making, crafts and commerce.[50] In 1910, most Germans were still employed in these categories. However, a great number of Germans was employed in industry (54.46% of all Germans), more than Slovaks (47.6%). This was caused by the development of industry and the growth of the number of industrial workers. In 1900 Pressburg had 10,163 workers, and in 1910 16,194 workers.[51] Germans were to be found especially among the skilled workers who were higher in the social hierarchy (sometimes equivalent to the lower middle classes) and were better paid than the non-skilled workers. (I will consider workers in more detail in Chapter three.) In the social hierarchy, Germans could be found in all social classes in Pressburg. They formed the core of the traditional middle classes, the *burghers* in the city.[52]

	1890	1900	1910
All population:			
Employed	31,519	34,849	41,835
Dependants	24,529	31,018	36,388
Total	56,048	65,807	78,223
Agriculture:			
Employed	1,639	1,348	1,354
Dependants	2,256	1,974	1,577
Forrestry, Fishing, Beekeeping:			
Employed	33	33	37
Dependants	80	81	91
Industry:			
Employed	10,836	12,931	18,082
Dependants	8,801	11,740	16,063
Commerce and Credit:			
Employed	2,288	2,880	3,552
Dependants	2,632	3,836	4,405
Transport:			
Employed	941	1,686	2,255
Dependants	1,625	3,349	4,129
Mining and metallurgy:			
Employed		-	1
Dependants		3	2
State employment, Free professions:			
Employed		2,544	3,154
Dependants		3,336	4,056
Army:			
Employed		4,330	4,764
Dependants		817	876
Day Laborers:			
Employed		1,680	847
Dependants		1,151	535
Servants:			
Employed		4,237	4,400
Dependants		315	268
Other:			
Employed		3,171	3,389
Dependants		4,407	4,386

Table 1: Main occupational groups in 1890, 1900 and 1910.[48]

Magyars were at first employed in agriculture. However, their proportion in transportation and in state employment also grew continuously. By 1910, most Magyars in Pressburg were employed in transport (74.1% of transport employees were Magyars) and in state employment (67.1%), and their proportion in agriculture had dropped to 27.4%. Also the proportion of Magyars in commerce and credit was quite high. Magyars were also employed as servants in city households. Their number in this category was almost three times higher than the number of Germans and Slovaks.[53] Many Magyars also worked in industry (30.75% of all Magyars) and were part of the proletariat. When considering the position of Magyars within the social hierarchy, one can say that Magyars could be found in all social strata, from the uppermost to the lowest. Most significantly, a new Magyar middle class was developing, which competed with the German middle class for power in the city.

Traditionally, Slovaks worked in agriculture, on their own fields but were also strongly represented among the day-labourers, agricultural and later industrial workers. There were also Slovaks among the craftsmen. In 1910, most Slovaks were employed in industry (47.6% of all Slovaks). There were many Slovak men within the army units located in Pressburg. Further Slovaks worked as servants. These were the typical occupational categories for Slovaks. Thus in the social structure of the city they were predominantly among the lower classes.

Jewish people were counted as speakers of one or another of the above mentioned mother tongues. (Their shift from German to Magyar will be discussed in more detail in Chapter two.) Until 1850 Jews mostly earned their living in commerce and credit since they were not permitted to own estates and were excluded from the intellectual professions as well as state employment. With the onset of industrialisation in the second half of the nineteenth century, their experience with trade, contacts and capital paid off and many became important entrepreneurs.[54] As a consequence of the compulsory education law of 1884, Jews also started to appear in the fields of law, education, medicine and journalism.[55] Most of the Jews in Pressburg were employed in commerce and credit as independent merchants (52.6% in this category were Jewish in 1900, 49.3% in 1910) and assistants in trade (34.3% in 1900, 30.8% in 1910). There was a considerable increase between 1900 and 1910 of the proportion of Jews in the categories 'Big- and middle estate owner' (from 14.9% to 23.7%) and 'Estate owner of 50–100 KJoch' (from 10% in 1900 to 25% in 1910). In 1900, the group of independent artisans had Jewish membership of 12.5% and in 1910 12.8%.[56] In the intellectual professions the strongest Jewish representation was in the cultural and economic life as well as law while in the public administration system they were of almost no importance.[57]

Germans and Magyars were located in occupational categories across the city's social hierarchy. Germans formed the bulk of the traditional middle class but their position was challenged by the new emerging Magyar middle class. Slovaks were a larger component of the lower and middle-lower classes in the city. Jewish people were represented among all social strata, entering the entrepreneurial and professional classes after 1867.

3.3. PARTICIPATION OF DIFFERENT ETHNIC GROUPS IN EDUCATIONAL PROFESSIONS

Mass education in the national language is of crucial importance for national mobilisation.[58] In Hungary after 1867, Magyars began to take a leading role in the provision of education. There was a corresponding decrease in the participation by non-Magyars in employment positions in the field of education (see Table 10 in Appendix). Of all the people employed in education in Hungary in 1900, 93.2% spoke Hungarian and in 1910 95.3%.[59] Similar tendencies can be noted also in Pressburg. Tables 2 and 3 show the participation of different ethnic groups in educational professions and their proportion in church schools and private schools in Pressburg in 1910.

	Men	Women
Magyars	211	198
Germans	39	79
Slovaks	4	2
Romanians	—	—
Ruthenians	—	—
Croats	—	—
Serbs	—	—
Other	4	18
Total	258	297
Jews	44	17

Table 2: Number of people employed in the main occupational groups in education in Pressburg in 1910.[60]

Priests	47.8
Chaplains and curates	50.0
Nuns	36.1
Kindergarten female teachers	29.4
Elementary school male teachers	4.4
Elementary school female teachers	4.4
Bürgerschule male teachers	11.8
Bürgerschule female teachers	20.0
Secondary school professors	3.6
Private teachers and Korrepetitors	54.5
Governesses	50.5

Table 3: Proportion of non-Magyar ethnic groups in the church and private school professions in Pressburg in 1910.[61]

As is obvious from the tables above, people with Magyar mother tongue were over-represented in the educational professions in Pressburg as well. Non-Magyars were mostly found among priests and chaplains, and also among private teachers and women educators. In the categories of priests and chaplains the proportion of Germans increased from 29.6% to 33.3% between 1900 and 1910 while at the same time the proportion of Magyars decreased from 55.6% to 51.5%. There was a corresponding decrease in those with knowledge of the Hungarian language from 92.6% to 84.8%.[62]

In contrast, the proportion of Magyars among elementary school teachers grew from 62.1% in 1900 to 95.6% in 1910 while the proportion of non-Magyar nationalities fell drastically, the number of Germans falling from 35.6% in 1900 to 4.4% in 1910, and Slovaks declining from 0.8% in 1900 to zero in 1910.[63] This change can be connected with the passing of the Ápponyi law of 1907 which introduced Hungarian as the language of instruction in all schools, including even private schools. All teachers were obliged to know Hungarian.

Finally some information about the literacy level of the Pressburg inhabitants according to ethnic groups.

Ethnic group	Magyar		German		Slovak	
1910	31,705		32,790		11,673	
Can read and write						
– absolute number	25,965		26,660		8,390	
– 20–29 years old	7,409	(28.5%)	5,379	(20.2%)	3,294	(39.3%)
From 100 people who can read and write:						
– 1890	78.1		74.6		57.5	
– 1910	81.9		81.3		71.9	

Table 4: Literacy level of Pressburg's population by ethnic group.[64]

The table shows that the number of literate people increased in all ethnic groups, with the largest increase happening among Slovaks. The biggest proportion of people who could read and write was in the age group 20–29.[65] Glettler draws the conclusion that young literate Slovaks were attracted to the cities (since this age group was also present in Budapest in numbers exceeding the average for the country as a whole).[66]

This part of the chapter has presented a brief overview of the changing relation between ethnic affiliation and occupation in Pressburg at the turn of the century. The next part considers the spatial location of different ethnic groups in the city.

4. SPATIAL DISTRIBUTION OF THE ETHNIC GROUPS

In this part I will describe the spatial location of different ethnic groups in the city. First I will show the growth of the city districts in 1869–1910. Then I will consider the distribution of ethnic groups in the city according to the 1910 census.

4.1. ADMINISTRATIVE DISTRICTS OF PRESSBURG

At the turn of the century, Pressburg was divided into five city districts: I. Old Town (*Altstadt*), II. Ferdinand's Town (*Ferdinandstadt*), III. Franz Joseph's Town (*Franz Josefstadt*), IV. Theresa's Town (*Theresienstadt*), and V. New Town (*Neustadt*) (see Figure 6). Until 1910, the census data do not contain information about the distribution of the ethnic groups in the city.

However, on the basis of information in the main city newspaper, the *Pressburger Zeitung*, one can reconstruct changes in population in separate city districts. The rapidity of the growth of some city districts confirms the trends described in the first section of this essay: industrialisation and urbanisation, especially after 1890.[67]

Districts	1869	1880	1890	1900	1910
I. Old Town	8,965	8,307	8,773	9,206	8,446
II. Ferdinand's Town	10,075	*10,028	10,340	12,576	12,523
III. Franz Joseph's Town	6,509	* 8,150	8,571	9,361	12,256
IV. Theresa's Town	9,928	9,642	11,055	12,525	13,156
V. New Town	11,067	12,157	13,705	18,152	27,078
Total	46,544	48,284	52,444	61,820	73,459

Table 5: Population of Pressburg by administrative districts.[68]

Apart from the Old Town, all other city districts grew continually. However, the Old Town's population had actually declined in 1910 when compared to 1900 or even to 1869. This decrease was caused by the demolition of some buildings in this part of the town and also because the face of the Old Town was changing from its original character as a residential district. As the well-to-do inhabitants moved into villas in *Védczölöp út* (Palisades street) and on the castle hill, offices began to replace apartments.[69]

The city district which grew most between 1869 and 1910 was the New Town, increasing in population from 11,067 to 27,078 inhabitants (by 144%, 2% per annum). This growth was caused by industrial development; as many new factories were constructed in this district as well as workers' housing for the increased number of workers.[70] The highest period of growth took place between 1890 and 1910, the years of extensive industrialisation of Pressburg. The other district with newly constructed factories was Franz Joseph's Town, where the population in 1910 had grown by 88% (1.5% per annum) compared to 1869. The growth of workers' housing will be discussed in more detail in Chapter three.

It is possible to reconstruct an approximate picture of the social structure of city districts on the basis of the electoral lists from 1892 and 1895 which list the voters and their occupation for each district. These people represented only a small part of the overall population. One must keep in mind that after the turn of the century there was a trend for well-to-do people to move out of the centre into the new villa districts. In 1892 and 1895, however, the Old Town was still the preferred residential district for most physicians, lawyers, higher city and county officials, engineers, insurance company employees, some professors, religious dignitaries and also some craftsmen who were necessary for the everyday comfort of the inhabitants (barbers, hairdressers, photographers, tailors, shoemakers, patisseriers). Franz Joseph's Town had also many professionals like lawyers, engineers, physicians, dentists, clerks, teachers, restaurant owners, some house owners and master craftsmen (all these fall into category *"jövedelem"* [income earners] and *"értelmiség"* [intelligentsia]).[71] Ferdinand's Town I also had many income earners: tradesmen, shop-owners, lawyers, some clerks, retired army men. Ferdinand's Town II had a similar composition but also had many landowners, wine-growers, teachers and clerks. Theresa's Town had many small craftsmen and shop-owners, smaller intelligentsia and also a strong Jewish presence. This was definitely the most working class district. Many workers' families lived under the castle in *Zukermandl, Vödricz, Váralja* which were very poor parts of the city (Theresa's Town).[72] After 1890, the number of workers in the city was growing. Most of them could be found in the New Town and Franz Joseph's Town where the factories were built. (See Chapter three, section 1.2.) In contrast to these other parts of the town, the New Town had the largest number of house and land owners, followed by the category of "income earners" (e.g. prosecutor, post employee, engineer, industry supervisor, some officials, bank employees, craftsmen) and factory owners.[73]

4.2. DISTRIBUTION OF ETHNIC GROUPS IN PRESSBURG

The census data for 1910 makes it possible to see the population distribution in the city according to class and ethnicity in some detail. It is obvious that there was no residential segregation according to ethnicity, although some districts had higher concentrations of some ethnic groups. This distribution, however, depended primarily on social position. This information is available only towards the end of the period 1867–1914, and it is therefore, not possible to determine the ethnic composition in earlier years with any certainty.

Districts	Proportion in Total population			Proportion in Their Own Population		
	Magyar	German	Slovak	Magyar	German	Slovak
I. Old Town	47.8	42.7	7.6	13.4	11.4	6.5
II. Ferdinand's Town						
Inner	44.8	42.2	11.1	16.6	14.8	12.6
Outer	49.9	38.9	8.9	2.3	1.7	1.3
III. Franz Joseph's Town						
Inner	48.5	39.2	8.8	19.1	14.6	10.6
Outer	26.2	52.8	18.8	0.4	0.7	0.8
IV. Theresa's Town						
Inner	31.4	49.0	18.1	13.2	19.4	23.2
Outer	16.0	51.3	31.1	0.3	0.9	1.8
V. New Town						
Inner	38.2	44.9	14.7	24.4	27.1	28.6
Outer	39.0	38.1	18.2	10.3	9.5	14.7
Total	40.9	43.3	13.4	100.0	100.0	100.0

Table 6: Population distribution by administrative district and mother tongue in Pressburg in 1910.[74]

This table clearly demonstrates the multi-ethnic character of the city's districts. For example, the New Town (which was the most populated district as a result of industrial development as mentioned above) included 43% of all Slovaks which would indicate that they were mostly migrant workers. However, this district also included 37% of all Germans and 35% of all Magyars.[75] In the best city districts (the Old Town and the inner II. and III. districts), the number of Magyars was actually higher than the number of traditionally dominant German speakers. Croats and Serbs could also be found in the Old Town and in the inner II., III. and IV. districts. These members of ethnic minority groups probably belonged to the upper strata in the city.[76] Class mattered more than ethnicity in determining spatial distribution.

Figure 6 shows the distribution of ethnic groups in the administrative city districts. Figures 7–12 show the proportion of Magyars, Germans and Slovaks in the administrative districts of the city. There are two figures for each ethnic group: one representing the ethnic group as a proportion in the total population of each administrative city district, and the other showing distribution of the total population of that ethnic group in administrative districts of Pressburg.[77]

5. LANGUAGE USE IN THE CITY AROUND 1867

This part looks at the languages used in the city around 1867. German had been for a long time the dominant language in the city. It was used already in the tenth and eleventh centuries as the official language along with Latin. But other languages had been used as well, including forms of Slovak and Hungarian. Multilingualism was characteristic of the inhabitants of Pressburg. After the Dual Agreement of 1867, the situation changed as strong Magyarisation pressures began to be felt in municipal affairs and other areas of city life. These pressures intensified in the 1890s.[78] These changes will be discussed in more detail in Chapter two. I will concentrate here on describing language use in 1867 in different areas of city life: in the municipal offices, in religious and cultural life, and in education. I will also consider language use in the different kinds of associations in the city and note the 'ethnic' affiliation and differentiation made possible by participation in these associations.

5.1. LANGUAGE USE IN MUNICIPAL AFFAIRS

In 1867, Pressburg's streets and city districts were named in German. The only city directory (the *Pressburger Wegweiser*) was written in German. Later linguistic changes in the area of nomenclature will be described in Chapter two.[79]

Hungarian started to be used rather early in municipal politics and in the activities of various municipal offices. Until 1885, minutes of municipal assembly meetings were written in both German and Hungarian, and the German version was officially approved as the original.[80] Between 1861–1876 the minutes of meetings of the City Magistrate were kept in both German and Hungarian, and between 1877–1918 only in Hungarian.[81] A review of Ministry of Interior materials from the period 1867–1914 suggests that some of the official correspondence between the city and Hungarian government ministries might have been conducted in German even into the 1870s.[82]

The bilingual minutes of the municipal assembly meetings are particularly revealing of the facility and ease with which *Pressburgers* switched languages: a few paragraphs discussing a particular matter might be in Hungarian while other matters might be recorded in German. It is not clear what the criterion was for choosing which language to use. The records may have reflected the languages used by speakers at these meetings.[83]

5.2. LANGUAGE IN RELIGIOUS AND CULTURAL LIFE

Most of Pressburg's inhabitants were Catholic (see Table 5 in Appendix). Most churches in the city were also Catholic. Pressburg was divided into three parishes.[84] Many members of the *Katholischer Patronat* (Catholic Patronage) were prominent city officials and personalities and municipal assembly deputies. Members of the Patronage served as patrons of the religious schools in different town districts. Within the Catholic community, masses and rituals were carried out in Latin. Only the sermons were in vernaculars, in Pressburg in three languages, Hungarian, German and Slovak. Sermons were most frequently delivered in Hungarian, especially after the turn of the century, at the cost of German. There were German and Slovak (*Slavisch*)[85] sermons every Sunday and on holidays and saints' days in the Franziskans' and Kapuziner churches. In other churches all sermons were Hungarian.

The city's Evangelicals had two churches, *Kleine* und *Grosse Kirche* (the small and big church). German masses were performed in the Big Church and Hungarian and Slovak masses took place in the Small Church. The Small Church had a pastor (who also served as theology instructor) who spoke both Slovak and Hungarian. On Sundays there were even two Slovak masses, one in the morning and one in the afternoon.[86]

The main locus of cultural life in the city, the City Theatre, had traditionally offered performances in German. This was the situation in 1867. However, the new Hungarian elite in the city was very unsatisfied with this status quo, and the struggle to magyarise the City Theatre was one of their principal activities, especially of the association *Toldy Kör*. This effort on the part of the Magyar elite to exert greater influence on the City Theatre will be analysed in greater detail in Chapter two.

An overview of the local press also shows the preponderance of German, even after the turn of the century when Magyars were becoming numerically stronger in the town. Around 1867, there were only German periodicals published in the city. Their number grew throughout the period. To these belonged *Pressburger Zeitung* (started in 1764, the main daily of the German middle classes), *Westungarischer Grenzbote* (an opposition daily started in 1872), *Pressburger Tagblatt* (a Catholic daily started in 1896), *Pressburger Presse* (weekly of the radical burghers started in 1898), *Reform* (democratic weekly started in 1898—defending the interests of small artisans and shopkeepers) and *Westungarische Volksstimme* (started in 1902 as the periodical of the Social-democratic party).[87] It was only in 1873 that a Hungarian periodical, the *Pozsonyvidéki Lapok* (Newspaper for the Pozsony area) began to be published. This was the only Hungarian newspaper in the city and it was published until 1890. In 1887 was started the *Pozsonymegyei Közlöny* which in 1890 was turned into the political daily *Nyugatmagyarországi Hiradó*. *Hiradó* remained the only Hungarian daily in the city until 1919. Around it concentrated the chauvinistic Magyar elite. The Slovak newspapers started to be published in 1904, these were *Slovenské robotnícke noviny* (Slovak workers' newspapers) and in 1906 the magazine *Napred* (Ahead) of the Slovak workers and from 1910 *Slovenské ľudové noviny* (Slovak people's newspaper).[88]

An analysis of classified advertisements in the *Pressburger Zeitung* and *Westungarischer Grenzbote* for 1867–1914 shows that many jobs in Pressburg required knowledge of both German and Hungarian. Knowledge of Slovak was also often required, mainly in jobs connected with trade and sales, but also in municipal offices. Individuals seeking jobs usually advertised their knowledge of "drei Landessprachen" ("three languages of the land," implying Hungarian, German and Slovak) or else explicitly specified their knowledge of all three languages. This is further evidence of the continued multilinguality of every-day life in Pressburg, even if Hungarian appeared to be becoming increasingly prevalent on the surface in municipal politics and public life.

5.3. Language Use in Schools

Elementary schools (*Volksschulen*) in Pressburg were almost all founded and administered by the religious communities until 1919.[89] In 1901, there were 35 schools in the city, half of which were Catholic. Of just over 10,972 children of school-age in the city, 9,353 attended school (85% of all school-age children). By mother tongue, all school-age children included 3,205 Hungarians, 6,827 Germans, 912 Slovaks and 28 others.[90] By 1918 there were 8 *Bürgerschulen* in Pressburg, 3 state-owned, one municipal, two Catholic and two Jewish.[91]

One of the most prestigious secondary schools was the Royal Hungarian Catholic gymnasium (*Kön. ung. katholisches Gymnasium* from 1862). The other middle-level education institutions were the Evangelic lyceum (*Ág. hitv. ev. liczeum, Lyceum*), Theological Academy (founded 1882) and the state *Realschule* (Állami főreáliskola). There were also six professional schools (wine-growing and gardening, commerce, crafts, art-crafts), all with Hungarian language of instruction, founded in 1880s and later. Post-secondary education in Pressburg took place at the Law Academy (*K. k. Rechtsakademie, Királyi akadémia*).[92] Most of Pressburg's institutions of post-elementary education were not only of local importance but were attended also by students from all of Western Hungary, who were accommodated in student residences.[93]

The language of instruction in schools in Pressburg before 1867 was mostly German but Hungarian and Slovak were used as well. In 1867 there was only one Hungarian school in Pressburg. The XXXVIII/68 law created by baron Josef v. Eötvös regulating language use in education had important consequences for the school system and from the national point of view as well.[94] The Hungarian language was incrementally allotted larger number of hours in teaching schedules and finally pushed out the German language almost totally.[95] The change of language of instruction in the city's schools will be discussed in greater length in Chapter two when the effects of Magyarisation on different areas of city life will be considered.

5.4. LANGUAGE USE IN ASSOCIATIONS

Language use in city associations depended on the specific character and purpose of the association. There were workers' associations, middle-class, intelligentsia groupings, as well as elite associations.[96] The middle classes in Pressburg were mostly German and Hungarian, and so their associations were mostly German and Hungarian in composition and character, with a very limited Slovak presence. In 1867, German was still the primary language used in most associations. As late as 1868, the statutes of the *Pressburger freiwilliger Feuerwehrverein* (voluntary firemen's association of Pressburg) declared German the official language of the association.[97] However, while such city associations used German as their primary language, the city's traditionally German elite publicly professed to be Hungarian patriots and tried to downplay the German character of their associations. (The adaptation strategies used by the traditional Pressburger elite will be discussed in Chapter two.) Hungarians, on the other hand, created their own national associations whose activities were directed towards both the Magyar and non-Magyar inhabitants in the city and sought to promote Magyar culture and language as the culture of the state-creating nation.[98] Slovak started to become more visible within associations only after the turn of century. (Attempts to develop Slovak associations will also be discussed in Chapters two and three)

5.5. CONCLUSION

This overview of language use in Pressburg's public and cultural life indicates the complex and changing character of cultural affiliation during the period. The next chapters will discuss these changes in greater detail, and will examine the attitude of different segments of the city's population towards these changes.

The last part of this chapter will provide a brief overview of municipal politics during the period.

6. MUNICIPAL POLITICS

This part of the chapter will describe the restructuring of municipal administration in Pressburg after 1867. I will also discuss the effect of electoral restrictions on municipal and state politics in Hungary.

6.1. RESTRUCTURING OF CITY ADMINISTRATION

The 1867 Dual Agreement brought Hungarians into dominant administrative positions in the Hungarian part of the Habsburg Empire. The new Hungarian state re-organised the administration of its territory. Power was centralised in Budapest. Pressburg became the seat of second degree institutions of state and public administration in 1869. In 1871 jurisdictional authority was taken away from the municipal administration. Royal courts of law became independent juridical organs subordinated to the Ministry of Justice.[99] With decentralisation in 1891 the Royal High Court of Justice (*királyi itélő tábla*) was established in Pressburg, whose sphere of jurisdiction included six counties with 36 district courts of law. In 1900 was established the Royal Supreme Prosecutor's Office (*királyi főügyézség*).[100]

In 1888 the municipal assembly approved the organisational statutes of the city. The municipal assembly consisted of 186 members, 93 of which were elected and the rest were the biggest tax payers of the city (virilists).[101] The members of the municipal assembly were elected every three years for six years.[102] The mayor and senior officials of the municipal administration were also *ex officio* members of the municipal assembly.[103] The municipal assembly met in public session once a month.[104] Pressburg did not technically fall under the jurisdiction of Pressburg (Pozsony) county's *főispán*; however, he had the title "főispán of Pressburg county and city of Pressburg" and chaired meetings of the municipal assembly of Pressburg city. He could be represented at the meetings by the mayor or the first *Magistratsrath* (magistrate advisor). The meetings were public. [105]

The executive organ of the municipal assembly was called the City Magistracy and included the mayor, city captain, *Magistratsrathe*, the principal notary and the city lawyer. The City Magistracy oversaw the everyday activities, supervised the economic functioning of the city, and administered municipal assets and income and the municipal funds and foundations.[106]

While in theory the municipal assembly had wide-ranging authority over city planning, administration and public works, minutes of all municipal meetings had to be sent to the Hungarian Minister of Interior. In this way he could control the decisions and suggest their change.[107] Apart from this there were defined areas in which the municipality had to ask approval of the Ministry of Interior.[108]

The state's authority and centralising tendencies were strengthened by an 1886 law restricting the independence of the mayor and county assemblies. A new administrative committee (*közigazgatási bizottság*) was created which had a co-ordinating function between the central state authorities and the county administration. The departments in the county administration basically mirrored the different ministries. The authority of the *főispán* (appointed by the Minister of Interior) was strengthened and his deputy and the county officials had only secondary functions.[109]

6.2. ELECTORAL RESTRICTIONS

Electoral restrictions in Hungary made it possible for the Hungarian landowner classes to maintain their grip on power after 1867. These restrictions took three forms: open ballots; limited suffrage; and manipulation of electoral district boundaries.

The Hungarian electoral system forced voters to openly disclose their vote, enabling pressure and blackmail to be applied to voters. Furthermore, suffrage was extremely restricted in scale. In 1867, 6.7% of the inhabitants had right to vote. By 1900 this number shrank to 5.9%. The poor, workers and the mostly uneducated masses of the nationalities were excluded from suffrage. Lastly, manipulations in setting boundaries of the electoral districts made it possible to exclude the oppositional middle classes and peasants. This practice was used especially under Kálmán Tisza. Those areas which were easy to influence and which were loyal to the governmental party could elect more deputies than those areas which were known to favour the opposition. All these restrictions were then topped off by all kinds of violence, bribery, blackmail and manipulation during the elections themselves.[110]

Municipal elections were also subject to similar constraints. In Pressburg in 1882, the right to vote was held by 5.5.% of the population.[111] The 1886 electoral law (XLII/1886) restricted the right to vote for the municipal assembly to owners of houses, land and those inhabitants who had at least 105 Gulden yearly pension or 700 Guldens yearly income. The lists of voters for the parliamentary elections were used also for the municipal elections. In the municipal elections in 1892 and 1895, the city was divided into electoral districts according to the city districts (Altstadt I and II, Franz-Joseph Stadt, Ferdinand Stadt I and II, Theresienstadt, Neustadt). In both of these elections less than half of those entitled to vote used this right.[112]

The city was also divided into several electoral districts with candidates who represented different political parties. These parties reflected the existing political party system on the national level.[113] The surrounding areas were included in the electoral districts of Bazin and Stomfa (which means that people from Ligetfalu, mostly workers, which was just across the bridge from Pressburg's city centre had to travel to faraway Bazin to vote).[114]

6.3. CONCLUSION

This part has described the structure of municipal politics and electoral constraints in Pressburg in order to show the elite character of the city's institutions and the extent to which they were subordinated to the centralising Hungarian state. Hungarian efforts to "magyarise" Pressburg will be discussed at more length in subsequent chapters of this study.

7. CONCLUSION

This chapter has provided a basic overview of Pressburg between 1867–1914. Economic development in the city was paralleled by the modernisation of city infrastructure and administration. Industrialisation and modernisation also affected the ethnic, occupational and social structure of the city's population. Language usage in various areas of public and cultural life changed in response to political and social developments. Finally, municipal politics in the period point towards the key role of the centralising Hungarian state in its efforts to control Pressburg. The next four chapters will consider each of these issues in greater detail.

∽ 2 ∾

THE IMPACT OF MAGYARISATION IN

PRESSBURG

0. INTRODUCTION

THIS CHAPTER DESCRIBES the Hungarian government's Magyarisation policies and their impact on Pressburg's nationalities.[1] After 1867, the Hungarian state's Magyarisation policies affected municipal politics and social and cultural life in Pressburg. Magyarisation was intertwined with the new Magyar elite's struggle to wrest control of the city away from the traditional German-speaking Pressburger elite. The Magyar elite used nationalist rhetoric in order to identify itself with the nationalising policies of the Hungarian state. Pressburg's inhabitants came under increasing pressure to identify themselves as members of the Hungarian nation or of a minority 'nationality' (such as German or Slovak), as opposed to a 'Pressburger' identity characterised by local patriotism rather than distinct 'ethnic' affiliation.[2] 'Pressburger' identity had often been used by the German speaking elite as a way to avoid exclusively identifying themselves with any one ethnic group. Pressburg's Slovaks also had to negotiate between the conflicting pressures of Magyarisation, the gradual emergence of an active Slovak national movement, and the local 'Pressburger' identity.

The first part of this chapter presents an overview of Magyarisation policies in Hungary from 1867 to 1914. The second part focuses on Magyarisation in Pressburg and its influence on cultural, social, associational and political life in the city. In particular, I will look in some detail at the association *Toldy Kör* whose primary objective was to make Pressburg a

Magyar town. The third part analyses the struggle between the traditional German speaking elites and the new emerging Magyar elite for control
over the City Theatre, the primary locus of cultural life for the middle
classes in the city.³ This struggle serves as a case study showing the manner and extent to which the traditional elites resisted and also adjusted
themselves to the demands of the nationalising state represented in the
city by the new Magyar elites. The fourth part discusses 'Pressburger'
identity. I will examine the interplay between this local identity and Hungarian patriotism. I will also consider whether 'Pressburger' identity was
restricted to a social elite or whether it cut across class and ethnic divides.
The last part of the chapter considers 'Slovakness' in Pressburg during the
period. In this context I will consider two Slovak lawyers, Michal Mudroň
and Vendelín Kutlík, and the different ways in which their Slovak activities
were accepted or rejected by Pressburger society.

1. MAGYRISATION IN HUNGARY 1867-1914

This part of the chapter provides a brief description of the nationalising
policies of the Hungarian state. These efforts to build one Hungarian political nation were the context for ethnic relations in Pressburg in the period
1867–1914. I will consider how assimilation pressures affected different
nationalities and groups in the city. Finally I will briefly assess the extent to
which the city served as a "melting pot" enabling the Hungarian state to "de-
nationalise" migrants from surrounding villages.

1.1. MAGYARISATION POLICIES OF THE
HUNGARIAN GOVERNMENT 1867-1914

After 1867, the Hungarian state started the process of nation-building and
of "national socialization," in an attempt to create a unified 'national' high
culture.⁴ However, in their efforts to build one political Hungarian nation,
Hungarian governments considered the cultures of other "nationalities" to
be inferior and reacted oppressively towards attempts by these nationalities
to foster their own cultural development. While the Hungarian government
of 1867 (including the individuals who negotiated the Dual Agreement) still
believed in the natural attractiveness of Hungarian culture and in the power
of persuasion, later governments implemented more forcible measures
especially in the area of education and culture as well as in the surveillance
of nationalities' movements. Greater coercive pressure by the state resulted

in a stronger reaction by the nationalities whose intelligentsias tried to mobilise mass support for their own national ideals.[5]

Magyarisation pressures began to emerge by the beginning of the nineteenth century, as a consequence of the emerging Hungarian national movement.[6] However, these pressures found expression in the realm of policy making only when Hungarians acquired their own (relatively autonomous) state in 1867. The nationalities' law of December 1868 set out the doctrine of one Hungarian political nation in Hungary. The law confirmed the individual rights of Hungarian citizens but did not acknowledge any other nations within Hungary, only "nationalities." Hungarian became the state language and the use of other languages was only allowed in some lower courts, church schools, and county and municipal governments.[7]

Even this relative tolerance was already waning by the beginning of the 1870s. Premier Kálmán Tisza (1875–1890) was convinced that reducing the number of non-Magyars was the key to achieving independence from Vienna. He was afraid that Emperor Franz Joseph might turn the non-Magyar nationalities against Magyars, as had happened during and after the revolution of 1848/9.[8] "Nothing less ambitious than the objective Magyarize all Hungarian national groups seemed to be the policy of Tisza's government."[9] Magyarisation policies were embraced by all successive Hungarian governments. While there were minor differences in the policies adopted towards nationalities (for instance, by Kálmán Széll's government in 1899–1903), the idea of one political nation and the dominance of the Magyar race was part of the ideology of all Hungarian governments.[10]

Magyarisation was primarily directed towards education and culture.[11] After 1870, a state elementary school system began to be formed in which the only language of instruction was Hungarian. Hungarian became an obligatory subject in church schools as well as municipal schools, and the number of hours per week of this subject increased. In 1879, the Hungarian language was introduced into elementary schools and kindergartens. After 1883, instruction in secondary schools was conducted exclusively in Hungarian. The 1907 Ápponyi law required all teachers in non-Magyar schools to demonstrate proficiency in the Hungarian language, and fourth grade elementary school pupils had to demonstrate knowledge of Hungarian. Two years later Hungarian became the sole language of instruction in non-Magyar schools as well.[12]

Magyarisation also took place in public life. In the mid-1870s, the Hungarian language became both the external and internal language of all state agencies and the courts. In 1890, Hungarian became the official language of the municipalities. Hungarian was the only language used in official documents. In 1895, the Hungarian Prime Minister Dezső Bánffy created a special department monitoring the activities of nationalities. The electoral law's exclusion of the uneducated and poor masses (thus most of the nationalities) from the franchise meant that the nationalities were unable to take any effective political action.[13] They were subjected to pressure from the authorities, and activists were persecuted as "Pan-Germans," "Pan-Slavs" and "enemies of the Hungarian state."

Different ethnic groups reacted in different ways to these powerful pressures to assimilate. The next section considers the idiosyncratic characteristics of Germans, Slovaks and Jews affecting the pattern and extent to which these groups assimilated.

1.2. Magyarisation, Assimilation and Ethnic Groups

In this study, assimilation is seen as "a more complex process covering several cumulative phases." The adoption of the dominant group's language is a relatively shallow 'cultural assimilation' or 'acculturation' as opposed to "structural assimilation" which requires a "structural type of social integration which is 'large-scale entrance into cliques, clubs, and institutions of host society on the primary group level'."[14] While Hungarian historians for the most part consider assimilation merely one aspect of the building of a civic society in Hungary during the nineteenth century (and thus as a positive phenomenon), historians from the erstwhile "nationalities" consider assimilation from the viewpoint of the developing national movements, and see assimilation as predominantly negative (except insofar as it widened the ranks of their own nationality).[15] Understanding assimilation as a complex process influenced by more factors than merely linguistic adaptation makes it possible to avoid falling into either of these extreme positions. This section considers the relative tendency of different ethnic groups to assimilate into the Hungarian political nation.[16] According to census data, Slovaks, Germans and Jews constituted the largest "assimilation gain" in favour of Magyars.[17]

1.2.1. Slovaks

The Slovak population in Hungary was particularly vulnerable to assimilation because of such factors as high out-migration, extensive internal migration from north to south and towards the main cities, distinctive features of the patterns of urban/rural settlement, and the relative lack of a Slovak middle class.[18]

Between 1880 and 1910, at a time when Slovaks had a much higher birth rate than Magyars, the proportion of Slovaks in the territory of present-day Slovakia decreased from 63% to 57.6%.[19] "Weaker Slovak [population] growth was caused firstly by a high rate of out-migration and also through assimilation."[20] Out-migration was very high from all parts of Hungary, primarily because of high unemployment. Most emigrants were non-Magyars.[21] "Between 1871 and 1914 some 500,000 Slovaks settled permanently in the United States."[22]

Slovak migration from the northern highlands to the southern parts of Hungary, mainly to towns in search for jobs, was also very large. By 1900, Pressburg county's population was 46% Slovak.[23] However, most Slovaks (72%) lived in rural settlements with no more than 2,000 inhabitants. While the proportion of Magyars living in cities reached 77% by 1910, the proportion of Slovaks living there was only 8%. From 1890 to 1910 the number of Slovak residents in cities declined more rapidly than in rural areas; in other words, "the cities become centers of assimilation, either voluntarily or as a result of Magyarisation policies."[24]

This picture of a mostly rural population drawn to big cities points to another important factor in Slovak assimilation. Slovaks were underrepresented in the middle and upper classes in Hungary.[25] The weakness of the Slovak middle class was also a hindrance to the development of the national movement.[26] The number of educated Slovaks was very low. Magyarisation had concentrated especially on the area of education; acquiring higher education in the Slovak language was, therefore, impossible after the three Slovak gymnasia were abolished in 1874. In 1875, the *Matica Slovenská* (an institution supporting Slovak culture) was also closed down.[27] By 1914, only 42,000 of 214,000 elementary school-age children in the territory of present-day Slovakia were taught even partly in Slovak.[28] As a result, many people from Slovak areas who came through the Hungarian education system were assimilated. This was especially the case since assimilation was a precondition for rising in the social hierarchy.

However, assimilation among Slovaks was by no means complete. An increasing number of young Slovaks went to university in Prague and established their own student society there in 1882 (*Detvan*). Funds were raised to send Slovak students to Czech gymnasia and professional schools throughout Bohemia.[29] Furthermore, the Magyarisation of elementary school education may have had an opposite effect than that intended. Since illiteracy among Slovaks was very high, especially in the villages, instead of learning perfect Hungarian, children may have failed to learn any Hungarian at all since they had problems understanding Hungarian speaking teachers in school.[30]

1.2.2. Germans

Although there were two million German-speakers in Hungary at the turn of the century, there was no organised German national movement.[31] Germans in Hungary varied in dialect, religion, class, place of origin and the "colonisation wave" in which their ancestors had arrived in Hungary.[32] As was also the case with Slovaks, part of the originally German bourgeoisie had been assimilated, and the rest considered themselves German-speaking Hungarian patriots. Kováč claims that Germans in the territory of present-day Slovakia "reconciled themselves to centralisation and Magyarisation almost without resistance."[33] Although this under-estimates the extent of German resistance (and Hungarian fears of Pan-Germanic tendencies), it is true that Germans throughout Hungary "vehemently acknowledged Hungarian patriotism as a basic value."[34]

German-speaking Hungarian patriots denoted their double identity with the term 'Hungarus' (used by Gerhard Seewann) meaning "Ethnically I am German but politically and culturally I am Hungarian."[35] This self-proclaimed Hungarian patriotism and public use of the Hungarian language was a reaction to the waves of "Deutschfeindlichkeit" (inimical feeling against Germans) throughout Hungary after the end of an era of neo-absolutism marked by Germanisation pressures.[36] However, this outwardly manifested Hungarian patriotism did not mean that Germans gave up their language altogether. While the Hungarian language was used in communication with the authorities and to demonstrate their Hungarian identity and patriotism, German was used inside their own ethnic group as well as in associations.[37]

The assimilation of Germans also reflected changes in social stratification in nineteenth-century Hungary. Until the middle of the nineteenth century, German-speaking burghers carried out the economic functions and social role of the middle class. Ethnicity was not an important or even relevant criterion for social differentiation.[38] By 1867, however, the "gentry" (or middle nobility) had assumed the leading role in Hungarian political life. Since the gentry saw itself as the embodiment of historical *Magyardom*, assimilation into this elite class also meant a rise in prestige. "To be a lord meant to be a Magyar."[39] Thus, social elitism, attraction to Magyar culture, and socio-economic changes such as the end of the traditional guild structure also contributed to the assimilation of Germans in Hungary.[40]

Nevertheless, the Hungarian authorities continued to fear "Pan-Germanism." Their fears were influenced by the founding in 1880 (in Vienna and Berlin) of the *Deutscher Schulverein* (German school association), which started a campaign to help Germans in Hungary. The *Allgemeiner deutscher Verband* (Universal German Association) was founded in 1890 (from 1908 called the *Verein für das Deutschtum in Ausland* [Association for Germans abroad]). This organisation tried to use German minorities outside Germany to promote the aims of German imperialist politics and criticised Hungary's Magyarisation policies. The German nationalistic daily *Deutsches Tagblatt für Ungarn* was founded in 1900 in Temesvár (Timisoara), and openly espoused the politics of German expansion and Germanisation of the Habsburg Empire. The Hungarian government reacted strongly to these activities, and carefully monitored the Pan-German movement (See Chapter five). Efforts to defend the use of the German language were considered "Pan-Germanism," just as Slovak activities were considered "Pan-Slavism."

While Germans in the territory of present-day Slovakia did not support the activities of the *Schulverein* or the *Verband*, campaigns against the Magyarisation of town names (after 1897) and against the Magyarisation of education (after the turn of the century) resonated amongst them as well. Western Hungary became one of the most important centres of the *Ungarländische deutsche Volkspartei* (the German People's Party in Hungary), founded in 1907 with the assistance of Steinacker. However, German nationalists generally felt that the level of "national consciousness" among Germans in the territory of Slovakia was very low, with the exception of Germans in Pressburg and its surrounding areas.[41]

1.2.3. Jews

In 1867, Hungary passed an Emancipation law granting full political and civil rights to Jewish people. In 1895, the law on the equality of the Jewish religion was passed. Greater social mobility led to considerable assimilation into Hungarian society.[42] Most Jews in Slovakia initially noted German as their mother tongue in censuses.[43] This preference probably changed in the period 1867–1914, with strengthening Magyarisation pressures, especially in education.[44] German remained the language of daily use among Jews, particularly in Western Slovakia, for a long time, although Hungarian was used with increasing frequency among the educated professional classes. In Eastern Slovakia, Yiddish was also still spoken.[45] Mannová believes that since Jews identified primarily with their religion, their recognition of any mother tongue was merely formal.[46] Rothkirchen concurs: "These figures...indicate language distribution rather than nationality...."[47] Multi-linguality, knowledge of the state language as well as the local languages, was a characteristic of Jewish families.[48]

"[A]ssimilated Jews, unlike the educated Slovak gentiles who assimilated and ultimately blended with the Magyars, still remained a class apart" because of the religious difference.[49] Furthermore, the economic differential between better-off Jews and lower-income local gentile populations caused a strong anti-Semitic reaction, especially in North-eastern Slovakia. Many Slovak historians consider Jews as having played a negative role in 1867–1918 since they adopted the Hungarian language and many of them became Magyarisers.[50] In actual fact, many Jews in the territory of present-day Slovakia sympathised with the Slovak national striving. The founders of *Matica Slovenská* (the main Slovak nationalist organisation) included two Jewish names, a fact which Rothkirchen claims is often forgotten in Slovak historiography.[51]

1.2.4. Conclusion

This section has considered some factors involved in the relative tendency of Slovaks, Germans, and Jews to assimilate into Hungarian society under the pressures of Magyarisation. The next section outlines another important dimension of assimilation in nineteenth-century Hungary: the extent to which cities served as "melting-pots" facilitating assimilation.

1.3. VILLAGE VS. CITY

Romantic nationalists often posited an opposition between the unspoilt ethnically "pure" countryside and "folk" cultures versus the cosmopolitan and "corrupt" life of the city.[52] This opposition leads to a notion of the city as the venue for "de-nationalising" ethnic minorities. Migration to the cities is then seen as facilitating assimilation into the dominant culture. This view requires closer examination as it has remained embedded in modern Slovak interpretations.[53]

For Slovak historians and social scientists like Svetoň and Tajták, cities were 'melting pots' enabling the Hungarian authorities to "de-nationalise" non-Magyar nationalities. This "de-nationalising" effect of cities is contrasted to the conservatism of villages which preserved their inherent Slovakness because of the inborn resistance and distrust of peasants towards new and foreign things.[54] Both writers claim that "the saddest example" of Magyarisation was the production of a layer of educated Slovaks in Hungary who 'de-nationalised' in order to rise in the social hierarchy. Svetoň and Tajták seem to see 'denationalising' as the result of a lack of morality or as the consequence of a weakness of character. Such moralising is typical for much of Slovak historiography.[55] However, Tajták does concede that assimilation was also connected with "objective" factors such as industrialisation and migration from villages to cities. In the 'melting pot' of the city, the language of the ruling nation tended to become the *lingua franca*, especially in a multinational empire with many different languages.[56]

Leading Hungarian politicians from the period also considered cities "strong bastions of our [Magyar] nationality" and "of linguistic-cultural Magyarisation."[57] However, specific historical analysis of assimilation shows that immigration to cities did not necessarily result in an increased tendency to assimilation. Cities acted as 'melting pots' only when they lay on the cross-roads of multiple inter-regional and inter-ethnic migration routes. Thus assimilation was more likely to happen in a city with many ethnic groups like Budapest rather than in cities when there were two ethnic groups opposing each other.[58]

Cities opened up multiple possibilities for revising self-identification and group affiliation. A migrant to the city might assimilate because he/she wanted to rise in the social hierarchy. In the case of the working class, learning Hungarian was an opportunity to participate in the Hungarian workers' movement. However, cities did not always act as 'melting pots.' For one thing, even shared ethnicity did not always overcome the divide between new migrants and earlier inhabitants of the city.[59] In the case of newcomers, it was probably class and cultural behaviour which distinguished them from other people of the same ethnic group who were already settled in the city. As Cohen points out, "[t]he special interest of a group and the impact on it of general social and economic development can motivate efforts to articulate, maintain, or abandon an ethnic identity.... Economic interest, class, and ideology may become integral elements in a group's identity, and ethnic solidarity will then not easily cross occupational, class, or ideological lines."[60] Readiness to assimilate was also influenced by the religious affiliation of members of an ethnic group.[61] Assimilation was a complex process influenced by many factors, and the mere fact of migration to cities did not necessarily lead to assimilation.

1.4. CONCLUSION

This part of the chapter has provided a brief overview of the nationalising policies of the Hungarian state as the context for a more detailed consideration of ethnic relations in Pressburg in 1867–1914. As this part has shown, assimilation was a complex process that affected Hungary's 'nationalities' in different ways. Even in big cities, assimilation was influenced by such factors as the multi-ethnic character of the city, settlement patterns and religious affiliations. The next part of this chapter specifically considers Magyarisation in the city of Pressburg.

2. MAGYARISATION IN PRESSBURG

This part analyses the influence of the Hungarian state's nationalising policies on different aspects of city life in Pressburg. I will first examine the extent of Magyarisation as shown in the census data from 1880–1910. I will then consider the effect of Magyarisation on municipal life and in language usage in the municipality, since the new Magyar elite used nationalistic rhetoric in its struggle with the traditional German-speaking city elite. I will study the influence of Magyarisation on associational life in the city, paying particular attention to the creation and activities of new Hungarian associations such as *Toldy Kör*. I will consider the change of languages of instruction in schools and the development of the Hungarian press in the city. Finally, I will show how the Magyarisation drive affected the city's physical appearance.

2.1. MAGYARISATION OF PRESSBURG AS
REFLECTED IN CENSUSES 1880–1910

Strong Magyarisation pressures began to be felt in Pressburg in the 1880s and 1890s. These pressures intensified at the beginning of the twentieth century.[62] This section will look at the progress of Magyarisation in Pressburg as reflected in official census statistics, while keeping in mind the problematic nature of this information (as discussed above in chapter one). The table below shows the ethnic composition of the city's population between 1890 and 1900, based on 'mother tongue.'[63]

As the table shows, Magyarisation in Pressburg affected Germans most of all. While the proportion of Magyars in the population of Pressburg increased by 10% in 1890s and by the same proportion in the following decade, the percentage of Germans dropped by almost the same proportion. The absolute numbers of Germans stayed almost the same throughout the period, with a slight decrease between 1900 and 1910. It is hardly possible that Germans did not reproduce at all. Yet between 1880 and 1910 German-speakers grew by only 0.03% per annum(while Magyar-speakers grew by 4.7% annually).[64] Large numbers of Germans, mainly from the lower classes, were being assimilated, at least linguistically.[65] By 1900 and 1910 a new generation had already sprung up, with a German speaking home environment but a Magyar education and the statistics reflect this to a large extent.

Although Germans remained the most numerous group in the city until 1900, Germans gradually lost their dominant position to the Magyars. Yet, despite occasional complaints, Pressburg's Germans stuck to their Hungarian patriotism. As mentioned in the first part of this chapter, a double identity called 'Hungarus' was quite typical of Pressburg Germans who considered themselves ethnically German but politically and culturally Hungarian.[66] This apparent contradiction meant that, despite their numerical strength, Germans did not assert themselves *against* Magyars and at least outwardly accepted the idea of one Hungarian political nation with Magyar supremacy.[67] Mannová states that the lack of assertiveness on the part of the Germans meant that there were no overt ethnic conflict in the city.[68] The subtle tensions between the German burghers and the new Magyar elite will be discussed in greater detail later in this chapter and in subsequent chapters of this study.

Between 1880 and 1910, Slovaks formed approximately 15% of the civil population of the city.[69] As can be seen from Table 7, the proportion of Slovaks did not change much during the period. The absolute number of Slovaks did not change very much either, as the figures show only a slight growth. But when put into the context of the enormous growth of the Magyar group, it is very probable that some part of the Slovak population was assimilated, although it is hard to judge to what extent. According to Lubor Niederle's calculations, the number of Slovaks dropped by 10–25% due to biased Hungarian statistics.[70] Svetoň also considers the bias in Hungarian census data as a kind of "*statistical Magyarisation*" i.e. Magyarisation as reflecting the wish of Hungarian authorities rather than reality.[71] The last part of this chapter discusses the position of Slovaks in the city in greater detail.

The rapid growth in the number of Magyars is evident after 1890. Their proportion grew from 16% of the city's population in 1880 to 41% in 1910. There is hardly any doubt that this growth was not achieved by "natural" growth especially when compared with the decline of Germans. Another factor was the shift in linguistic and political identification on the part of the city's Jewish population.

Pressburg played an important role for the Jews of Hungary. The city was called the "Hungarian Jerusalem."[72] There were both Orthodox and Reform

	Total	Magyar	German	Slovak	Roman.	Ruthen.	Croat.	Serb.	Other
1880—Civil Population									
Absolute Number	48,006	7,537	31,492	7,537	-	-	-144(+Serb)	-	1,296
Percent		15.7%	65.6%	15.7%			0.3%		2.7%
1890—Civil Population									
Absolute Number	52,411	10,433	31,404	8,709	18	16	205	27	1,599
Percent		19.9%	59.9%	16.6%	0.03%	0.03%	0.4%	0.1%	3.1%
1900—Civil Population									
Absolute Number	61,537	18,744	32,104	9,004	24	12	242	25	1,382
Percent		30.5%	52.2%	14.6%	0.04%	0.02%	0.4%	0.04%	2.2%
1900—All Population (incl. army)									
Absolute Number	65,867	20,102	33,202	10,715	32	16	267	28	1,505
Percent		30.5%	50.4%	16.3%	0.05%	0.02%	0.4%	0.04%	2.3%
1910—Civil Population									
Absolute Number	73,459	30,010	31,768	9,816	22	3	303	20	1,517
Percent		40.9%	43.2%	13.4%	0.03%	0.004%	0.4%	0.03%	2.1%
1910—All Population (incl. army)									
Absolute Number	78,223	31,705	32,790	11,673	33	9	351	24	1,638
Percent		40.5%	41.9%	14.9%	0.04%	0.01%	0.4%	0.03%	2.1%

Table 7: All ethnic groups in Pressburg, 1880–1910.

Jews in the city but most of them acknowledged themselves to be Orthodox. After 1862, Jews were allowed to leave the Ghetto under the Castle and the richer ones moved out into the centre of the city and mixed with the other parts of the city's population, mixing language and culture in a rich melange of multiple identities.[73] The proportion of Jews in the city's population remained the same throughout the period, around 10%, the average in Hungary as a whole was 4.5–5%.[74] The increase in the Jewish population of Pressburg from 4,552 in 1869 to 8,207 in 1910 kept pace with the growth of the city. (See Appendix, Table 5 for the growth of population according to religious affiliation 1869–1910.) During this period many Jews changed their linguistic identification from German to Hungarian. Similarly, in Prague towards the end of the nineteenth century, Jews shifted from German to Czech as the language of everyday use, and this was an important reason for the statistical decline in the number of Germans in that city.[75] The next table shows the number of Magyar speakers in different religious groups.[76]

	Roman Catholic	Evangelical	Reformed	Israelite
1880	16.0	12.5	54.6	13.7
1890	20.0	13.1	80.6	21.7
1900	29.7	21.9	81.0	38.2
1910	39.9	27.2	86.0	51.4

Table 8: Magyar speakers in different religious groups, 1880–1910 (%).

Table 8 above shows that the percentage of Jews with Magyar mother tongue grew from 13.7% in 1880 to 51.4% in 1910. The rise in the number of Jews with Magyar as their mother tongue can be explained by the shift in linguistic identification induced by official policies but also by the fact that the education system by this time was basically Magyarised, producing a new generation who had attended Hungarian schools. Even so, the proportion of Jews with Magyar mother tongue was just over half. The next table shows the distribution of different confessions by their mother tongue.[77]

	Roman Catholic	Evangelical	Reformed	Israelite
Magyar				
1900	29.7	21.9	81.0	38.2
1910	39.8	27.7	86.0	51.4
German				
1900	48.0	62.1	14.2	60.2
1910	39.6	58.8	8.3	47.1
Slovak				
1900	18.9	15.5	4.0	1.2
1910	17.6	12.6	2.4	1.0

Table 9: Inhabitants of Pressburg by religion and mother tongue, 1900 and 1910 (%).

While the number of Jews with German as mother tongue in 1900 was much higher than that of Jews with Magyar mother tongue, by 1910 this had reversed. (The same situation can be seen in the case of Roman Catholics with Magyar mother tongue whose numbers had grown by 1910 while the number of German-speaking Roman Catholics had dropped.)[78]

2.2. MAGYARISATION OF MUNICIPAL LIFE

After 1867, Magyarisation began to affect public life in Pressburg. Magyars moved into privileged positions in the city administration, and in public, cultural and societal life. Knowledge of Hungarian was necessary for prominence in any of these areas. Having concentrated political power in their hands after the 1867 Dual Agreement, the Magyar ruling class could carry out a targeted and purposeful assimilation policy, in accordance with the idea of there being only one political nation in Hungary.[79] In this section, I will look specifically at changes in language usage in municipal life. I will examine the shift from German to Hungarian language use in official communications, municipal records, municipal meetings as well as in daily encounters between municipal authorities and city inhabitants. Looking at language use in municipal life provides a revealing glimpse into the attitude of the traditional German elite towards Magyarisation.

As noted in the first chapter of this study, Hungarian began to be used quite early in the activities of different municipal offices. Until 1885, minutes of municipal assembly meetings were kept in both Hungarian and German. After 1885, these minutes were kept solely in Hungarian.[80] Similarly, the minutes of meetings of the City Magistracy were kept solely in Hungarian from 1877 to 1918.[81] Materials from the Ministry of Interior for the period 1867–1914 indicate that all official correspondence between the city and the ministries was conducted in Hungarian.

However, there are also some revealing indications that German remained in use in official city communications even into the 1870s and early 1880s. For instance, in a letter to the mayor in 1881, the *főispán* (head of the county government) attached a report from the city captain written in German.[82] The *főispán* passed on the order of the minister of interior that all reports from the city captain were first to go to the mayor and then to the minister and that all the official communication should be in the "state language" and not in German as it had been hitherto. The minister also pointedly expressed his view that it was the mayor's duty to ensure that all municipal officers and their staff knew Hungarian. The minister ordered the mayor to submit a list of those municipal employees who did not know Hungarian at the next municipal assembly meeting, so that appropriate measures could be taken.[83] This letter suggests that the transition from German to Hungarian use was not smooth. It is quite possible that only the official correspondence going to higher-ups such as the *főispán* was rigorously in Hungarian and that internal correspondence continued to be conducted in German. An example of this is the correspondence between the city captain and the workers' association *Vorwärts* (of 1890) which was in German. However, when the captain informed the minister of interior about the content of this correspondence, he did so in Hungarian.[84]

Furthermore, while Hungarian was supposed to be the only official language, German and Slovak were also used in day-to-day work in the municipal offices. This could result in occasional embarrassment: when one visitor (a Hungarian parliamentary deputy) entered the office of the mayor, the office attendant (*hajdu*) wished him good day in German before the visitor had even opened his mouth. The Hungarian visitor took this as evidence that Pressburg was not as sufficiently Hungarian as it should have been. Otto Sziklay, the parliamentary deputy for Pressburg, defended the attendant, and by proxy, the city: "Well, there are Germans there too, Magyars and Slovaks (*tótok*), so he has to speak all three languages in one day, and so it can happen that a German word slips out of his mouth. However, the office attendant Both István is as good a Hungarian as anyone else."[85]

Even after the turn of the century, the older *Bürger* class' understanding of Hungarian was not fluent. In 1903, German was still used by many speakers in municipal assembly meetings. The lawyer Károly Zernek's suggestion that only Hungarian be used in the municipal assembly meetings as well as in all the expert municipal committees created a huge negative reaction among the German-speaking population. Reporting on this case to the prime minister, the *főispán* declared that the agitation against the Hungarian language was the work of the German press in Pressburg, especially the *Pressburger Zeitung* which had been continuously printing articles against the government, *főispán* and the Hungarian state. The *főispán* was very annoyed at the whole affair because the Hungarian-language minutes of municipal meetings had led him to believe that the proposal should have been enthusiastically accepted by a majority of the municipal deputies.[86] In this case, as also in the case of the City Theatre (discussed in the next part of this chapter), there is an obvious discrepancy between the publicly declared Hungarian patriotism of the German elite and their actions in specific cases of contention.

While Zernek withdrew his proposal in 1903, Hungarian became the sole language used in the meetings of the municipal assembly in 1908. In a general meeting of the *Bürgerverein* (a middle class association with German preponderance) in 1908, one member pointed out that the inability of most *Bürgerverein* members to completely understand discussions in the municipal assembly meetings prevented them from fully participating in these meetings. As a result, only 30 of the 75 *Bürgerverein* members who were also members of the municipal assembly actually took part in its meetings. This was true also of municipal expert committees meetings. The chairman of the association, Daniel Molec, pointed out that the absence of the *Bürger* members diminished their influence on city affairs.[87]

The shift from German to Hungarian language use in municipal life met with some resistance on the part of the German speaking traditional city elites. However, since the use of the state language—Hungarian—in all official communications was fixed by law, the traditional elites did not have any choice but to adapt to the changes. In the daily communication of the municipal authorities with city inhabitants, the necessity of communicating in the languages of non-Magyar clients was also acknowledged and multilinguality was typical in every-day affairs. However, after the turn of the century, Hungarian became predominant in official municipal communications and meetings, and by the outbreak of the First World War, municipal life was becoming increasingly Hungarian.

2.3. EFFECTS OF MAGYARISATION ON ASSOCIATIONS
As in other nineteenth-century European cities, Pressburg's voluntary associations were an important social locale where the interests of different

groups intersected. Pressburg's inhabitants were involved in dense social networks. While the number of inhabitants of Pressburg grew 1.7 times in the second half of the nineteenth century, the number of associations grew eleven-fold. In 1878, there were eighty-one associations in Pressburg which had a total of 18,599 members. By 1915, the number of associations had risen to 125.[88] The associations were "the carriers of modernisation" and influenced the re-grouping of the different interest groups in the city. "In many instances, their rank was demonstrated in architecture, and exerted impact on the shape of the town (the City Enhancement Society, the building of monuments, the construction of union houses)."[89] The growth in the number of associations was also connected with the "increasing privatisation of leisure" in the nineteenth century. Women were mostly excluded, except for the charity associations.[90] The middle class took the leading role in these associations, thereby expressing its cultural and economic interests as well as making its impact on municipal politics.[91] "The integration of city officers and city office holders into the network of voluntary associations caused the distinction between the societies and the "city" to gradually be erased."[92] The middle class in Pressburg was mostly German and Hungarian with only a very limited Slovak presence, and the associations reflected this in their composition and character. Most associations had charitable or social mandates, although towards the end of the century a number of entrepreneurial, professional and sport associations were also founded.[93]

As Cohen says, belonging to the middle class in ninetenth century Central Europe was determined by "a composite test of occupation, wealth, lifestyle, and personal cultivation."[94] The middle classes (*Bürgertum*) valued *Bildung und Besitz* [cultivation and property]. Wealth was not always the decisive factor of inclusion into the middle classes. Physicians, lawyers and university professors also belonged to the middle classes on the basis of their university degrees. It was a certain life style, education or self-employment that mattered. Cohen points out that while membership in voluntary associations theoretically depended only on individual merit, in reality these voluntary associations perpetuated the already existing social cleavages.[95] The voluntary associations in Pressburg reflected the existing social hierarchy as well. The middle class associations distanced themselves from the lower class and workers' associations.

This section describes the impact of Magyarisation on civic associations in Pressburg. I will first look at the ways in which traditionally German-speaking associations in the city adapted themselves to the demands of Magyarisation. I will also examine the rise of new Hungarian associations which were oriented towards the development of Hungarian culture and language in the city. The goal of these associations was the linguistic and cultural assimilation of non-Magyar inhabitants.

2.3.1. German "Pre-National" Associations·fl

Pressburg's German speakers did not publicly propagate the German character of their societies. Although they preserved the use of German within their own circles, they used Hungarian in communication with official agencies and in contacts with the public. This sub-section will give a few examples of how the German and Hungarian languages were used in these associations.

The *Liedertafel* (male choir) used German in its internal communications. After 1880, Hungarian also started to be used in public performances. During the 1880s almost half of the choir's repertoire became Hungarian. After the turn of the century, however, the proportion of Hungarian songs decreased and public performances followed the same pattern: the introduction was in Hungarian and the rest was in German. Posters announcing concerts were bilingual. The association's yearly reports were published in German except for a brief period around 1888 when they were published in Hungarian. However, when travelling abroad, the association styled itself as patriotically Hungarian, using the Hungarian name *Pozsonyi Dalárda*, Hungarian customs, a flag using the Hungarian colours, and the Hungarian and Pressburg shields of arms. The association stuck to its Hungarian and local patriotism even at a time when German and Austrian choirs were already overtly nationalistic. In celebrations, the members of the *Liedertafel* always toasted the fatherland in both languages.[97] The values of the association changed over time: in the 1850s and 1860s the association stood for the "power of the song, friendship and hospitality," while by the 1890s the association stood in the service of "patriotism and local-patriotism" and the "solidarity of the *bürgerlich* circles." By 1905 the association stressed "the importance of art 'as an international bond which unites educated people of all countries regardless of their language or religion.'"[98]

In 1882, the *Pressburger freiwillige Feuerwehr* (Voluntary Firemen Association of Pressburg) agreed to accept Hungarian as its language of command with enthusiastic calls of 'Éljen!' (Bravo!). However, German was still used in the internal life of the association, as can be seen by the primarily German content of the association's library. When representing the city and Hungary, like the *Liedertafel*, the *Feuerwehr* also used Hungarian and city symbols.[99]

The first sports club in Pressburg, the *Pozsonyi hajós egylet* (Rowing Club) was composed of aristocratic and wealthy bourgeois members. This club has been represented as Hungarian from its very inception. However, a description of a ceremonial dinner at this club indicates that when the 'better society' of the city met, it was more common to use German rather than Hungarian.[100] Also in the *Pressburger Casino* (City Casino), the main club where Pressburg's 'high society' met, German was frequently used even in the early twentieth century.[101] The *Frauenverein* (Women's Association) which had aristocratic and bourgeois membership also probably used the German language. Its statutes were printed in German, although together with an obligatory Hungarian version. Baroness Jeszenák, the patroness of the association in 1879, "found it fitting that the state language would find an appropriate introduction into the institutions" founded by the association and hired a teacher of the Hungarian language for that purpose.[102]

The freemason lodge *Verschwiegenheit* (Secrecy) was German-speaking from its inception in 1869. In the 1880s, the records of the lodge were kept in Hungarian. However, at the request of its members, most of whom had German mother tongue, the lodge returned to German. The lodge was often accused of Germanomania (*Deutschtümelei*) and of being pan-German (*alldeutsch*), although its members voiced their loyalty to the Hungarian fatherland. In 1902, some of its Hungarian members left and founded the Hungarian lodge *Testvériség* (Brotherhood). This was the only example between 1867 and 1914 of such a split within a city association. However, Hungarian and German freemasons continued to cooperate and in 1913 they jointly sanctified the newly built freemason temple.[103] Although *Verschwiegenheit* supported the development of German culture in town (which might have caused a serious clash with such members as Gábor Pávai Vajna, a Magyar chauvinist whose role in city life is described in greater detail in the next part), at the same time the lodge was also one of the founding members of the *Pozsonyi közművelődési egyesület* (educational society for the development of Hungarian language and culture) in 1883.[104] *Verschwiegenheit* had very close contacts with Vienna since many Viennese freemasons had their lodges in Pressburg (as freemasonry was banned in Austria).[105]

However, there were also occasional exceptions to the transition from German to Hungarian. The *Natur und Heilkunde Verein* was founded in 1851 by Austrian professors and scientists. The use of the Hungarian language use was only allowed after 1861. After 1867 many German professors left for Austria, and Hungarian became prevalent in the association's activities, primarily in the medicine section of the association in the 1890s. However, when one of the founding members Andreas Kornhuber came back to Pressburg in 1898, German began to be used in the association's meetings again.[106]

These examples illustrate the ways in which Germans adapted to Magyarisation. Traditionally German-speaking associations retained German in their internal communications while adopting Hungarian for outer public use. On public occasions and when outside Hungary, these associations presented themselves as Hungarian patriots, using state symbols and the city's shield of arms. One cannot conclude from this, however, that the associations were fully Magyarised. Rather, they became more bilingual, albeit still with German predominance. This bilinguality is a feature of the "Hungarus" type of German identity defined in the first part of this chapter.

2.3.2. Magyar Associations

While the traditional city associations played down their German character, Pressburg's Hungarians created their own overtly national associations. As opposed to the non-ethnic character of the "pre-national" German associations, these new associations explicitly propagated Magyarisation and the primacy of the Magyar culture of the ruling state-nation.[107] However, at the same time these associations welcomed members from different ethnic backgrounds. Among these associations were *Nemzeti kör* (National association) founded in 1861—later *Nemzeti kaszínó* (National casino) in 1871, *Pozsonyi Toldy Kör* founded in 1874, *Széchényi kör* (1876), *Magyar kör* (1877), the *Magyar közművelődési egyesület* (Hungarian educational association) (1883) and *Magyar dalárda* (Hungarian choir) founded in 1885.[108] Although these associations were ethnically defined, many of their Magyar members were also members of the traditional associations dominated by Germans and used the German language when in 'high society.'[109]

The membership of these associations was mostly drawn from the new Magyar middle class (professionals, officials, teachers and professors) who entered into a struggle with the traditional German middle class for power in the city. Since much of the city's political life was played out in these associations, and many decisions about municipal affairs were taken here, these associations acted as an important instrument for the new Magyar elite in their fight for power. In its struggle for local power, the Magyar elite's rhetoric derived legitimacy from the demands of the nationalising Hungarian state. The discrepancy between the pronounced aims and rhetoric of the associations and the activity of some of their members, taken in conjunction with the disinterest of the majority of the membership in active participation in the life of these associations, suggests that these associations were used instrumentally by a narrow elite fighting for positions of power in city life. (This point will become more clear in the struggle for control over the City Theatre described in the next part of this chapter.) This issue is also considered in the next section which is a detailed examination of one of the most active new Hungarian associations, the *Toldy Kör*.

2.4. MAGYARISATION OF SOCIAL AND CULTURAL LIFE: TOLDY KÖR

The *Toldy Kör* (Toldy association) was founded in 1874 with the basic goal of promoting Hungarian culture and language in order to amalgamate the other nationalities into one Hungarian state-nation, especially by 'magyarising' urban populations. Public education was the primary field of *Toldy Kör* activities. As one of the founders of *Toldy Kör*, Sándor Vutkovich, noted, "public education is the most important shield in guarding the state creation and in maintaining supremacy."[110] The main areas of "Magyarisation work" in which *Toldy Kör* developed initiatives were: courses in Hungarian language, public lectures, efforts for the consolidation of the Hungarian theatre in Pressburg, collecting money for erecting national monuments, laying down memorial tablets, celebration of events of national importance, and inviting prominent Hungarian cultural and political personalities to the city. In 1888 a choir of nineteen men (called *Dalárda*) was also established to sing at special events.[111] This section discusses the aims and activities of the *Toldy Kör* as a case study showing the complex intertwining of Magyarisation processes and the struggle for power between the new Magyar and traditional city elites.

2.4.1. Founding of Toldy Kör and the city environment

The *Toldy Kör* was founded in 1874 in an environment lacking enthusiasm for nationalist activity. Fearful of provoking strife between the nationalities, *Pressburgers* were initially reluctant to join the new association. Through the subsequent decades, the founders of *Toldy Kör* retained a sense of being an embattled minority struggling to assert Hungarian culture in a sea of indifference. The following pages describe the founding moment of the association and the change in the city atmosphere as perceived by the *Toldy Kör* leaders. I will also identify some important rhetorical themes which persisted in *Toldy Kör* discussions.

The idea of founding *Toldy Kör* was first raised at festivities held in Pressburg in 1871 celebrating the noted Hungarian writer Ferenc Toldy's fiftieth anniversary as a writer. Two years later, in 1873, Sándor Vutkovich and Ferenc Nirschy started a Hungarian weekly *Pozsonyvidéki Lapok* which offered space for propagation and preparation of *Toldy Kör*.[112] The organisation's first meeting took place in 1874.[113] Like other associations of the period, from its inception, *Toldy Kör* had rules and statutes governing every aspect of the organisation, from admission regulations to management structures as laid down by law.[114] However, the association had to wait several months before it could gather the required number of members in order to begin functioning.[115] The founders of *Toldy Kör* repeatedly expressed their frustration at an environment which seemed at best indifferent. Noting the mistrust of *Pressburgers* towards any nationally-oriented association, Emil Kumlik describes the member-registration process in the restaurant *Zöld-fa*: "Though some of the people present thought that what is mentioned here was to be the start of a nationalities' struggle, and for this reason they left the room during the main county notary Jozsef Schott's enthusiastic speech; still quite a lot of people registered as *Toldy Kör* members."[116] Kumlik also refers to "difficult conditions" for establishing the association in the city at a time when no Hungarian newspaper had even been published until Vutkovich, a newcomer to the city, founded the *Pozsonyvidéki Lapok*.[117]

Throughout the whole period 1874–1914 these difficult beginnings were mentioned by different members of the association, especially by the chairmen of *Toldy Kör* in their opening speeches to the society's annual general assembly. In 1874, Sándor Vutkovich said that the Hungarian community in Pressburg and the surrounding area was still "in children's shoes."[118] Count István Eszterházy spoke of the danger faced by Hungarian culture in Pressburg from the majority German population and about spreading "Germanisation" on the borders of the homeland against which the city served as a "defensive bastion."[119] In 1879, chairman László Orosz spoke about the bad will and enemies which the association's founders had to fight.[120] In 1900, chairman Kálmán Thály stated that "deep-rooted Magyars" were still a minority in Pressburg. However, he remembered the 1850s when he had come to Pressburg as a child to learn German and could hardly hear a Hungarian word. According to Thály, by the 1860s the picture had become rosier but the German character of the city still prevailed since Pressburg was no better than a suburb of Vienna. Then the year 1867 "filled the people with joy" and Thály would repeat the heroic story of *Toldy Kör*'s founding.[121] In 1907, one of the most active members of *Toldy Kör*, Gabor Pávai Vajna (1851–1913, physician and later the director of the Hungarian royal state hospital) went even further by claiming that at the time of the founding of the association by Vutkovich "it was hardly permitted to speak Hungarian in Pozsony."[122] Curiously enough, in 1904 the same Pávai Vajna had declared that *Toldy Kör* was accepted with outstretched arms by the city's inhabitants when it was founded in 1874, since Pressburg was a "desert" as a Hungarian city, although through no fault of its inhabitants, who were patriots in their hearts.[123]

Toldy Kör was quite often compared to an oasis in the middle of the desert. In 1879, describing the success of the Károly Kisfaludy celebration, *Pozsonyvidéki Lapok* used this poetic comparison: "These efforts in a German city resemble those green oasis seeds which from time to time the wind carries away into the desert and these seeds sometimes spring up and a new oasis is created."[124] Complaints about the hostile atmosphere became rarer later, and in 1891 Vutkovich noted a more kindly disposition in the city towards *Toldy Kör*. He compared Magyardom to a young and muscular youth preparing for a leap and said that its sickly childhood had been left behind.[125] However, representatives of *Toldy Kör* continued periodically to accuse the city's inhabitants of mistrust and bad will. Special attention was paid to the lack of press 'objectivity' regarding the *Toldy Kör*. For example, the association complained vociferously that its activities on behalf of the Hungarian theatre had been completely misinterpreted by the local German press (*Pressburger Zeitung* and *Westungarischer Grenzbote*).[126] In fairness, however, *Toldy Kör* did not forget to highlight 'objective' reporting on other occasions and to express its gratitude to the local press.[127]

Apart from complaining about the hostile outside environment, the chairmen and leading members of *Toldy Kör* often complained about their own members' lack of interest in the association's activities. While it was only a matter of time before other ethnic groups became convinced about the supremacy of Magyar culture, ignorance on the part of Magyars and especially members of *Toldy Kör* was unpardonable and was setting a bad example for other nationalities. These complaints were repeated in 1882, 1884, and 1886 by the chairmen or standing committee members. When discussing how to make public lectures more appealing, Pávai Vajna remarked that it was high time to do something since "at present *Toldy Kör* could dance on its head and it would not attract any attention" from the public.[128] This problem will be discussed in more detail later in this section when describing the membership of *Toldy Kör*.

Pressburg in the 1870s was not a particularly welcoming environment for the establishment of a nationalist association like *Toldy Kör*. The city was ruled by German-speaking burghers who held municipal offices, and dominated economic, cultural and social life. The *Bürgertum* did not surrender their predominance easily. However, in the 1880s and especially towards the turn of the century, Magyarisation had forced Germans to adopt an attitude of Hungarian patriotism, and as the Hungarian language gained ground in municipal administration, culture and education, the activities of *Toldy Kör* also made headway. The next sub-section considers the interlocking relation between *Toldy Kör* and Pressburg's municipal and intellectual elite.

2.4.2. Membership of Toldy Kör: Merging with the Municipal Elite

Relations between the *Toldy Kör* and Pressburg's municipal elite grew closer over time as Magyarisation progressed. This closeness was decisive in shaping the outcomes of many struggles over the city's Hungarian character. While central government policies and *Toldy Kör* goals closely coincided from the very outset, the municipal elite's composition and outlook grew closer to that of the *Toldy Kör* over time.

The membership of *Toldy Kör* was mostly drawn from the middle and upper classes of the city and county.[129] The association's leaders put great weight on the participation of the aristocracy.[130] In addition, the admission into *Toldy Kör* of forty-six *honvéd* ("defenders of the fatherland": i.e., territorial soldiers), of "this distinguished class," aroused great excitement and approval among the local intelligentsia.[131] In 1901, many law students entered *Toldy Kör* as well.[132] The association stressed its cross-class networking function: "In the Kör's halls, at the Kör's parties, the aristocracy, Hungarian gentry, the military class and the bourgeois class often appeared as a homogeneous body."[133]

However, it is evident from the organisation's financial difficulties and the constant complaints of the standing committee members that being a member of *Toldy Kör* did not necessarily entail identification with the association's aims and ideas. For instance, the Slovak attorney Michal Mudroň was notorious in the city as the defender of representatives of the Slovak national movement in press lawsuits and was considered an "agitator of nationalities" by many Hungarian patriots.[134] Yet Mudroň was also a member of *Toldy Kör* in 1875.[135] An examination of participation in *Toldy Kör* activities by important public personalities shows that membership in the association (or other Hungarian patriotic organisations) was often instrumental as a precondition for a successful career. The membership of *Toldy Kör* included a high proportion of state employees and county and municipal officials—35.4% in 1879 and 36.3% in 1896. Conversely, these members increased *Toldy Kör*'s chances of influencing municipal politics. As one *Toldy Kör* chairman pointed out, if *Toldy Kör* managed to win over the most important personages of the city, then Magyarisation of public life would happen almost automatically.[136]

The association was treated with respect by almost all of Pressburg's mayors between 1873 to 1914.[137] Pressburg's mayors participated in many *Toldy Kör* events. In 1880, mayor Moritz Gottl took part in the Károly Kisfaludy celebration organised by *Toldy Kör*.[138] At the most important *Toldy Kör* event of 1883, the visit of *Petőfi Társaság* (Petőfi society) from Budapest, mayor Karl Mergl welcomed the society in the name of the city at a banquet given in honour of the distinguished visitors.[139] It is not known whether Mergl was a member of *Toldy Kör*. However, the next mayor, Gustav Dröxler, was a prominent member of *Toldy Kör*.[140] When Dröxler was elected mayor of Pressburg in 1889, a delegation from *Toldy Kör* visited him to offer congratulations. Dröxler responded with a short speech in which he observed that the city was standing on the threshold of national transformation and promised as mayor to fulfil his patriotic duty and help *Toldy Kör* in every way.[141] The next mayor, Paul Taller, was also a member of *Toldy Kör*, but died after only one year in office.[142] As a deputy mayor (1890–98), Taller had taken part in the event organised in 1890 by *Toldy Kör* and the municipality for the building of the Izabella orphanage.[143] Taller was succeeded by Theodor Brolly who served as mayor from 1900 until 1917.[144] Brolly and his wife had both been active members of *Toldy Kör* since the association's inception in 1874.[145] In 1890–92, Brolly was one of the deputy chairmen of *Toldy Kör*.[146] He was also an active member of the association's standing and special committees.[147] When Brolly was elected mayor after Taller's death, he promised to support the efforts of *Toldy Kör* in every way.[148] At a celebration of the association's thirtieth anniversary in 1904, Brolly made a speech in which he stressed that he had always been led by patriotic duty and he toasted the ideals of *Toldy Kör*.[149]

It is not clear whether the close connections of Pressburg's mayors with *Toldy Kör* had any real practical impact on municipal affairs. Although the mayors expressed their patriotism and support for *Toldy Kör*, when it came to matters like stabilising the Hungarian theatre, the mayors' membership in *Toldy Kör* (or for that matter the presence of around forty *Toldy Kör* members in the municipal committee) did not seem to have much influence on the outcome. It is hard to say that this was the result of active duplicity on the part of these *Toldy Kör* members. Certainly matters changed during the mayoral tenure of Theodor Brolly.[150] Under Brolly's rule the city became increasingly Magyarised and the municipal committee's resistance waned. However, it could also be argued that the shift in power had been happening on a large scale slowly over the whole period and that it were merely the results of this process which became visible during Brolly's tenure as mayor.

Even so, the participation of the city's elites in the activities of the *Toldy Kör* exercised a pervasive effect on municipal politics. Many members of the municipal assembly and municipal administration were also simultaneously members of *Toldy Kör* as well as of other associations. Most leading intellectuals were also members of *Toldy Kör*, including almost all the directors of educational institutions in Pressburg, many teachers, and also some journalists.[151] Most of the active *Toldy Kör* members were also members of the City Casino which included the city and county elites.[152] Membership of all the city societies was interconnected; the same elite participated in the structure and hierarchy of many societies, sometimes even as members of societies with seemingly different agendas and concerns.[153] Mannová is probably right to argue that the "integration of city officers and city office holders in the network of voluntary associations caused the distinction between the societies and the "city" to gradually be erased."[154] Municipal politics was shaped in the social life and committee meetings of influential societies like *Toldy Kör* whose members formed a large cohesive sociable elite. These connections between *Toldy Kör* and the city's municipal, intellectual, and opinion-forming elites suggest that *Toldy Kör* was able to press for more Magyar-friendly treatment in municipal politics.

The next few pages review *Toldy Kör*'s relation to other ethnic groups as expressed in speeches of its members as well as in their nationalist rhetoric.

2.4.3. Toldy Kör's *Relation to Other Ethnic Groups*

Patriotic rhetoric was used by the leaders of *Toldy Kör* in their struggle for power in the city. The association proclaimed tolerance of other cultures while also foreseeing the prospect of a 'nationalities fight.' *Toldy Kör* saw itself as having a special mission as a bastion of Magyardom in this ethnically mixed part of Hungary. In order to fulfil this mission the association's leaders believed that strong patriotism and even chauvinism were required.

2.4.3.1. *Germans: The Main Target*

Germans were the strongest and most influential ethnic group in the city when *Toldy Kör* was founded in 1874. As a result, *Toldy Kör* often referred to Germans and the danger of ceaselessly spreading Germanisation when justifying its existence.[155] On the other hand, the organisation's founder, Sándor Vutkovich also boasted in 1891 that *Toldy Kör* had always been a gentleman-like opponent of Germanism.[156] The aim of *Toldy Kör* was to make Germans into good Hungarian patriots not only in their "good Hungarian feeling" but also by language.[157] However, linguistic Magyarisation did not progress fast enough to satisfy *Toldy Kör*. In 1889, Vutkovich pointed out that according to the last census there were still 18,735 inhabitants of the city who spoke only German.[158] For Vutkovich, this meant that the Magyarisation efforts of *Toldy Kör* must get stronger. In 1898, Kálmán Thály also described the German inhabitants of the city as having become "stiff" and "narrow-minded" out of habit:

> In sharp contrast to this accepting and receptive inclination of the Magyar people is the rigid shutting in of the German population. This is the unfortunate consequence of the immigration politics of Saint Stephan whose main idea was that a unilingual country is fragile and vacillating. To this politics can be attributed the present state of Pozsony because the German citizens as a spoilt child defended their ancestors' language through centuries and in those times of need they did not consider it necessary to learn the language of the nation.[159]

Thály stressed that this German insistence on their "old habits" was selfish since it regarded only their own comfort and disregarded the change of the environment created by the idea of the Hungarian state. He said that thirty years had passed since 1867 and the new generation of Germans could not justify not knowing the Hungarian language. Loyalty, as understood in the right way, demanded that Pressburg be Magyar.[160]

According to *Toldy Kör* ideology, while Germans had the right to develop their own culture, it was still desirable that they should become patriotic Hungarians, especially in their adoption of the Hungarian language. The real test of *Toldy Kör's* tolerance came in 1909 when it joined the movement against German schools in Budapest at the request of the shrill Hungarian-nationalist journalist Jenő Rákosi.[161] A similar ambivalence was noticeable in regard to other nationalities as well.

2.4.3.2. Relationship to Other Nationalities

Toldy Kör's nationalist discourse was two-sided. On the one hand, *Toldy Kör* stressed the need to achieve understandings with other nationalities; yet, on the other hand, it also talked about a 'fight' of nationalities in which *Toldy Kör* and Magyars were involved, in which they were fighting for their very existence.[162] *Toldy Kör* chairman Orosz denied that the aim of the association was to push out other languages, pointing to the presence of books in languages other than Hungarian in the association's library.[163] In 1885

Canon Antal Pór stressed that *Toldy Kör* distanced itself from any kind of political, ethnic or religious hatred, claiming that its only aim was "fostering and developing the Hungarian national spirit, the Hungarian state idea, and Hungarian national public education."[164] In 1901, undoubtedly influenced by Social Darwinism, chairman Kálmán Thály declared that the new century would be profoundly shaped by the struggle of languages for hegemony. It was, therefore, important for *Toldy Kör* to sink deep roots of national ideas in the soil of Pressburg.[165] Thus *Toldy Kör* claimed to respect the right of other nationalities to their own language and culture while seeking to promote Hungarian language and culture to such an extent that no space was left for any other languages or cultures.

The embedded conflict inherent in *Toldy Kör*'s position becomes most evident when the association's leaders discussed the position of *Toldy Kör* in Pressburg. The peaceful picture of ethnic co-existence disappears, and the rhetoric turns gloomy or fierce. Pressburg is seen as a desert where "for the Magyar nationality there does not grow a single blade of green grass." Some pessimists did not believe that the fight in Pressburg could possibly end in a Magyar victory.[166] However, the same sense of embattlement could also lead to more fiery sentiments. Lying at the very western border of Upper Hungary (*Felvidék*), Pressburg was seen as a strategic location for the Magyar nation. *Toldy Kör* chairman Viktor Kramolin wanted Pressburg to be "the hearth of Magyar life" and "the place of assimilation of all the other [languages] speaking elements of goodwill."[167] Pressburg was particularly important because it was reached by many "nationality streams."[168] The city, then, was a bulwark against other encroaching nationalities, especially the Germans and Slavs; and the *Toldy Kör* leaders saw themselves as an embattled and valiant garrison fighting for Hungary.

In 1903, Thály talked about the growing indifference towards Magyar national feeling and about "hundreds" of Serb and Pan-Slav agitators supported from abroad (i.e. Russia) who were pushing forward in Hungary. According to Thály, the 1868 Nationalities' law had given too many liberties to the nationalities, rights that were not enjoyed by minorities in any other country besides Switzerland. The Slavs (from the North) were pushing more and more into the South and this had to be prevented.[169] In 1907, on the anniversary of 15 March (commemorating the 1848 revolution), Pávai Vajna noted that the celebration was taking place every year in an ever narrower circle of people, while the other nationalities did not miss any opportunity to express their love for their own "race."[170]

The *Toldy Kör* attitude towards the other nationalities was on the whole ambivalent. Although *Toldy Kör* expressed tolerant views at times, it also wished for an assimilation of minorities which it regarded as positive given the superiority of Magyar culture. Culture and education were the main battlefields for *Toldy Kör*, who realised, as did the central Hungarian government, the importance of these areas in the process of Magyarisation. Indeed, the association often even claimed to be carrying out the government's policies. The next few pages consider the association's activities in these areas.

2.5. Main Areas and Means of Magyarising Pressburg

Toldy Kör's activities were centred around "social, literary and artistic propaganda."[171] The association was determined to ensure a thorough Magyarisation of public and cultural life in the city.[172] *Toldy Kör* founder Sándor Vutkovich stressed that "the strongest shield" securing the supremacy of the state-nation was public education.[173] He also repeated on many occasions that it was "not politics but public education [which] is the capital of a nation and the main factor is literature which is the thermometer of its inner value.... The strength of a nation does not depend on its numerical strength but on the number of its intelligentsia." While science is international, "every race expresses its individuality in a different way so it grasps science from a general point of view but at the same time uses it in the interest of its homeland."[174] For Vutkovich, Magyarisation began with kindergarten. He believed that this early socialisation was already taking place: German burghers were hiring Hungarian nannies and putting their children into Hungarian kindergartens and so "the next generation will already be Hungarian."[175]

The main means for building the Hungarian national state were "Hungarian church, Hungarian school and Hungarian theatre," according to Vilmos Unghváry, the head of *Toldy Kör's* theatre committee. While only children learned Hungarian in the schools, Hungarian theatre performances also influenced adults.[176] *Toldy Kör* leaders also saw an increasing role for patriotic Hungarian journalism, especially in Pressburg where in 1895 there were three German newspapers but only one published in Hungarian. The *Toldy Kör* leaders were particularly concerned with securing the widest possible dissemination of Hungarian newspapers to the crucial target audience of school teachers in order to Magyarise these educators.[177] Despite their periodic outbursts of gloom and frustration at the indifference they faced in Pressburg, the *Toldy Kör* leaders were also convinced that even members of other nationalities could become true Hungarian patriots, if given the chance. In order to achieve this goal, ethnic chauvinism was justified, especially since Hungary was surrounded by alien masses. Magyar chauvinism was not as coldly exclusive as the chauvinism of other people (such as the Germanising rule of absolutist Habsburg monarchs like Joseph II).[178]

In many of their speeches the *Toldy Kör* leaders condemned the preference of the Hungarian public for "idegen" (foreign, alien) as opposed to "hazai" (domestic, "our own"). This preference ranged from foreign spas to foreign universities.[179] In 1903, Thály regretted that Hungarian youth did not consider ethnic chauvinism "elegant." Thály also deplored the aristocracy's lack of knowledge of their own (Hungarian) language.(Chapter four also considers this censure of the aristocracy's use of German rather than Hungarian.) The opposition between the "foreign" versus the "domestic" was also connected in *Toldy Kör* rhetoric with a strong concern for the purity of Magyar thought and language. Chairman Rényi expressed the need to safeguard the purity of the Hungarian language and to prevent it from becoming "contaminated" by the increasing use of Germanisms and the seductive influence of Western thought. The unity of the Hungarian people was of utmost importance in order to "preserve the treasure inherited from fathers—the nationality and the language." This guardianship was the *raison d'etre* of *Toldy Kör*, according to Rényi: especially in this border region where Magyars were surrounded by other nationalities it was imperative to preserve the "genius of the Hungarian language."[180] While *Toldy Kör* speakers were concerned with the protection of Hungarian culture and literature from foreign influences, they also desired the assimilation of other nationalities into the Hungarian nation. Patriotism and chauvinism were necessary for the "creation of the Hungarian empire with 30 million Magyars," as Pávai Vajna put it in 1904. He sought the blessing of "the God of Magyars" on this noble undertaking.[181]

2.5.1. Conclusion

This section has described the challenge posed by *Toldy Kör* and other similar organisations. The earlier multi-ethnic civic discourse (represented by the "pre-nationally" minded German associations) was contested by single-culture nationally-minded organisations like *Toldy Kör*. The association existed in a public space where the state and society intersected. Nationalism, as the fusion of state and culture, exists and is propagated in precisely this dual public space, the nexus of institutions and individuals, governments and societies. *Toldy Kör*, then, represented a key element in the increasing nationalisation of public life in Pressburg, the replacement of the earlier multi-ethnic discourse of hierarchical coexistence by a new nationalist discourse emphasising the hegemony of one culture, the culture of the ruling state-nation.

2.6. STRUGGLE FOR THE LOOK OF THE CITY

The rising Magyar elite's struggle for power in Pressburg extended into a concern for the physical appearance of the city. Associations like *Toldy Kör* wanted the city to physically reflect the reality of being a part of Hungary. This led to an intersection of interests with another city association, the *Stadtverschönerungsverein*. The two organisations differed in important ways in their approaches towards this issue.

The interests of the Magyar elite in altering the physical appearance of the city overlapped in some areas with the activities of the *Stadtver-schönerungsverein* (City enhancement society), founded in 1867. This association included all the prominent people in the city, as well as some aristocrats and municipal employees. The *Stadtverschönerungsverein* was first of all concerned with making the city look respectable, so that it reflected the values of the middle class and presented a good moral example for its inhabitants. (Chapter five describes the activities and goals of this organisation in greater detail.) Since the Magyar elite was mostly middle class too, its interests were similar to that of the *Stadtverschönerungsverein* in this regard. However, while ethnicity was not a consideration in *Stadtver-schönerungsverein* membership and activities, it was the most important criteria for *Toldy Kör* members. Unlike the *Stadtverschönerungsverein*, *Toldy Kör* was first and foremost interested in imprinting a Hungarian character upon the city. This interest found its expression in three forms: putting up commemorative tablets and statues, changing the shop signs and advertisements, and in naming and re-naming the streets of the city. *Toldy Kör* saw ceremonial occasions such as the unveiling ceremony of a statue of a Hungarian poet or writer as opportunities to rewrite the past of Pressburg and to re-define it as Hungarian Pozsony.

Putting up commemorative tablets on houses where prominent Hungarian patriots used to live was one way to remind inhabitants and visitors of the great Hungarian past of this city. *Toldy Kör* chairman Thály noted that there were commemorative tablets of Goethe and Schiller everywhere in Germany while in Hungary such tablets commemorating their own national heroes were altogether missing. In Hungary, such tablets were even more necessary since the Hungarian nation was numerically smaller and thus "the patriotic feeling must be more intense."[182] If Hungary were as a big nation as England or Germany, it could afford to neglect its speech but given the smallness of the Hungarian nation it could not give up its language.[183] The sense of competition for survival with other nations was very strong among the nationalist *Toldy Kör* members. They felt that they had to struggle for a homogeneous nation-state more fervently than the other nations which were already large both in size and territory, like the French or the English. These *Toldy Kör* members were undoubtedly influenced by social Darwinism.

Similarly, *Toldy Kör* was concerned with Hungarian-language signs in the city, including shop signs and inscriptions as well as commercial advertisements. In 1887, *Toldy Kör* even created a special committee whose task was to help craftsmen and shopkeepers with the translation of their signs and advertisements into proper Hungarian.[184] In 1889, at the suggestion of Vutkovich, *Toldy Kör* appealed to craftsmen and shopkeepers to use the Hungarian language when communicating with the public.[185] The success of these endeavours is unknown. However, in 1901 *Toldy Kör* again created a committee with the task of translating the names of firms, firm signs as well as their circulars since these were full of mistakes.[186] This shows that Pressburg's Magyarisers paid attention even to the details of the city's everyday physical appearance as well. Conversely, the fact that many signs and circulars were full of language mistakes even in 1901 indicates that *Pressburgers* either had an insufficient knowledge of Hungarian or refused to worry too much about this issue.[187]

Toldy Kör's city-shaping efforts were not restricted to putting up statues and laying down memorial stones. The association also initiated efforts to rewrite history by changing street names.[188] In 1880 *Kecske utca* (She-goat street) was changed to *Kisfaludy Károly utca* at the initiative of one of the most active members of *Toldy Kör*, the historian Mór Pisztóry.[189] In 1905 one of the main streets of the old centre, *Hosszú utca* (Long street) was changed to *Szilágyi Dezső utca* (honouring a minister of justice who was an honorary citizen of Pressburg) at the initiative of Pávai Vajna who was also a member of the municipal assembly.[190]

Even before the law of 1898 requiring Hungarian names in communities, the Pressburg municipal assembly had re-named some streets after prominent Hungarian cultural and political personalities.[191] The practice of the parallel naming of streets in German and Hungarian was begun in 1880.[192] The German speaking members of the municipal assembly do not seem to have objected to Hungarian street names, nor to the installation of various memorial tablets. Indeed, the traditional city elite eagerly participated in these ceremonies as a way to reclaim prominence for Pressburg, now that it no longer had the status of being the capital of Hungary.[193] One of the favourite activities of the municipal assembly was declaring prominent Hungarian personalities honorary citizens of Pressburg. For example Count Albert Ápponyi became an honorary citizen of Pressburg for all he had done for the "cultural interests" of the city and his "material as well as moral support of our patriotic mission here on the state border."[194]

Insofar as such Hungarian patriotic activities were restricted to such superficial concerns as the look of the city, there was no resistance from the traditional city elite. However, when in 1903 the language used in the municipal assembly itself came under discussion (as described above in the section on Magyarisation in municipal life), or in the matter of the City Theatre, issues surrounding Hungarian identity and language proved very sensitive. Furthermore, ordinary inhabitants like the small shopkeepers did not show even the same amount of Hungarian enthusiasm as the municipal elite but just the opposite: a remarkable ignorance of the efforts to implant correct Hungarian in their shop signs.

All the ceremonies mentioned above were organised in order to promote Hungarian culture and language and to bring them closer to the inhabitants of Pressburg in order to remind them that they lived on Hungarian territory. By placing memorial tablets and statues in the city, *Toldy Kör* was actively participating in creating the look of the city. Juxtaposing these little memorial plaques along with Hungarian translations of shop signs gives an image of a city of contesting signs.[195] In this way the city was the location of contradictory signs and social messages which expressed the contradictory identities present in the shared space. The very fact that Hungarian signs were grammatically incorrect even a generation after Magyarisation had begun indicates the persistence of local identity. Culture and power form a complex network of interactions that change in time, and the relation of Hungarian organisations like *Toldy Kör* vis-a-vis the older German elite (whose dominance they were contesting in myriad ways) illustrates the complex multi-dimensional character of this process. The next part of this chapter will look more closely at one very specific strand of the process of cultural politics determining identity in the city during this period: the long and determined effort on the part of *Toldy Kör* to consolidate the position of Hungarian theatre.

3. CHALLENGE TO THE GERMAN POWER HOLDERS IN THE CITY: THE CASE OF THE PRESBURGER CITY THEATRE

From its inception in 1874, *Toldy Kör* saw the consolidation of the Hungarian theatre in Pressburg as one of its principal objectives.[196] Along with schools and churches, the theatre was one of the most important public spaces laden with tactical and symbolic meaning for *Toldy Kör*'s program of spreading Hungarian national culture. From 1874 until the First World War, the association waged a campaign to consolidate the Hungarian theatre in Pressburg. The principal obstacles were the initial reluctance of the city authorities, the traditional predominance of the German theatre, and the lack of widespread public interest in Hungarian performances. *Toldy Kör*'s campaign on behalf of the Hungarian theatre struggled against these obstacles and against dissension within its own ranks. By 1911, however, the association could claim victory in its efforts to secure a permanent position for the Hungarian theatre in Pressburg. A detailed examination of *Toldy Kör*'s campaign on behalf of the Hungarian theatre shows the gradual and complicated nature of political action and propaganda in the nationalist discourse, revealing the complex textured intertwining relations of culture and power in the struggle to shape the identity of Pressburg as a city and the identity of its inhabitants.

German and Hungarian speaking strolling players troupes had struggled intermittently throughout the nineteenth century. The German theatre ensembles were dominant in the Pressburg theatre and also in the Slovak countryside. However, they were being pushed out by the Hungarian ensembles. In the last third of the nineteenth century the goal of cultural Magyarisation was key in securing the Hungarian state theatre organisational structure and a state grant.[197] The Hungarian theatre was continuously gaining ground in Hungary and in the period 1867–1918 only Pressburg managed to keep its German theatre.[198] However, the Pressburg theatre was also hotly contested by the new Hungarian middle classes in Pressburg.

In 1874, at the time when *Toldy Kör* was founded, most of the theatre season belonged to the German ensemble which was resident in Pressburg while the Hungarian ensemble was merely a guest ensemble performing for only a couple of months in spring and summer.[199] Regular attempts by the government authorities in Budapest to promote Hungarian performances usually failed because of the city inhabitants' insufficient knowledge of Hungarian. In 1868, *Pressburgers* even protested against attempts to offer regular theatre performances in Hungarian.[200] Theatre and culture at this time were clearly dominated by German-speakers.

Toldy Kör was not slow to express its dislike for this situation. After one Hungarian performance in 1874, *Pozsonyvidéki Lapok* (edited by *Toldy Kör* member Vutkovich) wrote: "But we admit that we were not able to plunge with all our soul into the principles presenting themselves: at each minute the question appears before us why must the Magyar muse *play as a guest* in one of the most renowned royal towns of *Hungary*?"[201] The previous spring, in 1873, together with the Hungarian theatre director Antal Bokódy and the actor Zádor, Vutkovich had gone to Pressburg mayor Heinrich Justi with the request that the Hungarian director should not have to pay the "blood-tax" (900 forints) to the German theatre director for each performance by the Hungarian troupe. The mayor received the delegation in a "very unfriendly and rather rude manner." Condescendingly, he explained to Dr. Vutkovich "who moved to Pozsony only a few years ago" that "the Hungarian director can under no conditions demand the use of the town theatre, at the most he can ask for it as a *favour* and he should be glad if for even a high rent he gets permission to play at all."[202] This impolite answer clearly indicates the balance of power in the city in the 1870s when a mayor could still afford to display such behaviour towards the Hungarian theatre director, given the importance ascribed to theatre by the Magyarisation policies of the Hungarian state.[203]

In 1878, the *Toldy Kör* standing committee decided to establish a joint *Magyar színi bizottság* (Magyar theatrical committee) with the City Casino.[204] This committee was tasked with visiting Pressburg families to ask them for material help and to urge attendance at Hungarian performances. György Fésűs (a lawyer and an active member of *Toldy Kör*) said that the Hungarian ensemble was in constant deficit and proposed to raise funds so that the Hungarian actors had something to live on while in the city. Such fund raising was repeated in later years as well. The Hungarian newspapers blamed the city's inhabitants for the failure of the Hungarian theatre. *Pozsonyvidéki Lapok* wrote that the German local press often attacked the Hungarian performances, and that, despite having the theatre now for free, the Hungarian theatre had the worst part of the season (spring and summer) when everyone preferred to be outside since the theatre was too hot.[205]

Toldy Kör developed a whole range of activities, in order to stabilise a Hungarian ensemble in the city. Before the end of the contract with the German theatre directors, the association sent delegation to the mayor with its proposals. Of course the mayors always promised their full support to the Hungarian culture and the development of city's culture in a patriotic direction. However, until 1899, the municipal Theatre Committee always decided to rent out the theatre to the German theatre director.[206] In 1890, on the basis of Count József Zichy's proposal, an Association for the Support of the Hungarian Theatre (*Magyar szinpártoló egyesület*) was established. Zichy felt it necessary that the Hungarian ensemble should function independently of the German one.[207] *Toldy Kör* financially supported this association.[208]

Meanwhile, construction was underway of a new theatre building in Pressburg. After the disastrous fire of the *Ringtheater* in Vienna in December 1881, the old theatre building in Pressburg had been torn down.[209] The well known architects Fellner and Helmer had designed a new building which was opened in 1886. The new theatre opened with a performance by the National Theatre and Magyar Royal Opera of the Hungarian opera "Ban Bánk" and with the dramatic prologue "Lidércfény" (Will-o'-the-wisp) written by Mór Jókai who was also present.[210] As Portisch remarks, "the inauguration [of the new theatre] was to show that Pressburg lay in Hungary where Hungarian was the state language."[211]

In the 1890s, an active members of *Toldy Kör*, Vilmos Unghváry, proposed a range of measures in support of the Hungarian theatre, including buying tickets at a bargain price and distributing them to *Toldy Kör* members, poor teachers and good pupils; inviting the Hungarian actors to the association's chambers; and setting up a special *Toldy Kör* committee for the consolidation of the Hungarian theatre (of which Unghváry was appointed head).[212] Perhaps as a result of this initiative, the issue of the theatre was constantly on *Toldy Kör*'s agenda in 1895.[213] Unghváry said that the theatre was one of the most effective means of Magyarisation since "everybody was convinced that to whom belongs the school and theatre in Pozsony, belongs the future!" The Magyar church, Magyar school and Magyar theatre were the most important means of Magyarisation. Unghváry claimed that he was merely reiterating the same views as the Hungarian Prime Minister Dezső Bánffy who had said that building a strong Hungarian nation and strengthening the Hungarian state idea were also in the Habsburg dynastic interest. Thus those who hindered the realisation of the Hungarian state idea were pursuing anti-state and anti-dynastic activity. As such, Unghváry claimed that the theatre committee was only fulfilling its patriotic duty in protecting the Hungarian theatre and Pressburg's theatre by preventing it from falling into the dangerous clutches of "foreign" culture.[214]

In 1896, Unghváry wrote a memorandum to the municipal authorities urging the consolidation of the Hungarian theatre.[215] The theatre committee suggested that the *Toldy Kör* standing committee should vigorously lobby in favour of this proposal to the already favourably inclined *főispán* Julius von Szalavszky, the mayor Gustav Dröxler, the municipal assembly, and the city council.[216] This memorandum had all the usual patriotic rhetoric of *Toldy Kör* but it is worth looking more closely at the justifications employed for their demands.[217] Five basic arguments are given in the memorandum: first, the need to consolidate a *lingua franca* in Hungary; secondly, the need to build the Hungarian state-nation by strengthening the Hungarian state idea; thirdly, the disgraceful condition of the Hungarian theatre (and by extension, Hungarian culture) in Pressburg; fourthly, the patriotic duty of other nationalities to adjust themselves to the Hungarian nation; and lastly, the patriotic duty of the municipal authorities in this millennial year to fulfil the important strategic role of Pressburg in Hungary by consolidating the Hungarian theatre.

As the memorandum noted, the government expected other nationalities to show enthusiasm and readiness to make sacrifices for the Hungarian state-nation especially now on the verge of the Hungarian millennium. The other nationalities could easily adjust themselves to this imperative: the German theatre would still perform for six months of the year, and in any case younger Germans and Slovaks (*tótok*) already knew enough Hungarian that "in the satisfaction of their artistic tastes they are not bound only to the foreign but can be satisfied by the Magyar Thália." *Toldy Kör* took a sterner line with die-hard proponents of the German theatre, that "small number" of inhabitants who "were not able or do not want to learn the state language and so estrange themselves from Hungarian culture":[218]

Whereas the German theatre performances have been established in Pozsony for 120 years, the Magyar theatre has been almost completely pushed in the background and paralysed, which has denationalised our magnates, nobility and civil population as well as had a decisive influence on their acceptance of foreign morals and foreign ideas and on the spread of feelings standing in contrast to the love of Magyar culture—now in the new circumstances in our country, in the present era of national awakening, the German theatre has no other aim than [merely] to entertain that German-Slovak audience which does not understand or even want to learn Hungarian; thus while the German theatre can have only a partial interest, at the same time the Hungarian national theatre has apart from uplifting entertainment and [truly] Magyar amusement a vital cultural-political and very serious patriotic duty.[219]

Toldy Kör was convinced that it would be a very impressive symbolic act if on the occasion of the Millennium festivities the City Theatre (*Városi színház, Stadttheater*) would go over to the Hungarian ensemble which still had a "nomadic, temporary and uncertain fate." The stabilisation of the Hungarian theatre was especially necessary because of the closeness of the Austrian capital. Thus it was a "vital national and political mission" that the Hungarian theatre became permanent in Pressburg. (Chapter four discusses Hungarian nationalist criticisms of *Pressburgers* travelling to Vienna to see theatre performances.)

Toldy Kör's rhetoric here illustrates a frustrated shrillness, especially in response to its critics. Thus, when the *Pressburger Zeitung*, the oldest newspaper in Hungary and the main newspaper of Pressburg's German middle class responded to the memorandum by remarking that the "local patriots" of the *Toldy Kör*'s movement to consolidate the Hungarian theatre were getting stronger every year, but that they "rushed after their aim without considering the conditions in Pressburg," the *Toldy Kör* reacted angrily, calling the newspaper's comment "a biased overreaction and misinterpretation."[220]

For all its impassioned rhetoric and patriotic appeals, *Toldy Kör*'s memorandum failed to win the support of the municipal committee. (This is not very surprising, when one considers that even *Toldy Kör*'s own members failed to attend performances of the Hungarian theatre ensemble.[221]) Despite Pávai Vajna's appeals to the forty *Toldy Kör* members who were also members of the municipal committee,[222] *Toldy Kör* had to admit defeat. The municipal committee decided on June 4 to rent out the theatre to the German theatre director (from Karlsbad in Austria) again.[223] According to the *Pressburger Zeitung*, this crucial municipal committee meeting had only "average attendance." Despite the vigorous support of the deputy Viktor Kramolin (chairman of *Toldy Kör* between 1891–1894), the association's demands were not accepted. The municipal committee accepted a lukewarm compromise that, while the contract with the German theatre director would be renewed for another three years, the municipal Theatre Committee would look for a new solution before the end of this period. The compromise was put forward by Daniel Molec, a member of *Toldy Kör* but also a municipal employee, and approved by the *főispán* Szalavsky (also a *Toldy Kör* member).[224]

From the discussion of the issue in the municipal committee, it is clear that even *Toldy Kör*'s own members did not support the association's proposal (except for Kramolin). Membership in the association was probably a good thing to show in a period when displays of Hungarian patriotism were necessary to rise in the social hierarchy. However, participation was no more than formal for many of the association's members. Molec's compromise barely made any concession to *Toldy Kör*'s wishes. Even *főispán* Szalavszky (who had earlier given a speech to *Toldy Kör* calling for the consolidation of the Hungarian theatre) chose the more rational and feasible path rather than the immediate fulfilment of his "patriotic duty."

Yet *Toldy Kör* did not give up its efforts to secure a permanent position for the Hungarian theatre ensemble in Pressburg. Having failed to win municipal backing for their goal, in 1896 *Toldy Kör* declared that the national government should pass a law securing the position of the Hungarian national theatre, as well as providing financial support for Hungarian theatres in the provinces.[225] In this way, *Toldy Kör* wanted to achieve by central *diktat* the aim which it had not succeeded in achieving by its own efforts. In 1898, facing the end of the three-year contract with the German director, *Toldy Kör* once again submitted another memorandum to the municipal authorities. Western Upper Hungary occupied a strategical position for "Hungarian national art" and if this was lost, the "foreign streams" would have free access all the way to the heart of Hungary: Budapest. The memorandum stated that the Germans' insistence on their "habits" was "selfish and narrow-minded." *Toldy Kör* once again demanded a permanent position for the Hungarian theatre.[226]

On 23 January 1899, the municipal committee agreed that from 1 October 1899 on, for the next three years, there would be a mixed theatre.[227] There would be one theatre director—the Hungarian Ivan Relle—who engaged two ensembles that would give performances alternately in Hungarian and in German.[228] At first sight, it would seem that *Toldy Kör* had finally won the battle. However, this new compromise was even worse than the previous situation of German dominance, from the association's point of view. For one thing, the German theatre played to larger audiences and its performances were therefore more frequent.[229] But more importantly, *Toldy Kör* was vehemently opposed to the mixing of languages represented by the new compromise. (The Hungarian association of actors in Budapest also protested against such mixing of languages.[230]) *Toldy Kör* resolved to fight even harder for the consolidation of a purely Hungarian theatre.[231]

After the turn of the century, the tide began to turn in favour of *Toldy Kör*'s long struggle on behalf of the Hungarian theatre. Resistance in the municipal assembly was finally dying away. In 1900 *Toldy Kör* won a symbolic victory when the name of the City Theatre was changed from *Stadttheater* in German into *Pozsony városi szinház* in Hungarian.[232] In April 1901 *Toldy Kör* again took a stand against the mixing of languages in the theatre, which "was declared fatal with regard to the Hungarian cause." The influential City Casino joined *Toldy Kör* in this stand. There were also demonstrations against the German theatre by Hungarian students. However, the German-speaking inhabitants gathered for a counter-demonstration in support of those members of the municipal committee who had voted for the German theatre. Police dispersed the student demonstration.[233] This small but telling detail indicates which side the city authorities supported in this confrontation. It also shows that the struggle in 1901 for the City Theatre was indeed a serious affair. In September 1901, the municipal committee unanimously decided to scrap the mixed theatre and to start an exchange program between Pressburg and Sopron in 1902.[234] This exchange was made possible by the generous financial support of the Hungarian government which finally acknowledged the critical state of Hungarian theatre in this important locale. The Hungarian ensemble received rights to the more profitable season from September until 15 January.[235] The new schedule of divided seasons shifted more and more over the next few years in favour of Hungarian.[236] In December 1911, the municipal assembly voted for the consolidation of the Hungarian theatre in Pressburg which meant that the Hungarian ensemble was now the main resident group in the city theatre.[237] The balance was shifting in favour of the Hungarian theatre which played most of the year including the winter season while the German theatre was limited to a few summer months. However, the theatre season never became exclusively Hungarian.[238] In March 1918 (ironically, just a few months before Pressburg became a part of the new state of Czechoslovakia) the theatre was renamed the *Magyar Nemzeti Szinház* (Hungarian National theatre).[239]

Toldy Kör's long struggle to entrench the Hungarian theatre in Pressburg illustrates how "Magyarisation work" took considerable effort and met with significant resistance in the city. This resistance was primarily covert, because all city representatives said that they wished for the stabilisation of the Hungarian theatre and consistently employed patriotic rhetoric. However, when it came to action, they were always trying to come to a compromise and to guard the previous identity and ethnic tolerance in the city. It is possible that even the nationalistic rhetoric of *Toldy Kör* was restricted to a small circle of members. Even mayor Theodor Brolly, who was an active *Toldy Kör* member, realised that he needed to take the wider picture into consideration and not merely try to fulfil *Toldy Kör's* ambitions. The City Theatre Committee appears to have decided about the rent of the theatre on purely pragmatic grounds. It was always first of all concerned that the performances were well-attended and thus the municipality did not have to deal with the financial difficulties of the Hungarian directors.[240] On the other hand, Brolly's tenure as mayor (1901–1917) also coincided with the period when the German theatre was losing its position in favour of the Hungarian theatre which could also indicate the shifting balance in the city in favour of the Hungarians.

3.1. Conclusion

This part of the chapter has examined the issue of the consolidation of the Hungarian theatre in Pressburg, an issue that was central to *Toldy Kör's* political and cultural agenda. Detailed examination of the interaction between the municipal authorities and *Toldy Kör* leaders shows both disparities in interests and reluctance to embark on radical change in the transition from the earlier civic discourse to the later nationalist discourse represented by *Toldy Kör*. The struggle for the consolidation of the Hungarian theatre shows that the traditional German-speaking elite did not relinquish power easily, even as they publicly proclaimed their Hungarian identity and patriotism. This seeming duplicity on the part of many members of the traditional city elite was one of the factors which most hindered Magyarisation. While Magyarisation (whether through state initiatives or through the activities of Hungarian patriotic associations like *Toldy Kör*) shaped the Magyar character of the city, Pressburg did not cease to be an ethnically mixed and, to a large extent, tolerant environment. In spite of the cultural and educational achievements of Magyar nationalists, Pressburg remained a city with a distinctively multicultural and pluralistic cultural 'Pressburger' identity. This local patriotism was an identity which overrode ethnic considerations. Its main characteristic was loyalty to the city. The next part of this chapter considers Pressburger identity in greater detail.

4. PRESSBURGER IDENTITY

This part of the chapter considers 'Pressburger' identity. Its main components were multi-linguality, lack of specific ethnic identification and ascription, and loyalty to Pressburg. I will briefly look at the origins of this identity as well as its use by the traditional city elites as a justification of their activities and as escape from the growing pressure to identify along ethnic lines. I will also consider whether this identity cut across class divides in the city or whether it was restricted to Pressburg's elites.

4.1. Multi-linguality

As noted in the first chapter of this study, multi-linguality was the norm in Pressburg. By one account, the Emperor Franz Joseph asked a delegation from Pressburg whether they were German or Hungarian. They answered: "Wir sind halt—Pressburger [We are *Pressburgers*]."[241] According to J. J.

Skalský, *Pressburgers* constituted "a peculiar nation for themselves."[242] Another often recounted description of Pressburg at the turn of the century claims that in the city Slovak could be heard in the morning, Hungarian in the afternoons and German in the evenings. (In the morning, when people from the nearby villages came to the market to sell their produce, Slovak was heard in the market places, in shops and in the streets. The afternoons belonged to the civil servants leaving their offices and pupils leaving their schools, and the evenings to the German middle class who met in restaurants, cafés and pubs.)[243] Thus, Pressburg/Pozsony/Prešporok was mainly a city of three languages, although the middle and higher social strata used Hungarian and German.

Census data from 1910 indicate the multi-linguality of Pressburg's inhabitants. Among inhabitants whose mother tongue was Magyar, 36% also spoke (in addition to Hungarian) German and/or Slovak; among those of German mother tongue, 39% spoke Hungarian and/or Slovak; and among inhabitants of Slovak mother tongue, 35% spoke Hungarian and/or German.[244] As Glettler notes, "Bi- or even trilingualism (Slovak-Hungarian-German) was a prerequisite of the age, especially for Slovak lawyers in Bratislava or Slovak working class leaders in Budapest."[245] A review of job advertisements in the local newspapers suggests that most people looking for jobs boasted a knowledge of the "three languages of the country (*drei Landessprachen*)," and job descriptions usually required knowledge of both German and Hungarian, and in some cases also of Slovak (especially in retail jobs). Multi-linguality is closely connected with the notion of a *Pressburger* (Prešpurák in Slovak), although latter-day descriptions of this identity are no doubt laden with nostalgia and romanticisation:

> A peculiarity of the city on the Danube was the so called *Pressburgers*. In a few sentences they could alternate Hungarian, German, and even Slovak. They were natives of Bratislava, of indefinite nationality who were connected with the city by history, family tradition, work, property, but also by its beauty. Their love and devotion to the native city were without limits. They had a long tradition of crafts, wine growing and commerce.[246]

A genuine *Pressburger* spoke all three languages. More precisely, he/she usually spoke at least two languages perfectly and also understood and possibly spoke a third one badly. This trilinguality meant a co-existence of languages, rather than giving them equal status.[247] Language choice is influenced by "the statuses of people with whom the speaker most often interacts." In this way "the speaker's linguistic behaviours are constrained and shaped by the sorts of social contacts they maintain and ... their speech influences other people's perception of their status."[248] One reason why many educated Slovaks assimilated was also the low social status of the Slovak language. "[L]inguistic varieties are evaluated by speakers as prestigious or stigmatized on the basis of the social groups with which they are associated."[249] It is doubtful whether one could expect a member of the German upper class to speak Slovak. Rich German merchants understood Slovak but they did not speak it unless they needed it. By some accounts, these merchants sent their sons to Slovak villages to learn Slovak which they needed to communicate with customers in their shops. Slovak was also necessary for communication in the markets and with domestic servants. However, people from the villages who came to sell their produce at the city's markets also learnt basic Hungarian and German, especially since many of them also sold their goods in the markets of Vienna.[250]

With growing Magyarisation, knowledge of the Hungarian language (at least according to the statistics) also increased among the Pressburg's populace. Census data (see Table 10 below) shows the spread of knowledge of Hungarian among non-Magyars (although it does not indicate the level of knowledge of the language).[251]

	1880	1890	1900	1910
Hungarian knowledge of non-Magyars				
Abs. Numbers	7,619	10,848	14,162	21,892
Percent	18.8	25.8	33.1	47.1
Hungarian knowledge of all population				
Abs. numbers	15,156	21,281	32,906	53,597
Percent	31.6	40.6	53.5	68.5

Table 10: Knowledge of Hungarian in Pressburg, 1880–1910.

4.2. Lack of Single Ethnic Identification
Pressburg was the site of multiple interactions between intersecting cultural groups. This led to complex forms of loyalty and identification. Thus,

Pressburg's inhabitants were integrated in multi-ethnic social networks and were not separated by rigid linguistic or ethnic categories.[252] The mixture of languages and identities was the result of centuries of co-existence of people of different languages and ethnic backgrounds. Local assimilation but also mixed marriages were primary vehicles for the coming together of individuals and families of different linguistic and ethnic backgrounds. As has been mentioned in Chapter One, more than one-third of the marriages that took place from 1880–1914 were ethnically mixed.[253]

It could be argued that it was exactly this amalgamation (which happened before the age of nationalism) that was the core of the specific 'Pressburger' identity. Thus, although the nineteenth-century city elites were German speaking and cultivated German culture, this did not necessarily mean that they were of German ethnic origin. As the Slovak nationalist demographer Svetoň disapprovingly notes, Pressburg was the site of "national de-concentration," a process whose characteristics included "from the view of language a process of linguistic accommodation with a strong tendency to tri-lingualism, from the viewpoint of mixed marriages a process of national amalgamation and from the viewpoint of spiritual content national instability leaning towards regional patriotism, albeit with a Hungarian imprint."[254]

4.3. Loyalty to the City

The third major component of 'Pressburger' identity was loyalty to the city. This loyalty expressed itself in many ways: in concern for the appearance of the city, in the activities of the traditional city elites, in the daily press, and in public events and celebrations. This notion of loyalty was perceived and expressed by the middle classes as behaviour directed towards the good of the city. Such civic-minded behaviour might even include displays of Hungarian nationalistic rhetoric and public approval of Magyarisation, given the political imperatives of dealing with the nationalising state.

The seeming duplicity of the traditional middle classes (noted above in the detailed discussion of the Magyarising activities of organisations like the *Toldy Kör*) derived in part from this underlying pragmatic loyalty to the city and also from the multiple identifications of many *Pressburgers*. Although a large number might have switched to Hungarian language use (as denoted in the census data), they still retained their more multi-ethnic 'Pressburger' identity. This identity did not exclude membership in different associations with contradictory aims, nor did it necessarily exclude Hungarian patriotism, either.[255]

'Pressburger' identity often acted also as an escape from the growing pressure to identify with only one ethnic group. In such situations the traditional elite would justify its actions as seeking the best outcome for their city, but would also state their Hungarian patriotism as wanting the best for the nation. (The clash between different understandings of Hungarian patriotism on the part of the traditional and new Magyar elites will be discussed in Chapter five.) 'Pressburger' identity could be used instead of a determinate ethnic identity.

Since a key component of 'Pressburger' identity was loyalty to the city, the traditional elite could use this identity to justify its activities. Even if their actions were driven by self-interest or class loyalty, they could still hide behind the phrase "the good of the city" since a good citizen of Pressburg was expected to feel loyalty towards his home town. The traditional burgher elite styled itself as "city fathers" taking care of the city as if it was their child. This particular parent-child relationship was that of an authoritarian father who knew best what is good for the child. Just as the new Magyar elite used Hungarian patriotism as an instrument in their struggle for power, in a similar way the traditional elite used local patriotism to reinforce and preserve their dominant position.

However, it is also important to note that the discourse of local patriotism was by no means confined only to the traditional elites. While 'Pressburger' identity was typical of the city's middle classes, it also extended to those inhabitants who were traditionally employed in wine growing, crafts and commerce. It is questionable how much this concept extended to lower classes and to the poor. Soňa Kovačevičová claims that this was also the identity of workers leaders and small craftsmen, thus of the 'folk' strata of population. She claims that the real *Pressburgers* were first of all the craftsmen and the workers' leaders who lived in Zuckermandl, Vödricz, under the castle (in Theresa's Town) and Ligetfalu (see Figure 4).[256] It is true that the workers' movement was multi-ethnic and its leaders were multi-lingual. However, workers did not necessarily demonstrate loyalty to the city. The primary concern of workers' leaders were class divisions. However, for many workers, the struggle for better living conditions was also connected with the value of leading a "respectable" lifestyle. To this extent, workers were closer to the values of middle-class *Pressburgers* than to the more radical values of activist leaders of the workers' movement. (Ethnicity and the workers' movement in Pressburg will be discussed in greater detail in the next chapter.)

Moreover, the traditional elites overlapped with the Magyar elite, and it would be misleading to demarcate the members of the Pressburg middle class into two polarised groups with clearly defined boundaries. 'Pressburger' identity could not be defined in the ethnic terms which were becoming prevalent especially around the turn of the century. This lack of ethnic identification by the *Pressburgers* was particularly irritating to the nationalists of each ethnic group, whether Magyar, Slovak or German. But then identity itself is a fluid concept whose boundaries are constantly shifting, creating overlaps, including and excluding different elements. This fluid concept of identity is especially visible when considering, for instance, membership by individuals of different associations with seemingly contradictory aims and agendas. (See footnote 147.) Such multiple affiliations might lead to the conclusion that these were merely self-interested individuals with no fixed character and a lack of values. Alternatively, these individuals could be regarded as possessing complex identities that required negotiation between overlapping and sometimes conflicting values and choices.[257]

4.4. Pressburger Identity and Magyarisation: Conclusion

When compared to 1867, Pressburg in 1914 seemed Magyarised to a large extent. The census data point to considerable linguistic Magyarisation. Municipal life had become increasingly Magyarised, with more Magyars occupying prominent positions in municipal life and with Hungarian as the official language of municipal communication. Even non-Magyar associations presented themselves publicly as Hungarian. Education in the city was almost totally Magyarised.[258] The theatre was substantially Magyarised, playing Hungarian performances for most of the year. The city looked more Hungarian in its physical appearance, with streets named after Hungarian political and cultural personalities, Hungarian monuments and plaques, and even shop names and inscriptions in Hungarian. Even the city directory, the *Pressburger Wegweiser/ Pozsonyi Útmutató* reflected the rising power of Hungarian.[259] According to the Slovak lawyer Ivan Dérer, Pressburg had a totally Hungarian character before the First World War.[260] However, all this does not mean that the city was in fact completely Magyarised.

Although municipal affairs were formally conducted in Hungarian, municipal offices used German and Slovak and not just Hungarian in their everyday communications with inhabitants and visitors. Associations may have kept their minutes in Hungarian and used more Hungarian (often badly) on public occasions, yet they continued to use German in their internal communications. Shops still had German names, although they came after the Hungarian versions. At the end of the period 1867–1914, although there were three German-language daily newspapers and three weeklies, there was only one Hungarian daily, the *Nyugatmagyarországi Híradó*.[261] This indicates that the Magyar elite remained in a defensive position in the city, as had been perceived by *Toldy Kör* at the beginning of the period. Efforts to Magyarise the city were partially successful but were not sufficient to change the 'Pressburger' identity of most city inhabitants.

5. SLOVAKS IN PRESSBURG (PREŠPOROK)

This part of the chapter considers the role of Slovaks in Pressburg during the period 1867–1914. I will first consider the role of Pressburg as a centre of the Slovak national revival. I will then describe some key events and features of Slovak nationalist politics during this period. I will also examine the extent to which Pressburg included a distinctive Slovak presence between 1867 and 1900. In this context I will look at the careers of two prominent Slovak lawyers, Michal Mudroň and Vendelín Kutlík, as contrasting case studies of identity politics in Pressburg during the period. Lastly, I will discuss the growing visibility of Slovaks in Pressburg after 1900.

5.1. PRESSBURG IN THE SLOVAK NATIONAL REVIVAL

Pressburg played an important role in the three waves of the Slovak national revival. This movement's beginnings can be traced to 1784 when Emperor Joseph II founded a general seminary for training Catholic priests in their vernaculars. A group of Slovak seminarians initiated the first wave of the Slovak national revival. While remaining Hungarian patriots, Anton Bernolák and his followers codified the first literary language based on the dialect used by educated people in western Slovakia and asserted the difference of their language from Czech. The second wave of the national revival consisted mainly of Slovak Protestants who had studied in German universities from where they imported Romantic ideas of the nation (influenced by Herder).[262] Ján Kollár and Pavel Josef Šafárik identified the nation with language and claimed that they belonged to a smaller community defined by language rather than the multicultural *natio hungarica*.[263] Both Kollár and Šafárik were "Czechoslovakists," admitting the existence of only one Slav nation. In the 1830s, a new generation of students emerged from the Evangelic lyceum in Pressburg, led by Ľudovít Štúr. This generation moved away from the "Czechoslovakist" idea (since Czech intellectuals refused to recognise Slovak as a separate language) and codified a new literary language based on the speech used by cultivated people in Central Slovakia. After 1843, three competing versions of the Slav/Slovak language were in use: biblical Czech (used by Evangelicals even before the national revival and in their religious periodicals until 1883), Bernolák's version and Štúr's version. After the 1860s, new Slovak (Štúr's version) spread among the Slovak intelligentsia and became the basis of modern Slovak. Although there were some Slovak intellectuals in Pressburg in the 1850s, the centre of Slovak national activity shifted towards Martin in Central Slovakia in the 1860s.

The revolutionary events of 1848 showed that national consciousness among Slovaks was limited to a small intellectual elite which was split along confessional lines. The masses were indifferent to nationalist appeals.[264] Slovak nationalists were unable to generate a mass movement with political demands (the critical Phase C in Hroch's developmental analysis of national movements.) In 1848, the Slovak intelligentsia did indeed compose a document demanding Slovak autonomy within Hungary with their own parliament, Slovak as the official language, cultural institutions and general voting rights, freedom of speech and the delineation of the borders of the Slovak territory. However, this was merely the programme of an intellectual elite with minimal mass support. A similar memorandum in 1861—*Memorandum slovenského národa* (which has been described by later Slovak historians as the national programme of the Slovak nation) also had no impact on the largely indifferent masses in a hostile climate of strengthening Magyarisation.[265] (See Chapter four, Part 6.)

5.2. SLOVAK POLITICS 1867–1914

After the Dual Agreement of 1867, the strong Magyarisation policies of the Hungarian authorities and their suppression of nationalities' movements brought the activities of Slovak nationalists to a halt. In the 1860s Slovaks had achieved some successes in education, establishing institutions of higher education with Slovak as the language of instruction, founding *Matica Slovenská* in 1863 to publish Slovak literature, and building up a national museum, archive and library. However, after 1867 Slovaks lost most of these gains.[266]

During this period Slovak politics split into two wings. The party responsible for the 1861 Memorandum became known as the *Stará Škola* (Old School). Its leaders were graduates of the Pressburg Evangelic lyceum: Jan Francisci, Štefan Marko Daxner, Jozef Hurban, and Viliam Paulíny-Tóth. This group was oriented towards co-operation with other non-Magyar nationalities in the Hungarian part of the monarchy. The other group, *Nová Škola* (New School), led by Ján Palárik and Jan Nepomuk Bobula, were more inclined to cooperate with the Hungarians. They rejected the Czech influence and also did not pursue the 1861 Memorandum's demand for a Slovak national territory. In 1869 the Old School's main activities moved to the small Central Slovak town of Martin where the *Slovenská Národná Strana* (the Slovak National Party) was founded in 1870. This continued to be the only Slovak party until the end of the nineteenth century, although it became passive after 1880 and did not participate in Hungarian elections until the early twentieth century.[267]

A new emphasis on Czechoslovakism came into Slovak political life towards the turn of the century.[268] The *Československá jednota* (Czechoslovak Unity) led by Vavro Šrobár was created in 1896. This association was influenced by Masaryk's idea of Czechoslovakism and opposed the National Party's pro-Russian orientation. In 1898, students returning from Vienna, Prague and Budapest gathered around the magazine *Hlas* (Voice), and later around the magazine *Prúdy* (Streams).[269] The *Hlas* movement did not succeed in building a mass movement but it did revitalise Slovak political life. Slovaks also became more involved in party politics at around this time, founding and splitting off into small more nationally oriented parties from the main Catholic and popular parties.[270]

The divisions and squabbles among the Slovak political parties and the nationalist intelligentsia during the period 1867–1914 do not point to a radically different level of political activity or mass mobilisation than in the earlier period.[271] The Slovak national movement was only able to make linguistic and cultural demands (Phase B of Hroch's developmental schema.) It took the upheavals of the First World War and a combination of fortuitous circumstances for Slovaks to attain independence from Hungarian rule, as part of the new Czechoslovak state. It took a further seventy years before the Slovak national movement attained its ultimate objective of full independence as a sovereign state.[272]

5.3. Pressburg after 1867–until the Turn of the Century

Slovak nationalist activity in Pressburg mirrored the level of activism in Slovak nationalist politics generally. After an initial burst of national activities in the 1860s, followed by the closing in 1873–4 of the three Slovak gymnasia and *Matica Slovenská*, Slovak national life stayed dormant until the beginning of the twentieth century. This section briefly considers the extent to which Slovaks were a tangible presence in Pressburg. I will look at expressions of 'Slovak-ness' in the city, and show the areas where a distinct Slovak presence was detectable: the markets, lower classes, middle classes, and Slovak students in the city. I will then look at two cases of negotiation between 'Pressburger' identity and Slovak national identity by comparing the careers of the Slovak lawyers and national activists Michal Mudroň and Vendelín Kutlík.

5.3.1. *Slovakness of Pressburg*

Although Pressburg played an important part in the initial phases of the Slovak national revival, nationalist activity had moved to Martin by the 1860s. Slovaks did not emerge as a visible group with a distinct group identity in Pressburg until the beginning of the twentieth century. Most Slovaks were part of the Pressburger masses, and did not take any interest in public displays of their ethnicity. Slovak was most often heard in the markets, and most *Pressburgers* knew some 'market Slovak.'[273] According to Štefan Krčméry who came to Pressburg in 1907, the city "was almost a desert" in terms of a visible Slovak presence. There were only a few nationally-conscious Slovak burgher families.[274] Slovaks could be found in markets, suburbs and around the factories. "The Slovak element was mostly poor and therefore shy, concealed. It was hard to get it together, since there was not enough cohesion, it [the Slovak element] was dispersed."[275] Slovaks were to be found especially among the workers, day-labourers, small entrepreneurs and craftsmen, peddlers and servants in burgher households.[276] Another large contingent of Slovaks were soldiers from the 72nd Infantry regiment which was resident in Pressburg. Many Slovaks from the surrounding areas served in this regiment.[277]

The Slovak middle class was not interested in advertising its Slovakness. Most members of this middle class displayed 'Pressburger' identity with its associated trilingualism and therefore did not feel it necessary to stress the particularly ethnic aspect of their identity. 'Nationalist life' was restricted to a few families where those interested would meet for entertainment and literary evenings. Certainly the Slovak members of the middle class must also have felt the increasing pressure of Magyarisation. According to Svetoň, acceptance of the Hungarian language and superficial Hungarian patriotism were enough for Slovak migrants and domestics, in terms of facilitating their inclusion and rise in the social hierarchy.[278]

The Slovak presence in the city was discernible in church activities. While there are no figures for church attendance, a clue to the substantial number of Slovaks in the city is provided by the number of sermons given in the Slovak language. The small Protestant church had Slovak sermons every Sunday until the First World War. In Catholic churches there were Slovak sermons every Sunday and on holidays and saint's days. The Franziskaner and Kapuziner orders had Slovak monks and some of the chaplains in St.

Martin's Cathedral were Slovak (for instance, Vincent Havlíček who served in the Cathedral from 1880–1899).[279]

It is also important to note the presence of Slovak students in Pressburg, studying at the Law Academy, the Evangelic Lyceum (which had previously been an important centre of nationalist activity, as noted above) and the Theological Academy. However, Slovak "national life" in Pressburg could not consolidate around the activities of these students, due to their temporary residence in the city.[280] These students were most active in the 1870s. In 1868 the Slovak students of the Law Academy created an association called *Naprej*. The aim of this association was to promote "the national spirit." The association only had about 22 members (although in 1870 half of the students in the Law Academy were Slovaks). Its members celebrated Slovak national 'holidays' such as 6 June (the date of the Memorandum of the Slovak nation) and 10 May (the 1848 declaration of the Requirements of the Slovak Nation). *Naprej* members also made trips to Devín castle ruin in remembrance of Štúr's group.[281] The association organised "komersy," larger entertainment events in which other Pressburger Slovaks also participated. These Slovak students were significantly influenced by the Slovak national activists Jozef Miloslav Hurban, Michal Mudroň and Vendelín Kutlík (the latter two are discussed in greater detail in the next sub-section.)[282]

These Slovak students cooperated with Serb students and were also in contact with other student associations in the territory of Slovakia. Consequently, some Slovak students were accused of forbidden "Pan-Slavism," were expelled from Pressburg and were unable to attend any educational institution in Hungary. By one account, Pressburg had the highest number of expelled Slovak students, 31 in total between 1882 and 1885.[283] These cases are considered in greater detail in the following discussion dealing with the activist lawyers Michal Mudroň and Vendelín Kutlík.

5.3.2. Michal Mudroň and Vendelín Kutlík

Michal Mudroň (1835–1887) and Vendelin Kutlík (1834–1904) were lawyers who worked and lived in Pressburg (Kutlík was later a lawyer in Malacka). They both came from families in which Slovak language and culture were cultivated. They were both active in the Slovak national movement and were considered "Pan-Slav" by the new Magyar elite but also by many members of the traditional Pressburger elite. However, Mudroň was highly regarded even by enemies of "Pan-Slavism" while Kutlík and his family were ostracised by Pressburger society. The reason for this may have been Mudroň's ability to incorporate a larger part of 'Pressburger' identity, so that he was not wholly defined by his Slovak ethnicity. Kutlík on the other hand, remained first of all a Slovak, and did not even try to incorporate anything from the 'Pressburger' identity.

Michal Mudroň came to Pressburg in the 1850s to study at the gymnasium and later the Law Academy. (Kutlík and other Slovaks who later became active in the national movement also studied at the Law Academy during the same time.) Mudroň received his advocate diploma in 1861, starting a successful career as a lawyer. Mudroň's nationalist activities included participation in national gathering of Slovaks, consciousness-raising among Pressburg's Slovaks by distributing books and journals in Slovak, and providing Slovak students with a meeting place in his home. Mudroň participated in the 1861 national gathering (consisting mainly of Slovak intelligentsia) in Martin which formulated the "Memorandum of the Slovak nation" and submitted it to the Hungarian parliament.[284] Mudroň also ran unsuccessfully as a candidate in the parliamentary elections in the predominantly Slovak districts, in 1865, 1869, 1872, 1876 and 1881. While proclaiming himself as a good Hungarian who loved his Hungarian homeland, Mudroň also stressed the need to remember "one's mother tongue and origin." Even after learning Hungarian and German, Slovaks should remember Slovak. Mudroň demanded the full implementation of the Nationalities' Law of 1868 which gave assurances of minority rights.[285]

Mudroň's argument that minority rights were no threat to Hungary was strengthened by the fact that he himself spoke German and Hungarian perfectly.[286] He defended clients of different nationalities in a wide range of different cases. He defended Slovak nationalist activists (Jozef Miloslav Hurban, Viliam Paulíny-Toth, Martin Kollár) in press prosecutions aimed at shutting down their activities, but he also defended ethnic Rumanians and other *Pressburgers*. In fact, Mudroň's first press lawsuit in 1871 was on behalf of a (Magyar) *honvéd* major against the owner of the *Pressburger Zeitung*.[287] In another sensational case Mudroň defended the chauvinistic Hungarian editor of the *Pozsonyvidéki Lapok* who was sued for slandering the Austrian anthem. In this case as Mudroň himself pointed out, "the accused was a Magyar, the defender a Slovak, the judges mostly German and the prosecutor an Austrian Hungarian [*rakúsky Uhor*]." He concluded his speech: "So go, gentlemen of the jury, and prove with your liberating verdict that all nationalities of Hungary are united against absolutism and central monarchy."[288] Mudroň also achieved fame through his rational responses to Hungarian chauvinistic pamphlets written by the *alispán* of Zólyom (Zvolen) county Béla Grünwald and by Ján Thébusz, an Evangelic priest from Zólyom.[289]

Mudroň's credentials as a "good Slovak" were clear even to his contemporaries.[290] In the 1860s he was a member (and legal representative) of the Slovak cultural association *Matica Slovenská*.[291] He also defended Slovak students in the 1870s against the chauvinism of their Hungarian colleagues at the Law Academy and Evangelic Lyceum. These activities caused Hungarian chauvinists to consider Mudroň a supporter of anti-state ideas.[292] However, Mudroň also figured on the membership list of *Toldy Kör*, which explicitly promoted the Magyarisation objectives against which Mudroň fought in his articles and lawsuits.[293] It is possible that Mudroň's participation in this Hungarian patriotic association was merely a precondition for his successful career. However, the high esteem with which Mudroň was regarded in Hungarian as well as German circles shows that he was considered a true *Pressburger*.[294] Even if Hungarians and Germans considered him a Pan-Slav and disapproved of his nationalist activities, they honoured his professional and human qualities.[295] As Iván Simonyi wrote in his obituary of Mudroň in the *Westungarischer Grenzbote*: "Mudroň was a character whom everyone must hold in esteem. In him died a generous ideal human of whom there are only a few in our centuries, and therefore every one, friend or enemy, pronounces the name of the dead [man] with respect."[296]

Vendelín Kutlík also studied law at the Pressburg Law Academy and worked in Mudroň's law offices from 1862–1866. Here he gathered a circle of Slovak students, and enthusiastically lectured them on the history and future of Slavs.[297] In 1867 he moved to Nagyszombat [Trnava] but returned to Pressburg in 1875 since "Trnava was too narrow for the agility of Vendko Kutlík."[298] This enthusiastic agility in the Slovak cause brought hostility against Kutlík to a head in 1885. Kutlík's household had become a meeting place for Slovak students. They also frequently went out to pubs together, and one such gathering was interrupted by Hungarian students who accused Kutlík of inciting the youth against the Hungarian state.[299] Although Mudroň had also been similarly accused a number of times, matters never went as far as in Kutlík's case which had an unhappy ending for both Kutlík and the Slovak students.

The whole case centred around a gathering of nineteen people in a brewery, celebrating the birthday of Kutlík's wife. They were singing Slovak and "Russian sounding songs." Kutlík was reported to have said that "the Magyar yoke is worse than the Turkish one but there will come a time when the Slav people will finally be liberated." The students were charged with Pan-Slav sympathies, participating in a secret meeting, isolating themselves from patriotic youth, and for possessing the prohibited Slovak book *Venček*.[300]

The Evangelical Lyceum disciplinary committee excluded Kutlík's son from all educational institutions, expelled some students from the Lyceum, and severely punished others.[301] This case was condemned by the Pressburg municipal assembly as well and the *főispán* of the county urged the minister of the interior to prosecute Kutlík.[302] However, neither the royal prosecutor in Pressburg nor the Hungarian minister of justice found enough evidence to prosecute since anti-state ideas had not been expressed publicly. The prosecutors could only forward Kutlík's case to the Pressburger Bar Association (*Pozsonyi ügyvédi kamara*) for disciplinary proceedings.[303]

Kutlík was examined by the Bar Association and found guilty for regularly meeting Evangelical youth and exerting a bad influence over them by participating in "pub debauches" (lyceum students were prohibited from visiting pubs.) He was also charged with incitement of the youth against the state and promoting hostility against Magyars and Germans.[304] Kutlík's defence—that he had never taken an oath to the constitution of the Hungarian fatherland—only provoked his judges further. Kutlík's conduct was condemned as "unworthy of respect and trust" since his acts "deeply insult the honour and authority of the legal profession." An initial ruling expelling Kutlík from the legal profession was changed (upon his appeal) to a one year ban preventing him from carrying out his profession as a lawyer.[305] As a result, Kutlík was financially ruined since Pressburger society boycotted him professionally and socially even after the ban had expired. This boycott and the animosity of the judges made it impossible for Kutlík to continue his practice. To add insult to injury, the Hungarian students broke the windows of his house.[306]

The contrasting fates of these two men are revealing in terms of the politics of identity in Pressburg. Mudroň, although acknowledged as a Pan-Slav agitator, was respected by Pressburger society as an excellent professional and a person of high human qualities. This means that he must have taken on some characteristics of *Pressburgers*. Kutlík, on the other hand, was ostracised because of his vehement insistence of the primacy of his Slovak identity. The next few pages briefly consider the revival of Slovak political activity in Pressburg after 1900.

5.4. PRESSBURG 1900–1914

Slovak political life revived in Pressburg after the turn of the century. After the 1881 elections, Slovak politics had fallen into a condition of dormancy and internal squabbling. After 1900, a new generation of Slovak politicians condemned this defensive inactivity and proclaimed the need for active work among Slovak people. Concurrently with this revival, Slovaks were also becoming more visible in Pressburg. This sub-section will discuss the areas of growing visibility: the activity of Slovak workers, burghers and students.

Many Slovak workers were organised in the *Robotnícky katolícky kruh*, the Catholic association of workers, which organised theatre performances and education for workers in 1903–5. This association had its own Slovak branch. However, the Hungarian newspaper *Nyugatmagyarországi Híradó* made a public scandal over these Slovak theatre performances.[307] Although the theatre group was banned from performing in the Catholic school, their performance went ahead in the room of the workers' association.[308] However, in the following year (1906), the Slovak branch of the association was closed because of the theatre performances. Since many workers were reluctant to join the Hungarian speaking central association, they decided to join the social democrats. Here they were not persecuted for being Slovak and the social democrats promised to respect the religious feelings of the Slovak workers.[309] The Slovak social democrats were organised in the Slovak section of the association *Vorwärts* (*Vpred*) and started to publish their own newspapers *Robotnícke Noviny* and *Napred*. (The activities of Slovak social democrats will be discussed in more detail in Chapter three.)

As discussed earlier in this chapter, theatre served an important educational and propaganda role in Pressburg. The nationalistic Magyar elite stressed its importance for Magyarisation. Despite giving in to Magyarisation in other areas of social and political life, the German-speaking middle classes resisted relinquishing their primacy over the City Theatre. Pressburger workers also recognised the symbolic importance of the theatre, managing in 1912 to appropriate the City Theatre, the domain of the middle classes, even if only for one day. *Vpred* also pursued theatre activities, preparing six Slovak performances between 1906 and 1914. These were pieces by Slovak authors and also included two German plays translated into Slovak.[310] However, these activities were few and far between. The Slovak workers' newspaper *Robotnícke Noviny* criticised this inactivity: although Slovaks also paid the theatre tax, "only we Slovaks in Prešporok are such that we do not even try to satisfy our cultural needs." The writer sourly noted that Slovaks seemed happy just to sing Slovak songs in a pub instead of joining forces to at least get a Czech theatre troupe for the summer off-season. "For that, however, there would have to be solidarity, of which there is very little among Prešporok's Slovaks. But this solidarity is needed if we do not want to be the last wheel on the carriage in Prešporok and the appendix of all possible and impossible factions and cliques or comfortable Slovaks-for-ourselves."[311] A subsequent article criticised the basic lack of solidarity among the city's Slovaks: "They can lament over the oppression of Slovaks but they do not want to solve the essential cultural tasks in favour of Slovaks even when it would be easy to do so."[312] The middle classes organised their own amateur theatre performances but not publicly.[313]

While there is little recorded information on the activities of the Slovak middle classes, Slovak newspaper reports and the memoirs of Slovak intellectuals like Ivan Dérer and Štefan Krčméry paint an interesting picture. Although Dérer's memoir begins in 1893 while Krčméry's memoirs start only in 1907, both name the same "Slovak" personalities in Pressburg. Although these two writers call these figures Slovak, there is no doubt that many of these people would have described themselves as *Pressburgers* as well.[314] Slovak activity only began to take place in public spaces in the years prior to the First World War. Public meetings and entertainment among the Slovak community took place in the pub of Ján Grajciar (regularly advertised also in the Slovak workers press as a meeting place) or in the rooms of another tavern owned by František Idzi.[315] The first big Slovak folk gathering took place in the Hotel Bellevue (which was also used for balls given by upper-class Pressburger society), owned by the Czech Dubský.[316] In 1901 Slovaks also organised trips into the countryside which brought together thirty, and on a later occasion, a hundred Slovaks.[317]

Some Pressburger Slovaks expressed their concern about the "de-nationalising" of Slovaks.[318] Except for a few families, children of Slovak parents often refused to speak Slovak and were becoming Germanised or Magyarised.[319] Dérer explicitly names those individuals whom he considered "good Slovaks (or Czechs)" as well as "renegades" and "Maďaróns" (those who had adjusted themselves to Hungarian and German ways of life). Anton Štefánek claims that there was a group of just seven active families and individuals in Pressburg between 1913 and 1918, among whom Slovak national life was concentrated.[320] In 1903, the Pressburger Slovaks (including Dérer) founded the *Slovenský vzdelávací spolok* (Slovak educational society). The statutes of this association were not approved by the minister of the interior since "it endangered the patriotic character of the city." However, this initiative revived Slovak community life in Pressburg.[321] From 1903 on, regular Slovak balls and theatre performances took place in Pressburg, which, in later years, were also attended by Slovaks coming from surroundings areas.

However, the class split among Slovaks in Pressburg affected these gatherings. In one entertainment evening in 1903, out of 400 Slovak participants there was only one person from the "intelligentsia," although they had all been invited.[322] Workers complained that the richer Slovaks were only interested in founding new banks which were even more exploitative than the "enemy institutions."[323] Slovak students residing temporarily in Pressburg also complained about the intelligentsia: "The whole Slovak intelligentsia in Prešporok has to be reproached for indifference and ignorance towards Prešporok's Slovak folk. This intelligentsia—except the studying youth—which has time for meetings if they concern entertainment and pleasure, should also remember the people, all the more since it promised this to the people and should a certain opportunity [of nationhood] arise it will want to count on the people."[324] The Slovak students felt that their nation was "dying out" in Pressburg because of neglect and a lack of education in the Slovak mother tongue.[325]

Throughout the whole period, between 15 and 30 students from other parts of Slovak territory attended the Theological Academy, and (to a lesser extent) the Law Academy in Pressburg.[326] These students tried to revive Slovak life in the city by attending and participating in amateur theatre, collecting money to found a Slovak people's library in Pressburg in order to enter into contact with "the people," and by organising literary evenings and lectures for self-education in the Slovak language.[327] These Slovak students complained of petty bourgeois chauvinism and physical violence in the city. In 1907, a Slovak law student was beaten up by his Magyar colleagues. Conflicts also took place between the Magyar and Slovak students of the Theological Academy.[328] The Slovak students were also attacked by the "chauvinistic circles of Prešporok" in the Hungarian daily *Nyugatmagyarországi Hiradó*.[329] Magyar chauvinists felt that the Theological Academy was "Pan-Slav" since its students had the right to use the Slovak language.[330] Many Magyar students (especially law students) exhibited little tolerance towards the use of other languages in the city. Many of these students even joined *Toldy Kör* in 1901.[331] Their ethnic chauvinism is understandable considering that many of these law students were aspiring to become central government officials or parliamentary deputies. These aspirations required demonstrations of fervent Hungarian patriotism in line with the government's emphasis on the dominance of the Magyar race in the Hungarian state. As will be shown in Chapter five, loyalty to the Hungarian state (ranging from Hungarian patriotism to Magyar chauvinism) was a pre-condition for state employment. However, not all teachers or Hungarian students at the Theological Academy were chauvinistic, and the Slovak students were not the sole target of Magyar chauvinism as they claimed.[332]

Slovaks became more visible and active as a group in the decade before the First World War. The Slovak *Ľudová banka* (People's bank) was founded in Pressburg in 1907 and became a branch of the *Úverová banka* (Credit bank) in Ružomberok in 1909.[333] In 1911, the *Nakladateľský kníhtlačiarsko-kníhkupecký spolok* (Publishing and book-printing-booksellers' association) was founded in order to publish the Slovak periodical *Slovenské ľudové Noviny*.[334] Large crowds of countryside Slovaks came to Pressburg to observe the trials of the Slovak nationalist activists Ferdinand Juriga (in 1906) and Andrej Hlinka (in1908).[335] Hlinka's People's Party had its centre in Pressburg. Milan Hodža, another important Slovak politician (a supporter of Masaryk and the Czechoslovak orientation) also planned (together with Miloš Štefánek, a Pressburg lawyer) to publish periodicals in Pressburg. Slovak social democratic activity was also growing (described in the next chapter). The important Slovak priests Juriga and Jehlička also served in Pressburg as chaplains for some time.[336] Chapter four will discuss in greater detail how the Slovak intelligentsia saw the place of Pressburg within the Slovak territory.

The growth of Slovak activity in Pressburg coincided with the growing activity and crystallisation of Slovak politics in the whole of the Slovak territory.[337] It is interesting that Slovaks in Pressburg should have become more active in the period after Magyarisation efforts had peaked. This might show that the harshness and extent of 'national oppression' (which has been blamed for the passivity of Slovak politics until the turn of the century) was not decisive in determining the fortunes of the Slovak national movement. What appears to have been more important was the rise of a new generation of Slovak intelligentsia and politicians who were more capable of attracting mass support. The growth of mass politics and the organisation of the social-democratic movement and its Slovak part also had an impact, as did support from Slovaks in Vienna and the Czech associations in Vienna. Even so, the level of national consciousness on a mass level remained low, and had to be built up within the new Czechoslovak state after 1919.

6. CONCLUSION

This chapter has described the effects of Magyarisation on Pressburg. Magyarisation was manifested in the city as a struggle for power between the new Magyar elite and the traditional, German speaking, Pressburger elite. This struggle extended into all areas of the city life, into municipal politics, into associational and cultural life, and it even affected the physical appearance of the city itself.

The chapter reviewed the Magyarisation policies of the Hungarian government and the settlement patterns, social standing and national activities of the German and Slovak ethnic groups as well as the Jews. I then considered the impact of Magyarisation in different spheres of city life in Pressburg, showing how the traditional elite resisted Magyarisation of the city while still proclaiming its Hungarian patriotism. This was most evident in the case of the City Theatre but also in language use in public life. The new Magyar elite's use of nationalist discourse in order to gain power in the city was demonstrated in the activities and rhetoric of *Toldy Kör* and its relationship to other nationalities. The gradual interlocking of the municipal elite and associations like *Toldy Kör* gradually moved power towards the Magyar elite. Yet, despite the successes of the Magyar elite in transforming multi-ethnic Pressburg into Hungarian Pozsony, the older 'Pressburger' identity persisted. While Hungarian had become the main language used in public life, German and Slovak continued to be used in more private contexts. Most *Pressburgers* still felt more comfortable using German rather than Hungarian, official census data notwithstanding.

In addition to the *Pressburger*/Magyar struggle, Slovaks were also a fluctuating presence in the city. Individual Slovaks had to negotiate and choose between a more multicultural 'Pressburger' identity and their ethnic identity. Slovak national activity in Pressburg after the turn of the century was connected to the revival of Slovak political life. In general, there was no mass support for Slovak national activity in the city. The most visible Slovaks were the Slovak workers within the social democratic movement in the city. This will be the topic of the next chapter.

⌁ 3 ⌁

INDUSTRIALISATION, URBANISATION
AND DEVELOPMENT OF THE
WORKERS' MOVEMENT

0. INTRODUCTION

PREVIOUS CHAPTERS OF THIS STUDY HAVE EXPLORED changes in ethnic identification in Pressburg between 1867 and 1914. This chapter examines the development of the workers' movement in order to better understand identity politics in the city. Industrialisation and urbanisation led to considerable growth in the number of working class inhabitants in the city between 1867 and 1914. The development of the workers' and later social democratic movement in the city reflected an important intersection between class and ethnicity and also represented an alternative mode of self-identification for the working class.[1] By the beginning of the twentieth century (especially in the years immediately preceding the First World War) the workers' and social democratic movement was a considerable force to reckon with in the city.

The first part of this chapter maps the industrial and urban growth of the city and considers the ethnic origins and background of the growing working class. The second part looks at the development of the workers' movement in Hungary and Pressburg between 1869 and 1914. The third part analyses the formation and activities of the workers' movement in Pressburg, especially the activities of the workers' educational association *Vorwärts*. The fourth part considers the repertoire of collective action (public

meetings and demonstrations) and the forms of challenge these represented. The fifth part concentrates on the question of ethnicity in the Hungarian workers' movement. The separatist efforts of Slovak workers serve as a
case study showing the tension between efforts to build an 'imagined community of class' as opposed to an 'imagined community of language.' The last
part looks at relations between the workers' movement, the city authorities,
and other inhabitants of the city in order to show the ways in which workers'
identities and views differed from the world view of the bourgeoisie.

1. CONDITIONS FOR THE DEVELOPOMENT OF
THE WORKERS' MOVEMENT: INDUSTRIALISATION
AND URBANISATION OF PRESSBURG

The Dual Agreement of 1867 accelerated industrial development in Hungary. By 1900, the territory of present-day Slovakia had become the second
most industrialised part of Hungary (next only to Budapest and its surrounding areas.)[2] About one third of the Hungarian state budget for industrial development was directed towards the Slovak territory, supported also
by tax and tariff concessions.[3] After the economic crisis and recession of
1873, previously numerous craftsmen and small factories were overshad-
owed by larger enterprises. In 1890, there were 51 factories in Pressburg
which employed 5,790 people, approximately 37.5% of the total population.[4]
In 1869 Pressburg ranked third in Hungary in its volume of industrial production, after Budapest and Kassa and by the turn of the century, Pressburg
was the most important industrial city in the territory of present-day Slovakia.[5] Rapid industrial growth led to an influx of workers from outside the
city. This part examines the ethnic background of these workers and considers the impact of industrialisation on urban growth and settlement patterns in Pressburg during the period 1867–1914.

1.1. BACKGROUND OF WORKERS: COMMUTING AND MIGRATION
As explained in Chapter one, the ethnic composition of Pressburg was
affected by the influx of workers during a period of considerable industrialisation. The multicultural environment of the city took in new cultural and
ideological elements brought in by immigrant workers. Depending on their
place of origin, immigrant workers varied in their knowledge of languages
and in the extent to which they were open to new influences. Workers who

commuted from surrounding areas varied distinctly from migrants from outside the Pressburg region.

The ethnic division of labour can be seen in the patterns of employment in new factories. The personnel of the factories were drawn from three groups of workers: a very small group of German, Austrian Czech and Moravian specialists; from Pressburg's proletariat of German, Magyar and Slovak nationality with some experience in manufacturing work; and, finally, from an untrained workforce drawn from villages to the north of Pressburg, some of whom commuted to work by bicycle or tram. (Récse, Szentgyörgy, Basin, even Igrám and Senkvic).[6] (Figure 5.) Most factories drew the majority of their workforce from the nearest neighbourhood and villages.[7] Thus changes in Pressburg's ethnic structure were affected by the ethnic structure of the surrounding villages.[8] Another important contributing factor was the ethnic background of workers coming from other counties. Between 1890 and 1910, more than 80% of Pressburg's population increase was due to immigration (in the period 1890–1900 the population grew by 9,126, of whom 8,727 were immigrants; between 1900 and 1910 the population grew by 11,922, of whom 9,546 were immigrants.)[9] The next table shows the distribution in 1900 and 1910 of the city's population according to their place of birth.

	1900	1910
Born in the place of registration	43.0	42.0
Born in the same county	19.2	21.0
Born in a different county	26.0	26.4
Born in Croatia/Slavonia	0.2	0.2
Born in Hungary	88.4	90.6
Born abroad:		
In Austria	10.7	8.5
In a different country	0.9	0.9
Total born abroad	11.6	9.4

Table 11: Population of Pressburg by place of birth in 1900 and 1910 (%).[10]

As the table shows, most of Pressburg's inhabitants were born in the Hungarian kingdom. Approximately 20% were born in Pressburg county which was predominantly Slovak (see Chapter two, Part 1). An additional 26% were born in other counties and might have been Slovak or Magyar. According to Goláň, the city's growth depended almost entirely on an influx of migrants from the area above the Danube. Pressburg also "caught" a part of the wave of workers passing through on their way to look for jobs in Vienna.[11]

Immigration made Pressburg a more proletarian city. By the beginning of the 20th century, Pressburg had the largest working-class population of any city in the territory of present-day Slovakia.[12] The city's ethnic and class character was also affected by a substantial out-migration from the city composed primarily of "grocers, merchants, railway and tram workers who for decades had been resident in Vienna."[13] (The special connection between Pressburg and Vienna will be more closely described later in this chapter as well as in Chapters four and five.) Significantly, out-migrants were primarily those with German mother-tongue.[14]

The ever-increasing working class became visible in Pressburg through their organised activities. However, even among the working class, the varied origins of migrants created cultural and class divides. While migrants from Austria (and workers from Pressburg itself) tended to be multi-lingual urbanised skilled workers, the unskilled working force was largely composed of rural immigrants who probably knew only their mother tongue when they arrived in the city.[15] Attempts to build a community of workers had to contend with this divide between cosmopolitan multi-lingual workers (and most of the leaders of the workers' movement belonged to this category) and those other workers who had to cope with a new environment, different languages and a loss of ties with their original communities.

1.2. Urbanisation

Industrial development at the turn of the century led to the growth of the city and its administrative districts (as described in Chapter one, Part 4). The fastest growing city districts were those with newly founded factories, since workers' housing and new apartment buildings were built in the proximity of the factories. These districts were the *New Town* and *Franz-Joseph Town*. These districts were ethnically very mixed. Many workers and low-income people also lived in Ligetfalu (which was technically not part of Pressburg) and the areas of the city referred to as "under the castle" (in Theresa's Town).

As in other parts of Europe during the Industrial Revolution, the need to accommodate large numbers of migrants to growing industrial cities had become a significant concern by the 1850s.[16] In Pressburg, workers tended to live in rented rooms in the historical centre.[17] In 1873, the soldiers' barracks were changed into workers' housing by Baron Walterskirchen as an act of philanthropy.[18] The first modern workers' housing was built in 1894–1902 by the philanthropist Georg Schulpe who had travelled around Europe and studied the social conditions of workers. (Chapter five describes Schulpe's activities in greater detail.) More housing was later built by the city (especially for municipal employees) and by factory owners in areas around their factories.[19] By 1905, employers had built 700 flats for their employees and workers.[20] (Figure 4 shows the location of this housing in the city.) Much of this accommodation was intended only for indispensable workers. Living conditions for the majority of the labour force remained grim.[21]

Growing urbanisation was not restricted merely to the growth of workers' housing and factories. There was also considerable building of new banks, schools, hospitals, apartment buildings, and villa districts. According to Obuchová, there was a growing tendency to exclude factories from residential areas.[22] Urban development in Pressburg followed two diverging trajectories: the dynamic of industrialisation and proletarian immigration, and the growth of an upwardly mobile middle-class. This growing middle-class joined with the city's traditional burgher elite in a strenuous effort to uphold aesthetic and moral standards in the midst of rapid industrialisation and urbanisation, whose negative aspects were associated with the influx of the working-class and the poor. (Chapter five takes up this "good city/bad city" dichotomy in greater detail.)

The workers' movement in Pressburg developed in a specific urban context. Initially educational activities evolved into political activities. The growing number of workers in Pressburg shifted the city's social and political balance, and opened opportunities for workers to act more as a collective force, although this unity was difficult to pull together and was often illusory. The next part describes the origins and development of the workers' movement in Hungary and Pressburg.

2. DEVELOPMENT OF THE WORKERS' MOVEMENT IN HUNGARY AND PRESSBURG

Between 1867 and 1914, the workers' movement in Hungary passed through waves of alternating activity and passivity that were also discernible in the progress of the workers' movement in Pressburg. This part of the chapter sketches the trajectory of the workers' movement as it evolved from small associations and self-help groups and grew to become trade unions and a mass political movement. This trajectory places the workers' movement in Pressburg into the wider contexts of Hungary and the Habsburg Empire, which in turn were nested in the wider European context.

Three stages can be identified in the development of the workers' movement in Hungary (and in Pressburg in particular) from the 1860s until the beginning of the 1890s: the foundation of educational and mutual support associations; the creation of a legal workers' party; and, finally, the evolution of this party into a mass movement.[23] The development of the workers' movement had to contend with setbacks and obstacles along the way. (Chapter five discusses the constant surveillance the workers' movement by the city and state authorities.) After 1890, modernisation, industrialisation, and urbanisation created an environment that enabled the gradual emergence of the workers' movement as a collective force. During the period 1900–1914, the workers' movement in Pressburg became a force which had to be taken into consideration by the city and state authorities who were seen by the workers as representatives of the dominant Pressburger 'bourgeois class.'

2.1. 1860s–1890: ESTABLISHING THE MOVEMENT

The Dual Agreement between Hungary and Austria radically re-shaped the political environment in both parts of the Habsburg Empire. New liberal legislation enabled the founding of workers' and craft associations, albeit with the consent of the Ministries of Interior and Agriculture. However, the right to collectively gather was not passed in the form of a law until the end of the empire, making workers dependent on the goodwill of the authorities responsible for the maintenance of law and order. The first workers' associations in Hungary were founded in 1867, with the formation of educational associations in Vienna, Prague and Liberec (and in 1868 in Budapest also). In Pressburg, the workers' educational association *Vorwärts* was founded in 1869.[24] (The activities of *Vorwärts* will be analysed in greater detail in the next part of this chapter.) German speaking workers assumed leadership roles in the emerging workers' movement in Pressburg because of the city's close contacts with Vienna and also because their educational level was higher than that of workers who spoke other languages.[25]

In June 1871, workers in Budapest staged a large march expressing solidarity with the defeated Paris Commune. This demonstration was followed by a wave of persecution. In 1872 the workers' association in Budapest was dissolved. The first attempt to establish a Hungarian workers' party (supported also by workers in Pressburg) took place in 1873 but its activities were banned by the authorities six weeks later. Because of the lack of a legal organisational framework, the workers' movement initially coalesced around the workers' weeklies *Munkás Héti-Krónika* (in Hungarian) and *Arbeiter Wochen-Chronik* (in German), (Workers' weekly chronicle) both published in Budapest.[26] Efforts to found a mass workers' party in Hungary started to materialise again after 1876 when Leo Frankel (1844–1896), who had been a member of the First International and a former minister of the Paris Commune, took over the leadership of the Hungarian workers' movement. In 1878, the first Hungarian workers' congress met in Budapest and founded the "Party of those not entitled to vote" (*A Nemválasztók Pártja*). This party had considerable support among Pressburg's workers. Two months later, the Workers' Party of Hungary (*Magyarországi Munkáspárt*) was founded by another group of workers led by Viktor Külföldy. This party's support was largely in Budapest and was concentrated around the newspapers *Népszava* (The word of the people) and *Volksstimme* (The voice of the people). The two parties amalgamated in 1880, establishing the Universal Workers' Party (*A Magyarországi Általános Munkáspárt*). The program of the new party was largely based on the Gotha program of the German social democrats.[27]

By 1883, the Universal Workers' Party was in crisis. Leo Frankel had been imprisoned by the authorities in 1881 and was subsequently forced to leave the country. The state's determination to prevent "anarchists" from establishing a foothold in Hungary also affected the workers' movement.[28] In Pressburg, the membership of the association *Vorwärts* decreased considerably.[29] At the founding congress of the Second International in Paris in 1889, the leaders of the newly founded Austrian Social Democratic Party discussed the decline of the Hungarian workers' movement. As a result, representatives of the Austrian and Hungarian workers' movements met in September 1889 and elected a new leadership for the Hungarian workers' movement, to be headed by Paul Engelmann (1854–1916), an Austrian social democrat. The founding congress of the Social Democratic Party of Hungary (*Magyarországi Szociáldemokrata Párt*) (henceforth SDPH) was convened in December 1890.[30]

2.2. 1890–1914: Increased Activity

The early 1890s were marked by increased activity by the social democratic and trade union movement in Hungary and Pressburg. The SDPH focused its efforts on achieving better living and working conditions for the workers as well as increasing their basic education and class consciousness.[31] The first trade union organisation in the territory of present-day Slovakia was founded in 1890 by Pressburg's tile and pottery producers, soon followed by workers from other industries.[32] Trades unions initially derived their membership from workers in bigger ethnically mixed cities such as Budapest, Pressburg, and Kassa. The first Slovak workers' periodicals *Nová Doba* (New Times) and *Zora* (Aurora) were published in 1897 with the help of Czech workers in Budapest.[33]

In 1893, the leadership of the SDPH became more moderate after the radical Paul Engelmann and his group were excluded from the party. Persecution of the social democratic movement increased after Dezider Bánffy became prime minister of Hungary (1895–1899). Bánffy established a special department in the Ministry of Interior to monitor the socialist and nationalities' movements.[34] The unionising activities of the SDPH decreased, and the party concentrated primarily on the fight for universal suffrage and on extending its reach beyond Budapest. By 1898, the social democrats had established twelve territorial organisations in Hungary.[35] However, internal divisions within the party continued to exist and the party was unable to capitalise on growing unrest among rural workers and poor people. Because of a lack of interest among the party leadership, agricultural workers split away from the SDPH and created their own independent socialist party espousing agrarian socialism.[36]

The efforts of the social democrats led the Hungarian government to pass laws improving the condition of workers to some extent: the 1884 (XVII) entrepreneur law establishing factory inspectors; laws in 1891 restricting work on Sunday and instituting obligatory health insurance; and the 1893 law giving greater authority to factory inspectors in order to prevent industrial accidents.[37] Even so, mass strikes took place in Budapest after 1 May 1897.[38] The SDPH became a mass movement after the beginning of the twentieth century.[39] An economic recession from 1900 to 1903 caused many factories to stop or limit production and the number of unemployed people in Hungary reached 100,000 in 1901.[40] Strikes become an instrument of the fight for better social conditions, and regular demonstrations showed off the numerical strength and organisation of the workers' movement. There was a whole wave of strikes in 1903 and the first general strike (of railway employees) in Hungary took place in April 1904.[41] The workers' critique of the existing class structure also became more vocal. This was particularly visible in Budapest but also in other industrial cities in the monarchy such as Pressburg.[42]

The number of organised workers swelled after the failed Russian revolution in 1905.[43] In 1906 the number of workers organised in trade unions increased two-fold, and outside Budapest, almost three-fold. However, these numbers decreased again after 1907, especially in the countryside.[44] In 1906, universal suffrage was passed in the Austrian half of the monarchy, and in the 1907 elections the Austrian Social Democratic Party gained 87 seats in parliament (out of a total of 455 seats). This victory acted as an incentive for the social democrats in Hungary to also fight for universal suffrage. A general strike was called for 10 October 1907, the day of the opening of the Hungarian parliament's autumn season.[45] Despite the mass character of the general strike, the workers did not achieve their objective, although the Hungarian parliament did pass a law about the health and accident insurance of workers.[46]

After this unsuccessful general strike, the workers' movement went into a period of decline that lasted until 1911. The number of strikes decreased and fewer workers were involved. The government banned the activity of some trades unions and several workers' organisations collapsed.[47] However, as in the earlier recession of 1900–1903, deteriorating economic conditions in 1912–1914 brought a sharp rise in unemployment and led to a wave of strikes and militancy. In 1912 there were 80,000 unemployed people in Hungary.[48] This was another period of active struggle for universal suffrage.[49] On 4 March 1912 there was a half-day general strike in the whole country, which was the largest public gathering that had ever taken place in Pressburg. New laws on military service and limited suffrage led to further waves of protest.[50] On 23 May 1912 there was a demonstration of 30,000 workers in Budapest. This gathering against the military service law in Budapest was bloodily crushed by the police and the army (on the so-called "bloody Thursday").[51] The SDPH called upon workers to prepare for a general strike against the limited suffrage law but it was forced to cancel the strike since Budapest was occupied by 60,000 soldiers and policemen.[52]

Left-oriented groups developed within the SDPH, one around the socialist intelligentsia and its leader Ervin Szabó (1877–1918), another around Gyula Alpári (1882–1944) and a third which consisted of functionaries of some countryside organisations. These groups were critical of the party leadership on the questions of general strike, political tactics and co-operation with the bourgeoisie and the government.[53] In 1910, Alpári was expelled from the party for his "slanders on the party."[54] Until the First World War the reformed evolutionary orientation which stressed the parliamentary way of achieving the set goals remained prevalent in the SDPH.[55]

As in other parts of Hungary, conditions for workers in Pressburg were harsh in this period. The unemployment office registered 6,800 people looking for jobs in 1912, of whom only 39% found employment. In 1913 the number of unemployed people in the city rose to 8,042.[56] The prices of food and rent also rose at this time. The city magistracy was unmoved by the difficulties faced by the unemployed, at first refusing to fund any relief for the unemployed, and finally, after many requests from the workers' leaders, approving a minimal amount of funding. Unsurprisingly, the Pressburg branches of the workers' movement were particularly strong before the First World War. In 1913, 2,132 workers were members of trade union organisations—the highest number in the territory of Slovakia.[57]

This part of the chapter has provided an overview of the development of the workers' and social democratic movement in Hungary and Pressburg. The movement gained strength gradually, moving through stages and waves of increased activity. Internal divisions and external persecution hindered the movement's growth but external economic conditions also led to greater solidarity among Hungary's working class. The social democratic movement in Hungary gained increasing mass support after the turn of the century. However, ethnic tensions within the social democratic movement also grew in this period. The next part of this chapter will look at the development of the workers' movement in Pressburg.

3. PRESSBURG AND DEVELOPMENT OF WORKERS' MOVEMENT

This part examines the activities of the workers' association *Vorwärts* as a case study of the workers' movement in Pressburg. While this association was one of the main actors of the workers' movement in the city, after the 1890s the activities of the social democrats also became important. The leading personalities from *Vorwärts* participated in the activities of the SDPH and were also involved in organising trade union activity in the city. This part will describe the foundation of the association, its membership and main activities. I will also examine the ideology and symbols used in the workers' movement. Lastly, I will consider the networks and mobilising structures of the workers' movement.

3.1. FOUNDING OF VORWÄRTS

> The founding of the smallest workers' educational association will have a far greater value for the future cultural historian than the great battle day of Sadowa.[58]
>
> —Karol Hanzlíček (former chairman of Vorwärts)

The idea of founding a workers' educational association in Pressburg arose in the cloth-factory of J. M. Mandel in 1868. The initiative was led by Philip Flexner, the commercial chief of the factory who was inspired by workers from Vienna where a similar association had been founded the previous year.[59] The inaugural meeting was held on 1 February 1869 in the City Casino, and was attended by a large number of workers as well as the city police chief.[60] (The law stipulated that a representative of the authorities had to be present at every public meeting to make sure that the meeting was peaceful.[61]) The programme of the association was almost literally copied from the programme of the Viennese workers' association.[62]

The most important aim of the association was "to increase and help the education of its members as well as to protect their material interests so that workers would not only be useful citizens of the state but become citizens capable of using state institutions which serve freedom."[63] The means designated for achieving this objective were popular lectures, establishment of a library and periodicals, and the foundation of a health and mutual support fund.[64] The main slogan of the association was: "Freedom through education!" However, at its inception the association lacked both financial means and intellectual capital. There were only a few workers who had rhetorical talent and these did most of the association's work. Many workers hoped for immediate improvement of their financial situation, and when this did not take place, they left the association.[65] After the initial burst of activity, the association fell dormant from 1882 to 1890. The association revived in 1890 with the foundation of trade unions and the organisation of the 1st of May celebrations.[66]

3.2. MEMBERSHIP

The membership of *Vorwärts* was very diverse. Workers comprised the majority but the membership included many small craftsmen, shopkeepers, clerks and even policemen. The number of industrial workers in Pressburg grew rapidly only after 1890 and as a result, the initial phases of the workers' movement also involved small craftsmen and artisans. This was typical for the workers' and social democratic movement in Hungary.[67] Industrial growth triggered a rise in the number of industrial workers but craftsmen and artisans remained an important part of the workers movement and later created their own trade unions as well.[68] The presence of craftsmen and artisans significantly influenced the ideological orientation (in particular, the prevalence of petit-bourgeois values) of the workers' movement.[69] Increasing industrialisation brought many more industrial workers into the organisation.[70] Nevertheless, craftsmen continued to constitute a considerable part of the membership, taking leadership roles in the association and also serving as editors of the workers' newspapers.[71]

Vorwärts had no more than 100 members in 1890.[72] These were primarily activists in the workers' movement. The remaining 7,261 workers in Pressburg in 1890 were not organised at all. By 1892, the association's membership had grown fourfold.[73] However, the association's membership fluctuated over the next decade, like other parts of the workers' movement. By 1906, *Vorwärts* had only 160 members, decreasing from 212 in the previous year.[74] By this time *Vorwärts* served purely as an educational association and the SDPH had taken over the task of organising public meetings and similar mobilisation activities.

3.3. ACTIVITIES

The association *Vorwärts* had from its inception four sections: for illness and mutual support, education, care for the unemployed workers, and for social events.[75] Members met in a rented room until they acquired a house (thereafter called the Workers' Home) on the Duna utca in 1902, where all meetings, lectures, discussions and public gatherings were subsequently held.[76] Records of the association for May 1869 show a busy schedule of events, including meetings of the standing committee on Tuesdays, the education committee on Wednesdays, the social events committee on Thursday, the health insurance section meeting on Fridays, and general discussions on Saturdays.[77] These general discussions were usually educational lectures.[78]

In 1869 the association also opened a library where workers could read newspapers and books.[79] In 1890, the association founded its own singing group (*Gesangsektion*) which in 1893 gave rise to the choir *Liedesfreiheit* (Freedom of the song).[80] These choirs performed at public and social occasions and at the May Day celebrations. Other workers' organisations also took on social and sporting activities.[81] Ethnic divisions can be seen to emerge in these activities. For example, the German construction workers founded the *Turnsektion der Bauarbeiter* for field athletics. In 1913, the Czech workers' association founded the *Dělnická telocvičná jednota* (Workers' physical exercise association) which organised trips and entertainment in which Slovak workers also participated.[82]

Although primarily focused on the education of workers, the association *Vorwärts* was also an agent of collective action in the city until almost the end of the nineteenth century. (The next part of this chapter considers the repertoire of collective action used by the workers' movement.) The following section considers the networks and mobilising structures that enabled collective action to take place.

3.4. Networks

This section describes how the workers' movement in Hungary and Pressburg was organised and how workers were brought into the movement. I will also look at the contacts of the association *Vorwärts* and Pressburg's social democrats with social democrats and workers' movements outside Hungary.

In the absence of the legal right to freely hold public meetings, the organisational activities of the SDPH took place within the frame of the trade union organisations and workers' education associations.[83] Political parties in Hungary were not allowed to found branch offices but were also not required to get the approval of authorities for their activity (unlike associations). Trade unions were not allowed to organise strikes or financially support strikers. Two organisational forms were created in order to overcome these hindrances. "Loose organisations" were the organisational basis of the party. (Their existence did not require the statutory permission of the authorities since they met primarily for informal discussions.) They consisted of "confidants" chosen by workers who collected money for "resistance funds" (the other organisational form) created for financial support of workers during strikes. "Confidants" basically represented the local party organisation. These "loose organisations" were a link between the party and trade unions. When the party was planning a strike or demonstration, it contacted its "confidants" who then carried out the actual mobilisation of workers. "Loose organisations" had the right to send delegates to the party congresses. County agitation committees also existed in those places where the movement was most active.[84]

These "loose organisations" consisted of trade unions' functionaries, functionaries of educational associations and the editorial boards of workers' newspapers. Their activities often merged with the activities of educational associations, as in the case of *Vorwärts*. These associations were the main agents of the workers' movement, organising public meetings, May Day demonstrations and other workers' activities.[85] The SDPH considered as a member anyone who was organised in trade unions and was paying his/her trade union fee. Apart from these, party members paid fees into the "resistance funds" and a majority also paid a party fee.[86]

By 1898 the SDPH had twelve territorial organisations in Hungary.[87] The social democratic organisations in Pressburg and Kassa also spread their agitation outside their respective cities. After 1893 Pressburg was the centre for one of the first regional workers' organisations in Hungary, the "Western-Hungarian social democratic organisation" which covered the territory of Pozsony and Trencsén counties and two counties on the right bank of the Danube (in present-day Hungary.) This Western Hungarian social democratic organisation, together with the trade unions, organised workers' activities in Pressburg, taking over the leading role previously played by the association *Vorwärts*.[88] This regional social democratic organisation was concentrated around the workers' newspapers published in Pressburg.[89] However, it probably did not function in this form for long and changed into Pressburg's social democratic party. In 1905, regional centres were established again. However, the territorial impact of the Pressburg regional organisation narrowed, by 1910 covering only Pressburg.[90] Within Pressburg itself, the main agents of the SDPH were the workers' educational association, the branch associations of the apprentices and the local groups of the Hungarian trade unions.[91]

The association *Vorwärts* was the main agent of the workers' movement in Pressburg from 1869 until the 1890s, taking a leading role in founding and organising trades unions in the city by craft and industry. In this capacity, *Vorwärts* had extensive contacts with the workers' movement in the Austrian part of the monarchy and also with some German social democrats. The help of the Viennese workers was crucial in organising *Vorwärts*, both at its inception and in subsequent activities.[92] The Viennese workers took an active role in many of the association's public meetings. Members of the Viennese trade unions were often present at the Saturday meetings and lectures of *Vorwärts*. Pressburg's workers frequently met Austrian workers in Hainburg (a village in Austria close to Pressburg). The Pressburg printing shop of Lowy and Alkalay which employed workers of social democratic conviction, printed not only the local workers' newspaper but also did a number of jobs for the Viennese workers.[93] The 1873 strike of typesetters was made possible by the financial support they received from Vienna.[94] Personal records of activists in the period indicate that the leaders of the Pressburg workers' movement also followed the Austrian workers' press.[95] Several of the workers' leaders in Pressburg were themselves originally from the Austrian part of the monarchy or from Germany. Pressburg was also important for Viennese socialists: when they wanted to escape surveillance of Austrian authorities or their meetings were banned, they organised their meetings in Pressburg.

The first chairman of *Vorwärts*, Eduard Niemczyk tried to actively spread the principles of the association and to make contacts with other similar associations. As the Pressburg police chief reported to the minister of interior, Niemczyk was in contact with both Viennese and Brno workers' associations where "he collects their ideas and brings them to the local association."[96] On 14 November 1869, the first conference of the social democrats of the Dual Monarchy with participation of the delegates of the First International took place in Pressburg, which was chosen not only because of its central geographical location but also because of the organisational abilities of the association *Vorwärts*.[97] In 1889, representatives of the Austrian and Hungarian workers met in Pressburg to take action against the existing leadership of the Hungarian workers' movement and to prepare the founding of the SDPH.[98]

Pressburg's social democrats had very close relations with Vienna, often even closer than with the Budapest centre of the party. However, the Pressburg group still belonged to the SDPH (initially the Workers' Party) and were also in frequent contact with the Budapest leaders. In the second half of the 1890s, the workers' movement in Pressburg developed its range of activities in accord with the Budapest leadership's efforts.[99] Pressburg's leaders participated in all the party congresses, and often represented Hungary at international workers' congresses. Therefore the Pressburger as well as the Hungarian social democratic movement was connected with the social democratic movement in other European countries. During the same period, Slovak workers who had started to participate in the Hungarian social democratic movement also developed close relationships with Czech workers in both Vienna and Budapest.[100]

The Hungarian authorities were aware of these close relations. In 1880, the minister of interior informed Pressburg's *főispán* of the decision of the Austrian social democrats to organise their meeting on Hungarian territory close to the Austrian border, in case of difficulties organising this meeting on Austrian territory.[101] In 1890, the minister of interior informed Pressburg's mayor that workers from his city were planning to go to Hainburg in Austria territory on the first of May to violently force a day off for workers there. The Pressburg police had to ensure that workers from Pressburg did not cross the Danube on this occasion.[102] The city and state authorities were also concerned by the trip of 1,700 Austrian workers from Florisdorf (Austria) to Pressburg in 1895.[103] The fifth chapter of this study describes the surveillance apparatus that was put into place to track the movements of social democratic activists and their foreign connections.

This part has examined the membership, activities and contacts of the workers' movement in Pressburg. The next part considers the repertoire of collective action used by the workers' movement in the city.

4. COLLECTIVE ACTION AND SOLIDARITY BUILDING IN PRESSBURG

Mass movements use a repertoire of collective action which "challenge opponents, create uncertainty, and build solidarity."[104] This part studies the ways in which Pressburg's workers challenged their opponents, created uncertainty in the city and built solidarity, especially through collective action. While the Hungarian workers' and (later) the social democratic movement gained organisational coherence only in the 1880s and 1890s and acquired mass support only in the twentieth century, the activities of the Pressburg workers' association *Vorwärts* were marked from its inception in 1869 by a consistent effort to organise public gatherings. This part will look at two forms of collective action used by *Vorwärts* and its social democratic allies: public meetings and demonstrations connected with the celebration of 1 May. I will then examine the ideological and cultural symbols used by the workers' movement in creating solidarity among Pressburg's workers.

4.1. PUBLIC MEETINGS

Hungary had no law regulating public gatherings. As a result, permissions for holding a public meeting were completely in the hands of local authorities who often consulted with the minister of interior (as discussed in Chapter five). Permissions were difficult to obtain and were often denied on arbitrary grounds.[105] In order to call a public meeting, the meeting's organisers had to fulfil several formalities. They had to announce the gathering to the city authorities at least eight days before it was supposed to take place. Furthermore, at least ten entrepreneurs had to vouch with their signatures that the meeting would have a peaceful character and that there would be no offences against public order, either before or after the gathering.[106]

Six weeks into its existence, the association *Vorwärts* organised (with the help of the Viennese workers) a public meeting which was the first socialist public gathering in Hungary.[107] The languages spoken at the meeting were German and Hungarian.[108] The meeting passed a resolution demanding rights for workers, the unlimited right of assembly and association, freedom of the press, universal suffrage, freedom of confession, and the abolition of the standing army in favour of general arming of all people.[109] These demands were frequently repeatedly until 1914. Meetings in the first years of the workers' movement focused on the need for workers to organise themselves, on the need for improvements in living conditions, and on the need for protection at times of illness and in the face of employers. The demand for universal suffrage was often repeated (becoming especially important after 1890). More specific concerns were also addressed at these meetings.[110]

In 1890 the celebration of 1 May began, trade unions were founded, and the number of active workers grew. Public meetings also became more frequent and their main demands were for universal suffrage and an eight-hour work-day. Until 1902, all of the public meetings in the city were held indoors within a closed space as the police found it easier to control such gatherings. However, in August 1902 there was a public meeting at the square Haltér where 3,000 workers demonstrated in favour of universal suffrage.[111] Increasing demands for universal suffrage (especially during the years 1905–1907, 1910–1912) even led to meetings with speakers from various social classes and ethnic backgrounds. For example in October 1907, 3,000 people participated in a public meeting in the garden of the Workers' Home, including 1500 peasants from rural areas around Pressburg. Speakers included the Slovak parliament deputies Pavol Blaho and Milan Hodža who spoke in Slovak. Their speeches were translated into Hungarian by Dezső Bokányi. Paul Wittich, the representative of the social democrats in Pressburg, spoke in German.[112] Public meetings after 1912 all concentrated on universal suffrage, critique of the governmental proposals for suffrage reform, and attacking militarisation laws.[113]

Public meetings in Pressburg were very peaceful for the most part. They did not provoke intervention by the authorities, except for some measure of censorship. The presence of police officials at meetings restricted what was permissible to say and did not allow for much radicalism. In one public meeting in 1877 the chairman even asked speakers to refrain from giving the authorities reasons to dissolve the gathering.[114] At another public meeting a police officer interrupted a speaker who had called local journalists "press hussars" and warned him to moderate his expressions.[115] On another occasion, László Balogh proposed the overthrow of the present class society and was promptly interrupted by the representative of the city police who considered the opinions subversive and provocative.[116] The police representatives were obviously willing to intervene in order to silence speakers attacking the existing social order, the government or the Hungarian state itself. However, even the city police chief noted the peaceful character of the workers' movement in Pressburg (as will be shown in Part 6 of this chapter and in Chapter five).[117]

The next section describes the annual effort by the workers to disturb the peace in Pressburg: the 1 May celebrations.

4.2. May Day Celebrations

In 1889, the Second International adopted 1 May as the day of the working people of the world, emphasising the international character of the proletariat. From 1890 onwards, the Pressburg workers' movement organised public gatherings with a social democratic agenda and tried to organise demonstrations in the city.[118] The leaders of the workers' movement sought to demonstrate the strength and organisation of the movement and to put forward their main demands, for an eight-hour work-day and for universal suffrage. 1 May celebrations became large public events in Pressburg only after the turn of the century. Until 1902 marches and street processions were not allowed in the city.[119] From 1902 on, an increasing number of workers marched through the city centre almost every year.[120] After 1903, the gatherings took place in the Workers' Home, which had become the main venue for workers' activities. As in the case of other public meetings, the workers were careful to stay on legal ground. They asked for permission to organise public meetings and demonstrations from the city police chief and always provided a detailed programme of the meeting and topics of speeches since the police chief would not give permission without a detailed itinerary.

It was only in the twentieth century that the May Day celebrations began to fulfil their purpose of demonstrating the strength of the workers' movement. In Austria, electoral reforms in 1897 and the introduction of universal suffrage in 1906 brought social democrats into the Austrian parliament.[121] By contrast, Hungarian proposals for suffrage reform prevented the masses from voting because existing elites were afraid of losing power.[122] As a result, the demand for universal suffrage acquired greater urgency at 1 May celebrations.[123] In 1912, workers marched in a large procession making a loop around the old town centre in order to demonstrate the force of the movement to the city's inhabitants (see Figure 4).[124] The symbolic connotations of workers occupying this upper class space (if only for an afternoon) were plain to see. This act of appropriation by the workers gave this public space a new meaning as a venue of social protest.[125] For a short time, the street became a part of the living space of the lower classes and this space was temporarily controlled by them and not the upper classes.[126]

Similarly, in 1911 (and then every year until the First World War) the City Theatre's German ensemble gave a performance of "Wilhelm Tell" for the workers. For one day in the year the workers had managed to appropriate the cherished domain of the Pressburger middle classes: the City Theatre. (Chapter two has shown the symbolic value ascribed to this venue during the struggle over "ownership" of the City Theatre between the city's traditional Pressburger elite and the new Magyar nationalist elite.)

From the outset, the worker leaders aimed to secure 1 May as a day off so that Pressburg's workers could demonstrate their solidarity with workers in other countries. However, this was difficult to achieve. In 1890 workers asked employers to release them from work on 1 May (which was a Thursday).[127] Only some employers gave workers a paid day off. Most workers had their wages reduced and some employers even threatened dismissal. In 1891, workers met and decided to categorically refuse to postpone the 1 May celebration to Sunday or to the evening hours of workdays.[128] In 1893, the minister of interior ordered state enterprises not to give their workers a day off; private employers could do as they pleased.[129] In the period 1894–1898 only a few factories stopped work on this day.[130] After 1901, typographers succeeded in getting a day off, so that no newspapers were published in Pressburg for the subsequent day.[131] Gradually, with the growing strength of trade unions and social democrats in Pressburg, more and more workers were allowed by their employers to celebrate 1 May.

May Day celebrations gradually became part of the city landscape. Until the turn of the century, these celebrations were smaller affairs that took place in closed spaces and outside the city. Police officials were always present. These extensive security measures illustrate the authorities' fear that these meetings could degenerate into disorder and create tension in the city. Over the years, the authorities relaxed their grip on the celebrations to some extent, allowing workers to march through the city centre. However, when the city authorities again wanted to ban these marches in later years, the workers were able to force the authorities to back down.[132] This shows both that the workers' movement was gaining more self-confidence and also that the city authorities were afraid to refuse the workers' demands. (The fifth part of this chapter considers the reactions of the city authorities and inhabitants to the growing workers' movement.) The next section considers the ways in which the leaders of the workers' movement succeeded in building solidarity among Pressburg's workers.

4.3. FRAMING COLLECTIVE ACTION:
USE OF CULTURAL AND IDEOLOGICAL SYMBOLS

This section looks at the ideological and cultural frames which were used by the leaders of the workers' movement in their efforts to build solidarity among the 'working class.'[133] I will consider the ideology of the workers' movement in Pressburg, briefly describing the workers' main demands which brought them together in a social movement and spurred their collective action. While public meetings and May Day celebrations challenged opponents by their very occurrence and the presence of large numbers of workers, the workers' demands posed an explicit challenge to the existing social system and structure. I will examine the symbols used in building solidarity among the workers. I will also examine the role of the workers' press in spreading these ideological and cultural symbols, in fomenting 'agitation' and thereby creating an 'imagined community' of class. Finally, I will also look at the "enemies" identified by the workers' leaders in order to determine the boundaries of this 'imagined community'.

4.3.1. Ideology

After the mid-nineteenth century Pressburg became an 'entrance gate' between the two parts of the Austro-Hungarian Empire. The development of transport between Vienna, Pressburg and Budapest accelerated the flow of migrants, primarily apprentices and workers looking for jobs in the new industries. This increased migration also resulted in a "migration of ideas."[134] Pressburg's workers were very much influenced by the Austrian social democrats and received ideological as well as organisational support from the Viennese workers' associations. They were also connected to the wider international workers' movement.[135]

The association *Vorwärts* initially had adherents of both Schulze-Delitzsch's and Lassalle's ideas. Hermann Schulze-Delitzsch believed that small producers should found cooperatives in order to defend themselves against competition from large capital deployed in mass production. Schulze-Delitzsch was against political activity by workers. Ferdinand Lassalle, on the other hand, wanted workers to join together in a political movement in order to gain universal suffrage and thus to improve the conditions of workers by bringing about legal change. Lassalle was against strikes and violence and imagined a transition to socialism through the foundation of production cooperatives set up with the help of the state.[136] In 1869 most *Vorwärts* members were followers of Lassalle and his views became the basic ideological basis of the association.[137] Marx's ideas did not acquire much support until the 1890s.[138] Some left-wing tendencies became visible within the Hungarian social democratic movement only in the twentieth century but the left wing orientation did not become dominant (as noted earlier in Part 2 of this chapter).[139] The leadership of the SDPH was strongly ideologically influenced by the German and Austrian social democracy, concretely by the theorists Lassalle, Karl Kautsky and later also Eduard Bernstein.[140]

The demand for universal suffrage and the use of legal means remained central tenets of the workers' movement in Pressburg throughout the period 1869–1914. Already in the first meeting organised by *Vorwärts* in 1869 the speakers stressed that the social question had to be solved in a peaceful way and that workers should gain power through general elections and refuse any violent forms of struggle.[141] The workers' leaders were always careful not to push the authorities too far, planning and organising their public meetings and demonstrations very carefully so as to contain any possible source of violent conflict.[142] This was even specified in the original statutes of *Vorwärts*: "Use of all legal means to achieve political and civic rights for the working class." This point had to be dropped on the demand of the minister of interior.[143] For the authorities, even this statement carried too much uncertainty as to the means workers might employ in their struggle for future objectives.

The workers' main demands were universal suffrage, the right to freely gather and associate, freedom of speech, an eight-hour work day and other improvements in the bad working and living conditions faced by workers, and the necessity of education for workers. The most immediate of these demands related to the miserable living conditions of workers. Workers' leaders raised this issue at every public meeting:

Despite all his diligence the city's proletarian lives in poverty, he starves with his wife and children whom he cannot feed. Used by the "better" society and chased until exhaustion, insulted and deeply hurt by public opinion, banished by society, the wretch is walking eternally sad in an earthly paradise, in mute desperation because humanity has driven him out.[144]

Feelings of solidarity grew among workers with discussions of the difficult conditions they faced in their daily lives. Many workers came to believe that they could change their living conditions for the better through collective action. For many workers the vision of a better life meant humane working conditions and shorter working hours, better pay, security in case of illness, accident and old age. They wanted to be self-respecting and respected at the same time.[145] Workers demanded better pay so that their wives did not have to work but could do "what nature meant them to be doing"—household upkeeping and bringing up their children.[146] Better pay also symbolised recognition by other social classes. The demand for an eight-hour workday became especially important after 1890, crystallising around the 1 May celebrations, together with the demand for universal suffrage.[147] Universal suffrage remained a key demand of the workers' movement until the First World War. Workers believed that only representation in parliament would ensure that their complaints would be heard and acted upon. Workers' representatives in the parliament could ensure that legislature on social reform would be passed. While power was held solely by "exploiters," workers had no chance for a better life. Thus exclusion from political power was seen as the cause of their social anomalies.[148] Furthermore, the right to vote was seen as a right that workers had earned through their labour.[149]

The need for a law specifying the right to freely gather and associate became more deeply felt as city and state authorities arbitrarily banned workers' meetings. The absence of a law was very advantageous for the authorities because it enabled a flexible response on each occasion. Indeed, the state authorities considered the absence of this right the very reason why the socialist movement in Hungary had not developed to such an extent as in Austria (see footnote 82). However, workers' leaders considered the freedom to gather and associate a basic right to which they were entitled. As Hanzlíček put it: "How can we give up our free right to association when we have so much to say about our position and working conditions?"[150]

The association *Vorwärts* was founded with the goal of educating the workers. The importance of this objective was also stressed at the founding congress of the SDPH: "we consider it our duty to spread self-confidence, education and enlightenment among proletarians so that the masses of workers prepare for their future cultural-historical mission and also in the interest of humanity."[151] The leaders of the workers' movement realised that ignorant workers were hard to organise. The ruling elites considered uneducated workers uncultured, primitive and unworthy of even the right to vote. Educating illiterate workers and teaching them how to articulate their demands was therefore an important task. *Vorwärts* chairman Niemczyk declared that: "Education makes us free, unity gives power and we fight with the weapon of education!"[152] However, the leaders had to struggle with the "ignorance" and "indifference" of the workers and meld them into a mass movement.[153]

The Pressburger workers' movement understood that solidarity among all workers in Hungary was necessary for fulfilling their demands. The leaders accepted the principle of internationalism and class based solidarity:

> The Pressburger comrades wish that the strength of the Hungarian workers' movement was born out of understanding and solidarity so that the necessary organisation could be secured. Our strong association is universal; every comrade may speak whatever language and belong to whichever confession, but he has to become part of this unity; as the same act leads us to the same goal.[154]

Despite the efforts made by the workers' movement to stress their commitment to legal approaches to change, their demands posed a significant challenge to the power holders since the challenged the basis of the social hierarchy.(The reactions of the city and state elites are discussed later in this chapter and in Chapter five.) The next few pages examine the symbols that were used in building solidarity among the workers.

4.3.2. Building Solidarity: The Use of Symbols

In addition to a shared ideology, workers were also brought together by symbols that expressed their solidarity and sense of belonging to an 'imagined community' of class. As discussed above, the 1 May celebrations were a symbol of the workers' participation in a world-wide community of oppressed workers. The demonstrations and marches through the city were symbolic acts insofar as they asserted the right of Pressburg's workers to "own" their city. (Equally, the dominant elites saw these marches as a form of "transgression," especially when workers paraded on the elite's own favourite walking space, the Promenade.) Similarly, the workers' "occupation" of the City Theatre in 1911 had important symbolic meaning in the context of the power struggle between the German and Magyar elites over the theatre. The next few pages identify some more key symbols that were used both to generate internal solidarity within the workers' movement but also to demonstrate the strength of the movement to outsiders. Some key symbols include the use of the colour red, distinctive badges and songs, the anniversary of the Hungarian revolution on 15 March, and the ritualisation of the workers' flag.

Workers adopted the colour red as a symbol of the blood shed in their struggle for a better future. At public gatherings and at 1 May celebrations workers wore red ribbons, red ties, and red carnations, and red May Day badges.[155] They also wore distinctive badges picturing a harvester and an industrial worker. The use of these symbols enabled workers to differentiate themselves from other inhabitants of the city. Since the First of May was also a day of celebration for the city's middle class, the use of the colour red provided an immediate visual marker differentiating one city inhabitant from another. These common symbols also built pride and self-confidence among the workers. In addition to the vibrant colour red, workers were also linked together through lively and distinctive forms of music. Workers joined together in singing revolutionary songs like the "Song of Work" or the *Marseillaise*.[156] Workers' marches and celebrations were usually accompanied by their own choirs. On several occasions workers were also accompanied by the local gypsy band., which was generally favoured in middle-class entertainment. This might indicate the workers' aspirations to became normal rather than distinct, a part of the 'respectable' petty bourgeoisie rather than a revolutionary force intent on changing the social system.[157]

In 1902 the local social democratic newspaper *Westungarische Volksstimme* published a special issue printed all in red for the First of May. The flag of the association *Vorwärts* itself was made from red velvet. The name of the association was in golden letters on a white field in the middle. The flag was suspended on a red pole. The pole ended in a silver workers' badge—two hands holding a hammer. (Even a new bakery advertised in the workers' press as having the cheapest bread, had a hammer as its symbol.[158]) The name of the association "Erster Pressburger Arbeiter-Bildungsverein Vorwärts" (The first Pressburger workers' educational association) was also embroidered on red ribbons with golden letters.[159]

The symbols above were used exclusively by workers to denote their belonging to the workers' movement. Workers also attached a distinct meaning to an important event whose symbolic value was contested by different strata of the city's population. This was the celebration of the anniversary of the Hungarian revolution on 15 March 1848. As Chapter two noted, the Hungarian patriotic association *Toldy Kör* celebrated this event every year with the substantial support of the Hungarian students in the city. Many German-speaking non-chauvinistic inhabitants of Pressburg had also been supporters and adherents of the ideals of the Hungarian revolution. Sándor Petőfi (the poet who was killed in the revolution and became a Hungarian national hero) had even lived in Pressburg for some time. However, workers saw the meaning of this anniversary and of Petőfi's "martyrdom" in a different light. While the bourgeoisie celebrated the Hungarian fight for freedom from Austrian oppression, the workers celebrated the fight for freedom from the oppressors of the poor. Petőfi was the "revolutionary of the oppressed," a "son of the people" since he had wished for a better life, for freedom and equality for the poor.[160] Workers described the bourgeois celebration of this anniversary as a "pious deception" (*frommer Selbstbetrug*) since the burghers and the students supported the reactionary nobility. The workers considered the Hungarian revolution incomplete: although feudal duties had been lifted, the revolution had preserved the power of the aristocracy and nobility. Thus workers did not celebrate the birthday of freedom "but the premonition of the dawn of a new day ... which shall bring us freedom."[161]

It is also interesting to note the ritualisation of certain practices in the workers' movement. As mentioned above, 1 May was charged with symbolic meaning for workers. The May Day celebrations acquired a ritualised quality. The symbols of unity and solidarity described above were one aspect of the ritual. Another aspect was the schedule of the day itself which workers tried to keep the same each year (depending on permission from the authorities): an early morning meeting in the park or near the bridge, a public gathering in the morning, and then a demonstration through the city in the afternoon and an entertainment in the evening. The sequence of events had a certain symbolic order: first, the consecration of the day, a gathering together of purpose, the demonstration of that purpose, and finally, the coming together again in good fellowship. The highlight of the day, the march through the city, was also put together in advance, assigning a place in the parade to all groups of workers, organised by industry or craft.

Even the consecration of the *Vorwärts* flag (at the inception of the association in 1869) was performed in a ritual manner. At the meetings founding the association, members wondered whether the flag should be consecrated by a priest. Most members were in favour; as one noted, "a flag which is not consecrated by a priest could be spat upon."[162] Since the association had members from several religious persuasions, it was finally decided that the flag would be unfolded by the association's chairman.[163] On the day of the ceremony, 400 people gathered in front of the Hotel National and marched across the pontoon bridge to Ligetfalu on the other bank of the Danube. The procession was accompanied by an army orchestra. The 'mother' and the 'godmother' of the flag (worker women) were appointed. After a speech by the association's chairman, the flag was raised up and then turned towards the four directions. Afterwards shots were fired and the army orchestra played the Lassalle march. After the consecration of the flag, the chairman read an oath that was repeated by twenty members standing in a circle together with the 'mother', the 'godmother' of the flag and six girls in white around the flag. The oath read:

> I raise my right hand and I swear here in God's free nature on my honour and my happiness to the flag of freedom that I will remain faithful to it on the principles of social democracy; that I will never misuse it for unworthy goals but I will raise it high in the fight for universal human rights. I promise that I would rather die under the flag of freedom than betray it. Amen![164]

In the evening there was a celebration attended also by some members of the Pressburg's elite and the colonel of the infantry regiment placed in Pressburg.[165]

The elements of this ritual (and the oath) were clearly borrowed from the church ritual. The whole ritual resembles the baptism of a newborn child. The discussion on priestly consecration of the flag also indicates the important role played by religion in the lives of workers at the time. Religion was still an integral part of the workers' world view. The turning of the flag in all four directions is also suggestive of another ritual, that of the coronation of kings. The freshly crowned king would flourish his sword in all four directions to indicate his protection of the country from all sides. Similarly, in this context, turning the flag in all directions could illustrate a sense of unity with workers in all parts of the world.

As the above discussion shows, workers used different symbols to denote their belonging to an 'imagined community.' Some of their activities (such as the celebration of 1 May) even acquired a ritual character through repetition over the years. This 'imagined community' of class was built on ideological and symbolic grounds. Solidarity was also built through agitation, through leaflets handed out in workers' gatherings and especially through the social democratic press. The next sub-section considers the role played by the workers' press in creating solidarity in the workers' movement.

4.3.3. Workers' Press

The workers' press played a crucial role in spreading social democratic ideas in Pressburg. The workers' leaders put great importance on creating their own workers' press so that the workers would not be contaminated by the biases of the 'burgher press.' Speakers at workers' meetings in the 1870s often discussed the need for the workers' press, declaring that while the press ought to be defending progress and truth, in reality it was misleading the people and serving the ruling class. "The burgher press always just denounces workers and still the workers support it and this must change." The *Pressburger Zeitung* (the main local daily of the German middle classes) was mockingly called the "Pressburg Auntie" (*Pressburger Tante*) because of its reactionary and conservative attitudes.[166] The only press "speaking pure truth that will not crawl before the rich adventurers is the social democratic press."[167] *Vorwärts* members read the Viennese workers' newspapers *Wiener Vorstadt-Zeitung* and *Brüderlichkeit* initially, and the association later subscribed to the *Arbeiter Wochen-Chronik* which was published in Budapest.[168] The leaders appealed to the workers to support workers' newspapers rather than the bourgeois press.[169] The leaders made an exception for Simonyi's *Westungarischer Grenzbote* which they considered objective and they had a positive relationship with this editor.[170]

However, although there were workers' newspapers printed in Budapest that were distributed all over Hungary, the Pressburg workers wanted their own newspaper which would actively counteract the local "burgher press."

In 1879, the worker's movement made its first attempt to publish its own newspaper, *Die Wahrheit*, but its editor, former *Vorwärts* chairman Hanzlíček was prosecuted because of the newspaper's political articles. He was sentenced and fined, and the newspaper banned. Another attempt, *Der Zeitgeist* (1881) had a similar fate.[171] It was only in 1893 that the *Neue Volkszeitung* began regular publication until 1895. In 1896 the *Westungarische Volkszeitung* was established until 1899 when its editor Zalkai left the Social Democratic Party.[172] After March 1902 the weekly *Westungarische Volksstimme* was the main newspaper published in Pressburg by organised workers, from 1910 by the local Social Democratic Party.[173] All these newspapers were published in German. At the beginning of the twentieth century, newspapers also began to be published in Slovak. However, this was already a time when class solidarity had started to split along language lines, as described in the next part of this chapter.

4.3.4. Enemies

Solidarity in the workers' movement was also defined and maintained by identifying 'enemies.' The main 'enemies' were the 'bourgeoisie' and the clergy as well as the police as the main defender of the "exploiters." The 'bourgeoisie' could be identified and attacked in various ways: most directly, as the city and state authorities who were suppressing workers' rights; grand capital; exploitative employers (on several occasions Jews in the city); and the bourgeois press (as described above). The workers' press also frequently attacked religion. The clergy were seen as having a strong interest in keeping poor people ignorant and submissive, thereby supporting existing power structures.

The city authorities were constantly criticised in the workers' press and in public meetings as inflexible, "stale" and oriented only towards their own self-interest and profit.[174] Municipal deputies were described as devoid of social feeling and lacking sensitivity towards the miserable conditions in which workers lived. The worker's press was especially indignant towards city expenses that were seen as "frivolous" and "absurd," while the poor were starving and forced to live in dank squalor. For example, one meeting of the municipal assembly allocated 5,000 guldens for organising horse races while giving just 50 guldens to support a construction worker's widow with six children.[175]

The workers' press was especially concerned about the serious lack of affordable accommodation for an ever increasing number of workers and their families. The press ironically described the selfish behaviour of "our city fathers" (*unsere Stadtväter*) whose main interest was in maximising the rent received from their properties and who were therefore uninterested in improving the disastrous housing situation which was turning into "a shame for the second city of the land."[176] Municipal representation was seen as clique-ridden, concerned solely with their own class-interests, and incapable of serving the good of the city's inhabitants.[177] The workers sarcastically called the city authorities "mamelukes" who could not see beyond their self-interest.[178] "These are patriots, clericals, Austrians, everything in one person."[179] Another derogatory name for the traditional Pressburger elite (which was also used by the Magyar nationalist elite) was "Kraxelhubers."[180] The burghers were seen as totally lacking any feeling for liberty and fraternity.[181] However, these self-interested burghers were also seen as a part of the class of oppressors which included the government and the ruling class. The social system as a whole was considered exploitative and its purported liberalism was just a lie.[182]

The other immediate enemy in the city was the Association of Catholic Workers (and by extension, the Catholic People's Party) and Christian socialists with whom the social democrats were engaged in a fight for the "souls" of the workers. The Christian Socialist Party (Országos Keresztény Szocialista Párt) in Hungary was founded in 1907. In February 1908 it merged with the Hungarian People's Party (active especially among peasants) which changed its name to Christian Socialist People's Party (Keresztény Szocialista Néppárt).[183] Many social democratic workers were also religious-minded. However, according to the social democrats, Christian socialists only taught obedience to enduring exploitation.[184] Feelings of injustice also grew rampant when the social democrats were not allowed to hold a gathering but the "black brothers" (*Schwarze Brüder*) received permission for a public meeting on the same day (another example of how the city and state authorities used their power to arbitrarily permit or deny public meetings). In this case the workers blamed the deputy mayor who was "inimical to workers and a clerical."[185] There were also cases when the Catholic workers held meetings on the same day as the social democrats and tried to lure workers away from the social-democratic meeting.[186] Most of the strike-breakers were also Christian socialists.[187] The workers' press abounded in descriptions of the immoral behaviour of priests and clerics. However, most workers probably wavered between Christian beliefs and social democratic ideas, in contrast to the firm ideological convictions of their leaders.

4.3.5. Conclusion

This part has considered the ways in which the leaders of Pressburg's workers built a mass community, generating solidarity through collective action in public meetings and demonstrations. This 'imagined community' of class developed a common ideology of interests and a shared vocabulary of symbols that were used to differentiate the workers from their 'enemies', in particular, the bourgeois elite and the ruling class. However, as the next part of this chapter shows, the attempt to build identity on the basis of class became increasingly difficult with the emergence of linguistic and ethnic divisions.

5. WORKERS AND ETHNICITY: THE ACTIVITIES OF THE SLOVACK SECTION OF VORWÄRTS AND THE SLOVAK SOCIAL DEMOCRATS

This part of the chapter is concerned with the impact of ethnicity on the workers' movement in Pressburg. The Hungarian workers' movement's efforts to reach the widest possible audience of workers (audiences speaking different languages) caused the movement to split along linguistic lines. The effort to build 'imagined communities' of class collapsed because of the need to incorporate 'imagined communities' of language. I will first look at the question of ethnicity in the Hungarian workers' movement. I will then concentrate on ethnicity within the workers' movement in Pressburg, taking as case studies the Slovak section *Napred* of the workers' association *Vorwärts*, and the Slovak social democratic group the Slovak Executive Committee (*Slovenský Výkonný Výbor*). I will examine the relationship of the Slovak social democratic leaders to the Slovak 'bourgeois' national movement. Finally I will consider the question of language use and how it appeared within the Slovak social democratic movement.

5.1. ETHNICITY IN THE HUNGARIAN WORKERS' MOVEMENT

At its inception in 1890, the SDPH defined itself as an "international party which does not acknowledge the privileges of nations just as it does not acknowledge the privileges of birth or wealth, and claims that the fight against exploitation must be as international as exploitation itself."[188] Internationalism was the basis of the workers' movement. For the most part, the idea of class and the definition of interests on the basis of class unity rather than nationality was predominant among social democrats in Hungary. Workers from minority nationalities considered their own respective nationalist movements 'bourgeois.' The leaders of the nationalities' movements were accused of being interested only in securing advantageous positions for themselves rather than in improving the plight of the poor who were merely "sacrificial lambs."[189] Workers' leaders were convinced of the "invalidity of the national principle; it is not capable of realising an organic whole. Instead of unity it brings fragmentation and mutual recrimination...." According to the workers' leaders, nationalities were all oppressed in the same way: "they have the same duties but don't have any rights." People were not divided by nationality but by their status as exploiters or the exploited. Strengthening national differences was something to be avoided.[190]

However, the question of language use became a divisive issue in the Hungarian workers' movement. Some Hungarian social democratic leaders held that Hungarian had to be the official (and even conversational) language of the movement.[191] Some even wanted an exclusively Hungarian socialist party which would try to achieve universal suffrage for only those who could read and write in Hungarian.[192] Ethnic tensions in the SDPH began to rise after the turn of the century as a growing number of workers from different nationalities began to become organised. The Hungarian leadership of the social democrats refused to deal with the question of other nationalities and to help them with financing their own workers' press (except the Germans who were from the very beginning an organic part of the workers' movement in Hungary). The Budapest leadership did not pay enough attention to the mobilisation of workers in the Hungarian hinterland who were totally left to their own devices. Conversely, these workers from other parts of the country had little reason to support the centre.[193]

The demand for equal treatment of all languages was difficult to carry out in practice. Hungarian and German were the main languages used in social democratic congresses and speeches in other languages were translated. The 1904 party congress (with around 700 participants) allowed speeches to be given in the mother tongue of the speaker. The result was described as "Babel" by the Slovak press. Few topics on the conference's agenda were actually discussed since most of the conference's time was taken by speeches and their translations.[194] In 1906, at the XII. congress of SDPH, Rumanian, Serbian and German agitation committees were set up.[195] Later congresses had fewer participants with the organisation of separate congresses for each nationality thus diminishing affiliation to the party centre.[196]

By the beginning of the twentieth century, while still proclaiming its solidarity on the basis of class, the Hungarian workers' movement had started to split along linguistic lines, although it did not split as openly as the social democrats in Austria.[197] Social democrats were still united on their main demand for universal suffrage. However, the pragmatic need to include as many workers as possible required agitation in languages that the workers could understand. Although the workers' leadership was multilingual, the largely unorganised masses of workers in rural areas and in smaller towns needed to be educated and convinced in their own mother tongue. The need to mobilise workers brought nationalities' workers' leaders closer to their own 'bourgeois' national movements in their common interest in demanding education in the mother tongue. Although the workers' leaders refused to give their allegiance to these bourgeois national movements, the stress on education in the mother tongue created a point of intersection and tension between an 'imagined community of class' and an 'imagined community of language.' The social democratic movement in Hungary did not manage to resolve the tension between these two different principles. As the First World War showed, social democrats in European countries denied their internationalism and supported their own national bourgeoisies, thus giving preference to their class enemies but national allies before their class allies and national enemies.[198]

5.2. ETHNICITY AMONG PRESSBURG'S WORKERS

The workers' movement in Pressburg in 1867 was largely German speaking (as were most of the city's inhabitants).[199] The leading personalities of the movement used German as their language of communication.[200] Although the workforce was diverse, consisting of workers speaking other languages (Hungarian, Slovak, Czech), an important factor determining German as the main language of the movement was the higher education level of the German speaking workers and the close contact and help from Vienna.[201] Although fewer in number, Slovaks and Czech workers also participated in the activities of the association *Vorwärts* and some of them were functionaries of the association.[202] Speeches to public meetings were delivered in the German and Hungarian languages until the turn of the century.[203] By the mid-1890s a group of Slovak workers had became more active in Pressburg and also participated in congresses of the SDPH where they demanded a workers' publication in the Slovak language, at least in the form of a weekly supplement of the Budapest workers' weekly *Népszava*.

In 1869 workers read German-language worker newspapers: at first newspapers printed in Vienna and then the *Volksstimme* from Budapest.[204] The increasing numbers of workers coming from different backgrounds had to be addressed in languages they understood. By the beginning of the twentieth century, Pressburg had workers' publication in three languages, German and Slovak journals published in Pressburg and the Hungarian newspapers from Budapest. In 1901, Hungarians, Germans and Slovaks were equally represented in Pressburg's seven trade unions. However, trade unions' activities used the German language and therefore those workers speaking only their mother tongue were unable to fully participate. The Slovak social democratic leader Emanuel Lehocký, therefore, urged the party congress to organise workers by language.[205] However, Paul Wittich, the German-speaking leader of Pressburg's social democrats warned against dividing workers according to their nationality. In a public meeting, Wittich said: "First we want to introduce prosperity for everyone, and only then will we ask what language they speak."[206]

The collective activities of Pressburg's workers indicate that they preserved the spirit of co-operation and internationalism through most of the period 1869–1914. The tension between the Slovak social democrats and the Budapest leadership was not strongly reflected in Pressburg's social democratic movement. Public meetings and May Day celebrations were joint gatherings, except for some public meetings which were organised by the Slovak social democrats and the Slovak bourgeoisie. No such separate meetings were organised by German or Hungarian social democrats (perhaps reflecting the linguistic dominance of their communities). It seems that the drive for separatism was stronger among Slovak social democratic leaders.[207] The next section describes their efforts to create an independent organisation.

5.3. SLOVAK SOCIAL DEMOCRATS IN PRESSBURG

The tension between class based and language based solidarity is clearly shown in the history of the Slovak social democrats in Pressburg. This section considers the growing separatism of Slovak social democrats from the Budapest-centred Hungarian movement and their growing co-operation with Czech and Viennese workers. I will also describe the activities of the Slovak social democrats in Pressburg: the education of Slovak workers, trade unions' activities, Slovak-language workers' publications, and organising Slovak gatherings in Pressburg. Finally I will consider the relationship between the Slovak social democrats and the Slovak national movement as their common language-related demands brought the Slovak social democrats closer to the Slovak bourgeoisie.

5.3.1. Struggle for Autonomy among Slovak Social Democrats

Slovak social democrats tried to bring class and language together in their efforts to organise Slovak workers. While still declaring solidarity with the workers' movement on the basis of class, Slovak social democrats had been demanding language-based activities and structures since the late 1890s. This attempt to bring together class and language only resulted in a growing separatism among Slovak social democrats that led them to eventually compromise on what they had claimed to be their primary interest—class based solidarity.

The Slovak workers' movement began to be more active in the mid-1890s. In 1897, the Slovak workers started to group around the magazine *Nová Doba* in Budapest and became active participants in SDPH congresses. In 1899, after *Nová Doba* ceased publication, Slovak workers demanded a social democratic publication in the Slovak language which they could use to organise workers in Slovak speaking areas.[208] Since the Hungarian party leadership had not kept its promise to publish a weekly Slovak supplement of the Hungarian *Népszava*, Slovak workers approached Viennese workers for help.[209] With the help of Czech workers in Vienna, the Slovak workers' newspaper *Slovenské Robotnícke Noviny* began to be published in Pressburg in 1904. In September 1906 another monthly called *Napred* began publication.[210] In 1909, the support of Czech social democrats was again crucial in enabling the publication of *Robotnícke Noviny* as a weekly.[211]

In 1904, the Central Committee of the organisation of Slovak workers was founded. In June 1905 Slovak social democrats went further and founded their own separate Slovak Social Democratic Party as a reaction to the Magyar chauvinism of the leadership of the SDPH. The Hungarian leadership did not recognise the separate Slovak party and, one year later, the Slovak social democrats re-joined the SDPH again and established the Slovak executive committee of the SDPH (*Slovenský Krajinský Výkonný Výbor*, referred to as the SEC).[212] The second congress of the Slovak social democrats in Pressburg stressed its support for the SDPH although "for special linguistic and national [*národnostné*] needs of the organised Slovak workers the congress elects the Slovak executive committee of the Social Democratic Party of Hungary."[213]

Relations between the SEC and the Budapest leadership of the SDPH were tense from the outset. The Slovak social democrats sought the federalisation of the social democratic movement in Hungary as had happened in Austria.[214] The Slovak social democrats demanded autonomy so that they could make decisions independently of the Budapest centre but in agreement "with brother parties in Hungary."[215] The SEC saw its *raison d'etre* as the promotion of social democratic ideas in the territory inhabited by Slovaks. Although formally a part of the SDPH, the SEC organised Slovak conferences of social democratic and trade organisations in Upper Hungary as well as congresses of Slovak social democrats in Hungary.[216] Most of these congresses and conferences took place in Pressburg. These congresses were also attended by representatives from the Budapest centre of the SDPH as well as Czech-Slav Social Democratic Party representatives from Vienna.

In the early twentieth century, there were some signs that the Slovak social democratic movement's centre might shift from Pressburg to Budapest.[217] However, Pressburg seemed a better location for the Slovak workers' press because of its geographical proximity to the predominantly Slovak areas and also because of the proximity of Vienna and its better educated Slovak as well as Czech socialists.[218] It is important to note that a new generation of workers met in Pressburg during this period, who took over the organising of the Slovak workers.[219] The Slovak social democrats' insistence that the SDPH be internally divided according to nationalities meant in practice that Slovaks did not always work together with other workers in Budapest. Conversely, Magyar social democrats in predominantly Slovak towns ignored the SEC and followed instructions from Budapest.[220] The Upper-Hungarian (in present-day Eastern Slovakia) regional organisation based in Kassa included workers of all nationalities, and these workers did not follow the instructions of the SEC. The Upper-Hungarian organisation also had more members and was more active than the solely Slovak group.[221]

The help of Czech workers was crucial for the Slovak social democrats and this tie became even closer with growing separatism among both groups of workers. Czech workers regularly visited Pressburg and Slovak workers regularly went to Vienna.[222] Slovak workers supported the separation of Czechs within the Austrian trade unions, which in turn undoubtedly influenced and fuelled Slovak separatism within the Hungarian social democratic movement.[223] There were also close contacts with Viennese Slovaks; however, Slovak workers in Vienna were not as active as the Czech workers.[224] The Slovak workers also co-operated with Czech workers living in Pressburg within the auspices of the educational association *Vpred*.

5.3.2. Slovak workers' activities in Pressburg

Slovak workers in Pressburg were organised in two principal groups: *Vpred*, the Slovak section of the workers' educational association *Vorwärts*, and the SEC which did organisational and political work not only in Pressburg but also in the wider territory of present-day Slovakia. This sub-section considers *Vpred's* educational work and the SEC's organisational activities.

5.3.2.1. Vpred Activities

Vpred, the Slovak section of the association *Vorwärts* concerned itself with educating Slovak workers by providing the basic elementary education which many workers lacked, and also educating them in social democratic ideas and values.[225] *Vpred's* activities were similar to those of *Vorwärts* (*Előre*), focused primarily on education but also entertainment evenings and balls (especially after the turn of the century), and group trips.[226] In the period immediately before the First World War, women increasingly became involved in *Vpred's* activities.[227] *Vpred* also built up a library of socialist literature (presumably mostly in Czech) for its members' use. In 1912 *Vpred* opened a "public reading room" which had periodicals.[228] In the same year, the group established its own choir which co-operated with the choir of *Bratrství*, Pressburg's Czech workers' association.[229] In 1913 *Vpred* founded the Slovak workers' physical training club.[230] As noted in Chapter two, the theatre was a particularly important educational and propaganda instrument for all layers of Pressburg society: *Vpred* also pursued theatre activities, preparing six Slovak performances between 1906 and 1914. These were mostly pieces by Slovak authors but also included two German plays translated into Slovak.[231]

5.3.2.2. SEC and the Organising of Slovak Workers

While *Vpred* concentrated on educational activities, the SEC focused on political mobilisation. The SEC organised public meetings and demonstrations, participation in May Day celebrations and helped in founding Slovak trade unions and social democratic organisations throughout the territory inhabited by Slovaks. The SEC also handled the editing and publication of Slovak workers' newspapers and other social democratic publications.

5.3.2.2.1. Trade Unions

In the early years of the twentieth century, workers in the territory of present-day Slovakia were best organised in the industrial cities of Pressburg and Kassa.[232] The editors of workers' newspapers regularly appealed to

Slovak workers to join trade unions: "every honest worker should become a member of his trade union organisation!"[233] SEC activists travelled to distant localities to offer advice and practical help in setting up trade union branches. The number of organised workers grew gradually, and in 1907 the Slovak social democratic organisations in Hungary had around 7,000 members.[234]

Pressburg's trade unions wanted to spread their activities beyond Pressburg but their statutes were not approved by the minister of interior and so they had to limit their activity to the Pressburg area.[235] The languages used in these organisations were probably German, Hungarian, and in the twentieth century Slovak as well.[236] Judging from press accounts, Slovak workers were not very interested in political organisation. SEC activists complained that younger workers were interested only in alcohol, playing cards, and bowling although workers in Pressburg had at their disposal a library, lectures, plays, and a choir.[237] In 1911 the editor of the *Robotnícke Noviny* exhorted Pressburger Slovaks to wake up from their passivity.[238] Direct activism appears to have been less successful in enlarging the Slovak social democratic 'imagined community' than the role played by the workers' press.

5.3.2.2.2. SEC and the Workers' Press

Slovak social democratic leaders considered the founding of the Slovak-language workers' press the most important step for spreading social democratic ideas and for building solidarity and unity among Slovak workers. The first editorial of the weekly edition of the *Robotnícke Noviny* declared that "the press is a great power whose acquisition will be decisive over all the treasures of the world, material as well as spiritual."[239]

Slovak-language workers' publications were necessary in order to banish the "stupefying burgher press" from workers' households. The goal was to get every Slovak worker to subscribe to the *Robotnícke Noviny* or to *Napred*.[240] The task of the workers' press was clear: "*Robotnícke Noviny* shall stir up every week every poor Slovak in his household from the sleep of indifference, call him into the fight for the rights of the people, teach him what people want, require and what they are fighting for."[241] Each conference of Slovak social democrats discussed the number of subscribers.[242] The SEC also published occasional pamphlets concerning specific situations.[243] The diffusion of these publications was also hindered by apathy and indifference among Slovak workers, many of whom were illiterate. Although the number of organised workers grew, apathy among Slovak workers continued to be a significant problem, not only in the Slovak territories but also in Budapest and Vienna.[244]

5.3.2.2.3. Slovak Public Meetings

Slovak social democrats organised a number of meetings for Pressburg's Slovaks. At some 1 May demonstrations Slovak workers held a public meeting separately from other workers.[245] On 1 May 1913 Slovak workers even had a separate ball while German and Hungarian workers celebrated together.[246] Other public meetings brought together Slovak workers and bourgeoisie and usually also Slovaks from the vicinity of Pressburg. Some of these planned meetings did not take place because the city captain banned speeches in Slovak "upon higher orders" because of the expected presence of Slovak peasants.[247] Speaking in Slovak was also prohibited at some social democratic meetings.[248]

Slovak workers and the Slovak bourgeoisie were brought together by the demand for universal suffrage and the idea of the national oppression of Slovaks. Speakers at a 1906 meeting at the Workers' Home included the "bourgeois" parliament deputy Milan Hodža and the workers Emmanuel Lehocký and Štefan Príkopa. All three speakers stressed that universal suffrage was "the necessary prerequisite for securing civil and national equality."[249] The Slovak social democrats were often very critical of the Slovak National Party (*Slovenská národná strana*).[250] However, the two groups came together at another large joint meeting with the Slovak National Party, resolving to reject partial suffrage reform because "the old injustice committed on the Slovak people in social, political, cultural and national terms would receive new support."[251] This statement shows how far Slovak social democrats had moved from the class-based solidarity of proletarian internationalism towards a politics based on linguistic and national divides. The next sub-section discusses the attitudes of Slovak social democrats towards the Slovak national movement and the gradual convergence of the two groups.

5.3.3. Slovak Workers and the Slovak National Movement

There was an ongoing competition between the social democrats and the Slovak national movement to win mass support for their ideas. The social democrats promoted changing the existing social order through class struggle. National requirements only followed after the main human requirement— universal suffrage—had been fulfilled. The Slovak intelligentsia and bourgeoisie, on the other hand, gave priority to the national idea, feeling that improved social conditions would follow from the building of a Slovak nation.

The social democrats often criticised the national movement. The Slovak workers' press complained about the Slovak intelligentsia's disinterest in the workers.[252] The Slovak intelligentsia did not help in educating the workers, with the exception of occasional lectures.[253] Pressburg's Slovak intellectuals very rarely participated in workers' entertainment or theatre performances. "It is against *bon-ton* to go to an entertainment which is organised by workers."[254] Slovak national parliament deputies were also often criticised for not fulfilling their duties towards their electorates by failing to appear at parliament meetings when important questions were discussed.[255] *Robotnícke Noviny* also criticised Slovak deputies in Pozsony county council for not taking their duties seriously and for not behaving like "deputies of the Slovak people."[256]

Slovaks were divided by class and by religious denomination (Catholics vs. Evangelicals). The attempt to build a cohesive national movement failed to sufficiently mobilise mass support. However, the workers' movement did come closer to the Slovak 'bourgeois' national movement in the years preceding the First World War. The ambiguous attitude of the Slovak social democrats towards the national movement reflected their differing views of the three principal components of the national movement: the conservative Slovak bourgeoisie as represented by the Slovak National Party, the clericals, and the liberal stream in the Slovak national movement.

5.3.3.1. Attitude towards the conservative bourgeoisie

The conservative bourgeoisie (centred in Martin) was traditionalist and relied on Russia as a guarantor of national liberation in the case of a conflict between empires.[257] Slovak social democrats criticised the Slovak national party for their passivity and unwillingness to do "tough, small-scale political work among the people," for their conservatism and for their passing themselves off as "the spiritual aristocracy of the Slovak nation."[258] *Robotnícke Noviny* also criticised the "national celebrations" held in Martin every August for falsely representing the Slovak nation as united. The newspaper noted that while these celebrations had once attracted ordinary Slovaks, this was no longer the case since national leaders looked down on simple Slovak people.[259]

The conservative nationalist leaders were equally opposed to the social democratic ideology. The periodical *Národnie Noviny* (the organ of the Slovak National Party in Martin) stressed the need to found a radical party which would be an antidote to the social democratic movement so that workers did not have to improve social conditions solely "according to the recipes of Lassalle and Marx." *Národnie Noviny* agreed that workers might work "for their rights but on a national basis."[260] This drew a sharp response from the social democrats: according to *Robotnícke Noviny*, the Martin's intelligentsia were accusing the social democrats of national treason since they themselves had not succeeded in winning over the workers. *Robotnícke Noviny* even called *Národné Noviny* a "famous national journal without a nation."[261]

5.3.3.2. Attitude Towards the Clericals[262]

The Hungarian Catholic People's Party was strongly anti-liberal and consistently opposed socialism as an "immoral Jewish liberal invention."[263] In 1905, many Slovak Catholics (represented by František Skyčák, František Jehlička, Ferdinand Juriga, and Andrej Hlinka) left the Catholic People's Party and created the Slovak People's Party (*Slovenská Ľudová strana*), which did not have its own organisational structure but was the Catholic wing of the Slovak National Party.[264] The Catholic People's Party and the Christian workers' movement were serious opponents for the social democrats. The Catholic workers' association in Pressburg even printed leaflets criticising the social democrats.[265]

A fight ensued between Slovak social democrats and Slovak clericals for "the souls" of the Slovak masses. Slovak workers saw national "clericalism" as one of their main enemies since its representatives were anti-liberal and thus hindered progress.[266] Slovak social democrats considered religion to be each person's private affair.[267] The workers' press also fought vehemently against "clerical stupefiers" who kept the people in ignorance and it railed against corruption and immorality in the Catholic Church, citing high-ranking members of the Church hierarchy who were themselves rich while preaching the virtues of poverty. The main proponents of the new Slovak People's Party were described as intolerant people of very low moral standing.[268] In order not to alienate the largely religious Slovak masses and to win their sympathies, the social democratic press quoted the Bible, arguing that Christ himself was poor and that early Christian communities had been "communist."[269]

5.3.3.3. Attitude towards the Liberal Bourgeoisie

This group consisted primarily of liberal urban bourgeois intellectuals who were trying to improve conditions for the Slovak masses. As opposed to the conservative leadership of the Slovak National Party, this group promoted democratisation of civic life, political activity and active work among different layers of Slovak population.[270] This group included prominent figures like Milan Hodža (founder of the Slovak agrarian movement), and the liberal Slovak bourgeoisie some of whom were adherents of Masaryk's ideas (Vavro Šrobár, Pavol Blaho, Fedor Houdek, Milan Rastislav Štefánik and Anton Štefánek).[271] The liberals developed co-operative relations with the Czech middle bourgeoisie and propagated modern Czech views of capitalism.[272] Slovak social democrats varied in their attitudes towards the liberal Slovak intelligentsia, ranging from allegations of corruption to positive comments.[273] The Slovak workers' press published opinion pieces by some leading Slovak liberals.[274] At the beginning of the twentieth century social democrats even organised joint meetings with the liberal representatives of the Slovak national movement calling for universal suffrage (1905–1907 and 1910–1912). However, for most of the period, Slovak social democrats believed that the Slovak masses could not count on the bourgeois parties or on personality politics to defend the interests of the masses.[275]

The social democrats thought that dominant class and family networks had an overwhelming interest in maintaining the existing social and economic system. "Politics is gentlemen's entertainment" (*pánske huncútsvo*).[276] *Robotnícke Noviny* portrayed the extensive nepotism and connections in Slovak financial institutions, banks, factories, and journals.[277] The Slovak proletariat could not expect help from the Slovak bourgeoisie or intelligentsia who had such strong vested interests in perpetuating the existing system. The only hope lay in the "progressives" of the younger generation which was, however, "cursed" by association with "the great political and literary inquisitors" of the conservative Slovak national movement.[278]

5.3.4. Slovak Workers and Their National Requirements
The Slovak social democrats saw themselves as the only representatives of the interests of the Slovak masses. *Robotnícke Noviny* listed the Slovak social democrats' demands in the economic, political and national areas and contrasted the national movement's positions on these issues. According to the *RN*, the Slovak National Party could not construct an adequate economic program as it could not defend the interests of both Slovak factory owners and Slovak workers. It could not have a cultural programme which would satisfy both the clericals and the liberal forces. And its political programme (which consisted solely of the demand for universal suffrage and respect for the 1868 Nationalities' Law) was otherwise no different from any other Hungarian democratic party. *Robotnícke Noviny* was also convinced that the bourgeois parties could not offer anything to poor Slovak immigrants coming to the cities.[279]

However, despite these criticisms, the Slovak social democrats came to co-operate with the Slovak bourgeoisie because of the convergence of key interests such as universal suffrage and "national requirements" that became more obvious over time. One of the requirements for which Slovak workers' leaders consistently pressed was education in the mother tongue. In order to effectively mobilise mass support, Slovak social democrats had to be able to talk intelligibly to migrant workers from monolingual rural areas. These pragmatic considerations brought the Slovak social democrats closer to the 'bourgeois' Slovak national movement and hurt efforts to build an imagined community of class in Hungary.[280] The separatist efforts of the Slovak social democrats were welcomed by the Slovak liberal representatives.[281]

The national question was first of all a social question for the Slovak social democrats, since what mattered "in the struggle of nationalities ... is the fight between the rich who have political rights over the poor who are politically without rights ... the fight of the socially powerful against the socially oppressed." A just solution of the national question was intrinsically connected with the elimination of social injustice.[282] However, Slovak social democrats also felt that Slovak workers faced additional persecution and discrimination because of their mother tongue, in addition to the social oppression faced by all workers in Hungary, including Magyars.[283] Slovak social democrats stressed that the 1868 Nationalities' law was not respected in reality and that equality of all nationalities could be achieved only after civil equality was enabled by direct universal suffrage. Slovak workers, peasants and burghers had an equal interest in acquiring universal suffrage.[284]

When writing about the national oppression of Slovaks, social democrats even used the clichés and myths of the Slovak nationalists: "we cannot understand why the Second International should deny independence to the social democratic movement ... [of] a nation that has been living its own life but which lost its state independence in the past and present because of the will of kings, nobles, army, capitalists."[285] The congress of the Slovak social democrats also stated its "national requirement": "Only such nationality politics in Hungary is healthy and sustainable which secures the Slovak people ... their rights in their own language, so that they can get education and assert themselves in public life in their mother tongue."[286] This demand brought Slovak social democrats close to the demands made in the 1861 Memorandum of the Slovak nation (which was the political platform of the conservative Slovak National Party), essentially asking for territorial autonomy. In this way the Slovak social democrats came closer to the position espoused by the Slovak national movement and split their class-based solidarity with the pan-Hungarian workers' movement.

6. THE WORKERS AND PRESSBURG

This part of the chapter considers the place of the working class in Pressburg. The workers saw the city primarily in class terms. They did not have friendly feelings towards the "bourgeois" middle classes, as represented by oppressive city authorities who restricted workers' rights (such as freedom of speech and the right to gather.) Workers saw the Pressburger elite as exploiters of their labour, who participated in and profited from an unjust social system. The attitude of the workers also was affected by the attitude of the city's authorities and middle-class inhabitants towards the workers. This part will first look at how city authorities, the burgher inhabitants and the 'bourgeois' press reacted to the appropriation of public spaces by workers in their public gatherings and 1 May celebrations. I will then examine multi-lingualism in workers' activities in Pressburg and consider whether it was possible for a 'Pressburger' identity to emerge among the city's social democrats.

6.1. ATTITUDE OF THE CITY INHABITANTS AND AUTHORITIES TOWARDS THE WORKERS' MOVEMENT
This section first briefly considers the attitude of the city authorities towards the workers' movement, and then analyses the attitude of Pressburg's middle-class inhabitants and mainstream press.

6.1.1. Attitude of City Authorities
The Hungarian state considered socialism especially dangerous since it threatened to overthrow the whole social system. The state and city authorities acted in close co-operation to monitor socialist activities and to prevent class conflict. (Chapter five considers these surveillance activities in greater detail.) Especially at the beginning of the period, relations between the workers and the city authorities were often fraught with mutual suspicion. In 1869, the workers had difficulty getting the city authorities' approval of the statutes of the association *Vorwärts*.[287] Some of the anniversary celebrations of *Vorwärts* were also banned when the city police captain felt unsure about whether the authorities would be able to maintain control. When workers did not follow the police chief's orders, they were summoned

for an interview.[288] The military was always kept on alert during large public meetings of the workers' movement.

However, class conflict in Pressburg was always negotiated peacefully and never led to violent intervention by the police or the army as happened in Budapest.[289] The attitude and behaviour of the city authorities towards the workers changed during the period, as the city authorities gradually learned that the workers always tried to stay within legal limits and did not provoke the authorities. The city police chiefs were well informed about planned social democratic activities and acted upon this knowledge. Reports from Pressburg's police chiefs to the minister of interior show a high opinion about the city's workers who were considered to have a "temperate way of thinking and a peaceful nature."[290] Furthermore, as the social democratic movement gained numerical and organisational strength, the city authorities felt less able to deny them the right to publicly demonstrate through the city centre.

6.1.2. Attitude of Inhabitants

The attitudes of Pressburg's middle-class inhabitants towards the workers' movement shifted from fear to acceptance. Different social strata and interest groups in the city varied in their attitudes towards the workers' movement. However, even those who considered the workers "uneducated barbarians" had to reconcile themselves to their presence in the city, and even to their appropriation of public spaces for short periods of time.

The founding of a workers' association in 1869 stirred up the calm waters of Pressburg life. As Hanzlíček wrote, the foundation of *Vorwärts* startled "burgher beer politicians" who were afraid of a social revolution. *Vorwärts* issued a reassuring declaration about its goals, stating that only legal means would be used in its activities and that it would not interfere violently with ownership rights or provoke reactionary elements by committing public disturbances.[291] However, the workers' demands (as described in Part 4 of this chapter) appeared as a threat to established elites since these demands expressed a desire to change the established order. Although the workers' movement had been developing for several decades throughout Europe, Pressburg's middle classes had not expected such a development in their sleepy city. The middle classes were mostly afraid of public disturbances, threats to their property by the poor masses, and of their loss of control over the public space of the city.[292] Any larger gathering of the poor posed the threat of potential violence.[293] As one *Pressburger* complained in 1877, "who knows what kinds of people" gathered in pubs for workers' meetings. This worried citizen wondered what the police was doing to counter this threat by socialist elements and foreign workers.[294] The city police's very visible supervision of workers' activities did not merely ensure public order, but was also meant to reassure the worried middle classes.

Most of the earlier public meetings of the workers' movement took place in enclosed spaces (such as pubs) and the number of participants was relatively small. In 1890, however, the proclamation of 1 May as the day of workers' solidarity and strength caused considerable fear among the burghers. The first May Day demonstration was marked by "strong security measures, a military emergency, fear and terror among the Pressburger burghers." More than two people were not allowed to walk together down the streets. Soldiers had loaded weapons. Many house owners did not even dare to go out at all.[295] The fears of the city authorities and inhabitants were based on the memory of the 1882 anti-Semitic riots in the city in which some workers and small craftsmen had also taken part. News of security measures in Vienna was also not reassuring.[296] A few days before 1 May, in Bielitz-Biala soldiers dispersed a gathering of workers with gunfire, resulting in several dead and injured.[297] The local press remarked that the authorities were not worried about local workers but about the "street rabble and foreign agitators."[298] In the event, 1 May 1890 passed off peacefully and the extensive security measures proved needless. However, these measures were implemented in later years as well.[299]

The entry of large numbers of workers into the city centre was the next step. In 1902 a large public meeting took place in the city centre, and for the first time workers were permitted to march through the city centre on 1 May. The police chief permitted the march on condition that the workers would keep to a pre-determined route and stay in a precise order.[300] During the next few years, the daily press published the exact route of the march in advance. In this way the movement of workers became predictable, ritualised and, therefore, unthreatening.[301] This ritualisation was helped by the way in which different groups of workers and their associations had assigned places in an exact order, creating an organised body in rows of four and six. "The impressive manifestation of the workers was generally acknowledged and everyone praised the order and discipline of the organised workers of Pressburg."[302] The 1902 public meeting (called the "monster rally" by the local press) had about 3,000 participants and was held in a square at the end of the favourite promenade of the Pressburger middle classes, followed by a march through the centre.[303]

In subsequent years workers regularly appropriated Pressburg's public spaces for short periods of time. These public demonstrations of their numbers and presence in the city showed that they were a force to reckon with. However, as the city's inhabitants gradually became used to the workers' presence, the workers became part of the urban landscape. After 1903 even the local press seldom gave much attention to the public gatherings of the social democrats or to May Day celebrations. The burghers certainly no longer felt their initial fear of the workers. Inhabitants lined the city streets and voiced exclamations of support during later workers' marches through the city centre.[304] Most shops on the routes of the marches were closed (perhaps to protect property rather than to demonstrate solidarity with workers).[305] Some burghers even participated in and spoke at workers' gatherings.[306]

The middle classes also became more comfortable with the social democrats because of their orderly behaviour. The first public meetings and marches represented a "transgression against the famous order."[307] However-er, the local press had to praise the "exemplary parliamentary manner" in which public meetings were conducted.[308] The *Westungarischer Grenzbote* even described participants at one meeting as "gentlemen in workers' clothes."[309] Organised workers in Pressburg went out of their way to demonstrate moderation and consideration for bourgeois values. Contem-porary photographs show how workers tried their best to look respectable at all public occasions. On the one hand, this showed the bourgeoisie that the workers were not a threat; but also tellingly demonstrated the real desire of most workers to become more like the respectable middle classes rather than like their own more radical leaders.[310]

6.1.3. Attitude of the Local Press

The local press was particularly influential in shaping attitudes towards the workers. The two main German middle-class newspapers, the *Pressburger Zeitung* and the *Westungarischer Grenzbote*, provided objective accounts of workers' meetings and 1 May celebrations. However, these relatively sympa-thetic accounts still represented typical middle class opinions. The *Westun-garischer Grenzbote* approved of the workers' objectives but claimed that social agitation was not the way to achieve these goals.[311] The *Pressburger Zeitung* dismissed the workers' demands as "utopian," supporting universal suffrage "not in a social democratic but in a burgher [*bürgerlich*] sense." The burghers sought peaceful evolution but not a revolution which would destroy the social system.[312]

The newspaper of the Magyar nationalist elite, the *Nyugatmagyarországi Hiradó*, was unsympathetic to the workers' movement, objecting particu-larly to the internationalism of the movement. The *Nyugatmagyarországi*

Hiradó thought that patriotic Magyar workers should stop celebrating 1 May, a festival connected with international socialism.[313] In addition to objecting to the lack of ethnic chauvinism among Pressburger Magyar workers, this newspaper also expressed its contempt for workers as the "lower classes, especially the factory workers." Only the education of these "barbarians" could prevent the "modern barbaric flood of people … breaking through from the lowest depths of the socialist organisation in order to mercilessly annihilate [and] overturn all that was created during the last century."[314] According to the *Nyugatmagyarországi Híradó*, workers lacked "responsibility and moral soundness."[315]

The Christian democrat daily, the *Pressburger Tagblatt*, was also hostile towards the social democrats. This newspaper declared that history was a struggle "between the banners of belief and unbelief, Christianity and freemasonry, solidarity standing on a Christian basis and atheistic, red and vengeful socialism."[316] This newspaper opposed any "violent" activities (such as general strikes) by the social democrats.[317] Another major daily, advocating the interests of the urban petty bourgeoisie and craftsmen, the *Pressburger Presse* had a largely objective and supportive attitude to the social democratic movement, but also opposed general strikes.[318]

6.2. Conclusion

Pressburg's authorities and inhabitants were initially afraid of the workers' movement but gradually came to accept the workers' presence in the city. The orderliness and peacefulness of the workers' movement in its pursuit of limited and moderate objectives played a significant role in furthering acceptance by the city authorities and middle classes.

6.2. Workers—Multiple Identities?

A distinct 'Pressburger' identity was typical of the city's middle classes, as well as among those inhabitants who were traditionally employed in wine growing, crafts and commerce. As Chapter two has discussed in detail, the main characteristics of this 'Pressburger' identity were multi-linguality, a lack of strong ethnic belonging, and an overriding loyalty and identification with the city. Kovačevičová claims that this identity was also shared by workers' leaders and small craftsmen, who belonged to the "Volk" strata of the city's population.[319] However, the extent to which the lower classes, workers and poor people also shared this 'Pressburger' identity is questionable.

The workers' movement was multi-ethnic and its leaders were multi-lingual, fulfilling the first condition for being considered a 'Pressburger.'

However, the existence of three linguistically divided sections of the workers' association *Vorwärts* suggests that multi-linguality did not extend to most workers. At one public meeting in 1902, when parts of the audience demanded speeches in Hungarian, both the German speaking leader Paul Wittich and the Slovak Pavol Černák explained the necessity for Hungarians, Germans and Slovaks to join together.[320] Leaflets in all three languages were distributed in Pressburg.[321] Even the Slovak section *Vpred* printed its invitations to a concert in all three languages. This led to controversy among Slovak social democrats. The editor of the *Robotnícke Noviny* considered these multi-lingual invitations needless "uncomfortable and repugnant ballast" and expressed his surprise at the concert's lack of "Slav character" with too many French, Hungarian and German songs.[322] As this comment shows, *Vpred* (as a section of *Vorwärts*) was more 'Pressburger' than leading Slovak social democrats might have preferred. It also shows that *Vpred's* activities were part of the multilingual atmosphere and traditions of the city.

The internationalism of the workers' movement also reflected a lack of strong ethnic or national attachment. At least at the beginning of the movement, workers' solidarity was based on class loyalty rather than identification with a national or ethnic group, although this changed as immigrant workers flooded into Pressburg from other parts of the country. Workers of all three nationalities in Pressburg co-operated for the most part: the separatism of Slovak workers was more apparent in their relationship with the Budapest leadership of the workers' movement than in inter-ethnic relations within Pressburg's worker community. While only Slovak workers marched as a separate ethnic group within demonstrations, Pressburg' social democrats did not seem to mind. In 1907, when the authorities banned a meeting because Slovak would have been spoken there, the other social democrats also protested against this decision.[323]

The workers' leaders were multi-lingual and did not have strong feelings of ethnic belonging. However, these leaders did not feel loyalty to the city in the same way as the middle classes. Many of them were immigrants, mostly from Germany or Austria.[324] The workers' leaders were primarily concerned with the living conditions faced by workers in the city and the extent to which these were worsened or improved through the decisions of the municipal authorities. Unlike the Pressburger elites, the workers' leaders had no power to actively affect the look of the city, apart from periodic public events such as marches and demonstrations that were symbolic appropriations of the city rather than an active re-shaping of its spatial contours. The workers' leaders did not share the burgher elite's patriotic or patronising relationship to the city. As such, even multi-lingual workers' leaders were not genuine *Pressburgers*. Insofar as most workers tried to achieve better living conditions for themselves and tried to be "respectable," ordinary workers were in fact closer to the Pressburger bourgeois world view than that of their leaders.

7. CONCLUSION

This chapter has examined the intersection of class and ethnicity in Pressburg between 1869 and 1914. Identification with class was an alternative to ethnic identity because of the internationalism of the workers' movement. This was the case for the multilingual leaders of Pressburg's workers' movement. However, new immigrants to Pressburg were not multi-lingual. Pragmatic considerations made the Pressburger workers' movement establish different sections by language. While this did not split solidarity among workers in the city, linguistic separation brought Slovak workers closer to the Slovak national movement. The effort to build an 'imagined community of class' in the Hungarian workers' movement finally collapsed because of the demand of the nationalities to divide this class-based community into 'imagined communities of language.'

Attempts to mobilise and consolidate workers' identity took place through spatially located practices such as marches through the city centre. Furthermore, working class identity and loyalties in Pressburg were affected by the city's key location between the Hungarian and Austrian parts of the Habsburg Monarchy. The next chapter considers the spatial contexts within which identity was formed in Pressburg between 1867–1914, the contested spaces within the city and within the national and imperial landscapes of the Hungarian kingdom and the Austro-Hungarian Empire.

✌ 4 ✌

BETWEEN VIENNA AND BUDAPEST:
PRESSBURG IN A NATIONAL LANDSCAPE

0. INTRODUCTION

THIS CHAPTER CONSIDERS Pressburg's geographical location and its impact on the politics of identity in the city. Physically situated between Vienna and Budapest, Pressburg was a strategic locus in the Hungarian and Slovak national landscapes within the still larger context of the Austro-Hungarian Empire. Identity in the city was intertwined with changing power relations that were reflected both in the contestation of spaces within the city and in the position of the city within national and imperial landscapes. Hungarian patriots saw Austria as a curb on Hungarian freedom and Pressburg was seen as a bastion of Magyardom on the western edge of Hungary.

The first part of this chapter describes the geographical position of Pressburg between Vienna and Budapest. I will briefly review Pressburg's connections with these two capitals and consider the relation between location and migration. The second part examines the Hungarian patriotic association *Toldy Kör*'s fear of "losing" Pressburg to other nationalities encroaching on this "bastion of the Hungarian nation." National monuments were used to symbolically incorporate this territory into the Hungarian national landscape. The third part looks at two such monuments: the monument of the Hungarian warrior facing Austria demarcating the border; and the monument of Maria Theresa in Pressburg, built as a reminder of the city's history as a Hungarian coronation city. The fourth part analyses the nationalist rhetoric employed by the *Pressburger* city elite in their efforts to attract the 'third' university in Hungary. The fifth part considers the debate over the proposal by the city authorities to build an electric railway (or "tram") line between Pressburg and Vienna. Many Hungarian nationalists took this proposal as a proof that Pressburg was essentially German and non-patriotic, and that the city authorities were more interested in becoming a suburb of Vienna than in connecting more tightly to "the heart of the nation"— Budapest. However, Magyar nationalists were not alone in seeking to appropriate the city and to embed it firmly into their national landscape. Pressburg (Prešporok) also played an important role in the mythologies of the Slovak national intelligentsia. Slovak nationalist discussions about the borders and centre of the Slovak 'national territory' intensified in the years leading up to the end of the First World War. The last part of this chapter considers the symbolic meaning of a capital for a nation and looks at the role played by Pressburg as an urban centre for Slovak national activities.

1. PRESSBURG'S LOCATION

Pressburg is located in the transition zone between the Alps and Carpathian mountain ranges and the lowlands of the Danube and Viennese valleys. The city was founded on the left bank of the Danube under the Castle hill, leaning onto the Small Carpathian Mountains hills, on the edge of a fertile lowland. From an early date the Danube was forded at this point. The main roads in the region fall into a strip passing between the Litavské Mountains and the Small Carpathian Mountains (see Figure 13). The city lies on an axis linking Budapest-Pressburg-Vienna-Linz which has been called "the second most important strategic direction in Europe."[1] (See Figure 14.)

Within the Habsburg Monarchy, Pressburg served as the capital of Hungary between 1536 and 1783 since large parts of Hungary (including the capital, Buda) were occupied by the Turks. Pressburg was able to play an integrating role in a nearly bifurcated Hungary.[2] According to Ján Buček, Hungary's geo-strategic core lay on the Danube axis between Budapest and Vienna marked by Esztergom, Komárom and Pressburg (Figure 15).[3] Beluszky also stresses the strategic importance of Pressburg's location in the "Budapest-Vienna corridor."[4] Pressburg became less important after the Turkish threat receded. The central institutions had already moved to Buda in 1783, and the Hungarian parliament went in 1848. After the Dual Agreement of 1867, Hungary became a nationalising state with its national 'heart' in Budapest. As a city somewhere between Vienna and Budapest, Pressburg was now in an ambiguous position. It was now within a nationalising state demanding constant evidence of Hungarian patriotism but was also close to Vienna which exerted a strong attraction.

Pressburg also served as an important "regional centre" attracting migrants from surrounding areas and other counties.[5] In 1900, Pressburg was the fourth most important urban centre in Hungary, after Budapest, Zagreb and Kolozsvár.[6] As the centre of Western Upper Hungary, nearly a million people lived within Pressburg's "sphere of influence" which included the counties of Pozsony, Nyitra, Trencsén, and in the border territory, the counties of Árva, Litptó, Turóc, and a part of the county Moson (Figures 16 and 17).[7] Pressburg's geographical location significantly influenced the city's ethnic structure. As Chapter one has noted, in the nineteenth century the city and its surroundings were primarily inhabited by three nationalities: German, Magyar and Slovak.[8] Pressburg's status as an important regional centre brought a large influx of migrants, especially after the 1890s with rapid industrialisation and urbanisation. More than 80% of the population increase between 1890 and 1910 came from in-migration.[9]

The development of rail transport also facilitated commuting and travel to Vienna and Budapest.[10] In addition to rail, a steamship left daily from Vienna for Pressburg and Budapest (twice a day after the turn of the century).[11] The good transport links between Pressburg and Vienna meant that it was even possible to commute to Vienna. Vienna's proximity meant that its influence on Pressburg was probably greater than that of Budapest, the "national" capital. For example, as the previous chapter showed, the workers' movement in Pressburg increasingly relied on their contacts in Vienna while contacts with the Hungarian workers' movement were loosening. Lively trade links had also developed over the centuries with the towns of Lower Austria. The Hungarian government was aware of Pressburg's location on the western border of Hungary, and also of Vienna's influence. The next part will look at the complicated relations that followed from Pressburg's ambiguous position within Hungary as a border town between Hungary and Austria.

2. PRESSBURG AS A BASTION OF MAGYARDOM

Pressburg played an important role in the ideology of Magyar nationalists as a border town on the western edge of Hungary. The city was seen as the western bastion of the Hungarian state. This image was often used by the leading elite of the Hungarian patriotic association *Toldy Kör*.[12] (As the fourth part of this chapter shows, this image was also later adopted by the municipal elite when arguing that the third Hungarian university should be located in Pressburg). The defensive posture of the nationalising Hungarian state gave special weight to the image of Pressburg as the bastion of a Hungary endangered by encroaching foreign nationalities. This part examines the key elements of this crucial image in *Toldy Kör* rhetoric.

Toldy Kör's political rhetoric and activities were grounded in an image of Pressburg which stressed the importance of the city for Hungary. This image of Pressburg as a crucial locale for Hungarian nation-building activities was no doubt partly inspired by the need to motivate the association's members. Three distinctive inter-related images of the city can be identified in *Toldy Kör* rhetoric: the image of Pressburg as a historic royal city with ancient and enduring links to the Hungarian kingdom; the image of the city as a bastion of Hungarian culture; and the image of Pressburg as a strategically important locale.

When Budapest became the capital of Hungary, Pressburg suffered a considerable drop in importance. In order to compensate for this decline, the Pressburg's elites began to refer to their city as the "second capital of Hungary." This designation was taken up also by Magyar nationalists stressing the crucial role of Pressburg in the Magyarisation process. (In seeing "Pozsony" as the second city of Hungary, *Toldy Kör* did not differ from the views of municipal leaders. However, as Chapter two has shown, in wanting to turn Pressburg into a Hungarian city in its looks, manners and language, *Toldy Kör* had different ideas about the future of the city than the municipal elite.) The reasons for awarding Pressburg this title were expressed on many occasions. "If any city, then certainly the coronation city of Pozsony which being the second capital of Hungary by virtue of its splendid history and its developed culture, is predestined to become a sanctuary for our own literature and art."[13] On another occasion, one leading *Toldy Kör* member, Antal Pór, described the association's objective as: "To see Pozsony completely transformed so that it shall be the second capital of our home not merely in name but also in reality."[14] József Komócsy, a member of the *Petőfi Society* delegation visiting Pressburg poetically noted that: "As Budapest is Hungary's head, so Pozsony is its brow."[15] *Toldy Kör* chairman Kálmán Thály went even further: "This city is a pearl in the Hungarian crown."[16]

Toldy Kör also ascribed a special mission to Pressburg because of the city's location on the western border of Upper Hungary in close proximity to Vienna. Pressburg was seen as a "defensive bastion on Hungary's frontier against the spreading *Germanisation* … especially for the development of domestic *literature* and of the *Hungarian spirit*, there is the greatest need here in Pozsony where our homeland's great treasures are constantly endangered by the preponderant German population."[17] *Toldy Kör* saw itself as having an especially important mission because of Pressburg's geographical location at an exposed tip of the country.[18] In 1893, the newly appointed *főispán* Julius von Szalavszky stressed the importance, "in this border city, of spreading and strengthening Hungarian culture."[19] In 1904, Thály darkly noted that there were still some people in Pressburg who would prefer the city to belong to Austria as a suburb of Vienna. For Thály, *Toldy Kör* was an "alarm clock" for those who were "patriotically lukewarm." He declared that "if there were no Toldy Kör it would be necessary to found it."[20]

Pressburg was important in the nationalist ideology of leading *Toldy Kör* members not only because of its position on the Hungarian border but also because of the city's position in an ethnically mixed territory of many "nationalities' streams."[21] Pávai Vajna declared that, "[i]n the same way as in past struggles when Pozsony was the strong border castle of the country where the sainted crown driven out from the destroyed country found sanctuary, so also today Pozsony must be the border castle of Hungarian national culture holding up the foreign tendencies pouring in from west and north and pounding against the Hungarian national culture, just as the Carpathian mountain range rising above the city breaks the destructive force of the harmful northern winds." Pávai warned that Pressburg was still "not strong enough [an] advance outpost."[22] Again, this sense of Pressburg as a bastion of Magyar culture enhanced the importance of *Toldy Kör* for its members: "Toldy Kör is the main military camp of Magyardom."[23]

Toldy Kör's image of Pressburg as a bastion rested on the city's historical importance as a strategic centre. The region around Pressburg had been the locale of many military conflicts. Since the eleventh century all attacks from the west had concentrated on the Pressburg castle and its surrounding settlement. Buček believes that "Bratislava was the most important and most western strong fortification of Hungary."[24] By describing the city in these military or geo-strategic terms, *Toldy Kör* rhetoric tried to re-awaken interest in the strategic importance of the city in the cultural battlefield. As a bastion of Hungarian culture, Pressburg had a "symbolic value" for these nineteenth-century nationalists, just as thirteenth-century rulers had struggled to capture the strong fortifications of Pressburg castle.[25] *Toldy Kör* rhetoric about Pressburg reflected an anxiety concerning this contested part of the Hungarian territory. The new Magyar elite felt the need to demonstrate their ownership of the city. This need found symbolic manifestation in the form of monuments. The next part considers the millennial monuments that were built as symbols of loyalty to the Hungarian nation.

3. MILLENIAL MONUMENTS—
SYMBOLIC APPROPRIATION OF THE TERRITORY

> Monuments, holidays, cemeteries, museums and archives…. These remain very effective in concentrating time in space, in providing many people with a sense of common identity no matter how dispersed they may be by class, region, gender, religion, or race.[26]
> —John R. Gillis

Since the nineteenth century public monuments "have been the foci for collective participation in the politics and public life of towns, cities and states." Their location gives monuments additional symbolic meaning.[27] The monuments built in Pressburg towards the end of the century were important moments in the symbolic appropriation of Pressburg by the nationalising Hungarian state and the city's Magyar patriotic elite. Towards the end of the nineteenth century, a group of statues was erected at strategically or historically important places in Hungary, as monuments of the millennial anniversary of the successful taking of this territory by Hungarians (*honfoglalás*) which lasted from 888 until 898.[28] Pressburg's importance in Hungary was reconfirmed by the millennial celebrations: Kálmán Thály, the prominent Hungarian historian and *Toldy Kör* member, successfully proposed building a monument honouring the Hungarian warrior from the Árpád period on Dévény hill near Pressburg.[29] This part will first consider the significance of the millennial monuments in Hungary, especially the Dévény (Devín) monument. I will then examine in detail the 1897 unveiling of the Maria Theresa millennial monument in Pressburg by Emperor Franz Joseph, as this occasion provides important insights into the politics of ethnic affiliation and dynastic loyalty in Pressburg.

3.1. MILLENNIAL MONUMENTS:
MARKING THE BORDERS OF THE HUNGARIAN TERRITORY
This section considers the millennial monuments erected in Hungary at the end of the nineteenth century.[30] I will briefly describe the placement of the monuments in strategic locations and then look in more detail at the

Dévény monument near Pressburg, as the design and iconography of this monument explicitly represented the Hungarian state's nationalising ideology. While ostensibly commemorating the thousandth anniversary of the Hungarian state, the millennial monuments also symbolically demarcated the border of the state and of Hungarian national space.[31] They served as a reminder to potential enemies of the country that this territory belonged to Hungary. The millennial monuments were locations dedicated to the confirmation of Hungarian identity.[32] "Monuments fostered and expressed the sacralisation of the nation, creating sacred spaces and symbols dedicated to the nation, which were very reminiscent of those used for religious practice."[33] Monuments mark the national landscape, they incorporate the landscape on which they are located into the national space, they make the landscape familiar and connected with national identity. In this way monuments are important for building national self-consciousness.

The millennial monuments were the idea of Thály, a prominent Hungarian historian and member of *Toldy Kör*. Participating in the Hungarian parliament's discussions on preparations for the millennial celebrations, Thály proposed that in addition to the millennial monuments built in major cities, monuments should also be built in strategic rural locations of the important events of the *honfoglalás*. Thály was inspired by German monuments such as the monument to Germania on the Rhine or Valhalla in Regensburg. He felt that such monuments were important for the nation since they "increased national self-consciousness."[34] Thály's suggestion was accepted by both the parliament and the emperor. Monuments were erected at seven places in Hungary, chosen by Thály himself. The reason for building these monuments was clear: "The national committee put special focus on the symbolisation of the state idea in areas inhabited by [other] nationalities..."[35] Thály was elected to the executive committee planning most of these monuments and was even given a secretary with whom he travelled across Hungary deciding on the exact location of the monuments.[36]

Thály gave careful thought to the symbolic meaning of the location of the rural monuments. Two monuments were located in the heartland of "pure" Magyardom.[37] Four more monuments were to be erected at the "gates" of Hungary so that foreigners approaching Hungary could "see from the columns standing on striking places that it is the Hungarian [Magyar] soil onto which they step; to remind the nationalities that it is the Hungarian soil on which they live even if that soil is shared with others;—and finally to encourage Magyars in the border counties."[38] In the north, the monument was located on Munkács (Mukachevo) castle hill, where the

Magyars had "entered" the country. This monument overlooked the main line of the Polish railway. In the south, the monument was located at Zimony castle hill (facing Belgrade) at the place where the Hungarian hero János Hunyady had died.³⁹ The Orient-Express from Paris to Constantinople passed this spot. In the south-west, a monument was planned for Czenk mountain overlooking Brassau (Brasov).⁴⁰ In the west, the monument was built on Dévény castle hill, (which, according to some Slovak historians, was the seat of the Great Moravian king Svätopluk and already had a castle when the Magyars arrived). (See Figure 2.)

Thály was quite clear about the symbolic function of these triumphalist monuments and their desired impact on the other nationalities of the Hungarian kingdom as well as on foreigners. All of the monuments were equipped with a brass coat of arms.⁴¹ The Munkács monument was dedicated to the Russian nationality (Ruthenes) to keep them faithful to the Hungarian state. The memorial in Zimony was to remind Serbs "only as far as Száva, no further." The memorial in the south-west was a warning to the Rumanians. The memorial in Dévény had to remind the Austrians that this was Hungarian territory.⁴² Thály stressed that he had not forgotten about the "Slovak sons," either. A monument was built on Zobor mountain overlooking Nyitra, once the seat of the Great Moravian rulers. This statue was meant to remind Slovaks that they had lived in Hungary peacefully for centuries. For those who persisted in refusing the Hungarian state idea, this monument was meant to inspire them to "better their ways."⁴³

The Dévény monument (called also Árpád monument) symbolically incorporated the Pressburg region into Hungarian territory. Built on a hill near Pressburg, the monument could be seen from the railway and the steamship coming from Vienna (Figure 18). The monument was a visible reminder for visitors that they were leaving Austria and entering Hungary. The symbols on the monument were carefully thought out to suggest Hungarian ownership while avoiding threatening gestures towards Austria. (The emperor resided in Vienna.) The monument consisted of a column on which stood a knight from the Árpád period, his left hand leaning on a shield bearing the Hungarian coat of arms so that foreigners coming from Vienna could see that this was "Hongrie" and not "Autriche." (Thály felt that this distinction was necessary to emphasise since the two parts of the monarchy were always confused abroad.) In his right hand the knight held a curved Hungarian sword. His hand pointed down, symbolising that "here is the border where the *honfoglalás* had been finished." However, the hand also meant: "Up to here, German, but not a step further! Because I can raise the sword any time for the defence of my homeland!... Honour the integrity of the Hungarian state!" It was decided not to depict a raised sword as Austria might consider this a provocation.[44]

The millennial monuments were designed as repositories of national memory and expression of Hungarian national identity.[45] As Thály put it: "These monuments will announce in the long years ahead the thousand years of existence of the Hungarian state and they will represent the Hungarian state idea to the nationalities who also have to become adherents [of the Hungarian state idea]."[46] Thus the millennial monuments were not only reminders of a glorified past but also were meant as a message for future generations. The monuments were concrete emblems of a posited historical continuity of ownership, stretching back a thousand years and potentially extensible into the distant future.[47] The location of the monuments also created a 'sacred circle' around the territory of Hungary in an attempt to ensure its inviolability in the future.[48] In this ritualised fashion, the Hungarian state tried to make the territory its own. The next section considers in greater detail another ceremony with important ritual and symbolic connotations: the unveiling of the coronation monument of Maria Theresa built by the city of Pressburg.

3.2. THE CORONATION MONUMENT OF MARIA THERESA

Pressburg decided to build the Maria Theresa monument to celebrate the millennial anniversary of the Hungarian state and to commemorate the city's historic role as a coronation city. The unveiling of the statue by Emperor Franz Joseph resembled the enactment of a ritual, re-connecting the city with its glorious (and now vanished) past. This section describes the location and construction of the Maria Theresa monument and discusses the symbolic aspects of the monument and its unveiling ceremony.[49] I will also briefly describe the reaction of the local press to the unveiling ceremony and consider the uneasy mix in Pressburg of Hungarian national loyalty and dynastic loyalty.

3.2.1. Location and Construction of the Monument

The Maria Theresa monument was built on the former location of Pressburg's "coronation hill." At this place, after his coronation the king would brandish his sword in all four directions to indicate that he would defend the country from its enemies.[50] After the capital was moved to Budapest, the Pressburg municipal authorities decided that the coronation hill had lost its function and that the only reason to preserve it was in "reverence" of its historical significance. However, Pressburg possessed other reminders of past coronations such as the coronation cathedral (St. Martin's Cathedral) which was already undergoing renovation. Moreover, the coronation hill was adjacent to the horse railway and steamship station and hindered local transport. The city, therefore, proposed to remove the coronation hill and to mark the location with a symbolic monument.[51] The Ministry of Interior approved the city's decision and the coronation hill was removed in 1870. This pragmatic decision clearly showed that the city authorities gave priority to the development of a modern city rather than to the preservation of the city's history.

This pragmatic attitude changed with the approaching millennial celebrations of the Hungarian state. The Hungarian state wanted to use the millennium celebrations to confirm its Magyar nationalist agenda.[52] In an effort to prove their Hungarian patriotism, the city authorities decided to honour the millennial anniversary in some substantial manner. An 1892 municipal assembly meeting enthusiastically supported the proposal of city deputy Karl Neiszidler to hold a special meeting on the 8 June, anniversary of the coronation "of our beloved king" to approve the erection of a monument at the location of the coronation hill to be unveiled in the millennial year.[53] The symbolism of this event is interesting. It was not enough that the municipal assembly finally decided to build the monument. The decision had to be formally made on the anniversary of the emperor's coronation. However, the Pressburg municipal assembly's decision to connect the millennial celebration with the coronation of the Habsburg emperor merely confirmed Magyar nationalist doubts about the mixed loyalties of *Pressburgers*. For Magyar nationalists, celebrating the coronation of Franz Joseph (in whose reign the 1848/9 Hungarian revolution fighting for independence from Austria had been crushed) was hardly an appropriate way to celebrate the Hungarian millennium.

The city authorities worked up a proposal for the 8 June 1892 special municipal assembly meeting.[54] The text of this proposal is worth analysing in some detail as it provides interesting insights into the city elite's motivations. The text starts by noting the immense importance of the king's coronation anniversary, celebrated wherever "Hungarian blood pulsates.... This celebration marks the great love and unshatterable loyalty of the Hungarian nation to our crowned apostolic king and its faithful attachment to the members of the glorious ruling house."[55] Most Magyar nationalists would probably not agree with these lofty sentiments, as their attachment to the Habsburgs was certainly shattered in 1848/9. The proposal goes on to mention the 300 years that Pressburg had been Hungary's coronation city. The coronation hill (which the city so eagerly removed in 1869) is now described as "the witness and sacred symbol of great historic importance and of the privileged position taken by our city in the country" which was removed "with deplorable haste."[56] The monument is to be erected as a correction of that previous error and as proof of the "sincere love of the king's subjects and their unshakable loyalty ... and finally also with regard to the approaching celebration of the thousand years of existence of our beloved homeland."[57] It is interesting to note that the millennial aspect of the monument is mentioned almost in passing while more emphasis is paid to the city's historic ties to the Habsburg dynasty and its rulers. The monument would testify to the "warmest love and loyalty of the Pressburger citizens to the kings and queens from the glorious house of Habsburg who were once crowned here, as well as to our dear homeland."[58] Again, the "dear homeland" comes as an afterthought: the principal aim of the monument (and of the *Festschrift* itself) is to invoke the glorious past when Pressburg was the coronation city of Hungarian kings and queens.

However, in order to prove that "the old crowning city has always felt, feels and will feel with the beloved homeland," the monument had to be ready in the millennial year.[59] The municipal assembly elected a committee including prominent city personalities, to oversee the preparation of the monument.[60] The committee agreed that a Pressburger artist should be given the commission for the monument.[61] The commission was eventually given to Johann Fadrusz, a famous Hungarian sculptor born in Pressburg. The committee specified that the monument "should embody loyalty to the homeland and the king."[62] In June 1893 Fadrusz's initial sketch for the monument was publicly exhibited in the city hall and won general admiration.[63] The artist had chosen an episode which took place in Pressburg. Threatened by enemies from all sides, young queen Maria Theresa came looking for help from the gathered Hungarian nobles who answered: "We live and die for our Monarch!" (*Vitam et sanguinem pro Rege nostro!*)[64] The group of statues proposed by Fadrusz represented the already fulfilled oath of the Hungarian Diet to the queen. The main figure was that of the queen on a horse. On her left stood a magnate (a Hungarian noble) with his outstretched left hand pointing towards the Danube as if saying: "See, there lies your loyal Hungary." On the right stood the figure of a *Bürger* fighter, with a threatening look and a lowered sword prepared for fight. His left hand held the coat of arms of Hungary.[65] (See Figure 19.) These two figures embodied the aristocracy and the bourgeoisie (*Bürgerschaft*) of Hungary. The monument tried to reconcile the idea of loyalty to the Habsburg dynasty and the Hungarian national idea.

The pedestal had in front the inscription "*Vitam et sanguinem*" and at the back the dedication (in Hungarian):"Erected in the thousandth year of the existence of Hungary by the inhabitants of the free royal town Pressburg in memory of the coronations that happened here. 1896."[66] The monument also had a dedication written by Kálmán Thály.[67] Thály put more stress on the occasion of the millennium rather than on past coronations. His dedication praised the "Hungarian love of the homeland, Hungarian respect of the law and unshakable loyalty of the nation to the staggering throne and the chivalrous support of Hungary...." The monument symbolised the "enduring and inviolable sanctity of the king's oath and of the laws." The inscription ended: "But you monument, into stone turned herald of the old Hungarian virtues, Hungarian loyalty, Hungarian heroic courage, Hungarian knighthood and respect of law, Stand unshakable! Stand in eternity! Stand as long as the thousand-year-old beloved homeland exists!"[68]

A new coronation hill was built where the old had been demolished. According to an old Hungarian tradition, the crowning hill had to be built from earth brought from all parts of the country. The Pressburg city authorities appealed to all counties to send a quarter cubic meter of soil. Although all the preparations were ready by 1895, the unveiling ceremony planned for 11 September 1896 had to be postponed to May 1897 because of difficulties with quarrying marble in Carrara.[69]

3.2.2. The Unveiling Ceremony

The 1897 unveiling ceremony of the Maria Theresa monument was one of the most significant public events in Pressburg during the period 1867–1914. As the *Westungarischer Grenzbote* excitedly noted, "Pressburg has not seen so much glitter and pomp since the last coronation which happened within the walls of this city...."[70] In addition to the king, many members of the royal family, aristocrats, members of the Hungarian government and prominent Hungarian public personalities were to participate in the ceremony. Advance preparations for the ceremony were extensive and time consuming. The route of the ceremonial procession and the positioning of the military were carefully planned. The city newspapers announced which streets would be closed down.[71] The city police chief asked his counterpart in Budapest to send reinforcements, "if possible German speaking" detectives and policemen.[72]

On the day of the ceremony, 16 June 1897, the whole city was richly decorated. A triumphal arch was built at Pressburg railway station. The king was welcomed there by Hungarian ministers, senior representatives of the church, civil and military offices, and representatives of the city. At the ceremony, choirs first sang Kölcsey's '*Hymnus*' and '*Szózat*' in Hungarian, thus symbolically bringing the city into Hungary. After the veil fell from the monument, the anthem was played and canons fired from the castle ruins.[73] The king and the city authorities spoke in mixed Hungarian and German.[74] Such mixture of languages was typical for Pressburg and in any case the emperor's knowledge of Hungarian was not very good anyway (as was also the case for many *Pressburgers* and local aristocrats).[75]

All the local periodicals celebrated the king's presence in the city and gave detailed accounts of his every move. The *Pressburger Zeitung* published a detailed history of the monument as well as the program of the ceremony. Days before the unveiling ceremony, the periodicals printed lists of arriving guests and where they would be staying. Most newspaper articles on the day of the royal visit stressed the undying loyalty of the city to the king. The articles idealised Pressburg, presenting the city as a peaceful happy big family, and proclaiming that ungratefulness and envy were totally alien to the "*Pressburger Bürger*."[76] The royal visit for the unveiling ceremony was a big event for the city and all the local newspapers were anxious to portray the event in a positive light.

However, there were significant differences in the attitudes of different periodicals as they represented different interest groups in the city. The *Pressburger Zeitung* and *Westungarischer Grenzbote* took a balanced approach, celebrating the emperor and the historic past of the city but also emphasising the thousand years of existence of the Hungarian state. The *Pressburger Tagblatt* (the local Christian Democrat periodical), on the other hand, concentrated totally on the person of the emperor, the Habsburg dynasty and its connection to the Catholic church and on the loyalty and love of inhabitants to their king. The *Tagblatt* even criticised Hungarian Prime Minister Bánffy for openly being in a foul mood and also criticised Hungarian ministers for their inappropriate dress at the festivity. Ministers were criticised for not bothering to put on their "Hungarian Gala" (richly decorated traditional Hungarian costumes) while the great magnates could wear their precious inherited costumes and risk their damage in bad weather so that "they could prepare joy for both the nation and the king." The *Tagblatt* was also critical of the rude and inappropriate behaviour of secret police agents from Budapest who had to be removed from the front lines by the local police chief.[77]

For its part, the *Nyugatmagyarországi Híradó* (the local newspaper of the Magyar nationalist elite) criticised non-Hungarian (especially Austrian) participants in the festivity for not recognising the importance of this day as a millennial celebration of the Hungarian state. What had been intended to be a national celebration had turned into a mere celebration of the king's visit to the city.[78] The *Híradó* tried to reconcile the Hungarian national idea with loyalty to the Habsburgs, claiming that at present "the national and dynastic interest is one and the same."[79] The *Híradó* stressed the romantic story of a "weak woman" (Maria Theresa) asking for help from the chivalrous Hungarian nation (embodied in the noblemen of the Hungarian parliament) which defended her from her enemies without hesitation.[80] According to the *Híradó*, even the statue showed clearly that Maria Theresa was "a Hungarian queen in her total stature" since her face bore the same heroic features as the faces of Hungarian national heroes.[81] The German press pointed out that the Maria Theresa monument was the first monument in Hungary dedicated to this ruler and had been built at the cost of the city.[82] "Bitter" memories of the past had led the Hungarian nation to first build monuments to their own national heroes. The *Híradó* felt that Pressburg's patriotic erection of this monument was evidence of the city's political maturity.[83]

The day of the royal visit made *Pressburgers* feel special and that their city had a glorious past which had been inherited by the present inhabitants. "For the city it was ... the greatest and most uplifting celebration which was celebrated by the municipality and its inhabitants."[84] *Pressburgers* were delighted to hear Emperor Franz Joseph say: "I always come with joy to this old coronation city which is so close to my heart."[85] Even the Hungarian press felt that no city was more appropriate for the construction of a monument expressing the unity of the nation and the dynasty than "the Magyar Versailles."[86] This was the reaction of the Pressburger middle class who saw themselves as heirs to the coronation tradition. This category of 'Bürger' did not include the masses of workers, most of whom were immigrants and were not citizens of Pressburg. Unfortunately, since the workers' local press for this period is not available, it is impossible to assess what the reaction of the workers was to the presence of the king in the city and to the monument itself. The trust placed by the workers in the emperor indicates that he was probably liked by the workers, as also by most poor people in the empire.[87]

While the Budapest press celebrated the monument as "the most beautiful monument of our fatherland," the Slovak press was more critical.[88] The Slovak publications felt that the artistic quality of the monument was poor and criticised its historical inaccuracies (such as the figure of the *kuruc* (the *Bürger* fighter) since these were actually seventeenth and eighteenth century rebels who had fought against the Habsburgs). Slovak newspapers also noted that Fadrusz, the creator of this monument celebrating the Magyar millennium, was not a Magyar artist but a "German Pressburger" who had learnt his craft in Slovak Nitra and who had crafted the statue in Italian Carrara and the cost had been met by German Pressburg.[89]

The reactions in the local press reflect variations in the reactions of different groups of inhabitants towards the monument.[90] While the German speaking press stressed dynastic loyalty and the city's glorious past, the Magyar elite was primarily concerned with celebrating the Hungarian nation. However, even the Magyar elite shared in the glory of Pressburg as the "Magyar Versailles." The message of the monument was mixed from the moment of its inception. Although it was meant to be also the monument celebrating thousand years of existence of the Hungarian nation, the monument expressed more the mixed loyalties and multiple identities of the city elite. Despite its inscriptions commemorating the millennial year of the Hungarian state, the monument remained more an embodiment of the pride of the city elite in the glorious past of their city.[91] This theme is further developed in the next part of this chapter describing the rhetoric used by the city elite in their attempts to attract Hungary's third university to Pressburg.

4. THE THIRD UNIVERSITY—
PRESSBURG AS "HUNGARY'S SECOND CAPITAL"[92]

Hungary's two universities were located in Budapest and Kolozsvár. The idea of creating a third university was first raised in 1878 by the Minister of Education, Ágost Trefort, who felt that Pressburg would be the right location. The issue became a topic of public debate as other Hungarian cities (Szeged, Győr, and Debrecen) competed to become the location for the university. In this debate, Pressburg was often accused in the Hungarian press of being insufficiently patriotic for the role of Hungary's third university town. Minister Trefort's successors also differed on the need for a third university. Overcrowding and insufficient capacity in Budapest university finally forced the foundation of new universities in Pressburg and Debrecen in 1912.[93]

The Pressburg city elite strategically used Hungarian nationalist rhetoric in order to get the third university located in the city. This part looks at the rhetoric employed in three pamphlets written in favour of the university: one by the Magyar nationalist and active *Toldy Kör* member Gábor

Pávai Vajna; a second written by the Pressburger philanthropist Georg Schulpe; and the third put forward by the municipality, with annexes written by another *Toldy Kör* member, Mór Pisztóry. These pamphlets reveal how Pressburg was perceived in Hungary and the position Pressburger citizens sought for their city.

The three pamphlets did not differ very much in their reasoning. Pávai's pamphlet was perhaps most patriotic and also included a convincing argument in favour of a medical faculty in Pressburg with supporting evidence since Pávai was the director of Pressburg's state hospital.[94] Schulpe was more philosophical and philanthropic.[95] The municipal pamphlet contained similar arguments. The pamphlet was signed by the mayor and had supplements which were written by Mór Pisztóry, a member of the Hungarian patriotic association *Toldy Kör*.[96] *Toldy Kör* itself also lobbied the members of the Hungarian government for the university.[97] In its 1895 memorandum on the Hungarian theatre, *Toldy Kör* stressed that Pressburg would not get the third university unless it showed its Magyarisation.[98] When Albert Berzeviczy (the deputy chairman of the Hungarian parliament) came to give a lecture in November 1897 to *Toldy Kör*, the association's representatives asked for his support in securing the university for Pressburg.[99] In 1906 a *Toldy Kör* delegation in Budapest met Education Minister Albert Ápponyi and Prime Minister Alexander Wekerle in order to lobby for Pressburg.[100]

Pávai's reasoning drew upon the arguments employed by *Toldy Kör* towards other nationalities (as described in Chapter two and in the second part of this chapter). The establishment of a third university was necessary in order to stop youth from flooding away to foreign universities. Pávai described the "competition for existence" in the areas of power, wealth and education where Hungary was lagging far behind other European nations and noted that "from the viewpoint of preserving the national independence [this was] a vital question."[101] The absence of "brothers of related language" (i.e. other languages of related origin) meant that there was no other country from which Hungarians could take scientific knowledge and "*if only from a national point of view, foreign scientific forces and universities must not be pampered.*"[102] Thus Hungarians had to create science and culture (education and civilisation) at home. "Science is not always *cosmopolitan* but has its *national direction* which it indeed must have under our special conditions."[103] Many of the students who studied medicine in Vienna were forever lost for the Hungarian nation or else returned from Vienna "with a foreign spirit" and were indifferent towards Hungarian culture. If Magyars wanted the non-Magyar nationalities to melt into the state-creating nation and to become real Hungarians then a new university was an imperative. Also, the overcrowded medical faculties of Vienna and Budapest, as well as their placement in "world-cities," distracted students from their studies.[104] As Pávai picturesquely put it, "The pretty metropolis of Upper Hungary wants a university primarily in order to build up the muscles of Magyar racial rule."[105] After these patriotic reasons, Pávai cited "objective" reasons which were also repeated in the other two pamphlets: Pressburg's advantageous geographic position, good air and beautiful natural conditions, "its well developed and refined feeling for humanism and warm interest in erudition, education and art," a well equipped hospital, many libraries with valuable collections, museums, the century-old Law Academy and schools of all levels, the high educational level of its inhabitants, many popular and scientific lectures, and a calm and studious atmosphere where parents would not have to worry about their children straying from good morals.[106] Pávai paid special attention to the excellent conditions for establishing a medical faculty in the city, supporting this point with ample evidence. However, Pávai's key argument was based on nationalism: the Magyarisation of Upper Hungary and the strengthening of the Hungarian state idea made Pressburg clearly the right choice as the location for the third university.[107]

Schulpe's arguments were similar to those of Pávai but somewhat more sophisticated. Schulpe called Pressburg the "stepchild of Hungary."[108] He also reminded his readers of Pressburg's ancient past as one of the pre-eminent cities in Hungary and noted that the city had participated in the struggle for Hungarian independence in 1848. Arguing against those who proclaimed that Pressburg was an inappropriate locale for the university because of the proximity of Vienna and pan-Slavic Upper Hungary, Schulpe declared that these were precisely reasons for locating a university in the city as the university would then be "the bastion of Hungarian national culture and its shining tower."[109] For Schulpe, a university served education in the broadest sense, which he considered important in forming responsible citizens. As opposed to Pávai, Schulpe considered the proximity of Vienna to be a positive factor for the development of science "since science was neither German or Hungarian "but remains a field of free competition for unrestricted endeavours."[110] Thus, unlike Pávai and other leading Hungarian intellectuals, Schulpe did not ascribe any particular 'national character' to science, showing more cosmopolitan Pressburger spirit than Hungarian nationalism. For Schulpe, Pressburg's Hungarian character was beyond doubt but he did not identify this Hungarian identity with the Hungarian language. Schulpe also highlighted "the pure moral character" of the city's inhabitants.[111]

The municipal pamphlet's main purpose was to highlight Pressburg's advantages as compared to the competing city of Szeged. The municipal pamphlet repeated many of the points made by Pávai and Schulpe. It claimed that a university in Pressburg would strengthen the Hungarian "race" in this area. In contrast to Szeged, Pressburg's geographical situation would enable the city to prevent a brain-drain of youth from Upper Hungary to Austrian universities. The pamphlet also mentioned the city's long tradition of supporting learning (citing the foundation of the *Academia Istropolitana* four hundred years previously) and noted the emperor's support for Pressburg's application. The city defended its Hungarian patriotism, indignantly refuting accusations that in "Pressburg we can be sure of the prospect that a university established there will establish in its bosom the Slovak Matica and the German Burschenschaften."[112] The memorandum also noted that founding the university in Pressburg would be relatively cheap because of already built up infrastructure (buildings, hospitals, libraries, etc.) In 1880 (thirty-two years before the university was finally approved) the city had already voted 100,000 forints for founding the university.[113]

The arguments in favour of siting the third university in Pressburg show a remarkable consistency in the views of the Pressburg elites on the image of their city and its place in Hungary. The Pressburg elite saw their city as a place of culture and education, as Hungary's second city.[114] Pressburg's boosters also used the "strategic" position of the city at an ethnic crossroads in their arguments. However, the fact that *Pressburgers* needed to explicitly defend their city's patriotism points to lingering doubts about the city's loyalty and place in Hungary. The question of where Pressburg belonged came to the fore also in the discussion in the Hungarian parliament over the construction of the electric train line from Bratislava to the Austrian border and Vienna, discussed in the next part of this chapter.

5. UNFAITHFUL POZSONY?
DISCUSSION OF THE ELECTRIC RAILWAY LINE
CONNECTING PRESSBURG TO VIENNA

This part describes the discussion in the Hungarian parliament in 1908 on the construction of an electric railway between Pressburg and Vienna. The project was the subject of heated debate from the end of the nineteenth century until the project's approval in July 1909. This debate concerned the position of Pressburg on the border of Hungary and reflected a fear of losing Pressburg to the economic and cultural orbit of Vienna and thus endangering Hungarian "national interests." Opponents of the line were concerned about the "weak" position of Hungarian culture in Pressburg and the danger that Hungarian culture in the city would succumb under the influence of Vienna and German culture. Budapest newspapers accused Pressburg of insufficient Hungarian patriotism, preferring its own selfish local interests to those of the nation, and in being more interested in attaching itself to Vienna rather than to the "heart of the country," Budapest. This discussion illustrates the ethnic atmosphere in Pressburg at a time when Magyarisation had made considerable headway and also sheds light on the city's image in Hungary due to its ambiguous position between Budapest and Vienna and its multiple loyalties. I will first give a brief history of the project and then I will discuss the arguments used by supporters and opponents of the project.

5.1. HISTORY OF THE PROJECT

The city of Pressburg first proposed building an electric train line to Hainburg (on the Hungarian-Austrian border) in 1897. The project was at this date approved by the Hungarian government but rejected by the Austrian government. In 1898, the Austrian Minister Wittek dismissed a petition by the town Hainburg on the grounds that he did not intend "to open gates for the Hungarians."[115] In 1900 an entrepreneur declared his willingness to build an electric train connection between Pressburg and Vienna and, in 1904, Pressburg's municipal government signed a contract with the approval of the Hungarian government.[116] In 1906 the Hungarian minister of commerce introduced a bill proposing the construction of the train line which was discussed by the Transport, Financial and Economic parliamentary committees. The Economic Committee rejected the project mainly on nationalist grounds, as posing a danger to Magyar culture in Pressburg. Both the Transport and Financial Committees approved the project and dismissed the argument that this railway would harm Hungarian interests.[117] However, the proposal did not get discussed in the parliament since at the end of the second parliamentary season the government withdrew all its previous bills. After the opening of the third season in May 1908, the Pressburg parliamentary deputy Otto Sziklai took on the task of introducing the proposal to the parliament.[118]

The parliamentary debate reflected the ongoing public debate in the pages of both the Budapest and Pressburger newspapers.[119] Supporters of the project in the Hungarian parliament included Otto Sziklai, Gyula Kubik (secretary of the minister of commerce), József Szterényi (on behalf of the minister of commerce), and Count Tivadar Batthyányi, a member of the Economic Committee who supported the project. The deputies György Nagy, Károly Kmety and Árpád Bozóky spoke against the project.[120] Both the supporters and opponents of the project used economic and national arguments related to the railway's impact on Pressburg's economy and local industries and Hungarian culture. I will consider arguments put forward by opponents and supporters of the project in turn in the following sections.

5.2. Opponents of the Project

The opponents of the electric railway linking Pressburg to Vienna were deeply concerned that Pressburg would fall into the orbit of Vienna, adversely affecting Hungarian national interests.[121] Pressburg was seen as a gateway into the country which had to be guarded with utmost care. As one opponent put it, the electric railway "will destroy Pozsony's trade and industry, increase the costs and spread the German spirit even more."[122] This suggested that Pressburg had already been poisoned by the German spirit. Opponents such as Pávai saw the electric railway as "a great danger not only for Pozsony but also for the country ... I am very afraid of the foreign influence on Pozsony as well as the Magyar homeland because the Magyar heroic, cavalier nature very fast and easily accommodates to everything foreign, whose language and customs it adopts very fast to its own detriment."[123] Such national interest arguments show a strategic picture of power relations in the Austro-Hungarian Empire with three key elements: fears about the attraction and ambitions of Vienna as a world city; the belief that Pressburg was not sufficiently Magyarised; and the political importance of the railway network connecting Pressburg to Budapest as a key element of the Hungarian nation-building enterprise.

The opponents of the project were particularly worried about the "attraction power" of Vienna as a world city. Even inhabitants of the Hungarian metropolis, Budapest, would "look for fulfilment of their both spiritual and material needs in the world cities" if Paris, Berlin or Vienna were nearby. This possibility was even more pronounced for Pressburg which was just a small countryside town near "big, glamorous" Vienna which had the additional attraction of a shared German language.[124] Károly Kmety was afraid that Vienna would completely draw Pressburg (and other smaller towns

connected by railway) into its economic, social and cultural life: "these localities will lose their social independence and individuality, because like a big
vampire, that world city will suck out the life force of these localities connected to it and it will turn their previously independently circulating blood
into part of its own blood-circulation." Kmety believed that "at present a
physiological process is underway by which the separate localities connected to Vienna by railway will assimilate to the big Vienna, into one united economic, cultural, aesthetic and political spirit, the greater Vienna of a united
blood circulation. In this way these localities will become "organic spare
parts of 'a being of a higher order.'" Kmety saw the same process taking place
around Budapest; however, in the case of the electric railway drawing Pressburg closer to Vienna, all the advantages would go to Austria and not Hungary.[125] Hungarian nationalists like Kmety believed that: "the Viennese treat
this railway like a part of *Gross-Wien* (Greater Vienna).... The Viennese press
always describes Pozsony as a pretty German garrison-town."[126]

For Hungarian nationalists, Vienna was a place where "anti-Hungarian
streams spring up." This image of Vienna was shaped by a visceral hostility towards Austria. Hungarian nationalists assumed that the Austrians
would not want to construct this railway if it did not enable them to further
exploit Hungary in some way. For nationalists like Kmety, economic protectionism and cultural prejudice went hand in hand, resulting in a pes-
simistic paranoia about both Hungarians and Austrians. According to this
view, Austria wanted "to turn Pozsony into Vienna's customer."[127] This was
possible because of the weakness of Hungarian patriotism which was "only
lip-service": Hungarian patriotism evaporated at the prospect of cheaper
or more chic foreign products. Austrian patriotism, however, was not a
"straw-flame" like Hungarian patriotism.[128] The inhabitants of Austrian
villages would never do their shopping in a "city of the hated Hungary ...
as they would rather see their beloved imperial city profit than a Hungarian one." Austria did not nurture its enemies with its own money as Hungary did by preferring Austrian products. Kmety even called for a
Hungarian boycott of Austrian products.[129]

In addition to economic protectionism, opponents of the electric train
connection feared its impact on Magyarisation in Pressburg. Parliamentary
deputy György Nagy found it "sad" that while Hungarian patriotic youth
were doing their utmost to make the Pressburg theatre Hungarian, parliament deputies were making a decision "which could totally annihilate Magyardom in Pozsony."[130] They argued that cheap and frequent travel to Vienna
would encourage the inhabitants of Pressburg to go to Vienna whenever they

needed to go shopping or even to arrange some petty matter.[131] The project's opponents also brought up the Pressburger middle classes' visits to theatre performances in Vienna.[132] Considering the long struggle of the Hungarians in Pressburg to secure the City Theatre for Hungarian performances (as shown in Chapter two), this was an important issue. Despite admitting that Pressburg's inhabitants were good Hungarian patriots, a fundamental fear of Pressburg's attachment to Hungary underlay the arguments of the project's opponents. As the Economic Committee sourly noted: "in Pozsony public opinion even today we find in a German daily published there [*Pressburger Zeitung*] notions that belittle Magyar culture, showing an inability to understand that for every nation only its own culture has value, and the borrowed culture is only a superficial layer, which hinders the realisation that Magyar culture can show, in every area of life, such creations as are totally sufficient for the great mass of the people and for their elevation to a higher spiritual level."[133] Kmety also referred to attacks in the Pressburg press against the tram's opponents and used the debate in the press to obliquely suggest that public opinion in Pressburg was split along ethnic lines on this issue.[134] The Hungarian daily press, of which "there is unfortunately only one in Pozsony" was against the railway in contrast to the "five or six" German dailies. Although Kmety did not explicitly deny the patriotism of Pressburg, the juxtaposition of one Hungarian periodical to five or six German publications suggested that the dominant linguistic and ethnic milieu in Pressburg was German. Kmety also noted that there had once been another Hungarian periodical that had folded "due to a lack of the necessary support."[135] Again, this lack of support implicitly questioned the extent to which Pressburg's inhabitants were real Hungarian patriots.

The Economic Committee was also not optimistic about the progress of Magyarisation in Pressburg: "There are some facts which it is impossible to ignore. And one such fact is that Pozsony is a city ... with a German character, and is one in which the Hungarian language is in its weakest position."[136] Social Darwinist members of the Economic Committee were worried that Magyars would lose in the competition with other nations: "Magyardom is continuing such a difficult fight, it is subjected to competition from nations that will see their populations increase to a hundred millions today or tomorrow, if they have not already reached this number, so that we have to count every decigram in the national scales.... Under these circumstances it is of utmost importance that in such an esteemed city of the country like Pozsony one does not bring into existence a transport institution which will not strengthen the working of the national strength and which will make more difficult the arduous struggle being waged by Pozsony's Magyardom in the interest of the national idea."[137] The Economic Committee argued that Magyars were in a minority among people employed in industry and represented less than half of the management personnel.[138] According to the committee, Pressburg did not need greater market access to Vienna as it already possessed a huge area where it could sell its products. The committee was convinced that Pressburg could develop only after the independent custom territory of Hungary was established. Pressburg would then develop "on an American scale."[139] In the meantime, competition with Vienna could only harm Pressburg's industry since Vienna would only allow as much access as was convenient for its own interests.[140]

The parliamentary debate also highlighted the political importance of the railways in the Hungarian nation-building enterprise. "The centralising and assimilationist impact of the railways mirror themselves also in the political formation."[141] The organic character of nationalist discourse is particularly striking in this context. The Economic Committee described the electric railway as an "illness of the transport system": "even within the area of transport ... one can observe the pathological symptoms of hypertrophy, when the traffic can cause a nervous illness, risking important interests and useless expense."[142] The committee quoted Count István Széchényi's statement comparing the country to a physical body and the capital to the heart of this body. "In order to make our trade glorious, strong and blossoming, its various branches must concentrate in one place, like the blood in the heart and the country's legal sovereignty and independence demand that the gathering point of the trade be located within the homeland ... in our homeland Pest was chosen as such a place."[143] Since Budapest was the "heart" of the country, the infrastructural network had to start from there. "the whole transport network must start from the country's heart in which the national spirit is at its strongest. That indifference which permits the peripheries to fall under foreign influences is dangerous since there is decided the question of national integrity."[144] Consequently Pressburg could prove its Hungarian patriotism only by strengthening its connection to Budapest rather than by building another connection to Vienna. "If the Pozsonyers really want to be Magyars in their hearts, souls and language, let them ask for an electric railway which will connect them to Pest."[145] Pávai expressed his wish that "Pozsony gravitate towards the country's heart. But, please, not towards Austria's but Hungary's heart. From there it shall win the nourishing warmth necessary for its bloom, so that it would not be Vienna's suburb, and finally, so that Vienna does not blackmail the honest, diligent citizens of this town with its illustrious past, predestined to fulfil a great role in future."[146]

The project's opponents stressed that the question of the railway was a matter of national interest. The people of Pressburg and its surroundings who wanted this railway did not realise that they were only defending their short-term interests (being too gullible to see the danger posed by Vienna) and had lost sight of long-term national interests.[147] National interests required that the Viennese influence be counter-acted, otherwise the Hungarian culture "will never take deeper roots in Pozsony."[148] Pressburg was predestined to become "the national capital of the Western Hungary, to be the defence bastion to the conquering path of the inimical German spirit from Vienna's direction. The city of Pozsony is destined to be the economic emporium of Western Hungary, its industrial and commercial centre...."[149] Hungary could not afford to lose such an important city to the influence of an alien nation.

5.3. SUPPORTERS OF THE PROJECT
In contrast to their opponents, supporters of the project focused primarily on pragmatic considerations such as the project's economic advantages. The electric railway's supporters also actively countered nationalist attacks against the project by noting the progress of Magyarisation in Pressburg.

The supporters of the electric railway put forward detailed analyses arguing that the project would bring considerable economic benefits to Pressburg and to the Hungarian hinterland. The 'tram' would strengthen the ability of agricultural producers in Pressburg and in the many small villages between Pressburg and Vienna to meet Vienna's growing demand for agricultural produce by enabling producers to take their goods directly to the Viennese market hall. Pressburg producers would also be able to sell their agricultural and industrial products in lower Austria, thus further developing local industry and trade. Furthermore, the tram would preserve traditional networks and connections of Pressburg's craftsmen and merchants with small towns in lower Austria, which remained an important component of Pressburg's economy. The tram's positive impact on Pressburg's macro-economic situation was also noted: unemployment would be eased since workers would be able to commute to Vienna in search of work and the railway connection would bring down prices by stimulating economic growth.[150] József Szterényi also noted that the tram could protect Hungarian exports from the negative impact of possible new Austrian tariffs and was, therefore, strategically important.[151] Supporters of the project also noted that the electric train would ease congestion on existing train services. The train to Vienna was usually full when it arrived at Pressburg from Budapest. The train would not adversely affect tourist traffic on the existing steam railway which cut across a beautiful landscape and was therefore preferable.[152] Although these economic considerations were decisive for building the railway, the supporters of the project spent more effort defending the project against nationalist attacks. This was necessary since even the economic arguments of the project's opponents had national interest as their basis.

Supporters of the electric railway tried to show the progress of Magyarisation and the strong position of Hungarian culture in Pressburg to counter arguments made by their opponents in the parliament and in the Budapest press that building the railway would open Pressburg to the German influence of Vienna and would weaken the Hungarian economy. Otto Sziklai explained that Pressburg had been completely German in the past when Vienna had been half a day's horse-ride away. However, now, despite ten daily train connections to Vienna and twice-daily links by ship, "Pozsony is rapidly Magyarising." Sziklai proudly noted that only one confessional and one communal school in Pressburg did not use Hungarian as the language of instruction. The only working language in Pressburg's municipal offices was Hungarian, the records of the municipal meetings had been kept in Hungarian for twenty years, and even the main theatre season had shifted in favour of Hungarians.[153] Szterényi also emphasised the patriotism of Pressburg's inhabitants: "the public and authorities of Pozsony city have known at all times what they owe to the country, to their homeland.... Just because a part of Pozsony's inhabitants are of German mother tongue, we have no right to assume that they are less patriotic than we who are of Magyar mother tongue."[154] Unlike their opponents, supporters of the railway did not equate Hungarian patriotism with knowledge and every-day use of the Hungarian language.[155] Szterényi quoted statistics on the changing ethnic composition of Pressburg (discussed in the first chapter) to demonstrate the massive success of Magyarisation in the city. The number of Magyars in Pressburg had grown by 143% in the last twenty years, Slovaks by 19.1% and the Germans only by 1.9%. According to Szterényi, this process would not be reversed by a local electric railway of minor importance.[156] Szterényi also produced statistics comparing the relative frequency of transport and traffic to demonstrate that contact between Pressburg and Budapest—"the heart of the country"—was more frequent than that between Pressburg and Vienna.[157]

The project's supporters also tried to actively counter their opponents' arguments. Ridiculing the purported threat Vienna presented to Hungarian culture in Pressburg, Sziklai asked: "Do you wish the Viennese to come in large numbers to Budapest? [By going to Pozsony] they won't be adding to the numbers of the capital's cosmopolites, of whom there are more here than in Pozsony."[158] Here again appears the image of Pressburg as a fortress deflecting the attack of the Viennese cosmopolites away from the Hungarian capital. The tram's supporters also criticised the Budapest press's accusations that Pressburg lacked patriotism. Sziklai pointed to the long-standing Hungarian patriotism of *Pressburgers*, reaching back to the era of Bach's absolutism and the 1848 Hungarian revolution. Pressburg had thirteen martyrs in the 1848 revolution and even a German priest had been hanged because he did not reject the Hungarian language.[159] Sziklai noted that even Budapest had been not sufficiently Magyarised either: German was still the main language heard in Buda's markets and promenades.[160] The tram's supporters also hotly denied the argument that the tram would enable *Pressburgers* to make even more frequent excursions to Vienna for shopping and going to the theatre: Tivadar Batthányi said that it was ridiculous to claim that people would travel two-and-half hours just to buy something a little cheaper. In any case, Pressburg's workers did not have enough money or free leisure time to go shopping in Vienna. Batthányi pointed out that Pressburg already had a "theatre train" which left Vienna after 11pm. However, even the middle classes had neither the money nor the time to go to Vienna's German theatre often enough that it "would influence their hearts."[161]

5.4. CONCLUSION

Both chambers of the Hungarian parliament eventually passed the bill and permission was given in 1909 for the construction of the electric railway.[162] The 'tram' was put into operation in 1914 just before the First World War. The electric train was in service until 1934 when its operation on Czechoslovak territory ceased. Until 1938, a public tram took passengers to the Austrian state border where they had to change to Viennese trains.[163]

The parliamentary debate on the electric railway illustrated the ambiguous position of Pressburg within the Austro-Hungarian Empire. Pressburg was accused by Hungarian nationalists of not being patriotic enough and of preferring to develop its relationship with Vienna rather than with the "heart of the nation," Budapest. Vienna was seen as a vampire and an exploiter trying to lure Pressburg within its sphere of influence. The opponents of the project feared the loss of Pressburg, an important "outpost" guarding the Hungarian nation from foreign influences. While supporters of the project pointed to rapidly progressing Magyarisation in Pressburg and the city's historical support for the Hungarian cause, opponents equated Hungarian patriotism and love for Hungarian culture with knowledge of the Hungarian language. While the project's opponents were thinking along national lines, the Pressburg authorities' considerations were primarily pragmatic. However, as in the case of the Maria Theresa monument, the ambiguity of Pressburg's position within the national landscape once again came to the fore.

This part has discussed the importance of the position of Pressburg within the Hungarian national landscape. As the parliamentary debate shows, the capital of Hungary, Budapest, was seen as the heart of the country and was of particular symbolic importance for the Hungarian nation-state. Although Pressburg was an important centre of the territory claimed by Slovak nationalists, the city was not, however, seen in similar symbolically charged terms by the representatives of the Slovak national movement during the nineteenth century. The last part of this chapter explores the discussion about the borders of the Slovak territory and its national centre during this period.

6. CAPITAL CITY AND TERRITORY

After the creation of Czechoslovakia, the new state's Czech and Slovak elites decided that Pressburg (renamed Bratislava) should become the unofficial capital of the Slovak part of Czechoslovakia (it was officially given capital status in 1928.) However, during the period 1867–1914, Pressburg was not seriously considered as a potential national capital by the Slovak national intelligentsia, although it was usually considered a part of the Slovak territory. The inability to exactly define the borders of a putative Slovak territory made Slovak nationalist claims to autonomy, let alone independence, problematic.[164] The lack of a national centre also made the position of the Slovak nationalist intelligentsia more difficult. This part examines different notions of 'national territory' and 'national centre' in the Slovak national movement. The first section looks at the development of ideas about the borders of the Slovak territory from 1848 until the First World War. The second section analyses the discussion about the 'national centre' of the Slovak nation.

6.1. TERRITORY

In the nineteenth century, the Slovak nation existed only in the writings and imagination of the Slovak national intelligentsia. The intelligentsia recognised the importance of defining their territorial claims to a living space and collective rights for "Slovaks" (defined as people living in this territory who were ethnographically different from other people in Hungary). As Mark Purcell points out, referring to Anderson's concept of nation as an 'imagined community', a nation's territory must be imagined as well. "The territory must be *imagined* to be a coherent, meaningful area."[165] Discussions of the Slovak national territory also led to discussions about the capital, considered as a 'national centre' for the co-ordination of cultural and political work.[166]

According to Bokeš, the feeling of Slovak 'otherness' came as a reaction to Magyarisation pressures: "the realisation of the necessity of a national territory not threatened by foreign aggression and surrounded by fixed borders against this aggression."[167] Most Slovaks merely differentiated the territory they lived in as *Vyšné okolie* or *Felvidék* (Upper Hungary) as opposed to *Alföld* (Lower Hungary).[168] At the end of the eighteenth century, the Slovak national revival's reminiscences of the Great Moravian kingdom led to a vague sense of a 'Slovak' territory stretching from the Danube to Tisza above a line between Vác and Szolnok (see Figure 2).[169] A series of attempts to define the Slovak territory were made by Slovak ethnographers between 1829 and 1842.[170] In their 1848 representation to the emperor demanding a Slovak parliament, the Slovak intelligentsia did not even specify the territory of the Slovak lands.[171]

The question of the Slovak territory arose again after the defeat of the Hungarian revolution in 1849 when the Austrian government was planning the administrative re-organisation of Hungary. Ludwig v. Rosenfeld (the court advisor) proposed attaching the city of Pressburg and portions of Pressburg county to Austria since there was a German population living there and also since "this part gravitates by virtue of the spiritual and material interests of its inhabitants towards Vienna and so it should be once and for ever torn away from the damaging influence of Magyarism."[172] Rosenfeld noted that most of the county's population was Slovak (in his report he used both terms 'slavisch' and 'slovakisch') and proposed that the central town for the Slovak territory should be Banská Štiavnica (see Figure 3).[173] The Slovak intelligentsia also repeatedly demanded a separate Slovak territory within the empire.[174] The Slovak national revival leaders Ľudovít Štúr (1815–1856), Jozef Miloslav Hurban (1817–1888) and Michal Miloslav Hodža

(1811–1870) approached the Viennese government on several occasions suggesting that the separation of Slovakia from Hungary would reduce Magyar influence. They claimed that Slovaks were a "three-million nation" and asked that "the counties and communities should be organised in the form of national councils composed of the Slovak *národovci* (Slovak national movement proponents)."[175] Thus the Slovak intelligentsia was already seeking a key governance role as the elite of a nation which did not yet exist.[176]

Another proposal by Ján Kollár (1793–1852) suggested determining the Slovak territory on the basis of a census, which would have included the areas of continuous Slovak settlement in Northern Hungary, including the Slovak part of Pressburg county and other ethnically Slovak areas in Hungary (Figure 20).[177] Kollár demanded cultural and administrative autonomy for these territories within the monarchy. The Viennese government eventually decided to divide Hungary into five districts that roughly reflected ethnic divisions.[178]

The end of neo-absolutism (1859) and the reinstatement of the Hungarian parliament in 1860 revived Slovak hopes that their aspirations might now be fulfilled within the framework of the Hungarian kingdom. The 1861 national gathering in Martin approved the 'Memorandum of the Slovak nation' for submission to the Hungarian parliament. However, the Slovak intelligentsia could not agree on how to determine the territory of the Slovak lands. Some members even rejected attempts to determine the borders of the Slovak national territory: as Ján Nemessányi put it, "nobody is pushing Slovaks out from their space."[179] It was eventually agreed that the "national personality" should be expressed in the space of continuous Slovak settlement under the name '*Hornouhorské slovenské okolie*' (Upper-Hungarian Slovak environs) to be determined by 'rounding up' the counties according to nationalities', determining the Slovak-ness of the counties on the basis of census data so that counties with a Slovak majority would be considered Slovak (Figure 21).[180] The Memorandum was perceived as an attack on the integrity of Hungary and did not produce any results.[181] This reaction on the part of the Hungarians was not surprising. The Slovak imagination of the Slovak territory competed with the Hungarian vision of the territory of the unitary Hungarian nation-state.

Another memorandum to the king (the so-called Viennese Memorandum) was therefore drawn up, which not only demanded that Slovaks be acknowledged as a separate nation within Hungary, but which also exactly determined the area of the Slovak territory created by the 'pure' and partially Slovak counties, strictly adhering to the ethnic principle. The centre of the claimed territory was in the Zvolen basin with Banská Bystrica at its heart. This memorandum claimed a continuity of the Slovak territory with the Great Moravian Empire (see Figure 22), suggesting that the patrons of the territory were St. Cyril and Methodius. As such, this memorandum tried to use the historical principle of national continuity to legitimise the Slovak claim to this territory.[182] The Viennese Memorandum was also not successful.[183]

The Slovak geologist Dionýz Štúr (1827–1893) made the first attempt to map the borders of the Slovak territory, considering the Beskydy mountains the western, northern and eastern borders, and the Danube and Tisza rivers as the southern borders. This area roughly corresponded "to the extent of the Slovak part of the Great Moravian Empire and historic Slovakia."[184] Jozef Hložanský's *Biele Uhorsko* (White Hungary) was another attempt to demarcate the borders of Slovakia. Hložanský proposed a federal structure for Hungary on historical and geopolitical grounds.[185] He proposed to divide Hungary into four provinces, one of which was Slovakia (called 'White Hungary') with its capital in Nitra. The Slovak territory would have stretched like the "historic territory of Slovakia" between the Morava and Tisza rivers and from the Tatra mountains to the Danube. Hložanský claimed sovereignty for the Slovak nation on the historical basis of the Great Moravian Empire, claiming that the sovereignty "of a nation of four millions ... has not been interrupted since 1300." Nitra was to be the capital because of its important position in the Great Moravian Empire.[186] Hložanský argued that that the borders of Slovakia could not be demarcated on a purely ethnic basis since there were Hungarian and German villages even in predominantly Slovak ethnic areas. Moreover, an ethnically determined province (*Okolie*) would be a disaster from an economic point of view since "everyone who is able to think a little must admit that we as a nation cannot live without the Danube and the Tisza."[187] According to Hložanský, Slovak trade was dependent on the cities Pressburg, Komárom, Vác, Pest and Szolnok (see Figure 2).[188] Unlike previous ethnically-determined proposals such as the memoranda of 1849 and 1861, Hložanský and Dionýz Štúr included Bratislava as part of the proposed Slovak territory. Hložanský's proposal, however, did not find support, not even among the Slovak intelligentsia.[189]

After 1867 the centralising Hungarian government reduced the authority of counties and royal towns since the counties were historical strongholds of local power and could have served as power bases for developing national movements.[190] (See Chapter five on counties as loci of power which did not always follow the state's interests because of their own local interests and

power struggles.) The law about the territorial borders of counties (including the amalgamation of some counties) was passed in 1876 but the counties did not actually change until 1918 (Figure 17). The Slovak territory was
hardly touched by this reform.[191] The Slovak political program for the 1868
elections demanded the "rounding up" of counties according to the ethnic
principle.[192] However, after 1880, Hungarian censuses used a different
method for dividing counties on a non-ethnic basis.[193] Bokeš claims that
this division was never really accepted since the inhabitants of Hungary
tended to define themselves locally.[194] Vavro Šrobár noted the detrimental
effect that the division of Hungary into counties had on the unification of
the Slovak nation: "This splintering means that the population of one county, having in its mind the interest of its own narrow county region, often for-
gets the general, all-national interest, and thus it was the cause of the often
harmful and exaggerated local (county) patriotism."[195]

This section has described the complex discussion on the borders of the
Slovak territory among the Slovak intelligentsia from the mid-nineteenth
century until the beginning of the First World War. Attempts to determine
the Slovak territory were for the most part based on the ethnic principle of
supposedly continuous Slovak settlement. In some cases these attempts
were partially supported by historicising references to the Great Moravian
Empire as an earlier Slovak state. This reference, however, was based on the
romantic ideas of the proponents of the Slovak national revival, and were
not acknowledged by the governing Austrian or Hungarian elites. The borders of the Slovak territory (as part of Czechoslovakia) were definitely
determined only in the peace conferences after the First World War. Disagreements about the borders of the Slovak territory were an important
issue for the Slovak intelligentsia in the process of building the idea of the
Slovak nation. The absence of a 'national centre' for the co-ordination of
nationalist activity was another important issue. The next section considers
discussions of the Slovak 'national centre' and capital.

6.2. CAPITAL

As the parliamentary debate on the electric railway illustrated, the capital was
seen as a crucial component of the nation-state in political discourse during
the period. The capital was seen as the "heart of the nation," as the place where
the 'national spirit' was strongest. It was even felt that physical infrastructure
(such as railways and transportation corridors) should run outwards from
the capital like the rays of the sun. Indeed, the capital was the "sun" of the
nation, nurturing it and giving it warmth and life force. The development of

the nation-state meant that "much of the explosive urban growth of the last two hundred years has been channelled into regional and national capitals."[196] After 1867 this role was assumed in Hungary by Budapest which consequently grew three-fold in population during the period 1867–1914. Pressburg, by contrast, was a historical capital, a former Hungarian coronation city and, for Slovaks, a former centre of the national revival. Although Bratislava eventually became the capital of the Slovak part of the new Czechoslovak state after the First World War, the city had not figured prominently in most previous discussions about the Slovak 'national centre.'

Pressburg was the largest town in Hungary until the end of the eighteenth century, with more than 33,000 inhabitants.[197] The city began to lose its importance with the removal of central institutions to Buda in 1783. However, Pressburg became the centre of the first phase of the Slovak national revival: in the eighteenth century there were more scholars of Slovak origin in Pressburg than in any other place. Pressburg's attraction for Slavic students was based, to some extent also, on its proximity to the Czech lands. In the years 1783–1787, the city's Slovak evangelical scholars published the newspaper *Prešpurské noviny* (Pressburger newspaper) in the so-called biblical Czech.[198] The first 'Slovak' novel written by I. J. Bajza in 1785 was also published in Pressburg. After the foundation in 1784 of the General Seminary (founded by Joseph II with the intent of educating priests in the "language of their people"), Pressburg became a place for Slovak Catholic scholars to come together. These scholars were the first group of the Slovak national revival movement. In Pressburg, Anton Bernolák published the first attempt to codify a standard Slovak based on the Slovak spoken by Western Slovakia's elite (*kultúrna západoslovenčina*). After Joseph II's death, the General Seminary ceased to exist and, with the dispersion of these priests throughout Slovakia, Pressburg ceased to be an important locale for the Slovak national movement for the next decade.

At the beginning of the nineteenth century there was another wave of the Slovak national revival movement concentrated around the Faculty of Czechoslovak language and literature, founded in 1803 in the Evangelical Lyceum. This faculty educated future Slovak evangelical priests in biblical Czech, and brought together many future leaders of the Slovak national movement and proponents of the Czechoslovak idea, including Ján Kollár, František Palacký and Pavel Jozef Šafárik (1795–1861). The Slovak students had their own associations and also published a 'Slovak' newspaper in biblical Czech. A third group of the Slovak national revival movement grew around Ľudovít Štúr when he became a professor in the Faculty of

Czechoslovak language and literature at the Evangelical Lyceum in 1837 (he was removed from this position in 1843). While there were also groups of Slovak intellectuals in Buda and Slovak students in priests' seminaries in other towns of Slovakia, the centre of gravity of the Slovak national revival moved to Pressburg and centred around Štúr's group. Literary Slovak was codified in Pressburg in 1843. This later became the norm although different groups of Slovak intelligentsia continued to use Bernolák's version or biblical Czech. In October 1851 these different groups met in Pressburg and agreed on one version of Slovak based on Štúr's Slovak. Martin Hattala subsequently published a Slovak grammar, also in Pressburg.[199]

After the *Slovenké národnie noviny* (published by Štúr) stopped being published in Pressburg in 1848, the city "lost touch with the Slovak national movement."[200] In September 1843, the poet Jan Matuška had called Pressburg a place "where the hope of the Slovak people will blossom." However, less than a year later, after Štúr's departure, Mikuláš Dohnányi called Pressburg "the grave of the Slovak kin."[201] In the 1860s the *Slovenský ústav* (Slovak institute) (previously the Lyceum's Faculty of the Czechoslovak language and literature) ceased to exist and 'national' activity in Pressburg took place only among the small circles of Slovak students studying law and theology in the city.[202] Slovak national activities did not find support among Pressburger society. Most burghers were not Slovak and those Slovaks who were permanently resident in the city were not involved in nationalist activity. Slovak national life in the second half of the nineteenth century moved away from the major urban centres of the period (Pressburg, Banská Štiavnica and Košice) and moved to Martin and other towns around the river Váh, in the area of Liptov (Liptovský Mikuláš, Ružomberok) around the riverHron in Zvolen and Banská Bystrica, and in the Gemer region (Figure 3).[203]

During his studies in Jena, Štúr had decided to devote himself to developing Slovak national activities in Pressburg. However, Štúr and his contemporaries realised that Pressburg could not become for Slovaks what Prague was for Czechs, because of Pressburg's mixed ethnic composition and social character.[204] While this issue was not very important at a time when there was no united Slovak national movement, the question of a national centre became more pertinent when the codification of literary Slovak entailed a break from the Czech national movement.[205] By 1848–9, the Slovak intelligentsia acutely felt the lack of a central town. As Štúr lamented: "If we had received from the national view that which we necessarily need, we could be totally free and satisfied. And we could have easily received it if we had been prepared for it and if we had had already one educated central town.... If we had had one central town, in which there would have been many educated and willing burghers living there who would be wishing us and our nation well.... Paris helped the French, Berlin the Prussians, Vienna the Austrians, Leipzig and Dresden the Saxons, Munich the Bavarians; however, we do not have even a small example of such big cities."[206] However, in discussions among Slovak intellectuals in 1848-9 on possible locations for the Slovak national centre, small towns like Banská Štiavnica, Banská Bystrica or Nitra were considered rather than Pressburg.[207] When the Viennese government was considering the territorial re-organisation of Hungary in 1848, the Slovak intelligentsia was unable to answer the question of where the capital of the Slovak territory should be located.[208]

The idea of founding the Slovak cultural institution *Matica Slovenská* (hereafter called *Matica*) gave further urgency to the selection of a town as the Slovak national centre. In the 1850s, Jozef K. Viktorin won the influential František Hanrich over to the idea of bringing together educated Slovaks in Vienna and Pressburg and founding *Matica Slovenská*.[209] Temporary statutes of *Matica* did not specify where the institution would be located. In March 1851 the *Slovenské noviny* noted that "a *Matica* in the sense of Czech, Serb or Croat *Matica* cannot be created by us at all ... since we have neither a central town like the Czechs and Croats, nor a [church] hierarchy to identify with and represent the nation like the Serbs."[210] Viktorin's proposal to make Pressburg the location was due to the presence of several Slovak scholars in the city and the city's historical role in the initial phases of the Slovak national revival.[211] In 1857, representatives of the Slovak national movement met in Pressburg to decide on where to locate the *Matica*. Palárik's group proposed Budapest but other groups rejected this suggestion, eventually agreeing instead on Banská Bystrica.[212] However, none of the proposed Slovak institutions came into existence during the Bach era of neo-absolutist rule from Vienna (1849-1859) and this attempt to bring together a larger group of Slovak intellectuals in an urban milieu was unsuccessful.[213]

By the 1860s, a larger number of Slovak intellectuals had coalesced in Buda where they started to publish the newspaper *Pešťbudínske vedomosti* (Budapest News) edited by Ján Francisci (1822-1905). Another group (including Štefan M. Daxner and Mikuláš Š. Ferienčík (1825-1881)) was in Banská Bystrica. In an atmosphere of political reconciliation between Vienna and Budapest, national activities began to revive and the Slovak intelligentsia worked together with the emerging Slovak petite bourgeoisie to find a town which would best support Slovak national efforts. However, the results of this search were unsatisfactory.[214] In 1860, Karol Kuzmány

(1806–1866), the new superintendent of the Slovak evangelic church, was received in a very unfriendly manner in Banská Bystrica where he should have been located. Kuzmány moved to Martin, which then became more attractive for the Slovak national intelligentsia since its efforts to find a better atmosphere in other towns had failed.[215] Martin was the venue for the 1861 meeting of the Slovak national movement which drafted the "Memorandum of the Slovak nation" (*Memorandum slovenského národa*). However, although this memorandum proposed the creation of an "Upper-Hungarian Slovak Environs" (*Hornouhorské slovenské okolie*), it did not mention the centre of this territory. The so called "Viennese Memorandum" of the same year nominatedBanská Bystrica as the centre of the desired Slovak territory because of its geographical position in the centre of Slovakia.[216]

Although the ethnic milieu was more favourable in Martin, new discussions in 1861 on where to locate *Matica* again named Buda, Banská Bystrica and Brezno as possible locations.[217] However, since "Martin had the most nationally conscious bourgeoisie,"[218] it was chosen as the seat of *Matica* which gave Martin "a seal of approval as the national-cultural centre of the Slovaks."[219] In practical terms this aim was not achieved because of disagreements among the Slovak intelligentsia.[220] However, other important institutions were located in Martin, giving it the semblance of a national centre not only in cultural but also in political and economic terms.[221] The *Ústredný slovenský volebný výbor* (Central Slovak election committee) was founded there in 1871. Martin's relative importance grew with the dissolution in 1875 of the Budapest-based *Nová Škola* and its newspaper *Slovenské noviny*. In the same year, however, the *Matica* was closed down. The National Museum and the headquarters of the Slovak communal libraries were also founded in Martin. Every year until the First World War (except 1875–8), Martin's Slovak intelligentsia organised the *Augustové slávnosti* (August national celebrations).[222] In 1870, *Matica's* vice-chairman Viliam Paulíny-Tóth (1826–1877) declared that Martin was "the centre of the national culture…, a centre which we were missing until now and without which no nation exists and so neither ours shall or can exist."[223] Martin's Slovak intelligentsia jealously guarded their monopoly position as the only national centre for Slovaks and felt that they were most qualified to speak in the name of the Slovak nation. However, these conservatives lost touch with the changing political environment and by the beginning of the twentieth century Martin had lost its leading position. Although lying in a Slovak ethnic area, Martin lacked good railway connections and lagged behind in its economic development. As Buček points out, Martin was a "defensive nucleus" under disadvantageous political conditions and its rise was connected with the need to maintain some sort of centre for the Slovak nation in conditions of Magyarisation.[224]

At the beginning of the twentieth century, the lawyer Miloš Štefanovič (1854–1904) argued that a new centre of Slovak national life was needed. Štefanovič argued that Martin and Banská Bystrica were no longer important because of the development of the rail network. Zvolen, on the other hand, was becoming an important transport junction and economic centre. Štefanovič also commented that "in the case of an advantageous turn" in political developments, the capital of Slovakia would be "Prešporok or Košice." While admitting the importance of these two urban centres, Štefanovič noted that both of these cities were at the edges of the Slovak territory, while Zvolen was more central. As Buček points out, this mention of Prešporok and Košice indicates a shift in thinking from a "national-cultural centre to a big capital city developed in more complex ways."[225]

After the First World War, in 1919 Bratislava (as Prešporok was renamed) became the unofficial capital of Slovakia. However, this decision was by no means an obvious one. In November 1918 a Czech writer and publisher proposed that Liptovský Mikuláš or Martin become the seat of the political administration of Slovakia. At the peace talks following the war, Pressburg was an important and disputed territory sought by both Hungary and Czechoslovakia. It was even suggested that Bratislava should constitute a neutral city-state.[226] It was only the third demarcation line drawn at the end of December 1918 which decided that Bratislava would become part of Czechoslovakia, although the exact border-line was definitely decided only at the later conferences of Saint-Germain and Trianon. In January 1919, the Czechoslovak army occupied Bratislava.[227] In February 1919, when Vavro Šrobár, the new Minister for Slovakia ("with full power over Slovakia") and his entourage arrived in Slovakia, they decided on Bratislava as the seat of government since no other town in Slovakia was capable of accommodating such a large number of state officials or had the required infrastructure.[228] Undoubtedly, the new government also wanted to appropriate this space immediately in order to dispel "a suspicion that the Czechoslovak republic does not intend to occupy permanently the town of Prešporok which would again become the seat of agitation against our republic and would provide gangs to threaten the richest part of Slovakia."[229] The Czechoslovak authorities staged a mass *Sokol* and Slovak folk costume performance which was intended to demonstrate the strength of the Slavs in Bratislava and symbolically incorporate the territory into Czechoslovakia (these Slavs were brought to the city specially for this occasion.)[230]

Bratislava's position as the capital was disputed by Martin in the 1920s since Bratislava "if only due to its location on the furthest bordering periphery of Slovakia, in the immediate proximity of two—to us racially foreign nations (and especially in the south always hostile), has always been and will be a certain especially commercial and thus also a cosmopolitan city."[231] Fedor Ruppeldt criticised the bad influence of the "idle and unhealthy" environment of Vienna at Bratislava: a capital had to "be the pride, joy and support of Slovaks which would attract all, impress all, which would be in the centre and could be the *heart of the nation, in the same way, as there is and must be a heart in every living organism.*"[232] As a cosmopolitan place, Bratislava could never become the right place for raising nationally aware young people, or for national education, national theatre, art or journalism. Ruppeldt wanted the new capital to be built in Martin located in the "strategically safest [place], in the purest Slovak district, in a county that has long been nationally most awakened, in the cradle of the literary Slovak...."[233] Ironically, these comments by a Slovak nationalist are reminiscent of the Hungarian nationalist distrust of Pressburg: again, Bratislava was seen as not patriotic or nationally homogeneous enough to constitute a proper capital.[234]

6.3. Conclusion

The Slovak intelligentsia became aware of the importance of a 'national centre' for their nation-building activities in the mid-nineteenth century. However, Slovak national leaders could not agree on where this centre should be located. The position of Slovaks in the cities was weak and Magyarisation pressure was stronger there as well. Martin eventually became this 'national centre', although its importance diminished gradually. Despite its historic role in the initial phases of the national movement, Pressburg (Prešporok) was never seriously considered as a possible Slovak 'national centre', although it was the site of many meetings of Slovak national leaders. However, after the First World War, Pressburg (now renamed Bratislava) became the unofficial Slovak capital because of its infrastructure and ability to accommodate the officials of the new nation-state. Even so, Slovak nationalists have continued to remain sceptical of Bratislava's national credentials.

7. CONCLUSION

This chapter has explored the position of Pressburg within the Habsburg Monarchy as an important city ambiguously located between Vienna and

Budapest. Throughout the period, Pressburg was repeatedly accused of insufficient Hungarian patriotism. The city's traditional economic ties with Vienna and Lower Austria as well as its prevailing ethnic milieu made the national Hungarian elite suspicious of Pressburg. The nationalising Hungarian state wanted to transform Pressburg into Pozsony, to make it a truly Hungarian city. The ambiguity of this border town's identity worried Hungarian nationalists as a potential violation of the homogeneous national identity which they were striving to build up within the Hungarian kingdom.

Bratislava eventually became the capital of Slovakia after the First World War. However, the Slovak intelligentsia had never regarded Pressburg (Prešporok) as an appropriate 'national centre' for the Slovak territory because of its multiethnic composition and lack of support for the Slovak national activities in the city. After the First World War pragmatic considerations led Pressburg (Bratislava) to become the unofficial capital of the Slovak part of the Czechoslovak Republic. Bratislava's position remained disputed because of its position at the border and its cosmopolitan character. These discussions about the appropriateness of Bratislava as the capital of the Slovak nation have been going on until the present day.

～ 5 ～

SURVEILLANCE IN PRESSBURG

We must cease once and for all to describe the effects of power in negative terms: it "excludes," it "represses," it "censors," it "abstracts," it
"masks," it "conceals." In fact, power produces; it produces reality; it
produces domains of objects and rituals of truth. The individual and
the knowledge that may be gained of him belong to this production.[1]
—Michel Foucault

0. INTRODUCTION

THE MODERN STATE DEVELOPS a range of different activities which
enable it to collect knowledge and information about its citizens and
the events in its territory. Surveillance of its citizens and their activities are carried out in the interest of maintaining the power of the
government and to promote the effective functioning of the state. After the
Dual Agreement with Austria in 1867, the Hungarian government was
involved in the project of building a modern liberal state after the example
of the Western states. This was reflected in both explicit legislation but also,
implicitly, in the increased surveillance of all social movements that could
subvert the power of the governing elites. However, power was not only
something being imposed by the central state as represented by its institutions. Power penetrated the whole society through its members internalising and adapting in different degree to accepted patterns of behaviour. As
Hungary strove to build up a unitary national state with Hungarian as the
state language and Magyars maintaining hegemony, this process of internalisation and adaptation required conforming to the desired models of
using the Hungarian language and being a Hungarian patriot.

This chapter will look at some ways in which the state reacted to and monitored social movements in Pressburg. First it will discuss how the Hungarian state established and enabled the functioning of surveillance. The state used legislation but it also disposed of a wide coercive apparatus, starting with the state appointed officials and ending with the police and armed forces. Afterwards I will look specifically at how the state reacted to the movements in Pressburg city and county, focusing on the socialist and nationalities' movements. I will show the connection of the city authorities with state power, especially with the Ministry of Interior. There was a constant flow of information between these two centres of power regarding all mass gatherings in the town and the measures taken in order to retain control. Suspicious individuals, whether socialists, anarchists or Pan-Slavs, were followed with utmost attention.

Preserving the *status quo* was also a strong interest of the Pressburger middle classes who feared violent upheaval. So surveillance and control were enacted also by the elite and middle classes of Pressburg in order to maintain their power and ownership of the city and control over all of its spaces. Competing with the older, mostly German speaking power holders was a new Magyar elite. Many of its members were state employees, dependent on the state for their livelihood, spreading the state supported ideas and monitoring the city in order to gather information and cleanse it of any disruptive elements. The traditional elite's ideas of what constituted a 'good city' and 'good citizens' intersected, overlapped, and clashed with the 'good Hungarian patriot' ideal of the nascent Magyar elite. The overlap and conflict between these two sets of ideals merely confirmed the protagonists in their original beliefs.

Surveillance penetrated Pressburg city and the county from the highest official places represented by the ministries (especially the Ministry of Interior) through the county and city officials and other state employees, to the lowest classes. The degree to which individuals were involved in adapting to the presented norms, internalised them and acted upon them depended on their social standing and status and not least the position in the social hierarchy to which they aspired.

In the first part of this chapter I will briefly describe the development of the modern state in Hungary and the way this state secured surveillance in its territory. I will then look at the routes and directions of information flow between Pressburg and the state. Further, I will look at the way the socialist and nationalist movements were monitored in Pressburg.[2] In the last part of this chapter I will consider the self-disciplining aspect of surveillance and how it influenced all layers of the social structure in Pressburg.

1. THE DEVELOPMENT OF
THE MODERN STATE IN HUNGARY

After the Dual Agreement the Hungarian part of the Austro-Hungarian Empire acquired the status of an independent state, bound with Austria, however, in several areas (foreign policy, common finances, army, and the person of the king.) The emperor himself interfered in Hungarian politics, and he had a "pre-sanctification right" (all law proposals had to be first approved by him) on all the laws passed in the Hungarian parliament.[3] Hungary thus entered the path of nation-state building, albeit not quite independent. The political elite in power envisaged this state as the state of one political nation with a Magyar hegemony. "Hungarian liberalism's own fear of the Germanising power of Habsburg rule, and of the predominance of other nationalities, was the main motivation behind its insistence on a homogeneous culture and national identity."[4] The more moderate views of Deák and Eötvös with respect to nationalities prevailed only until shortly after the Dual Agreement but did not take hold in Hungarian politics.[5] Despite its intolerance towards other nationalities and growing social discontent, the Hungarian political system proclaimed itself to be liberal. The Liberal party ruled from 1874 until 1905, although there were no major differences between the programs of the Liberal party and the opposition.[6] Gerő marks the post-1867 period as that of an anti-liberal political regime, although political modernisation was taking place, accompanied by capitalist economic transformation and the emergence of a bourgeois society. Post-Dual Agreement Hungary had a mix of a liberal regime with strong remnants of the conservative-feudal one.[7] The system was liberal in the sphere of economic development but restrictive in the sphere of political and individual behaviour.[8]

The transformation from a feudal to a bourgeois system in Hungary had started already after the suppression of the Hungarian revolution in 1848/9. After the compromise in 1867, Hungary concentrated on modernisation of the country. When discussing the content of liberalism among the elites in Hungary, Gerő claims that one consideration was the cost of the repressive apparatus. Under absolutism about one third of the state budget went on military expenditure. Taxes increased dramatically between 1848 and 1867; the national debt more than doubling.[9] It was not possible to maintain such an expensive repressive apparatus. In Western Europe, the economic changes in the eighteenth century resulted in a shift of power; now it had to get to individuals, their bodies and daily actions.[10] A similar shift was now happening in Hungary. However, the new Hungarian regime also found it necessary, if not to actually repress (although especially after the turn of the century repression did become a part of dealing mainly with the social democratic and agrarian socialist movements) then at least to monitor the population living within its territory. The Hungarian state too was governed by the basic principle of territoriality.[11] As the state's control over its territory was becoming more extensive, the state was increasingly involved in collecting information about this territory.[12]

Modernisation in Hungary, both economic and political, was supported by legislation and by state institutions securing the implementation of laws. The Hungarian parliament gradually passed laws on public administration, judicial affairs, municipalities, about the national defence, *honvéds* (the Hungarian home defence), about popular revolt, about the organisation of the national statistics, taxation, suffrage and many other areas regulating all aspects of the social and political life in the country.[13] Some of these laws were closely connected to surveillance and repression, such as the law about *honvéd* (defenders of the homeland) forces, police, or statistics which was rapidly developing in all European countries in this period. As Foucault notes, facts of population became increasingly important in the nineteenth century.[14] From the 1860s, international statistical congresses regularly met in order to discuss the rules of conducting census and statistical surveys. Hungarian statisticians and demographers participated in these congresses. In 1874, the national statistical bureau in Hungary was created and laid down the rules for conducting censuses as well as other statistical research.[15] As Taylor has noted, "[t]he state is at the heart of that social process as the prime producer of statistics in the modern world...."[16] Statistics was a very important means of information collection not only because of the sheer amount of data collected (often distorted, however, for various reasons, e.g. individuals' distrust of authorities) but also because of the statistical categories which were created, grouping together people and material objects according to defined criteria that did not always reflect the social reality. This categorisation in turn could then influence the forms of self-identification of groups, which had not been groups before or which had not conceived of themselves as such.[17]

1.1. The Hungarian State and Surveillance

The development of the modern state in Hungary as well as in Western Europe involved the state penetrating more into all areas of the lives of its citizens. However, it was not only the Hungarian state that created laws, institutions and organs carrying out surveillance. It was the individuals themselves who in different ways acted either as extensions of the state (although pursuing their own interests) or by internalising the presented norms became part of the larger surveillance and self-disciplining mechanism. Technologies of surveillance, self-discipline, taking up of education by the state: all these functioned as means to create good and responsible citizens. The power of the state was especially felt in the cities, the 'melting pots' and vehicles of industrialisation and modernisation since the Hungarian countryside was still very 'backward' and isolated, although parts of it were being connected with the railway and were also involved in agrarian reform movements.

I will now consider different layers and elements of the surveillance mechanism: the state institutions with their policies, laws and coercive bodies (army, police).[18] I will look at the intelligence network for gathering information, monitoring the whole country and at the preventive and repressive measures taken by the state in order to protect the existing order and the power of the elites.

The intermediaries of the state power were the county administrations with their bureaucratic apparatuses and the *főispáns* appointed by the minister of interior i.e. the persons supervising the whole state surveillance 'machine' in the counties.[19] The employees involved in the county administration as well as state employees and officials were carrying out this surveillance further even in their spare time by adopting certain modes of behaviour which were required from state employees thus self-disciplining themselves, and trying to discipline others by demanding that they also comply to these models. They also passed on information about those who did not comply.

In carrying out these activities, state employees were not always necessarily following the state's interests or merely obeying the orders of the minister of interior as they sometimes claimed. First, the regional gentry and Hungarian politicians were very sensitive towards interventions of the state and jealously guarded what they considered their area of interest and a certain independence. Also the state basically left the monitoring of nationality politics to the discretionary authority of *főispáns* and *alispáns*, through different instructions and orders which had no basis in existing laws. Secondly, they had their own interests to follow and were involved in different struggles for power. These power struggles also took place within the county administration and within different interest groups involved in carrying out Magyarisation policies as well. Thus, for example, any plans of the state for a complex re-organisation of the Magyarisation associations like FEMKE (Felvidéki Magyar Közművelödési Egyesület [Upper-Hungarian Magyar educational association]) fell apart faced with resistance on the part of the Hungarian politicians and activists working in these associations who did not want the state to interfere in their areas of interests and in the regions of their activity. These associations were founded in Upper Hungary in 1870s as an attempt to spread the Hungarian language and culture among Slovaks but were largely unsuccessful since they were not able to develop an effective counter-balance to the nascent Slovak national movement. The Pressburger Magyar educational association (*Magyar közművelődési egyesület*) also refused to be included into a united territorial (Upper Hungarian) organisation by insisting on its independence.[20] This is another example of competing grids of power and knowledge. Obviously the intelligentsia and politicians gathered in the Pressburger association had their own interests to pursue rather than the interests of the central state's nationalities' policies. This also makes clear how instrumental Hungarian patriotic rhetoric often was.

Thus surveillance did not work only in the hierarchical vertical direction but also on the horizontal level, between individuals who might have been seen from the outside as a homogeneous group enforcing state policies, but who, however, had their own agendas and interests to follow.[21] Conversely, this internal heterogeneity demonstrates how a surveillance system through which passed a huge amount of information also could become ineffective and arbitrary.

The *főispán* and county assembly were linked to the communities, cities and villages in their territories. The county assembly consisted of the representatives of these communities. Although Pressburg was an independent municipal town with its own municipal assembly, in addition to leading the sessions of the municipal assembly of the Pozsony county, the *főispán* also took part in all of Pressburg town's municipal assembly meetings, representing here the state authority. The main surveillance and information gathering agent in the city was the police, led by the police chief who undertook his activities and measures in consultation with the mayor. The mayor would then inform the *főispán* or, directly, the minister of interior. There was a network of information passing in the form of letters and telegrams between these representatives of power.

However, surveillance of the spaces of the city was carried out also by the city elites and middle classes who were concerned that only good and well-kept public spaces were presented to a spectator walking across the city. Securing the handsome appearance of the city, especially the centre, was the concern of the association *Stadtverschönerungsverein*. (See Chapter two.) This group of the traditional city elite was concerned with the control of the city and with the 'good city' image. On the other hand, the competing Magyar elite was monitoring the behaviour of city employees, people of importance and controlling how much they kept up the behaviour suitable for a good Hungarian patriot, criticising any who strayed. Many members of this new Magyar middle class were teachers and professors, therefore supervising the behaviour of their students and their choice of the language of use even in private.

The main aim of surveillance was collecting information so that possible future disturbances could be strangled at birth. The main threats to the *status quo* were the growing nationalities' and socialist movements. Although there was no threat of a nationalist movement in the city of Pressburg, the number of workers increased with the industrialisation of the town and this spurred the development of the social democratic movement. The number of inhabitants belonging to the lower classes increased; so did the technologies developed for their control. In this period one can see the growing interest of the responsible city authorities, especially the city doctor and medical staff generally, with the conditions of housing, the control of epidemics and illnesses, and also the control of the morality of the lower classes who dwelled in crowded and unhealthy living spaces.

One solution to this problem was to build philanthropic housing, such as those started by the philanthropist Georg Schulpe. Workers' housing, apart from providing the workers' families with more decent living conditions, also exerted control over their life-styles by the division of spaces, providing social facilities but also serving as a basis for possible blackmail when factory strikes took place.[22] Worker families living in these places had to control their behaviour, to 'discipline' themselves, especially if they aspired to higher social status. One can say that from the lowest levels of the city's inhabitants up to the middle classes and elite, one had to conform and bring one's behaviour 'in line' with a certain norm required from a person in a certain occupational category and of a certain social standing. These were not necessarily "modern" norms in that there had even previously been older sets of expectations linked to different social groups. However, the spatiality of the modern state and surveillance system as built up by the modern state made these norms more pervasive and unavoidable. Those who diverged from the concept of 'normality' were shut into institutions erected to normalise them. The state took over education in order to produce relatively homogeneous, 'normal' citizens. A whole range of disciplines developed in the nineteenth century which were concerned with systematising and arranging objects according to notions of 'normal' and divergence from these posited norms. Pressure to conform to norms was much greater than ever before. Thus surveillance and self-governance were intertwined and engaged the city inhabitants in a net of power relations which did not just pass from above downwards but rather penetrated all levels of the city society, as was true also of the state.

2. THE FLOW OF INFORMATION BETWEEN THE STATE AND THE CITY OF PRESSBURG

This part of the chapter maps information flows between the Hungarian state and the Pressburg city authorities. In this part I will describe the surveillance of events, individuals and information in order to delineate some of the main strands in the web of surveillance in the period.

2.1. SURVEILLANCE OF EVENTS AND INDIVIDUALS

The institution concerned with the surveillance of the territory of the country was the Ministry of Interior. A special section was created within the ministry in 1876 called "confidential agenda" which dealt with confidential materials concerning nationalities' movements, the Pan-German movement, anti-Semitism, the socialist movement, anarchist activities and similar potentially state-endangering matters.[23] All the information from counties, towns and communities passed through this section. The first attempt to introduce a complex system of policies dealing with the nationalities based on regular reports from the counties was made by Prime Minister Gyula Szapáry in 1890, by calling together a conference of *főispáns* of the Upper Hungarian region.[24] Under the premiership of Dezső Bánffy, the pressure on the nationalities' and socialist movements in Hungary increased, along with a more intensive organisation of their surveillance. Bánffy set up a new section within the prime minister's office which dealt with nationalities' and socialist movements. Proponents of both of these movements were placed under observation.[25] Also the press control was strengthened. The government pressured the social democrats into giving up larger and more ambitious activities.[26] Bánffy built up a complex system of surveillance based on regular reports about the nationalities from counties (first monthly, then every half-year). Efforts were also made to build up a specialised apparatus and information network (including detectives) which made quick interventions by the government possible.[27] By creating this information system, Bánffy created a basis for specialised regional nationalities' policies.[28]

There was active co-operation between the Hungarian, Austrian and German Ministries of Interior and police offices in following the social democratic movement. Photographs of suspicious persons and information about the movements were passed on. The Hungarian minister received yearly reports from Austria and Germany about the situation of the social democratic and revolutionary movements not only in the monarchy but in the whole of Europe and North America.[29] Incidentally, both reports from 1889 considered the Hungarian workers' movement very weakly developed, "fallen asleep." The only activity was noted in the workers' associations in Budapest, Novy Sad and Pressburg (the association *Vorwärts*.)

The flow of information between the Ministry of Interior and the counties worked in both directions. From the material available it appears that the Ministry followed the development of the social movements, nationalities' agitation, movement of people associated with socialists or suspected of anarchism, with great attention. Material produced by the Ministry of Interior included reports from Pressburg county and its different districts about the socialist movement and also the nationalities' movements for the "last year": it is therefore possible to assume that in this way yearly reports were passed on giving an overview of the developments and lists of suspicious people in different counties and their districts.[30] This material was always collected by the county office and sent with an attached letter from the *főispán* to the minister of interior. The minister also often informed the *főispán* about the events being prepared in his territory and the desired course of action. The minister often seems to have had information in advance without getting it from the local authorities. This was due to the very well organised system of informers and detectives which was more reliable and faster than the local authorities.[31] Although this applies especially in Bánffy's era (1895–99), who as the prime minister created a system of administrative and repressive measures—a tighter surveillance mechanism —this system was used also by the later governments.[32] According to Lehotský, while in the 1880s there were interventions into activities of the developing socialist movement, in the 1890s these interventions turned into systematic control.[33] Under Bánffy, not only control but also repression reached its height. In this period 51 workers were killed and 114 wounded in clashes with law enforcement agencies.[34] No doubt the developing social democratic and later also the agrarian socialist movement were considered the main danger to the existing social system in Hungary since they proclaimed a desire to change the existing social order albeit by peaceful means i.e. universal suffrage and participation in parliament. However, not only the socialist movements but also all other potentially state-endangering activities and persons were followed in the same way, especially the various nationalities' movements.[35]

There was also a direct link between the town and the Ministry of Interior, i.e. the information did not always pass through *főispán*. The city police captain informed the mayor of all happenings in the city; he submitted reports to the mayor which were often forwarded to the minister of interior. In some instances the mayor made the necessary investigation and informed the minister directly. As in the case of the county authorities, the minister of interior often informed the mayor of planned events in Pressburg and instructed him as to the way they should be handled. He also demanded from the mayor confirmation of his information from "other sources."[36]

Thus the minister of interior was informed about all the celebrations, gatherings and meetings in all parts of the country. His detectives always wrote him detailed accounts of the Social Democratic Party congresses and meetings, sometimes even of pub conversations. Also the students' movement especially in Budapest was followed. In this case the minister was receiving reports directly from the Budapest city police captain. In periods of possible unrest, as on the eve of elections, the minister of interior was receiving regular reports from the *főispáns* of counties about the situation there. They reported on the pre-election campaign and made requests for military assistance during the elections. This was connected to the way in which elections were carried out in Hungary when Hungarian governments used all the state bureaucracy as well as military help in the elections, and did not hesitate to use bribery and violence to secure victory for the governing party.[37]

2.2. Surveillance of Information: Press Control

Not only people but also the movements of objects—the press and mail were followed, and the mail of suspicious persons was controlled, for example Hanzlíček's mail.[38] Every three months the post office submitted a list of the campaigning nationalist press specifying how many of which of these newspapers penetrated into which community.[39] Also lists of banned press were circulated among the post officials—the directory boards of post and telegraph so that these materials could be confiscated when they arrived at the post office or when the right to circulate certain periodicals in the territory of Hungary was withdrawn.[40] Many other issues of periodicals printed in Hungary were confiscated on the basis of some offence, most often the nationalist and socialist press.[41] Authors of these articles were taken to court and usually prosecuted for inciting hate against other (mostly Magyar) nationalities.[42] Usually, it was a local authority such as the *főispán* or the *főszolgabiró* who draw the attention of the higher authorities towards incriminating articles, with the proposal that this publication should be put on the list of forbidden periodicals, or that the publisher be prosecuted if resident in Hungary.[43]

Apart from local authorities keeping an eye on everything printed in their area of jurisdiction, according to the law article XVIII/1848, its paragraph 40, two copies of all materials printed in Hungary had to be sent to the authorities, one of which had to go to the Hungarian national museum.[44] In this way an archive of all printed materials in Hungary was gradually consolidated. There was an exchange of letters between the Pressburg town council authorities and the responsible person from the National Széchényi library (part of the Hungarian National Museum) in which the library demanded that the missing issues of newspapers published in Pressburg be sent to them. The city authorities were responsible for ensuring that the printing enterprises in Pressburg sent two copies of all printed materials to the city magistrate who in turn forwarded these to the Hungarian Academy of Sciences and to the Hungarian National Museum. According to the decree 15865 from 20.12.1867 all publishing enterprises had to send quarterly lists of their publications to the Hungarian Ministry of Education as well.[45]

In my research, I concentrated on checking the law suits in the territory of present-day Slovakia, and the confiscation of Slovak press materials since this was connected to the development of the Slovak national movement.[46] I will give the main reasons for their confiscation and the consequences for the writers of the articles, members of the Slovak intelligentsia. Obviously, this was a standard procedure which was used against "inciting" articles of any nationality as well as against socialists. However, the law suits did not avoid other newspapers that were more in line with the ruling elite. Such conflicts were, however, much less frequent. Among the confiscated (not prohibited, however) Slovak periodicals were *Slovenský Týždenník* published in Budapest by the Slovak politician Milan Hodža and issues of *Národnie Noviny* published in Martin.[47] The main reason for their confiscation was their "Pan-Slav propaganda" which in these cases meant that the newspapers published articles demanding the use of the Slovak language in schools and public offices in the counties with a Slovak majority.

Offending articles usually concerned Hungarian oppression, appealing to people to overcome their passivity, and to fight for their "natural rights." Most of these articles stressed the will of Slovaks to stay within Hungary and their respect towards Hungarian culture. They demanded, however, the instruction of schoolchildren in their mother tongue. Several articles from *Národnie Noviny* were sent in by the Zólyom *főispán* to the minister of interior. What he minded most was the fact that this newspaper always wrote about Magyars only as "folk," a people (*nép*), while Slovaks were always called a "nation" (*nemzet*).[48] Other Slovak newspapers were also confiscated, although only a few of them were altogether banned from circulation. A significant number of Slovak periodicals appeared in Slovakia and Budapest as well, although subscriptions were low due to lack of interest among Slovak readers.[49]

Other confiscated publications of Slovak printing shops included, for example, an English-language booklet about the Csernova (Černová) shooting, publicising the Slovak case abroad.[50] Some children's literature was also confiscated. The Hungarian minister of education banned the use of the ABC instruction book *Šlabikár* for its "poems oriented against the learning of Hungarian language."[51] The minister of interior banned the distribution of the children's magazine *Noviny pre naše dietky* (Newspaper for our children) since this magazine "tries to nip in the bud love and loyalty towards the Hungarian homeland, and therefore it is extremely harmful and dangerous from the national point of view."[52] Suppression was also the fate of leaflets like the one commissioned by the parliament deputy Ferdinand Juriga appealing to the Slovak people to wake up and "to not let the Hungarian chauvinists be parasitic upon them."[53] There was also an examination of the *Dejepis Slovákov* (History of Slovaks) and a prosecution was started against the publisher of the book.

In another case, the entire Upper Hungarian administration apparatus and police were mobilised in order to find out the source and to gather information about the "Slovak catechism." The Catechism for Slovaks contentiously stated that there were three million Slovaks in Hungary, that the Magyars had learned all they knew from Slovaks, that the king Stephan made his oath in Slovak, but also gave practical advice on how to use rights given to Slovaks by the 1868 Nationalities Law.[54] One can see how the Hungarian nationalists felt threatened by the competing version of history represented in the Slovak Catechism. Every nationalist elite tries to impose its version of the history of people it rules and make it dominant. Therefore any challenge to this dominance is considered a threat to the power of the national elite.

Slovak newspapers printed in the USA, published by the American Slovaks, represented a special case. These were all forbidden in Hungary because of their Pan-Slav character and anti-Hungarian and anti-dynastic, inciting articles.[55] However, there were also periodicals and leaflets coming from the Czech Republic, Germany, Vienna, most of which were confiscated in other towns in the territory falling within the jurisdiction of the Pressburg royal post (for example Turócszentmárton, Nyitra, Holics, Zsolna.)[56] In 1896 the Hungarian minister of trade characterised Vienna as the source of large numbers of newspapers directed against the Hungarian state and nation.[57]

It is obvious that Hungarian authorities were well informed about all printed literature in Hungary or entering Hungarian territory, as well as about even small printing shops. On one occasion the minister of interior ordered an inspection of the Pan-Slav presses.[58] The consequences for the publishers and writers were press prosecutions which were very common in post-Dual Agreement Hungary. The common reason was "engendering hatred towards the Magyar nationality and incitement against the state language." In the case of the prosecutions reviewed in this research, sentences ranged from three days to one month imprisonment and fines ranging between 40 and 120 crowns. Many of the Slovak editors were accused and many were convicted. However, there were also cases when they were released by the higher appeals court.[59]

Another group of law suits were those against the editors of the socialist press. As was already mentioned, the active leaders of the socialist movement were spied on, information about them was passed on from one authority to the other as they moved within Hungarian territory or in and out of the country. There were also undercover 'detectives' who mixed with workers, sat in pubs and listened to what the workers talked about. The workers' associations and networks were also penetrated by police informants.[60] As mentioned previously in Chapter three, workers' publications was often confiscated since it was not difficult to find offence in the many articles openly criticising the government and the existing social system. Many of the attempts to start workers' presses collapsed due to a lack of financial resources since the government attempted to suppress potentially subversive press by demanding that press publishing political content more than twice a month should pay "bail" of 12,000 crowns. Some newspapers were then banned from publishing since they printed political articles without having paid the security.

The next part of this chapter will look more closely at the surveillance of the socialist movement and press, as well as national movements in and around Pressburg.

3. SURVEILLANCE IN PRESSBURG

The organisation of surveillance in Pressburg can be seen as a combination of preventive and repressive measures which were applied by the state but also by the city authorities themselves in order to preserve the status quo. By preventive measures I mean the gathering of information about potentially dangerous activities by the city authorities and passing them on to the higher authorities so that a course of pre-emptive action could be determined.

In this part, I will look specifically at the surveillance of those movements that were considered threatening by the authorities. I will look at the surveillance of the socialists, at the policing of the 1 May demonstrations and public meetings, as well as of the nationalities' meetings and activities in the city. This part will look especially at the repressive element of the surveillance, i.e., the presence of police at these gatherings, prohibition of some of these gatherings, and the press prosecutions. It must be said that even these repressive measures never went as far as the physical injuries and bloodshed which happened on several occasions in Budapest.

3.1. SOCIALIST MOVEMENT: SURVEILLANCE AND POLICING

When the workers' association *Vorwärts* was founded in Pressburg in 1869 and especially when their first public gathering took place (attended by some prominent city personalities), it took most of the public and city authorities by surprise. Workers proved that they were not as uneducated and immature as they were assumed to be and that they could organise themselves. This public gathering became the subject of an ongoing debate in the city, and awoke fear of social revolution in some of the respectable Pressburger burghers. These worries were so acute that *Vorwärts* considered it necessary to publish in the most popular local newspaper *Pressburger Zeitung* a resume of its aims, stressing its commitment to exclusively peaceful means for achieving these goals.[61] However, over the next few years the middle classes and city elites became more accustomed to the idea of organised workers. Although, there was fear again because of the planned 1 May demonstration, after the turn of the century, the first of May demonstrations and marches through the city as well as public meetings became an established practice and as part of the urban landscape did not seem to trouble the bourgeoisie over much. This growing bourgeois acceptance of the organised working class is revealed very clearly in press reports from the period.

The evolution of the attitudes of the authorities, especially of the city captain and police employees, towards the workers' movement followed a similar development. Although workers' leaders often complained about the authorities' arbitrary decisions in the issuing of permits for public meetings and marches as well as about their interventions during the public meetings, on the whole a relationship of mutual respect was established between the two sides. Workers respected the prohibitions of the police captain (although they complained about it and appealed against it they never defied a ban) and the local press often commented on the considerate and controlled behaviour of Pressburger workers. When any problems occurred, these were blamed on foreign workers, coming from outside Pressburg. In 1890 the city police chief in his report wrote that it was the workers from other towns who were inciting and corrupting, not the Pressburger workers.[62] The line between workers and authorities was never crossed, and no brutal suppression of the workers' gatherings or marches happened, partly because these happened without any violent upheavals. (See Chapter three.) The workers always carefully prepared and organised their activities.

Information passed between the city and the Ministry of Interior which kept close watch on the socialist movement. The higher authorities took a harder line towards the workers than did the local (city) authorities. Judging from the reviewed material, the socialist movement was considered even more dangerous for the existence of the state than were the nationalists (perhaps because Slovaks never expressed their desire for a separate state; the furthest they went was to seek autonomy.) In one of his reports to the minister of interior about Karol Hanzlíček (I will discuss this later), the Hungarian chief prosecutor pointed out that the present socialist movement was no longer fighting for economic reforms or the improvement of working conditions but wanted to overthrow the existing social system.[63] So to a large extent, measures taken against or the stance adopted towards workers were dictated by the orders of the minister of interior rather than just the will of the city captain or the mayor. On several occasions when the city captain informed the minister about a forthcoming event planned by the socialists and in fact recommended that it be permitted because of the good behaviour of the Pressburger workers, the minister modified what could be allowed and what not, (allowing the meeting on 1 May but banning demonstrations or marches.)[64]

The situation was similar with the May Day event in 1891. The association *Vorwärts* submitted its programme of the celebration which involved a workers' meeting in the morning in Pálffy's hall (the usual locale for big meetings) and in the afternoon a march on the other bank of the Danube, not in the city, to an establishment next to Ligetfalu where they would hear speeches in German and Hungarian (see Figure 4). In his letter to the mayor the city captain stressed the peaceful character of the association *Vorwärts*, especially of its standing committee. He proposed to permit the workers' celebration since the march would happen outside the city and would therefore not be a demonstration, or in the case of bad weather would take place in the city in Pálffy's hall where he could personally supervise the meeting. He did not recommend permitting the morning meeting which according to him had a purely demonstrative intent. He proposed to put up guards as in the previous year especially to guard against the "street rabble." (The city captain usually made a distinction between the good and controlled workers and bad "street rabble.")[65] However, the minister of interior banned any workers' meetings on 1 May, arguing that it was the foreign workers who had moved into Hungary who prepared these meetings and that the considerate Hungarian workers did not want to join this effort and be distracted from their work. On any other day workers' gatherings were permitted. Just in case, military forces were in a state of emergency.[66] Thus *Vorwärts* received a letter from the city captain which banned any gathering or march on 1 May either under the flag of *Vorwärts* or anyone else.[67]

There were also contrary situations, such as when the minister demanded an explanation of the reasons for banning the anniversary celebration of the association *Vorwärts* as a result of the association's complaint about the behaviour of the city captain.[68] Permission was usually granted every year for this celebration to take place. However, the captain explained in his letter to the city magistrate that foreign workers were planning to take part in the celebration and so one could expect "agitation hidden in the socialist disguise" which would threaten the public order. Thus the captain banned the event, as he said, for the benefit of the workers themselves as they had nothing to gain from the spread of these conspiratorial tendencies.[69] On another occasion, when the workers' association *Vorwärts* submitted a request for permission to hold a public gathering, the mayor Moritz Gottl turned to the Ministry of Interior describing all the details about the prepared meeting and seeking advice about the appropriate action to take. The Ministry allowed the meeting. The content of the meeting, however, awakened dissatisfaction, not only among the municipal authorities but also in the minister himself (he demanded a special report about the meeting.)[70]

There is evidence of at least annual reports from the city captain about the state of the social democratic movement in Pressburg. This report was made at the request of the *főispán*, sent to him and forwarded to the minister of interior. The city captain described the organisation of the Social Democratic Party in the city, its leaders, the public meetings and their contents, the 1 May demonstration, published leaflets, strikes in the city and their results, trade union organisations and the number of members of the *Vorwärts* association.[71] There probably were also monthly reports of the *főispán* to the minister of interior which described any more politically significant happenings in his county and the suspicious individuals.[72] The minister and the *főispán* regularly demanded from the mayor or the police captain reports about different aspects of the workers' movement, and information about their contacts with the workers in Budapest and Vienna.[73]

Apart from the presence of the police officers at all the public meetings, gatherings and celebrations of the workers, in cases like the First May celebrations there was also a considerable military force prepared to intervene if required. It was placed all around the city in strategic places and further military units stood by in their barracks in a state of emergency. The first celebration of May Day was especially feared, and extensive security measures were taken in advance. The mayor of the city described them to the minister of interior in his report about the events of the 1 May 1890. He stressed the peaceful and orderly quality of the workers' meeting outside the city. The report included a detailed account of the preventive measures and the placement of the military and police forces.

1. The army units in the town were in a state of emergency and they sent out five patrols into the suburbs in the evening. There were military patrols stationed next to the Dynamit factory, the cartridge factory, the gunpowder store, and next to the gasworks.

2. In order to prevent 700–800 workers, working in the quarry in Dévény, from entering the city, a military guard was sent to the locality near Dévény.

3. Police were monitoring the area by the Danube bridge and checking ships so that Pressburger workers or those workers only passing through Pressburg were not able to get to Hainburg. (The news about the plan of the workers to go to Hainburg was forwarded as Ministry of Interior information to the city authorities.)[74]

4. A police officer was present at the workers' meeting.

5. The police crew was in service in full force in each of the city districts

on 30 April from 6 to 12pm, and on 1 May from 5 to 10 am and from 4 to 12pm and they were checked in each district by two police clerks. The police clerks were in telephone connection with the police captain to inform him about measures they adopted and to receive the necessary instructions.

6. In the city council building there were twenty four firemen and three fire clerks on emergency standby.

7. It was ordered that the street lamps should be kept burning all night from 1 to 5 May.

8. On the evenings of the 2nd, 3rd and 4th May evenings the police was in service as on the 1st May in case there was unrest because of wage reductions as a consequence of absence from work on 1 May.

All these measures were checked by the mayor and the *főispán* personally.[75] The measures began on the day before the first of May. On the 30th April a company of soldiers arrived in Pressburg, and the barracks in the city were in a state of emergency.[76] On this first of May there were soldiers and police on every corner, and the inhabitants of the city did not dare to go out into the streets.[77] On other first of May days the police was again in a state of emergency during the whole day, although the security measures were not as tight as on the first May Day in 1890.[78]

The surveillance of movements in Hungary became more intense under Dezső Bánffy and this was reflected in Pressburg as well, in the way the socialists were treated. May Day celebrations were strictly banned in 1894–8.[79] In 1894 the Ministry of Interior ordered that lists of anarchists be compiled and one year later this was extended to social democrats. The representatives of the Social Democratic Party in Pressburg had to be followed (shoemaker Karol Krchnár, carpenter Alois Zalkai and Ján Orlík and painter Jozef Würstlein) as "dangerous socialist agitators." The city captain managed to get some workers dismissed from their work as a warning to others thinking of joining the social democrats.[80] In 1898 the persecution strengthened. The government dissolved some workers' associations, strengthened the censorship, and drastically limited the workers' right to associate. The functionaries of the workers' movement were forced to be photographed, and a police album with their photographs was distributed to all *főispáns*. (From Pressburg there figured Henrich Kálmár-Kohn.) The house searches became more frequent and many workers functionaries had to leave the industrial towns and were deported back to their places of origin.[81] The correspondence between the minister of interior and the city police chief was busy. The captain always informed the minister about the formal request submitted by the workers to hold public meetings and these were always banned by the minister. Public gatherings on 1 May were prohibited until 1899 when the 1 May celebration was finally permitted.[82]

There were detectives who infiltrated the workers' movement, and thus the city captain and the minister had information in advance of what was being prepared.[83] It seems that they both had independent sources of information as well. In 1895 the minister asked the Pozsony county *főispán* Szalavszky to investigate information he had received about a planned strike in the Dynamit factory. After investigating the case, the *főispán* found no support for this information and added the report of the police chief about the conditions in Dynamit factory since the workers' movement was thoroughly infiltrated here.[84] Similarly in 1898 the minister of interior drew the attention of the mayor of Pressburg to the fact that the Viennese workers were planning to have brass medals celebrating the 1848 revolution made in Pressburg and then to put them into circulation in Vienna. The mayor refuted this information, and referred to the report of the city captain whose informants were part of the "narrower" leadership of the Social Democratic Party and therefore would have known about such a thing.[85] In another case the minister informed the mayor that "in a confidential way" he had found out that a movement had begun in Pressburg to plan a general strike for 1 September. This movement originated in Austria. The Austrian workers' leaders were supposed to appear in Pressburg to help with preparations for the strike. The minister asked for an investigation of this case and for deportation of foreigners.[86] In 1910 the minister sent two detectives to Pressburg to observe the socialist movement.[87] There was also a flow of information between the Pressburg district represented by *főszolgabiró* and the minister of interior.[88] In 1907, the *főszolgabiró* was informing the minister of interior about the social democratic movements in the factories in Ligetfalu (lying behind the Franz-Joseph bridge on the right bank of the Danube.)[89]

The workers were well aware of the measures taken by the authorities, and made sure that they gave no opportunities to the authorities to use repressive measures. However, the surveillance obsession of the authorities made the work of the workers' association and workers' activities more difficult. Hanzlíček in his memoirs mentions that the police did everything possible to make the life of the workers' association harder. The police put pressure on those pub owners who rented out their rooms for workers' meetings and lectures so that they had to move from one locality to another.[90] Hanzlíček also protested to the city police chief against sending police officers not only to the public meetings but also to the monthly meetings of the association and their public lectures. Of course this protest was without result since the police captain maintained that if the workers respected law there was no reason why they should mind the presence of police. Also when one of the ten entrepreneurs who vouched for a prepared public meeting and their peacefulness suddenly changed his mind, the public meeting could not take place. According to Hanzlíček this 'change of mind' was brought upon them from outside as the consequence of the police pressure put on them.[91] On the other hand, there were also incidents when the police captain entered into the role of a mediator between the workers and their employers, in order to prevent a conflict.[92] In 1901, around 500 unemployed construction workers met at the bridgehead in order to pass through the city and demonstrate. The police tried to dissuade them but to no avail. At the end the police captain appealed to the workers to choose a committee to come to him with their grievances which the workers did and then dispersed. The city captain promised to the committee that he would talk to the construction masters and make sure that they would employ first of all local workers.[93]

There seemed to be a change in the antagonistic relationship after the turn of the century. In 1902 workers were allowed to march through the city with their posters and banners. Of course the route of the march was announced in advance to the city captain, as well as the detailed programme of the whole day.[94] (See Chapter three.) This became the rule for every year afterwards. The only time that there was a minor clash between the workers and police was in the 1908 May Day celebration, when the attention of police was caught by a banner "Down with the class parliament!" After the policeman had destroyed the banner by stamping on it, the march could go further. The other incident happened when a small unit of *honvéds* came into the path of the marching workers. The leader of the unit directed the *honvéds* to march straight into the middle of the procession and so the *honvéds* crashed into the cyclists at the front of the procession. This was regarded by the workers as a provocation. Only after some time and after the intervention of police did the *honvéds* get out of the way.[95] The local press which used to give more detailed accounts of the May Day happenings at the beginning of 1890s, after the turn of the century just gave short notices about workers celebrations which means that they probably became part of Pressburg life.

As is clear from the police reports as well as from Hanzlíček's memoirs, the police banned especially those public gatherings where the participation of workers from outside Pressburg could be expected (e.g. this was the reason for banning the public meeting on 16.9.1891.)[96] Obviously on the basis of his gathered knowledge, the city captain had an idea or could predict how the Pressburger workers would behave and was sure that they would stay 'under control.' However, the presence of workers from outside Pressburg and Vienna decreased the predictability of workers' behaviour. 'Control' seemed to be the key word in decision making about the public gatherings and in policing the workers' movement in Pressburg generally. When describing public gatherings, marches through city, demonstrations, all articles in local newspapers end with the reassurance that "there were no disruptions to order" and refer to the controlled manner of the event.[97] The police presence at the meetings could be at times very annoying since the police officers used to interrupt the speakers when (according to the police) speakers were inciting rebellion or attacking the state. They also threatened to deny orators their right to speak (which happened on several occasions) or to dissolve the whole meeting (which according to the reviewed materials never happened). Thus it was not only that workers wanted to be peaceful and controlled but also that they did not have much choice if they wanted to continue their activities.

This section has showed how surveillance and policing of the socialist movement in Pressburg worked. Reports from Germany on the socialist movement disturbed Hungarian governments, leading them to fear the prospect of socialist agitation long before the movement developed into a considerable force in Hungary.[98] The government wanted to prevent socialism from taking root, but were not successful. However, the authorities kept close watch on the activities of socialists, and tried to hinder them by taking preventive measures—gathering information on events that were being planned—but also by repressive measures—persecuting the socialist press, banning workers' gathering, restricting their right to associate and limiting workers' freedom of gathering and speech. While workers perceived this treatment as repression, at the same time it forced them to mobilise their resources, improve their organisation and implement discipline during public events so that they did not provoke violence on the part of the ever-present police. In the process of adapting to the situation of constant surveillance, workers also internalised some of the norms of their oppressors. Workers made an effort not to disrupt order but rather to prove to the middle classes that workers indeed could be disciplined, that they were not a disorganised elemental mass which could any moment erupt into violence and sweep away everything that stood for the solid, order-obeying middle classes. This self-disciplining aspect of surveillance (or self-surveillance) will be discussed later in this chapter.

3.2. SOCIALIST PRESS PERSECUTION

The government paid attention also to the circulation of the socialist press and to the kind of information that was being disseminated to the public. In order to limit the amount of disruptive socialist propaganda and its negative effect on the public, the government passed a law which set so high an amount of money required for starting a periodical that it was hard for workers to secure funds to pay for this exorbitant license fee. Despite this, workers periodicals in Budapest were appearing regularly, having a better financial basis and organisation than in provinces. The workers in Pressburg made attempts to start their own press. They went to great pains to do this since they considered the "bourgeois local press" ideological poison for workers, disguising its disruptive intention by a seemingly positive attitude towards the workers.[99] In 1879, the workers' leaders came up with an idea to publish their own bi-weekly publication. A small collection of money was made and on 1.3.1879 the newspaper *Wahrheit* was started as a social-economic newspaper. It did not have a long life though since on 26.3.1880 the seventh number's proofs were confiscated while still in the printing shop on the initiative of the state prosecutor. Hanzlíček who was the editor, was summoned for interrogation.[100] Proceedings against Hanzlíček began on the basis of the par. 31 of the law XXVIII/1848 which allowed the publishing of a political periodical only after paying a high bail. The charge was that Hanzlíček published articles with political content, inciting the poor against the wealthy, in a periodical of claimed non-political content. Hanzlíček was defended by the very skilled Slovak 'bourgeois' lawyer Michal Mudroň. However, he was sentenced to eight days in prison and 30 guldens fine and the further publishing of the newspaper was banned.[101]

Another newspaper, *Der Zeitgeist* was started on 16.5.1881 but after its fourth issue the newspaper ended in the same way as *Wahrheit*. Hanzlíček as its editor was again sentenced to eight days imprisonment and a fine of 30 guldens, this time for articles taken from other workers newspapers including *Arbeiter Wochen-Chronik* which were published without hindrance in Budapest.[102] This example illustrates the arbitrariness of decision making in these processes. It also shows that the various state authorities could have very different understanding of what was considered an 'offence to the state.' As has been stressed earlier, the county apparatus or even the state officials in Pressburg (court employees were considered state employees as well) who carried out the policies of the state and implemented the orders of the minister of interior did not necessarily do this in a straightforward way. The arbitrariness of their decision making was partly because much was left to the discretion of *főispáns* since the orders of the minister were not necessarily supported by existing laws. Another factor causing this arbitrariness was the self-interest of different levels of the state administration, following their own agendas besides that of the state, and using "state interest" as a cover for their own power struggles thus creating competing grids of power and knowledge.

Before 1 May 1893, there appeared another workers' periodical *Neue Volkszeitung* edited by the social democrat Alois Zalkai. It was supposed to have had 160–170 subscribers. At the end of June 1894 there was another press persecution, this time against Zalkai for his article against the dirty trading practices of a local coal trader. However, this time it was the workers who won and Zalkai was freed from the charges brought by this tradesman. During this process the state prosecutor declared that he had often had opportunities to act against the newspaper for publishing political articles without having paid the bail. This happened under the editorship of Karol Krauss who on 22.1.1895 was brought before the court. Krauss was prosecuted for the offence of anti-state agitation. He was found guilty and sentenced to one month in prison and a fine of 100 guldens. With his confinement this workers' newspaper also stopped being published.[103]

Other newspapers included two Slovak papers *Slovenské Robotnícke Noviny* (which began to be published in 1904) and *Napred* (in 1906).[104] These newspapers complained about the state persecution not only of Slovak workers press but also of the German *Westungarische Volksstimme*. The newspapers regularly published the newest press persecution cases and their outcome.[105] On one occasion *Robotnícke Noviny* even claimed that in the last fourteen days seventeen "comrades" had been sentenced to a total of 20 years in prison and fines of 4790 Crowns for "inciting activity."[106]

The authorities also paid attention to the leaflets and booklets published by socialists. They were considered "a very dangerous instrument of socialist and anti-state propaganda."[107] In 1894 the minister of interior wanted to know whether the printing of the anarchist magazine *Die Freiheit* was not prepared in Pressburg. Such a possibility was absolutely contradicted by the city captain since the local workers did not agree with the ideas of anarchism.[108] In February 1895, during the house search of the shoemaker's assistant Michal Kubík, "Magyarország jogtalan népéhez" (To the Hungarian right-less people) leaflets were confiscated. These leaflets had been printed in Budapest in Hungarian and German. In April, leaflets were again confiscated including "Egy kérdés a magyar nemzethez" (A question to the Hungarian nation) published by the Social Democratic Party and "A legyek és pókok" (Flies and spiders).[109] Minister Dezső Perczel reminded the mayor of the obligation of the printing shops to submit to the municipal authorities all the printed publications and of the duty of the authorities to control all the press, especially the socialists.[110]

Another example of how tightly Austria and Hungary co-operated in tracking the socialist and anarchist movements and how information moved between the authorities in the form of letters, reports and telegrams was the case of Karol Hanzlíček and the parcel including the magazine *Die Freiheit*, which was sent to him from London. First there was a report of the mayor of Pressburg that the Viennese police had informed the Pressburg police chief that there was a parcel containing the revolutionary magazine Freiheit from London addressed to Hanzlíček. The mayor immediately visited the post director board in Pressburg and instructed them that in future they should hand over all similar parcels to the police captain. The post director said that there was this parcel but they could not confiscate it until it was delivered or unless they had an order from the judge. The city captain turned to the *főispán* in order to learn what course of action was required. The *főispán* responded that only the minister of interior had the authority to decide what had to be done.[111] There was also a house search carried out at Hanzlíček's premises which did not yield any incriminating material.[112] The minister (in a telegram) instructed the mayor that the parcel should be detained, and gave instruction to the *főispán* that the parcel should be delivered to Hanzlíček with police presence and right after its handing over the parcel should be confiscated.[113]

The parcel was delivered and confiscated on 8 August. It included three copies of *Die Freiheit*.[114] These magazines were sent to the minister and submitted to the Hungarian chief state prosecutor who wrote a report to the minister. In his report the state prosecutor complained that the law was ineffective and could not really do much in such cases since anyone could start a printing shop and unless a periodical was printed at least twice per month, it could have political content without paying the bail and spread revolutionary ideas. The only thing one could do was to destroy the incriminating press and adjust the law so that suspicious people were not allowed to enter Hungary. According to the state prosecutor, the press law needed to be modified with regard to the smuggling of this kind of periodical into the country as well as widening the legal procedure for all the political press of Hungary. However, Hanzlíček could not be prosecuted for a periodical which was printed in London. Besides that, the city police chief considered him a "person with flawless behaviour."[115] This example is particularly revealing in its intertwining of knowledge and power, in the intersecting and competing networks of information flow that led to the safe delivery and simultaneous seizure of the offending periodicals.

These few examples show in what ways information about the socialists moved between authorities, the flow of letters, reports and telegrams in both directions, i.e. from the city authorities to the Ministry of Interior or vice versa. The government strove to control not only the movement of people but also of information, considering the press the most important instrument of the workers' movement for spreading propaganda and revolution.[116] One can say that both the government and workers were clear about the enormous role of the press and its potential for enlarging 'imagined communities' in the development of the socialist and nationalist movements. However, in trying to control and restrict the enlargement of these 'imagined communities', surveillance and repression led to the contrary result, stimulating oppositional groups to more carefully define themselves and to improve their organisation and mobilisation.[117] In the next part, I will look at the surveillance of the nationalist movements in Pressburg (although more in the sense of movements of small groups of people rather than as movements of increasing number and force as was the case with the socialist movement).

3.3. SURVEILLANCE OF NATIONALITIES

Apart from the socialist movement, the nationalities were another source of worry for the Hungarian government. The government's aim was to build a nation state with one political nation—Hungarian with the pre-dominance of the Magyar race. In the area of nationalities' policies the trend was set by Kálmán Tisza in 1875 and the main aims of this politics was to prevent the organisation of nationalities so that they could not become influential in political life, to minimise their cultural activities and to annihilate their partial educational or church autonomy by administrative measures.[118] Ferenc Glatz holds that Hungarian nationalism was relatively tolerant compared to the nationalisms of France, Germany and other European states and sprang from the demands of the modern industrial state which required one lingua franca for communication in a country inhabited by people of different languages. He also claims that Magyarisation was never enacted into a law or government policy, and was advocated only by the coalition government of 1906–1910.[119] However, the possibilities for the members of nationalities to be educated in their own mother tongue were limited, and the policies of the nationalising state were expressed in educational laws, a restrictive electoral law, press control (1878 law) and political trials.[120] Although there were slight differences in the policies of the governments towards the nationalities and some governments decreased the persecution of nationalist movements, one aspect in which all Hungarian governments were consistent was the Magyarisation of education. No Hungarian governments wanted to go back to the 1868 Nationalities Law on this subject.[121] As pointed out by Gellner, a modern society is characterised by the universal standardised education which is taken up and organised by the state in an increasing degree. "The monopoly of legitimate education is now more important, more central than is the monopoly of legitimate violence."[122] In this respect, the Hungarian state was in the process of building a modern state albeit with a homogeneous "Magyar" high culture.

There were also restrictions on the power of the local authorities. A law of 1898 allowed only one, Hungarian, name for each locality on the Hungarian territory. According to Sked, these policies were motivated by a sense of cultural supremacy, and a belief in the civilising mission of the Magyar culture as well as the belief of Hungarian elites in the role of Hungary as a balancing power in European international affairs.[123] The nationalism of the minorities in Hungary was, to a large extent, a reaction against the nationalising policies of the Hungarian state.[124] The Hungarian Ministry of Interior did indeed keep tabs on the activities of nationalists, albeit only as one of the many other activities happening in the territory of Hungary. The materials of the confidential agenda of the Ministry of Interior included a wide range of issues, proving that the Hungarian state (like any other modern state) was keen to gather information about its population in order to act upon this knowledge.[125]

The minister of interior kept a close watch on the different nationalities' movements. The *főispán* of each county sent the minister regular reports about actual developments in his county. The Hungarian government's policies towards Slovaks were generally dominated by negative and repressive practices like the intimidation of the Slovak national movement through prosecution and imprisonment as well as by police supervision.[126] Not much material is available on this subject for Pressburg city. Obviously, nationalities' movements were not a problem in the city of Pressburg itself. However, in its surrounding area and in the county itself there were towns with more nationally active communities—especially Slovak ones (over half of the county population was of Slovak mother tongue according to the census data). Pan-German activities were not at all noticeable in this area, and the government was worried first of all about the Pan-Slavs.[127] Slovaks in Pressburg did not develop such activity as to be considered a movement, although they were watched by state authorities but mainly by the local Magyarising elites who were very sensitive to any cultural events which did not celebrate Hungarian culture and language. They reacted in the same way also to the German theatre as Chapter two has shown; however, their reactions to theatre performances in Slovak and German language were different reflecting the different social standing of these languages and their proponents. In this part I concentrate on the official policing aspect of the surveillance while the next part will then look at the way in which the city elites in promoting some models of behaviour acted upon the self-disciplining aspect of surveillance.[128]

There was constant communication between the minister of interior and the *főispán* (or sometimes the mayor of Pressburg if relevant) about the development of the nationalities' movements in Pressburg county, in Pressburg city and about the movement of different 'nationalist agitators.' Mostly it was the *főispán* who kept the minister informed about nationalities, especially the Pan-Slav movement in the county. His information came from reports from the state representatives in different communities and towns of the county, and from Pressburg's city captain (for Pressburg). The *főispán* must also have had other sources of information, including more informal sources. The directions of the information flow were as described in the previous section. The Pan-Slav movement was observable especially in counties Nyitra, Trencsén, Liptó and in parts of the Pressburg county with a Slovak majority.[129]

As previously noted, the minister also had information from his own "confidential sources." So the minister of interior in his letter to the *főispán* of Pressburg wrote that he had received a "confidential piece of information" that one inhabitant of Pressburg Vanicsek was an agent of a russophile committee in communication with the Pan-Slav committee in Moscow. The minister asked the *főispán* to gather information about Vanicsek's work and behaviour in a "confidential way" and to forward this information to the minister. He ordered the *főispán* to assign a trustworthy person to follow Vanicsek continuously, at the cost of the Ministry.[130] Also in other cases the minister was confirming information from his own sources, not relying only on what he found out from the local authorities. Thus in 1899 he wanted to know whether there was any movement on the territory of Pozsony county for bringing the Slovak language into the public administration. The *főispán* investigated the case and refuted such claims.[131] In 1906, in connection with the Congress of Slav journalists, the *főispán* Kálmán Bittó did not observe any Pan-Slav movement in the county or city of Pressburg. The only person who left his place of residence in these days was Jozef Dérer, the Slovak lawyer from Malacka. The *főispán* even knew that Dérer took a train in the direction of Pressburg and came back from that direction.[132]

The information moved around between different ministries too, depending on the case. In 1904 the minister of justice informed the minister of interior that he had been closely following the periodical *Reform* published in Pressburg by Alois Zalkai, although "the periodical could not be classified yet for agitation." In 1902 in Pressburg there were altogether fifteen law suits and in 1903 only six law suits for press offences.[133] Of course public meetings connected with nationalities did not escape the attention of the authorities, and the police were always sending detailed accounts of these giving the number of the people present and contents of the speeches.[134] As was already mentioned, no nationalist movement developed in Pressburg during this period. However, after the turn of the century, there were occasional Slovak public meetings in Pressburg, often organised in co-operation between the social democrats and the 'bourgeois' Slovak parliamentary deputies.[135]

The exact method of information collection becomes clear from the report of the Hungarian border police, based in Pressburg, to the minister of interior. The police captain collected this information on the basis of detective work in the area. The detectives, who spoke Slovak (thus had probably been recruited from Slovaks), mixed with the inhabitants in pubs and conversed with them.[136] The same report gave information on the eager Pan-Slav agitator Florián Tománek who, however, had no Pan-Slav convictions but did it more for material gain than from deep belief. The captain asked the minister to remove Tománek into a purely German or Rumanian area where he would not be in contact with Slavs.[137] This used to be a common practice with priests who were suspected of agitation or dissemination of national ideas among the people. They were just moved into a different community, preferably with a different ethnic group.[138]

Pressburg itself was not fertile ground for national activities. Only after the turn of the century, with the development of the workers' movement and creation of its Slovak section, as well as within the Catholic workers' association and with some individual Slovak burghers' efforts, did Slovaks become more visible within the city itself. It was rather different in communities in Pozsony county, many of which were close to Pressburg and supplied the city with its work force. In 1890, the *főispán* Count József Zichy reported to the minister of interior that there was no organised effort of Slovaks in his county, and one could not talk about mass movements, although there were some "feeble ephemeral efforts" of individuals. The *főispán* named localities where the movements "took deeper roots" (Modor, Malacka, Basin and some villages at the outskirts of Pressburg—Récse and Lamacs.) He also named the active priests, and added lists of teachers who were not diligent enough and neglected the instruction of the Hungarian language and substituted it with Slovak. The list included also the degree of knowledge of Hungarian of the teachers themselves. However, these teachers were not considered agitators, although in some towns they had stronger national feelings (Modor, Basin). The *főispán* also reported with some satisfaction that there were no agitators found among the county or town officials. In his report the *főispán* even listed rich landowners like Count Pálffy and Count Csáky as people who employed "suspicious individuals" as forest and hunting staff. (This might indicate a clash of interests.) The *főispán* appealed to the minister not to use more intense measures than necessary since this would only produce stronger opposition on the part of the nationalities. (This report was prepared for a government meeting discussing nationalities.)[139]

The detailed character of the information passing between the authorities is remarkable. In 1895, the *főispán* of the Pozsony county Szalavszky wrote a report about all political movements concerning the state interest in the last month. The *főispán* described the national movements in Nagyszombat district and Modor, as well as the activity of priests who belonged to the People's Party and who gathered signatures in villages binding the villagers to vote for them in the election. Szalavszky also gave a description of the Slovak newspaper *Krestan* which was an instrument for "agitation." In similar language, he described the association *Vojtech* of Pan-Slav orientation consisting of Slovak priests and teachers who spoke at their meetings in Slovak. He gave the names of individuals in Modor who were developing Pan-Slav activities. About the city Pressburg itself Szalavszky wrote that, although there were the lawyers Miloš Štefanovič, Vendel Kutlík and Filip Hladký and a few craftsmen of Slovak origin who developed national activities, they did not have any followers. "Generally, the city of Pressburg is not suitable for the spread of the Pan-Slav movement."[140] However, in 1902 the *főispán* could now write about the influential leader of the Pan-Slav movement Miloš Štefanovič who was not a municipal committee member yet, but who however could become one at any moment and this fact could cause protests (probably from the other, Hungarian oriented deputies). In the Nagyszombat district the Pan-Slavism was spreading "in a horrifying way."[141] In one of its meetings in 1893, the county municipal assembly decided that all its official parts would follow the national movements in the county and any agitators would be punished.[142] Surveillance of the Pan-Slav movements extended as far as the USA where large numbers of Slovak immigrants lived. The Joint Ministry of Foreign Affairs followed the activities of the American Slovaks, their publications, associations and travels to Hungary.[143]

Pan-Germanism was another movement followed by the authorities but which was also not really present in Pozsony county. Nevertheless, the minister considered it important to spread governmental propaganda to reach the German speaking citizens and to direct them in the 'correct' way. In 1882 the minister of interior sent to the *főispáns* of various counties (including Pressburg county) the leaflets "Was der Schulverein will" (What the school-association wants) so that these leaflets were distributed among the "patriotic German population" in their territories.[144] While Slovak movements were observed in different parts of Pozsony county, and indeed there was fear among some *Toldy Kör* patriots that these movements could even 'infect' Pressburg city, the city itself did not have strong nationalities' activity of any kind (except among Magyars of course.) It was more characterised by an effort to assimilate and adjust than by the assertion of differences. Surveillance worked on a much more subtle level here, and was carried out by the city elites themselves, on different levels and aimed at different levels of the population.

4. SURVEILLANCE AND SELF-DISCIPLINING

This part considers some forms of internalisation of surveillance on the part of different social strata in Pressburg. In particular, I will draw attention to the dichotomy in images of the "good city" and the "bad city" that were prevalent in the civic discourse of the period. The first section considers the activities of civic and charitable associations such as the *Stadtverschönerungsverein*. I will note the different normative models of identity and value in the traditional elite and the Magyar elite. In the second section, I will briefly examine the attempt to secure control over the city's working class and poor populations through the activities of the police forces, network of spies and plain-clothes detectives, and also by the self-disciplining aspects of the help provided by charities and workers' housing.

4.1. City elites and the Middle Classes
Another distinctive aspect of surveillance is the self-disciplining and internalising of the presented values and models of behaviour.[145] Individuals

watch each other to see if they behave in accordance with the norm and apply sanctions on those who diverge from the norm. This sanctioning does not have to happen by legal means but can be expressed in social forms e.g. by denying entry into an association, or by hindering advancement up the social ladder. Indeed, social sanctions are powerful incentives for internalising the prevailing values. In this section I want to look at the ways in which power and knowledge were tied together by way of surveillance and self-disciplining in Pressburg, extending from the county to the city even to the lowest layers of the population, focusing especially on the connecting ties and the relations of interdependence and mutual watching.

There was a certain desired model of behaviour, presented by the state officials at the highest level and it was accepted that all the state employees should comply with it. To be a state employee meant that one had to openly demonstrate Hungarian patriotism, condemn nationalist activities, not be a socialist and simply make the government's aims one's own aims, at least outwardly.[146] The county (as the next level in the hierarchy of the state bureaucracy) controlled its employees and also the behaviour of the city (Pressburg) authorities. As has been described earlier, this was not always a straightforward process since individuals at each level of the hierarchy also followed their own interests, creating contradicting and competing grids of power and knowledge. Concretely, this control was carried out by the *főispán* himself and was extended down the hierarchy. However, the individuals within the system were checking upon each other continuously, too. The nature of the information in the materials of the *főispán* and minister of interior shows that this information must have been gathered by individuals spying on others and reporting on what they considered 'out of norm' behaviour. (See footnote 162.) The county in the person of the *főispán* was checking also on the municipal employees in the city Pressburg. The *főispán* was always present at the municipal assembly meetings of the city Pressburg, and so knew what was happening, what kind of deputies were there, what were their requirements, political affiliations, and power groups. Furthermore, many members of the county bureaucracy lived in Pressburg themselves and participated in its social and cultural life, extending these institutional practices more broadly across the city.

Surveillance and self-disciplining in Pressburg was happening in the context of competing city elites, the traditional, predominantly German speaking elite, and the new Magyar elite. In terms of social structure, the values of these two groups overlapped. Even in their Hungarian patriotism and loyalty to the Hungarian state, at least outwardly, there was no divergence. However, there was a competition for the positions in the city occupied traditionally by the German elite, in economic as well as cultural life and in municipal politics. This competition was often voiced in national terms, the Magyar elite complaining that the city was not Hungarian enough, that the knowledge of Hungarian in all areas of the city life was not sufficient and that there was a lack of enthusiasm for Hungarian theatre and culture in general. The German elite tried to maintain the *status quo* and their position, although giving in on the question of language usage as well as by manifesting their pronounced desire to embrace Hungarian culture and to help make the city Hungarian. Indeed their positions could be kept only by adhering to the model of the good Hungarian patriot, although in reality their actions did not always mirror this model.

One could say that there were two basic models of behaviour in the city. The traditional middle class elite espoused the model of the solid, reliable, non-revolutionary good citizen, the local patriot based on local civic pride. (See Chapter two, the section on 'Pressburger' identity.) This view found its representation in many middle class associations and charities. It was especially within the charities and philanthropic activities that these views spread to the lower classes. The new Magyar elite joined this stable bourgeois milieu, being part of the middle classes. However, there was another image which they aspired to: that of the good Hungarian patriot, presented especially by the Hungarian intellectuals and professionals. This model implied uncritical love for anything Hungarian (Magyar), starting with culture and a concern about the language spoken within families. Without knowledge of the Hungarian language, social climbing became almost impossible, thus this model was in a way self-reinforcing.

I want to stress that by 'model' I do not meant a rigid pattern of behaviour or presented values. On the contrary, there were many values which overlapped and shifted and it would be difficult to separate the two models in any rigid fashion. However, for the sake of analysis a certain degree of separation is necessary. In the sense of the existence of two prevalent models one could speak of competing surveillances in the city, of overlapping and contradicting grids of power and knowledge. The city authorities often acted in contradiction with what was considered patriotic behaviour by the Magyar elite (see Chapter two). At the same time the Magyar middle classes were entering the municipal assembly, and municipal offices, competing for power and becoming part of the power structures. The values of the local patriot could clash with that of the Hungarian patriot, when the Hungarian patriot specifically meant a Magyar patriot. Although speaking German, the prevalent traditional elite was non-nationalistically oriented, and the city had accommodated people of different languages in the past, without trying to force them into exalting one national culture at the expense of others. However, the traditional elites themselves were adapting to the Hungarian dominance, something which considering their numerical preponderance in the city seems quite difficult to understand.

The city authorities (mostly from the traditional elite) were thus both agents and objects of surveillance. They secured the surveillance of the workers' movement as well as of potential nationalist activities. They took care to be well informed about anything which might disturb the peaceful life of the inhabitants. In one way they acted as an extension of the state authorities to whom they passed on information about the happenings in the city. At the same time the city authorities collected all this information in their own interest, in the interest of keeping the *status quo*, promoting their city's image and keeping the potentially dangerous social classes in check. Simultaneously, the state authorities also watched the city authorities, and how far they complied to the desired patriotic model of behaviour. As the extension of the state in this case, the main actors were the zealous representatives of the Magyar elite in the city who wished to Magyarise Pressburg and were quick to notice if the city officials did not use or know Hungarian properly, or were associated with people who were suspected of being involved in nationalities' activities.[147] Their pressure on the Magyarisation of all spheres of the city life affected the internalisation of some of the values of the Hungarian patriotism by the city elites. The degree of internalisation was different with different people. It is questionable how deep it actually reached. However, at least at the superficial layer some degree of internalisation was necessary in order to maintain one's position in the social structure.

4.1.1. Traditional Elite: "Good City"

> It is in the city that one learns to be a citizen. There people acquire valuable knowledge, see many models to teach them avoidance of evil. As they look around, they notice how handsome is honor, how lovely is fame, how divine is glory.[148]
>
> —Leon Baptista Alberti

The traditional elite was concerned with a 'good city', a city which had easily controllable spaces containing a life lived in accordance with middle class values. "The physical form and shape of a city, its official plan and ceremonial places are articulated by political and social configurations that a nation or municipality wants to instil within its public."[149] In the case of Pressburg, there were both the efforts of the municipality and of the Hungarian nation represented by the local Magyarising elite's attempt to instil its own sets of ideas and models on the physical form of the city. These two models of sets of ideas competed but also overlapped. However, both models faced resistance when bigger crowds (socialist demonstrations, Slovak public meetings) gathered in the city and threatened the overthrow of order by their very presence. This shows that despite not having political power, the lower classes had ways to resist the dominant images instilled upon them.[150]

In order to secure the control of the city spaces there was the city police as well as various associations and charities concerned with the look of the city, its safety and presentability. One of those associations, the *Stadtverschönerungsverein* was directly concerned with the physical appearance of the city. It strove to make the city and its environment neat-looking.[151] Founded in 1868 by the mayor Heinrich Justi, the number of its members grew from 303 in 1868 to 1116 in 1914. The association included the most prominent personalities of the city life (city employees and representatives, intelligentsia, professionals, entrepreneurs) as well as aristocrats who did not actually reside in Pressburg but who usually presided over the association. A look at the membership list reveals that the city elite formed the primary membership of the association. The connection to the city governance was even defined in the statutes: the mayor, his deputy, the city engineer, the city main forester, the city administrator and gardener were permanent ex officio members as well as six members of the city beautification committee. All the improvements done by the association became a part of the city's property.[152]

The aim of the association was to enhance the environment of the city. The association was convinced that it was one of the most "magnificent and noble-minded associations in Pozsony...working...so altruistically and blessedly for all the inhabitants..."[153] What "a beautiful and enhanced environment" actually meant was defined by the largely middle-class membership of the association. Thus the 'city fathers' shaped the city in their own image.[154] However, to make "one of the most beautiful and important cities of Hungary...the second city of Hungary"[155] or "the most central city of the Central Europe" presentable so that it made good impression on visitors was not the only aim of the association.[156] It was believed that a pleasant city environment would influence its inhabitants in a positive way, and so would raise their cultural level. If the citizens formed their environment "after their image (*nach sich selbst*)," they became more cultivated. The city itself was considered a "natural high-cultured environment" in which people could be educated to be more cultured and civilised.[157] The well ordered environment had to 'order' also the way in which the inhabitants lived, the way they thought. The city itself should be the model for the citizens' efforts to shape their behaviour. Thus self-governance was an integral part of the ideology of the city environment enhancement. "To ensure acts of self-governance, citizens were represented with visual models to internalize, remember and apply."[158] A self-governed individual made his/her contribution to the wealth of the city, and so through the city contributed also to the flourishing of his/her own nation. "Our nation does not need only more wealth but also a higher level of culture... The future of our nation can be ensured first of all by continuous increase of its culture which is also the best weapon of the hegemony of Hungarians."[159] In this way the self-governance of the individual was connected to the hegemonic surveillance of the nation-state.

Despite the last quote, the city elites did not necessarily intend to make Pressburg a Hungarian looking city. (Here one has to consider the year of the writing of the association's history in 1918.) Because of its mixed membership and the participation of aristocrats, whose knowledge of Hungarian was not good or often was totally lacking, as well as of the traditional not nationally oriented elite, the 'national' character of the city was not so important for the local Pressburger elite. The city itself was important, and it was the duty of every good *Pressburger* to take care of it. The local patriotism of the elite was strong and it was very present in the daily press of the period as well as in other publications. Great care was taken of the history of the city, and one of the deeds of the association was to found the city museum.[160] It was in this period that many memorial tablets were put on the houses in which famous personalities used to live. This effort to bring out and stress the famous past of Pressburg was tightly connected with its lost position as the capital of Hungary and its degradation to a mere provincial city after 1867. While it had been a capital, there was no need to stress the fact, but once the city faded from its glory, retrieval and commemoration of the city's history became of utmost importance. Also the rapid urban changes in the nineteenth century brought about by modernisation made this need to preserve the past more urgent. The period 1867–1914 was the time when the first comprehensive history of the city of Pressburg was written, in six volumes, by the well-known Hungarian historian Tivadar Ortvay.[161]

However, the newly forming Magyar elite wanted Pressburg to be not only an ordered and safe city, a concern which overlapped with that one of the traditional elite, they wanted Pressburg above all to become a Hungarian city in its visual appearance as well as in its sounds (so that Hungarian was heard in the streets). Thus the surveillance and control of spaces of the city in order to make it more a presentable, controllable and educational space for the inhabitants, was joined by the ideal of Hungarian patriotism which in the understanding of the Magyar elite meant rather Magyar patriotism since Hungarian patriotism was not something the traditional elite lacked.

4.1.2. Magyar Elite: The Good Hungarian Patriot

The model favoured by the Magyar elite was oriented towards a national ideal, concerned with the qualities represented by a good Hungarian patriot. Previous chapters of this study, especially Chapters two and four have showed how this issue was central in Hungary during this period. In this way the Magyar elite was basically advancing the nationalising state's notions of the qualities that constituted a good Hungarian citizen. However, as the discussion about the electric train to Vienna showed, even among the parliament deputies there was no consensus on what or rather to what degree these qualities had to be present, and on what stance a good Hungarian patriot should adopt in different situations. Very often, patriotism served as a tool in the hands of different interest groups. In Pressburg, where the Magyar intelligentsia was trying to establish itself in a city where the power had traditionally been held by the German speaking elite, Hungarian patriotism was also an instrument in the power struggle. It happened to be so effective that to a degree Hungarian patriotism became internalised by the traditional elite, and was exhibited on public occasions. Indeed, it was necessary to exhibit it in order to move upwards in the new social order.

It can be said that the nationalistic Magyar middle class in Pressburg was an extension of the Hungarian state, in that they 'supervised' the implementation of its nationalising ideas, albeit for their own different reasons. This group drew first of all from the teachers and professors of the educational institutions in Pressburg but also from civil servants, lawyers and other professionals. These people also made up the kernel of the *Toldy Kör* membership. Their main organ was the newspaper *Nyugatmagyarországi Hiradó*, whose main concern was the unfavourable national milieu in Pressburg. In its articles, the newspaper pointed out any discrepancies between the model of the Hungarian patriot and the activities of the Pressburg's elites. The city authorities were criticised for their lack of Hungarian patriotism, and the Pressburger elites were often nicknamed "Kraxelhuber" which denoted a person speaking German. Especially in the professions which were connected to the state, spying on people was common. People employed in city and county administration, in the army or in education were expected not to mix with suspicious individuals, with people labelled socialists or with national agitators. While professing to follow the interest of the Hungarian state, these individuals often pursued their own interests and entered into power struggles which also influenced how and at whom they directed their disciplining and normalising activities. Evidence suggest that individuals were observed even during their holidays and spare time, and reported on if they showed 'improper conduct', i.e. conduct that deviated from the norm expected of people of a certain standing in the social hierarchy.[162]

Although the ideas of what was a good Hungarian patriot shifted and there were differences also between the governing parties in the definition of this ideal, the Magyar elite in Pressburg presented what it considered as the model of a good Hungarian patriot in all its various activities, whether in its newspapers, in the *Toldy Kör* association and on municipal assembly meetings. This model was in many ways opposed to what the traditional elite stood for, and thus could work as a means of exerting pressure in the struggle for power. The good Hungarian patriot had to have a good command of Hungarian language which was not typical for the traditional elite. Although they knew bits of Hungarian, this was not considered sufficient. The traditional elite, for its part, stressed its Hungarian patriotism and also the fact that there could be good Hungarian patriots speaking languages other than Hungarian. Thus there were different views of a patriot: the Magyar elite's which can be termed national or even ethnic since Hungarian in their thinking meant Magyar, and the traditional elite's which was associated with citizenship and belonging to the Hungarian state (Magyar vs. Hungarian patriotism).[163]

According to the Magyar elite a good Hungarian patriot had to love Hungarian culture and language. This meant that even if the Hungarian theatre was not profitable, it had to substitute for the traditional German theatre, no matter what. The very fact that the Hungarian ensembles continually failed to attract a full house in Pressburg was for the Magyar elite a proof of serious lack of that strong patriotic feeling in the hearts of the Pressburg's inhabitants. The German elite, however, did not see any conflict between going to see German theatre performances and at the same time feeling enthusiasm about Hungarian literature and culture in general. The Magyar elite wanted the Hungarian language to spread not only in the public life in Pressburg but to spread even into the private lives of inhabitants.[164] This was largely helped by state-implemented measures in the area of education. A new generation was growing up which attended schools with Hungarian language of instruction, thus not being 'deficient' in this sense like their parents. However, knowledge of Hungarian did not exclude knowledge of German, or Slovak. The traditional elite largely adapted itself to this model, being sometimes zealously patriotic on the outside. However, some of the resistances (e.g. the case of the city theatre but also continued use of more languages in the municipal offices, although all the official documents were in Hungarian—see the case referred to in Chapter two) which on the surface seemed like slowly changing underlying patterns persisted and only began to break down after the turn of the century, especially just before the First World War.

The Magyar elite also paid attention to any kind of nationalities' movement activities in Pressburg. With its strong focus on the Magyarisation of the theatre performances, the Magyar elite was indignant if any attempts were made to stage performances in any other languages besides Hungarian. So in 1905 the newspaper *Nyugatmagyarországi Hiradó* raised an outcry against the Slovak amateur theatre performance to be given by the Catholic workers' association, and the school inspector and the *főispán* went even to Nagyszombat and Esztergom where the religious authorities resided in order to hinder it. The performance was banned.[165] A year later even the Slovak section of the Catholic workers' association was closed down so as to put an end to the Slovak amateur theatre performances.[166]

The language the Magyar elite used (partly adopted by the traditional elite as well, especially by those aspiring for any public office) was strongly marked by social Darwinism and medical metaphors. (See also Chapter two and four.) So the school inspector Károly Dworak stressed that the Magyars themselves in their struggle for Magyarising Pressburg had to be careful, "so that the germ of Germanism does not stick to them as well." On a more positive note, he spoke about elementary schools as "hotbeds" of the state language. These hotbeds were the fertile ground for the new, Hungarian generation. The language of defence and xenophobia was also applied as was shown in Chapter two. The idea of Pressburg being an island in the sea of nationalities, and teachers being the vanguard of the Magyarisation, were used by Dworak as well.[167] The Hungarian nation was fighting for its survival with other European nations and had no one to rely on besides its own resources in this fight, and therefore it needed to strengthen its Hungarianness, its power to hold together, and its homogeneity. In the same way there was also a competition in the field of culture and literature where Hungary had to compete with more developed literatures.[168]

This model of the Magyar elite was directed at the whole population of Pressburg but mainly at the traditional elite and those individuals who influenced decisions on municipal policy and public life. However, it did seep through to the lower classes as well. The idea of the 'good city' which was common for both the traditional elite and the new Magyar one, had especially important implications for the lives of the lower classes. Models of good morality, as presented by the middle classes, were exemplary practices that had to be adopted if the lower classes wanted to get a share in the aid offered to them by those who were better off.

4.2. SURVEILLANCE AND SELF-DISCIPLINING—
MIDDLE AND LOWER CLASSES: THE "BAD CITY"

> Space is fundamental in any form of communal life; space is fundamental in any exercise of power.[169]
>
> —Michel Foucault

In the previous section I have analysed the activities of the *Stadt-verschönerungsverein* aimed at beautification of the city, increasing its presentability and uplifting its inhabitants to a higher cultural level as well as imprinting order on their minds. The activities of this association were aimed at creating a 'good city.' However, this at the same time meant decreasing the uncontrollable, shedding light on the dark areas, the 'bad city', where the lower classes and poor of the city dwelled and which was the source of vice.[170] The obsession of the bourgeoisie with cleanliness and dirt was part of a spatial sensibility about private and public places.[171] Control of the city was secured not only by making visible more parts of the city but also by the police forces, network of spies and plain-clothes detectives, and also by the self-disciplining aspect attached to different kinds of help provided for workers and lower classes by charities, and accommodation in workers' housing.

The basis for intervention was provided by gathering information about the living conditions of the poor. The authorities needed to know how bad those conditions were in order to take some measures for their enhancement but also in order to be aware whether the situation could erupt into a violent protest against the authorities. The main gatherers of information were the doctors, whom Foucault calls "the first managers of collective space." Doctors studied the local conditions, water and sewage problems, residences— the problems of accommodation and displacements—migration of men and diseases.[172] In this period, Hungarian statistics developed rapidly, and all kinds of surveys on living conditions and health were carried out.[173] In the city itself, gathering this information was the task of the city doctor who was a member of the city magistracy. The city doctor had to work out for the magistrate monthly reports about the health situation in Pressburg, about the illnesses, mortality and its causes. He also developed proposals against the spread of infectious diseases, for the enhancement of hygiene as well as reports about the cost of care for homeless and unemployed people who were ill.[174] In this way the city magistrate was well informed also about the 'bad city', about the shadowy area of city life, about the poor and their way of life. Within the municipal office there was a department for care of the poor, administration of homes for the poor and representation of the poor vis-a-vis institutions. There was also a special committee dealing with the institutions caring for the poor, charity and hygiene.[175]

The city police captain made regular reports to the city magistrate about the events in the city and its safety.[176] His office was responsible for checking safety in the city, and the functioning of transportation and all the public enterprises and institutions.[177] The city police captain gave permissions to public meetings but also for amateur theatre performances, if they used locales which were considered public. The city police was the first line of contact with the shadowy parts of the town, and its primary concern was to keep them "clean." So in his report for the second half of year 1902, the city police captain wrote that prostitution among worker women and house maids had reached large dimensions and that this posed a threat to the health and morals of families. He also gave reasons for this situation: low wages, relatively easy living, loosening of the family ties because of the worsening financial situation, almost no religious upbringing of girls in the workers' families and the military units stationed in the city providing regular customers. The captain claimed that this situation needed more drastic measures since also the numbers of tramps and child beggars had increased. The captain asked for an increase of his staff.[178] This report shows one concern of the city authorities about bad morals and the danger lurking in the shadowy parts of the city, where the poor lived which could infect the healthy moral life of the decent families. In the same way, tramps and beggars who did not reside in the city were transported out of the town. The city also had a workhouse whose name was changed in 1892 to the Asylum for the homeless (*Asyl für Obdachlose*).[179]

Apart from the municipal offices there was a net of charities and religious associations which were involved in the care of the poor. The activity of this kind of association went hand in hand with manifesting exemplary models of morality. So the *Frauenverein* (Women's association) which was founded as early as 1830, had as its aim not only to found kindergartens and homes for poor children, to exercise patronage over the children's hospital and to develop a range of charitable activities in favour of poor children and orphans, but also to ensure that they grew up into useful citizens with good morals who would not crowd the streets and beg, thus cleaning the streets of people who might "disturb" decent people.[180] This aim was put into words by the first patron of the association, Countess Therese Brunsvik: "... purposeful supervision and care for children of many poor people who are otherwise left quite to themselves, their protection from bad examples, their adaptation to obedience, customs and religious feeling, finally preparation for the elementary schools, and by this targeted prevention from begging on the street."[181] The idea was that "the greatest treasure of a community are good upright citizens" but this could not be achieved without "good upbringing."[182] The highest priority assigned to this goal was likened to a gardener sowing seed.[183] An improper upbringing and lack of good moral environment were considered direct sources of all the later vices.[184] The association proclaimed its "fight against idleness, emptiness of life, unregulated movement of the human spirit which were the basis of all those paths that ended in hospitals and lunatic asylums, poor houses and prisons."[185] Similarly as in Victorian England, "those with property assumed an intimate link between begging, crime and political disorder."[186]

The *Frauenverein* was only one of many charitable organisations in the city. There were also soup kitchens (*Volksküche*) offering cheap food to the poor; their menu was published in the daily local newspapers.[187] There was a large number of private charities and foundations, as well as charities of different religious communities.[188] In their power to distribute help, these institutions could also control and observe the behaviour of the poor, and act upon the internalisation by the poor of normative behaviour and good morals as defined by the middle classes.[189] Providing help was one of the reasons for the existence of these associations but other important considerations included preventing the poor from crowding the streets and integrating them into society by providing them means to be 'useful.' As Foucault has written, "their aims were religious (conversion and moralisation), economic (aid and encouragement to work) or political (the struggle against discontent or agitation.)"[190] Certainly the Catholic associations aimed at protecting their membership from atheism and the "evil" of social democratic ideas.[191] In nineteenth century Paris the members of charitable organisations even divided the city so that they could make regular visits to the poor and check their living conditions and also simultaneously inquire into morality and religious feelings.[192] Similarly, in Pressburg, the charitable organisations played their part in disciplining individuals so that they could become 'useful' for their community and nation, and did not undermine the accepted way of life and society by their abnormal behaviour, by their anomalies.

Another aspect of self-disciplining and mastery of the self was the great number of associations aimed at the physical improvement of the body. There were associations for gymnastics, cycling, football, fencing, rowing, tennis, horseback riding, shooting, winter sports. Typically, these associations were socially divided. For cycling there was a middle class as well as workers' association. Workers had their own gymnastics training. The rowing club was an elite club, connected with playing tennis. Similarly fencing, horseback riding, shooting had largely middle class membership.[193]

There were also a great number of lectures aimed at the improvement of the education level of Pressburg's inhabitants. These lectures were given by different associations, and every week there was an opportunity for the city's inhabitants to attend at least one (depending on the amount of leisure time which was again a matter of class.)[194]

The growing numbers of the poor especially workers in the city connected with increasing industrialisation required a solution. They had to be accommodated somewhere in order not to crowd the city. Thus at the turn of the century houses for the poor as well as workers' colonies were built. They were built by the city authorities, by factory managements or by private persons. It is important to consider their physical location in the city space. The houses of poor were built closer to the centre but not within the centre itself. The workers' colonies were mostly built around the factories which were out of the city, thus keeping the workers out of the centre as well as out of the richer parts of the town. The industrial areas expanded mostly into the north-eastern direction from the city while the new villa districts were built closer and on the southern hill of the Small Carpathian mountains.[195] Thus even the geographical location of these newer residential quarters was biased in favour of the rich, who lived in the southern parts of the town.[196]

By building houses for the poor and workers' housing (in Slovak referred to as 'workers' colonies'), neighbourhoods were created with their own rules and surveillance practices.[197] Neighbourhoods had their own rules and were usually 'transparent' places whose inhabitants could exert control over individuals' behaviour by sanctioning those who did not keep with the norms recognised by the dominant group. "Little tactics of the habitat" applied in these neighbourhoods. Small networks of relationships, knowledge and power were embedded and connected into the larger power networks and spaces of the city. Building the workers' housing also meant "prescribing forms of morality," and thus influencing the self-disciplining of the workers.[198] There were more workers than there were flats of a relatively high standard (especially in comparison with the crowded spaces the workers and poor usually inhabited). These better quality flats were often assigned to the qualified workers, perpetuating an upper strata even within the class of workers. While living in this accommodation meant an increase in the living standard of a working family, it also contained the possibility of blackmail on the part of the employer, especially in the case of strikes or demonstrations, by making the workers and their families even more dependent on the employer and therefore, vulnerable. It made them more liable to compromises in situations of conflict.

One of the most important philanthropists in Pressburg at this time who built the first model workers' housing in the city was Georg Schulpe.[199] His activities aiming at enhancing the living conditions of the workers are a good example of how the philanthropic and charitable activities of the elites contained also a self-disciplining and moralising aspect, and presented certain moral values. Schulpe's social model included all areas of life in which he strove for reforms. These areas were health (e.g. public hygiene, workers' living conditions, tuberculosis, alcoholism), economic protection and social care (insurance, Sunday- and night-work, women- and child-labour) and finally care for culture, morals and ethics (schools, cultural and educational institutions, libraries, associations, lectures.) He claimed that: "Only peaceful evolution, i.e. natural development without the use of violence is the path to the creation of a new social state ethical institutions which will be able to remove existing contradictions."[200] Schulpe strove to eliminate class conflict, and he wanted to do this by raising the standard of living of the workers by providing better living conditions which were not damaging to health but also by education carried out according to certain moral values. Schulpe was a member of the city municipal assembly and of the municipal social committee where he presented his reforms and proposals. His workers housing was exemplary. Every flat had a small garden. The housing area had also a library-reading room, washing room, a bath, room for the ill, museum and also a kindergarten. The reading room (or workers' casino) had on its walls colourful paintings with biblical themes. On the wall hung a portrait of the Saviour. The reading room had 3000 books and could be visited by workers on any evening or on Sunday.[201] Even the furnishing of the reading room was creating an atmosphere of morality.

Another important part of Schulpe's care for the culture and education of workers was the effort to found a so-called "People's home" (*Arbeiterheim, Népotthon*) so that the workers could be brought up to be as independent as possible. He envisaged a whole network of institutions—people's university, folk-libraries, cultural associations, committees for the education of workers associated to the Industrial and Trade chambers, and many more. The people's home was founded in Pressburg in 1911. In 1905 Schulpe brought into being another of his dreams—the workers' theatre, Urania.[202] These few examples show how humanitarian and philanthropic activities at the same time contained elements of control and moulded the ones who were objects of this help according to ideas of what was good and moral. Schulpe's aim was to shape the uneducated lower classes into independent citizens who would rely on the help of the community and state as little as possible.[203] According to Schulpe, living spaces shaped the character of individuals, and the atmosphere in the homes was decisive for children to acquire "noble and pure morals."[204]

It must be stressed that the lower classes did not constitute a homogeneous class or a solid group. On the contrary, the borders between different strata were constantly in flux. They were different individuals with different aspirations, caught in the net of surveillance, both the surveillance of the city authorities representing the better-off who felt threatened by the lower classes, and also in their own networks, neighbourhoods, small surveillances in their habitats. The lower strata as all other strata of the city population were subject to self-disciplining processes regulating their life and behaviour according to given norms, according to their various situations and aspirations. Thus those who aspired to move upward in the social structure, into the ranks of the qualified workers, clerks, maybe independent entrepreneurs, had to adapt more to the norm, to the Pressburger elite's notion of order: solid, hard-working, not wanting to overthrow the social order, not socialist, patriotic. The degree to which the lower classes had to adopt patriotism was different than it was for the middle classes. Although the national element played a role within the workers' movement especially after the turn of the century, and there were sections working in different languages within the workers' movement, putting themselves into the role of the Hungarian patriot was not necessary for upward social mobility, up to a certain point. And there was a diverse group of the poor who struggled just to survive, and who were not really forced to adopt such models of behaviour. They could afford to resist surveillances since they could not really afford anything else.

It is also important to keep in mind that there was a large number of the poor and workers who did not live in workers' housing and, therefore, did not have to deal with the kind of surveillance present in workers' housing and were less dependent on their employers. However, they also lived in neighbourhoods which had their own system of rules and norms. Most of them had to keep to regular rent payments and other rules present in common housing. They certainly were in need of help and, therefore, did not escape the normalising efforts of charitable organisations. However, the result of such normalising efforts was not always as the middle classes would have wished. As has been described in Chapter three, workers developed their own norm of 'respectability' which did not necessarily agree with middle class ideas of thrift and reasonable expenditure.[205] In this way the efforts of charitable organisations were not always successful and met with resistance which expressed itself in the adoption of different norms of respectability.[206] There was considerable diversity in circumstance and attitude among the popular strata which resulted also in different power relations and norms of behaviour. However, it is beyond the scope of this study to engage more than briefly with a topic which would require an entire study on its own. One can merely conclude that there were different degrees and extents to which internalisation occurred of presented models of behaviour, of reacting to surveillance, of watching neighbours. Individuals were caught in a web of power and knowledge relations, power and knowledge over them, over and about themselves and about other individuals to whom they related.

5. CONCLUSION

In this chapter I have looked at the ways in which surveillance worked in the Hungarian state and Pressburg county and city. By surveillance I mean not only the control of the state and city authorities over the population but also the self-disciplining aspect of this control which followed from the sanctioning of 'out of norm' behaviour, whether it happened in a legal way or by social discrimination.

However, power worked not only through the state and city authorities which were the most obvious carriers of power. Power is not only exercised over individuals but individuals themselves are submerged in a network of diffuse power relations. The connection between surveillance as control and the self-disciplining aspect can be seen both in the ideas of the elites about the desired models of behaviour of the citizens of Pressburg and in their own attempts to adjust themselves to norms accepted by state authorities. In this case it meant that the traditional power elite in Pressburg adapted to the model of the good Hungarian patriot, a requirement for upward social mobility presented as such not only by the state authorities but also by the new Magyar elite in the city.

Surveillance and self-governance worked not only between the county and city authorities and between the city elites and the middle classes but also downwards, to the lower strata of the population. The creation of a 'good city' meant getting rid of the 'bad city' which was not ordered, could run out of control and which was a hotbed of vice endangering the good morals of decent families. The good city was created not only by associations like *Stadtverschönerungsverein* which cared for the outward presentation of the city spaces and its neatness. There was also a network of humanitarian, charitable, religious associations and institutions who cared for the poor, their way of life and put their values in accord with the norm. The assistance provided by these institutions always went hand in hand with the 'normalising' of those who were being helped so as to make them self-reliant and good citizens. The municipality itself also possessed departments and committees dealing with the poor. The city doctor as well as other doctors of the Pressburg hospitals gathered information on living conditions and therefore, the 'moral conditions' in which the poor lived. The workers themselves accepted some of these elite and middle-class values and adapted to the norm, to varying degrees depending on their aspirations to social mobility. However, they also resisted surveillance and normalising efforts and created their own norms of respectability, different from the respectability of the middle class. In this way surveillance involved all of Pressburg's inhabitants in a interconnected and interdependent power network.

✂ CONCLUSION ✂

THIS STUDY HAS EXAMINED changing ethnic relations in Pressburg between 1867 and 1914, in a period marked by the onset of modernisation, industrialisation, urbanisation and developing mass movements. I have concentrated on the relationship between identity, politics and space in Pressburg and Hungary in order to show that Pressburg at this time was characterised by multiple loyalties and cultural identities, rather than the clear-cut ethnic identities that have often been assumed by nationalist historians and social scientists. The city was not segregated into ethnic neighbourhoods, was not violent, had its own "halt Pressburger" identity and was not receptive to the Pan-Slav or pan-German movement.

After the Dual Agreement between Hungary and Austria in 1867, like other nineteenth-century European states, Hungary began to build a nation-state. However, this goal came to mean a national Magyar state, rather than a Hungarian state defined by individual liberties and inclusive citizenship. While in Austria there was an effort to integrate minority nationalities (such as the Czechs) into the Empire, in Hungary integration meant assimilation and adoption of the Magyar language and culture. In the years before the First World War, the multicultural character of the Habsburg Empire came under increasing pressure. Ironically, the conflict appeared sharper in Austria with its more liberal policy towards nationalities than in Hungary, where the nationalities' movements were suppressed. The Habsburg Empire's dismemberment at the end of the First World War meant that new states were established on the principle of national self-determination but the new states themselves contained large ethnic minorities.

Amidst these growing conflicts and struggles Pressburg appeared to be a peaceful provincial town. However, the larger political struggles also affected local politics and power relations among the city's ethnic groups. The new Magyar elite in the city challenged the traditional German speaking elite, using the nationalistic rhetoric of the Hungarian state and its

Magyarising policies. Although the German speaking elites stressed their Hungarian patriotism and made no effort to counteract Magyarisation policies, they did not unconditionally accept the Magyarisation of the city. Power struggles and the renegotiation of conflicts and personal and collective identities were conducted on an everyday basis in Pressburg. The Magyar elite's attempt to Magyarise the city succeeded to some extent. However, many city inhabitants retained a specific, local 'Pressburger identity' characterised by loyalty to Pressburg, a lack of clear ethnic identification, and multilinguality.

Slovaks in the city could not be discerned as a special group and made no effort to assert themselves nationally. Thus they had more of a 'Pressburger' identity than a national identity. Those who did stand up for their Slovakness were mostly labelled 'Pan-Slavs' by the city elites. However, this was not always the case especially if those concerned were also *Pressburgers*. Very few members of the Pressburger Slovak middle classes were active in nationalist activity. Slovaks became most visible as a group within the workers' movement in Pressburg after the turn of the twentieth century which was also a time of renewal for Slovak politics in general.

The workers' and social democratic movement developed into a mass movement in Hungary after the turn of the century, becoming both an alternative form of identification and mobilisation for the working class as well as a source of concern for the Hungarian state. Growing industrialisation, in-migration of workers, and urbanisation in Pressburg from the 1890s onwards led to the growth of the workers' movement. The workers' educational association *Vorwärts* was founded in 1869, becoming the main agent of social democratic collective action in Pressburg until the foundation of the Social Democratic Party of Hungary in 1890. After the turn of the century, *Vorwärts* became a purely educational association and mobilisation of workers was done by the Social Democratic Party, albeit through informal networks. The leadership of the Social Democratic Party of Hungary did not pay enough attention to mobilising non-Magyar workers, who as a result created their own networks and periodicals. The ethnic question within the Hungarian social democratic movement created deep fissures within the movement: social democrats from the minority nationalities ended up supporting the ideas of their own 'bourgeois' national movements rather than supporting the international struggle against the bourgeois class and exploitative social system. By the onset of the First World War, the social democratic project of building an 'imagined community of class' had fractured into national 'imagined communities of language.'

However, the divisions between workers of different linguistic backgrounds were not very deep in Pressburg. German, Hungarian and Slovak workers coordinated their activities and cooperated amicably for the most part. Although most of the workers' leaders were multilingual, it is questionable whether they held 'Pressburger' identity since they did not have strong feelings of loyalty and ownership towards the city, tending instead to see the city more in terms of class conflict and unequal power relations that could only be resolved through universal suffrage. For their part, the city authorities and bourgeois inhabitants were initially afraid of the growth of the workers' movement, fearing violence and disruption of order. However, as peaceful and orderly gatherings of workers (such as the annual celebration of 1 May) became part of the city landscape and as the social democratic movement gathered strength, the initially negative attitude of the authorities began to take into account the demands made by the workers. Most conflicts were negotiated peacefully and bloody clashes with police or army did not occur in Pressburg.

'Pressburger identity' was also significantly influenced by the geographical location of the city within the national (Hungarian) and imperial (Habsburg) landscapes. Pressburg lay at the western edge of the Hungarian state and this frontier location gave the city a significant meaning in the iconography of Magyar nationalists. Efforts to incorporate Pressburg into the Hungarian national landscape can be seen on three levels: in the rhetoric employed by Hungarian patriotic associations like the *Toldy Kör*; more tangibly, in the form of the monuments that were constructed for the anniversary of the Hungarian Millennium, symbolically incorporating the city within the domain of the Hungarian kingdom and warning away outsiders; and in decisions that were made about infrastructure (such as the electric railway from Pressburg to Vienna) that emanated from geopolitical anxieties about Pressburg's ambiguous position at the Hungarian frontier. While Magyar nationalists envisaged Pressburg as a strong border castle defending Hungary from alien influences, they were also suspicious of the patriotism of *Pressburgers*. Pragmatic projects such as the proposed train line led to accusations that *Pressburgers* wanted to develop their relations with inimical Austrian Vienna rather than the "national heart" of Hungary, Budapest. Although the project was finally approved, the parliamentary debate shows how Pressburg was regarded as a place of multiple identities that was not considered "national enough" even as late as 1909.

A similar attitude of suspicion towards Pressburg's ambiguous identity can be seen in the debates on the borders and centre of the Slovak national territory that were taking place among the Slovak intelligentsia throughout the nineteenth century until the First World War. The Slovak national movement's inability to clearly demarcate the borders of its national territory was a major hindrance for the movement, as was the lack of a "national centre." While Martin partly fulfilled this role, it was more as a defensive nucleus rather than as the centre of Slovak national life. Although Pressburg had served as an important locale of national activity during the early period of the Slovak national revival, after the Slovak intellectuals and students left the city, national activity in Pressburg ceased and the city was not considered appropriate for a Slovak centre since it did not have a "nationally conscious" Slovak bourgeoisie. After the First World War, Bratislava's position as a capital was disputed again, mainly because of its multicultural character and the ambiguous character of identity and ethnic affiliation in the city.

Both the nationalities' and social democratic movements were closely monitored by the Hungarian state apparatus. As a modernising state, Hungary was keen to gather information on its inhabitants and territory, keeping an especially close watch on potential threats to the state's stability as represented by developing mass movements. The surveillance apparatus of the Hungarian state was particularly concerned with the social democratic and nationalities' movements because of the threat they posed (as alternative models of social organisation) to the nationalising state's ideal of a cohesive elite-led nation-state founded on Magyar culture. The state's surveillance activities entailed a constant flow of information between different levels of the bureaucratic apparatus, between the ministries, counties and towns and communities. However, this flow of information was not smooth and uninterrupted. The county elites often had their own agenda and power struggles, and did not necessarily implement the state's policies. Thus competing grids of power and knowledge were created, preventing the system from always functioning effectively.

In addition to external pressures exerted by the state (such as police forces, army, laws, and regulations) individuals themselves were key agents in making the working of power more effective by internalising social norms. Two normative models of socially acceptable behaviour were prevalent among the middle classes of Pressburg. One model (closely connected with 'Pressburger identity') was that of the 'good city', reflecting the values and ideals of the *burgher* 'city fathers.' This norm was expressed in the ideal of a "cultured person" who was actively involved in taking care of his city. However, actions taken for "good for the city" also often served the particular interests of the middle class. This model was multicultural, enabling the city's traditional elite to avoid growing pressures to identify with any one ethnic group. The other model, supported by the Magyar nationalist elite, was just the opposite in that it demanded ethnic identification and constant demonstration of Hungarian patriotism. This patriotism required uncritical love of Hungarian culture and language and increasingly also knowledge and active use of Hungarian. The Magyar nationalist elite was quick to point out if someone fell short of its model of a good Hungarian patriot, in this way acting as a non-institutional extension of the nationalising state's surveillance function. Both models operated flexibly in practice and people could identify with both or shift their loyalties. However, demonstration of Hungarian patriotism became a prerequisite for rising in the social hierarchy.

While the traditional and Magyar elites competed for power and positions in the city, they also projected their values upon the lower classes. In their attempt to banish the 'bad city' (thereby protecting their own social spaces and values), the middle classes tried to discipline and 'normalise' the working class and poor inhabitants of the city. Normalisation was achieved not only through municipal operations such as sanitation and city planning, but also through the growth of public departments caring for the poor and a net of charitable institutions and philanthropic projects which perpetuated and tried to instil the values of their supporters. These attempts to make the poor respectable were not always successful since the poor had their own norms of respectability that were often different from the values of respectability deployed by the middle class. Thus competing values and social norms penetrated in variable extents through different layers of the city's population, establishing competing and overlapping grids of knowledge and power.

This study has tried to show that the construction of identity is a complex process, involving the renegotiation of identification and affiliation in the context of everyday life. Attempts to categorise people into clear and mutually exclusive groups can be reductionist and simplistic perpetuations of Manichean historical visions. Certainly, this kind of categorisation of groups of people is convenient and desirable for those trying to gather people together in a collective movement. 'Othering' is an easy way to build cohesion among a group of people, by defining themselves against those who do not belong. Such approaches deny the diversity and richness of the possibilities of identification and how personal and collective identities change and shift. Conventional depictions of identity in the Austro-Hungarian Empire (such as traditional and communist historiography and social science, particularly in Central Europe) have tended to ignore the complexity of identity formation and the multiple possibilities for self-identification in the Habsburg *fin-de-siecle*. The dynamic interplay between the forces of modernity and the various reactions to modernity created space for diverse personal and group identities at the turn of the century. It is my hope that future studies will consider how the intellectual and cultural currents in this period coincided with the parallel processes of ethnic identification and the development of mass politics. Such an approach, intertwining the personal, political and spatial, might avoid and contest the ethnic reductionism prevalent in many discourses about nations and nationalism.

❧ APPENDIX ❧

Tables

Glossary of Names

Figures

Table 1: Population of Hungary by mother tongue, 1880–1910.

	1880		1890		1900		1910		1880–1910	
	Number	%	Number	%	Number	%	Number	%	Increase	%
Slovak	1,855,451	13.5	1,896,665	12.5	2,002,165	11.9	1,946,357	10.7	90,906	4.9
Magyar	6,404,070	46.6	7,357,936	48.5	8,651,520	51.4	9,944,627	54.5	3,540,557	55.3
German	1,879,772	13.6	1,990,084	13.1	1,999,060	11.9	1,903,357	10.4	23,585	1.3
Ruthenian	353,229	2.6	379,786	2.5	424,774	2.5	464,270	2.5	111,041	31.4
Other	3,263,081	23.7	3,538,567	23.4	3,760,736	22.3	4,005,916	21.9	742,835	22.7
Total	13,755,603	100	15,163,038	100	16,838,255	100	18,264,527	100	4,508,924	32.8

Source: Mésároš, 1995, p. 642. The total for 1880 and 1890 as well as some of the figures in the Increase column were incorrect in the original source and have been revised here.

Table 2: Population of (what became) Slovakia by mother tongue in 1880 and 1910.

	1880 Number	%	1910 Number	%	1880–1910 Increase	%
Slovak	1,489,707	61.2	1,684,681	57.7	194,974	13.1
Magyar	540,492	22.2	885,397	30.3	344,905	63.8
German	221,771	9.1	198,755	6.8	-23,016	-10.4
Ruthenian	78,781	3.2	96,528	3.3	17,747	22.5
Other	104,534	4.3	53,463	1.8	-51,071	-48.8
Total	2,435,285	100	2,918,824	100	483,539	19.8

Source: Mésároš, 1995, p. 643. Some figures in the Increase column were incorrect in the original source and have been revised here.

Table 3: Population of sixteen Upper-Hungarian counties by religion and mother tongue, 1880 and 1900.

| MOTHER TONGUE | Year | RELIGIOUS IDENTIFICATION | | | | |
		Roman Catholic	Greek Catholic	Evangel.	Calvinist	Israelite
Slovak	1880	1,142,701	87,160	298,024	9,426	19,115
	1900	1,314,195	94,803	320,736	9,833	9,603
Increase 1880–1910		15.0%	8.7%	7.6%	4.3%	-49.7%
Magyar	1880	440,408	32,073	30,127	169,434	59,283
	1900	621,757	52,526	55,860	197,977	88,183
Increase 1880–1910		41.2%	63.8%	85.4%	16.8%	48.7%
German	1880	107,707	228	46,026	694	82,393
	1900	113,629	305	39,226	622	73,812
Increase 1880–1910		5.4%	3.4%	-14.7%	-10.3%	-10.4%
Ruthenian	1880	790	115,418	14	11	3,441
	1900	1,647	135,578	7	73	2,284
Increase 1880–1910		108.5%	17.5%	-50.0%	563.6%	-33.6%

Source: Cambel et al., 1992, p. 494. Upper-Hungarian counties include all the counties listed in the Glossary except Komárom and Esztergom. In the following tables Calvinists are included in the category "Reformed."

Table 4: Population of Pressburg by administrative district of residence and by mother tongue, 1910.

Districts	Magyar	German	Slovak	Roman.	Ruthen.	Croat.	Serb.	Others	Total	Jews
I. Old Town	4,033	3,606	642	2	–	46	2	115	8,446	2,456
II. Ferdinand's Town										
Inner	4,992	4,705	1,240	2	–	42	2	156	11,139	1,170
Outer	691	538	123	–	–	2	4	26	1,384	56
III. Franz Joseph's Town										
Inner	5,744	4,642	1,038	8	–	69	4	346	11,851	1,109
Outer	106	214	76	–	–	8	–	1	405	–
IV. Theresa's Town										
Inner	3,954	6,172	2,275	2	1	41	5	150	12,600	2,135
Outer	89	285	173	–	–	–	–	9	556	11
V. New Town										
Inner	7,317	8,600	2,809	7	2	60	2	380	19,177	932
Outer	3,084	3,006	1,440	1	–	35	1	334	7,901	125
Total	30,010	31,768	9,816	22	3	303	20	1,517	73,459	7,994

Source: MSK, Vol. 42, p. 529. The table includes only civil population.

Table 5: Religious affiliations in Pressburg, 1869–1910.

	Roman Catholic	Greek Catholic	Greek Orthodox	Evangelical	Reformed	Unitarian	Israelite	Other	Total
1869	34,714	6	48	7,038	178	—	4,552	4	46,540
1880	35,308	25	53	6,939	509	—	4,966	206	48,006
1890	39,020	39	41	7,347	525	18	5,396	25	52,411
1900	49,107	100	49	8,292	1,139	18	7,110	52	65,867
1910	59,198	140	56	8,994	1,515	16	8,207	52	78,223

Source: Thirring, 1912, p. 64, MSK, Vol. 42, p. 155. For 1900 and 1910 total includes also army.

Table 6: Population of Pressburg by religion and mother tongue, 1900 and 1910.

	Roman Catholic	Greek Catholic	Greek Orthodox	Evangelical	Reformed	Unitarian	Israelite	Other
Magyar								
1900	14,594	28	8	1,813	923	15	2,717	4
1910	23,585	61	24	2,492	1,303	13	4,217	10
German								
1900	23,568	6	5	5,150	162	3	4,280	28
1910	23,445	10	19	5,288	126	3	3,865	34
Slovak								
1900	9,287	11	-	1,282	45	-	84	6
1910	10,403	11	4	1,129	37	-	86	3

Source: For 1900 MSK, Vol. 5, pp. 352–53, 356–57, 360–61. For 1910 MSK, Vol. 61, pp. 246–47, 250–51, 254–55.

Table 7: Marriages between members of the same ethnic group in Pressburg, 1900–1912.

| | | BRIDE AND BRIDEGROOM OF THE SAME MOTHER TONGUE | | | | |
	All Marriages	Magyar	German	Slovak	Other	Total
1900	631	102	240	66	8	416
1901	550	94	217	75	3	389
1902	596	82	232	71	6	391
1903	609	118	217	76	4	415
1904	664	153	230	89	7	479
1905	642	146	223	71	3	443
1906	645	180	229	67	4	480
1907	721	186	232	85	5	508
1908	671	178	234	81	3	496
1909	705	228	230	66	3	527
1910	647	202	208	53	5	468
1911	730	247	237	62	2	548
1912	759	247	230	66	5	548

Source: MSK, Vol. 7, pp. 30–31, 34–35, 38–39, 42–43, 46–47, 50–51, 54–55, 58–59, 62–63; MSK, Vol. 22, pp. 32–33, 36–37, 40–41, 44–45, 48–49, 52–53, 56–57, 60–63, 66–69, 72–73; MSK, Vol. 32, pp. 4–5, 36–37, 40–41, 44–45, 48–49, 52–53, 56–57, 60–63, 66–69, 72–73; MSK, Vol. 50, pp. 42–43, 46–47, 50–51, 54–55, 58–59, 62–63, 66–67, 70–71, 74–75, 78–79, 80–81, 84–87, 90–93, 96–97.

Table 8: Mixed marriages in Pressburg, 1900–1912.

	All marriages	Bridegroom with a Bride of Different Mother Tongue				Bride with a Bridegroom of Different Mother Tongue				Total
		Magyar	German	Slovak	Other	Magyar	German	Slovak	Other	
1900	631	87	68	41	19	46	97	58	14	215
1901	550	64	46	33	18	32	84	34	11	161
1902	596	92	56	35	22	47	111	39	8	205
1903	609	90	55	28	21	42	103	41	8	194
1904	664	90	51	20	24	37	101	38	9	185
1905	642	95	55	29	20	41	107	41	10	199
1906	645	82	45	20	18	27	96	36	6	165
1907	721	91	76	25	21	47	96	54	16	213
1908	671	83	49	21	22	38	82	40	15	175
1909	705	87	55	24	12	40	98	31	9	178
1910	647	88	55	20	16	41	94	38	6	179
1911	730	83	60	28	11	51	90	29	12	182
1912	759	100	57	26	28	39	110	48	14	211

Source: As for Table 8.

Table 9: Proportion of Jews in Pressburg in main occupational categories

	1900	1910
Agriculture	5.0	5.8
Mining, Metallurgy	—	—
Crafts	6.4	6.8
Commerce, Credit	49.3	45.8
Mining, Crafts, Transport	13.8	17.7
State & Church Employment, Public Employment, Free Professions	8.0	9.8
Army	6.3	4.4
Day Laborers	2.5	2.1
Servants	2.7	2.1
Pensioners, Other	12.0	9.9

Source: Glettler, 1988, p. 68.

Table 10: Proportion of different ethnic groups and Jews employed in education in Hungary.

ETHNIC GROUPS	1900	1910
Magyars	73.0	79.1
Germans	11.4	9.3
Slovaks	2.4	1.0
Romanians	8.0	6.2
Ruthenians	0.6	0.2
Croats	0.2	0.1
Serbs	1.7	1.7
Other	2.7	2.4
Jews	11.9	9.6

Source: Glettler, 1989a, p. 95.

Table 11: Proportion of ethnic groups and Jews in occupational categories in education in Hungary in 1910.

	Magyar	German	Slovak	Roman.	Ruthen.	Croat.	Serb.	Other	Jewish
Children reformatories	90.7	5.3	0.2	0.6	-	-	2.9	0.3	2.4
Elementary Schools	81.9	3.9	1.5	9.6	0.3	0.1	2.2	0.5	5.0
Higher public & Bürgerschulen	94.0	3.3	0.1	1.2	0.6	—	0.3	0.5	12.4
Teachers education Institutes	87.6	3.3	—	5.6	0.7	—	2.6	0.2	3.2
Higher girls' schools	90.5	4.3	—	—	—	0.2	2.1	2.9	5.9
Secondary schools	91.5	4.4	0.3	2.6	—	0.1	0.6	0.5	6.4
Universities	93.1	1.7	0.3	3.4	0.1	—	0.3	1.1	6.5
Professional Schools	91.8	5.3	0.4	1.6	—	0.1	0.2	0.6	15.2
Educators & Korrepetitoren	46.0	41.6	0.3	0.8	0.1	0.4	0.3	10.5	21.0

Source: Glettler, 1989a, p. 96.

Table 12: Proportion of Jews in intellectual professions in Pressburg in 1900 and 1910

	1900	1910
Employees in Economy	11.9	28.6
Employees in Crafts	24.8	24.6
Commerce Employees	42.7	42.2
Transport Employees	9.5	6.0
Lawyers	19.6	36.5
Employed in Public Administration	0.8	1.8
Employed in Juridical Apparatus	10.2	20.9
Church Employees	5.5	8.7
Employees in Education	12.6	11.6
Employees in Health Care	16.9	23.7
Physicians	30.8	45.9
Personnel in Public Service & Free Professions	10.3	10.6
Intelligentsia in Public Service & Free Professions	8.3	10.7

Source: Glettler, 1988, p. 67.

Table 13: Knowledge of Hungarian in different occupational categories in education in Pressburg in 1910.

	Magyars Speaking Only Hungarian	Non-Magyars Speaking Hungarian
Priests	none	8 (72.7%)
Chaplains	none	none
Nuns	3 (6.5%)	17 (65.4%)
Kindergarten Female Teachers	none	5 (all)
Elementary School Male Teachers	none	3 (all)
Elementary School Female Teachers	1 (1.5%)	3 (all)
Bürgerschule Male Teachers	3 (20%)	2 (all)
Bürgerschule Female Teachers	2 (8.3%)	4 (66.7%)
Secondary School Professors	3 (5.4%)	2 (all)
Private Teachers & Korrepetitoren	none	6 (all)
Governesses	4 (10.5%)	23 (59%)

Source: Glettler, 1989a, p. 99. Figures rounded to one decimal place.

Table 14: Participation of ethnic groups in main occupational categories in Pressburg in 1910.

	Magyar	German	Slovak	Other	Total
Traditional production					
Employed	367	703	265	56	1,391
Dependants	471	922	266	9	1,668
Industry					
Employed	4,933	9,214	3,320	693	18,160
Dependants	4,816	8,644	2,278	406	16,144
Commerce and Credit					
Employed	1,314	1,767	348	71	3,500
Dependants	2,037	2,011	277	47	4,372
Transport					
Employed	1,704	380	125	20	2,229
Dependants	2,970	871	224	16	4,081
Civil and church service & free professions					
Employed	2,064	687	281	122	3,154
Dependants	2,774	961	284	37	4,056
Army					
Employed	1,695	1,022	1,857	190	4,764
Dependants	383	433	23	37	876
Day Laborers					
Employed	197	351	286	13	847
Dependants	160	195	172	8	535
Pensioners, capital owners, self-employed					
Employed	889	1,276	105	69	2,339
Dependants	1,070	849	72	24	2,015

Table 14 (*continued*): Participation of ethnic groups in main occupational categories in Pressburg in 1910.

	Magyar	German	Slovak	Other	Total
Servants					
Employed	2,432	953	842	173	4,400
Dependants	115	107	41	5	268
Other					
Employed	358	411	252	29	1,050
Dependants	955	1,032	354	30	2,371

Source: MSK, Vol. 56, pp. 330–333, 346–349, 354–357, 362–365, 378–381, 386–389, 394–397, 402–405, 410–11, 418–419, 420–421. There are some differences between this and the Table 1 in Chapter one since here traditional production includes both agriculture and forestry, fishing and bee-keeping. Table 1 (Chapter one) in the category "Other" includes both "Other" and "Pensioners, capital owners, self-employed" from this table. There are also differences in the numbers in industry, commerce and credit and transport which, however, are also in the original source.

Table 15: Main occupational groups in civil service and professions in Pressburg.

	Total	Magyar	German	Slovak	Jewish	Magyars Speaking only Hungarian	Non-Magyars Speaking Hungarian
Civil service & free profesions	1,964	1,477	370	56	210	122	331
State administration	507	449	53	4	9	31	58
Judicial Affairs	263	236	20	5	55	7	27
Church Service	264	138	78	24	23	25	66
Education	555	409	118	6	61	27	95
Health Service	177	129	31	14	42	13	31
Science, Other Associations/institutions of Public Interest	46	26	19	1	1	2	19
Literature & Art	103	66	30	2	12	14	19
Other Free Professions	49	22	21	—	7	3	16

Source: MSK, Vol. 56, pp. 676–709. The category "Others" is not included in the table but is counted in the total. Similarly in Tables 16 and 17.

Table 16: Some important occupational subgroups in Pressburg in 1910.

	Total	Magyar	German	Slovak	Jewish	Magyars Speaking only Hungarian	Non-Magyars Speaking Hungarian
Magyars speaking Hungarian							
Landowners, above 1000KJ	19	15	4	—	1	1	2
Landowners, 100–1000KJ	40	26	12	1	13	—	12
Tenants, above 100KJ	29	16	13	—	27	—	9
Small landowners/tenants, 50–100KJ	12	7	5	—	3	2	2
Small landowners/tenants, 10–50KJ	71	16	50	5	1	4	42
Small landowners/tenants, 5–10KJ	86	14	71	1	2	5	65
Small landowners/tenants, under 5KJ	264	10	240	13	2	6	161
Agricultural Officials	42	33	5	2	12	4	4
Servants in Agriculture	183	68	35	78	—	25	81
Agricultural Workers	355	110	104	136	—	88	85
Officials in Forrestry/Coalburning	7	4	2	—	—	—	1
Help Personnel in Forestry/Coalburning	18	10	7	1	—	1	5
Officials in Mining/Metallurgy	—	—	—	—	—	—	—
Auxiliary Personnel in Mining/Metalurgy	1	—	1	—	—	—	1

(*Continued*)

Note: 1KJoch = 5,755m^2

Table 16 (*continued*): Some important occupational subgroups in Pressburg in 1910.

	Total	Magyar	German	Slovak	Jewish	Magyars Speaking only Hungarian	Non-Magyars Speaking Hungarian
Independent Craftsmen	2,905	753	1,688	374	373	108	1,056
Officials in Crafts	780	337	407	11	192	9	200
Auxiliary Personnel in Crafts	14,475	3,843	7,119	2,935	432	1,223	5,635
Self-employed in Commerce/Credit	1,239	294	816	64	611	10	492
Officials in Commerce/Credit	682	394	267	12	288	10	238
Auxiliary Personnel in Commerce/credit	1,579	626	448	233	487	100	619
Officials in Transport	419	375	288	2	25	21	39
Auxiliary Personnel in Transport	1,689	1,297	262	116	92	489	277

Note: 1KJoch = 5,755m2

Source: MSK, Vol. 56, pp. 434–605.

Appendix

Table 17: Some important occupational subgroups in civil service & professions in Pressburg in 1910.

	Total	Magyar	German	Slovak	Jewish	Magyars Speaking only Hungarian	Non-Magyars Speaking Hungarian
State officials	223	218	4	1	9	25	5
State small officials	38	36	1	—	—	2	2
County officials	50	46	4	—	—	1	4
County small officials	10	5	4	1	—	2	5
Municipal officials	130	102	26	2	—	1	28
Municipal small officials	40	29	11	—	—	—	11
Community/district notaries	—	—	—	—	—	—	—
Help notaries	1	1	—	—	—	—	—
Community small officials	—	—	—	—	—	—	—
Judges & attornies	42	41	1	—	1	1	1
Court/prosecutors/prison officials	52	51	1	—	—	4	1
Court/prosecutors/prison small off.	9	6	3	—	—	—	3
Lawyers	74	68	1	4	27	—	6
Assistant-lawyers/nominees	49	41	7	—	19	1	8
Law clerk/small officials	30	22	7	1	8	1	8
Priests	23	12	8	2	9	—	8
Chaplains & curates	10	5	3	2	2	—	3
Nuns	72	46	19	3	—	3	17
Kindergarten Female Teachers	17	12	4	1	—	—	5

(*continued*)

Table 17 (*continued*): Some important occupational subgroups in civil service & professions in Pressburg in 1910.

	Total	Magyar	German	Slovak	Jewish	Magyars Speaking only Hungarian	Non-Magyars Speaking Hungarian
Elementary School Male Teachers	68	65	3	—	3	11	18
Elementary School Female Teachers	68	65	3	—	4	1	3
Bürgerschule Male Teachers	17	15	2	—	6	3	2
Bürgerschule Female Teachers	30	24	6	—	5	2	4
Secondary School Professors	58	56	1	1	1	3	2
Private Teachers/Korrepetitors	11	5	4	2	4	—	6
Women Educators	77	38	33	1	6	4	23
Physicians	61	52	5	2	28	—	8
Chemists/Drugstore Owners	10	9	1	—	3	—	1
Chemists Assistants	30	26	2	2	3	5	3
Veterinary Surgeons	16	14	2	—	3	3	1
Midwives	43	17	16	9	4	2	12
Editors & Journalists	16	13	3	—	1	—	3
Actors	22	20	2	—	9	8	2
Actresses	21	21	—	—	2	5	—
Private Engineers	7	4	3	—	2	—	1

Source: MSK, Vol. 56, pp. 712–780.

Table 18: Out-migration from Pressburg, 1899–1913.

	Magyar	German	Slovak	Other	Together
1899–1904					
Absolute number	94	722	16	4	836
Percent	11.2	86.4	1.9	0.5	100
1905–1907					
Absolute number	109	186	89	—	384
Percent	28.4	48.4	23.2	—	100
1908–1913					
Absolute number	74	154	25	7	260
Percent	28.5	59.2	9.6	2.7	100
1899–1913					
Absolute number	277	1,062	130	11	1,480
Percent	18.7	71.7	8.8	0.8	100

Source: MSK, Vol. 67, pp. 18–19.

Table 19: Population of Budapest, Prague, Pressburg and Vienna, 1880–1910

	1869	1880	1890	1900	1910	Increase 1869–1910
Pressburg	46,544	48,006	52,411	65,867	78,223	31,679
% Increase		3.1	9.2	25.7	18.8	68.0
Prague	204,488	255,928	314,158	394,030	442,017	237,529
% Increase		25.2	22.8	25.4	12.2	116.2
Budapest	270,685	360,551	491,938	716,476	863,735	593,050
% Increase		33.2	36.4	45.6	20.6	219.1
Vienna	834,000	1,104,000	1,364,548	1,674,957	2,031,498	1,197,498
% Increase		32.4	23.6	22.7	21.3	143.6

Source: Cohen, 1987, p. 469, for Pressburg see MSK, Vol. 27, pp. 102–103 (for 1880 and 1890). For 1900: MSK, Vol. 1, p. 20*. For 1910: MSK, 1912, pp. 154–5 for all population, p. 529 for civil population.

GLOSSARY OF NAMES

HUNGARIAN	SLOVAK
Basin	Pezinok
Breznóbánya	Brezno
Dévény	Devín*
Dévényujfalu	Devínska Nová Ves*
Dunaszerdehely	Dunajská Streda
Förév	Prievoz*
Holics	Holíč
Hidegkút	Dúbravka*
Igrám	Igram
Károlyfalu	Karlova Ves*
Kassa	Košice
Komárom	Komárno
Körmöcbánya	Kremnica
Lamacs	Lamač*
Ligetfalu	Petržalka*
Liptószentmiklós	Liptovský (Svätý) Mikuláš
Malacka	Malacky
Malomliget	Mlynské Nivy*
Modor	Modra
Nagyszombat	Trnava
Német Próna	Nitrianske Pravno
Nyitra	Nitra
Oroszvár	Rusovce*
Esztergom	Ostrihom
(Pozsony)Beszterce	Záhorská Bystrica*
(Pozsony)Ivánka	Ivánka pri Dunaji
Récse	Račišdorf (Rača*)
Rózsahegy	Ružomberok
Ruttka	Vrútky

Szakolca	Skalica
Selmecbánya	Banská Štiavnica
Senkvic	Čaníkovce (Šenkvice)
Stomfa	Stupava
Szentgyörgy	Sv. Jur pri Bratislave
Szőllős	Vajnory*
Trencsén	Trenčín
Turócszentmárton	(Turčiansky Svätý) Martin
Vác	Vacov
Zólyom	Zvolen
Zsolna	Žilina

*These were separate communities (except Mlynské Nivy) which are at present part of the city Bratislava.

Hungarian counties which (or part of which) form the territory of present-day Slovakia:

HUNGARIAN	SLOVAK
Abaúj—Torna (megye)	Abovsko—Turnianska (župa)
Árva	Oravská
Bars	Tekovská
Gömör és Kis-Hont	Gemersko—Malohontská
Hont	Hontská
Komárom	Komárňanská
Liptó	Liptovská
Nógrád	Novohradská
Nyitra	Nitrianska
Esztergom	Ostrihomská
Hungarian	Slovak
Pozsony	Bratislavská
Sáros	Šarišská
Szepes	Spišská
Trencsén	Trenčianska
Turóc	Turčianska
Zemplén	Zemplínska
Zólyom	Zvolenská
Ung	Užská

HUNGARIAN	ENGLISH
Alsó—Ausztria	Lower Austria
Czehország	Bohemia
Felso Ausztria	Upper Austria
Stájerország	Styria
Karintia	Carinthia
Szilézia	Silesia
Horvát-Szlavónország	Croatia-Slavonia

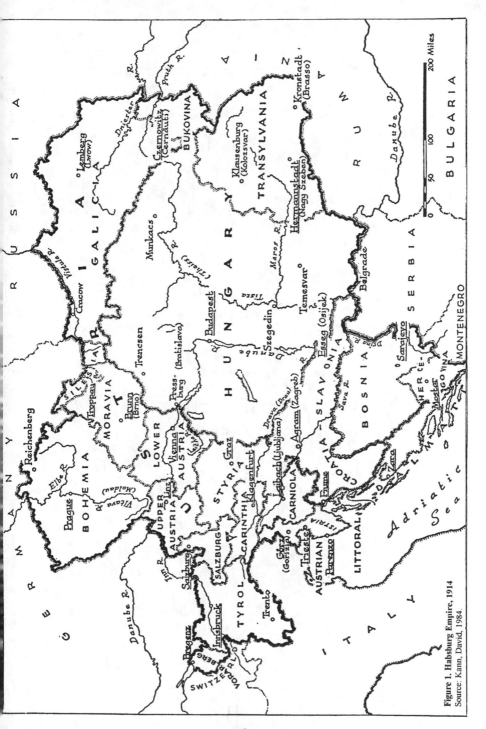

Figure 1. Habsburg Empire, 1914
Source: Kann, David, 1984.

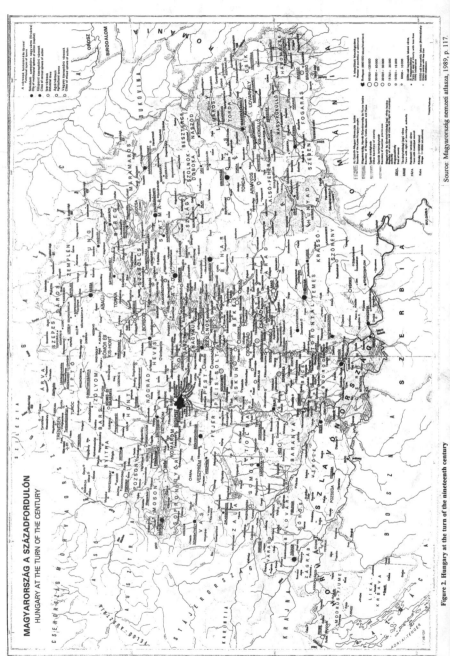

Figure 2. Hungary at the turn of the nineteenth century

Source: *Magyarország nemzeti atlasza*, 1989, p. 117.

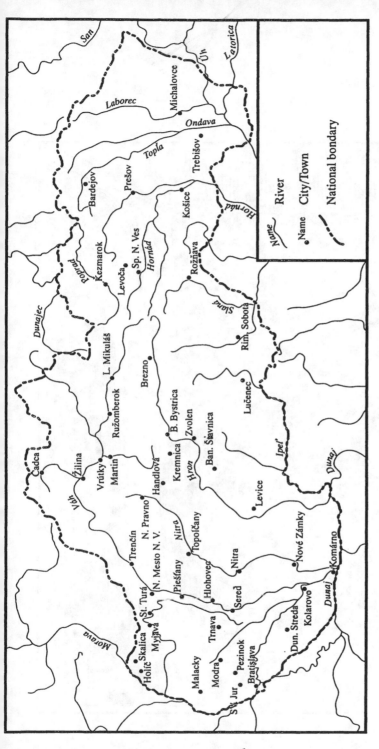

Figure 3. Present-day Slovakia

269

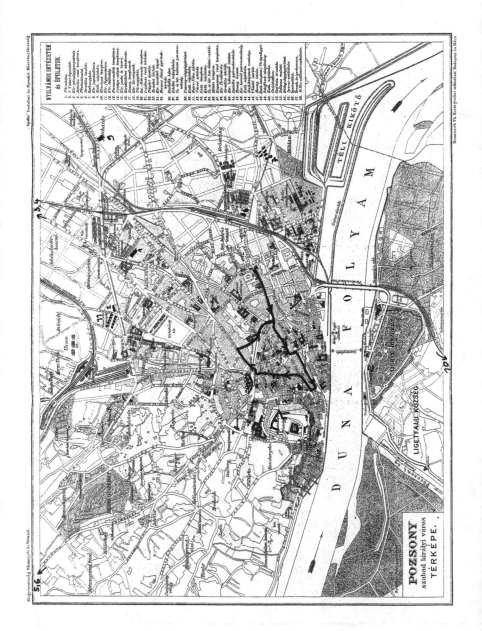

**NYILVÁNOS INTÉZETEK
és ÉPÜLETEK.**

1. *Városháza.*
2. *I. Vámház(pénztár.*
3. *Kir. pénzügyigazgatóság.*
4. *Zöldfa szálloda.*
5. *Államvasúti tanoda.*
6. *Pénzügyhivatal.*
7. *Postaszállás.*
8. *Kir. járásbíróság.*
9. *Kath. főgimnázium.*
10. *Kir. főgimnázium.*
11. *Kir. törvényszék.*
12. *Vármegyeház.*
13. *Ferencrendiek temploma.*
14. *Orsolya-zárda temploma.*
15. *Kir. posta és távírda.*
16. *Kereskedelmi akadémia.*
17. *Kaszinó-templom.*
18. *Kir. tanítónő-képző.*
19. *Kir. kórház.*
20. *Városmajor.*
21. *Szt. Háromság temploma.*
22. *Óváros.*
23. *Evangelikus templom.*
24. *Polgári dgszda.*
25. *Ferencrendi zárda.*
26. *Szidhh's háza.*
27. *Kir. honvéd parancsnokság.*
28. *Cs. és kir. hadmű parancsnokság.*
29. *Pannonia-szálloda.*
30. *Kath. székháza.*
31. *Matra-Táros-zárda.*
32. *Városi székháza.*
33. *Cs. és kir. közös hadsereg.*
34. *Hálda temploma.*
35. *Kir. tiszti és rendőr.*
36. *Izraelita iskola.*
37. *Evangelikus templom.*
38. *Evangelikus fögimnázium.*
39. *Izraelita gyermekmenhely.*
40. *Hegylakbeli vashálya.*
41. *Kir. honvéd parancsnokság.*
42. *Kath. népiskola.*
43. *Kath. templom (Virágvölgyi).*
44. *Városi szende.*
45. *Ligetfalu árvaház.*
46. *SzentJános-menhely.*
47. *Kath. népiskola.*
48. *Óváros.*
49. *Sürházak árvaház.*
50. *Izraelita kórháza.*
51. *Házakgyülekezet.*
52. *Iparos-emlékzah.*
53. *Kispalota.*
54. *Bersekö-ár parlamenta.*
55. *Redkézkárda szálloda.*

POZSONY
szabad királyi város
TÉRKÉPE.

LIGETFALU KÖZSÉG

D U N A   F O L Y A M

TÉLI KIKÖTŐ

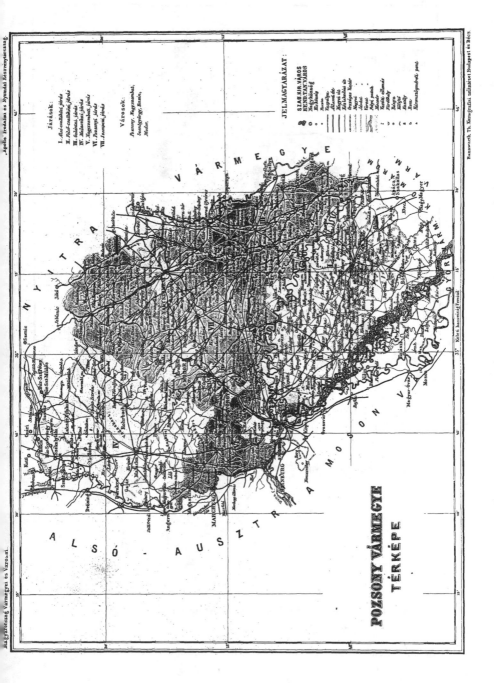

Járások:

I. *Alsó-csallóközi járás*
II. *Felső-csallóközi járás*
III. *Galántai járás*
IV. *Malaczkai járás*
V. *Nagyszombati járás*
VI. *Pozsonyi járás*
VII. *Szenpezi járás*

Városok:

*Bazin, Nagyszombat,
Szentgyörgy, Bazin,
Modor.*

JELMAGYARÁZAT:

SZAB. KIR. VÁROS
REND. TAN. VÁROS
Nagyközség
Kisközség

POZSONY VÁRMEGYE
TÉRKÉPE

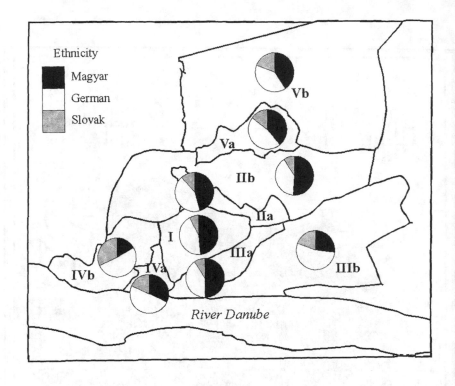

I. Old Town

II. Ferdinand's Town
   a) Inner
   b) Outer

III. Franz - Joseph's Town
   a) Inner
   b) Outer

IV. Theresa's Town
   a) Inner
   b) Outer

V. New Town
   a) Inner
   b) Outer

**Figure 6. Distribution of ethnic groups in the administrative districts of
Pressburg, 1910**

Source: Gletter, 1992, p.330 (figure outline), Table 6, Chapter one (proportions).

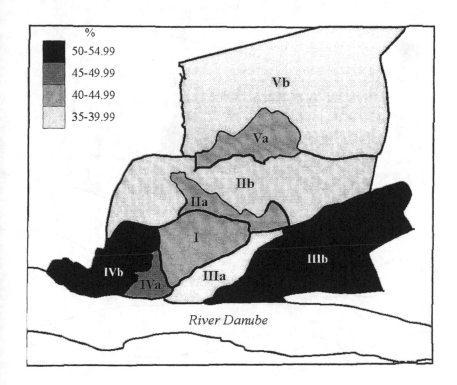

I. Old Town

II. Ferdinand's Town
   a) Inner
   b) Outer

IV. Theresa's Town
   a) Inner
   b) Outer

III. Franz - Joseph's Town
   a) Inner
   b) Outer

V. New Town
   a) Inner
   b) Outer

Figure 7. Proportion of Germans in total population of Pressburg by administrative district, 1910

Source: Gletter, 1992, p.330 (figure outline), Table 6, Chapter one (proportions).

Figures

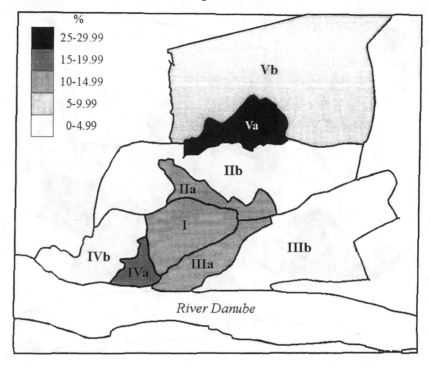

I. Old Town

II. Ferdinand's Town
  a) Inner
  b) Outer

III. Franz - Joseph's Town
  a) Inner
  b) Outer

IV. Theresa's Town
  a) Inner
  b) Outer

V. New Town
  a) Inner
  b) Outer

Figure 8. Distribution of the city's total German population in administrative districts of Pressburg, 1910

Source: Gletter, 1992, p.330 (figure outline), Table 6, Chapter one (proportions).

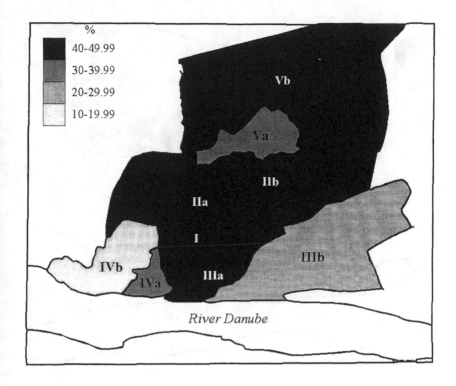

I. Old Town

II. Ferdinand's Town
   a) Inner
   b) Outer

III. Franz - Joseph's Town
   a) Inner
   b) Outer

IV. Theresa's Town
   a) Inner
   b) Outer

V. New Town
   a) Inner
   b) Outer

Figure 9. Proportion of Magyars in total population of Pressburg by administrative district, 1910

Source: Gletter, 1992, p.330 (figure outline), Table 6, Chapter one (proportions).

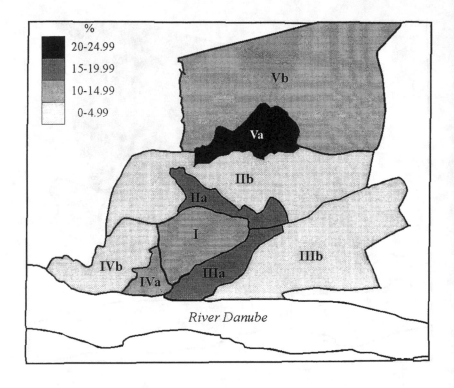

I. Old Town

II. Ferdinand's Town   IV. Theresa's Town
    a) Inner   a) Inner
    b) Outer   b) Outer

III. Franz - Joseph's Town   V. New Town
    a) Inner   a) Inner
    b) Outer   b) Outer

**Figure 10. Distribution of the city's total Magyar population in administrative
districts of Pressburg, 1910**

Source: Gletter, 1992, p.330 (figure outline), Table 6, Chapter one (proportions).

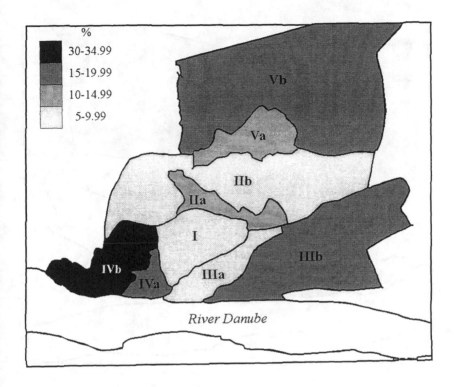

I. Old Town

II. Ferdinand's Town   IV. Theresa's Town
    a) Inner   a) Inner
    b) Outer   b) Outer

III. Franz - Joseph's Town   V. New Town
    a) Inner   a) Inner
    b) Outer   b) Outer

Figure 11. Proportion of Slovaks in total population by administrative district, 1910

Source: Gletter, 1992, p.330 (figure outline), Table 6, Chapter one (proportions).

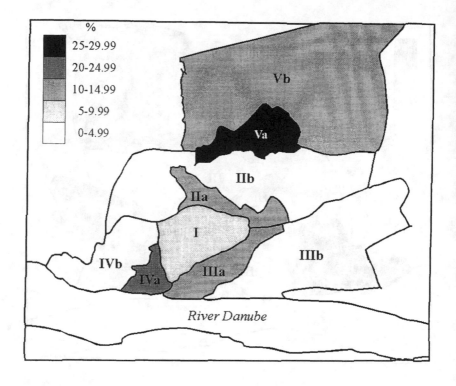

I. Old Town

II. Ferdinand's Town
    a) Inner
    b) Outer

III. Franz - Joseph's Town
    a) Inner
    b) Outer

IV. Theresa's Town
    a) Inner
    b) Outer

V. New Town
    a) Inner
    b) Outer

Figure 12. Distribution of the city's total Slovak population in administrative districts of Pressburg, 1910

Source: Gletter, 1992, p.330 (figure outline), Table 6, Chapter one (proportions).

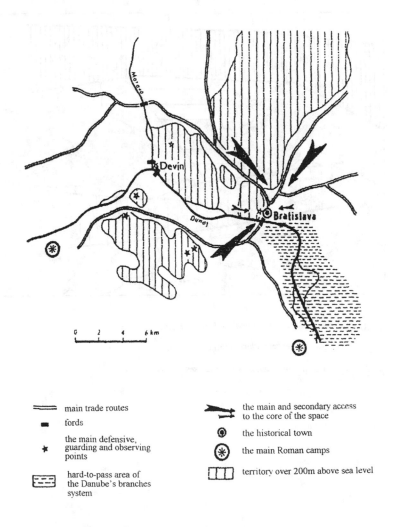

Figure 13. Historical static geostrategical situation in Bratislava's space

Source: Buček, 1995, p. 149.

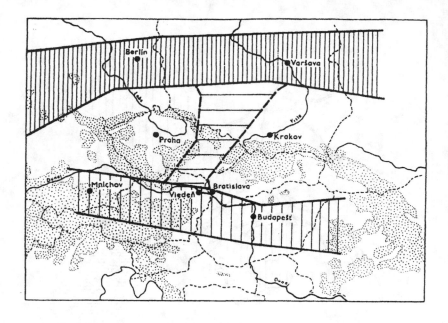

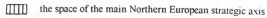

[IIII]   the space of the main Northern European strategic axis

[II]   the space of the secondary Southern European axis

[≡]   the space linking the two strategic axes

[:::]   territory over 500m above sea level

----   state border

●   selected towns

0   100   200 km

Figure 14. The main geostrategical axes in Central Europe

Source: Buček, 1995, p. 148.

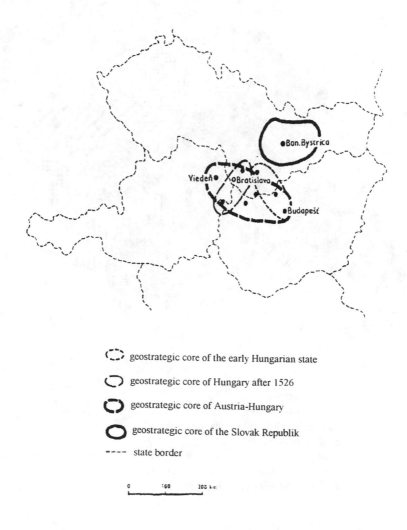

○⁼⁾ geostrategic core of the early Hungarian state

◯ geostrategic core of Hungary after 1526

◑ geostrategic core of Austria-Hungary

◯ geostrategic core of the Slovak Republik

- - - state border

0   100   200 km

Figure 15. Slovakia and the geostrategic cores in Danubian space

Source: Buček, 1995, p. 224.

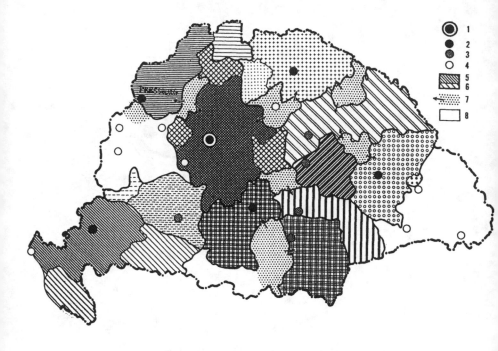

1. capital
2. full regional centre
3. partial regional centre
4. towns which also have regional functions
5. regional attraction areas
6. areas which are attracted with small intensity
7. areas which are attracted in more directions
8. undeveloped directions of attraction

Figure 16. (Hypothetical) attraction areas of the regional centres

Source: Beluszky, 1990, p. 53.

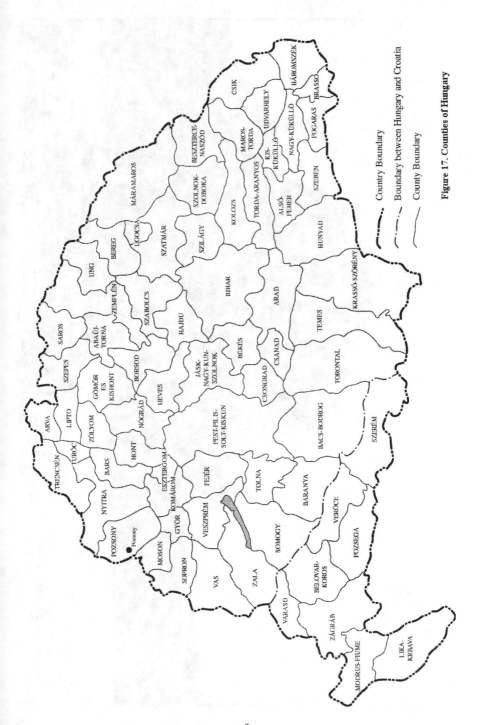

Figure 17. Counties of Hungary

Country Boundary
Boundary between Hungary and Croatia
County Boundary

Figure 18. Dévény millenial monument
Source: Mestské múzeum Bratislava

19. Maria Theresa monument in Pressburg.

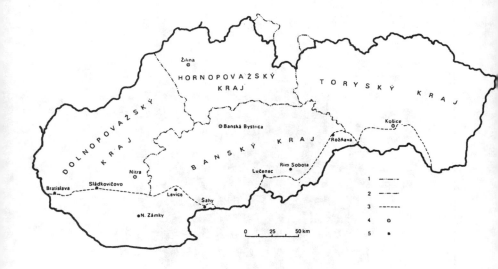

1. northern borders of Hungary different from the borders of Czechoslovakia
2. district boundaries
3. ethnic Slovak-Magyar border according to the Haufler's Sprachenkarte of 1845
4. district centres
5. settlements

Figure 20. Territory of the Slovak duchy (according to Ján Kollár's proposal in 1849)

Source: Žudeľ, 1980, p. 152, map 8.

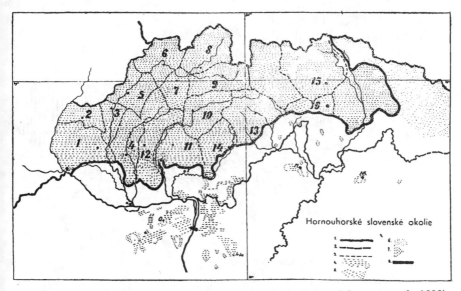

1. state border of Slovakia in 1920 (with correction in the Spiš and Orava areas in 1939)
2. boundaries of districts from the Bach era (southern boundaries of Bratislava and Košice districts)
3. boundaries of districts (counties) of the Upper-Hungarian Slovak Environs
4. continuous Slovak settlement
5. German settlement (the Spiš county remained indeterminate in terms of ethnic affililiation)
6. Ruthenian settlement
7. Magyar settlement
8. ethnic Slovak-Magyar border according to the nationalities' map of K. v. Czoerning of 1856

Arabic numbers mean districts:

1. Trnavský
2. Senický
3. Novomestský
4. Nitriansky
5. Trenčínsky
6. Žilinský
7. Turč.-sv.-martinský
8. Nižnokubínsky

9. Liptovskosvätomikulášsky
10. Banskobystrický
11. Bátovský
12. Zlatomoravský
13. Veľkorevúcky
14. Novohradský
15. Prešovský
16. Košický

Figure 21. Upper-Hungarian Slovak Environs

Source: Bokeš, 1945, p. 43.

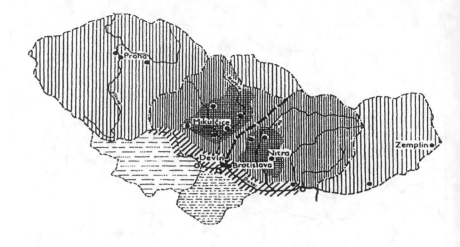

▥	the main territory of Great Moravia
▥	natural growth of Great Moravia
▨	geopolitical nuclei
▬ ▬	the boundary between the Moravian and Nitra parts
o	other important settlements
●	important settlements of Great Moravia
▭	the Eastern Mark
▦	province Avarorum
▨	the main conflict zone

0   50   100 km

Figure 22. Bratislava and the territory of the Great Moravian Empire

Source: Buček, 1995, p. 154.

↝ BIBLIOGRAPHY ↝

ARCHIVES

BRATISLAVA, SLOVAKIA
Archív mesta Bratislavy (Archive of the city Bratislava)

BRATISLAVSKÉ SPOLKY 1585–1956 (ZDRUŽENÝ INVENTÁR) (ASSOCIATIONS IN BRATISLAVA)

Toldy Kör, cartons 83, 84, 87, 88, 89, 91, 94, 96, 98, 99, 104

Meštianske Kasíno (City Casino), carton 54

MINUTES OF THE MUNICIPAL THEATRE COMMITTEE

Zápisnica zo zasadnutí divadelnej komisie, I. 1875–1880

Zápisnica zo zasadnutí divadelnej komisie, II. 1881–1885

Zápisnica zo zasadnutí divadelnej komisie, III. 1898–1919

MINUTES OF THE MUNICIPAL ASSEMBLY

Zápisnica municipálneho výboru, 1884, 1885, 1886, 1901, 1902, 1911

AMB, INVENTÁR SPISOVÉHO MATERIÁLU VII, 1790–1885 (INVENTORY OF THE CITY OF BRATISLAVA VII)

13298, 1878, 1370, List of persons who were permitted to change their name

13288, 1868, 1360, Decrees and instructions of the Ministry of Culture about the press and censorship of brochures, newspapers and books

Bibliography

AMB, Inventár mesta Bratislavy IX (Inventory of the city of Bratislava IX)

13718, 1886, 2112, Report of the mayor to the municipal assembly about important events which happened in the city in year 1903

13699,1904, 2113, Report of the mayor about important events in year 1904

13718, 1886, 2116, Elections into the municipal assembly (1892, 1895)

Pozostalosti bratislavských rodín a osobností, združený inventár (File Families and personalities of Bratislava)

Johann Nepomuk Batka

Štefan Fajnor st.

Slovenský národný archív (Slovak National Archive)

Uhorské ministerstvo vnútra v Budapešti, 1886–1918 (Hungarian Ministry of Interior)

UMV I. Prezidiálne spisy (tzv. Rezervátna agenda), inventory numbers 3, 6, 7, 8, 9, 11, 12, 14, 15, 16, 17, 18, 19, 20, 22, 23, 25, 41, 43, 53, 58, 63, 67, 69, 73, 77, 79, 81, 82, 83, 84, 88, 89, 90, 92, 121, cartons 1–22.

Sbierka Robotnícke hnutie na Slovensku a sociálna demokracia na Slovensku 1848–1919 (Collection Workers' movement in Slovakia and social democracy in Slovakia)

inventory numbers 8, 9, 10, 12, 13, 14, 16, 17, 18, 19, 20, 33, 34, 38, 39, 41, 44, 50, 57, 58, 61, 68, 70, 72, 77, 87, 109, 111, 113, 14, 116, 140, 141, 160, 167, 168, 184, 189, 269, 271, 276, 277, 281, 284, 287, 291, 293, 307, 311, 316, 317, 318, 319, 320, 321, 322, 323, 337, 352, 353, 361, 385, 387, 388, 390, 391, 392, 394, 399, 401, 403, 405, 406, 433, 434, 437, 439, 440, 442, 443, 452, 453, 454, 456, 457, 459, 460, 474, 477, 479, 481.

Budapest, Hungary

Magyar országos levéltár (Hungarian National Archive)

Thály család levéltára (Archive of the family Thály)

P 1747, Thály Kálmán

Szekció I. Belügyminisztérium (Ministry of Interior)

Bibliography

K 149 Rezervált iratok 1876–1914 (Confidential files)

Tétel 1 (Section 1): A munkás- és szegény parasztmozgalom, nemzetközi munkásmozgalom, anarchista mozgalmak (Workers and poor peasants' movement, international workers' movement, anarchist movement)

Tétel 2: Nemzetiségi és szomszéd országokkal kapcsolatos (irredenta) ügyek, pánszláv és pángermán mozgalom, német kisebbségi ügyek (Nationalities and matters concerning the neighbouring countries (irredenta), Pan-Slav and Pan-German movement, affairs of the German minority)

Tétel 6: Politikai mozgalmak, választási, gyülekezési ügyek. Dualizmus idején az egyetemi fiatalság mozgalmai. Antiszemita jellenségek, mozgalmak. Földvásarlási kérelmek. Szabadkőműves ügyek (Political movements, matters of elections and gatherings. Movements of university students during the dualism period. Anti-Semitic occurrences, movements. Applications for selling of land. Masonic matters)

Magyar Tudományos Akadémia, Történelemtudományi Intézet könyvtára (Library of the Historical Institute of the Hungarian Academy of Sciences)

Parliamentary sessions from the dualist period (published series)

Az 1906. évi május hó 19-ére hirdetett országgyülés képviselőházának naplója, Vol. XXI, Budapest, 1908:

334. parliamentary session 29.5.1908, pp. 282–283.

Az 1906–1911 évi országgyülés képviselő házának naplója, Vol. XXV, Budapest, 1909:

442. parliamentary session 19.3.1909, pp. 130–141.

443. parliamentary session 22.3.1909, pp. 142–163.

444. parliamentary session 23.3.1909, pp. 164–177.

445. parliamentary session 24.3.1909, p. 189.

450. parliamentary session 15.4.1909, p. 302.

453. parliamentary session 10.7.1909, p. 325.

STATISTICAL YEARBOOKS

Magyar statisztikai közlemények (1902, 1904, 1907, 1909, 1912, 1913, 1915, 1916, 1918), Volumes 1, 2, 5, 27, 42, 48, 56, 61, 67, Budapest: A Magyar királyi központi statisztikai hivatal.

MSK, the new series (used only for tables in Appendix):

MSK, Vol. 7, *A Magyar szent korona országainak 1900., 1901. és 1902. évi népmozgalma,* Budapest: A Magyar királyi központi statisztikai hivatal, 1905.

MSK, Vol. 22, *A Magyar szent korona országainak 1903., 1904. és 1905. évi népmozgalma,* Budapest: A Magyar királyi központi statisztikai hivatal, 1907.

MSK, Vol. 32, *A Magyar szent korona országainak 1906., 1907. és 1908. évi népmozgalma,* Budapest: A Magyar királyi központi statisztikai hivatal, 1910.

MSK, Vol. 50, *A Magyar szent korona országainak 1909., 1910., 1911. és 1912. évi népmozgalma,* Budapest: A Magyar királyi központi statisztikai hivatal, 1916.

LAWS

1868: XLIV. törvény-czikk a nemzetiségi egyenjoguság tárgyában (Law XLIV/1868 about the equality of nationalities), in Dezső Márkus (ed.), Magyar törvénytár, 1836–1868 évi törvényczikkek, Budapest, 1896, pp. 490–494.

1870: XLII o sriadení jurisdikcií, in Sbierka krajinských zákonov z r. 1870 (Law XLII/1870 about the establishment of jurisdictions), Vol. I, Budapešť, without the year of publication, pp. 175–201.

1898: IV. törvény-czikk a község és egyéb helynevekről (Law IV/1898 about the names of communities and other geographical names), in Dezső Márkus (ed.), Magyar törvénytár, 1898 évi törvényczikkek, Budapest, 1899, pp. 19–21.

1909: XIX. törvény-czikk a pozsony-országhatárszéli helyi érdekű villamos vasut engedélyézéséről (Law XIX/1909 about the Pozsony—state border electric railway of local interest), in Dezső Márkus (ed.), Magyar törvénytár, 1909 évi törvényczikkek, Budapest, 1910, pp. 332–341.

1912: XXXVI. törvény-czikk a debreczeni és pozsonyi magyar királyi tudomány egyetem felállításáról (Law XXXVI/1912 about the establishment of royal universities in Debreczen and Pozsony), in Dezső Márkus (ed.), Magyar törvénytár, 1912 évi törvényczikkek, Budapest, 1913, pp. 512–525.

CONTEMPORARY LITERATURE

...*A Toldy Kör...a pozsonyi egyetemért* (Toldy Kör ... for the university of Bratislava), Pozsony, 1908.

Magyarország vármegyei és városai. Pozsony vármegye. (Counties and towns of Hungary. County of Pozsony), series edited by Samu Borovszky, Budapest: Apollo irodalmi társaság, without the year of publication.

Pozsony sz. kir. város törvényhatóságának a magyar országgyülés képviselőházához intézett emlékirata a Pozsonyban fölállítandó egyetem tárgyában (Memorandum of the municipal assembly of Pozsony, royal free town, addressed to the house of the Hungarian parliament in the matter of the university that should be built here) (1880), Pozsony.

Presburger Wegweiser, 1867–1914

Révay Nagy Lexikon (1911) Vols. II, X, Budapest.

Angermayer, Károly (1896) *Pressburger Zeitung története* (History of the Pressburger Zeitung), Pozsony.

Celler, Ferdinand (1916) *Zur Geschichte der Loge "Verschwiegenheit" Orient Pressburg* (To the history of the masonic loge "Secrecy"), Pozsony-Pressburg.

Engyeli, Eugen (1897) *Festschrift zur Enthüllung des Pressburger Krönungdenkmales am 16. Mai 1897* (Commemorative volume to the unveiling of the coronation monument in Pressburg on 16 May 1897), Pozsony.

Fischer, Jakab (1894) *Legujabb statisztikai adatok Pozsony város lakosságáról* (The latest statistical data about Pozsony), Pozsony.

Fischer, Jakab (1902) *Pozsony város népességének haladása az utolsó évtizedben* (Changes in the population of the city of Pozsony in the last decade), Pozsony.

Bibliography

Fischer, Jakab, Ortvay, Tivadar and Polikeit, Károly (1907), *1856–1906 emlék-mű, kiadja a Pozsony Orvos-természettudományi egyesület fennállásának ötvenedik évfordulója alkalmából* (1856–1906 memorial work, issued by the Pozsony association for medicine and natural sciences on its fiftieth anniversary), Pozsony.

Geist, Karl (1882) *Die Strassentumulte in Pressburg* (Street riots in Pressburg), Budapest.

Győrik, Martin (1918) *Die fünfzigjährige Geschichte des Pozsonyer Stadtver-schönerungsvereins* (Fifty-year-history of the City beautification association in Pozsony), Pozsony.

Hirschmann, Nándor (1909) *A pozsonyi ágostai hitvallású evangelikus liceum értesitője az 1908–1909iki tanévről* (Yearbook of the Evangelic Lyceum in Pozsony for the academic year 1908–1909), Pozsony.

József Körösi (ed.) (1891) *Megyei monográfiák* (County monographies), Vol. I, Budapest.

Kumlik, Emil (1905) *A Pozsonyi Toldy Kör harmincéves története* (Thirty-year-history of the Pozsonyer Toldy Kör), Pozsony.

Lövö, Rudolf (1904) *Dreissig Jahre Pressburger Journalistik* (Thirty years of Pressburger journalism), Pozsony.

Ludwig, János (1911) *Pozsony mint a nyugatmagyarországi ipar támaszpont-ja* (Pozsony as the support point of the Western Hungarian industry), Pozsony.

Niederle, Lubor (1903) *Národopisná mapa uherských Slováků na základě sčítání lidu roku 1900* (Ethnographic map of the Hungarian Slovaks on the basis of the 1900 census), Praha: Lubor Niederle.

Ortvay, Tivadar (1884) *Száz és egy év egy hazai főiskola életéből* (Hundred and one years from the life of a home university) Budapest.

Ortvay, Tivadar (1892–1903) *Pozsony város története, I-IV* (History of the city of Pressburg), Pozsony.

Ortvay, Tivadar (1905) *Pozsony város utcái és terei* (Streets and squares of the city of Pozsony), Pozsony: Wigand.

Ortvay, Tivadar (1907) "Pozsony városának kulturális haladása az utolsó ötven évben (Cultural development of the city of Pozsony in the last fifty years)," in Fischer, Ortvay and Károly, *1856-1906 emlékmű, kiadja a Pozsony Orvos-természettudományi egyesület fennállásának ötvenedik évfordulója alkalmából*, pp. 1–44.

Pisztóry, Mór (1891) "Pozsony városa (City of Pozsony)," in József Körösi (ed.), *Megyei monográfiák*, pp. 57–130.

Pávai-Vajna, Gábor (1884), *Pozsony és a harmadik egyetem* (Pozsony and the third university), Pozsony.

Pávai-Vajna, Gábor (1887) *Hol állitsuk fel a harmadik egyetemet?* (Where shall we build the third university?), Pozsony.

Schmidt K. J., Ebner G., Markusovszky S., Freuszmuth F. (1906) *A pozsonyi ág. hitv. ev. egyházközség története, II. rész: Az egyház belső élete és intézményei* (History of the Pozsonyer Evangelical church, II. part, The inner life of the church and its institutions), Pozsony.

Schulpe, György (1893) *Pozsony és a harmadik egyetem* (Pozsony and the third university), Pozsony.

Stodola, Emil (1912), *Štatistika Slovenska* (Statistics of Slovakia), Turčiansky Svätý Martin.

Thály, Kálmán (1898) *Az ezredévi országos hét emlékoszlop története* (History of the seven millenial monuments), Pozsony.

Thirring, Gusztáv (1912) *A magyar városok statisztikai évkönyve* (The yearbook of the Hungarian towns), Vol. 1, Budapest.

Viator, Scotus (1908) *TheRacial Problems in Hungary*, London.

Wolff, Gregor (1903) *Die Pozsony-Wiener elektrische Bahn* (The electric railway Pozsony-Wien), Pozsony.

Wolff, Gregor (1907) *Die Entwicklung unseres Nordwestlichen Eisenbahn-Netzes* (Development of our northwestern railway network), Pozsony: A pozsonyi kereskedelmi—és iparkamara.

Wolff, Gerő (without the year of publication) *Előterjesztés a pozsony-határszéli villamos h.é.vasútról* (Proposal of the electric railway from Pozsony until the state border).

CONTEMPORARY ARTICLES

CIRKEVNÉ LISTY

CL, 24, 6, 1910, p. 206, "Kníhkupeckonakladateľský a kníhtlačiarsky spolok (Publishing, printing and book-selling association)."

CL, 24, 7, 1910, p. 221, "Z prešporskej teologickej akadémie (From the theological academy in Prešporok)."

KATOLÍCKE NOVINY

KN, 10.3.1905, N. 11, p. 5, "Prešporok."

ĽUDOVÉ NOVINY

ĽN, 16.1.1903, N. 3, pp. 3–4, "Prešporok."

ĽN, 14.9.1906, N. 38, p. 5, "Prešporok."

ĽN, 2.1.1908, N. 1, pp. 1–2, "Ruch Slovákov v Prešporku (Slovak life in Prešporok)."

NÁRODNIE NOVINY

NN, 30.4.1901, N. 50, p. 3, "Prešporskí študenti (Prešporok's students)."

NN, 28.3.1901, N. 37, p. 3, "Nemecké divadlo v Prešporku (The German theatre in Prešporok)."

NN, 3.1.1903, N. 1, p. 4, "Prešporok."

NN, 22.3.1904, N. 37, p. 3, "Z Prešporka (From Prešporok)."

NAPRED

Napred, 15.9.1906, N. 1, p. 1, leading article.
    pp. 1–2, "Bratia kresťanskí robotníci! (Brothers Christian workers!)."

Napred, 15.11.1906, N. 3, p. 3, "Chýrnik (News column)."
    p. 3, "Perzekúcia (Persecution)."
    p. 5, "Slovenské ľudové zhromaždenie (Slovak people's gathering)."

Napred, 15.12.1906, N. 4, p. 7, "Persekúcia (Persecution)."

Napred, 15.1.1907, N. 1, pp. 2–3, "Sociálna demokracia a náboženstvo (Social democracy and religion)."
    p. 3, "Slováci v uhorskej politike (Slovaks in the Hungarian politics)."
    pp. 3–4, "Čo chcú socialisti? (What do socialists want?)."

Napred, 15.2.1907, N. 2, p. 8, "Slobodná Škola (Free school)."

Napred, 15.4.1907, N. 4, pp. 1–2, "Žena a sociálna demokracia (Woman and social democracy)."

Napred, 15.5.1907, N. 5, p. 1, "Naša taktika (Our tactic)."

Napred, 15.6.1907, N. 6, pp. 2–4, "Konajte svoju povinnost (Do your duty)." p. 3, "Mäknutie mozgov (Softening of brains)."

Napred, 15.9.1907, N. 7, p. 3, "Klerikálna politika (Clerical politics)."

Napred, 15.10.1907, N. 10, p. 3, "Sloboda tlače a shromažďovania sa v Uhorsku (Freedom of press and gathering in Hungary)."

Napred, 15.11.1907, N. 11, p. 6, "Chýrnik (News column)."

Napred, 15.1.1908, N. 1, p. 1, "Ohlas na slovenských sociálnych demokratov Uhorska (Response to the Slovak social democrats of Hungary)."

Napred, 15.2.1908, N. 2, p. 1, "Pred zjazdom (Before the congress)." p. 10, "Naša tlač (Our press)."

Napred, 15.5.1908, N. 5, pp. 2–3, "Úvaha ku sjazdu sociálno-demokratickej strany Uhorska (Reflecting about the congress of the Social Democratic Party of Hungary)."

Napred, 16.9.1908, N. 9, p. 4, "Robotníctvo a náš program (Workers and our program)."

Napred, 15.10.1908, N. 10, p. 6, "Račišdorf."

Napred, 17.11.1908, N. 11, p. 8, "Organizačné záležitosti (Organisational matters column)."

Napred, 16.12.1908, N. 12, p. 8, "Chýrnik".

NYUGATMAGYARORSZÁGI HIRADÓ

NH, 6.2.1891, N. 29, p. 2, "Román tüntetés a kisdédóvó törvényjavaslat ellen (Romanian demonstration against the bill about kindergartens)."

NH, 30.4.1893, N. 99, pp. 1–2, "Május elseje (The first of May)."

NH, 20.4.1895, N. 91, pp. 1–2, "Szinügy (The matter of the theatre)."

NH, 1.5.1897, N. 99, pp. 1–2, "A munkásünnep (The workers' holiday)."

NH, 1.5.1902, N. 100, p. 1, "Május elseje."

NH, 1.7.1902, N. 148, p. 3, "Magyarosodunk (Magyarisation is progressing)."

NH, 10.10.1907, N. 232, p. 4, "Október tizedike Pozsonyban (10 October in Pozsony)."

Pozsonyvidéki Lapok

PL, 11.7.1875, N. 55, pp. 211–212, "A magyar szinészet ügye (The matter of the Hungarian theatre)."

PL, 18.7.1875, N. 57, pp. 219–220, "Még egyszer a magyar színeszetről (Once more about the Hungarian theatre)."

Pressburger Tagblatt

PT, 27.4.1906, N. 3533, p. 2, "Die nazionalistiche Agitation (Nationalistic agitation)."

PT, 27.9.1907, N. 4030, pp. 1–2, "Der moderne Kreuzzug! (The modern crusade!)."

PT, 10.10.1907, N. 4043, p. 2, "Zum 10. Oktober (To the 10th October)."

Pressburger Zeitung

PZ, 31.3.1869, N. 72, pp. 2–3, "Die Arbeiterversammlung in Pressburg am 29. März (Workers' public meeting in Pressburg on 29 March)."

PZ, 22.1.1870, N. 17, p. 3, "Resultate der Volkszählung (Results of the census)."

PZ, 30.11.1880, N. 275, p. 1, "Die 1881-er Volkszählung (The 1881 census)."

PZ, 30.12.1880, N. 304, p. 1, "Zur Volkszählung (About the census)."

PZ, 24.1.1881, N. 23, p. 1, "Volkszählung 1880."

PZ, 9.6.1882, N. 157, *Ab*, p. 3, "Volksversammlung im Speneder'schen Gasthaus vom 8. Juni (Public meeting in the Speneder's inn)."

PZ, 27.4.1890, N. 115, *Mb*, p. 1, "G'schossen hab'n's'! (They were shooting!)."

PZ, 29.4.1890, N. 117, *Ab.*, p. 2, "Der erste Mai (The first of May)."

PZ, 6.12.1890, N. 335, p. 3, "Zur Volkszählung."

PZ, 22.1.1891, N. 22, *Mb*, p. 2, "Volkszählung."

PZ, 1.2.1891, N. 32, *Mb*, p. 4, "Arbeiterball (Workers' ball)."

PZ, 19.4.1895, N. 106, *Mb*, p. 2, "Die Zukunft des Pressburger Theaters (Future of the Pressburger theatre)."

PZ, 15.12.1900, N. 342, *Mb*, p. 2, "Instruktionen zur Volkszählung (Instructions for the census)."

PZ, 16.12.1900, N. 343, *Mb*, p. 2, "Zur Volkszählung."

PZ, 1.9.1902, N. 241, *Ab*, pp. 2–3, "Der Demonstrationsumzug und die Monstre-Volksversammlung (Demonstration and monster-rally)."

PZ, 31.12.1903, N. 358, *Mb*, p. 2, "Zur Krise des ungarischen Theaters in Pozsony (To the crisis of the Hungarian theatre in Pozsony)."

PZ, 10.10.1907, N. 278, *Mb*, p. 1, "Allgemeines Wahlrecht (Universal suffrage)."

PZ, 9.1.1908, N. 8, *Mb*, p. 4, "Theater."

PZ, 13.1.1908, N. 12, *Ab*, pp. 1–2, "Ordentliche Jahresgeneralversammlung des städtischen Bürgervereines vom 12 Januar 1908 (The annual general assembly of the city's *Bürgerverein*)."

PZ, 17.1.1908, N. 16, *Mb*, p. 2, "Konferenz in Angelegenheit des Pozsonyer Theaters (Meeting in the matter of the Pozsonyer theatre)."

PZ, 2.10.1908, N. 271, *Mb*, p. 2, "Kultus und Unterrichtsminister Exzellenz Graf Albert Ápponyi—Ehrenbürger der kgl. Freistadt Pozsony (Minister of education and culture his excellency Count Ápponyi—honorary citizen of the royal free town of Pozsony)."

PZ, 24.1.1911, N. 24, *Mb*, p. 1, "Das Ergebnis der Volkszählung in Pozsony (Results of the census in Pozsony)."

PRÚDY
Prúdy, 1, 7, 1909/10, pp. 185–186, "Zo života prešporskej mládeže (From the life of the youth in Prešporok)."

Prúdy, 1, 9–10, 1909/10, pp. 287–289, "Z Prešporka (From Prešporok)."

Prúdy, 1, 1,1909/10, p. 19, "Prešporská mládež (The youth in Prešporok)."

Prúdy, 2, 2, 1910/11, pp. 80–83, "Vyhodenci (The expelled)."

Prúdy, 2, 2, 1910/11, pp. 79–80, "Z Prešporka."

Prúdy, 3 , 1, 1911/12, p. 35, "Z Prešporka."

SLOVENSKÉ ROBOTNÍCKE NOVINY (later only ROBOTNÍCKE NOVINY)
RN, 1.5.1909, N. 5, p. 1, "Náš týždenník (Our weekly)"
p. 5, "Zo súdnej siene (From the court room)."

RN, 17.6.1909, N. 12, pp. 2–3, "Jubileum memorandumu (Anniversary of the Memorandum)."

RN, 22.7.1909, N. 17, p. 5, "Chýrnik (News column)."

RN, 12.8.1909, N. 20, p. 6, "Organizačné záležitosti (Organisational matters column)."

RN, 9.12.1909, N. 37, p. 1, "Národnostná strana a jej politika (Nationalities' Party and its politics)."

RN, 30.12.1909, N. 40, p. 3, "Naša tlač (Our press)."
p. 5, "Dopisy (Letters column)."

RN, 13.1.1910, N. 2, p. 5, "Chýrnik."

RN, 24.2.1910, N. 8, p. 6, "Organizačné záležitosti."

RN, 7.4.1910, N. 14, pp. 1–2, "Krajinská konferencia (Hungarian conference)."

RN, 14.4.1910, N. 15, p. 4, "Z odborného hnutia (From the trade union movement)."

RN, 28.4.1910, N. 17, p. 6, "Májová oslava (May celebration)."

RN, 5.5.1910, N. 18, p. 4, "Bjönsterne Bjornson."

RN, 8.9.1910, N. 36, p. 1, "Medzinárodný socialistický sjazd v Kodani (The international socialist congress in Copenhagen)."

RN, 3.11.1910, N. 44, p. 1, "Čo máme robiť? (What shall we do?)."

RN, 2.3.1911, N. 9, pp. 2–3, "Od kosmopolitictva k nacionalizmu (From cosmopolitanism to nationalism)."

RN, 27.4.1911, N. 17, p. 7, "O sjazdoch sociálno-demokratickej strany v Uhorsku (About the congresses of the Social Democratic Party in Hungary)."

RN, 5.5.1911, N. 18, p. 1, "Májová oslava."

RN, 12.5.1911, N. 19, p. 3, "Milan Hodža."
p. 7, "Dľa martinských Národných Novín (According to the Martin's Národné Noviny)."

RN, 24.5.1911, N. 21, p. 3, "Ešte dva uprázdnené mandáty (Two more emptied mandates)."

RN, 3.8.1911, N. 31, pp. 5–6, "Viedeň (Vienna)."

RN, 10.8.1911, N. 32, pp. 1–2, "K martinským slávnostiam (To the celebrations in Martin)."

RN, 7.9.1911, N. 36, p. 2, "Český separatizmus a 'Népszava' (Czech separatism and 'Népszava')."

RN, 12.10.1911., N. 41, p. 2, "Shromaždenie ľudu v Prešporku (Public gathering in Prešporok)."

RN, 30.11.1911, N. 48, p. 6, "Slovenská zábava v Prešporku (Slovak entertainment in Prešporok)."

RN, 21.12.1911, N. 51, pp. 2–3, "Národnostná debata (Debate about nationalities),"

RN, 21.3.1912, N. 12, p. 2, "Čo konať? (What to do?)" ,

RN, 4.4.1912, N. 14, pp. 1–2, "Národnostní ľudia proti politike národnostnej strany (Nationalities' representatives against the politics of the Nationalities' Party)."

RN, 3.5.1912, N. 18, p. 1, "Májová oslava."
pp. 1–4, "Nová stanica našej kalvárie (A new station of our misery)."

RN, 27.6.1912, N. 26, p. 7, "Chýrnik."

RN, 1.8.1912, N. 31, p. 1, "Martinské národné slávnosti (National celebrations in Martin)."

RN, 26.9.1912, N. 39, p. 5, "Chýrnik."

RN, 3.10.1912, N. 40, p. 2, "Kongregácia prešporskej stolice odhlasovala (Prešporok's county assembly voted for)."

RN, 14.11.1912, N. 46, p. 6, "Chýrnik."

RN, 21.11.1912, N. 47, pp. 5–6, "Koncert slovenského a českého spevokolu (The concert of the Czech and Slovak choirs)."

RN, 16.1.1913, N. 3, pp. 2–3, "Národnostná strana (The Nationalities' Party [meaning Slovak National Party])."

RN, 6.2.1913, N. 6, p. 1, "Slovenskí národovci a sociálna demokracia (Slovak nationalists and social democracy)."

RN, 20.3.1913, N. 12, pp. 1–2, "Slovenské zhromaždenie v Prešporku (Slovak gathering in Prešporok)."

RN, 17.4.1913, N. 16, p. 1, "Májové oslavy (May celebrations)."

RN, 8.5.1913, N. 19, p. 1, "Májové oslavy."

RN, 29.5.1913, N. 22, pp. 3–4, "Slovenské úradníctvo (Slovak officials)."

RN, 3.7.1913, N. 27, pp. 4–5, "Dopisy (Letters column)."

RN, 10.7.1913, N. 28, p. 7, "Chýrnik (News column)."

RN, 31.7.1913, N. 31, p. 7, "Chýrnik."

RN, 29.1.1914, N. 5, p. 6, "O našej tlači (About our press)."

RN, 12.2.1914, N. 7, pp. 6–7, "Delnická telocvičná jednota (Workers' physical exercise association)."
p. 7, "Chýrnik."

RN, 26.2.1914, N. 8, p. 6, "Ženský obzor (Women's horizons)."

RN, 5.3.1914, N. 10, p. 3, "Rozhľady (Horizons)."
p. 6, "Divadlo v Prešporku (The theatre in Prešporok)."

RN, 12.3.11914, N. 11, p. 4, "Ženský deň v Prešporku (Women's day in Prešporok)."

RN, 16.4.1914, N. 16, pp. 1–4, "IV. sjazd slovenskej sociálnej demokracie (The IV. congress of the Slovak social democrats)."
p. 7, "Organizačné záležitosti (Organisational matters column)."

RN 4.6.1914, N. 23, p. 3, "Národná slovenská rada (National Slovak council)."
p. 6, "Slovenské divadlo v Prešporku (The Slovak theatre in Prešporok)."

RN 11.6.1914, N. 24, pp. 1–2, "Z psychológie slovenského života (From the psychology of Slovak life)."

Slovenské Listy
SL, 1.9.1901, N. 35, p. 2, "Prešporok."

SL, 22.9.1901, N. 38, pp. 2–3, "Prešporok."

Slovenský Týždenník
ST, 14.4.1905, N. 16, p. 4, "Jako nažívame (How we live)."

ST, 1.6.1906, N. 22, p. 7, "Z Prešporka… (From Prešporok)."

ST, 18.10.1907, N. 42, p. 7, "Beťársky život v Prešporku (Frivolous life in Prešporok)."

ST, 1.11.1907, N. 44, p. 9, "Na študentov fiškusa (A lawyer on students)."

ST, 15.11.1907, N. 46, p. 7, "Na študentov fiškusa."

ST, 12.5.1911, N. 19, p. 5, "Vzdelávací spolok v Prešporku (Educational association in Prešporok)."

Stráž na Sione, 1910, N. 6, p. 54, "Zosnulí (Obituaries)."

The Times
The Times, 9.12.1881, p. 3a (column a), "Burning of a theatre in Vienna. Great loss of life."

The Times, 10.12.1881, p. 6a, "The Burning of a theatre in Vienna."

The Times, 16.12.1881, p. 8a.

The Times, 17.12.1881, p. 5d.

The Times, 20.12.1881, p. 5e.

The Times, 21.12.1881, p. 5d.

The Times, 25.4.1882, p. 5b.

Bibliography

The Times, 19.5.1882, p. 5c.

The Times, 6.5.1882, p. 7c.

The Times, 2.10.1884, p. 4a.

The Times 3.10.1882, p. 5c.

The Times 5.10.1882, p. 3c.

The Times 7.10.1882, p. 5c.

WESTUNGARISCHER GRENZBOTE

WG, 20.10.1885, N. 4392, p. 1, "Die panslawischen Umtriebe (Pan-Slav machinations)."

WG, 12.11.1877, N. 1635, p. 1, "Pressburger Gewerbetreibende und die Sozial-demokraten (Pressburger craftsmen and social democrats)."
pp. 3-5, "Arbeiterversammlung in Speneder's Gasthaus vom 11. d. M. (Workers' gathering in Speneder's inn on the 11th of this month)."

WG, 2.5.1890, N. 5990, pp. 1-3, "Der Arbeitertag in Pressburg (The workers' day in Pressburg)."

WG, 3.2.1891, N. 6256, p. 2, "Freie Arbeiter-Volksversammlung (Free workers' public gathering)."

WG, 2.5.1893, N. 7043, pp. 1-2, "Der 1.Mai in Pressburg (1 May in Pressburg)."

WG, 2.5.1902, N. 10207, p. 3, "Die Maifeier der Arbeiterschaft Pressburgs (May Day celebration of the Pressburg's workers)."

WG, 1.9.1902, N. 10323, p. 1, "Demonstrationsumzug und Monstre-Volksver-sammlung (Demonstration procession and monster-rally)."

WG, 2.10.1907, N. 12105, p. 2, "Sitzung des Theaterkomites (Meeting of the Theatre Committee)."

WESTUNGARISCHE VOLKSSTIMME

WV, 23.8.1902, N. 25, p. 7, "Eröffnungsfeier der Petőfi Säle (Inauguration of the Petőfi rooms)."

WV, 4.9.1902, N. 27, p. 7, "Wahlrechtsversammlung in Pressburg (Public gathering for universal suffrage in Pressburg)."

WV, 21.4.1906, N. 16, p. 1, "Die Christlichsozialen und die Arbeiterfrage (The Christian socialists and the workers' question)."

WV, 5.5.1906, N. 18, p. 1, "Die Maifeier der Arbeiterschaft Pressburgs (May Day celebration of the Pressburger workers)."

WV, 5.10.1907, N. 40, pp. 1–2, "Die Pressburger Arbeiterschaft im Kampfe für das allgemeine Wahlrecht (The Pressburger workers in fight for universal suffrage)."

WV, 5.5.1906, N. 18, p. 1, "Die Maifeier der Pressburger Arbeiterschaft."

WV, 5.10.1907, N. 40, pp. 1–2, "Die Pressburger Arbeiterschaft im Kampfe für das allgemeine Wahlrecht (Workers of Pressburg in fight for universal suffrage)."

WV, 5.3.1912, N. 27, pp. 1–2, "Arbeitsruhe der Wahldemonstranten (A day off work for those demonstrating for universal suffrage)."

WV, 16.3.1912, N. 32, p. 1, "Petőfi's Weltanschaung (Petőfi's world view)."
p. 2, "Die Geburtsfeier der ungarischen Freiheit (Celebration of the birth of Hungarian freedom)."
p. 2, "Die Marzfeier der Pressburger Bevölkerung (March celebration of the Pressburg's inhabitants)."

WV, 4.5.1912, N. 52, pp. 1–2, "Der Maitag der Pressburger Arbeiterschaft (May Day of the Pressburg's workers)."
p. 3, "Die Maifeier (May Day celebration)."

Volksstimme Kalender, 1911, "Anno 1869. Eine Episode aus den Anfängen der deutschsprachigen Arbeiterbewegung Ungarns (One episode from the beginnings of the German-speaking workers' movement in Hungary)."

WESTUNGARISCHE VOLKSZEITUNG
WVZ, 18.4.1899, N. 142, p. 3, "Unsere 'Stadtväter' (Our 'city fathers')."

WVZ, 30.4.1899, N. 144, pp. 1–2, "Der 1. Maitag (The May Day)."

WVZ, 4.5.1902, N. 300, p. 3, "Die Maifeier (May celebration)."

WVZ, 6.5.1899, N. 145, p. 3, "Die Wohnungsnoth (Housing shortage)."

PUPBLISHED PRE-1918 DOCUMENTS

Bokeš, František (1965) *Dokumenty k slovenskému národnému hnutiu v r. 1848–1914, II. 1867–1884* (Documents on the Slovak national movement, II. 1867–1884), Bratislava: SAV.

Kemény, Gábor, *Iratok a nemzetiségi kérdés történetéhez Magyarországon a dualizmus korában 1867–1918* (Documents on the history of nationalities in Hungary in the age of dualism), Vol. I-VI, Budapest: Tankönyvkiadó, (1952) Vol. I: 1867–1892, (1956) Vol. II: 1892–1900, (1964) Vol. III: 1900–1903, (1966) Vol. IV: 1903–1906, (1971) Vol. V: 1906–1913, (1985) Vol. VI: 1913–1914.

Chovanec, Jaroslav, Mozolík, Peter (eds) (1994) *Historické a štátoprávne korene samostatnosti Slovenskej republiky* (Historical and state-legal roots of the independence of the Slovak Republic, documents), Bratislava: Procom.

Horváth, Vladimír, Rákoš, Elemír and Watzka, Jozef (1977) *Pripojenie Bratislavy k Československej republike roku 1918-1919, dokumenty* (Inclusion of Bratislava into the Czechoslovak republic 1918–1919, documents), Bratislava: Obzor.

LITERATURE AFTER 1918

UNPUBLISHED

Babejová, Eleonóra (1998) "Contesting the city: *Toldy Kör* in Bratislava 1874–1914," Unpublished manuscript.

Benyóová-Dudeková, Gabriela (1991) *Sociológ Juraj Schulpe a jeho činnosť.' Príspevok k sociálnym dejinám* (Sociologist Juraj Schulpe and his activities. A contribution to social history), Unpublished thesis, Bratislava: FFUK, Katedra československých dejín a archívnictva.

Csáder, Viliam (1971/1972) *Archívny fond Toldyho kruhu a pridružených fondov: spevokolu Bélu Bartóka, Meštianskeho kasína, Združenia katolíckej mládeže Slovenska a skautského oddielu Kiskarpátok* (Archival fund of Toldy Kör and of associated funds: the choir of Béla Bartók, City Casino, Association of the Catholic youth of Slovakia and the scout group Kiskarpátok), Unpublished thesis, Bratislava: FFUK, Katedra československých dejín a archívnictva.

Duka, Norbert (1967) *K histórii robotárne a jej budovy v Bratislave* (To the history of the workhouse and of its building in Bratislava), Unpublished manuscript in AMB, Bratislava.

Green, Abigail (1998) *Particularist State-Building and the German Question: Hanover, Saxony, Württemberg 1850-1866*, Unpublished Ph.D. thesis, Cambridge.

Hroch, Miroslav (1994) "The social interpretation of linguistic demands in European national movements," Unpublished article, Florence: European University Institute, pp. 1–37.

Kearns, Gerry (1997) "The history of medical geography after Foucault," Unpublished article, University of Cambridge, Department of Geography.

King, Jeremy (1998) *Loyalty and Polity, Nation and State: A Town in Habsburg Central Europe*, Unpublished Ph.D. thesis draft, Columbia University, Department of History, New York.

Kovács, Éva (1992) *A kassai zsidóság identitása a két világháború között* (Identity of the Jews of Košice between the two world wars), Unpublished candidate's thesis, in Teleki Lajos Alapítvány, Budapest.

Krug, Marven (1998) "Reports of a cop: civil liberties and associational life in Leipzig during the Second Empire," in Retallack, James (ed.), *Memory, Democracy, and the Mediated Nation, Political Cultures and Regional Identities in Germany, 1848-1998*, pp. 1–10.

Lehotský, Vladimír (1969) *Počiatky robotníckeho socialistického hnutia a boj o politické osamostatnenie robotníctva v Bratislave (1867-1900)* (Beginnings of the workers' socialist movement and fight for political emancipation of the workers in Bratislava), Unpublished candidate's thesis, Bratislava: FFUK, Katedra československých dejín a archívnictva, Bratislava.

Lehotský, Vladimír (1977) *Robotnícke socialistické hnutie v Bratislave od nástupu imperializmu do konca prvej svetovej imperialisickej vojny (1900-1918)* (Workers' socialist movement in Bratislava from the time of imperialism until the end of the First World War), Unpublished thesis, Bratislava: FFUK, Katedra československých dejín a archívnictva, Bratislava.

Mannová, Elena (1994) "Ethnic identity and the city (Bratislava in the 19th century)," Unpublished article, presented at the Second International Conference on Urban History, European Cities and Society, 8–10 September 1994 Strasbourg, pp. 1–13.

Mannová, Elena, Unpublished research "Ivan Dérer, Rozpomienky na starý Prešporok (Ivan Dérer, Reminiscences of the old Prešporok)," in Archív národního muzea Praha, Ivan Dérer, i.n. 358, c. 7, pp. 1–38 of the manuscript.

Obuchová, Viera (1986) *Vznik a vývoj robotníckych štvrtí a ich postavenie v rámci mesta Bratislavy 1848-1938* (Emergence and development of the workers' districts and their position in the city of Bratislava 1848–1938),

Unpublished candidate's thesis, Bratislava: FFUK, Katedra českosloven-ských dejín a archívnictva, Bratislava.

Pelikan, Egon and Uhl, Heidemarie (forthcoming) "Kultur-Identität-Politik: Kulturelle Aspekte nationaler Politik in Graz und Laibach/Ljubljana am Ende des 19. Jahrhunderts (Culture-identity-politics: aspects of the national politics in Graz and Laibach/Ljubljana at the end of the nineteenth century)," in *Slovanské štúdie*, pp. 1–18 of the manuscript.

Penny III, Glenn H. (1998) "Museum-building and nation-building in Leipzig: local needs, regional interests, international idioms," in Retallack, James (ed.), *Memory, Democracy, and the Mediated Nation, Political Cultures and Regional Identities in Germany, 1848-1998*, pp. 1–3.

Reckhaus, Christoph (1997) "Die Deutschen in Pressburg 1900–1920, Zur Analyse der relativen Bevölkerungsmehrheit in Pressburg/Bratislava (Germans in Pressburg 1900–1920, On the analysis of the relative population majority in Pressburg/Bratislava)," (Zwischenbericht nach neun Monaten an den Auswahlausschuss für die Vergabe des Immanuel-Kant-Promotionsstipendiums zum Stand der Arbeiten an der Dissertation), Unpublished manuscript, Köln, pp. 1–19.

Retallack, James (ed.) (1998) *Memory, Democracy, and the Mediated Nation, Political Cultures and Regional Identities in Germany, 1848-1998*, Conference Reader, An International Conference of the University of Toronto in collaboration with the German Historical Institute, Washington, D.C., Toronto, September 18–20, 1998.

PUBLISHED

Magyaroszág nemzeti atlasza/National Atlas of Hungary (1989) Budapest: Kartógrafiai vállalat.

Slovenský biografický slovník (Slovak biographic dictionary), Martin: Matica Slovenská, Vol. I (1986), Vol. II (1987), Vol. III (1989), Vol. IV (1990), Vol. V (1992), Vol. VI (1994).

Zlatá kniha Bratislavy (1928), Bratislava.

Župa bratislavská (1927), Bratislava.

Agnew, John (ed.) (1997) *Political Geography*, London, New York, Sydney, Auckland: Arnold.

Bibliography

Agnew, John (1997a) "Places and the politics of identity," in Agnew (ed.), *Political Geography*, pp. 249–255.

Agnew, John (1997b) "Geographies of nationalism and ethnic conflict," in Agnew (ed.), *Political Geography*, pp. 317–324.

Albrecht, Ján (1998) *Spomienky bratislavského hudobníka* (Memories of a Bratislava's musician), Bratislava: Vydavateľstvo PT.

Anderson, Benedict (1985) *Imagined Communities: Reflections on the Origins and Spread of Nationalism*, London: Verso.

Anderson, James (1988) "Nationalist ideology and territory," in Johnston, Knight and Kofman (eds) (1988) *National Self-Determination and Political Geography*, pp. 18–39.

Anderson, Kay J. (1991) *Vancouver's Chinatown, Racial Discourse in Canada, 1875–1980*, Montreal & Kingston, London, Buffalo: McGill-Queen's University Press.

Antolíková, Mária (1998) "Zdravotníctvo (Health care)," in *Bratislava (Annales)*, X, pp. 115–128.

Baker, Keith Michael (1990) *Inventing the French Revolution*, Cambridge: Cambridge University Press, 1990.

Balibar, Etienne and Wallerstein, Immanuel (1991) *Race, Nation, Class: Ambiguous Identities*, London, New York: Verso.

Barany, George (1969) "Hungary: from aristocratic to proletarian nationalism," in Sugar and Lederer (eds), *Nationalism in Eastern Europe*, pp. 259–309.

Becker, Edwin, Prahl, Roman and Wittlich, Petr (eds) (1999) *Prague 1900, Poetry and Ecstasy*, Amsterdam: Van Gogh Museum, Frankfurt am Main: Museum of Applied Art, Zwolle: Waanders Uitgevers (exhibition catalogue).

Beller, Steven (1989) "The role of Jews in Vienna culture and society at the turn of the century," in Pynsent (ed.), *Decadence and Innovation, Austro-Hungarian Life and Art at the Turn of the Century*, pp. 14–23.

Beluszky, Pál (1990) "A polgárosodás törékeny váza—városhálózatunk a századfordulón I. (The fragile outline of embourgeoisement—our town network at the turn of the century)," *Tér és társadalom*, 4, 3–4, pp. 13–56.

Bender, Barbara (ed.) (1993) *Landscape Politics and Perspectives*, Providence/Oxford: Berg.

Bender, Barbara (1993a) "Introduction: landscape—meaning and action," in Bender (ed.), *Landscape Politics and Perspectives*, pp. 1–17.

Beňušková, Zuzana and Salner, Peter (eds) (1995) *Stabilität und Wandel in der Grossstadt* (Stability and change in the metropolis), Bratislava: Ústav etnológie Slovenskej akadémie vied.

Bettelheim, Samuel (1932) "Geschichte der Pressburger Jeschiba (History of the Jeshiba in Pressburg)," in Gold (ed.), *Die Juden und die Judengemeinde Bratislava in Vergangenheit und Gegenwart*, pp. 61–67.

Bočková, Helena (1992) "Zusammenleben der Brünner Tschechen und Deutschen: Licht und Schatten (Co-existence of Czechs and Germans in Brno: light and shadow)," Salner and Luther (eds), *Ethnokulturelle Prozesse in Grossstädten Mitteleuropas, Adaptation im Stadtmilieu, Toleranz-Intoleranz in Grossstädten Mitteleuropas*, pp. 127–135.

Bokeš, František (1942) "Pokus o slovenskú mapu Uhorska r. 1866/67 (Attempt of a Slovak map of Hungary 1866/67)," in *Sborník matice slovenskej*, 20, 1–2, pp. 25–39.

Bokeš, František (1945) *Vývin predstáv o slovenskom území* (Development of the conceptions of the Slovak territory), Martin: Matica Slovenská.

Bokešová-Uherová, Mária (1958) *Bratislavský lekársko-prírodovedný spolok (1856–1945)* (The association of medicine and natural sciences in Bratislava), Bratislava: SAV.

Boyer, Christine M. (1994) *The City of Collective Memory*, Cambridge, Massachusetts and London, England: The MIT Press.

Breuilly, John (1982) *Nationalism and the State*, Manchester: Manchester University Press.

Brock, Peter (1976) *The Slovak National Awakening: An Essay in the Intellectual History of East Central Europe*, Toronto and Buffalo: University of Toronto Press.

Brubaker, Rogers (1996) *Nationalism Reframed*, Cambridge University Press.

Bruckmüller, Ernst, Ulrike Döcker, Hannes Steckl and Peter Urbanitsch (eds.) (1990) *Bürgertum in der Habsburger Monarchie* (Bourgeoisie in the Habsburg monarchy), Wien, Köln: Böhlau.

Buček, Ján (1995) "Mesto, štát a územie (City, state and territory)," in *Acta Facultatis Rerum Naturalium Universitatis Comenianae Geographica*, 36, Bratislava, pp. 132–250.

Burke, Peter and Porter, Roy (eds) (1987) *The Social History of Language*, Cambridge: Cambridge University Press.

Butvín, Jozef (1972) "The Great Moravian Cyril and Methodius tradition in the Slovak national revival," in *Studia Historica Slovaca*, Bratislava, 7, pp. 96–118.

Butvín, Jozef (1973) "Bratislava v slovenskom národnom obrodení a otázka slovenského národného strediska v rokoch 1848–1918 (Bratislava in the Slovak national revival and the question of the Slovak national centre in the years 1848–1918)," in *Historický časopis*, 21, 4, pp. 531–574.

Calic, Marie-Janine and Pazmandi, Susanne (1992) "Migration, Urbanisierung und Assimilation in der Vojvodina und der Slowakei (1880–1938) (Migration, urbanisation and assimilation in Vojvodina and Slovakia (1880–1938))," in Seewann (ed.), *Minderheitenfragen in Südosteuropa (Beiträge der Internationalen Konferenz: The Minority Question in Historical Perspective 1900–1990)*, pp. 211–235.

Cesnaková-Michalcová, Milena (1997) *Geschichte des deutschsprachigen Theaters in der Slowakei* (History of the German-language theatre in Slovakia), Köln, Weimar, Wien: Böhlau.

Chadwick, Owen (1990) *The Secularisation of the European Mind in the Nineteenth Century*, Cambridge, New York, Port Chester, Melbourne, Sydney: Cambridge University Press.

Chaloupecký, Václav (1930) *Zápas o Slovensko 1918* (Struggle for Slovakia 1918), Praha: Čin.

Cohen, Gary B. (1981) *The Politics of Ethnic Survival: Germans in Prague, 1861–1914*, Princeton, New Jersey: Princeton University Press.

Cohen, Gary B. (1987) "Society and culture in Prague, Vienna, and Budapest in the late nineteenth century," in *East European Quarterly*, 20, 4, pp. 467–484.

Colotti, Enzo (1990) "Nationalism, anti-Semitism, socialism and political Catholicism as expressions of mass politics in the twentieth century," in

Teich and Porter (eds), *Fin-de-Siecle and Its Legacy*, pp. 80–97.

Connerton, Paul (1989) *How Societies Remember*, Cambridge: Cambridge University Press.

Conversi, Daniel (1997) "Reassessing current theories of nationalism: nationalism as boundary maintenance and creation," in Agnew (ed.), *Political Geography*, pp. 325–336.

Cosgrove, Denis and Daniels, Stephen (1988) *The Iconography of Landscape*, Cambridge: Cambridge University Press.

Csáky, Moritz and Mannová, Elena (eds) (1999) *Kolektívne identity v strednej Európe v období moderny* (Collective identities in Central Europe in the modern period), Bratislava: AEP.

Csáky, Moritz (1999) "Úvod (Introduction)," in Csáky and Mannová (eds), *Kolektívne identity v strednej Európe v období moderny*, pp. 7–20.

Dangl, Vojtech (1977) "Vývoj, organizácia, vnútorná štruktúra a dislokácia pozemných síl rakúsko-uhorskej armády na území Slovenska v rokoch 1868–1914 (The development, organisation, inner structure and dislocation of the infantry regiments of the Austro-Hungarian army on the territory of Slovakia in the years 1868–1914)," in *Sešity příspěvků k sociálně politické a historické problematice vojenství a armády*, 6, 4–5, pp. 67–134.

Dangl, Vojtech (1996) "O vzťahu slovenskej spoločnosti k armáde na prelome 19. a 20. storočia (On the relation of Slovak society to the army at the turn of the nineteenth and twentieth centuries)," in *Vojenské obzory*, *H*, Vol. 3, Príloha 1/96, pp. 21–28.

Dann, Otto (1993) *Nation und Nationalismus in Deutschland 1770–1990*, München: Verlag C. H. Beck.

Deak, Istvan (1979) *The Lawful Revolution, Louis Kossuth and the Hungarians 1848–1849*, New York: Columbia University Press.

Deak, Istvan (1990) *Beyond Nationalism: A Social and Political History of the Habsburg Officer Corps, 1848–1918*, New York, Oxford: Oxford University Press.

Dennis, Richard (2000) "Historical geographies of urbanism," in Graham and Nash (eds), *Modern Historical Geographies*, pp. 218–247.

Döcker, Ulrike (1990) "'Bürgerlichkeit und Kultur—Bürgerlichkeit als Kultur.' Eine Einführung (*Bürgerlichkeit* and culture—*Bürgerlichkeit* as culture)," in Bruckmüller, Döcker, Steckl and Urbanitsch (eds), *Bürgertum in der Habsburger Monarchie*, pp. 95–104.

Driver, Felix (1991) "Political geography and state formation: disputed territory," in *Progress in Human Geography*, 15, 3, pp. 268–280.

Driver, Felix (1993) *Power and Pauperism: The Workhouse System, 1834–1884*, Cambridge: Cambridge University Press.

Dudeková, Gabriela (1994) *Juraj Schulpe: vedec a humanista* (Juraj Schulpe: scientist and humanitarian), Bratislava: YMCA.

Duncan, James S. (1990) *The City as Text: The Politics of Landscape Interpretation in the Kandyan Kingdom*, Cambridge: Cambridge University Press.

Duncan, James and Ley, David (eds) (1993) *Place/Culture/Representation*, London and New York: Routledge.

Dvořák, Pavel (1995) *Zlatá kniha Bratislavy* (The golden book of Bratislava), Bratislava: Slovenský spisovateľ.'

Elias, Norbert (1994) *The Civilising Process*, Oxford: Blackwell.

Edholm, Felicity (1993) "The view from below: Paris in the 1880s," in Bender (ed.), *Landscape Politics and Perspectives*, pp. 139–168.

Faust, Ovidius (1927) "Vývoj kultúrnych inštitúcií mesta Bratislavy (Development of the cultural institutions of the city Bratislava)," in *Župa bratislavská*.

Fekete, Štefan (1948) "Pôdorysný vývoj Bratislavy a národnostný vývoj obyvateľstva (Development of the ground plan of Bratislava and the national development of its inhabitants)," in Fiala (ed.), *Slovanská Bratislava I*, pp. 47–60.

Fiala, Alojz (ed.) (1948) *Slovanská Bratislava I.* (Slavic Bratislava), Bratislava.

Fiala, Alojz (1948a) "Činnosť akademického právnického spolku Naprej (Activity of the academic lawyers' association Naprej)," in Fiala (ed.), *Slovanská Bratislava I.* pp. 354–386.

Forest, Benjamin (1997) "West Hollywood as symbol: the significance of place in the construction of a gay identity," in Agnew (ed.), *Political Geography*, pp. 287–315.

Foucault, Michel (1977) *Discipline and Punish: The Birth of the Prison*, Harmondsworth: Penguin.

Foucault, Michel (1979) "Governmentality," in *Ideology and Consciousness*, 6, pp. 5–21.

Foucault, Michel (1984) "Space, knowledge, and power," in Rabinow (ed.), *The Foucault Reader*, pp. 239–256.

Foucault, Michel (1986) *Power/Knowledge*, Brighton: The Harvester Press.

Foucault, Michel (1988a) "Technologies of the self," in Martin, Gutman and Hutton (eds), *Technologies of the Self*, pp. 16–49.

Foucault, Michel (1988b) "The political technology of individuals," in Martin, Gutman and Hutton (eds), *Technologies of the Self*, pp. 145–162.

Francová, Zuzana (1998a) "Obyvatelia—etnická, sociálna a konfesijná skladba (Inhabitants—ethnic, social and denominational structure)," in *Bratislava (Annales)*, X, 1998, pp. 17–38.

Francová, Zuzana (1998b) "Z histórie dopravy (From the history of transport)," in *Bratislava (Annales)*, X, 1998, pp. 81–92.

Francová, Zuzana, (1998c) "Školstvo (Education system)," in *Bratislava (Annales)*, X, 1998, pp. 101–114.

Franz, Anton Richard (1935) *Pressburg*, Berlin und Stuttgart: Verlag Grenze und Ausland.

Franek, Jaroslav, Kamenec, Ivan, Baruch, Myers, Salner, Peter and Trabalka, Valerian (1997) *Židia v Bratislave* (Jews in Bratislava), Bratislava: Inštitút judaistiky FFUK, Ústav etnológie, Židovská náboženská obec.

Gajdoš, Peter (1987) "K problematike demografického vývoja Bratislavy od konca 19. storočia do súčasnosti (To the problems of the demographic development of Bratislava from the end of the nineteenth century until present)," in *Slovenský Národopis*, 35, 2–3, pp. 259–266.

Gal, Susan (1979) *Language Shift, Social Determinants of Linguistic Change in Bilingual Austria*, New York, San Francisco, London: Academic Press.

Gašparec, Miloš (1998) "Urbanistický rozvoj (The urban development)," in *Bratislava (Annales)*, X, pp. 39–48.

Geary, Roger (1985) *Policing Industrial Disputes: 1893–1985*, Cambridge University Press.

Gellner, Ernest (1983) *Nations and Nationalism*, Oxford: Basil Blackwell.

Gerő, András (1995) *Modern Hungarian Society in the Making: The Unfinished Experience*, Budapest, London, New York: Central European University Press.

Gerő, András (1997) *The Hungarian Parliament (1867–1918), A Mirage of Power*, Boulder: Social Science Monograph, Highland Lakes: Atlantic Research and Publications Inc., New Jersey, New York: distributed by Columbia University Press.

Giddens, Anthony (1985) *The Nation-State and Violence*, Cambridge: Polity Press, 1985.

Gillis, John R. (ed.) (1994) *Commemorations: the Politics of National Identity*, Princeton, New Jersey: Princeton Universty Press.

Gillis, John R. (1994a) "Memory and identity: the history of a relationship," in Gillis (ed.), *Commemorations: The Politics of National Identity*, pp. 3–24.

Glatz, Ferenc (ed.) (1995) *Hungarians and Their Neighbors in Modern Times 1867–1950*, New York: Columbia University Press.

Glatz, Ferenc (1995a) "Preface," in Glatz (ed.), *Hungarians and Their Neighbors in Modern Times 1867–1950*, pp. xi-xx.

Glatz, Ferenc (1995b) "Bourgeois transformation, assimilation, and nationalism," in Glatz (ed.), *Hungarians and Their Neighbors in Modern Times 1867–1950*, pp. 33–43.

Glettler, Monika (1988) "Ethnische Vielfalt in Pressburg und Budapest um 1910, Teil I. (Ethnic diversity in Pressburg and Budapest around 1910, Part I)," in *Ungarn Jahrbuch*, Band 16, München, pp. 46–71.

Glettler, Monika (1989a) "Ethnische Vielfalt in Pressburg und Budapest um 1910, Teil II. (Ethnic diversity in Pressburg and Budapest around 1910, Part II)," in *Ungarn Jahrbuch*, Vol. 17, München, pp. 95–152.

Glettler, Monika (1989b) "Minority culture in a capital city: The Czechs in Vienna at the turn of the century," in Pynsent (ed.), *Decadence and Innovation, Austro-Hungarian Life and Art at the Turn of the Century*, pp. 49–60.

Glettler, Monika (1992) "The Slovaks in Budapest and Bratislava, 1850–1914," in Max Engman (ed.), *Comparative Studies on Governments and Non-dominant Ethnic Groups in Europe 1850-1940. Ethnic Identity in Urban Europe*, Vol. VIII, Dartmouth: New York University Press, pp. 295-330.

Goláň, Karol (1957) "Prvé roky robotníckeho hnutia na Slovensku (First years of the workers' movement in Slovakia)," in *Historický časopis*, 5, 2, pp. 165-184.

Goláň, Karol (1958) "Organizačný rozmach robotníckeho hnutia v Bratislave v prvej polovici deväťdesiatych rokov 19. storočia (Organisational expansion of the workers' movement in Bratislava in the first half of the 1890s)," in *Historický časopis*, 6, 4, pp. 524-539.

Gold, Hugo (ed.) (1932) *Die Juden und die Judengemeinde Bratislava in Vergangenheit und Gegenwart* (Jews and the Jewish community of Bratislava in the past and present), Brünn.

Gordon, Milton M. (1964) *Assimilation in American Life: The Role of Race, Religion, and National Origins*, New York: Oxford University Press.

Gosiorovský, Miloš (1956) *Dejiny slovenského robotníckeho hnutia (1848-1918)* (History of the Slovak workers' movement (1848-1918)), Bratislava: Slovenské vydavateľstvo politickej literatúry.

Graham, Brian and Nash, Catherine (eds) (2000), *Modern Historical Geographies*, Longman.

Graham, Brian (2000) "The past in place: historical geographies of identity," in Graham, Nash (eds.), *Modern Historical Geographies*, pp. 70-99.

Green, David R. (1985) "A map for Mayhew's London: the geography of poverty in the mid-nineteenth century London," in *London Journal*, 11, 2, pp. 115-126.

Grexa, Ján (1997) "Sport- und Turnvereine als Bestandteil der Ausformung der bürgerlichen Gesellschaft in der Slowakei 1900-1945 (Sport- and physical culture associations as part of the formation of the bourgeois society in Slovakia 1900-1945)," in Mannová (ed.), *Bürgertum und bürgerliche Gesellschaft in der Slowakei 1900-1989*, pp. 259-273.

Grusková, Anna (1999) "'Duša zostala Židovská', O bratislavskom medzivojnovom divadle, Arthurovi Schnitzlerovi a reflexii židovskej identity ('The soul remained Jewish', On Bratislava's interwar theatre, Arthur Schnitzler and the reflection of Jewish identity)," in Csáky and Mannová (eds), *Kolektívne identity v strednej Európe v období moderny*, pp. 101–114.

Grünsfeld, Josef (1932) "Geschichte der orth. israelitischen Kultusgemeinde," in Gold (ed.), *Die Juden und die Judengemeinde Bratislava in Vergangenheit und Gegenwart*, pp. 109–114.

Grünsfeld, Josef (1932) "Neue Geschichte der Jeschiba," in Gold (ed.), *Die Juden und die Judengemeinde Bratislava in Vergangenheit und Gegenwart*, pp. 67–68.

Guiraudon, Virginie (1991) "Cosmopolitanism and national priority: attitudes towards foreigners in France between 1789 and 1794," in *History of European Ideas*, 13, 5, pp. 591–604.

Gyányi, Gábor (1993) "Az asszimiláció fogalma a magyar társadalomtörténetben (The concept of assimilation in the Hungarian social history)," in *Valóság*, 36, 4, pp. 18–27.

Gyányi, Gábor (1995) "Ethnicity and acculturation in Budapest at the turn of the century," in Zimmermann (ed.), *Urban Space and Identity in the European City 1890-1930s*, pp. 107–113.

Gyányi, Gábor and Kövér, György (1998) *Magyarország társadalomtörténete a reformkortól a második világháborúig* (Social history of Hungary from the age of reform until the Second World War), Budapest: Osiris.

Hall, A. John and Jarvie, I. C. (eds) (1992) *Transition to Modernity, Essays on Power, Wealth and Belief,* Cambridge: Cambridge University Press.

Hanák, Jozef (1992) *Bratislava na pohľadniciach z prelomu storočia* (Bratislava on postcards from the turn of century), Bratislava: Obzor, 1992.

Hanák, Péter et al (1978) *A Magyarország története 1890-1918* (History of Hungary 1890-1918), Vol. 7 (Part 2), Budapest: Akadémiai Kiadó.

Hanák, Péter (1984a) *Ungarn in der Donaumonarchie. Probleme der bürgerlichen Umgestaltung eines Vielvölkerstaates* (Hungary in the Danube Monarchy. Problems of the bourgeois transformation of a multinational state), Wien: Verlag für Geschichte und Politik, München: Verlag R. Oldenbourg, Budapest: Akadémiai Kiadó.

Hanák, Péter (1984b) "1898 a nemzeti és az állampatrióta értékrend frontális ütközése a Monarchiában (1898 frontal clash of the value hierarchy of the national and state patriot in the Monarchy)," in *Medvetánc*, 2-3, pp. 55–72.

Bibliography

Hanák, Péter (1985) "A letűnt alkotmányosság nyomában (On track of the vanished constitutionalism)," in *História*, 7, 5–6, 1985, without page numbers.

Hanák, Péter (1997) "Társadalmi struktúrák a 19. századi Közép-Európában (Social structures in the nineteenth century Central Europe)," in *Történelmi szemle*, 34, 2, pp. 159–177.

Hanák, Péter (1998) *The Garden and the Workshop*, Princeton, New Jersey: Princeton University Press.

Handler, Richard (1994) "Is "identity" a useful cross-cultural concept?," in Gillis (ed.), *Commemorations: The Politics of National Identity*, pp. 27–40.

Hanzlíček, Karol (1970) *Spomienky na začiatky robotníckeho hnutia v Bratislave* (Memories of the beginnings of the workers' movement in Bratislava), Bratislava: Práca.

Hapák, Pavol (1970) "Úvodom (Introduction)," in Hanzlíček, *Spomienky na začiatky robotníckeho hnutia v Bratislave*, pp. 10–15.

Hapák, Pavol (1970) "Doslov, Poznámky a Slovenské oddelenie spolku Napred (Epilogue, Endnotes and the Slovak section of the association Napred)," in Hanzlíček, *Spomienky na začiatky robotníckeho hnutia v Bratislave*, pp. 102–140.

Hapák, Pavol (1973) "Priemyselná revolúcia a vývin miest za kapitalizmu (Industrial Revolution and the development of towns in capitalism)," in *Historický časopis*, 21, 2, pp. 161–187.

Hapák, Pavol et al (1986) *Dejiny Slovenska IV (od konca 19. storočia do roku 1918)* (History of Slovakia (from the end of the nineteenth century until 1918)), Bratislava: Veda.

Harrison, Mark (1988) "Symbolism, 'ritualism' and the location of crowds in early nineteenth century English towns," in Cosgrove and Daniels (eds), *The Iconography of Landscape*, pp. 194–213.

Harvey, David (1985) *Consciousness and the Urban Experience*, Oxford: Basil Blackwell.

Haslinger, Peter (1992) "Die Ungarnrezeption in der burgenländischen Presse 1921–1934 (Attitude towards the Hungarians in the Burgenland's press 1921–1934)," in *Burgenländische Heimatblätter*, 54, 4, Eisenstadt, pp. 153–169.

Heffernan, Michael (1998), *The Meaning of Europe: Geography and Geopolitics*, London, New York, Sydney, Auckland: Arnold.

Hobsbawm, Eric J. and Ranger, Terence (eds) (1983) *The Invention of Tradition*, Cambridge: Cambridge University Press.

Hobsbawm, Eric J. (1992) *Nations and Nationalism since 1870*, Cambridge: Cambridge University Press, second edition.

Hödl, Klaus (1995) "Viennese Jews and the question of ethnicity at the turn of the century," in Zimmermann (ed.), *Urban Space and Identity in the European City 1890-1930s*, pp. 115-129.

Hohenberg, Paul M. and Lees, Lynn Hollen (1985) *The Making of Urban Europe 1000-1950*, Cambridge, Massachusetts and London, England: Harvard University Press.

Holčík, Štefan (1988) *Korunovačné slávnosti Bratislava 1563-1830* (The coronations in Bratislava 1563-1830), Bratislava: Tatran.

Holec, Roman (1993) "Tulipánové hnutie ako forma ekonomického nacionalizmu a Slovensko (The tulip movement as a form of economic nationalism and Slovakia)," in *Historický časopis*, 41, 5-6, pp. 567-582.

Holec, Roman (1997a) *Tragédia v Černovej a slovenská spoločnosť* (The tragedy in Černová and the Slovak society), Martin: Matica Slovenská.

Holec, Roman (1997b) "Bürgerliche Wohnkultur in der Slowakei vor dem Ersten Weltkrieg (Bourgeois habitat culture in Slovakia before the First World War)," in Mannová (ed.), *Bürgertum und bürgerliche Gesellschaft in der Slowakei 1900-1989*, pp. 197-211.

Holec, Roman (1999) "Hospodárska politika Uhorska z pohľadu slovenských ekonomických záujmov (Economic politics of Hungary from the viewpoint of the Slovak economic interests)," in Podrimavský and Kováč (eds), *Slovensko na začiatku 20. storočia*, pp. 66-79.

Horváth, Vladimír, Lehotská, Darina and Pleva, Ján (1978) *Dejiny Bratislavy* (History of Bratislava), Bratislava: Obzor.

Horváth, Vladimír (1998) "Správa mesta (City administration)," in *Bratislava (Annales)*, X, pp. 11-16.

Hrabovcová, Emília (1999) "Slovenskí národne uvedomelí rímskokatolícki kňazi v zrkadle rakúsko-uhorskej diplomacie (Slovak nationally conscious Roman Catholic priests in the mirror of Austro-Hungarian diplomacy)," in Podrimavský and Kováč (eds), *Slovensko na začiatku 20. storočia*, pp. 180–200.

Hroch, Miroslav (1985) *Social Preconditions of National Revival in Europe*, Cambridge: Cambridge University Press.

Hroch, Miroslav (1992) "Language and national identity," in Rudolph and Good (eds), *Nationalism and Empire, The Habsburg Empire and The Soviet Union*, pp. 65–76.

Hromádka, Ján (1933) *Zemepis okresu bratislavského a malackého* (Geography of the districts of Bratislava and Malacky), Vol. I, Bratislava.

Hronský, Marián (1975) "K politickému profilu generácie okolo časopisu Prúdy (prúdistov) (1909–1914) (The political profile of the generation around the magazine Prúdy (1909–1914))," in *Historický časopis*, 23, 4, pp. 509–531.

Islamov, Tofik M. (1992) "From *natio hungarica* to Hungarian nation," in Rudolph and Good (eds), *Nationalism and Empire, The Habsburg Empire and The Soviet Union*, pp. 159–183.

Ivanka, Milan (1948) "Vendko B. Kutlík," in Fiala (ed.), *Slovanská Bratislava I*, pp. 343–386.

Jankovics, Marcell (without year, probably 1939) *Húsz ezstendő Pozsonyban* (Twenty years in Pozsony), Budapest: Franklin Társulat.

Jelinek, Yeshayahu A. (1995) "Židia na Slovensku v 19. storočí: poznámky k dejinám (Jews in Slovakia in the nineteenth century: comments to history)," in *Slovenský národopis*, 41, 3, pp. 271–296.

Jeszensky, Géza (1990) "Hungary through World War I and the end of the Dual Monarchy," in Sugar, Hanák and Frank (eds), *A History of Hungary*, pp. 267–294.

Jeszenszky, István (1927) *A "Testvériség" páholy 25 éves története* (25 years history of the masonic loge "Fraternity"), Budapest: Testvériség páholy.

John, Michael (1996) "Strassenkravalle und Exzesse (Street riots and excesses)," in Melinz and Zimmermann (eds), *Wien-Prague-Budapest: Blütezeit der Habsburgmetropolen*, pp. 230–244.

Johnson, Nuala (1997) "Cast in stone: monuments, geography, and nationalism," in Agnew (ed.), *Political Geography*, pp. 347–364.

Johnson, Nuala C. (2000) "Historical geographies of the present," in Graham and Nash (eds), *Modern Historical Geographies*, pp. 251–272.

Johnston, R. J., David B. Knight and Eleonore Kofman (eds) (1988) *National Self-Determination and Political Geography*, London, New York, Sydney: Croom Helm.

Johnston, R. J., David B. Knight and Eleonore Kofman (1988a) "Nationalism, self-determination and the world political map: an introduction," in Johnston, Knight and Kofman (eds), *National Self-Determination and Political Geography*, pp. 1–17.

Johnston, R. J. (1989) "The state, political geography, and geography," in Peet and Thrift (eds), *New Models in Geography (The Political-Economy Perspective) Vol. 1*, pp. 292–309.

Jones, Gareth Stedman (1983) *Languages of Class*, Cambridge University Press.

Joyce, Patrick (1991) *Visions of the People: Industrial England and the Question of Class 1848–1914*, Cambridge University Press.

Kalesný, František (1974) "Poznatky z národopisného výskumu robotníkov v Bratislave (Conclusions from ethnographic research of workers in Bratislava)," in *Múzeum*, XIX, pp. 184–190.

Kalesný, František (1985) "K otázke historických premien a etnickej mnohorakosti spôsobu života a kultúry ľudu Bratislavy (To the question of historical transformations and ethnic diversity of the way of life and culture of the people of Bratislava)," in *Slovenský národopis*, 33, 1, pp. 7–30.

Kalesný, František (1987) "Slováci v starej Bratislave (Slovaks in old Bratislava)," in *Slovenský národopis*, 35, 2–3, pp. 247–255.

Kamenický, Miroslav (ed.) (1997) *1867–1997, 130 rokov od založenia prvého Dobrovoľného hasičského spolku v Bratislave* (1867–1997, 130 years from the founding of the first Voluntary firemen's association in Bratislava), Bratislava: Okresný výbor Dobrovoľnej požiarnej ochrany SR Bratislava a Dobrovoľný požiarny zbor Bratislava-Staré mesto.

Kann, Robert A. and David, Zdeněk V. (1984) *The Peoples of the Eastern Habsburg Lands, 1526–1918*, Seattle and London: University of Washington Press.

Bibliography

Kantár, Ján (1987) "Ľudové stavby v prímestských častiach Bratislavy (Folk-architecture in the suburbs of Bratislava)," *Historický časopis*, 35, 2–3, pp. 281–292.

Karády, Viktor (1993) "Asszimiláció és társadalmi krízis (Assimilation and crisis in society)," in *Világosság*, 34, 3, pp. 33–60.

Karády, Viktor (1994) "A magyar zsidóság regionális és társadalmi rétegződéséről (1910) (On the regional and social stratification of the Hungarian Jewry)," in *Régió*, 5, 2, pp. 45–70.

Kearns, Gerry and Philo, Chris (eds) (1993) *Selling Places: the City as Cultural Capital, Past and Present*, Oxford: Pergamon.

Keith, Michael and Pile, Steve (eds) (1993) *Place and the Politics of Identity*, London and New York: Routledge.

Keith, Michael and Pile, Steve (1993a) "Introduction part 2: the place of politics," in Keith and Pile (eds), *Place and the Politics of Identity*, pp. 22–40.

Kemény, Ludwig (1930) *100 Jahre der Wohltätigkeit gewidmet 1830–1930, Rückblick auf die Vergangenheit des Pressburger Wohltätigen Frauenvereines* (130 years devoted to charity, Looking back at the past of the charitable association of Pressburger women), Bratislava-Pressburg.

Kertész, János (1935) *Pozsony város és Pozsony vármegye bibliográfiája* (Bibliography of the city and county of Pozsony), Komárom.

Kischke, Horst, Andicz, Helmut and Haubelt, Josef (1997) *Svobodní zednáři* (Freemasons), Praha: ETC Publishing.

Klimko, Jozef (1980) *Vývoj územia Slovenska a utváranie jeho hraníc* (Evolution of the territory of Slovakia and the formation of its boundaries), Bratislava: Obzor.

Komora, Pavol (1996) "Milenárne oslavy v Uhorsku roku 1896 a ich vnímanie v slovenskom prostredí (Millenial celebrations in Hungary in 1896 and attitude towards them in the Slovak environment)," in *Historický časopis*, 44, 1, pp. 3–16.

Koshar, Rudy J. (1994) "Historic preservation and identity in twentieth century Germany," in Gillis (ed.), *Commemorations: The Politics of National Identity*, pp. 215–280.

Kováč, Dušan (1987) "Nemecká menšina na Slovensku medzi uhorským patriotizmom a všenemeckou expanziou (The German minority in Slovakia between Hungarian patriotism and Pan-German expansion)," in *Slovanský přehled*, 73, 2, pp. 118–126.

Kováč, Dušan (1991) *Nemecko a nemecká menšina na Slovensku (1871–1945)* (Germany and the German minority in Slovakia (1871–1945), Bratislava: Veda.

Kováč, Dušan (1996) "Die slowakische Historiographie nach 1989 (The Slovak historiography after 1989)," in *Bohemia Band*, 37, pp. 169–174.

Kováč, Dušan (1998) *Dejiny Slovenska* (History of Slovakia), Praha: Nakladatelství Lidové Noviny.

Kováč, Dušan (1999) "Zahranično-politické koncepcie a alternatívy riešenia slovenskej otázky na prelome storočí (Foreign-political conceptions and alternatives for the solution of the Slovak question at the turn of the century)," in Podrimavský and Kováč (eds), *Slovensko na začiatku 20. storočia*, pp. 17–24.

Kovács, Endre et al (1979) *Magyarország története 1848–1890* (History of Hungary 1848–1890), Vol. VI (Part 2), Budapest: Akadémiai Kiadó.

Kovačevičová, Soňa (1976) "K problematike životného prostredia robotníkov na Slovensku v minulosti (The question of habitat of workers in Slovakia in the past)," in *Slovenský národopis*, 24, 1, pp. 1–29.

Kovačevičová, Soňa (1985) "K etnografickej charakteristike ľudových štvrtí a kolónií Bratislavy v minulosti (Ethnographic characterisation of the folk districts and colonies of Bratislava in the past)," in *Slovenský národopis*, 33, 1, pp. 33–85.

Kovačevičová, Soňa (1987) "Ľudové byty, štvrte a centrá Bratislavy v 19. storočí a v 1. polovici 20. storočia (Folk flats, quarters and centres of Bratislava in the nineteenth century and in the first half of the twentieth century)," in *Slovenský národopis*, 35, 2–3, pp. 267–280.

Krajčovič, Milan (1999) "Slováci v emancipačnom pohybe nemaďarských národností (Slovaks in the emancipation movement of the non-Magyar nationalities)," in Podrimavský and Kováč (eds), *Slovensko na začiatku 20. storočia*, pp. 48–65.

Kraus, František (1927) "Dejiny mestského sociálno-humanitného oddelenia (History of the municipal social-humanitarian department)," in

Župa bratislavská, pp. 136–139.

Krčméry, Štefan (1931) "Slovenská rozpomienka na Bratislavu (Slovak reminiscence of Bratislava)," in Medvecký (ed.), *Slovenský prevrat IV.*, pp. 63–73.

Kršáková, Dana (1997) "Das Bild des gesellschaftlichen Lebens der bürgerlichen Schichten in der slowakischen Literatur an der Wende vom 19. zum 20. Jahrhundert (An outline of the social life of the bourgeois strata in Slovak literature at the turn of the nineteenth and twentieth centuries)," in Mannová (ed.), *Bürgertum und bürgerliche Gesellschaft*, pp. 105–112.

Kühn, Ludvík (1928) *Buditelia v župe bratislavskej* (National awakeners in the county of Bratislava), Bratislava.

Kusý, Miroslav (1998a) *Čo s našimi Maďarmi?* (What to do with our Hungarians?), Bratislava: Kalligram.

Kusý, Miroslav (1998b) "Slovenská pravda (The Slovak truth)," in Viktor, *Roky meruôsme*, pp. 163–166.

Kutlík III, Felix (1931) *Dejiny Kutlíkovcov* (History of the Kutlík family), Bratislava.

Lehotská, Darina (1948) "Zástoj Michala Mudroňa v kultúrno-politickom živote slovenskom (The role of Michal Mudroň in Slovak cultural-political life)," in Fiala (ed.), *Slovanská Bratislava I*, pp. 290–342.

Lehotská, Darina (1952) "K začiatkom robotníckeho hnutia v Bratislave v XIX. storočí (About the beginnings of the workers' movement in Bratislava in the nineteenth century)," in *Historický sborník Slovenskej akadémie vied a umení*, X, pp. 95–115.

Lehotská, Darina et al (1955) "Bratislavské prvé máje (Bratislava's May Days)," in *Sborník archivních prací*, 5, 2, pp. 3–25.

Lehotská, Darina (1973) "Vývin buržoáznej mestskej správy do roku 1918 (The development of the bourgeois city administration until 1918)," in *Historický časopis*, 21, 4, pp. 575–592.

Lehotský, Vladimír (1970) "K niektorým otázkam z dejín robotníckeho hnutia v Bratislave v období Bánffyho teroru (1895–1900) (On some questions of the history of the workers' movement in Bratislava in the period of Bánffy's terror (1895–1900))," in *Bratislava (Annales)*, VI, pp. 267–280.

Bibliography

Lipták, Ľubomír et al (1992) *Politické strany na Slovensku 1860-1989* (Political parties in Slovakia 1860-1989), Bratislava: Archa.

Lipták, Ľubomír (1996) "Die Freimaurer und die Modernisierung in der Slowakei im 20. Jahrhundert (Freemasons and modernisation in Slovakia in the twentieth century)," in *Bohemia (Zeitschrift für Geschichte und Kultur der böhmischen Länder, A Journal of History and Civilisation in East Central Europe)*, 37, 1, pp. 55-68.

Lipták, Ľubomír (1997) "Elitenwechsel in der bürgerlichen Gesellschaft der Slowakei im ersten Drittel des 20. Jahrhunderts (Change of elites in the bourgeois society in Slovakia in the first third of the twentieth century)," in Mannová (ed.), *Bürgertum und bürgerliche Gesellschaft in der Slowakei 1900-1989*, pp. 67-80.

Lipták, Ľubomír (1998) "Naším najväčším problémom sme my sami (We are our biggest problem)," in *Domino-Fórum*, 38, pp. 4-5.

Lipták, Ľubomír (1999a) *Storočie dlhšie sko sto rokov* (A century longer than a hundred years), Bratislava: Kalligram.

Lipták, Ľubomír (1999b) "Slovenská otázka na prelome 19. a 20. storočia (The Slovak question at the turn of the nineteenth and twentieth centuries)," in Podrimavský and Kováč (eds), *Slovensko na začiatku 20. storočia*, pp. 11-16.

Lipták, Ľubomír (1999c) "Kolektívne identity a verejné priestory (Collective identities and public spaces)," in Csáky and Mannová (eds), *Kolektívne identity v strednej Európe v období moderny*, pp. 117-131.

Lowenthal, David (1994) "Identity, heritage and history," in Gillis (ed.), *Commemorations: The Politics of National Identity*, pp. 41-57.

Luther, Daniel (1992) "Soziale Kontakte in den Strassen der Stadt" (Social contacts on the streets of the city)," in Salner and Luther (eds), *Ethnokulturelle Prozesse in Grossstädten Mitteleuropas, Adaptation im Stadtmilieu, Toleranz-Intoleranz in Grossstädten Mitteleuropas*, pp. 51-56.

Mackey, William F. (1988) "Geolinguistics: its scope and principles," in Williams (ed.), *Language in Geographic Context*, pp. 20-46.

Mann, Michael (1992) "The emergence of modern European nationalism," in Hall and Jarvie (eds), *Transition to Modernity, Essays on Power, Wealth and Belief*, pp. 137-165.

Mannová, Elena (1987) "Spolky v Bratislave koncom 19. a začiatkom 20. storočia (Associations in Bratislava at the end of the nineteenth and the beginning of the twentieth century)," in *Slovenský národopis*, 35, 2–3, pp. 363–369.

Mannová Elena (1990) "Spolky a ich miesto v živote spoločnosti na Slovensku v 19. stor. Stav a problémy výskumu (Associations and their place in social life in Slovakia in the nineteenth century. The condition and problems of research)," in *Historický časopis*, 38, 1, pp. 15–27.

Mannová, Elena and Daniel, Paul David (eds) (1995) "A guide to historiography in Slovakia," *Studia Historica Slovaca*, XX.

Mannová, Elena (1995a) "Transformácia identity bratislavských Nemcov v 19. storočí (Transformation of the identity of Bratislava's Germans in the nineteenth century)," in *Historický časopis*, 43, 3, pp. 437–449.

Mannová, Elena (1995b) "Identitätsbildung der Deutschen in Pressburg/Bratislava im 19. Jahrhundert (Construction of identity of Germans in Pressburg/Bratislava in the nineteenth century)," in *Halbasien, Zeitschrift für deutsche Literatur und Kultur Südosteuropas*, Frankfurt am Main, 5, 2, pp. 60–76.

Mannová, Elena (1995c) "Sebaprezentácia nemeckých stredných vrstiev v Bratislave v 19. storočí (Self-presentation of the German middle classes in Bratislava in the nineteenth century)," in *Slovenský národopis*, 43, 2, pp. 167–174.

Mannová, Elena (ed.) (1997) *Bürgertum und bürgerliche Gesellschaft in der Slowakei 1900–1989* (Bourgeoisie and bourgeois society in Slovakia 1900–1989), Bratislava: Academic Electronic Press.

Mannová, Elena (1997a) "Entwicklungsbedingungen bürgerlichen Schichten in der Slowakei im 20. Jahrhundert (Conditions for development of the bourgeois strata in Slovakia in the twentieth century)," in Mannová (ed.), *Bürgertum und bürgerliche Gesellschaft in der Slowakei 1900–1989*, pp. 11–18.

Mannová, Elena (1997b) "Meštianstvo na Slovensku v 19. a 20. storočí ako predmet historického výskumu (Burghers in nineteenth and twentieth century Slovakia as a subject of historical research)," *Historický časopis*, 45, 1, pp. 85–90.

Mannová, Elena (1997c) "A transition from social to national values in association activity (German union balls in Bratislava)," in *Journal of Urban*

Ethnology 2, Warsaw: Muzeum Niepodleglosci, pp. 49–55.

Mannová, Elena (1999a) "Elitné spolky v Bratislave v 19. a 20. storočí (Elite associations in Bratislava in the nineteenth and twentieth centuries)," in Salner and Beňušková (eds), *Diferenciácia mestkého spoločenstva v každodennom živote*, pp. 52–69.

Mannová, Elena (1999b) "Dobročinné spolky a konštruovanie kolektívnych identít (Charitable associations and the construction of collective identities)," in Csáky and Mannová (eds), *Kolektívne identity v strednej Európe v období moderny*, pp. 195–212.

Martin, Luther H., Gutman, Huck and Hutton, Patrick H. (eds) (1988) *Technologies of the Self*, London: Tavistock Publications.

Massey, Doreen (1993) "Politics and space/time," in Keith and Pile (eds), *Place and the Politics of Identity*, pp. 141–161.

Medvecký, Karol A. (ed.) (1931) *Slovenský prevrat IV.* (Slovak coup), Bratislava: Komenský.

Melinz, Gerhard and Zimmermann, Susan (eds) (1996) *Wien-Prague-Budapest: Blütezeit der Habsburgmetropolen* (Vienna-Prague-Budapest: Flourishing time of the Habsburg metropolises), Wien: Promedia.

Mésároš, Július (1995) "Pramene a literatúra k vývoju národnostného zloženia obyvateľstva Uhorska v 18. a 19. storočí (Sources and literature to the development of the ethnic composition of the population of Hungary in the eighteenth and nineteenth centuries)," in *Historický časopis*, 43, 4, pp. 628–650.

Mésároš, Július (1997) "Maďarizácia a asimilácia v Uhorsku od konca 18. storočia do roku 1918 (Magyarisation and assimilation in Hungary from the end of the eighteenth century until the year 1918)," *Historický časopis*, 45, 2, pp. 295–304.

Mezey, László Miklós (1995) "A pozsonyi Toldy Kör három korszaka (Three periods of the Pozsonyer Toldy Kör)," in *Limes, Komárom-Esztergom megyei tudományos szemle*, 8, 3, pp. 57–64.

Minár, Pavol (1997) "Die Stadt in slowakischen Fiktionen der Zwischenkriegszeit. Voraussetzungen, Regeln, Kodes und die Logik der Textproduktion (The town in Slovak fiction of the interwar period. Conditions, rules, codes und logic of the text's production)," in Mannová (ed.), *Bürgertum und bürgerliche Gesellschaft in der Slowakei 1900–1989*, pp. 123–151.

Mucsi, Ferenc (1985) "Haza csak ott van, hol jog is van... (Home is only there where there is law...)," in *História*, 7, 5–6, pp. 46–49.

Nash, Catherine (2000) "Historical geographies of modernity," in Graham and Nash (eds), *Modern Historical Gepgraphies*, pp. 13–40.

Nimni, Ephraim (1991) *Marxism and Nationalism*, London, Concord, Mass.: Pluto Press.

Ogborn, Miles (1993) "Ordering the city: surveillance, public space and the reform of urban policing in England 1835–56," in *Political Geography*, 12, 6, pp. 505–521.

Ormis, Ján V. (1948) "Zo zápisiek Krištofa Chorváta (From the memoirs of Krištof Chorvát)," in Fiala (ed.), *Slovanská Bratislava I.*, pp. 387–399.

Paríková, Magdaléna (1985) "Obchod so zeleninou a ovocím v prímestských obciach Bratislavy (Trade with fruits and vegetables in villages on the outskirts of Bratislava)," in *Slovenský národopis*, 33, 1, pp. 179–194.

Paríková, Magdaléna (1987) "Služobníctvo v Bratislave v prvej polovici 20. storočia (Servants in Bratislava in the first half of the twentieth century)," in *Slovenský národopis*, 35, 2–3, pp. 331–340.

Pašiak, Ján (1997) "Bürgertum und bürgerliche Gesellschaft in der Slowakei im Kontext der Siedlungsentwicklungen 1900–1989 (The bourgeoisie and bourgeois society in Slovakia in context of the development of settlements 1900–1989)," in Mannová (ed.), *Bürgertum und bürgerliche Gesellschaft in der Slowakei 1900–1989*, pp. 19–35.

Pekník, Michal (1999) "K profilu slovensko-českých vťahov pred prvou svetovou vojnou (On the profile of Slovak-Czech relations before the First World War)," in Podrimavský and Kováč (eds), *Slovensko na začiatku 20. storočia*, pp. 87–99.

Peet, Richard and Thrift, Nigel (eds) (1989) *New Models in Geography (The Political-Economy Perspective) Vol. 1*, London, Boston, Sidney, Wellington: Unwin Hyman.

Periwal, Sukumar (ed.) (1995) *Notions of Nationalism*, Budapest, London, Prague: Central European University Press.

Periwal, Sukumar (1995a) "Conclusion," in Periwal (ed.), *Notions of Nationalism*, pp. 228–240.

Petruf, P. (1996) "Die slowakische Historiographie in 1990–1994 (The Slovak historiography in 1990–1994)," in *Bohemia Band*, 37, pp. 153–168.

Pichler, Tibor (1997) "Nationaleiferer oder Bürger: Institutionalisierung als Problem (National zealots or burghers: institutionalisation as a problem)," in Mannová (ed.), *Bürgertum und bürgerliche Gesellschaft in der Slowakei 1900-1989*, pp. 61–66.

Pichler, Tibor (1999) "Hľadanie stratenej pamäti: K politike spomínania v strednej Európe (Looking for the lost memory: On the politics of remembering in Central Europe)," in Csáky and Mannová (eds), *Kolektívne identity v strednej Európe v období moderny*, pp. 51–58.

Pile, Steve (1996) *The Body and the City: Psychoanalysis, Space and Subjectivity*, London and New York: Routledge.

Písch, Mikuláš (1966) *Ohlas ruskej buržoáznodemokratickej revolúcie na Slovensku (1905-1907)* (The response to the Russian bourgeois-democratic revolution in Slovakia (1905–1907)), Bratislava: Vydavateľstvo politickej literatúry.

Podolák, Ján (1985) "Niektoré poznatky z etnografického výskumu prímestských osád Bratislavy (Some conclusions from ethnographic research on villages on the outskirts of Bratislava)," in *Slovenský národopis*, 33, 1, pp. 136–149.

Podrimavský, Milan (1972) "Oszkár Jászi a národnostná otázka (Oscar Jászi and the question of nationalities)," in *Historický časopis*, 20, 1, pp. 65–88.

Podrimavský, Milan (1977) "Program Slovenskej národnej strany v rokoch 1900–1914 (The program of the Slovak national party in years 1900–1914)," in *Historický časopis*, 25, 1, pp. 3–25.

Podrimavský, Milan et al (1992) *Dejiny Slovenska III (od roku 1848 do konca 19. storočia)* (History of Slovakia III (from the year 1848 until the end of the ninettenth century)), Bratislava: Veda.

Podrimavský, Milan and Dušan Kováč (eds) (1999) *Slovensko na začiatku 20. storočia* (Slovakia at the beginning of the twentieth century), Bratislava: Historický ústav SAV.

Podrimavský, Milan (1999) "Slováci a uhorský štát na prelome 19. a 20.

storočia (Slovakia and the Hungarian state at the turn of the nineteenth and twentieth centuries)," in Podrimavský and Kováč (eds), *Slovensko na začiatku 20. storočia*, pp. 25–35.

Potemra, Michal (1958) *Bibliografia slovenských novín a časopisov do roku 1918* (Bibliography of Slovak newspapers and magazines published before 1918), Martin: Matica Slovenská.

Potemra, Michal (1963) *Bibliografia inorečových novín a časopisov na Slovensku do roku 1918* (Bibliography of other-language newspapers and magazines in Slovakia until the year 1918), Martin: Matica Slovenská.

Potemra, Michal (1964) *Bibliografia slovenských kníh 1901–1918* (Bibliography of Slovak books 1901–1918), Martin: Matica Slovenská.

Potemra, Michal (1975) "Uhorské volebné právo a voľby na Slovensku v rokoch 1901–1914 (Hungarian suffrage and elections in Slovakia in the years 1901–1914)," *Historický časopis*, 23, 2, 1975, pp. 201–239.

Potemra, Michal (1980) "Prejavy supremácie maďarských vládnych kruhov v politickom živote Slovenska v rokoch 1901–1914 (Expressions of supremacy of the Hungarian ruling circles in the political life of Slovakia in the years 1901–1914)," in *Historický časopis*, 28, 1, pp. 41–73.

Potemra, Michal (1983) *Kultúrna a osvetová práca na Slovensku, 1901–1918* (Cultural and advanced educational work in Slovakia, 1901–1918), Vols. I-IV, Košice: Štátna vedecká knižnica.

Potemra, Michal (1990) *Školstvo na Slovensku v rokoch 1901–1918* (Education in Slovakia in the years 1901–1918), Košice: Štátna vedecká knižnica.

Potemra, Michal (1993) *Školstvo na Slovensku v rokoch 1901–1918* (Education in Slovakia in the years 1901–1918), Martin: Matica Slovenská, 1993.

Portisch, Emil (1933) *Geschichte der Stadt Pressburg-Bratislava* (History of the city of Pressburg-Bratislava), Pressburg-Bratislava: S. Steiner.

Purcell, Mark (1998) "A place for the Copts: imagined territory and spatial conflict in Egypt," in *Ecumene*, 5, 4, pp. 432–451.

Profantová, Zuzana (1999) "Tendencie v slovenskej folkloristike na prelome storočí (Tendencies in Slovak folklore studies at the turn of the centuries)," in Podrimavský and Kováč (eds), *Slovensko na začiatku 20. storočia*, pp. 252–266.

Pynsent, Robert B. (ed.) (1989) *Decadence and Innovation , Austro-Hungarian Life and Art at the Turn of the Century*, London: Weidenfeld and Nicholson.

Rabinow, Paul (ed.) (1984) *The Foucault Reader*, Penguin.

Reichensperger, Richard (1999) "Umenie pamäti medzi Parížom a Viedňou, Maurice Halbwachs, Walter Benjamin, Alfred Schütz a viedenská Ringstrasse (Art of memory between Paris and Vienna, Maurice Halbwachs, Walter Benjamin, Alfred Schütz and the Viennese Ringstrasse)," in Csáky and Mannová (eds), *Kolektívne identity v strednej Európe v období moderny*, pp. 23–44.

Rothkirchen, Livia (1968) "Slovakia: I., 1848–1918," in *The Jews of Czechoslovakia*, Vol. I, Philadelphia: Jewish Publication Society of America, pp. 72–84.

Rose, Nikolas (1990) *Governing the Soul*, London and New York: Routledge.

Rudolph, Richard L. and Good, Davod F. (eds) (1992) *Nationalism and Empire, The Habsburg Empire and the Soviet Union*, University of Minnesota: St. Martin's Press.

Ruppeldt, Fedor (1927) "Srdce národa (The heart of the nation)," in *Slovenské Pohľady*, 43, 1, pp. 70–86.

Russell, Mark (2000) "The building of Hamburg's Bismarck memorial," *The Historical Journal*, 43, 1, pp. 133–156.

Salner, Peter et al (1991) *Taká bola Bratislava* (How Bratislava used to be), Bratislava: Veda.

Salner, Peter and Luther, Daniel (eds) (1992) *Ethnokulturelle Prozesse in Grossstädten Mitteleuropas, Adaptation im Stadtmilieu, Toleranz-Intoleranz in Grossstädten Mitteleuropas* (Ethno-cultural processes in the big cities of Central Europe, Adaptation in the urban environment, Tolerance-intolerance in the big cities of Central Europe), Bratislava: SAV, Národopisný Ústav.

Salner, Peter (1992) "Die Stadt zwischen Mensch und Politik (The town between humans and politics)," in Salner and Luther (eds), *Ethnokulturelle Prozesse in Grossstädten Mitteleuropas, Adaptation im Stadtmilieu, Toleranz-Intoleranz in Grossstädten Mitteleuropas*, pp. 69–78.

Salner, Peter (1993) "Tolerancia a intolerancia vo veľkých mestách strednej Európy (model Bratislava) (Tolerance and intolerance in the big cities of the central Europe (model Bratislava))," in *Slovenský národopis*, 41, 1, pp. 3–15.

Salner, Peter (1997) "Die Juden in der bürgerlichen Gesellschaft der Slowakei (Jews in bourgeois society in Slovakia)," in Mannová (ed.), *Bürgertum und bürgerliche Gesellschaft in der Slowakei 1900-1989*, pp. 153–163.

Salner, Peter and Zuzana Beňušková (eds) (1999) *Diferenciácia mestského spoločenstva v každodennom živote* (Differentiation of urban society in everyday life), Bratislava: Ústav etnológie SAV.

Savage, Kirk (1994) "The Politics of memory: Black emancipation and the civil war monument," in John R. Gillis (ed.) *Commemorations: the Politics of National Identity*, pp. 128–149.

Schama, Simon (1995) *Landscape and Memory*, London: Harper Collins Publishers.

Schorske, Carl E. (1981) *Fin-de-Siecle Vienna—Politics and Culture*, Cambridge University Press.

Seewann, Gerhard (ed.) (1992) *Minderheitenfragen in Südosteuropa (Beiträge der Internationalen Konferenz: The Minority Question in Historical Perspective 1900-1990, Inter University Center Dubrovnik)* (Minority questions in Southern and Eastern Europe (Contributions of the international conference)), München: R. Oldenbourg Verlag (Südost-Institut, Band 27, München).

Seewann, Gerhard (1992a) "Siebenbürger Sachse, Ungarndeutscher, Donauschwabe? (*Siebenbürger* Saxon, Hungarian German, Danube Swabian?)," in Seewann (ed.), *Minderheitenfragen in Südosteuropa: Beiträge der Internationalen Konferenz: The Minority Question in Historical Perspective 1900-1990*, pp. 139–155.

Seliger, Maren (1996) "Wien im Zeichen bürgerlicher Vorherrschaft (Vienna in the sign of the bourgeois rule)," in Melinz and Zimmermann (eds), *Wien-Prague-Budapest: Blütezeit der Habsburgmetropolen*, pp. 84–92.

Sennet, Richard (1994) *Flesh and Stone: the Body and the City in Western Civilisation*, London: Faber and Faber.

Sidler, Lia (1995) "Koncepty identity a etnické vzory identity v Bratislave (Concepts of identity and ethnic examples of identity in Bratislava)," in *Slovenský národopis*, 43, 2, pp. 5–18.

Sked, Alan (1989) *The Decline and Fall of the Habsburg Empire 1815-1918*,

London and New York.

Smith, Anthony D. (1981) *The Ethnic Revival*, Cambridge: Cambridge University Press.

Smith, Anthony D. and Colin H. Williams (1983) "The national construction of social space," in *Progress in Human Geography*, 7, 4, pp. 502–518.

Smith, Anthony D. (1986) *The Ethnic Origins of Nations*, Oxford: Basil Blackwell.

Smith, Anthony D. (1991) *National Identity*, Penguin.

Smith, Graham, Law, Vivien, Wilson, Andrew, Bohr, Annette and Allworth, Edward (1998) *Nation-Building in the Post-Soviet Borderlands: The Politics of National Identities*, Cambridge: Cambridge University Press.

Soja, Edward and Hooper, Barbara (1993) "Some notes on the geographical margins of the new cultural politics," in Keith and Pile (eds), *Place and the Politics of Identity*, pp. 183–205.

Špiesz, Anton (1992) *Dejiny Slovenska na ceste k sebauvedomeniu* (History of Slovakia on the road to self-consciousness), Bratislava: Perfect.

Štefánek, Anton (1944) *Slovenská vlastiveda III.* (Slovak sociology), Bratislava: Slovenská akadémia vied a umení.

Steinberg, Jonathan (1987) "The historian and the *Questione della lingua*," in Burke and Porter (eds), *The Social History of Language*, pp. 198–209.

Stoličná, Rastislava (1987) "Bratislavské 'ľudové kuchyne' v prvej štvrtine 20. storočia (Bratislava's soup kitchens in the first quarter of the twentieth century)," in *Slovenský národopis*, 35, 2–3, pp. 341–346.

Stoličná, Rastislava (1992) "Die Judengemeinde in Bratislava (The Jewish community in Bratislava)," in *Ethnokulturelle Prozesse in Grossstädten Mitteleuropas, Adaptation im Stadtmilieu, Toleranz-Intoleranz in Grossstädten Mitteleuropas*, pp. 100–108.

Sugar, Peter F. and Lederer Ivo J. (eds) (1969) *Nationalism in Eastern Europe*, Seattle, London: University of Washington Press.

Sugar, Peter F. (1969) "External and domestic roots of Eastern Euroepan nationalism," in Sugar and Lederer (eds), *Nationalism in Eastern Europe*, pp. 3–54.

Bibliography

Sugar, Peter F., Hanák, Péter and Frank, Tibor (eds) (1990) *A History of Hungary*, Bloomington and Indianapolis: Indiana University Press.

Sundhaussen, Holm (1973) *Der Einfluss der Herderschen Ideen auf die Nationsbildung bei den Völkern der Habsburger Monarchie* (Influence of Herder's ideas on the nation-building of the peoples of the Habsburg Monarchy), München: R. Oldenbourg Verlag.

Svetoň, Ján (1942) *Slováci v Maďarsku, Príspevky k otázke štatistickej maďarizácie* (Slovaks in Hungary. Contributions to the question of the statistical Magyarisation), Bratislava: Vedecká spoločnosť pre zahraničných Slovákov.

Svetoň, Ján (1948) "Od maďarizácie k reslovakizácii Bratislavy (From Magyarisation to re-Slovakisation of Bratislava)," in Fiala (ed.), *Slovanská Bratislava I*, pp. 268–289.

Szabad, György (1982) "A polgári jogegyenlőség elleni támadás és kudarc a század végi Magyarországon (Attack on and defeat of the citizen's legal equality in Hungary at the end of the century)," in *Társadalmi szemle*, 37, 8–9, pp. 68–78.

Szabó, Dániel (1985) "Választás és csalás Magyarországon a századfordulón (Elections and fraud in Hungary at the turn of the century)," in *História*, 7, 5–6, pp. 44–46.

Szabó, Dániel (1991) "Századfordulás azonosulásformák (Turn of the century identification forms)," in *Valóság*, 34, 11, pp. 23–31.

Szabó, Miklós (1981) "Nemzetkarakter és resszentiment, Gondolatok a politikai antiszemitizmus funkcióiról (National character and re-sentiment, Thoughts about the functions of political anti-Semitism)," in *Világosság*, 22, 6, pp. 58–62.

Szarka, László (1999) *Szlovák nemzeti fejlődés—magyar nemzetiségi politika/ Slovenský národný vývin—národnostná politika v Uhorsku* (Slovak national development—Hungarian nationalities' politics), Bratislava: Kalligram, Kultúrny inštitút maďarskej republiky, (bilingual Hungarian/Slovak edition, page numbers used in the text from the Slovak version).

Száz, Zoltán (1995) "Government policy and the nationalities," in Glatz (ed.), *Hungarians and Their Neighbors in Modern Times 1867-1950*, pp. 23–32.

Tacke, Charlotte (1995) *Denkmal im sozialen Raum* (Monument in social space), Götingen: Vandenhoeck&Ruprecht.

Tajták, Ladislav (1980) "Vývin, pohyb a štrukturálne zmeny obyvateľstva na Slovensku v predvojnovom období (1900-1914), (Development, movement and structural changes of the population of Slovakia before the war)," in *Historický časopis*, 28, 4, pp. 497-524.

Tajták, Ladislav (1981) "Vývoj robotníckeho hnutia na Slovensku na začiatku 20. storočia (Development of the workers' movement in Slovakia at the beginning of the twentieth century)," in *Slovenský národopis*, 29, 6, pp. 820-856.

Tajták, Ladislav (1995) "K niektorým otázkam dejín robotníckeho hnutia na Slovensku do roku 1918 (On some questions of the history of the workers' movement in Slovakia until the year 1918)," in *Historický časopis*, 43, 4, pp. 723-742.

Tamás, Lajos (1938) *A Toldy Kör története (1906-1935)* (History of Toldy Kör (1906-1935)), Pozsony: A Pozsonyi Toldy Kör kiadása.

Tarrow, Sidney (1994) *Power in Movement*, Cambridge University Press.

Taylor, Peter J. (1997) "World-systems analysis and regional geography," in Agnew (ed.), *Political Geography*, pp. 17-25.

Teich, Mikuláš and Porter, Roy (eds) (1990) *Fin de Siecle and Its Legacy*, Cambridge: Cambridge University Press.

Thomas, Julian (1993) "The politics of vision and the archaeologies of landscape," in Bender (ed.), *Landscape Politics and Perspectives*, pp. 19-48.

Tibenský, Ján (1972) "The function of the Cyril and Methodius and the Great Moravian traditions in the ideology of the Slovak feudal nationality," in *Studia Historica Slovaca*, VII, pp. 69-95.

Tóth, Zoltán (1990) "Transformation und Abstieg der alten städtischen Kleinbürger (Transformation and decline of the old urban petty bourgeoisie)," in Bruckmüller, Döcker, Steckl and Urbanitsch (eds), *Bürgertum in der Habsburger Monarchie*, pp. 105-113.

Tóth, Zoltán (1996) "Was wird im Schmelztiegel geschmolzen? (What is melting in the melting pot?)," in Melinz and Zimmermann (eds), *Wien-Prague-Budapest: Blütezeit der Habsburgmetropolen*, pp. 210-218.

Tóth, Zoltán (1998) "What is melting in the melting pot?," in *Regio, A Review of Studies on Minorities, Communities and Society (Budapest)*, 1998, pp. 187–217.

Trančík, Martin (1996) *Zwischen Alt- und Neuland. Die Geschichte der Buchhändlerfamilie Steiner in Pressburg* (Between the old and new land. History of the bookshop owner family of Steiner), Bratislava: Vydavateľstvo PT.

Uhl, Heidemarie (1999) "Kultúrne stratégie politiky národnej identifikácie v Grazi okolo roku 1900 (Cultural strategies of the politics of national identification in Graz around 1900)," in Csáky and Mannová (eds), *Kolektívne identity v strednej Európe v období moderny*, pp. 133–153.

Viktor, Gabriel (1998) *Legenda rokov meruôsmych* (Legend of the years 1848/9), Bratislava: Sursum.

Weber, Eugen (1979) *Peasants into Frenchmen: the Modernization of Rural France 1870-1914*, London: Chatto and Windus.

Weeks, Theodor R. (1999) "Monuments and memory: immortalizing Count M. N. Muraviev in Vilna, 1898," in *Nationalities Papers*, 27, 4, pp. 551–564.

Williams, Colin H. (ed.) (1988) *Language in Geographic Context* (Multilingual Matters 38), Clevedon, Philadelphia: Multilingual Matters Ltd.

Williams, Colin H. (1993) *Called Unto Liberty!* (Multilingual Matters 97), Clevedon, Philadelphia, Adelaide: Multilingual Matters Ltd.

Wolff, Janet and Seed, John (eds) (1988) *The Culture of Capital: Art, Power and the Nineteenth-Century Middle Class*, Manchester: Manchester University Press.

Wolff, Janet (1988) "The culture of separate spheres: the role of culture in nineteenth century public and private life," in Wolff and Seed (eds), *The Culture of Capital: Art, Power and the Nineteenth-Century Middle Class*, pp. 117–134.

Woolf, Penelope (1988) "Symbol of the Second Empire: cultural politics and the Paris Opera House," in Cosgrove and Daniels (eds), *The Iconography of Landscape*, pp. 214–235.

Zajac, Peter (1999) "Pamäť, zabúdanie a pripamätúvanie ako problém utvárania kolektívnej identity slovenského národa (Memory, forgetting and remembering as a problem in constructing the collective identity of the Slovak nation)," in Csáky and Mannová (eds), *Kolektívne identity v strednej Európe v období moderny*, pp. 45–50.

Zerubavel, Yael (1994) "The historic, the legendary, and the incredible: invented tradition and collective memory in Israel," in Gillis (ed.), *Commemorations: The Politics of National Identity*, pp. 105–123.

Zimmermann, Susan (ed.) (1995) *Urban Space and Identity in the European City 1890-1930s*, Working Papers Series 3, Budapest: CEU History Department.

Zigmundík, Ján (1926) *Rozpomienka na Vendka Bohboja Kutlíka.* (Recollection of Vendko Bohboj Kutlík.) Bratislava: Ústredná Slovenská Liga.

Žudeľ, Juraj (1980) "Sprievodný text k mapovým prílohám (Accompanying text to the map enclosures)," in Klimko, Jozef, *Vývoj územia Slovenska a utváranie jeho hraníc*, pp. 135–154.

Yeoh, Brenda S. A. (2000) "Historical geographies of the colonised world," in Graham and Nash (eds), *Modern Historical Geographies*, pp. 146–166.

✧ NOTES ✧

INTRODUCTION

1 'Ethnic groups' here does not denote ethnic communities with sharply defined boundaries. Boundaries between groups were flexible and many people shifted between different groups. German, Magyar and Slovak 'ethnic groups' are used here as these categories were used in the Hungarian censuses, referring mainly to language usage. However, a person's identity was often not characterised by exclusive belonging to one of these 'groups.'

2 Connerton, 1989, p. 7.

3 Pisztóry, 1891, Ortvay, 1907. Ortvay's history of Bratislava's streets and squares contains much valuable information. (Ortvay, 1905.) An extensive monograph on Bratislava city and county *Magyarország vármegyei és városai. Pozsony vármegye* (without the year of publication) also includes invaluable information about the city. However, this monograph is marked by the idea of Hungarian dominance. For example, its section on education and journalism is heavily concerned with the spread of the Hungarian language in education and the periodical press in Bratislava. In addition to these works there is a whole range of books, bulletins, booklets concerned with different aspects of the city life, associations, culture, church, education, etc. See the bibliography by Kertész, 1935.

4 Portisch, 1933.

5 See *Zlatá kniha Bratislavy*, 1928, Hromádka, 1933 (on the geographical and demographic situation). For example, the author Ovidius Faust in his brief history of the city museum and library (in *Župa bratislavská*) claims that activity of both institutions was insufficient, haphazard and unsystematic, unlike the new, improved and better conditions in the Czechoslovak Republic. (Faust, 1927.) Similarly, in his article on the municipal social-humanitarian department, Kraus is primarily interested in describing the functioning of the new department. Kraus, 1927.

6 Lipták, 1999a, pp. 142–152. Historians and publicists would criticise the ruthless Magyarisation policies of the Hungarian state in this period, failing to see positive

developments. For example, although the number of Slovak schools decreased, there was a rapid increase in the number of school-going pupils and rising literacy levels. The Slovak territory had a good network of secondary schools and four higher education institutions. Bi- and tri-lingualism made growing information accessible to wide layers of population. (Ibid., p. 147.) Lipták also refers to the so-called "cut-off hands" connected with the frequent changes of elites in Slovakia (1918, 1938, 1948, 1968) which always meant new requirements on history writing (for example in terms of "de-Hungarisation, de-Czechisation, Slovakisation, internationalisation") depending on the power elite. Ibid., pp. 159–165.

7 Kalesný, 1985, 1987, Fekete, 1948.

8 Lehotská, 1973.

9 Kovačevičová, 1976, 1985, 1987, Obuchová, Unpublished thesis, 1986.

10 Goláň, 1957, 1958, Gosiorovský, 1956, Hapák, 1973, Kalesný, 1974, Lehotská, 1952, 1955, Lehotský, Unpublished thesis, 1969, Lehotský, 1970, Lehotský, Unpublished thesis, 1977, Tajták, 1981. There were also different studies and works on other aspects like for example music life in the city, trade in Bratislava. However, these were not so relevant for this study.

11 Horváth et al, 1978.

12 Lipták, 1998.

13 Lipták, 1999a, p. 272.

14 See Pichler, 1999. As Pichler writes, Jozef Miloslav Hurban, a leading intellectual in the nineteenth-century Slovak nationalist movement said: "We don't have history…only 'prologues' to it…we are the first persons." The new beginning was connected to the "prologues" of the Great Moravian state and the collective memory was based on "tradition of suffering." Ibid., p. 53. See also Pichler, 1997, Zajac, 1999.

15 Salner et al, 1991. See also Salner 1992, 1993 generally on tolerance, intolerance and co-existence of people in the urban environment, also Luther, 1992. See Franek et al, 1997 on the Jews in Bratislava.

16 Mannová has some extensive research on the German middle classes and their associations in Bratislava (1995a, 1995b, 1995c, 1997c) but also on the city's associational life in general (1999a,b).

17 Glettler, 1988, 1989a, 1992.

18 Szarka, 1999, p. 157.

19 However, Hungarian social scientists also hold differing views of assimilation and factors that influence it. For an overview see Gyányi, 1993.

20 Hanák, 1984a.

21 Mésároš, 1995, 1997. On so-called "moral Magyarisation" and definitions of a "renegade" and "Magyaron" see Štefánek,1944, pp. 166–168.

22 Mannová, Unpublished article, 1994.

23 Glatz, 1995a, p. xiv.

24 Williams, 1993, p. 19.

25 Brubaker, 1996, p. 14.

26 On the discussion whether one can at all use the '*terminus technicus*' "Slovak society" before 1918 see Pichler, 1997.

27 Lipták, 1999, p. 282. Lipták talks about the effort of Slovak historiography to "de-Hungarise" the Slovak history and concentrate on the "anti-Hungarian dissidents." (Ibid., p. 287.) See for example *Historický časopis* 1, 45, 1997 on the discussion about the Slovak historiography on the 11th convention of the Slovak Historical Society. Also see Petruf, 1996, Kováč, 1996.

28 Csáky, 1999.

29 Pichler 1997, 1999, Kusý, 1998a, 1998b, Zajac, 1999.

30 Kusý, 1998b, p. 163.

31 See Mannová, Daniel (eds), 1995.

32 See Csáky, Mannová (eds), 1999. However, many articles of the recent collection on history of Slovakia at the turn of the nineteenth century (Podrimavský, Kováč (eds), 1999) are very similar to those published in previous years.

33 See for instance Gellner, 1983, Hobsbawm, 1992. While modernists consider nations to be modern phenomena whose emergence takes place as late as after the eighteenth century, primordialists claim that nations have always been around and that people have always had a feeling of belonging together, of an identity which could be associated with today's national identity. In this sense tribes were predecessors of today's nations, and there is a connection between the two.

34 Periwal, 1995a.

35 Smith, A., 1986, pp. 179–183. See also Smith, A., 1981, 1986. "The history of nations…is always presented to us in the form of a narrative which attributes to these entities the continuity of a subject." In Balibar, Wallerstein, 1991, p. 86.

36 Smith, A., 1986, p. 192. Seewann points out the importance of the "genesis-myth" which involves claiming that the land was empty prior to the arrival of a certain group of people and that they therefore have a historical right to claim ownership. Such statements lead to competing mythologies between several groups of people inhabiting a certain territory. Seewann, 1992a, pp. 145–146, footnote 9. On invention of tradition see

Hobsbawm, Ranger (eds), 1983. On competing myths of ethnogenesis in Post-Soviet states see Smith, G. et al, 1998. Slovak nationalist myths include: Slovaks have been in the Carpathian valley for 1500 years (as a continuous entity), thousand years of Hungarian oppression (denying that the Hungarian state was based on class not ethnic principle), the peacefulness of Slovaks as a national characteristic (as opposed to the invading barbaric hordes). See also Lipták, 1998, p. 5.

37 Smith, A., 1991, p. 100. This kind of distinction is very wide-spread. Miroslav Hroch also distinguishes between the large and small nations on a somewhat similar premise. The 'large' nations are those which had their own state and when the new class the bourgeoisie emerged it declared itself having the same interest as the whole nation already given as existing within this state. The 'small' nations are those which did not have their own state in the period of the formation of the nations. The criteria for 'large' or 'small' is the very fact of an existing bureaucratic state. Hroch, 1985.

38 See, for instance, Weber, 1979 and Hobsbawm and Ranger (eds), 1983.

39 Tacke, 1995, pp. 16, 296.

40 Smith, A., 1991, pp. 157–161.

41 Hroch, Unpublished article, 1994. See also Hroch, 1992. On language myths see Smith, G. et al., 1998, Chapter eight.

42 Anderson, B., 1983.

43 Gellner quoted in Hroch, 1985, p. 27, italics in original.

44 Hroch, 1994, pp. 25–26, italics in original.

45 Breuilly, 1982, p. 1. Similarly also Michael Mann sees the emergence of the modern state with its administration as one of the two principal causes of the emergence of nationalism. (The other condition is the emergence of universal social classes in commercial capitalism.) Mann, 1992.

46 Breuilly, p. 90. For his analysis of Hungarian nationalism, see pp. 92–99.

47 See Brubaker, 1996, p. 63, footnote 12, p. 5, italics in original.

48 Hroch, 1985, p. 189.

49 Agnew, 1997b, p. 318. See Driver, 1991, for a critique of theories of state formation in political geography, and Elias on the formation of states in Europe (Elias, 1994), Giddens on nation-state (1985). See also Johnston, 1989.

50 See Johnston, Knight, Kofman (eds), 1988.

51 Johnston, Knight, Kofman, 1988a, p. 14.

52 Anderson, J., 1988, p. 25.

53 Purcell, 1998, p. 433.

54 Graham, 2000, p. 77.

55 Smith, A., Williams, 1983.

56 Ibid., p. 502.

57 Ibid., pp. 504–512. Boundary creation is important on three levels: geopolitical, bureaucratic and ethnic. (Ibid., p. 508.) Chapter four of this study deals with geopolitical and ethnic boundary creation. Chapter five is concerned with the bureaucratic control of the state within its borders.

58 Williams, 1993, p. 45.

59 Buček, 1995.

60 Graham, 2000, p. 79.

61 Baker, 1990, p. 56.

62 Lowenthal, 1994, p. 50.

63 Gillis, 1994a, pp. 6–7.

64 For a review of recent literature on the topic see Johnson, 1997, pp. 348–351, Agnew, 1997a, pp. 249–252.

65 Johnson, 1997, p. 349. See Duncan and Ley (eds), 1993.

66 Agnew, 1997a, p. 251.

67 Handler, 1994, p. 30.

68 Keith, Pile, 1993a, p. 28.

69 Soja, Hooper, 1993, pp. 184–185.

70 Graham, 2000, p. 79. On "place and politics of identity" see essays in Keith, Pile (eds), 1993.

71 Harvey, 1985, p. 22. On landscape politics, and landscape as intersection of knowledge and power see Bender, 1993a, Thomas, 1993 as well as the collection of essays by Daniels and Cosgrove, 1988.

72 Boyer, 1994, p. 343.

73 On the city as a body from a psychoanalytic perspective see Pile, 1996. See also Sennett, 1994.

74 Thomas, 1993, pp. 22–23. On "power-geometry" of space see Massey, 1993. Since space is "created out of social relations" it is "full of power and symbolism, a complex web of relations of domination and subordination, of solidarity and

cooperation." Ibid., p. 156.

75 On the development of mass movements see Schorske, 1991 (in Vienna), Colotti (1990), from a theoretical perspective Tarrow, 1994.

76 On the use of city spaces in street demonstrations see Harrison, 1988. On the construction and manipulation of identity of the other (in this case the "racial identity" of Chinese in Vancouver) by the municipal elites and the use of this construction in order to consolidate and perpetuate their power see Anderson, K., 1991.

77 On the relationship between collective memory, remembrance, urban space and power see Boyer, 1994.

78 See Schorske, 1981, on the construction of the *Ringstrasse*; Edholm, 1993 on Hausmann's redesigning of Paris; Hanák, 1998, on Budapest.

79 See Harvey's study of the Basilica the Sacre Couer in Paris (Harvey, 1985), Woolf (1988) on the construction of the Paris opera house, Uhl's analysis of conflicting representation of spaces and monuments in Graz (Uhl, 1999) and Duncan, 1990 on readings of Kandyan landscape by different social groups. On monuments and urban space see also collection of essays by Kearns and Philo (eds), 1993.

80 Johnson, 1997, p. 361. On the relationship between monuments and national identity see also Tacke, 1995.

81 See Lipták on the connection between collective identities, public spaces and monuments. Lipták, 1999a, pp. 311–350, Lipták, 1999c.

82 Lipták, 1999a, pp. 247–252.

83 Jones, 1983, Joyce, 1991.

84 Szarka, 1999, pp. 158–159. Szarka points out that this is not merely a problem of translation. Different terms often express different interpretations of the history of multi-national Hungary.

85 For a bilingual use of Laibach/Ljubljana see Pelikan, Uhl, Unpublished article. A similar form to "Bratislava" was used by the codifier of the Slovak literary language in the nineteenth century, Ľudovít Štúr, who used "Břetislava." This name referred to a Slav prince from the Great Moravian period. This use did not become common in Slovak until 1919 when Pressburg was re-named Bratislava by the Czechoslovak authorities. See Horváth, Rákoš, Watzka, 1977, p. 317, document 165. On the difficulties in using the geographic and proper names in Habsburg histories see Deak, 1979, pp. xviii-xx. Deak also discusses the problem of how to refer to Bratislava, and the city's many names in the period. He decides to use the German "Pressburg" since this is the name by which the city was known in nineteenth century Europe.

86 Cohen, 1981, p. 12.

87 Ibid.

88 I am indebted to Professor Jonathan Steinberg for pointing this out as "the oddest piece of evidence" uncovered in my research.

89 Distinctive differences between different dialects are indicated also by the fact that 'Slovak' books were published not only in literary Slovak but also in different dialects for specific audiences. (Potemra, 1964, pp. 471.) This suggests that indeed people coming from different parts of present-day territory of Slovakia had a distinguished local identity and found literary Slovak as well as other dialects hard to comprehend. Here I can only add that I myself found it almost impossible to understand my grandmother from Northeastern Slovakia when she spoke in her dialect and not in literary Slovak.

90 See Grusková, 1999. Anti-Semitism in Bratislava appears to have been rather weaker than in Vienna during the period. For instance, the Reform synagogue was constructed right next to the Catholic Cathedral of Saint Martin.

CHAPTER 1

Pressburg 1867–1914: Overview

1 The terms 'Slovak', 'German' and 'Magyar' nationalities are used in the sense of the categories of Hungarian censuses which divided nationalities by their professed mother tongue. However, these categories are considered only inventions for the sake of statistical measurement since in reality such neat groups did not exist. Especially in Pressburg, which had for centuries been characterised by the coexistence and intermingling of different ethnic 'groups', drawing such borders would be impossible. Although in 1867 the city appeared predominantly 'German', this merely meant that the language used in city politics and culture was predominantly German; it did not, however, express the identification of individuals with any one ethnic 'group.' Since the main source of information for the social and occupational structure were census data, I will use these 'ethnic groups' in this sense throughout this study.

2 For an excellent overview of the economic and cultural development in the city between 1856 and 1906 see Ortvay, 1907.

3 Buček, 1995, p. 190.

4 The Dual Agreement meant that Austria and Hungary were connected by the person of the emperor. The two states had common foreign affairs, army and financial policies. Hungary received full authority of a state (except areas mentioned above), it had a prime minister and government, a parliament with legislative power and autonomy of counties and cities. Horváth et al, 1978, p. 163.

5 The close connection to Vienna is noticeable also in the announcements of engagements and marriages. Glettler, 1988, pp. 50–51.

6 In 1873, the towns of Buda, Pest and the market places Obuda and Margaret's island (*Margit-sziget*) were joined into one city, Budapest. (Glettler, 1992, p. 295.) The city's population grew from 280,349 in 1869 to 880,371 in 1910, especially because of migration. Glettler, 1988, p. 49.

7 Gašparec, 1998, p. 40.

8 Horváth et al, 1978, pp. 165–173.

9 Ibid., p. 73.

10 Gašparec, 1998, p. 42.

11 Komora, 1998, p. 66.

12 Horváth et al, 1978, pp. 174–175.

13 *Stadtverschönerungsverein* (City beautification society) was concerned with enhancement of the city environment. See Chapter five, Part 4.

14 Gašparec, 1998, p. 42, selected issues of *PZ*, Portisch, 1933.

15 Gašparec, 1998, p. 46.

16 Ibid., p. 40.

17 Francová, 1998b, p. 83.

18 Gašparec, 1998, p. 46.

19 Győrik, 1918, p. 32.

20 Ibid., pp. 32–33. Justi also planned other things for the city such as, for example, a permanent bridge over the Danube (there was only a pontoon bridge until 1898), slaughterhouse, water piping system, market hall, construction of schools, increasing of the tourism in the city. However, none of these long-term plans was carried out since Justi did not always find support among the city representatives. Justi managed to increase the city incomes and the city property and was a great administrative talent. For the most part, he ruled the city in an autocratic manner with the support of the majority of the city representatives led by the banker Theodor Edl and the Catholic city priest Karl Heiler. However, Justi's autocratic manners often brought him into conflict, and when he got into a conflict with the new institution of the főispán (head of the county government) he had to withdraw and was not even granted the full pension to which he was entitled. When he died only the freemasons praised Justi's work for the city although he had been their opponent. Ibid.

21 Gašparec, 1998, pp. 40–46.

22 Komora, 1998, p. 65.

23 Podolák, 1985, p. 136.

24 I use *Magyar* when I talk about ethnicity and *Hungarian* when I mean the Hungarian part of the monarchy or Hungarian as a state nation. It was and is in this sense differentiated by speakers of Slovak and other languages. However, there is no such differentiation in Hungarian language where 'Magyar' means an ethnic group but also the Magyar nation-state, the Magyar part of the monarchy, Magyar language, culture, etc. I think that this differentiation plays a crucial role in the way in which Magyars related towards the Hungarian (for them meaning Magyar) state and in their attitudes towards other nationalities inhabiting this state.

25 Hromádka, 1933, pp. 80–81; Podolák, 1985, p. 136.

26 Dvořák, 1995, p. 364. Nevertheless, as Dvořák says, it is important to keep in mind that the defeat of the 1848/9 revolution and the following persecution of Magyars could be also reflected in their proportion in the city since many of them fled.

27 *MSK*, Vol. 27, pp. 102–103. There are no data about ethnic structure available for the period between 1850 and 1880. Also different authors provide a little different numbers. See Francová, 1998a, p. 19.

28 Glettler, 1988, p. 46.

29 Kantár, 1987, p. 281.

30 Ludwig, 1911, p. 4. Ludwig praised the workers for their diligence and wrote that they adjusted themselves very well to the new environment.

31 Horváth et al, 1978, p. 165.

32 Glettler, 1988, p. 49. Budapest was the most attractive centre for immigrants within Hungary. In 1880 the proportion of those born in Budapest was 42.3%, in 1910 only 35.4%. See Gyányi, 1995, p. 107.

33 Gajdoš, 1987, p. 260.

34 Svetoň, 1942, p. 10. The 1880 census was for the first time carried out on the basis of the conclusions of the International Statistical Congress, similar statistical categories used across Europe. In *PZ*, 30.11.1880, N.275, p. 1, "Die 1881-er Volkszählung [The 1881 census]." About Hungarian statistics also see Mésároš, 1992, pp. 472–506, Mésároš, 1995, pp. 628–650, Mésároš, 1997, pp. 295–304 and Svetoň, 1969. See Tables 7 and 8 in Appendix for mixed ethnic marriages.

35 In *PZ*, 15.12.1900, N. 342, *Mb*, p. 2, "Instruktionen zur Volkszählung [Instructions for the census]" inhabitants were asked to fill in the forms if possible in Hungarian. In 1911 some inhabitants complained that they spoke only German or Slovak which indicates that the forms were in Hungarian only. In *PZ*, 24.1.1911, N.24, *Mb*, p.

1, "Das Ergebnis der Volkszählung in Pozsony [Results of the census in Pozsony]."

36 The technique of data collection is described in *PZ*, 6.12.1890, N.335, p. 3, "Zur Volkszählung [About the census]."

37 *PZ*, 30.12.1880, N. 304, p. 1, "Zur Volkszählung ."

38 As stressed by William F. Mackey, the question itself has a great influence on the outcome of the census: "The value of language data from census sources depends on the questions, responses and the records. The usefulness of the language question depends on what is meant (its semantic coverage) and what is understood (like the degree of specificity and possible ambiguity of the responses)." Mackey, 1988, pp. 23–24.

39 *MSK*, Vol. 27, p. 2*. "This question was for reasons of political carefulness omitted because it could eventually have offered the possibility for agitation on the part of the nationalities."

40 Svetoň, 1942, p. 10.

41 *PZ*, 16.12.1900, N. 343, *Mb*, p. 2, "Zur Volkszählung"; Svetoň, 1942, p. 11. Svetoň shows the enormous drop in the number of Slovaks and argues that such huge numbers could not have been assimilated.

42 Gyányi, 1995, p. 109.

43 Mannová, Unpublished article, 1994, p. 3. As Gary B. Cohen says, when in Prague the spouses put down in census forms different language of everyday use it indicated different political preferences, but it did not mean that they had to communicate through translators. In Cohen, 1981, p. 90.

44 Brubaker, 1996, p. 56, footnote 1.

45 Glettler, 1988, p. 47.

46 *MSK*, Vol. 2, pp. 32*-34*. It is impossible to use these categories for comparison for earlier censuses since those used different groupings of professions.

47 Glettler, 1988, p. 68.

48 *MSK*, Vol. 2, pp. 32*-33*, 118–119; *MSK*, Vol. 48, pp. 306–307. On the pages 32*-33* there is information for some occupational categories. It is impossible to compare directly the numbers for 1890 and 1900 since some occupations were taken out and put in different groups (p. 9*). Thus in some categories data for 1890 are not available. Dependants were the persons in the household who did not earn any money and so they were dependent on the income of the head of the household.

49 For the participation of different ethnic groups in main occupational groups in 1910 see Table 14 in Appendix.

50 Francová, 1998a, p. 25. Wine growing was the traditional domain of Germans. They were dominant in wine producing still in the first half of the twentieth century. German wine-growers and producers community was relatively closed and its members did not marry persons of other ethnic background. In Salner et al., 1991, p. 93.

51 Francová, 1998a, p. 28.

52 This and the next two paragraphs are informed by a variety of sources: Francová, 1998a, pp. 25–26; *MSK*, Vol. 2, pp. 402–403; *MSK*, Vol. 42, pp. 346–347, 362–363, 378–379, 386–387, 394–395; *MSK*, Vol. 56, pp. 330–331; Glettler, 1988, pp. 68–70; Glettler, 1992, p. 304.

53 According to Glettler, the extremely high number in this category could indicate the better way of life in Magyar households, preference of servants of own ethnic background or manipulation by the households' heads when filling in the census forms. Glettler, 1988, pp. 69–70. More on servants in Pressburg see Paríková, 1987. Most servants were women, and most of these were single girls between 20–24 years of age, from the countryside which was the preference of Pressburg's families.

54 Glettler, 1988, p. 66.

55 Rothkirchen, 1968, pp. 75–76.

56 Glettler, 1988, p. 66. 1Kjoch (Katastral Joch) =5,755 square meters.

57 Ibid., p. 67. For the proportion of Jews in different intellectual professions see Table 12 in Appendix.

58 Gellner, 1983.

59 Glettler, 1989a, p. 95. From all the employed people of non-Magyar nationality in 1900 74.7% and in 1910 77.6% spoke Hungarian.

60 Glettler, 1989a, p. 132. Jewish people are at the bottom of the table since they were not acknowledged as a separate nationality or ethnic group. Therefore they were already included in one of the ethnic groups above.

61 Glettler, 1989a, p. 98. Figures rounded to one decimal place.

62 Ibid., p. 98.

63 Ibid., p. 98.

64 Ibid., p. 99, *MSK*, Vol. 61, pp. 278–279, 282–285. Figures rounded to one decimal place.

65 Ibid., p. 100.

66 Ibid., pp. 63–64. In Pressburg two thirds of the Slovaks were unmarried which would indicate immigration of single Slovaks into the city. However, according to Fischer, the immigrant workers increased the number of illiterate people in the city.

Fischer, 1894, p. 23.

67 On the spatial growth of the city see Fekete, 1948.

68 Data for 1869 are from *PZ*, 22.1.1870, N.17, p. 3, "Resultate der Volkszählung [Results of the census]"; for 1880 from *PZ*, 24.1.1881, N.23, p. 1, "Volkszählung 1880"; for 1890 from *PZ*, 22.1.1891, N.22, *Mb*, p. 2, "Volkszählung"; for 1900 from *PZ*, 24.1.1911, N. 24, *Mb*, p. 1, "Das Ergebnis der Volkszählung"; for 1910 *MSK*, Vol. 42, p. 529. The total number of inhabitants is usually higher than the numbers in the statistical yearbooks. These numbers were the first official results which were corrected later after thorough data processing and were then published in the statistical yearbooks. All numbers are for the civil population only, excluding soldiers.

*In 1880 the houses in *Korház utcza* (Hospital street) were re-numbered and some of the houses were taken out from Ferdinand's Town and included into Franz Joseph's Town. Thus the number of the inhabitants in Ferdinand's Town did not actually decrease but increased by 807 (10,882) while in Franz Joseph's Town the real increase was only 729 (7,238).

69 *PZ*, 24.1.1911, N.24, *Mb*, p. 1, "Das Ergebnis der Volkszählung."

70 Ibid. This article also mentions that it would only be possible to assess the total number of workers after the census results for the villages Ligetfalu, Récse and Szőllős would be known since most Pressburg-workers came from these villages (see Figure 5).

71 The voters were divided into these categories: historical right (*régi jog*), land- or house-owner, income, intelligentsia. These categories designated the basis for their right to vote.

72 Kovačevičová, 1985, p. 36. At the end of the nineteenth century the old houses were rebuilt into small flats in order to accommodate workers' families.

73 AMB, Inventár Mesta Bratislava IX, 1886, c. 2116.

74 Proportions counted on the basis of *MSK*, Vol. 42, p. 529. For absolute numbers see Table 4 in appendix.

75 Glettler, 1988, pp. 62–63. Glettler stresses that Slovaks did not settle as a united community, either in Pressburg or in Budapest. Glettler, 1992, p. 305. See also Gyányi, 1995.

76 Ibid., p. 62.

77 The outline of the city districts in figures 6–12 is based on Glettler, 1992, p. 328, shading and proportions (from Table 6) are mine.

78 Mannová, Unpublished article, 1994, p. 2, Mannová, 1995a, p. 438.

79 *Pressburger Wegweiser* was an address-book published yearly for the use of the

inhabitants of Pressburg. It contained much useful information about city life: calendars for Catholics, Protestants, Greek Orthodox and Israelites (Jews), the schedule of masses in the Catholic churches for the whole year, lists of all the state institutions and public offices in the city, municipal administration and offices, lists of the *Religionsgemeinde* (religious communities) and their functionaries, schools, a list of associations in the city, also the administration and associations of the neighbouring communities, lists of different shops, craftsmen, cafes, hotels, and newspapers. It also contained directories of house owners, professionals and their addresses. The directory also contained schedules for the steam ship, trains and trams, and markets in Pressburg and surrounding areas. The last part included advertisements for local businesses.

80 Kumlik, 1905, pp. 153–154.

81 AMB, Inventár knižných rukopisov AMB I; minutes from the meetings of the City Magistrate available only until 1888, then 1912 and 1914–20.

82 MOL, K149, 1876–1914, UMV I, 1886–1914.

83 AMB, Inventár knižných rukopisov AMB I.

84 There were three parishes: 1. Parish of the St. Martin Cathedral for the inner city, 2. Parish of the St. Trinity and 3. Parish in *Blumenthal* (*Virágvölgy*). Parishes were centred around the Catholic churches in different town districts: Dreifaltigkeitkirche (Trinity church), Neustadtkirche (New Town church), Kirche zu St.Salvator, Kirche z. h. Ladislaus, Kirche zur Dreifaltigkeit (in Zuckermandl), Franziskaner-Convent, Jesuitenkirche, Kapuzinerkirche, Notre-Dame, Ursulinenkirche, Elisabethkirche, Barmherzigenkirche. *Magyarország vármegyei*, pp. 487–488, *PW*, 1867–1914.

85 In some years, the chaplains of the St. Martin Cathedral community (*Collegiat—Dom kapitel zu St.Martin*) were Slovak, e.g. Vincent Havlíček (1880–9, 1890–9 the administrator of the Neustadtkirche zur Maria Himmelfahrt), Johann Juriga (1900–1 administrator of the Neustadtkirche), even proponents of the Slovak national movement such as Ferdinand Juriga (in Blumenthal church as cooperator 1903–5, in 1905 in Neustadtkirche Blumenthal) and František Jehlička (1906 cooperator of the St. Martin Cathedral community). There were also Slovaks among the Franziskaner order and Kapuziner order. In *PW*, 1867–1914.

86 *PW*, 1867–1914, Schmidt et al, 1906, pp. 105–108. In 1864–June 1875 these were performed by Lajos Szeberényi, from June 1875–March 1876 by Pavol Zelenka and in 1876–1910 by Franz Trsztyénszky. Afterwards there were still Slovak masses, also in 1914 but the name of the priest is unknown. Slovak Evangelicals grieved the death of Trsztyénszky (1.5.1910). They called him "one of the most eminent men of the church." As a teacher at the Theological Academy, Trsztyénszky put great weight on the education of really truthful preachers and criticised the empty patriotism of the Hungarian theological students and their cursing of the Slovak students. His honesty

often angered the ruling classes. "We honestly grieve after Trsztyénszky since in him we have lost a priest, a professor who not only held offices but fulfilled them conscientiously with all his ability, we have lost a courageous and determined defender of truth of whom we have very few." ("My srdečne žialime za Trsztyénszkym, lebo v ňom utrácame farára, profesora, ktorý nie len že nosil úrady, ale ich dľa vsetkých schopností i svedomite plnil, utrácame smelého a odhodlaného zástupcu pravdy, akých málo máme.") In *Stráž na Sione*, 1910, N. 6, p. 54, "Zosnulí [Obituaries]." Other denominations were also represented in the city, however, their numbers were small and therefore they are not discussed here. See Table 5 in Appendix.

87 On the history of *Pressburger Zeitung*, the most popular newspaper in Pressbug, see Angermayer, 1896. The social democratic press will be described in more detail in Chapter three.

88 In Francová, 1998a, p. 23, *Magyarország vármegyei és városai. Pozsony vármegye*, without the year of publication, pp. 474–480, Potemra, 1963, *PW*, 1867–1914. There were published also some scientific and specialist journals, both in German and Hungarian.

89 In the 1860s, the lower school system was organised as follows. 1. Elementary schools with two classes (grades) for children from 5 to 8 years; 2. General (*allgemeine*) *Bürgerschulen* with two classes for children over 8 year old; 3. Higher (*höhere*) *Bürgerschulen* (*Unterrealschulen*)—these were considered equivalent to the *Untergymnasien*. After the 1868 reform of education, school attendance was obligatory for children from 6 to 15 years of age: children between 6–12 years of age attended the *Volksschulen* and from 13 to 15 years the so-called Repetition schools (*Wiederholungsschulen*). In Portisch, 1933, pp. 183–184.

90 *Magyarország vármegyei*, p. 353.

91 Portisch, 1933, pp. 183–184. Pressburg was also an important centre of Jewish learning. *Jesode Hatora-Schule* was founded in 1885 by R. Chajjim Wolf Grünhut and prepared the boys for Talmud studies. Pressburg's *Rabbinatsschule Jeschiba* existed already in the Ghetto and had a very good reputation in Hungary and abroad also thanks to the activity of Rabbi Chatam Sofer. (Ibid., p. 196.) In 1872, the Jewish community split into Orthodox majority and Reform minority. Francová, 1998a, p. 29, Bettelheim, 1932, Grünsfeld, 1932.

92 Portisch, 1933, p. 184–196, *Magyarország vármegyei*, pp. 354–371. See Ortvay, 1884 on the history of the Law Academy.

93 *Magyarország vármegyei*, pp. 354–371.

94 This law introduced compulsory education for all children aged 6 to 15 and set out the minimal range of subjects to be taught. From the national point of view this law was important since it introduced the teaching of Hungarian language also in German schools. (In 1868 there was only one elementary school in Pressburg with

Hungarian language of instruction.) The law was obligatory only for the every-day schools (Alltagsschulen) which had to be attended by all children aged 6 to 12. In Portisch, 1933, p. 172.

95 Portisch, 1933, p. 172.

96 Mannová, 1987, p. 367.

97 Kamenický, 1997, p. 9.

98 Mannová, 1995a, pp. 440–441, Mannová, Unpublished article,1994, pp. 8–9.

99 Horváth et al, 1978, p. 164. Pressburg became a municipality in 1870 according to the municipal law XLII/1870. In the administration hierarchy municipal towns were independent administrative units and equal to the counties in the state administration (county municipalities). The next step down were the towns with a magistrate equal to the districts in state administration (districts headed by *szolgabiró* [lord lieutenant]). The lowest level were the communities (*községek*) subordinated to districts. According to the 1870 law, there were 71 municipal towns (basically the previous free royal towns) in Hungary, of which there were 24 on Slovak territory. Lehotská, 1973, p. 585. Also *Magyarország vármegyei*, pp. 334–341.

100 *Magyarország vármegyei*, p. 337–338.

101 Horváth, 1998, p. 12. The number of the members of the municipal assembly was determined on the basis of the number of inhabitants, one member per 250 inhabitants in municipal towns and one member per 500 inhabitants in other municipalities. The law determined the minimal and maximal numbers, in municipal towns 48–400 and other municipalities 120–600. In "XLII. zákonný článok," par. 21, also Lehotská, 1973, p. 586.

102 "XLII/1870," par.28. In practice this meant that only half of 93 elected members were elected at the same time, and the other half was elected after three years, although for six years. The same principle applied in the election for the county assembly members. Lehotská, 1973, p. 587.

103 Lehotská, 1973, p. 588, "XLII/1870," par. 47.

104 Lehotská, 1973, p. 588.

105 Lehotský, 1998, pp. 12–13.

106 The administration was carried out by five departments: I. Department for the citizenship matters, treatment costs, censuses and police; II. Department for economy, administration of beneficiaries, accommodation of military units, administration of forest, property, city constructions, fees, maintenance of streets, municipal buildings and parks, conscription and relieving from military service; III. Department for taxes and public works; IV. Department for the care for the poor, administration of the institutes of the poor and their representation in the public

offices; V. Department for matters not falling under the authority of the other departments. The Magistracy created expert committees and different organs and offices in order to carry out its work. Lehotský, 1998, p. 13.

107 Lehotská, 1973, pp. 588–589, "XLII/1870," par.51.

108 "XLII/1870," par. 3.

109 Lehotská, 1973, pp. 590–592. Already in the XLII/1870 law (53. par.) the function of the *főispán* was defined as follows: "*Főispán* is the representative of the executive power; as such he supervises the self-administration of the municipality and he guards the interests of the state political administration carried out through the municipality." *Főispán* was appointed by the Minister of Interior and approved by the emperor. While the *főispán* was the representative of the political power, his deputy *alispán* was responsible for the every-day work of the county administration. See also Lehotská, 1973, pp. 575–592.

110 Hanák, P., 1985, without page numbers. See also Lehotská, 1973, pp. 575–592. On the electoral system in Hungary see Gyányi, Kövér, 1998, pp. 105–116.

111 Horváth et al, 1978, p. 181.

112 AMB, Inventár Mesta Bratislavy IX, 1886, c. 2116.

113 There is absolutely no literature available on political life in Pressburg during this period. The only clue for this can be found in the local press of the period. A thorough study of at least one daily periodical throughout the whole period would be necessary in order to gain an approximate picture of the political parties in the city. Some information can be found in Michal Potemra's bibliographies, especially in his *Bibliografia inorečových novín*. About the political parties in Hungary in 1867–1914 see Lipták (ed.), 1992. Information in this section is based on selected issued of the daily press and Potemra. It can be said though that the Hungarian intelligentsia, especially those who were state employees or officials, always represented the opinions of the governing party.

114 Horváth et al, 1978, p. 165.

CHAPTER 2

The Inpact of Magyarisation in Pressburg

1 "Magyarization can be viewed as a belated and coercive effort to turn a state formed on the basis of a historical and geographical principle (loyalty to the Crown of St. Stephen and hegemony over the Carpathian basin) into a 'modern' nation-state on the Romantic model, held together by ethnic and linguistic homogeneity." Gal, 1979, p. 42.

2 As the previous chapter pointed out (see Chapter one, footnote 1), the terms 'Slovak' and 'German' nationalities are used in the sense of the categories of the Hungarian censuses which divided nationalities by their professed mother tongue. In reality such neat groups did not exist. The assimilation of the city's Jewish population will also be considered in this chapter.

3 I use new "Magyar" elite instead of new "Hungarian " elite throughout the text. This does not denote Magyar ethnic origin of members of this elite but rather their political opinions. For the members of this elite "Hungarian" meant Magyar and they equated Hungarian with Magyar patriotism, in contrast to the traditional elite.

4 The term "national socialization" is used in Smith, A. and Williams, 1983, p. 514.

5 National revival movements among the nationalities in Hungary came after the Hungarian national revival movement; however, by 1867, some of these national revival movements were already in the second or third phases of Hroch's typology of the development of national movements, in the phase of disseminating the national ideas among the masses and the masses becoming increasingly responsive to these ideas. For the phases of national movements see Hroch, 1985. On nationalism as a counter-reaction to the nationalism of the state see Breuilly, 1982. Integration efforts of the Hungarian governments directed at unification of the social and economic structure of Hungary met with resistance of nationalities which increased when at the turn of the century the idea of integration was exchanged by the idea of creation of a unitary Magyar state. Szarka, 1999, p. 200.

6 Slovak historians place the beginning of Magyarisation into the end of the eighteenth century. In 1840, the Hungarian parliament voted for the substitution of Latin by Hungarian as the official language of the state. According to some Slovak historians this marked a "new wave" of Magyarisation of Hungary as Hungarians started to force Magyar culture and language upon all the inhabitants of Hungary. (See Špiesz, 1992, Chapter seven.) This is a common view in the Slovak historiography. Mésároš considers as the first wave the assimilation of the polyglot feudal class to its Magyar "kernel." The extent of assimilation, however, grew after 1850 and especially after 1867. Mésároš denies the conclusions of the Hungarian historian Péter Hanák that all assimilation was "natural," caused by solely economic transformation of the country and not by "forceful de-nationalising." See Mésároš, 1997, pp. 300–303.

7 Špiesz, 1992, p. 105, Kováč, 1998, pp. 138–139. See also Kann and David (eds.), 1984, p. 352. The law talks about "oszthatatlan egységes magyar nemzet" (the indivisible unified Hungarian nation) since there is no distinction between Hungarian and Magyar in the Hungarian language. (In *1868. évi XLIV. törvényczikk a nemzetiségi egyenjogúság tárgyában* [Law XLIV/1868 about the equality of nationalities], also Gyányi, Kövér, 1998, pp. 139–140.) On differences in understanding of the "Hungarian political nation" between the Hungarian politicians and non-Magyar nationalities see Szarka, 1999, pp. 164–177.

8 Kann, David, 1984, p. 354.

9 Ibid., p. 380.

10 For more detailed evaluation of the politics of different Hungarian governments towards nationalities see Kemény, G., 1952–1971 and Szarka, 1999. According to the leading Slovak nationalists, there was no difference between the attitudes of different Hungarian political parties to the nationalities' and Slovak question. Podrimavský, 1999, p. 32.

11 For the reactions of the Slovak press to the policies of the Hungarian state in education after 1900 as well as on the number of Slovak students in the Hungarian educational institutions see Potemra, 1990 and 1993. For brief characterisation of Hungarian laws in the area of education and their impact on assimilation of nationalities see Gyányi, Kövér, 1998, pp. 141–143. Gyányi and Kövér point out that education was not as effective in assimilation of non-Magyar nationalities as it is often assumed.

12 Kann, David, 1984, pp. 354–359. The brochure of the *alispán* (deputy of *főispán*) of Zólyom county Béla Grünwald called "Felvidék" (Upper Hungary) had a great impact on Magyarisation policies on the present-day Slovak territory. Grünwald was a popular Hungarian author of historical works and parliament deputy. He was one of the leading proponents of Magyarisation in Upper Hungary. The Slovak secondary schools (gymnasia) were abolished as a result of his initiative in 1874–5. Grünwald was convinced that Upper Hungary poses a serious threat to the Hungarian state (because of the growing political and cultural organisation of Slovaks and foreign Pan-Slav agitation) and therefore it is necessary to co-ordinate the Magyarisation activities of the government, local administration and intelligentsia and Magyarise the Slovak population. Szarka, 1999, p. 221.

13 Kann, David (eds.), 1984, pp. 354, 359. See Szarka, 1999, p. 235–246 for more details on Bánffy's cabinet politics. This special department was created within the office of the prime minister.

14 This notion of assimilation is derived from the argument expressed in Milton Gordon, 1964, especially Chapter three, and used by the Hungarian historian Gyányi, 1995, pp. 109–110. Gyányi also discusses why the census data cannot reflect ethnicity and how it obscures rather than explains the assimilation processes by over-stressing the criteria of language. For a similar view, especially with regard to the assimilation of Hungarian Jews, see Kovács, Unpublished thesis, 1992, pp. 21–22. Kovács argues that census data measured by mother tongue does not have much explanatory value as to the identity of individuals. See also Brubaker, 1996, p. 56, footnote 1.

15 Gyányi, 1993, p. 26.

16 Hanák, P., 1984a, p. 284. In contrast to Gyányi, Hanák believes that one can judge the extent of assimilation on the basis of statistical data, and mere increases or decreases in the numbers of people of a certain mother tongue.

17 Tables 1 and 2 in Appendix show ethnic groups as a proportion of the population of Hungary and of the territory of present-day Slovakia between 1880–1910.

18 On assimilation of Slovaks see also Szarka, 1999, pp. 191–197. For a comparison of assimilation in Vojvodina and Slovakia see Calic, Pazmandi, 1992.

19 Kann, David, 1984, p. 384.

20 Glettler, 1992, p. 298.

21 Kann, David, 1984, p. 366. Between 1880–1900 some 500,000 emigrants left Hungary, and in the period 1900–1914 this number was even larger, 1,400,000.

22 Ibid., p. 384.

23 Podrimavský et al, 1992, p. 489. The ethnic composition of Pressburg county in 1869 was: 42% Slovaks, 39.7% Magyars and 18.3% Germans. In 1900 there were 38.6% Magyars and 15.6% Germans.

24 Glettler, 1992, p. 298.

25 Kann, David, 1984, p. 384. In 1910 out of 230,000 civil servants, officials and members of free professions only 2,911 were Slovaks (or admitted to being Slovak). In Slovakia, out of 6,185 civil servants only 154 were Slovaks.

26 On the importance of the middle class in the development of the national movement see Hroch, 1985.

27 Kann, David, 1984, p. 380.

28 Ibid., p. 384.

29 Ibid., p. 382.

30 This fact is very often mentioned in the Slovak workers' press. Their explanation is that it was the objective of the ruling classes to keep the masses illiterate since it is easier to exploit and rule over uneducated people not knowing their rights.

31 The only attempt to organise a German movement in Hungary was led by Edmund Steinacker (coming from Pressburg) in 1875 and was unsuccessful.

32 Mannová, Unpublished article, 1994, pp. 4–5, Kováč, 1991, pp. 14–17. In Slovakia there were three main areas with German inhabitants: 1. Pressburg and its surrounding, 2. the area of Spiš (Szepes county), 3. Central Slovakia with centres in Körmöcbánya (Kremnica) and Németpróna (Nitrianske Pravno) (see Figure 3). Apart from these concentrated areas, Germans were scattered also through other areas and they lived in most of the Slovak towns.

33 Kováč, 1991, p. 19.

34 Mannová, Unpublished article, 1994, , p. 6.

35 Ibid., p. 5.

36 Mannová, 1995c, p. 170.

37 Mannová, Unpublished article, 1994, , p. 7.

38 Mannová, 1995a, p. 438. See also Mannová (1997b) on factors which influenced the development of middle classes in Hungary. In terms of occupation, the middle class ("bürgerlich" social strata) included those practising free professions, teachers in secondary educational institutions and universities, tradesmen, lawyers, physicians and some of the richer craftsmen or shop owners. This social strata was characterised by distinct values, patterns of behaviour , life style and social and cultural values. The main values were independence and self-reliance. An important part of this "bürgerliche Kultur" was to attend the theatre. (Salner, 1997, p. 154, Pašiak, 1997, p. 19). On "Bürgerlichkeit" as culture see Döcker, 1990.

39 Hanák, P., 1984a, pp. 292–295. See also Hanák, P., 1997 on the structure and multiple identities of the Hungarian middle classes. Hanák considers the urban German burghers "conservative and prestige-conscious," while describing the Hungarian gentry as "liberal, sich verbürgerlichende." Towards the end of the nineteenth century, there was an increasing anti-Semitism among the Hungarian gentry. At this time assimilation policies were denounced as permitting foreign elements (especially Jews) to corrupt the pure original Magyar character. (See Szabó, 1981, Szabad, 1982.) On anti-Semitism in Vienna and the reactions of Viennese Jews at the turn of the century see Hödl, 1995, pp. 115–129, Schorske, 1981, Chapter three and Beller, 1989.

40 Mannová, Unpublished article, 1994, p. 5. In the period 1867–1918 there were three discernible processes in the development of elites: 1. shifts in the ownership basis and the economic base of elites, 2. institutionalisation of elites (influence of new prestige symbols like participation in the leadership of associations, joint-stock companies, financial institutions, from the turn of the century membership in the committees of political parties) and 3. homogenisation of elites (through V*erbürgerlichung*, education, assimilation.) Unfortunately there is a lack of analytic work which would show continuity or discontinuity between the "old" (i.e., guilds-bound burghers and traditional patrician families) and the "new" burghers at the end of the nineteenth century. (Lipták, 1997, pp. 67–80.) Tóth offers analysis of the generational transformation of, and mobility within, a petite-bourgeois family in Buda (part of Budapest). Tóth, 1990.

41 The whole part is informed by Kováč, 1991, pp. 13–34. On the German minority in Slovakia see also Kováč, 1987, pp. 118–126.

42 It must be stressed that when speaking about assimilation of Jews, I mean only Reform Jews. After the Jewish community split into Orthodox and Reform (1872), there were two almost totally different communities with very different attitudes towards assimilation. In Hungary at the turn of the century, about 60% of the Jew-

ish population were Reform. This groups included approximately 200,000 Jews living in Budapest. (Trančík, 1996, pp. 91, 100.) According to Jelinek, most of the Jews in the territory of present-day Slovakia were Orthodox. However, its is important to keep in mind that the Jewish community in the Slovak territory was very heterogeneous, different ethnically and geographically. Jelinek, 1993, pp. 280–284.

43 Mannová, Unpublished article, 1994, p. 12, Tajták, 1980, p. 521.

44 Svetoň states that in 1880 and 1890 censuses only one third of the Jews claimed Hungarian as their mother tongue, the rest German, and later they shifted to Hungarian. (Svetoň, 1942, p. 25.) Rothkirchen confirms this shift, pointing out that the 1867 Dual Agreement was a serious inconvenience for the Jews of Slovakia since they had to change from German to Hungarian language. (Rothkirchen, 1968, p. 73.) According to Glettler, Magyarisation of the Jews began around 1900. (Glettler, 1988, p. 66.) In Prague most Jews adopted the culture of the Austrian middle classes between the 1840 and the mid-1880s. However, unlike their counterparts in Vienna and Budapest, the Prague Jews could rise in the social hierarchy without the need to cut their ties to the Jewish religious community. In Vienna the lower Austrian Catholic society showed less tolerance; thus, socially upwardly mobile Jews had to abandon their religious identity. In Budapest, Jews had to identify with Magyar society and give up most of their Jewish traditions. (Cohen, 1981, pp. 60, 178.) On the assimilation of Hungarian Jews see also Jelinek, 1993, pp. 279–289, Karády, 1993 and 1994.

45 Rothkirchen, 1968, p. 80.

46 Mannová, Unpublished article, 1994, , p. 12.

47 Rothkirchen, 1968, p. 80.

48 Salner, 1997, p. 155.

49 Rothkirchen, 1968, p. 76.

50 This was typical behaviour for many eager assimilants, whether they were of Jewish, German or Slovak origin. The Slovak historians use for such people the word 'renegát' (renegade), for those of the Slovak origin there is a special word 'maďarón.' It is the use of such (negative) value-loaded words which mark the continuity of a nationalistically minded historiography, building on the post First World War historiography based on the opposition between "suffering Slovaks vs. Hungarian oppressors." This term is used even by those historians who otherwise take a more objective, non-nationalist stand. The term "Magyaron" was also used in the Burgenland after the First World War, to denote those members of the Hungarian minority who retained their loyalty to the Hungarian state, although now they had become Austrian citizens. (See Haslinger, 1992, p. 157, footnote 16.) Similarly in Ukraine, the word "Little Russian" is used to denote Russophone Ukrainian intelligentsia whom Ukrainian nationalists considered "the product of weakness of character." The Ukrainian nationalists (especially in the interwar period) saw the denationalisation

of the intelligentsia as the main reason for the weakness of the Ukrainian national movement. In post-Soviet Central Asian states also, Russified co-ethnics (called *"Mankurty"*) are seen as traitors to the national cause and are targets of the nationalising policies (together with ethnic Russians). Smith, G. et al, 1998, pp. 128, 140.

51 Rothkirchen, 1968, p. 73. See also Jelinek, 1993, pp. 271–296, Bokeš, 1965, pp. 315–316.

52 Williams, Smith, 1983, p. 505: "Their [romantic nationalists'] aim, of course, is to use these folk cultures based upon local communities tied to the soil, in order to purify the decadent, cosmopolitan urban civilization they deplore, and so endow their nation and countrymen with a vivid sense of their roots in their natural surroundings."

53 The works of Slovak writers at the end of the nineteenth century show the same split. The big city was seen as the centre of national oppression. Budapest represented the disintegration of virtues and morality. However, many authors wrote about the small city environment in which they passed judgement on the petit-bourgeois life style and "maďarónstvo" (meaning Slovaks assimilated to Magyars). (See Kršáková, 1997, pp. 105–112.) The Slovak politician Pavol Blaho saw peasants as "the root of the nation…uranium of all classes." (Pichler, 1997, p. 63.) A parallel current in Hungary at the end of the nineteenth century was characterised by the rise of neo-conservativism as a reaction to the assimilationist enthusiasm of the liberals. For the neo-conservatives (agrarians and clericals) Pest was also corrupt, most of all because of its cosmopolitanism, which meant too many assimilated (and successful) Jews. This stream of thought was also reflected in the literature in which countryside was seen as "the bastion of the nationality" and not the city. (In Hanák, P., 1984a, pp. 313–319.) For a similar romanticisation of peasants as the only source of true uncorrupted national spirit in the Slovenian nationalistic movement in the nineteenth century see Pelikan, Uhl, Unpublished article, pp. 11–12.

54 In Svetoň, 1942, p. 122; Podolák, 1985, pp. 141–142; Tajták, 1980, p. 504. Glettler also sees Hungarian cities as 'melting pots', without attaching any negative connotation to this. She writes that "cities were the workshops of linguistic-cultural Magyarisation." (Glettler, 1988, p. 52.) See also Glettler, 1992, p. 298.

55 There is, however, a different, more objective attitude in the generation of Slovak historians and social scientists represented by Mannová, Holec and Salner as well as in the works of Lipták.

56 Tajták, 1980, pp. 513–514. The numbers of Magyars in the cities on the present-day Slovak territory grew also because around 25% of 500,000 of Magyars who moved to this territory (from the central Magyar areas of country) settled in towns. The migration statistics of Pressburg, Kassa and Selmecbánya shows high number of people coming from the central Magyar areas of the country. Szarka, 1999, p. 195.

57 Hanák, 1984a, p. 313.

58 Gyányi, 1993, p. 24. Similarly assimilation was happening also in Vienna. Glettler describes the assimilation of Viennese Czechs and the dissatisfaction of Czech nationalists in Bohemia about this. In March 1914 they were informed that in the tenth district in which lived 18,500 Czechs, Czech candidates got only 160 votes. The number of nationally active Czechs in Vienna was small since most Czechs preferred social mobility rather than the discrimination they had to face when being nationally active. After Karl Lueger became the mayor of Vienna, immigrants who wanted to become citizens could do so only if they swore an oath to "do their utmost to preserve the German character of the city of Vienna." Viennese of Bohemian descent even had to swear that they would not join any Czech associations or form such associations. Glettler, 1989b, pp. 53–54.

59 Gyányi mentions the importance of the date of arrival to the city as a divide between members of the same ethnic groups. "It is obvious that there have been no close connections between the German and Slovak communities living in Budapest for centuries and the newly arriving German and Slovak immigrants." Gyányi, 1995, p. 111.

60 Cohen, 1981, p. 13. As Gordon states, "[w]ith regard to cultural behaviour, differences of social class are more important and decisive than differences of ethnic group." People of the same social class shared values which may not have been shared by people of the same ethnic origin but different class. Gordon, 1964, p 52.

61 Tóth showed the influence of religious affiliation on assimilation in his research on intermarriage in Pest and in selected localities in the vicinity of Pest. By 1895, Calvinists were the most closed group in terms of ethnic intermarriage but the most open one in the confessional intermarriage. It was just the opposite with the Catholics. The most closed group regarding the confession was the Jewish one. (Tóth, 1996, pp. 216, 218.) This is demonstrated by the fact that until the religious emancipation of Jews in 1895, Christian-Jewish marriages were invalid. All churches forbade denominationally mixed marriages. The civil marriages and state registers were introduced in 1894. (Tóth, 1998, p. 209.) Tóth points out that assimilation was not as straightforward a process as is often assumed by both Slovak and Hungarian historians.

62 Mannová, Unpublished article, 1994, , p. 8; Franz, 1935, p. 20.

63 For 1880, 1890: *MSK*, Vol. 27, pp. 102–103. For 1900: *MSK*, Vol. 1, p. 20*. For 1910: *MSK*, 1912, pp. 154–155 for all population, p. 529 for civil population. These numbers were used for determining the proportions.

64 Glettler, 1988, p. 54.

65 Horváth et al, 1978, p. 231. Similarly in Prague, it was mainly Germans from the lower classes who assimilated into the Czech population. (See Cohen, 1981 and Cohen, 1987, pp. 476–479.) However, it is important to keep in mind that it was mostly Germans who emigrated out of Pressburg, although this number for 1899–1913

(1,062) does not seem so significant when compared with the enormous growth of Magyars (see Table 18 in Appendix for out-migration). In *MSK*, Vol. 67, pp. 18–19.

66 Mannová, Unpublished article, 1994, p. 6. Seewann defined 'Hungarus' type ("conscious carrier of a double identity") as someone who stresses "subjective characteristics of his ethnic consciousness i.e. he cultivates ethnic customs and his mother tongue culture from his own conviction; strives towards cultural exchange and negotiation of interests with the majority society, shows himself as realistic, open and adaptable; has a positive-critical relationship to the past (of his minority as well as the majority); sees himself tied 'organically' as well as a group to the majoritarian society, who interprets himself as the part of the Hungarian nation in the sense of state- and constitutional patriotism." Seewann, 1992a, p. 154.

67 However, the extent to which Germans truly accepted Magyar culture is open to question. *Pressburger Zeitung* in January 1908 repeatedly wrote that the theatre (at this time with Magyar performances) was almost empty despite the good quality of performances, e.g. *PZ*, 9.1.1908, N. 8, *Mb*, p. 4, "Theater," *PZ*, 17.1.1908, N. 16, *Mb*, p. 2, "Konferenz in Angelegenheit des Pozsonyer Theaters [Meeting in the matter of the Pozsonyer theatre]." Given the importance of the theatre for burgher culture, one might ask why neither the German burghers nor the growing number of Magyars attended these performances in Hungarian language.

68 Mannová, Unpublished article, 1994, p. 6.

69 Glettler, 1988, p. 54.

70 Niederle, 1903, p. 1. According to Niederle, Slovak patriots claimed that the bias in Hungarian statistics in favour of the Magyar nationalities caused the "loss of as many as 200,000 souls" in Slovakia. (See Chapter one on Hungarian censuses.)

71 Svetoň, 1942, p. 21. According to Svetoň, only a part of the big drop in Slovak numbers could be assigned to real and finished Magyarisation which resulted in complete assimilation. He states that Magyars won in these ways 1/4 million people, Slovaks, Germans and Jews. (Ibid., p. 21.) "The essence of being Slovak has not been and is not made up only by the language but by a totality of blood, territorial and cultural bonds." (Ibid., p. 123.) Similarly, Svetoň differentiates between assimilation and Magyarisation: "It [Magyarisation] means to *over*nationalise but not *de*nationalise. It is an active change of the national-biological character as opposed to assimilation which means passively adapting to a new folk environment.... Practically this change means the exchange of the inherited and by nature and social environment given feeling and intellectual life for a different, strange (foreign) life." Ibid., p. 121.

72 Mannová, Unpublished article, 1994, p. 11.

73 It is extraordinary how little has been written about the Jews of Pressburg in this period despite the fact that the city served as an important place of Jewish learning. (For basic information see Franek et al, 1997, Gold, 1932, Stoličná, 1992.) This

lack of coverage was obviously caused by an excessive emphasis on class in the Communist period, neglecting other aspects of social life that fell into the "bourgeois" category. Another reason was the anti-Semitism of the power elites prevalent in this period. An interesting family history of the Pressburger antiquarian family Steiner encompassing the years 1848–1948 has recently appeared which provides some background information about the life of the Jewish community in the city. See Trančík, 1996. Unlike Trančík, Jelinek claims that in Pressburg which had richer Jews, Reform were in a strong position. Jelínek, 1993, p. 284.

74 Trančík, 1996, p. 100.

75 See Cohen, 1981, especially Chapter three, pp. 100–111. However, one must bear in mind that the situation in the Hungarian part of the monarchy was different. In the more liberal Austrian situation, national mobilisation was possible while in Hungary all developments seemed to be delayed. Also the fact that in Prague there were two ethnic groups standing against each other, made the conflict much sharper. For a similar analysis of the conflict between Germans and Czechs in České Budějovice see Jeremy King, Unpublished thesis draft. In Brno (Brünn) as well, there were conflicts between the Czechs and Germans which often led to open fights on the streets of the city. At the turn of the century, Brno even acquired the image of a "nationally unbearable city." (Bočková, 1992, p. 127) In Laibach/Ljubljana there were also two ethnic groups competing for positions, the Slovenians and the Germans. See Pelikan, Uhl, Unpublished article.

76 MSK, Vol. 27, p. 134, Glettler, 1988, p. 56.

77 For 1900 see MSK, Vol. 5, pp. 352–353, 356–357, 360–361. For 1910 see MSK, Vol. 61, pp. 246–247, 250–251, 254–255. Both for 1900 and 1910 the entire population (civic+army) of Pressburg is considered. For absolute numbers see Table 6 in Appendix.
  Distribution of religious identification by mother tongue (Magyar, German, Slovak) within Hungary was as follows (in %): 1880 (1910) – Roman Catholics: Magyar 55.14 (64.78), German 18.87 (14.07), Slovak 19.7 (15.52); Greek Catholics: Magyar 9.39 (15.16), German 6.83 (less than 5); Reformed – almost exclusively Magyar, 97.67 (98.42); Evangelicals – Magyar 23.43 (31.92), German 35.01 (31.44), Slovak 39.57 (34.58); Jewish – Magyar 58.48 (76.89), German 34.56 (21.62), Slovak less than 5. Gyányi, Kövér, 1998, p. 135. For distribution of the population of the sixteen Upper-Hungarian counties (what Slovak intelligentsia referred to as "Slovak territory" within Hungary, see Chapter four, footnote 165) by mother tongue in 1880 and 1900 see Table 3 in Appendix.

78 This confirms the conclusions of Tóth's research showing that Roman Catholics were the most open denominational group in terms of ethnic intermarriage (see footnote 59) and consequently were more prone to assimilation.

79 Mannová, Unpublished article, 1994, p. 7. Some authors distinguish between

the attitudes of the different Magyar social strata towards the other nationalities. While the higher strata of Magyar society nourished the dream of a linguistically unified Hungarian nation, the Magyar proletariat did not have any reasons to consider its nationality as an advantage. See Horváth et al, 1978, p. 232.

80 Kumlik, 1905, AMB, Inventár knižných rukopisov AMB I., I.B.2.b., pp. 2–7.

81 AMB, Inventár knižných rukopisov AMB I., I.B.2.a., pp. 19–24. From 1851–1860 the minutes were kept in German only, from then in both German and Hungarian until 1877.

82 See Chapter one, footnote 109 on definition of the responsibilities of *főispán*.

83 SNA, UMV I, i. n. 18, c. 2, letter from *főispán* to the mayor Moritz Gottl from 28.12.1881.

84 SNA, SRH, i. n. 316, c.13. For much of the material in the records grouped in the SRH in the SNA it is hard to judge as to the language used. Many of the original documents are missing and only typed Slovak transcripts are available (in some cases there are attached copies of original documents). I have however verified the reliability of the translations wherever possible. Obviously, since the workers' movement was one of the main areas of interest for Slovak socialist historiography, the materials were translated so that even historians not speaking Hungarian or German could work with them. These records also included many of the materials which were listed in the inventory of the AMB. They were not available in AMB since in the first years of socialism all materials dealing with workers' movement were taken out and grouped together into the collection SRH—*Sbierka Robotnícke hnutie* (Collection workers' movement). The practice of making such collections was later abandoned.

85 MTA, 443. országos ülés (parliamentary session), 22.3.1909, p. 146: "Hát vannak ott németek is, magyarok és tótok, mind a három nyelvben kénytelen napjában beszélni, megesik, hogy német szó csuszik a szájából, de Both István, az a hajdu, van olyan jó magyar, mint akárki." The need to know Slovak when dealing with the Slovak population was indicated by the Hungarian lawyer from Pressburg, Lajos Ejury, who claimed that even the district judge for the area required that judges in this district should know this language. Ejury himself claimed to speak Magyar, German, Slovak, French and a little English. See MOL, P1747—Thály Kálmán, 5.cs. 6.t., letter dated 5.5.1891.

86 Kemény, G., 1964, pp. 113–116. Zernek proposed that 1. Everyone should speak Hungarian in the meetings except those whose mother tongue was German, 2. the City Magistrate should discuss the different subjects only in Hungarian and that 3. Hungarian should be the only language also of all the municipal expert committees. The *főispán* even suggested some severe punishment of the *Pressburger Zeitung*.

87 Linguistic incomprehension resulted in comic situations when people kept standing up or sitting down (the way of voting) at inappropriate times. This also

took place in committees' meetings. *PZ*, 13.1.1908, N.12, *Ab*, pp. 1-2, "Ordentliche Jahresgeneralversammlung des städtischen Bürgervereines vom 12 Januar 1908 [The annual general assembly of the city's *Bürgerverein*]."

88 Mannová, 1995a, pp. 439-440.

89 Mannová, 1997c, p. 50. The original German name of the City Enhancement society was *Stadtverschönerungsverein*. For more detailed information on associations see Mannová, 1987, 1990.

90 This went hand in hand with the growing division of the public/private spheres. Wolff, 1988, p. 126.

91 Mannová, 1995a, p. 440. See Cohen, 1981, pp. 53-60 on voluntary associations in nineteenth century Central Europe.

92 Mannová, Unpublished article, 1994, p. 12.

93 Mannová, 1995a, p. 439.

94 Cohen, 1981, p. 57. See footnote 38 of this chapter.

95 Ibid., p. 53.

96 Mannová, Unpublished article, 1994, p. 8. Mannová calls German dominated traditional associations "pre-national 'German'" associations.

97 Mannová, 1995a, pp. 443-445. More on *Liedertafel* and its social structure see Mannová, 1995c. While the association felt flattered when invited to perform for aristocratic audiences, it kept its distance from the lower classes and from workers. Its members were members of many other middle class associations and elite clubs like *Kasino* or freemasons. (Mannová, 1995c, pp. 168-169.) Symbols were very important for these associations, as expressed through the use of colours, association uniforms (Rowing association), flags (important for workers', firemen, sport and religious associations). Salner et al, 1991, pp. 78-79.

98 Mannová, 1995a, p. 449.

99 Mannová, 1995a, p. 445. Members of the association were mostly German wine growers and craftsmen which would also indicate the continued use of German. The number of officials in this association's membership was rather small.

100 Mannová, 1995a, pp. 445-446. On the basis of analysis of much material on German associations in Pressburg in this period, Mannová came also to the conclusion that even by the end of the nineteenth century the German middle class's knowledge of Hungarian was weak. (Ibid., pp. 443, 445-446.) I draw the same conclusion with regard to municipal life.

101 Mannová, Unpublished article, 1994, p. 9. The Casino (founded in 1837) was a gentlemen's club where men from the middle and upper classes of the city and coun-

ty met to discuss different issues like politics, to read the daily press, play pool, for entertainment or just to chat. The *Casino* included on average 200–300 of the wealthiest and most influential men of the city and county. In 1880s, one of the members was also the Slovak politician Miloš Štefanovič, who was recognised as an excellent lawyer despite his 'Panslavism' (similar to Michal Mudroň, see footnote 131). Mannová, 1999a, p. 58.

102 "Schutzfrau Baronin Jeszenák fand es für opportun, dass die damalige Staatssprache in den Anstalten gebührende Einführung finde...," in Kemény, L., 1930, p. 12. Mannová, 1995a, p. 446. According to Mannová this might have happened as the result of pressure from the city administration.

103 Celler, 1916. The splitting away of the Hungarian membership was brought also by the pressure of the city and the pressure from the Budapest lodges. Mannová, 1995a, p. 446.

104 Mannová, 1995a, p. 446, footnote 49.

105 MOL, K149–1877–6, correspondence between the minister of interior and *főispán* Count István Eszterházy of Pressburg county where the *főispán* informs the minister about the Viennese lodges in Pressburg. Their meetings were organised by their local representatives (it had to be announced to the city police chief) and took place mostly in the rooms of the *Verschwiegenheit*. On freemasonry in Hungary see Jeszenszky, I., 1927, Lipták, 1996 and Kischke, Andicz and Haubelt, 1997.

106 Mannová, 1995a, pp. 446–447, Bokešová-Uherová, 1958, p. 19. On the history of the association see also Fischer, Ortvay and Polikeit, 1907.

107 Mannová has described this kind of Magyar nationalism as *integral nationalism*. (See Mannová, 1995a, pp. 440–441, Mannová, Unpublished article, 1994, pp. 7–9). Integral nationalism is a type of nationalism when an ethnic group starts to believe that "it is the 'chosen people', and that all individual or class demands and complaints must be subordinated to the national interest." Sugar, 1969, p. 43. Integral nationalism is described by Otto Dann as nationalism that looks for the enemies of the nation within the borders of the national community. Dann, 1993, pp. 193, 201.

108 Mannová, 1995a, p. 441, *PW*, 1867, 1877, 1887, 1897, 1910.

109 Mannová, Unpublished article, 1994, pp. 8–9.

110 Kumlik, 1905, p. 176.

111 Ibid., pp. 216–217.

112 An active role in recruiting members was also taken by the lawyer and Law Academy professor György Fésüs, the Pressburger provost Jácint Rónay, the historian Tivadar Botka, the *alispán* (deputy of *főispán*) of Pozsony county Kálmán Bittó, and the gymnasium professor József Óvári. (Kumlik, 1905, pp. 4–11.) One Pressburg jour-

nalist wrote of Vutkovich: "Freund Vutkovich den die Regierung dazu erkor, kam schon ein Jahr bevor, das Terrain zu nivelliren und die Kraxelhuber zu magyarisieren." ("Friend Vutkovich, who was chosen by the government to level the terrain and to Magyarise the Kraxelhuber, came here one year earlier.") (In Lövö, 1904, p. 7). *Kraxel-huber* was the slightly derogatory name given to German speaking *Pressburgers*.

113 AMB, Toldy Kör, c. 83, Statutes from 1875 and 1903.

114 According to the decree of the Ministry of Interior 1394/1873 the associations were supervised first of all by the municipal authorities and then by the Ministry which could dissolve an association. (Budapest Fővárosi Levéltár XI, Leonardo da Vinci kör 3, p. 187.) Nominally, anyone with two recommendations from existing members could join *Toldy Kör*. (Even women.) The requirements were merely that the prospective member should be able to support himself and be of good charac-ter. However, as Csáder points out, "proper education" was an important criterion in admission to *Toldy Kör*. (Csáder, Unpublished thesis, 1971/72, p. 16.) Furthermore, as a letter from the *Toldy Kör* member Vilmos Unghváry shows, proof of *Toldy Kör* membership (and consequent cultural services) counted as evidence of patriotism in "higher places." This might indicate that *Toldy Kör* membership was useful and therefore sought after. In *AMB*, Toldy Kör, c. 89.

115 Although the statutes of *Toldy Kör* had already been approved by the minister of the interior in December 1873, the founding assembly gathered only in March 1874 when the association had the 100 members required by law.

116 Kumlik, 1905, p. 11: "Jólehet néhányan a jelenlevők közül azt hitték, hogy holmi nemzetiségi harc meginditásáról van szó, s azért Schott József megyei főjegyző lelkes felszólalása alatt a teremből távoztak, mégis elég sokan beiratkoztak a Toldy Kör tagjai sorba."

117 Ibid., p. ix. Potemra, 1963, p. 96.

118 Kumlik, 1905, p. 34.

119 Ibid., p. 38: "elnémetesülés" (Germanisation), "védbástya" (defence bastion).

120 Ibid., p. 59.

121 Ibid., p. 462: "tősgyökeres magyarság" (deeprooted Magyars).

122 AMB, Toldy Kör, c. 84, Minutes of the Toldy Kör standing committee meeting from 21.2.1907: "...mikor még beszélni is alig volt szabad Pozsonyban magyarul."

123 Kumlik, 1905, p. 538.

124 Ibid., pp. 62–63: "Ezen törekvések a német városban hasonlítanak azon zöld oázokhoz, melyeknek magvát időnkint elhordja a szellő a sivatagra és ez ott néha kikel és új oáz keletkezik."

125 Ibid., pp. 286–290.

126 AMB, Toldy Kör, c. 84, Minutes of the *Toldy Kör* standing committee meeting from 7.4.1895.

127 Kumlik, 1905, pp. 209, 223 (1888), 266 (1890), 328 (1904).

128 AMB, Toldy Kör, c. 84, Minutes of the *Toldy Kör* literary section meeting of 29.10.1895.

129 Csáder, Unpublished thesis, 1971/72, Table. In 1879 *Toldy Kör* had 197 members (430 in 1896): 35.4% (36.3% in 1896) state employees and county and municipal bureaucracy; 20.2% (20% in 1896) intelligentsia: medical doctors, lawyers, journalists, writers, engineers, artists; 18.5% (6.3% in 1896) landowners, aristocracy, mayors, parliament deputies; 8.8% (12.1% in 1896) professors and teachers; 7.4% (8.83% in 1896) royal officers and gendarmes; 5.4%(7.9%) entrepreneurs and trade bourgeoisie; 2.7% (2.6% in 1896) clergy; and 1.7% (4.4% in 1896) women (teachers, wives of landowners and entrepreneurs). Most of the nationalist intelligentsia in *Toldy Kör* supported the governing Liberal Party (Vutkovich as well as other leading journalists of the *Nyugatmagyarországi Hiradó* were members of the Pressburger Liberal Party). In the crisis 1905–6 they supported the oppositional coalition and later the Gyula Justh's fraction in the parliament. Potemra, 1963, pp. 222–228.

130 For example see Kumlik, 1905, p. 435, commentary to the lecture of Count Géza Zichy (in 1897).

131 Ibid., p. 480.

132 Ibid., p. 486.

133 Ibid., p. vi: "Hisz a kör termeiben, a kör mulatságain az aristokrácia, a magyar gentry, a katonai osztály és a polgári osztály nem egyszer jelent meg, mint homogén testület."

134 Ibid., p. 575: "nemzetiségi agitátor."

135 See AMB, Toldy Kör, c. 83, List of *Toldy Kör* members attached to the statutes from 1875. Mudroň was also a member of the *Forschrittsverein/Haladó Kör*—a middle class club which consisted of "men of every profession, regardless religion and nationality, for purpose of social encounters, mutual learning and for support of ideas of political and social progress." The association had its own library, organised Hungarian language courses, lectures and fortnightly entertainment—"Bürgerabende." See Mannová, 1999a, pp. 59–60.

136 Kumlik., 1905, pp. 323–324.

137 With the exception of Heinrich von Justi who did not remain mayor very long after (although this was probably not why he retired).

138 Kumlik, 1905, p. 60. Information about the municipal government is from *Pressburger Wegweiser* (after 1890 also *Pozsonyi Útmutató*), the Pressburg directory published every year in German and after 1890 also including some Hungarian translations, 1867–1914.

139 Ibid., p. 131. Both Kisfaludy and Petőfi were Hungarian poets.

140 In 1889, 1894, and 1895 Dröxler was also a member of the association's standing committee. Ibid, p. 341 for 1894; AMB, Toldy Kör, c. 84, Minutes from *Toldy Kör* general assembly from 6.1.1895.

141 Kumlik, 1905, p. 237.

142 Ibid., p. 471.

143 Ibid., p. 268.

144 In municipal administration since 1881, Brolly was first vice-notary, then after 1885 the main notary. In 1899–1900, he was the deputy mayor and from 1900 to 1917 he was the mayor of Pressburg. See *PW*, 1869–1914.

145 In 1874 Brolly's wife even acted in and helped to organise an amateur play performed by *Toldy Kör* members. In 1891 Brolly gave an enthusiastic speech to *Toldy Kör* extolling the deeds of the association's founder, Vutkovich. In response, Vutkovich called Brolly his right hand. Kumlik, 1905, pp. 282–287. Even during his tenure as mayor, Brolly continued to serve on the association's special committees. In 1910, he was on the committees for Hungarian language courses and theatre. AMB, Toldy Kör, c. 84, Minutes from *Toldy Kör* standing committee meeting from 27.1.1910.

146 For an overview of the functionaries of *Toldy Kör* see Csáder, Unpublished thesis, 1971/1972, pp. 86–108.

147 Kumlik, 1905, pp. 300, 341, 376; AMB, Toldy Kör, c. 84, Minutes from the general assembly of *Toldy Kör* from 6.1.1895.

148 Kumlik, 1905, p. 472.

149 Ibid., p. 546.

150 However, the deputy mayor after 1900 was Theodor Kumlik, whom the Hungarian chauvinist Pávai called a "German spirited ultra." (MOL, P1747, Thály Kálmán, 14cs., 6.t, Pávai-Vajna Gábor, letter from 10.5. 1900.) Pávai also blamed Brolly for the failure to push out the German theatre: "In Pozsony the theatre question caused a national scandal again, and Brolly and the City Magistrate are guilty for this. They derogate everything that is Magyar." ("Pozsonyban a szinház kérdés ismét országos botrányt okozott s ennek oka Brolly és a tanács. Ezek megnyirbálnak mindent ami magyar.") Ibid., letter from 18.7.1901.

151 Daniel Molec, for instance, was a member of *Toldy Kör*, for some time a mem-

ber of *Toldy Kör*'s standing committee, and of its entertainment committee. Later he also became a member of *Pozsonyer städtischer Bürgerverein*, indeed the president of this society when the 1908 general assembly complained about the use of Hungarian in the municipal committee. Molec was also the municipal lawyer in 1881–83, 1901 and 1908–14. He was also municipal deputy. He was a member of *Polgári Kaszinó* (City Casino), and in 1879–88 its librarian. Other examples of *Toldy Kör* members who were also working in the municipality include: Johann Hosztinszky (1868–7 *Magistratsrath*, later parliament deputy), Johann Batka (city archivist), Theodor Kumlik (1885–90 deputy notary, 1890–1900 *Magistratsrath*, 1900–14 deputy mayor), Karl Ejury (chief municipal lawyer), Ludwig Kemény (member of *Toldy Kör*'s standing committee, municipal accountant). Other prominent members of *Toldy Kör* were Károly Neiszidler (1885–88: deputy chairman of *Toldy Kör*, after 1913 honorary member of Toldy Kör, 1888–1919 a director of *Polgári Kaszinó* also a member of the *Pozsonyer Bürgerverein*, municipal deputy, Hungarian parliament deputy), Bertalan Klempa (deputy chairman of *Toldy Kör* in 1888–June 1896, chairman of *Toldy Kör* 1896, *alispán*-1886–98, 1900–7), Julius von Szalavszky (*főispán* 1894–99), Graf István Eszterházy (chairman of *Toldy Kör* 1876–78, *főispán* 1876–89), Graf József Zichy (he entered *Toldy Kör* when he became *főispán* from 1889–93), Graf Géza Zichy (chairman of *Toldy Kör* 1910–18). Prominent intellectuals included Tivadar Ortvay (member of the Hungarian Academy of Sciences, a prominent historian and scholar), Sándor Vutkovich (professor at the Law Academy, owner and editor of *Nyugatmagyarországi Híradó*) and Kálmán Thály (prominent Hungarian historian, member of the Hungarian Academy of Sciences, Hungarian parliament deputy, honorary citizen of Pressburg). Some journalists were also members: Károly Angermayer, older and younger (after 1874 owner of *Pressburger Zeitung*, in 1874–5, 1883–85 also the editor in chief, at the beginning of the twentieth century—Angermayer younger the editor), Alajos Pichler, Deutsch Ignác (editor of *Pozsonyvidéki lapok*, later editor of *Pressburger Zeitung*.)

152 In addition to their cultural, educational and social functions, casinos were the locale of city and county-politics, especially as the venue for questions of personality politics. Lipták, 1997, p. 74.

153 See Babejová, Unpublished manuscript, 1998.

154 Mannová, Unpublished article, 1994, p. 12.

155 For example see Kumlik, 1905, p. 3.

156 Ibid., p. 290.

157 Ibid., p. 296: "jó magyar érzelmű."

158 Ibid., p. 225.

159 Ibid., p. 436: "A magyar nép eme befogadó, recepiáló hajlamával élénk ellentétben állt a városok német polgárságának merev elzárkozottsága. Ez Szent István

azon szerencsétlen betelepitési politikájának következménye, a melynek az volt a főelve, hogy az egynyelvű ország törékeny és ingadozó. Ennek tulajdonítható Pozsony jelenlegi állapota is, mert a német polgárság évszázodokan át mint elkényesztetett gyermek védte őseinek nyelvét s az akkori viszontagságos idők közepette nem látta be a szükséget annak, hogy a nemzet nyelvét megtanulja." Saint Stephan I. (975–1038) was the first Hungarian king.

160 Ibid., pp. 448–449.

161 AMB, Toldy Kör, c. 84, Minutes from *Toldy Kör* standing committee session from 4.2.1909. Jenő Rákosi was a leading Jewish journalist—*Pressechef* in Budapest. He belonged to a group of writers and journalists *Kávéforrás* (Coffee source) who met regularly in the Café Richelieu in Pest from the 1860s onwards and who after the Dual Agreement became zealous promoters of political and linguistic Magyarisation. See Hanák, 1984a, p. 296.

162 Kumlik, 1905, p. 477.

163 Ibid., p. 60. The same argument was repeated by Vutkovich in 1888 and 1891. Ibid., pp. 203, 283.

164 Ibid., p. 155: "a magyar nemzeti szellem, a magyar állameszme és a magyar nemzeti közműveltség ápolása és fejlesztése."

165 Ibid., p. 477.

166 Ibid., pp. 110–111: "a Szahara sivatagja, mely a magyar nemzetiség számára egy zöld szálat meg nem termett."

167 Ibid., pp. 315–316: "Legyen tűzhelye a kedélyes magyar életnek és legyen egyszersmind asszimiláló helye a jóindulatú idegenajkú elemeknek."

168 Tamás, 1938, p. 18: "nemzetiségi áradatok."

169 Kumlik, 1905, pp. 496–497. A similar position was ascribed to Graz in Styria. According to its daily, *Grazer Tagblatt*, the geographic position of the city "so close to Slav barbarism" predestined it for the specific national duty of being "the guardian of the borders of Great Germany (*Alldeutschland*)." Graz was "the southeastern bastion of German culture." In 1880, 96% of the city's population had German as their language of communication while the proportion of population speaking Slovenian was 1.02%. Uhl, 1999, pp. 151, 133.

170 AMB, Toldy Kör, c. 84, Minutes from the *Toldy Kör* standing committee session from 11.3.1907.

171 Kumlik, 1905, p. 155: "a társadalmi, irodalmi és művészeti propaganda."

172 This aim was proclaimed openly throughout the period. Kumlik, 1905, Vutkovich—pp. 244 and 247, Krampolin—p. 339.

173 Ibid., p. 176.

174 Ibid., pp. 202, 205: "A nemzetnek a politika nem tőkéje, de igenis tőkéje a közműveltség és ennek főtényzője az irodalom, mely a nemzet belértékének fokmérője." (Ibid., p. 202.) " ...a nemzet nagysága nem a nemzet számerejétől függ, hanem az értelmiség mennyiségétől." (Ibid., p. 205.) "...de minden nemzetiség, minden faj külön fejti ki sajátságát, mindegyiknek meg van individualitása, mely szerint a tudományt általános szempontból fogja föl, de egyszersmind hazai cél érdekében érvenyesiti." Ibid., p. 205.

175 Ibid., p. 209: "A legközelebbi nemzedék már magyar lesz." *Toldy Kör* had patronage over the first Hungarian kindergarten (*Pichler-féle "Első magyar gyermekkert"*) and contributed every year to its support.

176 AMB, Minutes of the *Toldy Kör* theatre committee meeting from 30.1.1895: "Magyar egyház, magyar iskola és magyar szinház."

177 AMB, Minutes of the *Toldy Kör*'s standing committee's preparatory meeting form 3.1.1895. *Nyugatmagyarországi Hiradó* was the Magyar daily owned and edited by Sándor Vutkovich. In 1873 Vutkovich had started the *Pozsonyvidéki Lapok*. At this time, there was no Hungarian newspaper published in the city. A few years later it passed from Vutkovich onto other editors and later ceased to exist. The *Pozsonymegyei Közlöny* weekly began publication in 1887. Vutkovich took over editorship in 1888 and in 1890 he changed it into a political daily *Nyugatmagyarországi Hiradó* which he edited until 1902 when his son Ödön became the editor. *Nyugatmagyarországi Hiradó* remained the only Hungarian language daily in the city until 1914. On the periodical press in Pressburg see *Magyarország vármegyei*, pp. 474–480, *PW*, 1867–1914 and Potemra, 1963.

178 Gábor Pávai Vajna in Kumlik, 1905, pp. 360–361. Also see Pávai-Vajna, 1884 and Pávai-Vajna, 1887.

179 Kumlik, 1905, p. 494.

180 AMB, Toldy Kör, c. 84, Minutes from *Toldy Kör* standing committee meeting from 6.1.1895.

181 Kumlik, 1905, pp. 535, 540: "a magyar impérium megalkotása 30 millió magyarral." This was no isolated dream: "Magyarisation and economic progress, predicted the [Hungarian] publicists, would lead to the rebirth of the empire of Matthias Corvinus, which, with its thirty million Hungarians, would dominate the Balkans." In Jeszensky, G., 1990, p. 270.

182 Kumlik, 1905, p. 470.

183 Ibid., p. 510. In the nineteenth century, Friedrich Ratzel's theory of the state as a living organism was very popular as well. In Ratzel's view, size was the main virtue of the state since large states dominated history. See Williams, 1993, p. 29.

184 Kumlik, 1905, pp. 192–193.

185 Ibid., p. 251.

186 Ibid., p. 477. Similarly, in Graz the municipal council even founded the "Committee for the protection of German existence in Graz" (in 1910) which had to "suppress foreign attack right in its inception." This committee was formed in order to restrict the number of Slovenian commercial signs in the city. Uhl, 1999, p. 153.

187 Even so, it was a fact that the Hungarian language was taking more and more hold in the city. This was also helped by the policies of the Hungarian government. In 1898, the Hungarian parliament passed the bill requiring that every community can have only one official name and that had to be in the state language. (1895: IV törvény-czikk a községi és egyéb helynevekről [Law IV/1895 about the names of communities and other geographical names].) The Prime Minister Bánffy said: "For the Hungarian state idea cannot be served only by feeling and words but by strong will, continuous effort, permeated with the most extreme chauvinistic 'national idea' one has to want to create a unitary Magyar national state that in order to be unitary and national in both language and feeling, needs formalities…it needs that not only its sons but also its mountains and valleys had Magyar names." The law came into effect in the Upper-Hungarian counties in 1901. (Szarka, 1999, p. 244) This law evoked a great dislike on the side of nationalities. Some German communities on present-day Slovak territory also protested against the Magyarisation of community names. (Kováč, 1991, p. 25.) Even the Hungarian historical association condemned this law since its members thought that one should preserve the original local names which are an important source for the study of multinational Hungarian history. Szarka, 1999, p. 244.

188 Similarly in Graz, the German nationalist *Verein der Deutschvölkischen* (Association of German people) initiated change of street names. This change symbolised the nationalist radicalisation in Graz after 1897. In 1899, when 79 streets were to acquire new names, the German nationalists stipulated that these should be named after "German heroes, poets, thinkers, artists." (Uhl, 1999, pp. 139–140.) In formerly Polish territories of Russia, the authorities banned Polish signs in the streets using Russian signs instead. It was forbidden to speak Polish in public and official spaces and all efforts were made to turn public spaces into Russian in appearance. (Weeks, 1999, pp. 555–556.) Replacement of place names has accompanied most changes of power elites and regimes, recently in the Central and East European as well as in the Balkan and Post-Soviet states.

189 Kumlik, 1905, p. 63. This year was also marked by the Kisfaludy celebration in *Toldy Kör.*

190 Csáder, Unpublished thesis, 1971/72, p. 15, Ortvay, 1905, p. 512.

191 Many streets were re-named at the municipal meeting on 28.7.1879. The re-

named streets and squares included Batthyányi Tér (Hungarian aristocrat and politician), Eszterházy Tér (Hungarian aristocrat and politician), after 1876 Deákutca (Hungarian politician), after 1893 Jókai Mór-utca (Hungarian writer), Erkel Ferenc-utca (Hungarian composer). (Ortvay, 1905, pp. 19, 50, 192, 45.) However, the streets were also named after the prominent citizens of the city, for example, Petzlutca (after 1879), commemorating the founder of the *Suppenanstalt* (Soup kitchen) in Pressburg, also Justi sor commemorating the Pressburger mayor Heinrich von Justi, Kempelen Farkas-utca, a well-known engineer and polymath born in Pressburg. (Ibid., pp. 434, 196, 233.) Thus the streets and squares were re-named after prominent personalities which included Hungarians but also *Pressburgers*.

192 Francová, 1998a, p. 31, endnote 2.

193 For more detail on efforts to reclaim the past, founding of museums and the historical sense of the nineteenth century see the discussion in Chapter five on the activities of the *Stadtverschönerungsverein*. The choice of personalities for naming the streets reflects the so called "hierarchy of memories," a concept used by Pierre Nora. (Uhl, 1999, p. 140.) This hierarchy reflects a ranking of the importance of personalities for a certain representation of the city history as seen by the city elites.

194 *PZ*, 2.10.1908, N. 271, *Mb.*, p. 2, "Kultus und Unterrichtsminister Exzellenz Graf Albert Ápponyi—Ehrenbürger der kgl. Freistadt Pozsony [Minister of religion and education his excellency Count Ápponyi—honorary citizen of the royal free town of Pozsony]": "unserer patriotischen Mission an der Landesgrenze hat er auf Schritt und Tritt moralische und materielle Unterstützung angedeihen lassen." The whole article contains limitless admiration of this "ravishing" man. It even praised Ápponyi for the 1907 education law hated by all nationalities. The proposal to elect Count Ápponyi an honorary citizen was signed by 106 municipal deputies. He was the third honorary citizen who was a member of the government. Also the chairman of *Toldy Kör* Kálmán Thály became a honorary citizen. Ortvay, 1905, p. 25.

195 "There is an intimate connection between the social process that forms personal and group identities, and the symbolic aspect of place....Places, since they are experienced as wholes, organize meaning in such a way that contradictory ideas can be held simultaneously." Forest, 1997, p. 308.

196 Cesnaková-Michalcová writes that *Toldy Kör* (especially its theatre committee) was "the most agile and important" element in the struggle for Magyarisation of the Pressburger Theatre and Pressburg. See Cesnaková-Michalcová, 1997, pp. 159–160.

197 From 1879 there was published in Kassa (whose theatre was quickly Magyarised although it had also first been German and Hungarian) a weekly *Színészeti Közlöny* (Dramatic art gazette). Hungary was divided into thirty theatre districts so every Hungarian theatre director knew when his troupe would play in which part of Hungary. Later the number of the theatre ensembles was reduced in order to improve quality. Hungarian towns created theatre committees which decided the theatre sea-

son for towns within each district (larger towns got better ensembles). The theatre directors had to report every week on the expenses and incomes of their ensemble to the central administration in Budapest. From 1883 until 1914 the *Színészek lapja* (Actors' magazine) was published in Budapest. This was the magazine of the Association of Hungarian actors which gave information about the movement of the ensembles on the Hungarian territory. Cesnaková-Michalcová, 1997, pp. 149–151.

198 Cesnaková-Michalcová, 1997, p. 160.

199 Kumlik, 1905, p. 25.

200 Portisch, 1933, p. 262.

201 Kumlik, 1905, p. 20: "De mi, megvalljuk, nem birtunk egészen lélekkel a kinálkozó élvekbe merülni: minden percben azon kérdés merült föl előttünk, hogy miért kell *Magyarországnak* egyik legnevezetesseb királyi városában a magyar múzának *vendégszerepelni*?" (italics in original)

202 Ibid., p. 25: "a magyar direktor a városi szinház átengedését semmi szin alatt nem követelheti, legfőlebb *kegyelemképen* kérheti és örulhet, ha bármi drága bér fejében a játszási engedelmet egyáltalán megkapja." (italics in original)

203 On Heinrich von Justi who is called by Győrik "the greatest mayor of Pozsony in the nineteenth century" (Győrik, 1918, pp. 32–33) see Chapter one, footnote 20.

204 *Toldy Kör* created special committees for different areas: theatre, literary, courses of Hungarian language, organising entertainment, and the Magyar kindergarten. AMB, Toldy Kör, c. 84, Minutes of *Toldy Kör's* general assembly from 6.1.1895.

205 Kumlik, 1905, pp. 48–53.

206 Ibid., pp. 148–150. The only compromise was renting the theatre to the Hungarian ensemble for limited periods of time, which happened during the summer.

207 Ibid., pp. 254–256. At a joint meeting on 28.5.1885 (together with *Toldy Kör*, *Magyar Közművelődési Egyesület* and *Kasino*), the City Theatre Committee suggested that these associations should jointly found an association fighting for the Hungarian theatre in the municipal assembly. *AMB*, Minutes of the City Theatre Committee II (1881–85).

208 Kumlik, 1905, p. 286.

209 The *Times* reported extensively on the Ringtheater fire and the trial with those held responsible for this catastrophe. See issues on 9.12.1881, p. 3a (column a), 10.12.1881, p. 6a, 16.12.1881, p. 8a, 17.12.1881, p. 5d, 20.12.1881, p. 5e, 21.12.1881, p. 5d, 25.4.1882, p. 5b, 19.5.1882, p. 5c, 6.5.1882, p. 7c.
It would be interesting to know whether there were other than security concerns involved in the decision by Pressburg's elite to build a new theatre. This was a period when many European cities acquired new theatres and thus the Pressburger elite's

decision might have been driven out of a sense of competition or the need for a more elaborate expression of the power and culture of the city elite and of bourgeois culture. The old theatre building was built in 1776 by an aristocrat, Count György Csáky. In Paris, the temporary opera building was condemned by the press as dangerous since it could collapse any moment and was "architecturally unworthy of Paris.... A disgrace to a city internationally respected as the queen of arts." The work on the new opera house started in 1862 under the Second Empire and was supposed to be its historical document testifying to the achievements of this period (it was finished in 1875). (Wolff, 1988, pp. 217, 222) In Prague, the new Czech National Theatre was completed in 1881. (Becker et al, 1999, p. 12.) In Graz, the discussions began in 1887 on which style to adopt for the new theatre building in order to best express German culture (reflecting the German nationalism of the Graz city elite). The theatre was eventually built in baroque style by the same architects responsible for the Pressburg theatre. (Uhl, 1999, pp. 149–151) In Vienna, the *Burgtheater* was also built in the baroque style, "commemorating the era in which theater first brought together clerics, courtiers, and commoner in a shared aesthetic enthusiasm." For the Viennese *haute bourgeoisie*, the patronage of arts and the sponsorship of theatre began as an "avenue to aristocratic culture," although by the end of the nineteenth century there was a real enthusiasm for theatre which could not be found elsewhere in Europe. (Schorske, 1981, pp. 8, 17.) In Pressburg in the eighteenth century as well as at the beginning of the nineteenth century there were still aristocratic families residing in the city (since it was formally the capital of Hungary). Thus it is conceivable that the middle class enthusiasm for the theatre developed as a way of becoming at least in this way a part of aristocratic culture, similarly as in Vienna. There was also very close connection to the Viennese theatre, and the ensembles in Viennese theatres had regular performances in the Pressburg theatre. (See Chapter four.)

210 Mór Jókai was one of the greatest Hungarian poets and writers of the nineteenth century.

211 Portisch, 1933, pp. 253: "schon die Eröffnungsvorstellung sollte zeigen, dass Pressburg sich in Ungarn befindet, in dem die Staatssprache die ungarische ist." (Also Kumlik, 1905, p. 181.) Similarly, the opening of the new theatre in Graz symbolised its dedication to German culture. The opening performances were Schiller's "William Tell" and Wagner's "Lohengrin." (Uhl, 1999, p. 151.) The new Pressburg theatre's facade was decorated by the busts of J. W. Goethe, M. Vörösmarthy, J. Katona, F. Liszt and W. Shakespeare. The theatre had the Hungarian inscription *Városi Szinház* (City Theatre) on its front. (Cesnaková-Michalcová, 1997, pp. 107, 109.) The balance of busts was numerically in favour of Magyars: one German writer, two Hungarian writers, one Hungarian music composer (a regular visitor to Pressburg) and an English writer. The theatre building received its Hungarian inscription at the demand of *Toldy Kör* and other similar associations. This was decided on the meeting of the municipal Theatre Committee on 28.5.1885. However, the committee refused to inscribe the theatre building facade with the declaration that this theatre

was dedicated to the Hungarian muse as "needless" although acknowledging this as its purpose. (AMB, Minutes of the City Theatre Committee II (1881–85).) In 1876 the centenary of the existence of the Pressburg's City Theatre was celebrated by a German play (Johann Ch. Brandes: "Die Medicäer") performed by the German theatre troupe then residing in the city. See Cesnaková-Michalcová, 1997, p. 106.

212 Kumlik, 1905, pp. 348–354.

213 My analysis of minutes from all *Toldy Kör* standing committee meetings in this year shows regular discussions of the theatre issue. In the absence of complete minutes from other years, it is impossible to assert that this level of interest existed at other times as well. Since Unghváry was also the main notary of standing committee minutes at this time, his interest in theatre issues may perhaps have influenced his coverage of the subject in standing committee meetings as well.

214 AMB, Toldy Kör, c. 84, Minutes from the *Toldy Kör*'s theatre committee meeting from 30.1.1895. In the same year *Toldy Kör* also announced a literary competition for writing up the history of the Hungarian theatre in Pressburg, with a prize of 400 forints. Ibid., Minutes from the *Toldy Kör* standing committee meeting from 7.3.1895.

215 The memorandum was also printed in the local newspapers. The main Hungarian newspapers in which it was printed in full were *NH*, 20.4.1895, N. 91, pp. 1–2, "Szinügy [The matter of the theatre]" (edited by Sándor Vutkovich) and *Magyar Ujság*. The memorandum was also mentioned in ten or twelve other newspapers; according to *Toldy Kör*, it was completely misunderstood in the local *Pressburger Zeitung* and *Westungarischer Grenzbote*. Ibid., Minutes from the *Toldy Kör* special general assembly meeting from 7.4.1895. Reports on the newspaper coverage seem to have been added to these minutes of the meeting itself.

216 In particular, the theatre committee suggested that the *Toldy Kör* standing committee seek the support of other similarly minded associations such as the *Pozsony vármegyei magyar közművelődési egyesület* (Hungarian educational association of the Pozsony county), *Pozsonyvárosi polgári kör* (Pozsonyer *Bürger* association), *Haladás kör* (Forschrittsverein), *Polgári kaszinó* (Casino), *Magnás klub* (Club of magnates), *Magyar polgári kör* (Hungarian *Bürger* association), *Országos szinészi egyesület* (Hungarian association of actors) and also make direct appeals to those members of *Toldy Kör* who were members of the municipal assembly to vote in favour of the consolidation of the Hungarian theatre. AMB, Toldy Kör, c. 84, Minutes from the *Toldy Kör* theatre committee meeting from 28.3.1895.

217 AMB, Toldy Kör, c. 84, Memorandum.

218 "csekély…azon szinházlátogatók száma, akik bár Magyarországban kösztünk laknak, de nem voltak képesek, vagy nem is akarják a magyar államnyelvet megtanulni és igy a magyar kultúrától, a magyar szinészettől is, oktalanúl idegenkednek."

219 "Tekinttetbe kell vennünk továbbá azon körülményt is, hogy mig a német

szinielőadásoknak—melyek a történet tanuság szerint Pozsony sz. kir. magyar városában már 120 év óta állandositva, a magyart csaknem teljesen hátterbe szoritva és megbénitva, főurainkat, nemességünket és polgárságunkat elnemzetlenitették és idegen erkölcsök és idegenszerű felfogások és a magyar kultura szeretetével ellentétes érzelmek terjesztésére is döntő befolyással voltak—most már hazánk uj viszonyok közt s a nemzeti felébredés jelen korszakában, nem lehet más céljuk, mint a még magyarul nemértő, vagy magyarul megtanulni nem is akaró német-tót ajkú közönség szórakoztatása, vagyis míg a német szinészet csak is részleges érdekkel birhat, addig a magyar nemzeti szinészetnek—az imént felsorolt fontos okokból—a nemes mulattatáson és magyaros szórakoztatáson kivül, felette fontos kulturpolitikai és igen komoly hazafias kötelességei is vannak, minélfogva annak fontossága nemcsak helybeli, hanem országos jellegű is."

220 *PZ* 19.4.1895, N.106, *Mb*, p. 2, "Die Zukunft des Pressburger Theaters [Future of the Pressburger theatre]," AMB, *Toldy Kör*, c. 84, association's assembly meeting 17.4.1895.

221 At *Toldy Kör's* literary committee meeting on 20.4.1895, Árpád Berczik appealed to the members to come to the Hungarian performance in the evening. These appeals were often made before performances of the Hungarian ensemble which were poorly attended. (This particular performance was very successful with a large audience.) Even so, Pávai Vajna reproached members for their lack of interest in the Hungarian theatre by referring to a performance on 30 March which was attended only by 25 members (in 1895 *Toldy Kör* had 452 members). Thus even *Toldy Kör* members showed a lax attitude towards the Hungarian theatre at a time when the association was doing its utmost to entrench the Hungarian theatre in Pressburg. *AMB*, Toldy Kör, c. 84, Minutes from the *Toldy Kör* committee meeting from 20.4.1895 and minutes from the *Toldy Kör* standing committee meeting from 2.5.1895.

222 Twenty of these were elected municipal deputies, while twenty more were appointed "virilists" (rich tax-payers). Pávai Vajna suggested issuing a confidential appeal to these forty members to ask them to support *Toldy Kör's* memorandum, hoping that these votes would secure the balance in *Toldy Kör's* favour. Pávai Vajna noted that in 1893 when municipal committee voted on this issue, there were 60 deputies for stabilisation of the Hungarian theatre, 70 deputies against it—even then more than 11 members of the *Toldy Kör* did not participate in voting and 9 members voted against. AMB, Toldy Kör, c. 84, Minutes from the *Toldy Kör* standing committee meeting from 2.5.1895.

223 AMB, Toldy Kör, c. 84, Minutes from the *Toldy Kör's* committee meeting from 5.10.1895.

224 *PZ*, N. 152, 5.6.1895, *Mb*, p. 2.

225 AMB, Toldy Kör, c. 84, Minutes from the *Toldy Kör* standing committee meeting from 7.11.1895.

226 Kumlik, 1905, pp. 436–449.

227 Ibid., p. 412.

228 Portisch, 1933, p. 255.

229 Ibid.

230 Reckhaus, Unpublished manuscript, 1997, pp. 13–15.

231 Kumlik., 1905, p. 456.

232 Portisch, 1933, p. 255.

233 *NN*, 30.4.1901, N. 50, p. 3, "Prešporskí študenti [Pressburg's students]." "Strong opposition" against the removal of German theatre performances was mentioned even earlier in *NN*, 28.3.1901, N. 37, p. 3, "Nemecké divadlo v Prešporku [The German theatre in Prešporok]."

234 Kumlik, 1905, p. 480.

235 *Magyarország vármegyei*, p. 401.

236 Reckhaus, Unpublished manuscript, 1997, p. 16.

237 Tamás, 1938, p. 32.

238 Cesnaková-Michalcová, 1997, pp. 159–163. See pp. 216–220 for the list of different theatre troups residing or hosting in the city. It must be mentioned that many foreign theatre ensembles performed in the City Theatre including Russian ballet, Italian opera, opera ensemble from Brno (with Czech operas) as well as different Austrian ensembles. Ibid. For the division of the seasons in the City Theatre see also *PW*, 1867–1918.

239 Reckhaus, Unpublished manuscript, 1997, p. 16. See Pelikan, Uhl, Unpublished article, about the struggle for the City Theatre in Laibach/Ljubljana between the Slovenians and Germans.

240 Several times the Theatre Committee exempted Hungarian directors from payments of fees for the theatre rental since they could hardly cover their expenses. The failure of the Hungarian performances to attract audiences and the lack of state subsidies to financially support the stabilisation of the Hungarian theatre were the main reasons given by the Theatre Committee. Discussion in the Theatre Committee and in the daily press suggests that Hungarian performances were poorly attended even in 1900–2. In 1900, the Theatre Committee complained about the poor standard of Hungarian performances and feared further deterioration. See AMB, Zápisnica zo zasadnutí divadelnej komisie I. 1875–80, II. 1881–85, III. 1884–87, IV. 1898– 1919. The first two records (I-II) have meeting minutes either in Hungarian or in German, with German prevailing. III. Has the records from meeting of the *Theaterbau-Comite* (Theatre construction committee) and is solely in German. The IV. is only in Hun-

garian. See also *PL*, 11.7.1875, N.55, pp. 211–212, "A magyar szinészet ügye [The matter of the Hungarian theatre]," *PL*, 18.7.1875, N.57, pp. 219–220, "Még egyszer a magyar színeszetről [Once more about the Hungarian theatre]," *PZ*, 31.112.1903, N. 358, *Mb*, p. 2, "Zur Krise des ungarischen Theaters in Pozsony [To the crisis of the Hungarian theatre in Pozsony]" (a polemics with *Hiradó*), *WG*, 2.10.1907, N.12105, p. 2, "Sitzung des Theaterkomites [Meeting of the Theatre Committee]."

241 Francová, 1998a, pp. 20–21, (capitals in original).

242 Grusková, 1999, p. 105. According to Skalský, Pressburg's inhabitants traditionally submitted to the powerful if formalities were preserved and their honour as burghers was respected. He also claims that the Pressburger mentality was very close to Viennese optimism and frivolity. "The Viennese 'der dumme Kerl' is the brother of the Pressburger 'Kraxelhuber'." Skalský quoted in ibid.

243 Kalesný, 1987, pp. 251–252, Kalesný, 1985, p. 16, Hanák, J., 1992, p. 1. According to M. Korman who was born in Pressburg, in the years 1918–1919 Pressburg was still mainly German and Hungarian, Slovak was heard only in the market and some poorer areas under the castle. Shop assistants refused to speak Slovak. Salner et al, 1991, p. 11.

244 Thirring, 1912, p. 110.

245 Glettler, 1992, p. 315.

246 Hanák, J., 1992, p. 1: "Zvláštnosťou mesta na Dunaji boli tzv. Prešpuráci. V niekoľkých vetách vedeli vystriedať maďarčinu, nemčinu ba aj slovenčinu. Boli to tunajší rodáci, národnosti neurčitej, s mestom spätí históriou, rodovou tradíciou, prácou, majetkom, ale i jeho krásami. Ich láska a oddanosť k rodnému mestu boli bezhraničné. Odpradávna sa zamestnávali najmä remeslom, vinohradníctvom a obchodom."

247 For factors influencing the status of a language see Mackey, 1988, pp. 34–41.

248 Gal, 1979, p. 131.

249 Ibid., p. 13. The Slovak language was associated with the lower classes even in the first years of the Czechoslovak Republic. In Trnava in the 1920s the daily press regularly complained that when a well-dressed person entered a café or shop, the personnel automatically greeted him/her in Hungarian. "Majority of the businessmen do not know or cannot imagine that a Slovak could also belong to intelligentsia." (Lipták, 1997, p. 76, footnote 33.) This was similar in Bratislava. See footnote 243. Many Russians in the post-Soviet Central Asian states refuse to learn Uzbek or Kazakh as they consider these languages "underdeveloped" and of lower status. Smith, G. et al, 1998, p. 144.

250 Paríková, 1985, p. 188.

251 Thirring, 1912, p. 28*.

252 Mannová, Unpublished article, 1994, p. 6.

253 Ibid., p. 3. Some Slovak historians even expressed concerns that the Slovak population in Pressburg was very easily Magyarised and that it was threatened (especially through intermarriage among the three nationalities) with the loss of its 'national consciousness.' In Horváth et al, 1978, p. 231.

254 Svetoň, 1948, p. 273. "S hľadiska jazyka objavuje sa nám tu proces ako jazyková akomodácia so silným sklonom k trojrečovosti, s hľadiska smiešanej sobášnosti ako proces národnostnej amalgamácie a s hľadiska duchovného obsahu ako národná labilizácia smerom k regionálnej patriotizácii, pravda, uhorského razenia."

255 Hungarian patriotism was characteristic for many Germans living in the territory of Hungary throughout the nineteenth century, it was not something that developed only after Hungary became a quasi-independent state. Nor was local patriotism peculiar to Pressburg. Similar phenomena were typical also for other cities such as Hamburg (at least in the claims of local elites.) See Russell, 2000.

256 Kovačevičová, 1985, p. 52, endnote 21.

257 "People have multiple identities and loyalties that derive from the overlapping social worlds in which they live their lives." Craig Calhoun quoted in Agnew, 1997a, p. 250. On multiple identities of the members of Hungarian middle class during this period see Hanák, 1997, pp. 169–176. See Sidler, 1995 on concepts of identity in Bratislava.

258 Education was one of the areas which became almost completely Magyarised in Pressburg. In 1893, the Catholic elementary schools voluntarily adopted Hungarian as the language of instruction as did the evangelic and Jewish elementary schools (népiskolák). In the middle school system where both German and Hungarian had previously been the languages of instruction, in the 1880s Hungarian became the only language of instruction, German being taught as a foreign language (Royal Higher Catholic Gymnasium after 1885, State Realschule after 1886, all professional schools). Only the Evangelic Lyceum preserved more extended use also of German and limited use of Slovak in the theological courses. (Evangelic Lyceum had also a small Slovak library. See Hirschmann, 1909.) At the Law Academy, the only language of instruction after 1861 was Hungarian. In Magyarorszg vármegyei, pp. 351–371, Portisch, 1933, pp. 172–208, Francová, 1998c, pp. 101–114. The extent of Magyarisation of education is shown also by the fact that until 1918, among the many German professional journals there was not one concerning education. Potemra, 1963, p. 197.

259 Pressburger Wegweiser was an address-book published yearly for the use of the inhabitants of Pressburg. (See chapter one, footnote 79.) At the beginning of the period, Pressburger Wegweiser was German with Hungarian gaining ground in the 1890s. It was, however, not consistent in its use of both languages. In 1890, the title page was already bilingual, and so were the names of the listed schools and institu-

tions. Then in 1894, although the title page was bilingual, the whole address-book was in German. In 1898, the entire *Pressburger Wegweiser* was in German and the 1898 version lacked the Hungarian translations as well (apart from Hungarian associations). In 1900, the listed schools and offices were also in Hungarian, the rest was German, unless it was a Hungarian association. In 1905 the *Pressburger Wegweiser* was bi-lingual, German-Hungarian. In 1908, some of the associations were already called *Pozsonyer* even in the German version but some still *Pressburger* (depending probably on the date of founding). In 1913, the Hungarian version was first and afterwards followed the German one and similarly in 1914. See *PW*, 1867–1914.

260 Mannová, Unpublished research, p. 1.

261 This daily concentrated all the intellectually and conceptually capable Magyar individuals in Pressburg, and so the publishing of another newspaper was excluded since this would have split the forces. This did not mean there was no political differentiation among Magyars in Pressburg. There were attempts to publish other Hungarian newspapers but these never survived for very long. Potemra, 1963, pp. 216, 228.

262 See Sundhaussen, 1973 on the influence of Herder's thought on the national movements in the Habsburg Empire.

263 See Islamov, 1992 on *natio hungarica* and its transformation into the 'Hungarian nation', also Barany, 1969.

264 The statements of leading Slovak intellectuals from this period are evidence of the extent of their disappointment and the fear of a small nation of being forgotten, disappearing from "historical memory." Zajac, 1999, p. 46.

265 As Anton Špiesz writes, "one has to take into account that at least as many of the Slovaks who welcomed the Memorandum refused it or saw it as irrelevant to them. The Slovak political leaders who composed the Memorandum used for the Slovaks the expression nation. In reality the Slovaks were not yet a nation because not all of those who spoke Slovak had a sense of belonging to this nation." Špiesz, 1992, p. 96.

266 Hungarian politicians considered Slovaks (together with Ruthenians) the weakest nationality, incapable of asserting its rights. The Slovak National Party did not manage to mobilise mass support and it was seen by the Hungarian government and counties as weak and lacking inner cohesion, and not a suitable partner for negotiation. Szarka, 1999, pp. 159, 209–210. Also "[t]he legalistic Hungarian nobility could recognize claims based on ancient constitutional privileges; it rejected claims based on nationalism." Deak, 1979, p. 122.

267 Špiesz, 1992, pp. 105–109; Glettler, 1992, pp. 309–310.

268 Co-operation between Slovaks and Czechs increased after the turn of the century. This was caused by external factors such as the Austro-Hungarian dualism

and the agreement between Germany and Habsburg Empire, both of which had a negative impact on the development of the Czech and Slovak national movements. Pekník, 1999, p. 87.

269 See Hronský, 1975 on the political opinions of people gathered around the magazine *Prúdy*.

270 Thus, for instance, Slovaks split away from the main *Katolikus Néppárt* (Hungarian Catholic Party) in 1905 and became a wing of the (Slovak) National Party to contest the Hungarian elections as a new joint Slovak Party. However, the discord in this alliance grew and in 1913 the People's Party broke away and the *Slovenská Ľudová strana* (Slovak People's Party) was founded under the leadership of Andrej Hlinka who later played an important role in the Slovak autonomist movement during the 1930s.

271 The Slovak nationalist intelligentsia did not succeed in winning over the Slovak speaking gentry (before 1867) or most of the Slovak speaking middle classes who preferred cultural and political "Hungarismus." Since the Slovak nation-building process did not offer any immediate advantages in terms of social mobility, these layers of the population refused to participate and were called "renegades." Pichler, 1997, p. 63.

272 However, the Slovak nation (defined in terms of Hroch's periodisation) was constituted already by the 1930s, with its own intelligentsia, educational and cultural institutions, and ministries. In 1992 the Slovak nation acquired its own "roof," its state. See Gellner, 1983.

273 Mannová, Unpublished research, pp. 1, 4.

274 Krčméry, 1931, p. 65.

275 Ibid., p. 63. "Slovenský element bol zväčša chudobný a preto aj zakríknutý, utajený. Ťažko sa dostával pospolu, nebolo v ňom dosť kohezie, bol rozsypaný."

276 Svetoň, 1948, p. 273.

277 Mannová, Unpublished research, p. 20. The language of command in this regiment was German. On the Habsburg army on the present-day Slovak territory see Dangl, 1977 and Dangl, 1996. On nationalism and the Habsburg army see Deák, 1990.

278 Interestingly, Svetoň attributes this to the romantic character of Hungarian nationalism. Svetoň, 1948, p. 273.

279 *PW*, 1867–1900. The "struggle for the church" was important in the Slovak national movement. "The language used in church was considered an important means of assimilation and also public demonstration of the ethnic situation in the town or village." Lipták, 1999, p. 125.

280 See Pichler, 1997 on whether one can appropriately use the term "Slovak society" for the pre-1918 context. Pichler differentiates between a merely language-based community and a constitutional nation of citizens.

281 When Štúr was in Pressburg, a group of enthusiastic Slovak youth was concentrated around him. All of them used to make trips to the nearby castle ruin Devín. Representatives of the Slovak national revival were convinced that it used to be the centre of the Great Moravian Empire. Trips to this place then were in remembrance of the glorious past when the 'Slovak nation' had its own state.

282 Fiala, 1948a, pp. 354–386. The year until when the association existed is not known, the last report for its activity is available from November 1873.

283 Prúdy, 2, 2, 1910/11, "Vyhodenci [The expelled]," p. 81. It is not clear, though, whether the reason for expulsion in all cases was the charge of "Pan-Slavism." The article assumes that this was true of all cases in Hungary. In total, 122 Slovak students were expelled from all educational institutions in Hungary between 1857 and 1906.

284 Lehotská, 1948, pp. 292–294.

285 Lehotská, 1948, pp. 297–302. The law XLIV/1868 about the equality of nationalities ensured especially the right for usage of the nationalities' mother tongues, depending on their numerous strength in different communities, esp. their municipal offices. E.g. the municipal meeting minutes had to be led in the state language but besides that they could be led also in a language demanded by the one fifth of the municipal deputies. Everybody who had the right to speak in municipal assembly meetings could do so in Hungarian or any other language, if Hungarian was not his mother tongue. Although municipalities were required to use state language in communication with state authorities, in their internal communication they were allowed also other languages. The law also regulated the use of mother tongue in courts of law. (See "1868. évi XLIV. törvénycikk a nemzetiségi egyenjogúság tárgyában.") After the turn of the century there was a movement in more counties demanding that the Nationalities' law be revised since it was too liberal. See Kemény, G., 1964, the leading article in the independent (*függetlenségi*) press of the Independent Party, pp. 116–117; letter of the county municipal assembly of Pozsony, pp. 118–119. See Szarka, 1999, p. 175.

286 Mannová, Unpublished research, p. 10. According to the chair of the Bar Association Theodor Rochlitz, at this time even Hungarians did not have a better orator than Mudroň who not only spoke Hungarian and German but also knew their literature and philosophy and used a wide range of quotations in the original.

287 Lehotská, 1948, pp. 302–304.

288 Ibid., p. 307. "Choďte teda páni porotci, a dokážte svojím oslobodzujúcim výrokom, že v obrane proti absolutizmu a centrálnej monarchii sú všetky národnosti Uhorska svorné."

289 Ibid., pp. 313–339. See Bokeš, 1965, pp. 427–437 on Mudroň's response to Grünwald. Thébusz' pamphlet on the Pan-Slav character of the Evangelic church in Slovakia used similar argumentation as Grünwald who in his chauvinistic pamphlet

wrote about the need for Magyars in Upper Hungary to defend themselves. In response Mudroň asked "whether there is any need for the defence of a nation which has in its hands the whole state apparatus and all power." These words resonate in the contemporary context, when many Slovak politicians suffer from a similar fear of the Slovak nation somehow being swallowed up by the Hungarian ethnic minority which has 10% of Slovakia's population.

290 Mudroň is also considered a "good Slovak" by Ivan Dérer who categorises Slovaks as "good" or "bad" on the basis of their loyalty to the Slovak national idea. Mannová, Unpublished research, p. 10.

291 Lehotská, 1948, pp. 290–291. The members were some Slovak lawyers, Catholic priests and burghers.

292 Ibid., pp. 310, 311.

293 AMB, Toldy Kör, c. 83, List of members attached to the statutes from 1875.

294 See also Mannová, Unpublished article, 1994, p. 1, the ceremonial address given by Mudroň (in German) at the ceremony in which the flag of the German choir of typographers was sanctified in May 1882. He concluded his speech with "God bless the homeland!" and was answered by enthusiastic calls of "Éljen! [Bravo!]" in Hungarian from the audience.

295 For example, Mudroň was elected to the standing committee of the Pressburger burgher association *Haladó Kör*. Mannová, 1999, p. 60.

296 Lehotská, 1948, pp. 340–341. Mudroň died in 1887 in Martin. At the end of his life he came into financial difficulties since he often took on law suits for poor people free of charge.

297 On Kutlík's activity among students see Žigmundík, 1926.

298 Ivánka, 1948, pp. 343–350. He married Božena, the daughter of another representative of the Slovak national movement Michal Miloslav Hodža. (*Slovenský biografický slovník*, 1989, p. 319.) Before that, he worked as the secretary of the *főispán* of the Zólyom county Ján Francisci. (Žigmundík, 1926, p. 36.) In 1872, Kutlík ran unsuccessfully for the post of parliamentary deputy in the district of Szombathely. Kutlík III, 1931, p. 27.

299 Ivánka, 1948, p. 350.

300 *WG*, 20.10.1885, N. 4392, p. 1, "Die panslawischen Umtriebe [Pan-Slav machinations]." *Venček* was a collection of Slovak national songs. Their subject was usually national oppression and the necessity to fight against it. Slovak students were well aware that they could be prosecuted by the Hungarian authorities for singing these songs. Žigmundík, 1926, p. 10. For the texts of these songs see ibid. See also Potemra, 1964, pp. 540–541.

301 Ivánka, 1948, p. 351.

302 SNA, UMV I, i. n. 7, 1885, c.1. letter dated 20.11.1885. The *főispán* in his letter stated that the royal prosecutor avoided answering him in this matter, and indeed put doubt on competency of the municipal assembly. (".".sőt kétségbe vonta a közigazgatási bizottságnak jogosultságát.") According to the *főispán*, the royal prosecutor did not show enough initiative and waited always for orders from above.

303 SNA, UMV I, i. n. 6, 1885, c.1, letter from 28.12.1885, i. n. 7, 1885, c.1, letter from 10.12.1885.

304 SNA, UMV I, i. n. 8, 1887, c.2, letter from 20.10.1887; the verdict in ibid. See also AMB, "Pozostalosť Štefana Fajnora st.", c.2.

305 SNA, UMV I, i. n. 8, 1887, c.2, the verdict, i. n. 9, 1888, c.2, letter from the Budapest royal prosecutor.

306 Ivánka, 1948, p. 352. One year of suspension from his practice cost Kutlík his last clients who had remained with him despite the fact that he was continuously persecuted by authorities for his 'Panslav' conviction. Žigmundík, 1926, p. 38.

307 *ST*, 14.4.1905, N. 16, p. 4, "Jako nažívame [How we live]." In his memoirs Krčméry calls theatre performances "the most effective means of awakening." In this opinion he does not differ from the opinion of *Toldy Kör*. In this light the almost hysterical behaviour of the Hungarian chauvinists and Hungarian press is not so surprising, especially considering how much effort they put into Magyarising the City Theatre.

308 *KN*, 10.3.1905, N. 11, p. 5, "Prešporok."

309 *ĽN*, 14.9.1906, N. 38, p. 5, "Prešporok."

310 Potemra, 1983, Vol. I, p. 340.

311 *RN*, 5.3.1914, N. 10, p. 6, "Divadlo v Prešporku [The theatre in Prešporok]."

312 *RN*, 4.6.1914, N. 23, p. 6, "Slovenské divadlo v Prešporku [The Slovak theatre in Prešporok]."

313 Krčméry, 1931, p. 67. Slovak students in the city also prepared amateur theatre performances. They played in the pub of Ján Grajciar. (Ibid., pp. 66–67.) However, the number of amateur performances given by Slovak workers was not large either. "One could count on one hand which organisations organise theatre performances….The reasons [are] unwillingness to read, aversion to any intellectual activity and devaluation of mental work—these are basic problems which do not allow the springing up of purposeful cultural work in our organisations." ["Na prstoch jednej ruky odpočítať si môžeme, ktoré organizácie usporiadajú divadelné predstavenia. Príčiny toho sú rozličné…. Nechuť ku čítaniu, odpor ku každej duševnej činnosti a znehodnocovanie duševnej práce—to sú hlavné chyby, ktoré nedajú vzkrsnúť

cieľavedomej kultúrnej práci v našich slovenských organizáciách." Edmund Borek (editor of the workers' press in Pressburg) quoted in Potemra, 1983, Vol. I, p. 342.

314 This kind of identification comes across in the memoir of the Slovak music composer Ján Albrecht, when writing about music composers who studied at the Royal Catholic Gymnasium in Pressburg, and about the music life in the city in general. Albrecht's father was a member of the traditional middle class, and he was the conductor of the prestigious choir *Kirchenmusikverein*. Albrecht, 1998, pp. 22–49.

315 Before 1918, Slovaks could be found mainly in pubs but also some cafés. While Germans were traditionally found especially in wine-taverns, Magyars tended to gather in cafés. Salner et al, 1991, pp. 15–16.

316 Mannová, Unpublished research, pp. 4, 18, 33. Krčméry, 1931, pp. 63–67. The first public gathering with Slovak speeches took place in 1893, on the gathering of the Hungarian Catholic People's Party. Mannová, Unpublished research, p. 15.

317 *SL*, 1.9.1901, N. 35, p. 2 and 22.9.1901, N.38, pp. 2–3, "Prešporok."

318 *ĽN*, 16.1.1903, N. 3, pp. 3–4, "Prešporok."

319 *NN*, 22.3.1904, N. 37, p. 3, "Z Prešporka."

320 Štefánek, 1944, p. 140. Štefánek counted these numbers on the basis of subscribers of the Slovak periodical press. According to the official Hungarian documents, until 1918 there were in Slovakia 526 members of Slovak intelligentsia with their families and from this number 101 people were capable of leading a movement. (Chaloupecký, 1930, p. 20.) Dérer felt there were more than just seven families, but the fact that he could list all nationally active Slovaks suggests that their number was small. Mannová, Unpublished research.

321 Mannová, Unpublished research, p. 22, *ST*, 14.4.1905, N.16, p. 4, "Jako nažívame [How we live]," also *ST*, 1.6.1906, N. 22, p. 7, "Z Prešporka…." The association was re-founded in 1911. *ST*, 12.5.1911, N.19, p. 5, "Vzdelávací spolok v Prešporku [Educational association in Prešporok]."

322 *NN*, 3.1.1903, N. 1, p. 4, "Prešporok."

323 *ĽN*, 2.1.1908, N. 1, pp. 1–2, "Ruch Slovákov v Prešporku [Slovak life in Prešporok]."

324 Prúdy, 1, 7, 1909/10, p. 185, "Zo života prešporskej mládeže [From the life of the youth of Prešporok]": "Ľahostajnosť a nevšímavosť proti prešporskému slovenskému ľudu nutno vytýkať i celej slovenskej inteligencii v Prešporku. Tá inteligencia — tu vynímame študujúcu mládež—, ktorá má čas na schôdzky, keď ide o zábavu a pôžitok, mohla by pamätať i na ľud, tým viacej, že mu to sľúbila a že pri danej príležitosti chce rátať na jeho dôveru."

325 Prúdy, 1, 9–10, 1909/10, p. 288, "Z Prešporka."

326 In the academic year 1909/10 there were 30 Slovak students studying in Pressburg (24 theology, 6 law). (Prúdy, 1, 1,1909/10, p. 19, "Prešporská mládež.") In 1910/11 18 students (17 theology, 1 law). (Prúdy, 2, 2, 1910/11, p. 80, "Z Prešporka.") In 1911/12 there were 19 students (12 theology, 3 law, Evangelic Lyceum 4). Prúdy, 3 , 1, 1911/12, p. 35, "Z Prešporka."

327 For small reports about the activity of Slovaks students in Pressburg see *Prúdy* published in Budapest from 1909.

328 *ST*, 18.10.1907, N. 42, p. 7, "Beťársky život v Prešporku [Frivolous life in Prešporok]"; *ST*, 1.11.1907, N.44, p. 9, "Na študentov fiškusa [Lawyer to students]," *ST*, 15.11.1907, N. 46, p. 7, "Na študentov fiškusa." Slovenian students in Graz after the turn of the nineteenth century were victims of similar attacks by German nationalists. Speaking or singing in Slovenian in public was considered a "provocation." However, the scale of expressing anti-Slovenian sentiments was much larger than that of anti-Panslav sentiments in Pressburg and these sentiments were supported by the Graz city representation itself. Uhl, 1999, p. 152.

329 Prúdy, 1, 1, 1909/10, p. 19, "Prešporská mládež"; Prúdy, 2, 2, 1910/11, p. 79, "Z Prešporka."

330 Prúdy, 1, 9–10, 1909/10, p. 289, "Z Prešporka."

331 Kumlik,1905, p. 486. They also gathered in large numbers outside the association's rooms when the anniversary of the Hungarian revolution 1848 was celebrated to demonstrate their patriotism. Ibid., pp. 533–534.

332 Prúdy, 1, 2, 1909/10, p. 40, "Z Prešporka." In one case of disciplinary examination of four Slovak and two German students which happened on the basis of a false accusation, while the Slovak students were merely rebuked, the German students were expelled from the Academy. In *CL*, 24, 7, 1910, p. 221, "Z prešporskej teologickej akadémie [From the theological academy in Prešporok]." Also Prúdy, 2, 2, 1910/11, p. 80, "Z Prešporka."

333 *ĽN*, 25.5.1907, N. 21, p. 7, "Vyzvanie [Appeal]"; Krčméry, 1933, p. 66. Among the founders in Pressburg were Adolf Mačalka (house owner), Anton Skitsák (landowner), Ján Grajciar (tavern owner), Josef Papánek (tailor), Andrej Zedník (shopkeeper), Pavel Havlík (craftsman), Mat. Šramek (wine-grower), Ján Duroška (craftsman), Michal Špaček (craftsman). The rest of founders were from the communities surrounding Pressburg. In *ĽN*.

334 Potemra, 1983, Vol. I, pp. 119–121. The association should have been founded in 1910 but was postponed into 1911. The main activists were Andrej Hlinka (the founder of the Slovak People's Party), Ferdinand Juriga, Ferko Skyčák, Florián Tománek, Jozef Závodský—all of them already managers of different Slovak banks. The association had Catholic, anti-socialist, anti-Masaryk and anti-Semitic character. See also *CL*, 24, 6, 1910, p. 206, "Kníhkupeckonakladateľský a kníhtlačiarsky

spolok [Publishing, printing and book-selling association]."

335 Mannová, Unpublished research, pp. 26–27.

336 Ibid., p. 17, *PW*, 1900–1914.

337 It is necessary to stress that there have always been geographical differences in the strength of the Slovak national movement and support for it. While the areas of Central Slovakia and Western Slovakia were generally supportive (although not totally either—see Chapter four regarding the search for a Slovak centre), Eastern Slovakia was largely unreceptive to Slovak national ideology. The strength of nationalism changes and is different in different places and times. (R. J. Johnston et al, 1988, p. 11.) However, in present-day Slovakia one can still discern these nationally more receptive areas or regions in the voting patterns. The populist and nationalist parties have much larger support in these areas. On regionalism and its causes see Mannová, 1997a, p. 17. See Kühn, 1928 about the personalities of the Slovak national movement in county of Pozsony. Kühn claims that this county had many active nationalists.

CHAPTER 3

Industrialisation, Urbanisation, and Development of the

Workers' Movement

1 "Class" here is understood "less as objective reality than a social construct, created differently by different historical actors." Joyce, 1991, p. 9. There is no strict division between the 'working class' and the 'middle classes' or 'bourgeoisie.' As Wallerstein notes, there are no "pure classes...Not only is there a constant discontinuity between the practices, movements and organizations that make up a 'class' in its relative historical discontinuity, there is an essential impurity in each of these terms....Similarly no significant social movement, even when it took on a definite proletarian character, was ever founded on purely anti-capitalist demands and objectives, but always on the combination of anti-capitalist objectives and democratic, or national, or anti-militaristic objectives, or cultural ones (in the widest sense of term)." (Balibar, Wallerstein, 1991, p. 171.) However, the socialist historiography of the workers' movement is marked by a monolithic understanding of the 'working class' as well as 'class consciousness.' Everything is judged from the Marxist perspective, or rather Lenin's interpretations of it. Thus workers' 'class consciousness' is considered not sufficiently developed if they did not propagate class struggle and use of violent means to overthrow the capitalist society. Also 'the working class' comes across as a homogeneous body. These descriptions lack any discussion of actual values and behaviour. Such reductionist understanding stands in sharp contrast to the richness and diversity of discourses prevalent in the working class as pictured in western working class histories, like Joyce's *Visions of the people*.

2 Gosiorovský, 1956, pp. 90–91.

3 Rothirchen, 1968, p. 76.

4 Horváth et al, 1978, p. 172.

5 Glettler, 1988, p. 51, also Horváth et al, 1978, p. 168. Chapter one of this study has described the different kinds of industry in Pressburg.

6 Kalesný, 1985, pp. 18–19.

7 In the case of the Roth cartridge factory most workers were from Hidegkút, Lamacs, Beszterce; in the Matador factory (rubber products) there were many workers from Ligetfalu; in the thread factory (*Magyar cérnagyár*) the workers from Förév, Malomliget, and so on. Ibid., p. 19.

8 Similarly see Obuchová, Unpublished thesis, 1986, p. 71. For a description of the ethnic structure of surrounding villages see Horváth et al, 1978, pp. 357–421, *Magyarország vármegyei*, pp. 23–130.

9 Glettler, 1992, pp. 296–297. According to Glettler, as a border town, Pressburg attracted mostly immigrants from abroad while Budapest was attractive mainly for migrants from inside Hungary. Pressburg's inhabitants left their city for Austria while immigrants from Austria came mostly from Lower Austria and Styria. (Glettler, 1988, pp. 52–53.) Glettler does not mention Slovak migrants to Pressburg, although, according to Slovak authors, Slovak workers were the core of the immigration to the city. (Horváth et al, 1978, p. 165.) Glettler only mentions that the settlement patterns of Slovaks show that they were mostly migrant workers. She does not mention their proportion of all immigrants. In the case of Budapest, the increase of population due to immigration was more dramatic, from 134,000 in 1851 to 930,666 in 1914. Gyányi, 1995, p. 107.

10 Glettler, 1988, p. 53.

11 Goláň, 1957, p. 165. Unfortunately there are few precise figures for the origins of these immigrants besides a few sources like Jakab Fischer who described in detail the results of the 1890 census in Pressburg. Fischer gives exact numbers for immigrants (people residing in the city but not residents) from each county as well as their mother tongue. In 1890, large number of immigrants came from the predominantly Slovak counties Pozsony, Nyitra, Trencsén and these were mostly workers. However, there was high immigration also from the Magyar dominated counties (Moson, Sopron, city of Budapest) (Figure 17). From the Austrian citizens, the majority was Czech and Moravian, many immigrants were from Lower Austria, Galicia and Silesia (Figure 1), mostly workers. (Fischer, 1894, pp. 9–12.) Often one can only estimate origins on the basis of the counties from which immigrants came.

12 Gajdoš, 1987, p. 260.

13 Glettler, 1992, pp. 296–297.

14 The proportion of out-migrating Germans on all out-migration for 1889–1913 was 71.7%. The out-migration of the Magyars and Slovaks was not as high as that of the Germans. *MSK*, Vol. 16, pp. 18–19.

15 The workers' housing built by factories brought together in the same domicile workers of different nationalities which could cause communication problems. (Kovačevičová, 1976, p. 24.) For the Slovak territory it was typical that commuting workers were more numerous than those residing in the city. Some workers remained in the city during the week but during the weekend they went back to their villages where they worked on their fields. (Ibid., p. 29.) Another reason for commuting was that many factories in the territory of present-day Slovakia were placed in the countryside, not in urban centres. (Tajták, 1981, p. 821.) Such commuting workers certainly differed in their outlook from the urban workers in that they had preserved traditional ways of thinking and conservative values. These workers were also harder to organise.

16 Obuchová, Unpublished thesis, 1986, pp. 51–66.

17 Ibid., p. 71. Hapák, 1973, p. 171. As the rich moved out, the houses became shabby and rents went down. Thus the centre became proletarianised although here were constructed new office-buildings, banks, hotels, schools and institutions.

18 Obuchová, Unpublished thesis, 1986, p. 72.

19 These included the Stollwerck housing, Kühmayer housing, Durvay housing, Klinger housing, Guttenberg housing. (Kalesný, 1985, pp. 20–21.) Flats were constructed for the railway employees, and the Szamek housing was built in Ligetfalu. Similar workers' housing also grew around the factories Apollo (oil-refinery), *Kabelgyár* (production of cables), Roth cartridge factory and Dynamit Nobel factory (explosives' production). See Kovačevičová, 1987, p. 271. See *Magyarország vármegyei*, pp. 323–327 for the list of most important factories in Pressburg. In 1907, there were more than 700 workers' houses in Pressburg. Ortvay, 1907, p. 16.

20 Obuchová, Unpublished thesis, 1986, p. 183, endnote 191.

21 Ibid., p. 80, Kalesný, 1974, p. 185.

22 Obuchová, Unpublished thesis, 1986, p. 168, endnote 35.

23 Horváth et al, 1978, p. 182.

24 Hanzlíček, 1970, p. 17. However, this association was not the first workers' association in Pressburg. The Pressburg's typesetters had created their own self-help association in 1867. Horváth et al, 1978, p. 176.

25 Horváth et al, 1978, p. 176, Goláň, 1957, p. 167, Lehotská et al, 1952, p. 100. The number of illiterate people in the city in 1870 was 16,541, and according to Goláň this

number was mostly made of Slovak workers. Goláň, 1957, p. 168.

26 Horváth et al, 1978, pp. 180–181.

27 Gosiorovský, 1956, pp. 47–55, Horváth et al, 1978, pp. 180–181. There were a few differences between the two programmes. Unlike the Gotha programme, the programme of the Social Democratic Party of Hungary included the demand that large estates be given over to communal ownership. Other demands included universal suffrage for all citizens over twenty years, separation of state and church, freedom of speech and press, ten hour work day, and rights to freely associate and congregate. In Gosiorovský, p. 1956, p. 54.

28 The influence of anarchism was felt in Pressburg in 1881–1890 due to the appearance of the anarchist periodical *Die Freiheit* (published in London). In 1882–1884, anarchist periodicals were also published in Hungary but the movement never gained as much importance as in Austria.

29 Horváth et al, 1978, p. 182.

30 Ibid., pp. 181–182, Gosiorovský, 1956, pp. 59–68, Lehotský, Unpublished thesis, 1969, pp. 71–87. The programme of the party was based on the programme of the Austrian Social Democratic Party. The main aim was "to achieve liberation from chains of dependence, removal of political injustice and uplifting from spiritual stuntedness." The programme designated the proletariat "organised as a party" as the carrier of historically necessary development. The party's demands included universal suffrage, legislation for protection of workers, adoption of the First of May as a day for expressing solidarity with workers of the world, and the use of all means for the spread of socialist ideas. (Gosiorovský, 1956, pp. 75–76.) In 1903 the program was revised on the basis of the Erfurt program of the German social democrats. It stressed the need to fight against the governing regime until the power in the state was taken over and it declared the equality of all nationalities in Hungary. (Lipták et al, 1992, pp. 81–82.) This program also included a demand for an eight-hour work-day. Gosiorovský, 1956, p. 141.

31 The organisational structure of the party will be described in Part 3, Section 'Networks.'

32 Horváth et al, 1978, p. 183, also Hanzlíček, 1970, pp. 81–92 about the founding of trade union organisations according to the industry or craft branch.

33 Gosiorovský, 1956, pp. 91–102. In 1897, the Slovak socialist newspaper estimated that 60,000 Slovak labourers lived in Budapest while the Ministry of Interior estimated this Slovak population at up to 80,000. Glettler, 1992, p. 303. However, many of these Slovaks were only seasonal workers.

34 Horváth et al, 1978, p. 184, Lehotský, 1970, p. 267, Hapák et al, 1986, pp. 731–732, Gosiorovský, 1956, p. 78.

35 Horváth et al, 1978, p. 184.

36 Gosiorovský, 1956, pp. 82–90. While the SDPH acknowledged the importance of the agrarian question and of co-operation with small farmers, it did not support the small farmers' demands for ownership of land, believing that large production would ruin the small farmers and proletarianise them (as was happening to craftsmen and small entrepreneurs) upon which small farmers would then co-operate with industrial workers. The XIV. congress of the SPDH in 1907 stressed that there would be common ownership of the means of production under socialism, and that therefore any promises of land to small farmers were unjustified. Opinions on the agrarian question in Hungary reflected the views prevailing in the German and Austrian social democratic movement based on the conclusions of Karl Kautsky (1854–1938) and his opponent E. David. Tajták, 1981, pp. 848–849.

37 Lehotský, Unpublished thesis, 1969, p. 61.

38 Gosiorovský, 1956, p. 106.

39 Ibid., p. 132.

40 Ibid., p. 134.

41 Tajták, 1981, pp. 822–823.

42 Horváth et al, 1978, p. 184.

43 For a detailed analysis of the period 1905–1907 see Písch, 1966.

44 Gosiorovský, 1956, pp. 162–166. Písch, 1966, pp. 153–174.

45 Gosiorovský, 1956, p. 167.

46 Horváth et al, 1978, p. 187.

47 Gosiorovský, 1956, pp. 195–212.

48 Horváth et al, 1978, p. 187.

49 Tajták, 1981, p. 846.

50 Horváth et al, 1978, pp. 187–188. The reform of the suffrage law restricted the numbers of those eligible to vote by age, literacy, level of tax payment, length of employment, etc. Moreover, there was still no secret ballot.

51 Horváth et al, 1978, p. 188. Similar violent clashes between the demonstrating workers and armed forces resulting in many casualties also occurred in other cities of Central, Eastern and Southern Europe at the beginning of the twentieth century: Vienna (17.9.1911), Warsaw (1905), Petersburg (1905), Naples (1911), Turin (1917). John, 1996, p. 242.

52 Tajták, 1981, p. 846, Gosiorovský, 1956, pp. 222–223. Similarly in 1913 the planned general strike for universal suffrage against the new government proposal of limited suffrage did not take place because the government strengthened the

police forces and the military was on stand-by. Tajták, 1981, p. 847.

53 Tajták, 1995, pp. 726–729.

54 Gosiorovský, 1956, pp. 195–212.

55 Tajták, 1995, pp. 726–729. Marxist historiography described the evolutionary direction as "opportunism, reformism and revisionism" since it did not advocate revolutionary class struggle and violent means of winning the political power in the state. Ibid., p. 727.

56 Horváth et al, 1978, p. 188.

57 Horváth et al, 1978, p. 189. The Hungarian average for workers organised in trade unions was 10–15%, for Slovak workers 9%. (Tajták, 1981, p. 843.) In 1912, the number of organised workers in Hungary reached 111,966 (of whom 4,854 were in Slovak-language organisations—6.3% of the Slovak workers in the present-day Slovak territory). Ibid., p. 841.

58 "Die Gründung des kleinsten Arbeiterbildungsverein wird für den künftigen Kulturhistoriker von weit grösserem Wert sein, als der grosse Schlachttag von Sadowa." Volksstimme Kalender, 1911, "Anno 1869. Eine Episode aus den Anfängen der deutschsprachigen Arbeiterbewegung Ungarns [One episode from the beginnings of the German-speaking workers' movement in Hungary]," p. 41 (also in SNA, SRH, i. n. 8, c. 9). I will use the Slovak orthography of Hanzlíček's name since his memoirs referred to in this text (Hanzlíček, 1970) are a re-edition and edited translation (by Pavol Hapák) of his memoirs published originally in Volksstimme Kalender. Authorities as well as newspapers used the form Hanslitschek or Hanslitsek while "Hanzlíček" is used in Slovak historiography. Although the name sounds Slavic, I have not encountered any claim that Hanzlíček spoke Slovak.

59 Hanzlíček, 1970, pp. 17–18. Eduard Niemczyk as well as typographers also joined the initiative. Niemczyk became the first chairman of the association. Niemczyk (1838–1897) came to Pressburg from Opava (Troppau) in Silesia. He got permission to open a shop with chemical products but his shop was sold in an auction. He was elected the first chairman of the workers' association. He married a Slovak woman and on 6 June 1870 he even took part in the celebration of the Memorandum of the Slovak nation which was organised at Devín castle ruins by the Slovak law students' association Naprej. As a leading personality of the workers' movement in Pressburg, he kept contacts with workers' associations in Brno and Vienna and took part in their meetings. He left Bratislava in 1893 for Bosnia. In one report to the mayor of Pressburg, the police chief described Niemczyk as a "boaster" who wanted to become the leader of the Vorwärts association at any price and who was looking for a rich bride without success. In SNA, SRH, i. n. 13, c. 1, report of the police chief Johann Kozsehuba to the mayor of Bratislava dated 5.8.1869; Gosiorovský, 1956, pp. 38, 385. The city police chief had Niemczyk interrogated on several occasions on sus-

picion that he was connected with the First International. Hanzlíček, 1970, p. 29.

60 Hanzlíček, 1970, pp. 17–18. There were difficulties with obtaining approval by the authorities for the association's statutes. These will be discussed in Part 6 of this chapter. SNA, SRH, i. n. 9, c. 1, Statutes of *Vorwärts*, also in Hanzlíček, 1970, pp. 141– 147.

61 Tajták, 1995, p. 740.

62 Lehotský, Unpublished thesis, 1969, p. 26. The programme will be considered in the following discussion on the ideology of the association.

63 Hanzlíček, 1970, p. 141.

64 SNA, SRH, i. n. 9, c. 1, Statutes of *Vorwärts*, also in Hanzlíček, 1970, pp. 141–147.

65 Hanzlíček, 1970, p. 33.

66 Hanzlíček, 1970, p. 32.

67 A high proportion of craftsmen and artisans was also typical for Vienna, although the Austrian part of the empire was economically more developed than the Hungarian part. In 1910, 83% of all enterprises in Vienna had no more than five employees. John, 1996, p. 242.

68 At the beginning of the twentieth century, many workers in large industry in Hungary were still not organised while workers in small production already had thriving trade unions. In Tajták, 1981, p. 841.

69 Horváth et al, 1978, pp. 175–191, Goláň, 1957, p. 167. As a result, the association's membership policy was that "every worker with good reputation" above 16 years of age could join the association. (See statutes of the association *Vorwärts*, SNA, SRH, i. n. 9, c.1.) The statutes specified that entrepreneurs or shop keepers could become members only when they did not employ more than one worker. See footnote 157 of this chapter on petit-bourgeois values in the workers' movement.

70 Many of these workers were newcomers to the city. As has already been mentioned, large numbers of artisans and workers passed through Pressburg on their way to Vienna. Pressburg also absorbed those foreign workers who did not find jobs in Vienna. Lehotský, Unpublished thesis, 1969, pp. 17, 23. See also Hapák, 1970, p. 10.

71 Hanzlíček, 1970, pp. 32–33. Karol Hanzlíček, later chairman of the association, felt that although some of the members belonged to the petit-bourgeois strata, all members were poor and subsisted from day to day. The association's members were united by their opposition to the dominant classes: "The so called intelligentsia hated the association… as well as the 'caring' police." Karol Hanzlíček (1850–around 1931) was born in Szentgyörgy near Pressburg (in this time a pre-dominantly German village). Hanzlíček came to Pressburg as a carpenter apprentice. Later he owned a small shop. Hanzlíček worked in the association for many years as its chairman or secretary. In 1893 he left Bratislava for Budapest where he worked for the

General workers' and invalids' fund. After his departure the leaders of the association were the typesetter Heinrich Kalmár (1870–1931) and then Alois L. Zalkai (1866–1938). Kalmár left for Budapest in 1895 and Zalkai at the beginning of the century left the social democrats and founded the *Radikale Bürgerpartei* (Party of Radical Citizens). The chairman then became Rudolf Kordík. Hapák, 1970, pp. 8, 102, Gosiorovský, 1956, p. 378.

72 Goláň, 1958, p. 527.

73 Ibid., p. 532, speech of Zalkai at the II. congress of the Social Democratic Party of Hungary in Budapest 6–8 January 1893. By this time there were about 10,000 workers in the city, and trade unions were being organised by trade (e.g., construction workers, carpenters, tailors, shoemakers). There were even 200 women participating in the union movement.

74 MOL, K149–1907–1t-679. In 1906 the city police chief reported that only a small number of workers attended the weekly lecture (there were 16 lectures scheduled between 15 September and 29 December 1906), and some of the lectures did not take place because there were too few participants. The number of trade unions' members also did not increase, which the police chief ascribed to rising membership fees.

75 Horváth et al, 1978, pp. 176–177. The educational courses were later divided into five groups: 1. reading, writing, arithmetic, geography, biology, history; 2. languages: Hungarian, German, Slovak, English, French; 3. shorthand writing,, accounting, correspondence; 4. course for reporters including lectures from world history, literary and social science; 5. lectures and discussions with members of the scientific association *Zukunft*. Ibid., p. 204.

76 The association moved from inn to inn at first, meeting especially frequently in the City brewery. The association's chairman Kordík eventually proposed that the association rent a permanent room where the association met until the beginning of the twentieth century when the Workers' home was built. Hapák, 1970, pp. 102–103; for the exact location of the room & reading room see ibid., p. 121, footnote 24. *WV*, 23.8.1902, N. 25, p. 7, "Eröffnungsfeier der Petőfi Säle [Inauguration of the Petőfi rooms]."

77 Goláň, 1957, p. 175.

78 SNA, SRH, i. n. 14, c. 1; Goláň, 1957, p. 170. In 1876, the association had 10 monthly meetings, 12 meetings of the standing committee and one general assembly. (In SNA, SRH, i. n. 18, c.2.) In 1893–5, more than fifty workers attended the Saturday meetings. Lehotská claims that social and political lectures were given for workers of all three nationalities. (Lehotská et al, 1952, p. 106.) However, at first, more of the lectures were probably given in German and fewer in Hungarian. The lecturers were mostly workers from the Viennese association *Zukunft*. (MOL, K149–1907–

1t-679.) The topics for these lectures included, for example, the French revolution, self-help, workers' associations and their importance, science and art in Middle Ages, and various statesmen. Goláň, 1957, p. 170, footnote 16.

79 Goláň, 1957, p. 175. At the beginning, the library had less than 100 volumes. In 1899, the library had almost 400 volumes of books and together with newspapers and magazines, this number was almost 4000. Hapák, 1970, p. 103.

80 The Slovak section *Napred* founded its own choir in 1906. There were several other workers' choirs in the city. *Typographenbund* (1872, typesetters), *Einigkeit* (1904, construction workers), the Czech workers' association *Bratrství* had a choir (1907), *Magnet* (1909, steel workers), *Immergrün* (1912.) One of the branches of the association had its choir in the area under the Castle called *Schlossberger Gesangsektion*. Horváth et al, 1978, p. 204.

81 Ibid., p. 204. In 1898 the first workers' association of cyclists (*Erster Pressburger Arbeiter Radfahrklub*) was founded. The workers' tourist association (*Naturfreunde*) organised trips for workers.

82 Horváth et al, 1978, p. 204.

83 The Hungarian government was not interested in passing a law enabling the right of public gathering. No such law was passed in Hungary until the end of the monarchy. In an 1895 letter to the minister of interior, Prime Minister Dezső Bánffy noted that it was exactly the absence of such a law that had prevented the socialist and nationalist movements from taking deep root in Hungary. Decisions about whether to permit public gatherings were within the competence of the local police. While the absence of a law enabling freedom to publicly gather was questionable from the constitutional point of view, the prevention of the development of socialist and nationalist movements was worth it. "In the name of the Hungarian nation one must not take risks." Bánffy also mentioned that Hungary was accused abroad by its "enemies' of being illiberal, however, international public opinion seemed to have calmed down. MOL, K149–1895–6t.

84 Tajták, 1981, pp. 824–826, 1995, pp. 732–734.

85 Hapák et al, 1986, pp. 724–725.

86 Tajták, 1981, p. 826.

87 Horváth et al, 1978, p. 184.

88 Hapák, 1970, p. 103.

89 Hapák et al, 1986, pp. 724–725.

90 Tajták, 1995, pp. 731–732. Paul Wittich (1878–1957), the leading German social democrat in Pressburg ascribed this lack of success to persecution of authorities.

91 MOL, K149-1907-1t-679, report of the Pressburg police chief on the socialist movement in Pressburg in the year 1906 to the *főispán*.

92 Goláň, 1957, p. 165. Lehotský, Unpublished thesis, 1969, pp. 18, 22–23. Viennese socialists helped to organise the first meeting of *Vorwärts* in 1869. (Hapák, 1970, p. 107, endnote 7.) Contacts with the Viennese socialists was kept up especially by the Viennese socialist Andreas Scheu who kept *Vorwärts* informed about the activities of the First International.

93 Lehotský, 1970, p. 269.

94 Lehotská et al, 1952, pp. 99–100, Typographia, 9.5.—12.9.1873 and 28.11.1873, in SNA, SRH, i. n. 33, c. 2.

95 Lehotská et al, 1952, p. 106.

96 Goláň, 1957, p. 179; Hanzlíček, 1970, pp. 26–27; Lehotský, Unpublished thesis, 1969, p. 33.

97 Horváth et al, 1978, p. 178.

98 Goláň, 1958, p. 525.

99 Lehotský, 1970, p. 272.

100 Ibid., p. 273.

101 MOL, K149-1880-1t-17.

102 Lehotská, 1955, p. 11.

103 Lehotský, 1970, p. 270.

104 Tarrow, 1994, p. 101. "The magnitude and duration of these collective actions depend on mobilizing people through social networks and around identifiable symbols that are drawn from cultural frames of meaning." Ibid., p. 6.

105 However, there were periods when persecution decreased, for instance, during the governments of Kálmán Széll (1899–1903) and Géza Fejérváry (June 1905–April 1906). During this last period all previously forbidden meetings were permitted although they still had to be announced to the authorities twenty four hours in advance. Tajták, 1981, p. 820, 1995, p. 740.

106 Sometimes the city captain pressured some of these ten signatories into withdrawing their support and consequently the gathering could not take place. Hanzlíček, 1970, p. 55.

107 Horváth et al, 1978, p. 177, Hanzlíček, 1970, p. 21, Goláň, 1957, p. 171. Approximately 1000 people took part in this meeting (29 March 1869).

108 Sources differ on the languages spoken at this meeting. The Hungarian mag-

azine *Aranytrombita* claimed that one of the speakers, Nándor Szmolényi spoke only in Hungarian. (See Aranytrombita, 31.3.1869 in SNA, SRH, i. n. 10, c. 1.) However, the Slovak translation of Hanzlíček's memoirs claims that Szmolényi spoke in both Hungarian and Slovak. (See Hanzlíček, 1970, p. 22.) Similarly in *Dejiny Slovenska* the authors state that Szmolényi spoke in Slovak. (Hapák et al, 1986, p. 571.) Goláň (basing his information on the *Pressburger Zeitung*) mentions speakers speaking only Hungarian and German. Goláň, 1957, pp. 171–172, footnote 17.

109 Aranytrombita, 31.3.1869 in SNA, SRH, i. n. 10, c.1. Lehotský, Unpublished thesis, 1969, p. 26.

110 In February 1873, for example, *Vorwärts* organised another meeting which passed a resolution seeking the abolition of the employer-controlled Fund for the Ill (*Krankenkasse*) giving the workers control instead. Other specific demands included a working day of ten hours, prohibition of child labour, protection of apprentices, and limiting female work. (Gosiorovský, 1956, pp. 45–46; Hapák et al, 1986, p. 577.) The workers' activists who spoke most often at these meetings included Karol Hanzlíček and Jakub Grundstein. Hanzlíček's background has been described above in footnote 71. Grundstein was born in Kelsterbach near Frankfurt am Main. He came to Pressburg as a journeyman (*tovariš*) and became a member of *Vorwärts*. He also acted as chairman of the association. After the law suit with the newspaper *Die Wahrheit* he was first imprisoned and expelled from Pressburg and later transported with his family to Frankfurt under police supervision. Hapák, 1970, p. 126, footnote 29.

111 Horváth et al, 1978, p. 185.

112 SNA, SRH, Az Újság, i. n. 140, c. 6. While most gatherings were ethnically mixed and primarily marked by class solidarity, there were also a few purely Slovak meetings (which will be considered in the last part of this chapter). In 1912, the demand for universal suffrage brought together the workers and the parliamentary opposition led by Gyula Justh. A half-day general strike took place in Hungary on 4 March 1912 which saw the largest public meeting in Pressburg to that date. Horváth et al, 1978, p. 187. Pavol Blaho (1867–1927) and Milan Hodža (1878–1944) belonged to the prominent liberal Slovak politicians. In this period, they were both parliamentary deputies.

113 There was a large demonstration in Pressburg to protest the death of workers killed by the police in Budapest at the demonstration on 23 May 1912. The most prominent representatives of the social democratic movement in Pressburg expressed their indignation about the distorted reporting on the Budapest demonstration in the "bourgeois" press and publicly ripped to shreds issues of the *Westungarischer Grenzbote*. The meeting was conducted in three languages by the leading social democrats in Pressburg. (Horváth et al, 1978, p. 188.) On 12 January 1913 there was a public meeting in the Workers' Home attended by 300 people who expressed dissatisfaction with the governmental suffrage reform proposal. The meeting expressed its willingness to join a general strike for universal suffrage should this be

announced by Budapest. MOL, K149–1913–6t-230.

114 Arbeiter Wochen-Chronik, 28.10.1877 in SNA, SRH, i. n. 18, c.2.

115 Arbeiter Wochen-Chronik, 28.10.1877 in SNA, SRH, i. n. 337, c.14.

116 László Balogh was a carpenter from Budapest where he made very radical speeches after 1876. (Hapák, 1970, p. 129, endnote 36.) Balogh was against Frankel's group of social democrats and he joined the opposition group around Viktor Külföldy. Lehotská et al, 1952, pp. 102–103; SNA, SRH, i. n. 18, c. 2, police report about the meeting.

117 MOL, K149–1912–1t-332. In June 1912 the Budapest workers' leadership demanded that Pressburg's social democrats call a strike in response to the events of "bloody Thursday" on 23 May 1912. However, the Pressburg movement could only muster up a peaceful and not very intense demonstration of 500–600 people. As the *főispán* noted, politics did not stir up life very much in the county or city of Pressburg.

118 1 May had been celebrated by Pressburg's middle class society as the arrival of spring since 1862. Music played in the popular café *Au-Park* (located on the right bank of the Danube in a park) from early morning onward. The summer theatre *Arena* offered a theatrical performance, there was dancing in the park, and also horse races. As this section shows, the workers' May Day celebrations had a totally different character. (Lehotská, 1955, pp. 4–5.) Pressburg was the only city in the territory of present-day Slovakia where the workers celebrated 1 May 1890. Goláň, 1958, p. 530.

119 However, there was a public meeting on Haltér in 1893. (Lehotská, 1955, p. 12, SNA, SRH, i.n. 319, c. 13.) For a description of the 1 May celebrations see Lehotská, 1955, pp. 3–25, SNA, SRH, i.n.316, c. 13, Horváth et al,1978, pp. 182–185, Hanzlíček, 1970, pp. 77–81, Goláň, 1958, pp. 527–530 and the contemporary daily press. Chapter five deals with surveillance of the workers' May Day celebrations .

120 In 1902, speeches were made for the first time in all three languages, German, Hungarian and Slovak. In 1906 and again in subsequent years, there were separate meetings for the German and Hungarian workers (in the big hall of the Workers' home) and for Slovak workers (in the small hall). The need for this separation arose primarily from an influx of workers coming from areas where only one language was spoken and who, therefore, could not understand other languages. In 1913, Slovak workers celebrated May Day together with Czech workers from the city, and were also joined by Slovak and Czech workers from Vienna. Lehotská, 1955, pp. 3–25, contemporary daily press, especially W*estungarische Volkszeitung* and *Robotnícke Noviny*.

121 Hanák, P., 1985, without page numbers.

122 In 1912, out of Pressburg's 80,000 inhabitants only 4,733 had the right to vote. Lehotská, 1955, p. 21.

123 In 1906, approximately 4000 people (also workers from the surrounding villages, both Hungarian and Austrian) participated in this march. (MOL, K149–1907–1t-679.) The 1908 celebration was on a similar scale. Lehotská, 1955, p. 20.

124 The march took the workers through the city centre, from Duna-utca, Lőrinczkapu utca across the Halászkapu, across the Promenade to the Haltér, returning through the Ventur utca, Mihály-utca, Széplak-utca, and across the Pósta-utca back to the Workers' home in the Duna-utca. (The route of the march is marked on Figure 4 with red.) In 1902, the procession was led by the workers' choir *Liedesfreiheit*, followed by a gypsy orchestra , then the flag of *Vorwärts* and the members of the association, followed by workers organised by trade union and industry. Various slogans were shouted during the march. (Lehotská, 1955, pp. 17, 22.) The routes were similar, with slight changes. See *WG*, 2.5.1902, N. 10207, p. 3, "Die Maifeier der Arbeiterschaft Pressburgs [May Day celebration of the Pressburg's workers]," *WV*, 5.5.1906, N. 18, p. 1, "Die Maifeier der Pressburger Arbeiterschaft," *WV*,18.8.1906, N. 33, p. 1 (announcement of a demonstration for universal suffrage), *WV*, 1.5.1913, N. 50, p. 2, *WV*, 4.5.1912, N. 52, pp. 1–2, "Der Maitag der Pressburger Arbeiterschaft [May Day of the Pressburg's workers]."

125 Harrison, 1995, p. 210.

126 John, 1996, pp. 241–242.

127 Hanzlíček, 1970, pp. 68–71; Goláň, 1958, p. 527.

128 Goláň, 1958, p. 531, Horváth et al, 1978, p. 183.

129 SNA, SRH, i. n. 319, c. 13.

130 Lehotská, 1955, pp. 12–16.

131 Ibid., pp. 16–17. This was in 1901 but happened also in the consequent years.

132 In 1905, the workers forced the city authorities to reverse their ban on a march through the city by threatening to start a general strike. Lehotská, 1955, p. 19.

133 Tarrow, 1994, p. 22.

134 Hapák, 1970, pp. 10–11. According to Hanzlíček, the workers' and socialist movement was born in Germany and came through Austria into Hungary. Hanzlíček, 1970, pp. 8, 102.

135 For example, at the May Day celebration in 1890, *Vorwärts* chairman Hanzlíček read out the resolution of the international workers' congress in Paris in 1889 and there was a vote on its approval. Hanzlíček, 1970, p. 71.

136 Hapák, 1970, pp. 14–15. Ferdinand Lassalle founded the General German Workers' Association in 1863 (*Allgemeiner deutscher Arbeiterverein*).

137 Hanzlíček, 1970, pp. 20–21. After Niemczyk and his supporters accepted Las-

salle's principles, a group of members left and founded a different association *Eintracht* (including Flexner.) However, the two associations soon joined again, and those who strongly opposed Lassalle's views left the association.

138 Around 1907, a more radical left wing began to form within the Hungarian social democratic organisations. However, there is no evidence of a similar development in Pressburg. (Lehotský, Unpublished thesis, 1977, p. 173.) An opposition group criticising the activity of the Slovak social democrats also developed within the Slovak workers' movement. Tajták, 1995, pp. 727–728.

139 Tajták, 1995, pp. 726–729.

140 Potemra, 1963, p. 204. The Pressburg socialist periodical *Westungarische Volksstimme* re-printed whole articles taken from the German and Austrian social democratic press.

141 Aranytrombita, 31.3.1869 in SNA, SRH, i. n. 10, c.1.

142 This is obvious from a review of newspapers from the period which usually noted the organised and orderly manner of the workers' meetings as well as marches through the city.

143 Statutes, SNA, SRH, i. n. 9, c. 1, also in Hanzlíček, 1970, pp. 141–147.

144 Hanzlíček, 1970, p. 57.

145 On this issue among English socialists trying to overcome the resignation of working people, see Joyce, 1991, p. 83.

146 Hanzlíček, 1970, p. 57.

147 In Hungary in 1869 the workday lasted 15 hours while in Austria it was 11. In Hanzlíček, 1970, p. 37.

148 For a relevant discussion of this point see Jones, 1983, pp. 100–110: "[B]ecause the institutions of the country are in the hands of the oppressors, because the oppressed have no voice in the formation of the laws that rule their destiny—the masses are socially—because they are politically—slaves." Ibid., p. 108.

149 Hanzlíček, 1970, pp. 93–94.

150 Ibid., p. 59.

151 Potemra, 1983, Vol. I, p. 38.

152 Goláň, 1957, p. 180.

153 Workers' leaders were especially frustrated by the indifference of ordinary workers in the 1870s and 1880s.

154 Goláň, 1958, p. 531, footnote 24.

155 For example in 1894. (Lehotská, 1955, p. 13.) See also descriptions of the 1 May celebrations in the local press, especially *Westungarische Volksstimme*, *Napred*, *Robotnícke Noviny* and *Westungarischer Grenzbote*.

156 Hanzlíček, 1970, pp. 68–71.

157 It should be noted that although socialist historians stated that 'petty bourgeois' values were prevalent among workers in Pressburg and in Hungary in general, there is no substantial study discussing these values and how they were reflected in the behaviour of workers. It is, therefore, difficult to come to any definite conclusions on this important point. More research is required on this issue which is beyond the scope of this present study.

158 *RN*, 30.6.1910, N. 26, p. 6.

159 Hanzlíček, 1970, pp. 30–31, Horváth et al, 1978, p. 179.

160 *WV*, 16.3.1912, N. 32, p. 1, "Petőfi's Weltanschauung [Petőfi's world view]."

161 "...sondern das Ahnen und Gähren und Werden einer neuen Zeit...die uns die Freiheit bringen soll." (*WV*, 16.3.1912, N. 32, p. 2, "Die Geburtsfeier der ungarischen Freiheit [Birthday celebration of the Hungarian freedom].") There was a workers' march to the *Petőfi statue* and a program. Workers laid their garland of red carnations next to the palm-leaf garland of the students. Also see ibid., "Die Marzfeier der Pressburger Bevölkerung [March celebration of the Pressburg's inhabitants]."

162 Hanzlíček, 1970, p. 29.

163 Ibid., pp. 29–30.

164 Volksstimme Kalender 1911, "Anno 1869. Eine Episode aus den Anfängen der deutschsprachigen Arbeiterbewegung Ungarns," p. 46 (in SNA, SRH, i. n. 8, c. 9): "Ich erhebe meine Rechte und schwöre hier in Gottes freier Natur beim Heile meiner Ehre und meines Glückes zur Fahne der Freiheit, und der Prinzipien der Sozialdemokratie festzuhalten und früher mit ihr zu sterben, als sie zu verlassen. Amen!" Hanzlíček was one of the members taking the oath.

165 Hanzlíček, 1970, pp. 30–31, also Horváth et al, 1978, p. 179, SNA, SRH, i. n.8, c.1.

166 Hanzlíček, 1970, p. 38.

167 Ibid., p. 37, public meeting on 12.11.1877.

168 Ibid., p. 33.

169 Arbeiter-Wochen-Kronik, 14.7.1878, "Pressburg, 7. Juli," in SNA, SRH, i. n. 337, c. 14.

170 The workers' movement's sympathy for Iván v. Simonyi is indicated in several places. Niemczyk mentions Simonyi in an article in the *Allgemeiner Arbeiter*

Zeitung (15.5.1870, in SNA, SRH, i. n. 8, c.1) and also Hanzlíček in his memoirs. (Hanzlíček, 1970, p. 100) This connection points to the darker aspect of the worker's movement: a latent anti-Semitism. Simonyi was also the owner and editor of the *Westungarischer Grenzbote* which later started to print anti-Semitic articles. Simonyi himself was suspected and held partly responsible for fuelling the anti-Semitic riots in Pressburg in September 1882. (MOL, K149–1882–6, report of the chief of the state police Lajos Jekelfalussy sent by the government to Pressburg to re-establish order dated 7.10.1882. *PZ*, 28.9–5.10.1882 reported in detail about the riots. See also Geist, 1882.) Workers participated in the demonstrations against the Jews in Pressburg in 1887. (Many craftsmen also participated. The craftsmen movement was crucial in the developing anti-Semitism in Vienna in 1880s. See Seiliger, 1996, p. 88) The *Westungarischer Grenzbote* excused workers and wrote that they only wanted to draw attention to their miserable living conditions and to scare entrepreneurs. (See Lehotský, Unpublished thesis, 1969, p. 69 and *WG* 27–29.5.1887.) However, workers' sympathy towards Simonyi later faded: at a public meeting in 1912 workers publicly tore this newspaper to pieces because of its distorted reporting about the Budapest demonstration and they also broke the newspaper's office windows. (Horváth et al, 1978, p. 188, *RN*, 30.5.1912, pp. 1–4, "Nová stanica našej kalvárie [A new station of our misery].") See also obituary of Simonyi in *Westungarische Volksstimme*. (*WV*, 8.7.1904, N. 28, p. 2, "Iván v. Simonyi.")Anti-Semitism was more visible among the Slovak workers. For example the leaflet explaining the meaning of the May Day celebration in 1895 in the Slovak language had anti-Semitic slogans added which were totally missing in the German and Hungarian version. (SNA, SRH, i. n. 321, c. 13.) Anti-Semitism was typical also of much of the Slovak national movement. Jewish pub owners in Slovak villages were seen to support and benefit from the alcoholism of poor Slovaks. There was a prevalent view of Jews as usurers and exploiters.

171 Horváth et al, 1978, pp. 180–181, Gosiorovský, 1956, pp. 55–58.

172 Horváth et al, 1978, pp. 183–184. After leaving the party, Zalkai gathered together a group of small craftsmen and entrepreneurs and concentrated on the fight against big capital. (Potemra, 1963, p. 207.) The editor of *Westungarische Volksstimme* became Heinrich E. Kalmár. Kalmár (1870–1931) was a member of the Social Democratic Party in Germany and he came to Pressburg from Germany in 1891. Potemra, 1963, p. 205.

173 Tajták, 1995, pp. 730–731.

174 Horváth et al, 1978, p. 185, public gathering on 31.8.1902.

175 Lehotský, 1977, p. 86.

176 *WVZ*, 18.4.1899, N.142, p. 3, "Unsere 'Stadtväter' [Our 'city fathers']," *WVZ*, 6.5.1899, N. 145, p. 3, "Die Wohnungsnoth [Housing shortage]." In municipal assembly meetings, the philanthropist Georg Schulpe supported projects to construct workers' housing. However, these plans took a long time to materialise and even then

were unavailable for poorer workers. Problems with housing and high rents were also common in *fin-de-siecle* Vienna. Rent strikes and unrest often resulted in conflicts with the police. Such unrest was a form of "traditional protest culture" typical of a certain part of the lower classes. Typical of this culture was also *Fremdenfeindlichkeit* [aversion against foreigners]. Many of these rent protests were aimed against the Jews. (See John, 1996, pp. 240, 243.) It would be interesting to see whether there was a similar layer among Pressburg's lower strata, considering the desperate housing and rent situation in the city. Vienna at this time was characterised by the coexistence between a disciplined and controlled workers' movement and these older more spontaneous forms of protest. Ibid., pp. 243–244.

177 *PZ*, 9.6.1882, N. 157, *Ab*, p. 3, "Volksversammlung im Speneder'schen Gasthause vom 8. Juni [Public meeting in the Speneder's inn]."

178 Those MP's who just carried out the orders of their 'general', Kálmán Tisza, were called "Mamelukes." These MP's owed their parliamentary seats to Prime Minister Tisza (1875–1890) and therefore were reluctant to take any stand of their own and were very susceptible to corruption from above. These "faceless Mamelukes " formed the bulk of the Lower House of the Hungarian Parliament. Gerő, 1995, p. 118. See Gerő's Chapter 7 on elected representatives in Hungary.

179 Napred, 16.12.1908, p. 8, "Chýrnik [News column]": "Tí sú vlastenci, klerikáli, Rakúšania, všetko v jednej osobe."

180 *RN*, 24.5.1911, N. 21, p. 3, "Ešte dva uprázdnené mandáty [Two more emptied mandates]."

181 *WVZ*, 30.4.1899, N. 144, pp. 1–2, "Der 1. Maitag [The May Day]."

182 *WVZ*, 4.5.1902, N. 300, p. 3, "Die Maifeier [May celebration]."

183 Hanák, P. et al, 1978, p. 1260. Lipták et al, 1992, p. 90. In the last two decades of the nineteenth century in Vienna, the lower classes which until then could be characterised as part of one "plebeian" culture, started to split into two 'camps', the social democratic proletarian and the Christian-socialist petit-bourgeois (*kleinbürgerlich*).

184 *WV*, 21.4.1906, N. 16, p. 1, "Die Christlichsozialen und die Arbeiterfrage [The Christian socialists and the workers' question]."

185 *WV*, 5.10.1907, N. 40, pp. 1–2, "Die Pressburger Arbeiterschaft im Kampfe für das allgemeine Wahlrecht [Workers of Pressburg in fight for universal suffrage]."

186 Napred, 15.10.1908, N. 10, p. 6, "Račišdorf."

187 Písch, 1966, p. 86. In Vienna, many of the strike-breakers were Slavs so conflicts among the Viennese workers concerning strike-breaking brought up anti-Slav elements. John, 1996, p. 240.

188 Gosiorovský, 1956, p. 76.

189 Arbeiter-Wochen-Chronik, 24. December 1876, in SNA, SRH, i. n. 385, c. 15.

190 Népszava, 22.8.1880, N. 34, p. 2, in SNA, SRH, i. n. 385, c. 15, Tajták, 1981, p. 851.

191 Népszava, 19.11.1882, N. 48, p. 2, in SNA, SRH, i. n. 387, c. 15.

192 This opinion was fiercely criticised by the Slovak press who believed that all nationalities ought to have the right to vote no matter what language they spoke: "it is a human not a Magyar right." Nová Doba (1897), in SNA, SRH, i. n. 392, c. 16.

193 This disconnection was noted by Lehoczky, one of Pressburg's representatives to the party's VIII. congress in 1901. MOL, K149–1901–1t (II.part)-655.

194 *RN*, 27.4.1911, N. 17, p. 7, "O sjazdoch sociálno-demokratickej strany v Uhorsku [About the congresses of the Social Democratic Party in Hungary]."

195 Hanák, P. et al, 1978, p. 1258.

196 Napred, 15.5.1908, N.5, pp. 2–3, "Úvaha ku sjazdu sociálno-demokratickej strany Uhorska [Reflecting about the congress of the Social Democratic Party of Hungary]." In 1908 there was a congress of the Rumanian and Serbian social democrats and later also a congress of the German social democrats. All these congresses discussed the question of equal participation of non-Magyar workers in the leadership of the trade unions as well as the linguistic and other needs of non-Magyar workers. See Tajták, 1981, p. 844.

197 In Austria the Social Democratic Party turned into a federation of national parties in 1897. Gosiorovský, 1956, p. 150.

198 After the beginning of the First World War the Second International fell apart. In 1915, leaders of the socialist movement came together in Zimmerwald, Switzerland, to discuss the future of the Euroepan workers' movement. This conference supported Kautsky's resolution demanding the end of the war.

199 According to the official statistics in Pressburg's population in the period of the Dual Agreement (1867) there were 7/12 Germans, 3/12 Hungarians and 2/12 Slovaks. In Goláň, 1957, p. 167.

200 As noted above, an interesting example of latter-day historical revisionism is the practice among Slovak historians of the workers' movement in the nineteenth century of adopting Slovak spellings of the names of workers' leaders (especially in cases where their names sound Slavic) who probably did not even speak Slovak (like Hanslitschek—Hanzlíček).

201 Goláň, 1957, p. 167; Lehotská et al, 1952, pp. 100–101; Horváth et al, 1978, p. 176. According to some authors, the association *Vorwärts* had its name written in three languages *Vorwärts-Napred-Előre* from the very beginning and had three sections— German, Slovak and Hungarian. (Lehotská et al, 1952, pp. 98–99.) However, these authors do not give the source of the information and I have not come across such

use in the beginnings of the workers' movement in Pressburg. They probably derive this conclusion from the statutes of the association which state that the statutes can, if needed, be translated into any of the country's languages (*Landessprachen*) which included all the languages spoken in Hungary.

202 Here the authors of *Dejiny Bratislavy* include Niemczyk who was actually of Polish (Silesian) origin, and Michal Sklárik as treasurer of the association. (Horváth et al, 1978, p. 178.) According to Goláň, Niemtzyk (Slovak historians use 'Nemčík') had a mixed Slavic-German upbringing. Goláň, 1957, p. 175.

203 The use of the Slovak language is not mentioned except at the first public meeting of workers in 1869 by a speaker from Budapest where there was a large number of Slovak workers. (Hanzlíček, 1970, p. 22.) Lehotský writes that speeches at a public meeting in 1902 were made in three languages "as was customary in the ethnically mixed environment of Bratislava." However, I have not come across such practice before the beginning of the twentieth century. Lehotský, Unpublished thesis, 1977, p. 91. See footnote 120 above.

204 In 1873 Pressburg had only one subscriber of the *Arbeiter Wochen-Chronik* (after 1873 also the Hungarian version), Karol Hanzlíček, who subscribed to 25 copies, in 1875 it was 60 copies. Hapák, 1970, p. 125, endnote 28.

205 MOL, K149–1901–1t-655.

206 Horváth et al, 1978, p. 185.

207 Písch claims that the German social democrats in Pressburg were also affected by the Slovak separatist tendencies and that their leader Kalmár demanded the creation of an autonomous German party organisation in 1907. Písch, 1966, pp. 171– 172.

208 Gosiorovský, 1956, pp. 90–123. By this time all other nationalities already had their own socialist press: from 1900 there was the German *Volksstimme* as supplement of *Népszava*, the Serbian *Narodna reč* first as supplement of *Népszava* and later independent, and the Rumanian workers had from 1903 on the periodical *Votul Poporului* later *Adeverul*. (See Tajták, 1981, p. 828.) According to Tajták, the main reason why the leadership of the SDPH did not pay attention to the demands of Slovak workers for their own press was the fact that Slovak workers in the cities were rapidly becoming assimilated. This process of assimilation was supported by the SDPH. (Ibid.) In Budapest, the Slovak workers assimilated rapidly because of their low level of residential segregation. Thus mobilisation of Slovak workers on an ethnic basis repeatedly failed. Research has shown that those setting up the Slovak workers' association in Budapest in 1899 all came from "three major residential clusters" within the city. Many of the association's organisers shared accommoddations with those constituting the hard-core membership. Gyányi, 1995, pp. 112–113.

209 Slovak workers in Vienna founded the educational association *Slovenská Vzdelávacia Beseda* in 1901. However, the existence of such an association did not

mean much as its members complained repeatedly about the small interest of Slovak workers in the activities of the association. (*Napred, Robotnícke Noviny*). Later the Slovak organisation of the *Czech-Slav Social Democratic Workers' Party* in Vienna was also created. Gosiorovský, 1956, pp. 148–149.

210 If a newspaper with political content was published once a month, its publishers did not have to pay the large deposit of 12,000 crowns that was required for more frequently published newspapers with political articles. (Gosiorovský, 1956, p. 101, Horváth et al, 1978, p. 185, *RN*, 29.1.1914, N. 5, p. 6, "O našej tlači [About our press].") With *Napred* and *Robotnícke Noviny* printed on different days, the Slovak workers' press appeared fortnightly, without paying the deposit.

Napred was systematically read for years 1906–1908, *Robotnícke Noviny* for years 1909–1914.

211 This happened through the fusion of the monthlies *Napred* and *Slovenské Robotnícke Noviny* on 1.5.1909. (Potemra, 1958, p. 36.) The exact financial extent to which Czech social democrats helped in changing *Robotnícke Noviny* into a weekly is not known. (Horváth et al, 1978, pp. 185–186, Gosiorovský, 1956, pp. 148–149.) *Robotnícke Noviny* realised the necessity of this step and it issued shares for 5 and 10 crowns which it offered to its readers. (Napred, 15.10.1908, N. 10, pp. 1–2.) The editors of *Robotnícke Noviny* also issued *Slovenský májový spis* (Slovak May booklet) for 80 hellers (1 crown=100 hellers) and money from its sales was also to be used towards interest payments. Napred, 15.4.1907, N. 4, p. 4.

212 Horváth et al, 1978, pp. 185–186. The leadership of SDPH did not attack the decision of the Slovak social democrats. However, it banned the access of Slovak social democrats to trade unions which were basically the financial basis of the SDPH. Since trade unions were paying money into the centre in Budapest, Slovak social democrats remained without financial support. When they saw that the Budapest leadership was not going to support them, the only solution was to join the SDPH again. Tajták, 1981, pp. 831–832.

213 Gosiorovský, 1956, p. 184.

214 Ibid., pp. 184–185.

215 *RN*, 8.9.1910, N. 36, p. 1, "Medzinárodný socialistický sjazd v Kodani [The international socialist congress in Copenhagen]." Slovak social democrats declared that the congress of the Second International in Copenhagen ignored the rights of "small nations." See footnote 223.

216 As mentioned earlier, the SDPH was not organised as a political party but carried out its activities first of all through 'loose organisations', its press, in the trade unions and through educational workers' associations. Thus Slovak social democratic congresses could bring together trade union organisations whose members included Slovaks, 'loose' organisations of Slovak workers (also Viennese

workers), subscribers of *Napred* and *Robotnícke Noviny* and Slovak workers from places where no trade union organisation existed yet. Napred, 15.1.1908, N.1, p. 1, "Ohlas na slovenských sociálnych demokratov Uhorska [Response to the Slovak social democrats of Hungary]."

217 See *RN*, 7.4.1910, N. 14, pp. 1–2, "Krajinská konferencia [Hungarian conference]" and Milan Frič's essay on socialism in Slovakia in *RN*, 22.1.1914, N. 4, p. 5, *RN*, 29.1.1914, N. 5, p. 5 and *RN*, 5.2.1914, N. 6, p. 5. According to Frič, a long-cherished dream of the Slovak workers was to shift the *Robotnícke Noviny* to Budapest and turn it into a daily. *RN*, 29.1.1914, N. 5, p. 5.

218 *RN*, 29.1.1914, N. 5, p. 6.

219 Tajták, 1981, p. 829. This new generation included Emanuel Lehocký (1876–1930), Ferdinand Benda (1880–1952), Ján Pocisk (1870–1941), all of whom were self-educated workers.

220 Gosiorovský, 1956, p. 185.

221 Ibid, 1956, pp. 186–187.

222 For example, Slovak workers organised a trip to Vienna in 1910 to take part in the celebration of the twentieth anniversary of the Czech workers' newspaper *Dělnické Listy*. *RN*, 24.2.1910, N. 8, p. 6, "Organizačné záležitosti [Organisational matters]."

223 In 1910 the Austrian trade unions split on national lines when the Czechs founded their own trade unions despite the Copenhagen resolution of the Second International which decided that in a multi-national state trade unions should preserve their organisational unity (therefore nationalities should not created their own trade unions). In this case, Slovak social democrats supported the Czech decision and were therefore accused of separatism by the leadership of the SDPH. (Tajták, 1981, p. 840.) However, the Slovaks defended themselves on the grounds that they only demanded equality. See *RN*, 7.9.1911, N. 36, p. 2, "Český separatizmus a 'Népszava' [Czech separatism and 'Népszava']." See other issues of *RN*, especially starting 1910. The separation of Slovak social democrats was heavily influenced by the financial as well as organisational support of Czech workers. (Tajták, 1981, pp. 830–831.) The politics of the Slovak nationalist movement also had an effect.

The 1908 conference of lower Austrian Slovaks in Vienna was also open to Slovaks from Vienna and its surroundings (including Pressburg) who were politically organised or active in trade unions. Napred, 17.11.1908, N. 11, p. 8, "Organizačné záležitosti [Organistional matters]."

224 Vienna's Slovaks were organised in the association *Slovenská vzdelávacia beseda*. The program of its events was printed in both Slovak workers' newspapers published in Pressburg. The Viennese correspondents complained repeatedly about the passivity and ignorance of the Viennese Slovaks whose life was "alcohol and

bread." In contrast, Vienna's Czechs were cited as a positive example. *RN*, 3.8.1911, N. 31, pp. 5–6, "Viedeň [Vienna]."

225 It is unclear when the Slovak section of *Vorwärts*, *Vpred* was founded. While most authors state that it was around 1905–6, Potemra gives 1902 as the approximate date. Horváth et al, 1978, p. 186, Potemra, 1983, Vol. I, p. 201.

226 Potemra, 1983, Vol. I, p. 201. Also see issues of *Robotnícke Noviny* and *Napred*. The lecture topics were diverse: F. Lassalle, K. Marx, evolution of human society, women and socialism, social topics but also personalities of the Slovak national movement like Anton Bernolák, the founder of literary Slovak, and figures from Czech history like Jan Hus. In 1914 *Vpred* began organising courses in Slovak orthography. (*RN*, 16.4.1914, N. 16, p. 7, "Organizačné záležitosti [Organisational matters]".) Balls took place in the traditional carnival season. Slovak workers also held some traditional rural balls—e.g., St. Catherine's day. (See *RN* and Napred.) Slovaks from the vicinity of Pressburg were also invited to these balls. The number of entertainments organised by different trade unions in Pressburg also grew in the twentieth century. *RN*, 16.12.1909, p. 6, "Chýrnik [News]," *RN*, 6.1.1910, N. 1, p. 5, *RN*, 27.1.1911, N. 4, pp. 6, 8, *RN*, 30.11.1911, N. 48, p. 6, *RN*, 1.2.1912, N. 51, p. 7, *RN*, 9.1.1913, N. 2, p. 8, *RN*, 23.10.1913, N. 43, p. 7, *RN*, 22.1.1914, N. 4, p. 7, *RN*, 12.2.1914, N. 7, p. 7, announcements of balls.

227 The social democrats were for full political and social equality of men and women. (Napred, 15.4.1907, N. 4, pp. 1–2, "Žena a soc. dem. [The woman and social democrats]") *RN* in 1913 had already new columns—"Ženský obzor" [Women's horizons] and "Prehľad mládeže" [Youth's overview]. On 8.3.1914 in the Workers' Home there was a demonstration by women seeking their political rights. *RN*, 26.2.1914, N. 8, p. 6, "Ženský obzor ," *RN*, 12.3.11914, N. 11, p. 4, "Ženský deň v Prešporku [Women's day in Prešporok]."

228 *RN*, 12.2.1914, N. 7, p. 7, "Chýrnik." Out of 2,700 books in Slovak (or its different dialects) published in Hungary between 1900 and 1918, only 27 had socialist content. About 1,200 of these published works were religious texts. Potemra, 1983, Vol. I, pp. 110–111. On book publishing on the present-day Slovak territory between 1901–1918 see Potemra, 1964.

229 *RN*, 26.9.1912, N. 39, p. 5, "Chýrnik."

230 *RN*, 10.7.1913, N. 28, p. 7, "Chýrnik." The newly founded club had 30 members. (*RN*, 31.7.1913, N.31, p. 7, "Chýrnik.") A women's section was also founded later. The club was preparing for a public performance in 1914. *RN*, 12.2.1914, N.7, pp. 6–7, "Delnická telocvičná jednota [Workers' physical exercise association]."

231 Potemra, 1983, Vol. I, p. 340. In 1903–1905 Slovak workers in the Catholic workers' association also performed amateur theatre but after Slovak performances were banned in 1906 by the Catholic priest, most Slovak workers left the association

and joined *Vpred*. Ibid., p. 341. See Chapter two, section 5.4.

.232In the first years of the twentieth century, the number of members (from all nationalities) of trade unions and socialist organisations in Pressburg oscillated between 1000–2000. Gosiorovský, 1956, pp. 188–189.

233 For example Napred, 15.6.1907, N.6, p. 6, Napred, 15.11.1907, N. 11, p. 4: "Každý čestný robotník, neni-li ešte, tak stane sa členom svojej odborovej organizácie."

234 Napred 15.2.1908, N. 2, p. 6. The largest numbers of organised Slovak workers in 1907 were in Ruttka (528), Zsolna (350), Liptószentmiklós (211), Dévényújfalu (168) and Pressburg (135) (see Figures 2 and 5). (Tajták, 1981, p. 835.) The trade union of the construction workers (which was the second strongest trade union in Hungary in 1913) had many Slovak workers who also participated in the congresses of this trade union. Therefore, in the West-Slovakian trade union groups the agitation was trilingual—Slovak, Hungarian and German. Tajták, 1981, p. 843–844.

235 Hanzlíček, 1970, pp. 81–92.

236In 1910 at the foundation of the trade union of coachmen all three languages were used. Many of the 55 coachmen present were Slovaks. *RN*, 14.4.1910, N.15, p. 4, "Z odborného hnutia [From the trade union movement]."

237 *RN*, 12.8.1909, N. 20, p. 6, "Organizačné záležitosti [Organisational matters]."

238 *RN*, 5.5.1911, N. 18, p. 1, "Májová oslava [May celebration]."

239 *RN*, 1.5.1909, N.5, p. 1, "Náš týždenník [Our weekly]": "Tlač je veľmoc a kto nadobudne si tejto, bude rozhodujúcim nad všetkými pokladami, jak hmotnými tak i duševnými celého sveta." The editor of *Napred* and also *Robotnícke Noviny* was Emanuel Lehocký, a tailor's assistant in Pressburg. Later the editors of *Robotnícke Noviny* became Štefan Príkopa (from *RN* 23.3.1911) and Andrej Kubál (from *RN* 19.6.1913). Another important editor was the Czech social democrat Edmund Borek (1880–1924), born in Vienna. He came to Pressburg specifically to help edit the Slovak workers' press. However, his name did not appear on the editing board since he was a foreigner in Hungary. Borek also published a number of pamphlets on social democratic ideology under different pseudonyms. Gosiorovský, 1956, p. 375.

240 Napred, 15.12.1906, N.4, p. 7, "Persekúcia [Persecution]."

241 *RN*, 30.12.1909, N. 40, p. 3, "Naša tlač [Our press]": "Robotnícke Noviny majú v domácnosti každého chudobného Slováka každého týždňa burcovať ho zo spánku ľahostajnosti, volať do boja za práva ľudu, poučovať ho, čo ľud chce, si žiada a začo bojuje."

242 In 1906 *RN* had 2,000–3,000 published issues, in 1907 4,000–4,600, in 1908 3,760. Napred, 15.2.1908, N. 2, p. 10, "Naša tlač." In 1912 there were 1,412 subscribers in all of Hungary, 93 in Pressburg and 148 in Budapest. Subscribers were

often trade union organisations rather than individuals. *RN*, 4.9.1913, N. 36, p. 2, table "Stav slovenského členstva v organizáciách [Number of the Slovak membership in organisations]."

243 For example, "About the condition of the miners in B. Štiavnica."

244 A correspondent from Vienna complained that despite the relative lack of persecution in Austria (compared to Hungary), Austrian Slovaks still failed to understand the importance of organisation. The same few people attended meetings in one district of Vienna. A few people worked on distributing *Robotnícke Noviny* but the rest did not care. (*RN*, 30.12.1909, N.40, p. 5, "Dopisy [Letters]."") The Hungarian workers were very successful in agitating on behalf of their press, which consequently was at a completely different level. There were thousands of Slovak workers in Budapest but nobody tried to spread *Robotnícke Noviny. RN*, 21.3.1912, N.12, p. 2, "Čo konať? [What to do?]," also *RN*, 3.11.1910, N.44, p. 1, "Čo máme robiť? [What shall we do?]."

245 *RN*, 28.4.1910, N. 17, p. 6, "Májová oslava [May celebration]"; *RN*, 3.5.1912, N. 18, p. 1, "Májová oslava," *RN*, 17.4.1913, N. 16, p. 1, "Májové oslavy."

246 *RN*, 8.5.1913, N. 19, p. 1, "Májové oslavy."

247 Napred, 15.10.1907, N. 10, p. 3, "Sloboda tlače a shromažďovania sa v Uhorsku [Freedom of press and public gathering in Hungary]," *WV*, 5.10.1907, N. 40, p. 2, "Die Pressburger Arbeiterschaft im Kampfe für allgemeine Wahlrecht [The Pressburger workers in fight for universal suffrage]."

248 Napred, 15.10.1908, N. 10, p. 6, "Račišdorf."

249 Napred, 15.11.1906, N. 11, p. 5, "Slovenské ľudové zhromaždenie [Slovak people's gathering]."

250 At another meeting (8.10.1911), small traders and craftsmen denounced the activities of the Slovak National Party. (*RN*, 12.10.1911., N. 41, p. 2, "Shromaždenie ľudu v Prešporku [Public gathering in Prešporok]."") At this time the social democrats supported Justh's opposition against the Károly Khuen-Hedérváry government since Justh advocated universal suffrage. The Slovak National Party instead made an agreement with the government.

251 *RN*, 20.3.1913, N.12, pp. 1–2, "Slovenské zhromaždenie v Prešporku [Slovak gathering in Prešporok]" (meeting on 16.3.1913): "ktorým stará krivda na slovenskom ľude v sociálnom, politickom, kultúrnom a národnostnom ohľade páchaná má dostať novú podporu."

252 One exception was the lawyer Michal Mudroň who defended the Slovak workers' press editors in the court. See Chapter two.

253 Potemra, 1983, Vol. I, p. 35, *RN*, 3.7.1913, N. 27, pp. 4–5, "Dopisy [Letters]," *RN*,

29.1.1914, N. 5, p. 5. The magazines *Nová Doba* and *Zora* in Budapest stopped being published because of the lack of subscribers and contributors. These magazines frequently criticised the Slovak intelligentsia who retaliated by refusing to support the magazines. *RN*, 22.1.1914, N. 5, p. 5, *RN*, 29.1.1914, N. 6, p. 5.

254 *RN*, 21.11.1912, N. 47, pp. 5–6, "Koncert slovenského a českého spevokolu [The concert of the Czech and Slovak choirs]." When "progressive" intellectuals came to these performances, it was always noted in the press. *RN*, 30.11.1911, N. 48, p. 6, "Slovenská zábava v Prešporku [Slovak entertainment in Prešporok]."

255 Napred, 15.2.1908, N.2, p. 1, "Pred zjazdom [Before the congress]," Napred, 15.6.1907, N. 6, pp. 2–4, "Konajte svoju povinnost [Do your duty]," *RN*, 16.1.1913, N. 3, pp. 2–3, "Národnostná strana [The Nationalities' Party (meaning Slovak National Party)]." In 1914 only Pavel Blaho spoke out in the parliament against the new division of the electoral districts which was disadvantageous to the Slovak electors while other Slovak deputies were not present in the parliament. *RN*, 5.3.1914, N. 10, p. 3, "Rozhľady [Horizons]."

256 *RN*, 21.12.1911, N. 51, pp. 2–3, "Národnostná debata [Debate about nationalities]," *RN*, 3.10.1912, N. 40, p. 2, "Kongregácia prešporskej stolice odhlasovala [Prešporok's county assembly voted for]." Slovak county deputies were also often criticised in the Slovak national press.

257Their position remained that of the 1861 Memorandum of the Slovak nation. (Lipták et al, 1992, p. 42, Kováč, 1999, p. 20.) On the program of the Slovak National Party in 1900–1914 see Podrimavský, 1977.

258 Napred, 15.5.1907, N. 5, p. 1, "Naša taktika [Our tactic]." Napred, 15.6.1907, N. 6, p. 3, "Mäknutie mozgov [Softening of brains]." The tactics of the old conservative leadership were also criticised by liberal Slovak intellectuals, such as the Pressburger lawyer Ivan Dérer who expressed his dissatisfaction with the politics of the Pressburger group of the Slovak National Party when even the social democrats supported Justh's opposition on the issue of universal suffrage while the representatives of the Slovak national movement did not. (*RN*, 4.4.1912, N. 14, pp. 1–2, "Národnostní ľudia proti politike národnostnej strany [Nationalities' representatives against the politics of the Nationalities' Party].") The conservative leadership in Martin was also criticised by the young Slovak intelligentsia grouped around the magazine *Hlas* (1898) which had studied in Prague, Vienna and Budapest as well as by the young liberal intelligentsia gathered around the magazine *Prúdy* in 1909. Their criticisms centred on the lack of organisation and of active political work on the part of the Slovak National Party. Lipták et al, 1992, pp. 41–42, 44.

259 *RN*, 10.8.1911, N. 32, pp. 1–2, "K martinským slávnostiam [To the celebrations in Martin]," *RN*, 1.8.1912, N. 31, p. 1, "Martinské národné slávnosti [National celebrations in Martin]." The general assembly of the Slovak's women association *Živena* was also held during these celebrations.

260 Quoted in Gosiorovský, 1956, pp. 108–109.

261 *RN*, 12.5.1911, N. 19, p. 7, "Dľa martinských Národných Novín [According to the Martin's Národné Noviny]." See also Napred, 16.9.1908, N. 9, p. 4, "Robotníctvo a náš program [Workers and our programme]."

262 I use the word 'clericals' here which was used in the Slovak socialist press to denote Catholic clergy. However, at present this word carries a negative connotation since it is connected with "ľudáci" who were the members of the fascist Hlinka's Slovak People's Party (*Hlinkova slovenská Ľudová strana*) in the Slovak fascist state during the Second World War.

263 Catholic People's Party made its own contribution to the politicisation of the village inhabitants of the present-day Slovak territory in 1890s since in the years 1893–94 it fought against the laws about civil marriage and state birth registers. The later Slovak People's Party sprang up within the Hungarian People's Party. (Krajčovič, 1999, p. 49). This was important because "the Slovak-Hungarian antagonism was concentrated in the struggle for the village or peasant." Holec, 1999, p. 69. On political Catholicism and other mass movements in this period see Colotti, 1990.

264 Gosiorovský, 1956, p. 110. The Hungarian Catholic People's Party (*Katolikus Néppárt*) was founded by Count Ferdinand Zichy in 1894 and promised to fight for respect of the 1868 Nationalities' Law. An independent Slovak People's Party was founded in 1913. See Lipták et al, 1992, pp. 88–96.

265 Napred, 15.9.1906, N. 1, pp. 1–2, "Bratia kresťanskí robotníci! [Brothers— Christian workers!]." Since many Slovak workers were religious, the Catholic workers' association was one of the main enemies of the Slovak social democratic workers. See also Napred, 15.11.1906, N. 3, p. 3, "Chýrnik [News]," Napred, 15. 1. 1907, N. 1, pp. 3–4, "Čo chcú socialisti? [What do socialists want?]."

266 Potemra, 1983, Vol. I, p. 30: "Protislovenská politika nepripúšťa slovenské vzdelávanie a klerikály hatia prúdy pokroku."

267 Napred, 15.2.1907, N. 2, p. 8, "Slobodná Škola [Free school]." This article declared that counting and reading were the same for children, regardless of religious affiliation. This was in answer to an article in the Catholic *Ľudové Noviny* which called schools without prayer "worse than pagan."

268 Napred 15.9.1907, N. 7, p. 3, "Klerikálna politika [Clerical politics]." See Potemra, 1958, pp. 39–42 on periodical press expressing opinions of the representatives of the Slovak People's Party and on the scandal around the bribery of some of these representatives by the Hungarian government that had to be finally resolved by a Slovak "national court" (meaning representatives of Slovak intelligentsia).

269 Napred, 15.1.1907, N. 1, pp. 2–3, "Sociálna demokracia a náboženstvo [Social democracy and religion]." The Slovak (and Hungarian) social democrats were not

exceptional in this regard. The French and German communists (led by Wilhelm Weitling) also appealed to scripture. Their favourite axiom was "Christianity is Communism." (Chadwick, 1990, p. 75.) Chadwick argues that secularisation in the nineteenth century hardly touched the working man. Discussions about Darwinism entered middle classes and educated circles. Ibid., p. 106.

270 Lipták et al, 1992, pp. 42, 44. Different streams arose within the Slovak National Party around the turn of the century (the liberal, people's—Catholic and agrarian) and so at the beginning of the second decade of the twentieth century the Slovak National Party was transformed and it lost it homogeneity. Szarka, 1999, p. 208.

271 See footnote 258. The Slovak socialist workers' press called them "progressives." Slovak socialist historians considered the liberals as most dangerous for the workers, infecting them with opportunism and nationalist ideas. (Gosiorovský, 1956, pp. 111, 113.) It must be stressed that "urban intellectuals" refers to those intellectuals who studied and lived for several years in big cities like Budapest, Prague and Vienna. (Those who studied in Prague were strongly influenced by Masaryk's ideas). Consequently the views of these intellectuals largely differed from those espoused by the traditionalist intelligentsia spending most of its life in a small town like Martin. In this period the towns in Slovakia (except Pressburg and Kassa) were very small with a few thousand inhabitants. See Mannová, 1997a, pp. 13–15 on the preponderance of small towns and petty bourgeoisie in the social structure of present-day Slovakia. See also Holec, 1997, pp. 197–211.

272 Gosiorovský, 1956, pp. 113–116.

273 In 1911 *Robotnícke Noviny* published a number of articles about the liberal Milan Hodža's alleged misappropriation of money *RN*, 12. 10. and 19.10.1911 (N. 41 and 42). However, *Robotnícke Noviny* wrote positively about his lecture on the nationalities' question to a Budapest group of progressive students called *Galilei*. *Robotnícke Noviny* wondered whether this lecture would be considered a betrayal by the conservative Martin politicians. *RN*, 12.5.1911, N. 19, p. 3, "Milan Hodža." The association *Galilei* co-operated with students of non-Magyar nationalities. Its main ideology was that of Oscar Jászi, the editor of a sociological periodical *Huszadik Század* (Twentieth century). Jászi represented the democratic stream in the Hungarian politics. He wrote number of works on nationalities in Hungary in which he refused the forceful assimilation policies of the Hungarian governments. Jászi was one of the leaders of the *Országos Polgári Radikális Párt* (Hungarian Citizens' Radical Party) founded in 1914. See Podrimavský, 1972, Lipták et al, 1992, pp. 190–191.

274 For example by the liberal Slovak lawyers Ivan Dérer and Milan Ivánka. *RN*, 27.6.1912, N. 26, p. 7, "Chýrnik [News]."

275 *RN* 11.6.1914, N. 24, pp. 1–2, "Z psychológie slovenského života [From the psychology of Slovak life]." *RN* 4.6.1914, N. 23, p. 3, "Národná slovenská rada [National Slovak council]": "We were always ruled by two or three individuals and there were

times when the whole of Slovakia worshipped one person. We always needed an idol in front of which we were crawling in the dust, always our martyrs illuminated by Bengali fire. Not the will of the nation, not the society of the good and the best decided but one or two of the greatest giants. And the nation brought up in slavery and mental dependence looked at its leaders as at saints and did not dare to point out to the martyr his mistakes, did not dare to reprove him or to halt him with a firm hand (even if it should hurt) when he went astray....All men were forgiven everything."

276 *RN* 11.6.1914, N. 24, pp. 1–2, "Z psychológie slovenského života."

277 *RN*, 29.5.1913, N. 22, pp. 3–4, "Slovenské úradníctvo [Slovak officials]."

278 *RN*, 6.2.1913, N. 6, p. 1, "Slovenskí národovci a sociálna demokracia [Slovak nationalists and social democracy]."

279 *RN*, 2.3.1911, N. 9, pp. 2–3, "Od kosmopolitictva k nacionalizmu [From cosmopolitanism to nationalism]," *RN*, 16.4.1914, N. 16, pp. 1–4, "IV. sjazd slovenskej sociálnej demokracie [The IV. congress of the Slovak social democracy]." However, the program of the Slovak National Party in 1913 had already concrete goals in political, economic and cultural areas. These goals were based on the requirement for autonomy of different nations within Hungary. Lipták et al, 1992, p. 46.

280 *Robotnícke Noviny* published a very positive article on the death of Björnsterne Björnson, "the great son of the Norwegian nation and defender of all oppressed ones...he stood up for the Slovaks against their enemy [Magyars] in front of the whole world" and therefore the Slovak proletarians would be grateful to him." *RN*, 5.5.1910, N. 18, p. 4, "Bjönsterne Björnson."

281 Gosiorovský, 1956, p. 183.

282 *RN*, 9.12.1909, N. 37, p. 1, "Národnostná strana a jej politika [Nationalities' Party and its politics]": "Národnostná otázka je konec koncov predsa len otázkou sociálnou, lebo v boji národností ide o boj bohatých, ktorí obdarení sú politickými nadprávami, proti chudobným, ktorí sú politicky bezprávni alebo menej cenní, o boj sociálne mocných proti sociálne potlačeným."

283 Napred, 15.1.1907, N. 1, p. 3, "Slováci v uhorskej politike [Slovaks in the Hungarian politics]."

284 *RN*, 17.6.1909, N. 12, pp. 2–3, "Jubileum memorandumu [Anniversary of the Memorandum]." The exact requirements were: 1. Universal equal direct suffrage in all elections for every Hungarian citizen aged 20 of both sexes. Secret voting according to communities. Every voter can be elected. The elections take place on a non-working day. Parliament, county and communal elections every two years; 2. Dissolution of the chamber of lords; 3. Total self-government. Independence of the state county and communal administration, election of all corporations' and administrative employees, their responsibility. Dissolution of all hereditary offices and ranks.

285 *RN*, 8.9.1910, N. 36, p. 1, "Medzinárodný socialistický sjazd v Kodani [International socialist congress in Copenhagen]," for national history myths which Slovak workers shared with the Slovak nationalists see also *RN*, 16.4.1914, N. 16, p. 3, "IV. sjazd slovenskej sociálnej demokracie [The IV. congress of the Slovak social democracy]." On the views of the leading representatives of the Second International Karl Kautsky, Rosa Luxemburg and Eduard Bernstein on nationalism see Nimni, 1991, pp. 44–69.

286 *RN*, 16.4.1914, N. 16, pp. 1–4, "IV. sjazd slovenskej sociálnej demokracie," p. 3.

287 The association sent a deputation to the minister of interior and then to state secretary József Szlávy, and eventually discovered that the statutes had been approved by the state authorities but were languishing in the mayor's office. The workers' leaders believed that mayor Heinrich Justi was trying to prevent the consecration of the flag of the association. (Hanzlíček, 1970, pp. 23–26.) However, when Justi sent the statutes to the Ministry of Interior for their approval he noted that the city authorities did not object to these statutes. SNA, SRH, i. n. 9, c. 1, letter from Justi to the minister of interior, 24.3.1869.

288 The police captain Stefan Kutsera summoned the chairman of *Vorwärts* and flew into a rage for having ordered 1 May posters to be printed, although the police chief had banned their distribution in Pressburg (in 1891). Hanzlíček, 1970, p. 77.

289 I have not come across a case of large-scale conflict of workers with the police or military as happened in Budapest. However, Písch mentions a collision of workers with the gendarmerie on 27.5.1907 during a public gathering organised by the SDPH to protest the dismissal of 2,500 construction workers in Pressburg from their jobs (the authorities had dissolved the trade union organisation of construction workers who then refused to obey the new employers' rules). The gendarmerie attacked a procession of several thousand workers and arrested many of them. The gendarmerie also raided the Workers' home and confiscated workers' publications. (Ibid., p. 83, 131.) At this public meeting, the speaker Paul Wittich was interrupted by workers shouting: "We will continue in the Russian way!," referring to the 1905 Russian revolution. (Ibid., p. 55.) 1905–1907 was a period in the Hungarian social democratic movement marked by many strikes and increased fight for universal suffrage.

290 SNA, SRH, i. n. 317, c.13, Letter from the city police captain to the minister of interior from 20.4.1890: "... józan gondolkodás módját és békességet szerető természetét."

291 Hanzlíček, 1970, pp. 22–23. The main local periodical *Pressburger Zeitung* also noted that the social democrats wanted to achieve their goals in legal ways. *PZ*, 31.3.1869, N. 72, pp. 2–3, "Die Arbeiterversammlung in Pressburg am 29. März [Workers' public meeting in Pressburg on 29 March]."

292 *NH*, 10.10.1907, N. 232, p. 4, "Október tizedike Pozsonyban [10 October in Pozsony]." On the day of the general strike in Hungary, this newspaper expressed its

hope that the workers would not attack private property or disturb order.

293 This uncertainty about the outcome of even non-violent demonstrations was threatening to Pressburg's burghers and power elites. "Uncertainty results not from the uncertain *length* of a protest, ... but from the indeterminacy of its cost." Tarrow, 1994, p. 102.

294 *WG*, 12.11.1877, N. 1634, p. 1, "Pressburger Gewerbetreibende und die Sozialdemokraten [Pressburger craftsmen and social democrats]."

295 *WG*, 2.5.1893, N. 7043, pp. 1–2, "Der 1.Mai in Pressburg [1 May in Pressburg]": "Strenge Vorsichtsmasregeln, militarische Bereitschaft, Angst und Schrecken unter der Bürgerschaft Pressburgs."

296 *PZ*, 29.4.1890, N. 117, *Ab*, p. 2, "Der erste Mai [The first of May]." The big market in Vienna did not take place because of security fears.

The anti-Semitic riots in Pressburg took place on the 27th, 28th and 29th September 1882. Crowds of what was later termed 'street rabble' including mainly poor artisans, day laborers and workers shouting "Éljen Istóczy!" ("Long live Istóczy!") and "Éljen Simonyi" ("Long live Simonyi!") plundered Jewish shops, taverns and broke windows. Minister of Interior sent in the Chief of the State Police, Counsellor Lajos Jekelfalussy with unlimited power to restore order. Jekelfalussy ordered in three battalions of infantry and three squadrons of cavalry to the city. No one was seriously injured during the riots. Acording to Pressburger Zeitung on the 28th there were around 400–500 rioters. They were also ignited by anti-Semitic propaganda in the local daily, Ivan Simónyi's *Westungarischer Grenzbote*. G. Istóczy was an anti-Semitic parliament deputy who stirred up anti-Semitic moods in Hungary in 1882 by the case of Tisza-Eszlár "ritual murder" in which Jews were accused of the ritual murder of a young girl. The riots in Pressburg took place at the same time as the trial. Jekelfalussy pointed out that the main organisers were surely not from the working class. He was convinced that if the municipal magistracy had acted decisevely the very first night (despite having only a tiny police force of 52 men), they could have prevented further plundering. MOL, K149–1882–6, report of Jekelfalussy to the minister of interior dated 7.10.1882. *Pressburger Zeitung* reported widely on the events. Quite detailed information can be found also in The Times, 2.10.1884, 4a, 3.10.1882, 5c, 5.10.1882, 3c and 7.10.1882, 5c. See also Grünsfeld, 1932, p. 110.

297 *PZ*, 27.4.1890, N. 115, *Mb*, p. 1, "G'schossen hab'n's'! [They were shooting!]."

298 *WG*, 2.5.1890, N. 5990, pp. 1–3, "Der Arbeitertag in Pressburg [The workers' day in Pressburg]": "Pöbel und auswärtige Agitatoren."

299 *WG*, 2.5.1893, N. 7043, pp. 1–2, "Der 1.Mai in Pressburg [1 May in Pressburg]"

300 *WG*, 2.5.1902, N.10207, p. 3, "Die Maifeier der Arbeiterschaft Pressburgs [May Day celebration of the Pressburger workers] ."

301 A change in the route of the procession "could itself induce panic among the upper classes because of the implications of a break in routine." Knowing the route of the procession in advance made workers' crowds avoidable for the upper classes. See Harrison, 1988, p. 195.

302 *WV*, 5.5.1906, N.18, p. 1, "Die Maifeier der Arbeiterschaft Pressburgs May Day celebration of the Pressburger workers]": "Allgemein wurde die imposante Kundgebung der Arbeiterschaft anerkannt und überall lobte man die Ordnung und Disziplin der organisierten Arbeiterschaft Pressburgs."

303 *WG*, 1.9.1902, N. 10323, p. 1, "Demonstrationsumzug und Monstre-Volksversammlung [Demonstration procession and monster public gathering]," *WV*, 28.8.1902, N.26, p. 7, announcement of the "Monstre-Versammlung," *WV*, 4.9.1902, N.27, p. 7, "Wahlrechtsversammlung in Pressburg [Public gathering for universal suffrage in Pressburg]," *PZ*, 1.9.1902, N.241, *Ab*, pp. 2–3, "Der Demonstrationsumzug und die Monstre-Volksversammlung." As Mark Harrison points out, "Celebratory processions (particularly those around the principal streets of the city centre) were a rather more direct declaration both of a crowd's social constituency and its symbolic control of space." Harrison, 1988, p. 203.

304 *WV*, 5.5.1906, N.18, p. 1, "Die Maifeier der Arbeiterschaft Pressburgs [May Day celebration of the Pressburger workers]." In 1911, state employees and officials joined workers in public gatherings protesting against increasing prices and living costs in the city. Lehotský, Unpublished thesis, 1977, p. 150.

305 *WV*, 2.3.1912, N.26, p. 1, program of demonstration for universal suffrage on 4 March 1912.

306 *WV*, 5.3.1912, N.27, pp. 1–2, "Arbeitsruhe der Wahldemonstranten [A day off work for those demonstrating for universal suffrage]." One speaker was a local dentist and he stressed that there were many supporters of universal suffrage among the burghers [Bürgerschaft] as well.

307 *WV*, 4.5.1912, N.300, p. 3, "Die Maifeier [May Day celebration]": "eine Renitenz gegen die famose Ordnung"

308 *WG*, 3.2.1891, N. 6256, p. 2, "Freie Arbeiter-Volksversammlung [Free workers' public gathering]."

309 Hanzlíček, 1970, pp. 63–64.

310 Jones describes a different kind of 'respectability' apparent among the poor in nineteenth-century London, which was also concerned with keeping up appearances but had different priorities than middle class 'respectability.' Rather than being concerned with such values as thrift and self-help, it "meant the possession of a presentable Sunday suit, and the ability to be seen wearing it." In Jones, 1983, p. 201.

311 *WG*, 12.11.1877, N.1635, pp. 3–5, "Arbeiterversammlung in Speneder's Gasthaus

vom 11. d. M [Workers' gathering in Speneder's inn on the 11th of this month]." The editor even considered workers' requirements somewhat selfish since he claimed to know hundreds of small clerks and teachers who made less money than workers. And while workers could dress simply and eat in cheap people's canteens, white-collar employees could not indulge in such behaviour since they could not afford the loss of status.

312 *PZ*, 1.2.1891, N. 32, *Mb*, p. 4, "Arbeiterball [Workers' ball]," *PZ*, 10.10.1907, N. 278, *Mb*, p. 1, "Allgemeines Wahlrecht [Universal suffrage]": "nicht im sozialdemokratischen sondern im bürgerlichen Sinne."

313 *NH*, 1.5.1897, N.99, pp. 1–2, "A munkásünnep [The workers' holiday]."

314 *NH*, 30.4.1893, N.99, pp. 1–2, "Május elseje [The first of May]": "…az a modern barbar népözön, mely a szociális szervezet legalsóbb mélyéből akar előre törni, hogy kegyetlenül megsemisitse, egyszerűen halomra döntse a százados fejlődés minden alkotását." Such an opinion of the working classes was certainly not restricted to the Magyar nationalist middle classes but was present among the middle classes regardless of language. Similarly, in nineteenth century London the term 'working class' carried only negative connotations, signifying "*ir*religion, *in*temperance, *im*providence or *im*morality." Middle class observers and charity members visiting poor districts conceived of themselves as "missionaries of civilisation." (Italics in original.) Jones, 1983, pp. 184–185.

315 *NH*, 1.5.1902, N.100, p. 1, "Május elseje."

316 *PT*, 27.9.1907, N. 4030, pp. 1–2, "Der moderne Kreuzzug! [The modern crusade!]": "Banner des Glaubens und Unglaubens, des Christentums und Freimauerertums, des auf christlicher Grundlage stehenden Solidarismus und des gottesfeindlichen, roten, rachedurstenden Sozialismus."

317 *PT*, 10.10.1907, N. 4043, p. 2, "Zum 10. Oktober [To the 10th October]." Christian socialists stayed with their employers during general strikes called by the social democrats.

318 Another periodical of the radical burghers was called *Reform* and was edited by the previously well-known social democrat Alois Zalkai. Potemra, 1963, pp. 220–221.

319 Kovačevičová, 1985, p. 52, footnote 21.

320 *WG*, 1.9.1902, N. 10323, p. 1, "Demonstrationsumzug und Monstre-Volksversammlung [Demonstration procession and monster public gathering]."

321 *WV*, 14.9.1907, N.37, p. 2, small announcement.

322 "However, to give this possibility [to hear Slav songs] to Pressburger (prešporským) Czechs and Slovaks and the whole music loving audience is the most noble task of the Slovak and Czech choirs. In this they must see the real reason of their existence. …[The] audience which came on Sunday to the concert is evidence

of the uselessness of more-lingual invitations and posters." *RN*, 21.11.1912, N.47, pp. 6–7, "Chýrnik [News]."

323 *WV*, 5.10.1907, N. 40, pp. 1–2, "Die Pressburger Arbeiterschaft im Kampfe für das allgemeine Wahlrecht [The Pressburger workers in fight for universal suffrage]." The gathering was banned because the "nationalistic" parliament deputy Milan Hodža was supposed to be one of the speakers. Another social democratic meetings with a Slovak social democratic speaker was permitted by the authorities, although later banned by the deputy mayor.

324 Lehotský, Unpublished thesis, 1969, p. 23.

CHAPTER 4

Between Vienna and Budapest: Pressburg in a National Landscape

1 Buček, 1995, pp. 146–147. According to Buček, the most important strategic direction in Europe connects Belorussia, Poland and northern Germany. The northern strategic direction connects to the southern strategic direction in the vicinity of Bratislava.

2 Ibid., p. 190. From 1563 until 1830, Pressburg also served as the coronation city for the Hungarian kings and queens. See Holčík, 1988.

3 Buček, 1995, p. 223.

4 Beluszky, 1990, p. 24.

5 Ibid., pp. 17–18. Beluszky divides Hungarian towns into five groups according to their functions and existing institutions. A regional centre was characterised by the presence of universities, royal courts, Hungarian insurance companies' agencies, district industrial supervision offices, the post directors' board, royal supreme prosecutor's office, etc. There were ten regional centres in Hungary in 1900, five of "full importance" and five of "partial importance."

6 Ibid., p. 31.

7 Ibid., pp. 23–24.

8 See Chapter one, Part 2. For more details on migration, see the first part of Chapter three.

9 Glettler, 1992, pp. 296–297.

10 See Part 1 of Chapter one for more on the development of rail transport. In 1867

there were two trains daily to both Vienna and Budapest. (*PW*, 1867.) By 1877 there were already four trains daily both to Vienna and Budapest. (*PW*, 1877). In 1898 trains departed from Pressburg in seven different directions (Budapest, Vienna, Zsolna, Szakolca, Szombathely, Sopron, Dunaszerdeheky-Komárom). There were ten trains daily to Vienna and six trains to Budapest. (*PW*, 1899.) In 1914, there were eleven trains daily to Vienna and nine to Budapest. The train ride to Vienna took between 1.5–2 hours, while the train ride to Budapest lasted around three hours. *PW*, 1914.

11 *PW*, 1867, 1901.

12 As noted in Chapter two, the association *Toldy Kör* included the chauvinistic Magyar elite but also had German speaking middle class members who used their membership in the association to publicly demonstrate their Hungarian patriotism. Therefore the expressions of the association's members usefully reflect the ideology of an interest group using Magyar nationalism for political purposes in the city.

13 Kumlik, 1905, p. 9: "Ha valamely város, úgy bizonyára koronázó Pozsony városa az, mely mind fényes története, mind előhaladt műveltségénél fogva Magyarország második fővárosa lévén, hivatva van arra, hogy a hazai irodalomnak s művészetének szentélyt nyisson."

14 Ibid., p. 110: "Pozsony várost teljesen átalakítva látni, hogy nemcsak névleg, hanem valójába hazánk második fővárosa legyen."

15 Ibid., p. 123, *Petőfi Társaság* [Petőfi Society]: "Ha Budapest Magyarország feje, úgy Pozsony annak homloka."

16 Ibid., p. 510: "A magyar koronának egyik gyöngye ez a város."

17 Count István Eszterházy in ibid., p. 38: "... mintegy védbástyáúl szolgál honunk határán a mindegyre tovább harapodózó *elnémetesüléssel* szemben ... különösen a hazai *irodalom* és *magyar szellem* fejlesztésére itt Pozsonyban van leginkább szükség, a hol a hazának e legnagyobb kincsei a túlnyomó németajku lakosság által állandóan veszélyeztetvék." (italics in original)

18 Ibid., p. 185.

19 Ibid., p. 334: "A Toldy Kör felé sok szív dobog az országban, munkásságát méltányolják és nagy eredményt várnak még tőle ebben a határszéli városban a magyar kultura elterjesztésének és erösítésének érdekében."

20 Ibid., pp. 510, 518.

21 Marcel Jankowicz in Tamás, 1938, p. 18: "nemzetiségi áradatok." In Hungarian, there is a difference between 'nationalist' and 'nationalities.' "Nationalities'" is used as an adjective here, since the Hungarian authorities referred to the movements of different nationalities in the Hungarian state as "nationalities' movements" rather than "nationalist movements."

22 Kumlik, 1905, p. 538: "Valamint a mult harcai között Pozsony volt az ország erős végvára, ahol menedéket talált az elpusztított országból kiszorított szent korona: ugy Pozsonynak ma is a magyar nemzeti kultura végvárának kell lennie, amely felfogja és megállitsa a nyugatról és északról betóduló s a magyar nemzeti művelődés ellen törő idegen áramlatot, miképen a város fölött emelkedő Kárpátok hegylánca is megtöri a káros északi viharok romboló erejét." Ibid., p. 535: "… még mindig nem elég erős határszéli előörs."

23 Kumlik, 1905, p. 324: "Legyen a Toldy Kör a magyarság főhadiszállása." *Toldy Kör* reflected the ideas of the *alispán* of Zvolen conty Béla Grünwald: "Our mission is within the borders of the country, and it lies in that we fill this state until its furthest borders, that we take up in it that position which we have the right to occupy by virtue of our numerical and property preponderance as well as our moral and spiritual superiority and historical significance: let's permeate the whole country with Magyar national spirit: in our interest as well as that of humanity, let's elevate to our level and refine the alien and backward races living in our country." ["A mi missiónk az ország határain belül van, s abban ál, hogy töltsük be ezt az államot legvégső határaig, foglaljuk el benne azt az állást, melyet elfoglalni számunk, vagyoni, erkölcsi és szellemi túlsúlyunk, történelmi jelentőségünknél fogva elfoglalni jogosultak vagyunk: hassuk át az egész országot a magyar nemzeti szellemmel: a magunk s az emberiség érdekében emeljük magunkhoz és nemesítsük meg az országban lakó idegen s elmaradt népfajokat."] (Quoted in Szarka, 1999, p. 70.) Although *Toldy Kör* was created before Grünwald's work was published (1878), the rapid spread of other similar associations with the aim of Magyarising local populations after 1881 was spurred on by Grünwald's ideas. See Smith, G. et al, 1998, pp. 125–126 on Ukrainian self-perception as an outpost of European civilisation against the 'other', in this case "Asia" (Russians) and Islam. This is also the case for Estonians. See footnote 31.

24 See Buček, 1995, p. 157.

25 Ibid., p. 157.

26 Gillis, 1994a, p. 14.

27 Johnson, 1997, p. 348.

28 Thály, 1898, pp. 4–5. There was a discussion among Hungarian historians on the precise year to be considered the year for the millennial celebrations since the whole process of taking the territory had taken ten years. 1895 was initially suggested but since preparations for the celebrations were not complete by that time, the year 1896 became the "millennial" year.

29 This hill is in the vicinity of Bratislava, and there are remnants of a fortification which according to the Slovak historians played an important role within the Great Moravian Empire. The leading personality of the Slovak national revival, Ľudovít

Štúr, who codified literary Slovak in 1843 used to make trips with his students to this site. Juraj Papánek and Juraj Sklenár (representatives of the first wave of the Slovak national revival: see Part 6) introduced one of the central ideas of the Slovak national mythology, the idea of the Great Moravian medieval state as a Slovak entity. Papánek considered Great Moravia the first Slovak state, "the kingdom of Slovaks, in which Slovaks were an independent nation and they had a great and highly developed culture." This account stressed that Slovaks were the original inhabitants of their territory and that Hungarians came only much later and were civilised by the Slovaks. (Brock, 1976, p. 8.) "When recent history denies their claim for nationhood, these groups turn to a more remote past to provide evidence of their distinct historical roots." (Zerubavel, 1994, pp. 107–108.) On the Great Moravian tradition in the Slovak national revival see Butvín, 1972, pp. 96–118. In this way, the Dévény castle hill was the site of alternative explanations or competing histories. It had different meanings in the Magyar and Slovak national mythologies. "Nationalist movements do not just operate territorially, they interpret and appropriate space, place and time, upon which they construct alternative geographies and histories." (R. J. Johnston et al, 1988, p. 14.) For competing versions of history of the arrival of Hungarians into this area and their relationship with Slav people in the Slovak and Hungarian national mythology see Tibenský, 1972. See Smith, G. et al, 1998, chapter three on competing myths of ethnogenesis in Transcaucasia (Armenia, Azerbaijan, Georgia, Abkhazia and South Ossetia). On contested "representations of the past" see Nash, 2000, p. 27. In this connection one could also talk about "discursive fields" as "a range of competing discourses constituted by a set of narratives, concepts, and ideologies relevant to a particular realm of social practices." (Duncan, 1990, p. 16.) In this case the official Hungarian version would constitute the dominant discourse which was contested by the Slovak discourse of the historical significance of the Dévény hill.

30 Kirk Savage notes: "The increasing tendency in the nineteenth century to construct memory in physical monuments—to inscribe it on the landscape itself— seems symptomatic of an increasing anxiety about memory left to its own unseen devices. Monuments served to anchor collective remembering, a process dispersed, ever changing, and ultimately intangible, in highly condensed, fixed, and tangible places." Savage, 1994, p. 130.

31 On the construction of "geographies of belonging" and links between nationalism, identity and place see Graham, 2000. On nationalist anxieties about the borders of the national territory and conflicting histories of mutual borderlands in Belorussia and Ukraine see Smith, G. et al, 1998, Chapter two, esp. pp. 36–37. Justifying his country's new alien laws in 1993, Estonian president Lennart Meri stressed the importance of a secure state border: "It is precisely in the name of European values that Estonia needs a secure border...Our border is the border of European values." Ibid., p. 102.

32 As Daniele Conversi stresses, "all the processes of identity construction are

simultaneously border-generating and border-deriving." In this way the millennial monuments also symbolically constructed the borders of Hungarian national identity. The Magyar nationalism connected with the millennial celebrations and presenting the multi-national thousand-year-old Hungarian state as essentially a state of one—Magyar culture, denoted the content of this identity. "[n]ationalism simultaneously strives at the reinforcement of external borders and the elimination of internal borders. The consequence of this is the notorious homogenizing pressure of nationalism, a steam-rolling action which devours and destroys all anti-entropic actors and forces." Conversi, 1997, pp. 328–329.

33 Green, A., Unpublished thesis, 1998, p. 178.

34 Thály, 1898, pp. 6–7: "...mennyire emelik a nemzet öntudatot." Thály became a member of the "millennial national committee" (millenáris országos bizottság). This committee primarily concentrated on preparations of the celebrations in Budapest but also handled preparations for the rural monuments after Thály's proposal was accepted.

35 Ibid., pp. 7–9, p. 14: "...az országos bizottság különös súlyt fektetett az állameszmének a nemzetiségi vidéken ajánlott szimbolizására..."

36 Ibid., pp. 16–19. Simon Schama notes, "National identity...would lose much of its ferocious enchantment without the mystique of a particular landscape tradition: its topography mapped, elaborated and enriched as a homeland." (Schama, 1995, p. 15). Schama also talks about "fluvial geography" and its significance for national myths. In the context of the Habsburg Empire, the river Danube flowing through German, Slav and Magyar lands was used by the "apologists of the polyglot Habsburg Empire since they could pretend that it bound the several nations together like an imperial ribbon." Ibid., p. 363. On the relation of landscape and power, see Duncan, 1990.

37 One of these was located at Pannonhalma where the honfoglalás was completed. This area was supposed to have been a Roman territory and was considered "the most educated part of the country." The second monument was at Pusztaszer, the place where the first Hungarian constitution was drawn up and where the first parliament met. Thály, 1898, pp. 11–12.

38 Ibid., p. 10. "Különösen az ország négy kapuját, északon, délen, nyugaton és keleten egy-egy emlékoszloppal jelöljük meg; a minek czélja, hogy valamint az ott lakó nemzetiségek, úgy az országba bejövő idegenek is lássák azokban a magyar állameszme kifejezését; lássák a feltünő helyen álló oszlopokról, hogy az magyar föld, melyre lépnek; emlékeztessék azok a nemzetiségeket, hogy az magyar föld, melyen laknak, és valamennyi nemzetiségnek kijusson belőllük;—végre biztatóul szolgáljanak azon a magyarságnak, pl. a határszéli székelyeknek."

39 János Hunyady was a Hungarian general (1385–1456) who became famous in the battles against the Turks in the fifteenth century. He defended the border against

the Turks. *Révay Nagy Lexikon*, 1911, Vol. X, pp. 389–392.

40 Thály, 1898, pp. 10–12.

41 Ibid., p. 45.

42 Ibid., p. 10.

43 Ibid., pp. 11–12, "Slovak sons [*tót atyafiak*]."

44 Ibid., pp. 20–21. The iconography of the other monuments was equally suggestive. In the south and west were statues of a flying turul bird which had in its beak the sword of Attila. (Attila was the great king of the Huns, who built up a great empire stretching from the river Volga to the Rhine, from the Lower Danube river to the Baltic Sea. He ruled from 433 to 453. *Révay Nagy Lexikon*, Vol. II, 1911, pp. 271–273.) The sword in the southern monument was directed at the Serbs.

The importance of iconography of the monuments, the direction the statues look or point, is suggested also in two other monuments. One is the monument of Prince Eugen in Budapest built in 1900 in front of the royal palace. Prince Eugen freed large parts of Hungary from the Turks and this statue was constructed in order to remind Magyars of this. Prince Eugen is looking in the south-eastern direction towards the territories he liberated. He symbolises the "apostolic function of Habsburg dynasty as defenders of the Christian faith." (Uhl, 1999, pp. 171–173.) The other is the statue of Josip Jelačič in the centre of Zagreb. Jelačič was the leader of Croatian uprising in 1848 and he fought against Hungarian revolutionaries. At the time when the statue was constructed (1866), Jelačič's raised arm with a sword pointed towards Hungary. The statue was removed by the communists in 1945. After Croatia gained independence, the statue was restored to the square; however, Jelačič now points in the southern direction towards the territories which Croatia demanded during the Yugoslav war. (Ibid., p. 169, footnote 17.) Competing representations of history are evident again in the person of Prince Eugen. When the fascists came to power in Germany in 1933, there arose a competition between Germany and Austria for the symbolic representation of Prince Eugen. Thus, ironically, Prince Eugen who was of French aristocratic descent, who led an army constituted of many different nationalities, who preferred to use Italian in his private life and who signed himself using three languages (Eugenio von Savoy), became the personification of the idea of Greater Germany. (Ibid., pp. 173–174.) See also Charlotte Tacke (1995, especially pp. 29–50), on the Hermann monument in Germany, pointing west towards the enemy—France. Hermann was the historic leader of the Germanic tribes in a victorious battle against the Roman army. He was seen as the unifier of the Germanic tribes against their enemy and this was then considered as the birth of the German nation. While Hermann's sword should on historical grounds have been pointing towards the south, in the nineteenth century the enemy was elsewhere. Using the example of the Hermann monument and the Vercingetorix monument in France, Tacke explains very well the construction of national myths, both directed outside—

Notes to Chapter 4

towards the outside enemies (for unifying the nation) but also inwards, defining those who are not considered part of this nation.

45 On the links between memory and national identity see Johnson, 2000, p. 253, also Gillis, 1994a. "Modern memory was born not just from the sense of break with the past, but from an intense awareness of the conflicting representations of the past and the effort of each group to make its version the basis of national identity." Gillis, 1994a, p. 7.

46 Thály, 1898, p. 47: "A fölállított emlékművek hirdetni fogják hosszú időkig Magyarország ezredéves fönnlétét, és jelképezni a nemzetiségek előtt a magyar állameszmét, a melyhez híveinek kell lenniök nekik is."

47 "Just as the past informed the present through the medium of existing monuments, so the future could be informed of the present through the construction of new monuments." Woolf, 1988, p. 216. See also Weeks, 1999 on the construction of the monument of Count Muraviev in Vilna in 1898, as a way to delineate the Northwest Russian territory (provinces returned from Poland) as Russian in its national character.

48 In this way then, a link was created between memory and space, in this case the Hungarian national space. "Thus memory orients experience by linking an individual to family traditions, customs of class, religious beliefs, or specific places." The link between memory and space is crucial since "when memories could not be located in the social space of a group, then remembrance would fail." Boyer, 1994, p. 26.

49 On monuments and national identity see Uhl, 1999, pp. 133–153 and Tacke, 1995.

50 The coronation hill was originally in the care of the Hungarian state. The city and the Ministry of Finance corresponded between 1867–1869 about who should take care of the monument. The Ministry proposed to hand it over to the city. However, the city administration could not guarantee that the hill would remain in the same place because of future urban development. A municipal committee decided that the city could finance the necessary preservation costs. However, the city engineer felt that the city could not afford the adaptation costs. Engyeli, 1897, pp. 6–8.

51 This proposed monument was continually postponed because of lack of money. In 1871 Mayor Justi proposed the erection of a column of Silesian marble. The municipal committee decided that the construction of the monument should be postponed until the condition of city finances improved. At the beginnings of the 1880s the Stadtverschönerungsverein considered the issue of the monument. The association considered two alternatives in the Gothic and Renaissance styles. However, this project was not realised either. Engyeli, 1897, p. 9.

52 It was this aspect of the millennial celebration which provoked protests from the nationalities living in Hungary. They protested against the representation of the historic Hungarian state as an essentially Magyar state. See Komora, 1996.

425

53 Engyeli, 1897, p. 10. Karl Neiszidler (1832–1916) was a parliament deputy for Pressburg in the years 1884–1916. (See *Slovenský bibliografický slovník*, 1990, p. 286.) The proposal for the monument itself came from the city archivist Johann Batka in a discussion in the middle class association *Bürgerklub*. The chairman of the association Neiszidler introduced the proposal in the municipal assembly. (See *WG*, 16.5.1897, N. 8465, p. 2, "Zur Enthüllungs-Feier unseres Krönungsdenkmales [To the unveiling ceremony of our coronation monument].") As Uhl points out, the impetus for construction of monuments and statues usually did not come from the city but different associations, committees and groups of people who asked for financial support of the city, for a location for the monument or for its patronage. (Uhl, 1999, p. 141.) This was the case in Pressburg where the impetus came from the *Bürgerverein* but the project was then taken over by the city. Since all the prominent personalities of the city were members of the city associations whose membership was interconnected, associations were often the places where such decisions were made. (See Chapter two on the interconnection of city elites with the *Toldy Kör* association.) Many social projects in the city were initiated in some of the philanthropic associations, especially the freemasons' lodges in Pressburg. (See Jeszenszky, I., 1927, Celler, 1916, Mannová, 1999b, p. 208.) Several associations and institutions of Pressburg contributed to the cost of the monument of *honvéd* (defender of the homeland) in Buda. (MOL, K149–1894–6.) On the organisation of subscriptions for monuments through middle class associations see Tacke, 1995, Chapters two and three. Tacke points out that most members of the association for the construction of the Hermann monument were mobilised through personal contacts or bureaucratic ruling structures. Only after they were persuaded and "morally obliged" did new members join the association. This shows that although newspapers played an important role in "homogenisation of the national ideologies" finally it was more the social position of the potential subscribers in the regional and local society and their connections which was decisive in choosing to join the list of subscribers. The decisive factor was not necessarily the strength of national conviction or level of national consciousness but rather the fear of social ostracism.

54 Engyeli, 1897, p. 10.

55 Ibid., p. 11: "Überall wo ungarisches Blut pulsiert, empfindet die Brust jedes Patrioten voll tiefer Ergriffenheit die grosse Bedeutung des heutigen Freudenfestes. Dieses Fest bezeichnet die grosse Liebe und unerschütterliche Treue der ungarischen Nation zu unserem gekrönten apostolischen König und ihre treue Anhänglichkeit an die Mitglieder des glorreich regierenden Herrscherhauses."

56 Ibid., p. 11: "Bis zum Jahre 1869 stand hier der Krönungshügel als Zeuge und heiliges Symbol der grossen historischen Bedeutung und der im Lande eingenommenen priviligierten Stellung unserer Stadt; in dem gedachten Jahre wurde mit bedauernswerter Übereilung die sofortige Abtragung desselben beschlossen..." On the day of unveiling of the monument, the *Westungarischer Grenzbote* even

wrote that "the best citizens" protested in the press against the removal of the crowning hill as "an act of vandalism" but to no avail. In *WG*, 16.5.1897, N. 8465, p. 2: "Zur Enthüllungs-Feier unseres Krönungsdenkmales [To the unveiling ceremony of our coronation monument]."

57 Engyeli, 1897, p. 11: "Einerseits um den begangenen Fehler und das bisherige Versäumniss gutzumachen, anderseits, um an diesem im ganzen weiten Vaterlande mit der grössten Begeisterung gefeierten Landes-Freudentage auch unserseits der für unseren schwärmerisch verehrten guten König Sr. Majestät *Franz Joseph I.* empfundenen aufrichtigsten Unterthanenliebe und unerschütterlichen Treue, sowie der für das angestammte Herrscherhaus Jahrhunderte hindurch fleckenlos und unverändert bewahrten treuen Anhänglichkeit nicht nur in Worten sondern *auch mit Thaten* dankbaren äusseren Ausdruck zu verleihen, schliesslich auch mit Rücksicht auf die herannahende erhebende Feier des tausendjährigen Bestandes unseres Vaterlandes,..." (italics in original).

58 Ibid., p. 11: "...[Zeugniss] von der wärmstens gepflegten Liebe und Treue der Bürgerschaft Pressburgs für die hier gekrönten Könige und Königinennen aus dem glorreichen Hause Habsburg, als auch für unser theures Vaterland."

59 Ibid., pp. 11–12 "...die alte Krönungsstadt jederzeit mit dem geliebten Vaterlande gefühlt hat, fühlt und fühlen wird..."

60 Ibid., pp. 11–12.

61 Such preference for city artists and craftsmen was typical for other public projects carried out by the *Stadtverschönerungsverein*. See Győrik, 1918.

62 Engyeli, 1897, p. 12. The cost was to be no more than 30,000 gulden.

63 Ibid., p. 12.

64 Ibid., p. 12.

65 Ibid., pp. 12–13. The monument was made from Carrara marble. The figures were twice life-size. The pedestal was of dark shiny granite and the whole monument stood on an earthen hill as a reminder of the previous crowning ceremonies. The monument was constructed in baroque style.

66 Engyeli, 1897, p. 14. The monument was 11 meters high. The pedestal was 4.35 meters high. The construction of the monument cost 85.000 florins. The monument committee decided that the monument would be surrounded by a wrought-iron railing. This work was also done by a famous Pressburger iron-working firm in the baroque style. Ibid., pp. 14–15.

67 This dedication further specified that the city Pressburg had decided on the day of the 25th anniversary of the coronation of Franz Joseph (8 June 1892), on the occasion of the coming 1000th anniversary of the existence of the Hungarian state

to erect a monument on the place of the old coronation hill. The monument was ready already in 1896 but unveiled in the presence of the king on 16 May 1897. Engyeli, 1897, p. 16, the German translation of Hungarian text.

68 Ibid., p. 16. "...[Andenken] *an ungarische Vaterlandsliebe, ungarische Gesetze-sachtung und jene unerschütterliche Treue,* mit welcher diese Nation den schwankenden Thron und die dem ritterlichen Schutze der Ungarn empfohlene allerhöchste Familie...[gerettet hat.]"; "...*die beständige und unverletzliche Heiligkeit des königlichen Eides und der Gesetze...*"; "Du aber Denkmal, zu Stein gewordener Herold altungarischer Tugenden, ungarischer Treue, ungarischen Heldenmuthes, ungarischer Ritterlichkeit und Gesetzachtung, *Steh' unerschütterlich! Steh' in Ewigkeit! Steh', so lange das tausendjährige, angegebete Vaterland besteht!"* (italics in original)

In the left over free space of the monument the artist expressed his gratitude to the "city fathers" for the financial support which he had received as a young artist for his studies in Vienna from the I. Pozsonyi Sparkasse (Pressburger savings bank) In *PZ,* 16.5.1897, N.134, *Mb,* p. 6, "Der dankbare Künstler [The grateful artist]": "Itt vésem be hálámat a városi atyái iránt, a kik engem mindannyian a szobor készítésénel lelkesen és áldozatkészséggel támogattak." Thály's attitude towards these monuments is similar to that of R. de Corval (the author of an 1867 guidebook on Paris) who considered monuments "historical witnesses." Corval said: "étudier les monuments d'une ville, c'est d'étudier son histoire dans ce que les siecles passés ont laissé de vivant et de palpable." Quoted in Woolf, 1988, p. 216.

69 The preparation of the monument involved considerable work. First, Fadrusz made a life-size model of the whole group which took eighteen months. For this purpose, the artist had to procure costumes and other necessities from Budapest and Vienna. Archduke Friedrich gave Fadrusz a recommendation letter to the court steward Count Hohenlohe so that all the necessary parts from the emperor's collection were made available to the artist. The head of Maria Theresa was modelled on the basis of many paintings and the costume of the magnate was made on the basis of a costume of Count Festetich which one of his ancestors had actually worn at the court of Maria Theresa. (In Engyeli, 1897, pp. 13–14.) The monument itself was then made in Carrara on the basis of the model. However, difficulties with cracking in the marble postponed the construction of the monument. The transport of the marble blocks was supervised by Fadrusz and the pieces of the monument were transported to Pressburg at the beginning of September 1896. Ibid., p. 14.

70 *WG,* 17.5.1897, N. 8466, p. 1, "Zur Enthüllungs-Feier unseres Krönungsdenkmales [To the unveiling ceremony of our coronation monument]": "Seit der letzten Königskrönung, die in den Mauern dieser Stadt erfolgte, hat Pressburg nicht so viel Glanz und Pracht gesehen als gestern."

71 *PZ,* 10.-15.5.1897.

72 This request points to the prevailing ethnic or rather linguistic character of the city in 1897. It was generally perceived that the public present at the unveiling would speak preponderantly German. The request for reinforcements also suggests that the Pressburg police force was not very large. The police chief asked for 8 detectives and 40 plain-clothes policemen. The Budapest police sent 3 detectives, 6 non-commissioned officers and 32 policemen. MOL, K149-1897-6-384.

73 Engyeli, 1897, p. 17, *WG, PZ, PT* on 16.5. and 17.5.1897.

74 The mayor ended his German-language speech at the unveiling ceremony with the Hungarian exclamation "Isten hozta felségedett!" (God brought his majesty!) and spoke German at the reception given by the king, again ending in Hungarian "Éljen a király!" (Long live the king!). The head of the Franziskaner church welcomed the king in German, and the king praised the winery of the cloister in Hungarian. *WG*, 16.5.1897, N. 8465, pp. 2–3, "Zur Enthüllungs-Feier unseres Krönungsdenkmales," *PZ*, 17.5.1897, N.136., pp. 1–6, "Zum Enthüllungstag [To the unveiling day]."

75 The *Nyugatmagyarországi Hiradó* reproached Archduke Friedrich (who resided in the city) for not sufficiently strongly supporting Magyar cultural efforts in the city. The newspaper felt that the Archduke "could make fashionable the cult of Hungarian national education before the higher circles in Pozsony who follow and respect the example given by the court." *NH*, 16.5.1897, N.112, p. 4, "Pozsony jövője [The future of Pozsony]."

76 *PZ*, 16.5.1897, N. 135, p. 7, *Mb*, "Vir probus et integer [A man of virtue and integrity]."

77 *PT*, 17.5.1897, N. 395, pp. 1–5, "Der Festtag in Pressburg [Day of festivity in Pressburg]."

78 *NH*, 18.5.1897, N. 113, p. 1, "Post festa [After festivity]."

79 *NH*, 15.5.1897, N. 111, p. 1, "A 'Sedes sacrae coronae' ékességének leleplezése előtt [Before the unveiling of the jewel of the home's sacred crown]."

80 *NH*, 16.5.1897, N. 112, pp. 1–2, "A mit ez a szobor beszél [What this monuments tells]."

81 *NH*, 15.5.1897, N.111, p. 1, "A 'Sedes sacrae coronae' ékességének leleplezése előtt."

82 *PZ*, 17.5.1897, N. 136, *Ab*, p. 1, "Der Enthüllungstag [The unveiling day]."

83 *NH*, 15.5.1897, N.111, p. 1, "A 'Sedes sacrae coronae' ékességének leleplezése előtt."

84 *PZ*, 17.5.1897, N. 136, *Ab*, p. 1, "Der Enthüllungstag": "Für die Stadt Pressburg war es, wie schon gesagt, das grösste und erhebendste Fest, welches das Munizipium und die Bevölkerung je feierte."

85 *PZ*, 17.5.1897, N. 136, *Ab*, p. 1, "Der Enthüllungstag."

86 *NH* 15.5.1897, N.111, p. 1, "A 'Sedes sacrae coronae' ékességének leleplezése előtt": "the Magyar Versailles which has grown up in the shade of the Habsburgs...with the only difference that Versailles of that time was German while now even if not rapidly but undoubtedly, in its whole population and its educational institutions, magyarising Pozsony, the shield of which got worn down a little by time, but is gilded by industry, even midst the changed times has managed to remain grateful, but at the same time national [a Habsburg árnyékában nevekedett magyar Versailles...a különbség csak az, hogy az akkori magyar Versailles német volt, mig most egész lakosságában, tanintézeteiben ha nem is rohamosan, de biztosan haladó Pozsony, melynek cimerét elkopta kissé az idő, de megaranyozza az ipar, a megváltozott idők közepette is hálásnak, de egyszersmind nemzetinek tudott maradni.]"

87 E.g. Napred, N. 6, 15.6.1907, p. 2, "Jubileum [Anniversary]," p. 3, "Nemilé prekvapenie [An unpleasant surprise]," *RN*, 25.11.1909, N. 35, p. 3, "Král' a národnosti [The king and nationalities]," Napred, N. 2, 15.10.1906, "Boj za všeobecné volebné právo [The fight for universal suffrage]." During the constitutional crisis in 1905–1906, the workers hoped that the king would force the Hungarian government and parliament to adopt universal suffrage. However, when one considers the use of different spaces in the city by different groups of inhabitants and the symbolic meaning of these spaces, one could conclude that the Maria Theresa monument or the ceremony connected with it was not important for the workers. A more symbolic site for the workers was the statue of the poet Petőfi (see Chapter three) where the anniversary of the Hungarian revolution was commemorated. (Workers in Budapest gathered at the Petőfi statue as well. MOL, K149–1904–464.)

88 *WG*, 19.5.1897, N. 8468, pp. 3–4, "Nachklange zur Enthüllungfeier [Impressions from the unveiling ceremony]."

89 *NN*, 23.6.1897, N.141, pp. 2–3, "Niekoľko slov o pomníku Márie-Terézie v Prešporku [A few words about the Maria Theresa monument in Prešporok]." This article pointed out some discrepancies in the design of the statue (the cloak of the figures moving with the wind in a different direction than the tail of the horse, weak anatomical work by the artist as well as the empty expression in Maria Theresa's face). Whatever the artistic value of the monument, its important symbolic value for the inhabitants of Pressburg was proved after the end of the First World War. After the Czechoslovak army occupied the city, the Maria Theresa monument was often the location of public gatherings. By coming to this monument the inhabitants of the city re-connected to Pressburg's past (when there was a strong sense of belonging to the Habsburg Empire and Hungary) in order to overcome the uncertainty of the present. Although occupied by the Czechoslovak army after January 1919, the fate of Bratislava was definitely decided only in 1921. In response to the return of the deposed Habsburg Emperor Karl I to Hungary (20 October 1921), the Czechoslovak government declared partial mobilisation and the very next night

Czechoslovak legionaries broke the Maria Theresa monument into pieces (despite the promise of the Czechoslovak government to the city authorities that no such acts would take place). Pressburgers were outraged and terrified by "this barbaric act." According to an eye-witness, many inhabitants carried away pieces of the statue and preserved them up to the present day. (Based on interview with Katarína Löfflerová and Dvořák, 1995, pp. 501–505.) Some of the marble was re-used in other monuments and fragments of the monument were taken to Budapest. (Lipták, 1999, p. 323.) The statue of the Árpád warrior standing on the hill Dévény was also knocked down into the Danube. However, the statue of Maria Theresa provoked the dislike of Czechs right after their arrival into the city. Maria Theresa was disliked for her Germanisation efforts and so someone threw a bag over her head and the whole statue was planked. The statues of the "renegade" Petőfi and the "German" Johann Nepomuk Hummel were also covered up at the same time. (Dvořák, 1995, pp. 501–505.) See Jankovics, 1939, pp. 109–123 for a personal account of the destruction of both millenial monuments.

90 As symbolic spaces monuments often carry conflicting messages and representations. For an interesting description of the construction of Basilica Sacré-Coeur in Paris see Harvey, 1985, pp. 221–249. The construction of the basilica took forty years (it was finished in 1919) and the whole period was marked by tensions between supporters and opponents of its construction. Originally conceived as an atonement for the "national crimes" of the French people, it was also widely seen as the symbol of the alliance between Catholicism and reactionary monarchism. However, the space of the basilica was not only the site of the murder of generals Lecomte and Thomas at the hands of the Parisian crowds but also of the slaying of the socialist Eugene Varlin and the communards by the Versailles troops in 1872. Among the chapels in the crypt is one towards which the Catholic workers contributed; however, this chapel is exactly at the place of the execution of the leftist Varlin.

91 On the mix of political symbols in German territorial, state-national and regional loyalties see the description of the unveiling ceremony of the Hermann monument in Detmold (1875) in Tacke, 1995, pp. 216–229. On different readings of the Kandyan landscape in Sri Lanka see Duncan, 1999. Duncan points out that both "production" and "reading of landscapes" are political because they reflect the interests of different social groups. Consequently, there are many readings of the same landscape. Ibid., p. 182.

92 Mór Pisztóry noted that Pressburg was on the fifth place among Hungarian cities in number of inhabitants. However, in the areas of industry, trade and lively social life—it was the second city. Pisztóry, 1891, p. 128.

93 *Pozsony szabad királyi város törvényhatóságának a magyar országgyülés képviselőházához intézett emlékirata a Pozsonyban fölállitandó egyetem tárgyában* (Memorandum of the municipal assembly of Pozsony, royal free town, addressed to the house of the Hungarian parliament in the matter of the university), 1880. For the

genesis of this problem see Márkus, 1913, pp. 512–525.

94 Pávai Vajna, 1887, Pávai Vajna, 1884.

95 Schulpe, 1893.

96 *Pozsony szabad királyi város törvényhatoságának*, 1880.

97 There was another booklet published by *Toldy Kör* called ...*A Toldy Kör...a pozsonyi egyetemért*, 1918. This was a reprint from the *Nyugatmagyarországi Hiradó* from 1908.

98 Kumlik, 1905, p. 437.

99 Ibid., p. 433.

100 Tamás, 1938, pp. 10–11.

101 Pávai, 1887, p. 6: "...a nemzeti önállóság fenmaradása szempontjából életkérdés."

102 Ibid., p. 7: "rokonnyelvű testvérek"; " *idegen tudományos erőket és egyetemeket pedig már csak nemzeti szempontból sem szabad dédelgetni...*" (italics in original)

103 Ibid., p. 7: "A tudomány sem mindig *kozmopolitikus* jellegű, annak is megvan a maga *nemzeti iránya*, sőt meg is kell lennie a mi különleges viszonyaink közepette." (italics in original)

104 Ibid., p. 7: "idegen szellem."

105 Ibid., p. 16: "Az Alföld derék metropolisa főleg a magyar faji uralom megizmosodásának szempontjából óhajtja az egyetemet."

106 Ibid., p. 17: "... lakósainak a humanismus iránt kifejlett élénk és finom érzéke, a tudományosság, művelődés és művészet minden ágában tanusított meleg érdeklődése és műizlése, továbbá a társadalmi élet és érintkezés simasága...."

107 Ibid., 1887, pp. 17–21.

108 Schulpe, 1893, p. 5: "a Magyarország mostoha gyermeke"

109 Ibid., p. 17: "... a Magyarország nemzeti kultura egy védbástyája és világító tornya legyen."

110 Ibid., p. 21: "... hanem marad az a korlátlan törekvéseknek szabad versenytere."

111 Ibid., p. 21: "tiszta erkölcsiség."

112 *Pozsony szabad királyi város törvényhatoságának*, 1880, p. 11: "Pozsonyban bisztos kilátásunk lehet arra, miként egy ott fölállitandó egyetem tót maticát és német burschenschaftokat fog teremteni az egyetem hebelében." *Matica Slovenská*, the cultural institution for developing Slovak culture and society, and the German

Burschenschaften (student societies) were considered hotbeds of nationalist propaganda by conservative Hungarians. The Slovak periodical *Národnie Noviny* claimed that Pressburg was eventually chosen so as to counteract the attraction of the university in Brno where many Slovaks studied. It also said that the best thing would be to give a university to each nation and that the university in Pressburg would be Slovak anyway one day. *NN*, 2.5.1911, N.51, p. 1, "Tretia univerzita [The third university]."

113 *Pozsony szabad királyi város törvényhatoságának*, 1880, p. 19.

114 In 1883, the renowned historian and archaeologist Tivadar Ortvay published an article describing the enormous spiritual and intellectual potential of Pressburg. Ortvay argued that this potential needed to be propagated because nobody knew about it. Kumlik, 1905, pp. 132–137.

115 MTA, 334. parliamentary session, 29.5.1908, p. 282.

116 Ibid., p. 282. The whole line was to be 70.7 km long, of which only 7.5 km were on Hungarian territory. The cost of the construction of the Hungarian part was 1,440,000 crowns and the city of Pressburg had laid down a guarantee of 70,000 crowns. The railway was to have 18 stops, connecting Pressburg with small Austrian towns and villages (e.g., Hainburg, Petronell, Wolfsthal, Berg) and finally Vienna market hall. The whole journey took 2.5 hours because of the frequent stops. Ibid., p. 282; MTA, 442. parliamentary session, 19.3.1909, pp. 130–131; 1909: XIX. törvénycikk a pozsony-országhatárszéli helyi érdekű villamos vasut engedélyézéséről (Law XIX/1909 about permission of the Pozsony-country border electric railway of local importance), pp. 332–333.

117 Law XIX/1909, pp. 332–334, 340–341.

118 MTA, 442. parliamentary session, 19.3.1909, p. 130.

119 There were several booklets and reports written in Pressburg in support of the electric railway, listing all its advantages and denying the supposed dangers. Some of these (written by the members of the Commercial and Industrial Chamber) were used to counter-attack the report of the Economic Committee. See Wolff, G., 1903, Wolff, G., 1907, Wolff, G., without the year of publication.

120 Kmety presented himself as an expert on the situation in Pressburg since he had lived there and taught at the Law Academy for several years. During this time he was an active member of *Toldy Kör*.

121 The opponents of the project also used the economic argument that the electric railway would destroy Pressburg's industries which would be unable to compete with Vienna. The city of Budapest and the Industrial and Commercial Chamber of Budapest were convinced that the railway would even harm the industry and commerce of Budapest. They were greatly supported by the Budapest press. MTA, 443. parliamentary session, 22.3.1909, p. 143.

122 MTA, 442. parliamentary session, 19.3.1909, p. 132: "Ennek a vasutnak lelkes felkarolása csak arra lesz hivatva, hogy Pozsony kereskedelmét és iparát tönkre tegye, a drágaságot fokozza és a germán szellemet még nagyobb mértékben terjeszsze." 123 Ibid., p. 133: "A külföldi befojástól nagyon is féltem mind Pozsonyt, mind a magyar hazát és pedig azért, mert a magyar hősi, gavallér természeténél fogva gyorsan és könnyen simul az idegenhez, annak nyelvét és szokásait a saját magáéi rovására gyorsan sajátitja el."

124 Ibid., p. 138: "Budapest világváros, de képzeljük el, hogy egy órányi távolságban volna hozzá Bécs, vagy pláne Berlin vagy Páris, nem-e a népesség nagy része e nagyvárosok körében keresné gazdasági, szellemi, de talán politikai szükségletének kielégitését...." Also Law XIX/1909, pp. 334–340.

125 MTA, 443. parliamentary session, 22.3.1909, p. 152: "[H]ogy azok a helységek elvesztik társadalmi önállóságukat, individualitásukat, mert az a világváros mint egy nagy vámpir kiszivja ezeknek a vele összekapcsolt helységeknek életerejét és saját vérkeringésének alkatrészeivé teszi ezeknek az eddig külön vérkeringéssel biró városoknak a vérét."; "[M]ost megy végbe az a fiziológiai proczessus, hogy azok a Bécscsel vassinekkel sürűn összekapcsolt külön helységek lassanként áthasonulnak egy nagy Bécscsé, egy egységes, gazdaságilag, kulturailag, erkölcsi és politikai szellemben egységes vérkeringésű nagy Bécscsé."; "[E]gy magassab rendű lénynek valnak szerves alkatrészeivé."

126 Ibid., p.148:"Ezt a tervezett pozsony-bécsi vonalat a bécsiek úgy kezelik, mint a Gross-Wien, a jövendő Nagybécs szomszédos közuti vasuti hálozatához tartozót...Mindig ugy ir a bécsi sajtó Pozsonyról, hogy a szép német garnizon-város." The fear of Pressburg becoming part of greater Vienna was not completely unfounded. Otto Wagner, the leading Viennese architect, was convinced that "a modern economy made the infinite expansion of the city inevitable." In 1911, he worked out a modular plan for the expandible city. Schorske, 1992, pp. 96–100.

127 MTA, 443. parliamentary session, 22.3.1909, pp. 154–157.

128 MTA, 442. parliamentary session, 19.3.1909, p. 134–138. Nagy's ideas on the unstable nature of the Hungarian patriotism echoed Kmety's ideas: "That's how we stand with the question of patriotism,—and this is a very sad sign of the present times—that a person when going to bed in the evening does not know whether he will get up as a good patriot or a bad patriot." ("Ugy vagyunk különben a hazafiság kérdésével,—és ez nagyon szomorú jele az időknek—hogy az ember a mikor este lefekszik, nem tudja, hogy mint jó hazafi vagy mint rossz hazafi kel fel.") Ibid., p.138.

129 MTA, 443. parliamentary session, 22.3.1909, pp. 154–157. P. 155: "...hogy a gyűlolt Magyarország városában szerezze be ipari szükségletét, hanem elmegy szeretett császárvárosába és ott áldozza filléreit." There was in Hungary a patriotic movement which called for boycotting Austrian products and promotion of Hun-

garian products instead. However, this movement had very little success. See Holec, 1993, pp. 567–582.

130 During the debate Nagy even read parts of a pamphlet written by the eager Hungarian patriot and *Toldy Kör* member Gábor Pávai Vajna, the content of which ran along the same lines as *Toldy Kör*'s ideology. (MTA, 442. parliamentary session, 19.3.1909, pp. 132–134, p. 132: "hogy a magyarságot Pozsonyban teljesen megsemmisitse.") *Toldy Kör* and the *Nyugatmagyarországi Hiradó*, the local newspaper of the Pressburg's Magyar elite, opposed the railway because they feared the Germanising influence of Vienna. However, not all Magyars or even all *Toldy Kör* members opposed the railway. Sziklai himself was a member of *Toldy Kör*. In an article in the *Hiradó* Vutkovich even attacked Sziklai for defending the railway, because supposedly he was against it nine years ago. He demanded that Sziklai behaved as a proper "Magyar person" and as a member of *Toldy Kör*. He sarcastically wrote that despite 44 years of going to municipal meetings, Sziklai did not recognise how much German was spoken there even at present. Vutkovich accused Sziklai of being a "local patriot" and supporting "Kraxelhubers." In NH, 26.10.1910, N. 244, pp. 1–2, "Már megint kisért a pozsony-wieni villamos vasut [The Pozsony-Viennese electric railway haunts again]."

131 MTA, 442. parliamentary session, 19.3.1909, p. 133.

132 MTA, 443. parliamentary session, 22.3.1909, pp. 147–148. This point must have seemed particularly important to Kmety since he was a teacher at Pressburg's Law Academy and a member of *Toldy Kör* when the association was fighting for the consolidation of the Hungarian theatre in Pressburg. Kmety reflected on this in his speech when he pointed out that Sziklai and he had "for one decade shoulder to shoulder had the pleasure to work together so that the matter of the Hungarian language and especially of the Hungarian theatre in Pozsony progressed somewhat." (MTA, 443. parliamentary session, 22.3.1909, p. 147.) Thus the prospect of Pressburg's inhabitants attending theatre performances in Vienna when the performances in Pressburg would be Hungarian must have seemed particularly threatening since it meant that Pressburg's inhabitants actually managed to escape the Magyarisation efforts.

133 MTA, 442. parliamentary session, 19.3.1909, p. 138: "... Pozsony közvéleményében még ma is érvényesülnek oly felfogások, melyek a magyar kulturát kicsinylik, melyek,—mint egy ott megjelenő német lap—képtelenek annak felismerésére, hogy minden nemzetre nézve csak a saját kulturája bir értekkel, a kölcsönvett kultura pedig csak külső máz, megakadályozza annak felismerésében, hogy a magyar kultura minden téren olyan alkotásokat mutat, melyek a népesség nagy összességének az élet egy magasabb fokára való emelésére teljesen elegendők." Also Law XIX/1909, pp. 334–340.

At this time Pressburg served as a Viennese "theatre suburb" (and the Viennese have again recently re-discovered Bratislava's theatre). The German theatre director

Paul Blasel regularly invited Viennese ensembles to play in Pressburg (between 1903 and 1919). Blasel organised a theatre festival (the so-called *Juni-Künstlerspiele* [June art festival]) at which Viennese theatre ensembles performed. Pressburg prided itself on being more liberal than Vienna: plays which were banned in Vienna could be performed in the Pressburg theatre (for example, Hauptmann's 'Wavers' [*Die Weber*]). The *Pressburger Zeitung* claimed that this performance was attended by three steamship-loads of Viennese theatre-goers. Similarly, in 1913, Arthur Schnitzler's play "Professor Bernardi" was banned in Vienna and was to have been performed in Pressburg. (The play was attacked as anti-religious, and the whole attack had an anti-Semitic character.) However, at the last moment, the Pressburg's City Theatre Committee banned the performance. Schnitzler referred in his diary to "strings between Vienna and Pressburg." Grusková, 1999, pp. 102–108.

134 By associating census statistics showing the number of Magyars in Pressburg with the *Hiradó*' s strong propaganda against the railway, Kmety gave the impression that all Pressburg Magyars were against the electric railway. Thus he divided the reading communities in Pressburg according to their language of use by drawing on the census data on ethnicity (mother tongue). In fact, the other two Pressburg deputies, Marcel Jankovics and Aurél von Bartal, were both Magyars who supported the project. (MTA, 443. parliamentary session, 22.3.1909, p. 158.) According to census data there were 18,744 inhabitants of Magyar mother tongue in 1900. See Chapter two.

135 MTA, 443. parliamentary session, pp. 156–158.

136 According to the statistics put forward by the Economic Committee, only one third of the non-Hungarian population in Pressburg knew Hungarian (33.1%) as compared to Sopron (39.7%), Temesvár (47.7%) and Buda (49.0%). Law XIX/1909, p. 337: "Ilyen tény az, hogy Pozsony a nagyobb és régebben német jellegű városok között az, melyben a nem magyar ajku népesség között a magyar nyelv leggyengébben van képviselve."

137 Ibid.: "A magyarság oly nehéz küzdelmet folytat, oly versenynek van kitéve mindenütt oly nemzetekkel szemben, a melyek maholnap száz millióra látják népességük számát szaporodni, vagy e számot már elérték, hogy nekünk nemzeti mérleg minden decigrammját is számon kell tartani....Ilyen körülmények között nagy fontogsággal bir az, hogy az országnak egy ilyen tekintélyes városában, mint Pozsonyban, oly forgalmi intézményt létesittetik, mely a nemzeti erő működését semmi esetre sem fokozza és mely azt a nehéz küzdelmet, melyet a pozsonyi magyarság a nemzeti eszme érdekében folytat, megnehezíti." It was quite typical for European states around the *fin-de-siecle* to worry about the size of their population since this was an indicator of power. In France, for instance, there were worries that the size of the population, "always a crucial sign of national well-being" was stagnating. Heffernan, 1998, p. 53.

138 In Pressburg, 45.4% of inhabitants worked in industry and trade while in

Fiume 46.8%, in Győr 47.1%, Budapest 53.7%. Pressburg had only 51 enterprises with more than 20 employees, and of these out of 250 management personnel only 104 were of Magyar mother tongue, and from the auxiliary personnel from 2,531 only 784 were of Magyar mother tongue. Law XIX/1909, p. 336.

139 Ibid., p. 338. Until then, the Magyars in Pressburg could strengthen and gain numerical strength also among the lower classes. It should be noted that the Economic Committee rejected the project by just one vote.

140 Ibid., p. 336.

141 MTA, 442. parliamentary session, 19.3.1909, p. 138: "A vasutak központositó és asszimiláló hatása a politikai alakzatokban is visszatükröződik." Also report of the Economic Committee in Law XIX/1909, pp. 334–340.

142 MTA, 442. parliamentary session, 19.3.1909, pp. 140–141, p. 140: "…hogy forgalmi téren is képzelhető egy pont, melyen már a hypertrophia kóros tünetei észlelhetők, a hol a forgalom ideges betegséget és fontos érdekek koczkáztatását, fölösleges költekezést idézhet elő." Law XIX/1909, pp. 334–340.

143 Law XIX/1909, p. 339: "Hogy kereskedelmünk nagyszerű, szilárd s virágzó legyen, különböző ágainak egy helyen, mint a vérnek a szivben kell összpontosulni s az ország törvényes önállásának és függetlenségének tekintete kivánja, hogy a kereskedés gyülpontja benn a hazában legyen…hazánkban ily helyül sz. k. Pest városát jelölték ki."

144 Ibid., pp. 338–339.

145 MTA, 442. parliamentary session, 19.3.1909, p. 137: "Ha a pozsonyiak igazán szivben, lélekben, nyelvben magyarok akarnak lenni, kérjenek egy villamos vasutat, a mely a Pesttel köti őket össze."

146 Ibid., p. 133: "…hogy Pozsony az ország szive felé gravitáljon. De, kérem, nem Osztrákország, hanem Magyarország szive felé. Onnan nyerje a felvirágozásához szükséges éltető meleget és hogy ne legyen Wien külvárosa, s végül, hogy Wien ne zsarolja ki e fényes multú és a jövőben nagy szerepre hivatott város becsületes, munkás polgárságát."

147 Ibid., p. 136.

148 Law XIX/1909, p. 338.

149 MTA, 443. parliamentary session, 22.3.1909, p. 147: "…Nyugatmagyarország nemzeti fővárosának szerepére van hivatva, a védbástya szerepére a Bécs felől hóditó utra kelő ellenséges germán szellem ellen…hivatva van arra is, hogy Nyugatmagyarországnak gazdasági empóriuma legyen, ipar- és kereskedelmi góczpontja."

150 MTA, 444. parliamentary session, 23.3.1909, pp. 169–170.

151 MTA, 444. parliamentary session, 23.3.1909, p. 175. The contract secured the same conditions for both the Hungarian and Austrian parts of the railway. (442. parliamentary session, p. 131.) The Hungarian part stretched from Pressburg to Hainburg at the Austrian border and the Austrian part was between Hainburg and Vienna. The railway was to be connected in Ligetfalu to other Hungarian railways, thus even in the case of higher Austrian railway tariffs (which were a possible consequence of the planned privatisation of the Austrian railway), the Hungarian side would not be affected. A similar argument also in the minister's of commerce report, in Law XIX/1909, pp. 332–333.

152 MTA, 334. parliamentary session, 29.5.1908, p. 282, 443. parliamentary session, pp. 143–145. The electric train was also much slower, taking 2.5 hours to get to Vienna while the regular train took only 1.5 hours. MTA, 443. parliamentary session, 22.3.1909, pp. 144–145.

153 MTA, 334. parliamentary session, 29.5.1908, p. 283.

154 MTA, 444. parliamentary session, 23.3.1909, pp. 171–172, p. 172: "[mert] Pozsony város közönsége és hatósága minden időbe tudta, mivel tartozik az országnak, hazának....Azért, hogy Pozsony város lakosságának egy része német anyanyelvű, nincs jogunk erről a lakosságról feltételezni azt, hogy kevésbé volnának hazafiak, mint mi, a kik magyar anyanyelvűek vagyunk."

155 This was stressed by Szterényi and also by Batthányi and Sziklai: "It is true that that one who does not know Hungarian has the right to speak German but one cannot insult anyone; he who does not speak Hungarian shall speak German; the new generation will be Hungarian anyway." MTA, 443. parliamentary session, 22.3.1909, p. 145, Batthyányi and Szterényi in MTA, 444. parliamentary session, 23.3.1909, pp. 169,172.

156 MTA, 444. parliamentary session, 23.3.1909, p. 173.

157 Ibid., pp. 173–175. Between 1904–6 the transport of persons between Pressburg and Vienna grew by 8.5% while transport between Pressburg and Budapest grew by 16.8%. Every year around 50–55,000 Austrian tourists came to Pressburg. (Ibid., pp. 174–175.) The transport of goods between Pressburg and Vienna grew by 11.8% and between Pressburg and Budapest by 20.5%. In absolute numbers though the transport between Pressburg-Vienna was larger than that of Pressburg-Budapest. (Ibid., p. 174.) The yearly number of letters from Pressburg to Vienna and Budapest in the last year (1908) was as follows. Pressburg to Vienna 2,700,000 and Pressburg to Budapest 3,100,000. There were 1,000,000 letters from Vienna to Pressburg and 1,300,000 from Budapest to Pressburg. These numbers did not include official correspondence. Ibid., p. 174.

158 MTA, 334. parliamentary session, 29.5.1908, p. 283: "Vagy azt kivánják, hogy Budapestre jőjjenek a bécsiek nagy tömegekben? Igy nem rontják a fővárosi ugy is rengeteg sok kozmopolitáját, mert itt több van ilyen mint Pozsonyban." Vienna was

seen as a cosmopolitan place despite "political extremism, social problems and the rise of political mass movements." Stefan Zweig in his study of Vienna around 1900 wrote that "every inhabitant of this city was unwittingly brought up as supranationalist, cosmopolitan citizen of the world." (Becker et al, 1999, pp. 9–10.) No wonder Magyar nationalists were worried about Pressburg 'catching' cosmopolitanism as a disease from the Viennese. On cosmopolitanism and its rejection in France between 1789 and 1794 see Guiraudon, 1991, pp. 591–604. The Revolutionary Committee of the Section of the Armed Man in Paris defined a cosmopolitan as "a man, strictly speaking, without a country, unable to identify himself with any government" on the grounds that a cosmopolitan cannot be recognised as a citizen of any country since the government of a country is the expression of the general will. Ibid., p. 596.

159 MTA, 443. parliamentary session , 22.3.1909, p. 145.

160 Ibid., p. 146.

161 MTA, 444. parliamentary session, 23.3.1909, pp. 170–171.

162 MTA, 445. parliamentary session, 24.3.1909, p. 189, 450. parliamentary session, 15.4.1909, p. 302, 453. parliamentary session, 10.7.1909, p. 325.

163 Dvořák, 1995, pp. 450–451.

164 "The Slovak intelligentsia always tried to determine and keep in mind the borders of the territory with the Slovak majority. However, the differences between ethnic 'Slovakia' and the geographical-historical Upper Hungary or 'historical Slovakia' which was created by the Slovak 'national revivalists' with a generous spatiality, always had a disturbing effect on the self-perception of Slovaks." Szarka, 1999, p. 158.

165 Purcell, 1998, p. 433, (italics in original). "National territory is socially constructed, and as such it is contested among those with different ideas of the nation and its territory."

166 Slovak territory within Hungary would have been composed of sixteen counties of which seven had a Slovak majority (Trencsén, Árva, Turóc, Zólyom, Liptó, Szepes and Sáros) and another nine counties that had a Slovak majority living on the territory above the Slovak-Magyar linguistic border (Pozsony, Nyitra, Bars, Hont, Nógrád, Gömör és Kis-Hont, Abaúj-Torna, Zemplén, and Ung). Szarka, 1999, p. 183. (See Figure 17.)

167 Bokeš, 1945, p. 8.

168 According to Bokeš the name *Slovensko* (Slovakia) was used for the first time in 1809 in Josef Dobrovský's linguistic work *Lehrgebäude*. It was used again in 1842 in the letter of Pavol Jozeffy (1775–1848), the leader of the delegation to the Emperor Ferdinand. Jozef Miloslav Hurban (1817–1888) used it repeatedly in his writing (1842, 1847). (Ibid., p. 15, footnote 7.) In the period before the mid-sixteenth century and from the eighteenth century until 1918, 'Upper Hungary' included all the areas

north of the rivers Danube and Tisza. This area, therefore, included the territory of present-day Slovakia but was larger. The 'Lower Hungary' included the southern part of Hungary. In the period of occupation of Hungary by the Turks (from the mid-sixteenth century until the end of the seventeenth century) 'Upper Hungary' included eastern and north-eastern part of Hungary and the 'Lower Hungary' included western and north-western territories of Hungary. Žudeľ, 1980, p. 151.

169 When defining the Slovak territory, two approaches were used: the historical one going back to the time of the Great Moravian kingdom and the ethnic, trying to define which were the Slovak counties. However, the ethnic or ethnographic approach prevailed. Ibid., pp. 9–11. On the Great-Moravian tradition see Tibenský, 1972, pp. 69–95 and Butvín, 1972, pp. 96–118.

170 In 1829 Ján Čaplovič produced a nationalities' map of Hungary. In 1830 and 1838 József Aszalay published a map which covered the topographic, ecclesiastic and ethnographic characteristics of the Hungarian kingdom. In his *Slovanský národopis* (Slovak ethnography) published in 1842, Pavol Jozef Šafárik defined the borders of the Slovak territory according to the Slovak dialects. (See Klimko, 1980, p. 62.) Šafárik even estimated the total number of Slovaks as 2.75 million, including 800,000 Evangelicals and 1.95 million Catholics in Austria (probably meaning the whole Habsburg Monarchy.) Bokeš, 1945, p. 15.

171 See "Žiadosti slovenského národa z 10.5.1848 zostaveného v L. S. Mikuláši [Requirements of the Slovak nation from 10.5.1848 composed in L. S. Mikuláš]" in Chovanec, Mozolík, 1994, pp. 72–75.

172 Bokeš, 1945, p. 20.

173 Rosenfeld also noted that "a wise internal administration of the Slovak territory could govern over fates of Slovaks among whom the consciousness of otherness has not been awoken yet." (Ibid., pp. 20–21.) This seemed to have been a general view among the Austrian government officials. In 1848 Windischgrätz divided Hungary into military districts on a geographical basis and noted that military districts would be divided according to nationalities only after Slovaks had reached a stage of development like the Croats and Serbs which made it necessary to differentiate them from Hungarians. Otherwise one faced the threat of a general uprising. Ibid., p. 17. I use Slovak geographical names in Part 6 since this is how they appeared in the discussions of the Slovak intelligentsia.

174 Ibid., pp. 23–24. I use 'Slovak intelligentsia', although Bokeš writes that "Slovaks demanded…" However, this generalisation does not seem justified since it was the Slovak intelligentsia who put together these petitions and who claimed to speak in the name of all Slovaks.

175 Ibid., pp. 26–27.

176 There was, however, some popular support already for the Slovak national

movement: one petition called 'Promemoria' was signed by 30.000 inhabitants of Slovakia. Ibid., p. 28.

177 Ján Kollár was the main representative of the second wave of the Slovak national revival (See Chapter two). During the era of neo-absolutism of Bach (1849–1859) he became the advisor of the Viennese court on the Slovak matters. Kováč, 1998, p. 122.

178 However, it was impossible to divide Hungary strictly according to the nationalities' principle because of the extent of ethnic intermingling. (Klimko, 1980, pp. 67–68.) Two districts in Slovakia (Prešporok and Košice), had southern borders that were consistent with the "natural and historic borders of Slovakia in the mountain range Matra." Bokeš, 1945, p. 33.

179 Bokeš, 1945, pp. 38–39.

180 There was co-operation between the Serbian, Rumanian and Slovak national parties in the 1860s when these three parties tried to co-ordinate their programs for territorial autonomy (unsuccessfully until 1918). The most important demand made in the political programs of these nationalities was for territorial autonomy. These three parties also co-operated closely later despite their political passivity. Their most effective co-ordinated event was the Congress of nationalities in Budapest in 1895 which protested against the representation of the multinational Hungarian state as a state of one nation. The nationalities claimed that "the right to identify with the state has only the whole of the nations of Hungary." After emerging from the period of political passivity, the elected members of these three nationalities created the Nationalities' parliamentary club in the Hungarian parliament (1905–1914). Szarka, 1999, pp. 166, 172–173.

181 Bokeš, 1945, pp. 39–40, Klimko, 1980, pp. 68–70. See also "Memorandum národa slovenského prijaté v Turčianskom Svätom Martine dňa 7.6.1861 [Memorandum of the Slovak nation accepted in T. S. Martin on 7.6.1861]" in Chovanec, Mozolík, 1994, pp. 79–87. On the spatial conflict between the Copts and Islamists in Egypt see Purcell, 1998, pp. 432–451. Here also, these two groups came into conflict "because they attempted to realize their imaginations in the same physical space." (Ibid., p. 444.) Hungarian authorities could not allow another territorial imagination to disrupt their imagination of the Hungarian state. As the militant Islamists think that "[o]nly a pure and unified Muslim territory can stand against the hostile forces of the Christian West" (Ibid., p. 441), similarly the Hungarian nationalists thought that only a unified national territory, territory having one unitary Hungarian (or rather Magyar) nation would be able to hold its place in the competition with other nation-states and in its fight with Vienna for independence. Slovaks were not allowed to build monuments of their own national heroes in public spaces or name the streets after them since this would have "polluted" the Hungarian national space.

182 Slovak nationalists had difficulty overcoming the perceived lack of a legitimising national history such as, for instance, evidence of a medieval Slovak state.

The Slovak newspaper *Národnie Noviny* printed in Martin claimed that the Upper-Hungarian Slovak environs was necessary in order to establish the separateness of the Slovak nation on the territory which had long since been the Slovak homeland.. Slovak nationalists claimed that the national existence of Slovaks could not be secured without this territory. Szarka, 1999, p. 207.

183 Bokeš, 1945, pp. 40–45.

184 Ibid., p. 46, Bokeš, 1942. However, Dionýz Štúr's geographical work *Slovenské okolie* (Slovak Environs) was a popular rather than a scientific work. When *Matica Slovenská* was later founded, it attempted to publish Štúr's map of the *Slovenské okolie*. Due to financial difficulties and changed political conditions after 1867, this plan did not materialise.

185 In 1850 the leader of the Hungarian revolution Lajos Kossuth together with Count László Teleki as representatives of the Hungarian revolutionary party abroad proposed the federalisation of Hungary and its division on the nationalities' principle which would have meant a separate Slovak territory. Bokeš, 1945, pp. 28–29, footnote 32.

186 Klimko, 1980, pp. 72–73, Bokeš, 1945, pp. 49–52.

187 Bokeš, 1945, p. 51, footnote 53.

188 Ibid., p. 102.

189 Ibid., p. 52.

190 Ibid.

191 Ibid., p. 61. This reform abolished twenty free royal towns, leaving only Pressburg and Kassa.

192 This demand was also made by the Nationalities' congress in Budapest in August 1895. Ibid., p. 63, part of the resolution of the congress pp. 137–138. This congress took place in protest against the Millennial celebrations of the Hungarian state and stressed that the Hungarian state in all its past had been made up of many nationalities and thus it could not be appropriated by only one (the Magyars) who were not even a majority. See also Komora, 1996. At the beginning of the twentieth century the Slovaks dropped this demand and instead asked for administrative reforms in the territories inhabited by the Slovak nationality. Bokeš, 1945, pp. 64–65.

193 This method developed by the Hungarian statistician Károly Keleti had two counties that included the Slovak territory but there were also extensive Hungarian counties stretching into what was considered Slovak territory. This division was used until 1918 which shows the power of statistics in creating new categories, whether ethnic or territorial. Ibid., pp. 64–65.

194 Ibid., p. 64. Vavro Šrobár (1867–1950) was one of the representatives of the

"Czechoslovak" orientation in Slovakia. He was influenced by the ideas of T. G. Masaryk. *Slovenský biografický slovník*, 1992, pp. 499–500.

195 Quoted in Buček, 1995, p. 197: "Z tohoto rozkúskovania vyplýva i to, že obyvateľstvo jednej stolice, majúc na mysli záujem svojho úzkeho kraja, často zabúda na záujem všeobecný, všenárodný a tak ono bolo príčinou neraz škodlivého a prehnaného lokálneho (stoličného) patriotizmu." On importance of regionalism in Slovakia see Mannová, 1997a, pp. 11–18.

196 Hohenberg, Lees, 1985, p. 217.

197 Butvín, 1973, p. 533.

198 Ibid., p. 537.

199 Ibid., 534–563. About the Slovak national revival see Brock, 1976.

200 Butvín, 1973, p. 559.

201 Ibid., pp. 554–555: "mohila rodu slovenskjeho."

202 Ibid., p. 561.

203 Buček, 1995, p. 195.

204 Butvín, 1973, pp. 548–549.

205 In 1846, Palacký criticised the Slovak movement for not coming together around one language for Czechs, Moravians and Slovaks and noted that the absence of a 'national centre' hindered the development of the national movement and the spreading of national consciousness. However, Štúr believed that the Slovak nation first had to be united in its own language which he called "the symbol of national unity." Ibid., pp. 549–552.

206 "Keby sme i z ohľadu národnieho to, čo nám je nevyhnutne potrebnô, boli dostali, to by sme už mohli byť úplne slobodní a spokojní. A ľahko by sme aj boli dostali, keby sme k tomu boli pripravení bývali a keby sme mali už jedno vzdelanô centrálnô mesto.... Keby sme mali jedno centrálnô mesto, v ktorom by bolo veľa vzdelaných a ochotných mešťanov, mysliacich dobre s nami a národom našim.... Paríž Francúzom, Berlín Prušiakom, Viedeň Rakúšanom, Lipsko a Drážďany Sasom, Mníchov Bavorčanom pomohli, my ale ani len ešte malieho vzoru z týchto veľkých miest nemáme." Štúr quoted in Buček, 1995, p. 193.

207 Butvin, 1973, pp. 555–559.

208 Ibid., p. 559. Ján Kollár's proposal from 1849 considered the towns Nitra or Banská Bystrica as potential centres for Slovak education. As an ethnically mixed city, Pressburg did not figure as a centre of any Slovak institutions. See Buček, 1995, p. 193.

209 Butvín, 1973, p. 562. František Hanrich became the general prosecutor of

the royal law court in Pressburg. After the end of his term as a Slovak adviser to the Viennese government in 1850; he proposed the division of the Slovak territory into three language areas.

210 "[U] nás Matica ve smyslu Čechu, Srbu a Chorvátu povstati naskrze nemůže…, protože my nemáme ani žádneho centrálniho města, jako Češi a Chorváti, ani s národem se stotožňující a představující ho hierarchii, jako Srbi." Ibid., p. 562.

211 Ibid., p. 562.

212 Ibid., p. 563. Also in the second request for the permit of *Matica* at the end of 1851 Kollár's group proposed Banská Bystrica as its seat. Ibid., pp. 564–565.

213 Ibid., pp. 564–565.

214 On the difficulties in finding a proper Slovak centre see also Holec, 1997b, especially pp. 198–199.

215 Butvín, 1973, pp. 565–569.

216 Buček, 1995, p. 194, Butvín, 1973, pp. 567–568.

217 Butvín, 1973, pp. 565–570.

218 Ibid., p. 569: "… v národnom povedomí relatívne najvyrovnanejšie meštianstvo Martina…."

219 Ibid., p. 569.

220 The *Stály slovenský národný výbor* (Standing Slovak national committee), which was to be "the only institution with national responsibilities [jediný národný úrad, ktorého vlastným a prísnym povolaním bolo by zodpovedne pracovať na roli národa]," did not manage to turn Martin into a national centre. The committee later broke up. After 1867, the Slovak national politics split into *Stará* and *Nová Škola* with different ideas about the direction of national politics and newspapers. Ibid., pp. 569–571.

221 In 1868, the *Sporiteľňa* (Savings bank) was founded, in 1869 *Kníhtlačiarsky účastinársky spolok*—the Slovak national book-printing association and *Živena*— the association of Slovak women and the *Slovenský spevokol* (Slovak choir). In 1870, the newspaper *Pešťbudínske vedomosti* was moved from Buda to Martin under the name *Národnie Noviny*.

222 Butvín, 1973, pp. 571–572. However, as the Slovak workers' press pointed out, these celebrations were occasions for the intelligentsia to get together rather than really representative assemblies of the Slovak 'people.' During these celebrations the Slovak national intelligentsia presented an illusion of a united Slovak nation which did not exist in reality. (See Chapter three, Part 5.) *RN*, 10.8.1911, N. 32, pp. 1–2, "K martinským slávnostiam [To the celebrations in Martin]," *RN* 1.8.1912, N. 31, p. 1,

"Martinské národné slávnosti [National celebrations in Martin]."

223 Butvín, 1973, p. 572: "... stredovište národnej kultúry..., centrum, akého sme dosial' vcele postrádať museli a bez akého žiaden národ nie je a ani náš byť nemá a nemôže."

224 Buček, 1995, pp. 194–195.

225 Ibid., pp. 196–197.

226 Ibid., p. 197.

227 Czechoslovakia was in a better position at the peace talks than Hungary, and stressed the importance for Czechoslovakia of this economic-administrative centre and of access to the Danube and thus to the Balkans. Buček, 1995, pp. 167–168.

228 Ibid., pp. 197–198.

229 Vavro Šrobár quoted in ibid., p. 198: "vzniklo podozrenie, že Československá republika nehodlá trvale obsadiť mesto Prešporok, ktoré by sa stalo znovu sídlom agitácie proti našej republike a ohrozovalo by bandami najbohatšiu časť Slovenska."

230 Horváth, Rákoš and Watzka, 1977, pp. 250–251. There were 2000 Sokols in folk-costumes coming from Prague. (Document 118, p. 250.) For the program of the festive welcoming of the representatives of the Czechoslovak government in Pressburg see document 108, pp. 237–238.

231 Ruppeldt, 1927, pp. 74–75:"už i len pre svoju polohu na najkrajnejšej periférii Slovenska, v bezprostrednej blízkosti dvoch nám rasove cudzích národov (a najmä na juhu vždy nepriateľského) ... vždy bolo a bude akýmsi špeciálne obchodným a tak i kozmopolitným mestom." The geographer Ján Hromádka's description of the "metropolis" (when writing about Bratislava's transformation into a metropolis between 1920 and 1930) is reminiscent of the arguments of the Hungarian nationalists in the Hungarian parliament describing Vienna as a vampire: "Metropolis is a parasite which empties the countryside of people, which takes advantage of it economically so that it can create new values both material and spiritual, good and bad and with this values it [metropolis] feeds again the countryside." ("Veľkomesto je parazit, ktorý odľudňuje vidiek, koristí z neho hospodársky, aby tvorilo nové hodnoty hmotné i duševné, dobré i plané, a nimi napájalo zase vidiek.") (Hromádka, 1933, p. 56.) The idea of the city as a parasite is present also in the work of the Slovak writer Štefan Gráf. See Minár, 1997, p. 130.

232 Ibid., 1927, p. 72: "[srdce národa], ktoré by bolo hrdosťou, radosťou a oporou Slovákov, ktoré by priťahovalo všetkých, imponovalo by všetkým, ktoré by bolo v ústredí a mohlo by byť *srdcom národa, tak, ako je a musí byť srdce v každom živom organizme.*" (Italics in original.) Fedor Ruppeldt (1886–1979) was a Slovak national activist, Evangelic bishop, writer, translator, politician.

233 Ibid., pp. 76–77. Bratislava was seen inappropriate as a capital despite the active support of Slovakisation of the city by the authorities and the increasing number of Slovak intelligentsia residing there. See Minár, 1997, pp. 134–135 on Slovakisation of Bratislava.

234 Ruppeldt, 1927, pp. 70–86.

CHAPTER 5
Surveillance in Pressburg

1 Foucault, 1977, p. 194.

2 As I have explained in Chapter four, footnote 21, the Hungarian state authorities used the word *nemzetiségi* which in English translation means "that of various nationalities living in Hungary" or "nationalities'" as an adjective rather than 'nationalist.' I retained the use of "nationalities'" in most cases, changing it to "nationalist" where it seems appropriate. As Szarka points out, Hungarian historiography also uses the term 'nationality' to denote the other ethnic groups living on the territory of Hungary in the period 1867–1918. Lajos Kossuth put it this way: "Nation is the state itself; nationality is in the state." ("A nemzet az állam maga; a nemzetiség az államban van.") Thus all citizens living in Hungary created the Hungarian nation which was within the state divided into different nationalities with their own cultures and languages. See Szarka, 1999, p. 157, footnote 2.

3 Gerő, 1995, p. 171.

4 Ibid., p. 190.

5 See Chapter two, footnotes 7 and 285 on the discussion of the 1868 Nationalities Law.

6 Gerő, 1995, pp. 109–144.

7 According to Gerő, Hungarian liberalism was a combination of French (strong anti-absolutist thrust), English (dominated by utilitarianism) and German (liberalism in order to improve the conditions of the nation) liberalisms. (Gerő, 1993, pp. 73–75.) The compromise in 1867 strengthened the utilitarian trend within Hungarian liberalism. This was caused also by the fact that the "politically minded nobility consisted almost exclusively of law graduates." Ibid., pp. 72, 89.

8 Ibid., p. 128.

9 Ibid., p. 170.

10 Foucault, 1986, p. 151. See also Kearns, Unpublished article, 1997, Section "Governmentality and subjectivation."

11 A fundamental principle denoting the state is its territoriality characterised by "the attempt by an individual or groups (x) to influence, affect or control objects, people and relationships (y) by delimiting and asserting control over a geographic area." R. Sack quoted in Johnston, Knight and Kofman, 1988, p. 5.

12 See Foucault, 1988b, on the development of a new political rationality from the end of the eighteenth century when the state increasingly intervenes in the lives of individuals using new political technology. The emergence of the social sciences is connected to this new political rationality.

13 See historical chronology in Hanák et al, 1978, pp. 1233–1281, Kovács et al, 1979, pp. 1510–1541. According to Lipták, although not the only source of knowledge, unified Germany was an inspiration to the Hungarian government, nevertheless. Initiatives like "Kulturkampf, fight against socialists, social reforms initiated from above, universal military service, organisation of railways, school reforms, universal suffrage" were well known and many were copied either indirectly from Austria, or directly from Germany. Lipták, 1999, p. 14.

14 Foucault, 1986, p. 150. Foucault talks about "biopower" as a specific state technology which is concerned with managing populations in both urban and rural spaces. In Kearns, Unpublished paper, 1997, Section "Governmentality and subjectivation."

15 Law XXV/1974 on the organisation of the national statistics. Kovács et al, 1979, p. 1524. On the development of statistics in Habsburg Monarchy and Hungary see Mésároš, 1995.

16 Taylor, 1997, p. 18.

17 "State building not only made the national government a target for citizens' claim; it led to broader framing of citizen actions. The standardisation of taxation, of administrative regulations and of census categories encouraged formation of groups which had been previously opposed or indifferent to one another's existence."Tarrow, 1994, pp. 72–73.

18 At the beginning of the seventeenth century in France, various theories held that the central government should think of the territory of the state on the model of a city. Many projects developed "on the premise that a state is like a large city; the capital is like its main square, the roads are like its streets. A state will be well organized when a system of policing as tight and efficient as that of the cities extends over the entire territory." Foucault, 1984, p. 241.

19 The *főispán* was the main representative of the state in the county, and its head. He was appointed by the minister of interior and approved by the emperor. His deputy was elected by the county municipal assembly and organised the actual work and agenda of the county office. The *főispán* therefore had the responsibility of protecting the interests of the government and keeping an eye on potential dangers to the state in his area of jurisdiction. About the legal organisation of the counties and

municipal towns see Lehotská, 1973, Horváth, 1998.

20 Szarka, 1999, pp. 176, 225–231. On the difference between nationalism of gentry and nationalism of the middle-class clerk see Glatz, 1995b, pp. 39–42. On middle-class mentality see Gyányi, Kövér, 1998, pp. 148–153.

21 For example see the correspondence of G. Pávai Vajna to Kálmán Thály. (Thály was a member of the parliament and an influential man.) It is obvious from these letters that Pávai Vajna is competing with other "Hungarian patriots" for a position since he describes why he is better than the others. So on one level, as a member of *Toldy Kör* within the city of Pressburg Pávai claims to be just carrying out the policies of the Hungarian state and talks constantly about Hungarian patriotism. However, when the position of the director of the hospital is involved, he is just pursuing his self-interest and even criticises how the Hungarian patriotism is just an empty phrase not being carried into practical life by anyone (after his efforts to be appointed a teaching position at the Law Academy are unsuccessful). Thály's correspondence includes more letters from different members of *Toldy Kör* who in their letters are pursuing their own interests and usually asking for help in getting appointed to a certain position. MOL, P1747—Thály Kálmán, letters of 17.12.1891, 9.3.1900, 28.11.1900, 22.10.1902.

22 The strike in the Kühmayer factory in Pressburg lasted from 17.4.-14.5.1906 and there were 262 striking workers. The strike ended (strikers' conditions were refused by the employer) because workers were threatened with eviction from factory housing and dismissal from their work. (Písch, 1966, p. 70.) Such threats were quite common during these conflicts. See Joyce, 1991, p. 27.

23 Most of the papers of this agenda are now deposited in the Hungarian National Archive (Magyar Országos Levéltár). I have checked sections 1, 2 and 6 of the agenda for every year until 1918. The first section is called 'Workers and poor peasants' movement, international workers' movement, anarchist movement'; the second section is called 'Nationalities and matters concerning the neighbouring countries (irredenta), Pan-Slav and Pan-German movement, matters concerning the German minority'; and the sixth section is called 'political movements, matters of elections and gatherings; movements of university students during the dualism period; anti-Semitic occurrences, movements; applications for selling of land; masonic matters.' The first report about monitoring the workers' movement in Pressburg is from 1877. Lehotská et al, 1952, p. 101.

24 The main points were: the influence of nationalities on the religious situation in Upper Hungary, the attitude of regional officials, the financial institutions of nationalities, elementary schools, nationalities' press and associations. The *főispán* of Pressburg, Count József Zichy, was appointed the government's representative for Upper Hungary and he was commissioned to work out a complex system of policies including Hungarian kindergartens, surveillance of the priests who disrupted the

nationalising policies of the state by their activities, inspection of the books of the Slovak church owned schools. Szarka, 1999, pp. 232, 234.

25 Száz, 1995, p. 30.

26 Lehotský, 1970, p. 267.

27 Szarka, 1999, pp. 235–246. Reports about nationalities were worked out by the municipal county committees and *főispáns*. These reports are available in the MOL in a special section. See ibid., p. 237, footnote 57.

28 Ibid., p. 245.

29 For e.g. MOL, K149–1882–1: "Allgemeine Übersicht über die Lage der sozialdemokratischen und revolutionären Bewegung [General overview of the state of the social democratic and revolutionary movement]" from the Viennese police director board; K149–1890–1: "Die sozial-demokratische und anarchistische Bewegung im Jahre 1889 [The social democratic and anarchist movement in 1889]" from Vienna and "Übersicht über die allgemeine Lage der sozialdemokratischen und revolutionären Bewegung [Overview of the general situation in the social democratic and revolutionary movement]" from Berlin.

30 As has been mentioned earlier, these reports became regular and obligatory under the government of Dezső Bánffy.

31 Lehotský, 1970, p. 270.

32 Although in 1900 Prime Minister Kálmán Széll dissolved the "nationalities' department" (nemzetiségi ügyosztály) set up by Bánffy, socialist and nationalities' movements were still closely watched as materials in the agenda of the Ministry of Interior show. (Kemény, 1964, p. vii.) Even when in 1905 the Minister of Interior József Kristóffy ended the so-called "police supervision" of the SPDH, still the Decree 128/1868 of the Ministry of Interior which stipulated that a representative of the authorities be present at every public meeting and dissolved it if the order was disturbed remained valid. (Tajták, 1981, p. 821, Tajták, 1995, p. 740.) The following Hungarian governments tried to stop all the processes with nationalities and to take a more reconciliatory attitude (except the coalition government between 1906–1910 which was very repressive). However, the basic direction of the nationalities' policies and of Magyarisation adopted by the Hungarian governments could not be stopped after the turn of the century either. Prime Minister István Tisza (June 1913–June 1917) tried to keep the extreme nationalism prevalent especially at the county level in check. In Slovakia, it was the county apparatus which was the strongest supporter of linguistic and cultural assimilation and therefore more positive procedures could not be implemented. Szarka, 1999, pp. 247–275.

33 Ibid., p. 270.

34 Sked, 1989, p. 211.

35 However, the county apparatus was not always effective and able to provide the necessary information. The circulars and decrees from the minister of interior just often induced panic and forced upon the county authorities the idea of imminent nationalist danger. In order to provide positive answers the members of the state apparatus checked hundreds of villages. Szarka, 1999, pp. 250–251, 262.

36 All this correspondence was written in Hungarian, although there are indications that in the 1870s until early 1880s there might have been some of it, or even most of it in German. See Chapter two, section on the Magyarisation of municipal life.

37 On the Hungarian elections see, for example, articles in *História* 1985/5–6 by Mucsi, Hanák, P. and Szabó, Gerő, 1995, pp. 109–144, Gerő, 1997, Potemra, 1975, Potemra, 1980. See also Kann, David, 1984, pp. 344–375, Szarka, 1999, p. 240–241.

38 MOL, K149–1880–1–412, Hanzlíček was the chairman of the workers' association *Vorwärts* in Pressburg. See Chapter three.

39 For e.g. MOL, K149–1907–2–315, the list of all "Pan-Slav" periodicals subscribed to in communities in the Pozsony county. In Pressburg city there was subscription to 102 issues of various periodicals, a very small amount compared to almost 15.000 Slovaks in the city according to the census.

40 SNA, UMV I, i. n. 53, 1903, c. 8, monthly lists of confiscated press at Pressburg post and telegraph director board office.

41 SNA, UMV I, i. n. 67, 1907, c.1, i. n. 69, 70, 73, 77, 1907, c.12. In SNA, the fund of the Hungarian Ministry of Interior abounds in letters informing about the confiscated newspapers and magazines, as well as giving information about the incriminating articles, their author and about the newspaper editor or the owner.

42 Hungarian law specified that the order of responsibility in the case of lawsuits against the press was first the author, then the editor, then the publisher, and finally the printer. Potemra, 1964, p. 535.

43 According to Szarka it was the county apparatus which proved more nationalistic than the government itself, incapable to bring about any positive changes in the nationality policies, even if government initiated them.Szarka, 1999, p. 269. *Főszolgabíró* (Lord lieutenant) denominates the person who was managing the administration of districts and smaller communities.

44 AMB, Mesto Bratislava, Inventár spisového materiálu VII, 13288,1868,1360.

45 Ibid., the whole carton contains correspondence of a similar character between other authorities.

46 Between 1901 and 1918, there were four main publishers of Slovak press and books in the territory of what is present-day Slovakia: *Kníhtlaziarsky úzastinársky spolok* in Turócszentmárton, *Ján Páriska* in Rózsahegy, *Spolok svätého Vojtecha* (for Catholics) in

Nagyszombat and *Tranoscius* (for Evangelical population) in Liptószentmiklós. Apart from these publishers there were 133 different publishers and print shops in the present-day Slovak territory, Czech lands, Lower Hungary and in Budapest. Authors wishing to avoid the censorship of the Hungarian state and religious authorities but also the Slovak national censorship (the so called „inquisition court" consisting of the Slovak national intelligentsia in Martin who felt that they were the only legitimate representatives of the interests of the Slovak nation) published their work in Czech lands. Books were published not only in the literary Slovak but also in different dialects for certain population groups. However, Slovak books did not meet with great interest among general public, partly because of the old-fashioned distribution methods and lack of publicity, partly also because many Slovaks read Hungarian (Popular titles were often condemned by the Slovak intelligentsia as spoiling the literary taste of the Slovak public.) Potemra, 1964, pp. 471–560.

47 For decades *Národnie Noviny*, the press organ of the Slovak National Party (published from 1870), had an almost monopoly position in Slovak public life. Its representatives considered themselves the exclusive representatives of the Slovak interests and criticised any new ideas or movements as "splintering of national forces and betrayal of the nation." They had a negative attitude towards both workers' and Hlas movements (with a Czechoslovak orientation, see Chapter three, footnote 258). Their Pan-Slavism was expressed in their sympathies towards the Russian tsarist regime. From 1881 until the First World War *Národnie Noviny* received annual financial support of 5,000 Rubles from Russia. *Národnie Noviny* (published three times week) were a periodical directed at Slovak intelligentsia. It had 1200 subscribers in 1898, 1000 in 1908 and 600 in 1917. (Potemra, 1958, pp. 28–30.) *Slovenský Týždenník* was published by the agrarian Milan Hodža in Budapest from 1903. The weekly was written in a popular style and had articles on national, economic and cultural questions as well as anecdotes and pictures. It was oriented towards the mass audience. The weekly had around 14,000 subscribers and managed to evoke interest also in the richer Slovak peasants. Ibid., pp. 38–39.

48 SNA, UMV I, not placed, 1882, c.1, letter from the *főispán* of Zólyom county to the minister of interior of 3.10.1882. It must be noted that Hungarians always used the word 'tót' instead of 'Slovak.' Sometimes they would use 'Slav language' instead of 'tót' language. A similar interchange is noticeable in the German press in Pressburg; when it wrote about Slovaks, it would use sometimes 'Slovaks', other time 'Slavs' and the same applied when writing about the language i.e. the local press used interchangeably 'Slovak' and 'Slav' language.

49 Holec, 1997a, p. 21, Potemra, 1983, Vol. I, pp. 111–112.

50 This event happened in 1907 and made the Slovak case known also to other European countries, not least by the Norwegian writer Björnsterne Björnson. (Another defender of Slovaks was the Scottish historian and publicist Robert W. Seton-Watson. See Viator, 1908.) In the village Černová (part of Ružomberok) a

church built from the villagers' money was to be sanctified by a Hungarian priest and not by the Slovak Andrej Hlinka whom the villagers demanded. When the villagers gathered around the carriage with the priest and threatened him, the gendarmes started shooting into the crowd and fifteen people were shot. (See Špiesz, 1992, pp. 118–119.) A less biased explanation can be found in Szarka, 1999, pp. 259–262 (since Slovak historians don't mention that Hlinka was also partly responsible for the bloodshed and instead blame the whole case on the Hungarian authorities, although the violence was closely connected to the power struggle between the representatives of the Slovak People's Party—a wing of the Slovak National Party—and the Hungarian People's Party). For a detailed analysis of this event see Holec, 1997a. This event had a huge echo abroad, although the bloodshed was not initiated by the government itself which before the First World War had never given an order to use armed forces against the nationalities . On the contrary, the central government tried to lessen the anti-nationalities' politics of the county apparatus which was liable to panic. (Szarka, 1999, pp. 259–260.) See Kemény, G., 1971, pp. 100–136 for documents connected to this case. The Times also reported on Hlinka, his speech in Prague (where he spoke about three million Slovaks living in Hungary "beneath Tatra hill") and his imprisonment. (The Times, 5.11.1907, 5b, 6.5.1908, 7d, 5.1.1910, 3d.) The Times brought periodically news about the nationalities in Hungary. In 1907 the English press was even accused by former Prime Minister Kálmán Széll of "disseminating calumnies against Hungary" and of stating that "citizens of non-Magyar tongue area treated with the greatest tyranny." At this time foreign public opinion was turning against Hungary and its ways of treating minority nationalities. The Times, 12.12.1907, 5a.

51 SNA, UMV I, i. n. 25, 1902, c. 6, Letter from the minister of religion and education to the prime minister of 5.2.1902: "...a magyar nyelv tanulása ellen irányuló verseért." See Potemra, 1964, p. 536.

52 SNA, UMV I, i. n. 82, 1911, c. 14: "... a magyar haza iránti hűséget és szeretetet már csirájában igyekszik elfojtani s épazért magyar nemzeti szempontból igen káros és veszedelmes."

53 SNA, UMV I, i. n. 67, 1906, c.11.

54 Szarka, 1999, pp. 238–239. Both of these cases happened under Bánffy.

55 SNA, UMV I, i. n. 14, 1893, c.3, i. n. 19, 1898, c. 5, i. n. 25, 1902, c. 6, i. n. 67, 1906, c. 11.

56 SNA, UMV I, i. n. 23, 1902, c. 6, i. n. 53, 1903.

57 SNA, UMV I, i. n. 17, 1896, c.4.

58 SNA, UMV I, i. n. 16, 1895, c.4.

59 SNA, UMV I, i. n. 43, 1903, c. 8. All materials in this carton contain information

about different press persecution cases. See Potemra, 1964, pp. 534–548 on censorship of the Slovak press and books.

60 The mayor of Pressburg, Gustav Dröxler, in his letter to the minister of interior mentioned that there was a *polgári* (civilian) detective who was a part of the leadership of the Social Democratic Party, thus the authorities were informed about all the actions planned by the social-democrats. MOL, K149–1898–1–238.

61 Hanzlíček, 1970, pp. 22–23.

62 SNA, SRH, i. n. 316, c. 13, the letter from the police chief to the minister of interior of 20.4.1890.

63 MOL, K149–1880–1–698.

64 SNA, SRH, i. n. 316, c. 13, the letters of 20.4., 22.4. and 29.4.1890. In this case it seems that the city police chief Kutsera acted on his own initiative. The mayor of Pressburg Dröxler received a letter from the *főispán* which gave permission to the meeting of workers but warned the mayor that in future he wished all similar request to be accompanied by the opinion of the mayor or his deputy. SNA, SRH, i. n. 316, c. 13, letter from the *főispán* Szalavszky to the mayor of Pressburg dated 22.4.1890. Both mentioned letters were written in Hungarian language. However, the request from *Vorwärts* to the police captain Kutsera was written in German. Ibid.

At the end the Ministry of Interior refused the original plan of the celebration. The minister even announced to the mayor, Dröxler, that according to his information the Pressburger workers wanted to go to Hainburg and force the interruption of work which was not permitted there. He instructed the police chief to prevent such an event, if necessary with the use of military force. SNA, SRH, i. n. 316, c. 13, letter from the minister of interior to the mayor Dröxler of 29.4.1890; see also Lehotská et al, 1955, p. 7.

65 SNA, SRH, i. n. 317, c. 13, letter from the city captain Kutsera to the mayor of 16.4.1891.

66 Ibid., letter from the minister of interior to the mayor Dröxler of 25.4.1891.

67 SNA, SRH, i. n. 317, c. 13, letter from the city captain Kutsera to *Vorwärts* of 25.4.1891.

68 SNA, SRH, i. n.19, c. 2, letter from the minister of interior to the city magistrate of 1875.

69 SNA, SRH, i. n.19, c.2, letter from the city captain to the city magistrate of 12.5.1875.

70 Hanzlíček, 1970, p. 129, footnote 37.

71 MOL, K149–1907–1–679, 24.1.1907.

72 MOL, K149–1895–6–29, 29.9.1895. Some of these reports are available but only bits and pieces for the whole period (in MOL and SNA, UMV I). It is assumed here that a similar informing system worked also in other years. There might be more reports in the "elnökségi iratok" (prime minister's documents) and more information about different movements in counties in "közigazgatási bizottsági jelentések 1895–1918" (reports of the municipal committees) in MOL. In Bratislava I have not checked the material in the Štátny oblastný archív (Regional Archive) relating to the *föispán* and *alispán* since it does not contain much material on the city of Bratislava itself but it certainly has valuable information about surveillance in the Pozsony county and in Hungary generally.

73 Lehotský, 1970, p. 268.

74 Lehotská et al, 1955, p. 7.

75 SNA, SRH, i. n. 316, c. 13, letter from the mayor Dröxler to the minister of interior of 4.5.1890.

76 Lehotská et al, 1955, p. 7.

77 *WG*, N.7043, 2.5.1893, pp. 1–2, "Der 1.Mai in Pressburg [1 May in Pressburg]."

78 SNA, SRH, i. n. 322, c.13, letter from the mayor Dröxler to the minister of interior of 4.5.1896.

79 They were banned between 1891 and 1898. The city captain refused to permit them on the basis of the instructions coming from the Ministry of Interior. The workers met anyway outside the town where they had entertainment. The minister in 1893 also gave specific instructions that the state factories must not give a day off for their workers on 1 May. SNA, SRH, i. n. 319, c. 13, letter from the minister of interior to the mayor Dröxler of 26.4.1893.

80 Lehotský, 1970, pp. 270–271, see also Sked, 1989, p. 211.

81 Lehotský, 1970, pp. 274–275.

82 Lehotská, 1952, pp. 110–118.

83 At the beginning, the association *Vorwärts* had a very diverse membership, including policemen. Shortly after the founding of the association its members accepted the chairman Niemczyk's proposal that policemen be not allowed to be members. However, this did not prevent the infiltration of the association and the leadership of social democrats with detectives who could not be found out by workers, although on a few occasions this happened. This practice became common especially under the city police chief Stefan Kutsera who came into this position after the death of Johann Kozsehuba in the first quarter of 1890. Hanzlíček, 1970, pp. 78–79.

84 SNA, SRH, i. n. 277, c.5, letter from the *föispán* to the minister of interior of 2.8.1895; Lehotský, 1970, p. 270.

85 MOL, K149–1898–1–238, 12.3.1898, 15.3.1898; Lehotský, 1970, p. 276.

86 MOL, K149–1895–1–1370.

87 SNA, UMV I, i. n. 81, 1910, c. 14, letter from the minister of interior of 10.5.1910.

88 *Főszolgabiró*'s area of responsibility lied beyond the Pressburg city territory which was taken care of by the city police.

89 SNA, SRH, i. n. 121, 1907, c. 22, report from the *főszolgabiró* to the minister of interior, 26.1.1907.

90 Hanzlíček, 1970, pp. 33, 52.

91 Ibid., p. 55.

92 See Greary, 1985 on similar negotiations between miners and their employers. Also see his description of the intelligence network involved in gathering information about the labour movement in England.

93 SNA, SRH, i. n. 281, c.11, from *Népszava* 2.3.1901, N.30, p. 3.

94 Similarly in Saxony, social democrats had to give the purpose and an accurate and detailed description of the program of their meetings. The Ministry of Interior even ordered police forces to reject the registration of meetings which had in their program the vague topic "discussion and questions" since this could lead to discussion of questions which would have otherwise been grounds for banning the meeting. Krug, Unpublished article, p. 5.

95 Lehotská, 1955, p. 20. Písch mentions a quite major clash between the police forces and the demonstrating workers which ended up with the police raiding the Workers' home and arresting workers. See Chapter three, footnote 289. I have reviewed only a small part of materials on strikes in Pressburg which did not mention any case of violent conflict. However, conflicts between striking workers and authorities could have happened.

96 Hanzlíček, 1970, p. 78.

97 This obsession with order was typical also for the Saxon government which facing 1 May 1890 expected that "the majority of order-loving workers will avoid and prevent anything liable to disturb the public peace" and proclaimed that "the government is obliged to preserve public peace and order with all means available." (See Chapter three for analysis of the 1 May celebrations in Pressburg.) In Krug, Unpublished article, p. 4.

98 Lipták, 1999, p. 14.

99 Goláň, 1958, p. 535.

100 The whole thing started earlier in a rather accidental way on 25.3. when a bar-

ber's assistant Heinrich Wicker was arrested on the claim that he put the leaflet "*Die Zeiten sind schlecht* [Times are bad]" (an anarchist leaflet coming from London) into the sixth number of *Wahrheit* and the police officer Breier who was just at the barber shop happened to read exactly this newspaper. The next day at one of the publishers—Jacob Grundstein's house a police search was carried out and he was immediately arrested and sentenced for eight days although the house search did not provide any evidence of state endangering material. After his arrest Grundstein and his family were deported under supervision to Frankfurt am Main where they originally came from. Wicker who came from Moravia also had to leave the city. In Hanzlíček, 1970, p. 39; SNA, SRH, i. n. 453, c. 18, letter of 8.4.1880. The minister confirmed the deportation in his letter. SNA, SRH, i. n. 453, c. 18, letter of 11.4.1880.

101 Hanzlíček, 1970, pp. 39–44.

102 Ibid., pp. 47–48.

103 Goláň, 1958, p. 537. Then on 5.4.1896 Zalkai started *Westungarische Volkszeitung*. This newspaper was published until 1902. In 1902 *Westungarische Volksstimme* was started by Zalkai, later when he left the Social Democratic party the editor changed to Henrich Kalmár. *Westungariche Volksstimme* was published until the year 1938. It was not a purely local newspaper but directed at the whole workers' movement of Western Upper Hungary, with local news. Zalkai started to publish also the periodical *Reform* which was also followed by the public prosecutor. As a counter-weight to the socialist press one of the *főispáns* proposed to publish a state-supported "proper direction" press. MOL, K149–1904–1–732, report from the *főispán* of Moson county of 31.8.1903.

104 Both of these newspapers although giving some information about the local workers' movement were oriented towards Slovak audience in the Slovak areas.

105 Napred, 15.9.1906, N. 1, p. 1, leading article; Napred, 15.11.1906, N. 3, p. 3, "Perzekúcia [Persecution]," Napred, 15.12.1906, N. 4, p. 6, "Perzekúcia," Napred, 15.11.1907, N. 11, p. 6, "Chýrnik [News]," *RN*, 1.5.1909, N.5, p. 5, "Zo súdnej siene [From the court room]," *RN*, 13.1.1910, N. 2, p. 5, "Chýrnik," *RN*, 14.11.1912, N. 46, p. 6, "Chýrnik."

106 *RN*, 22.7.1909, N. 17, p. 5, "Chýrnik."

107 Lehotský, 1970, p. 269.

108 Ibid. In his report the police captain Kutsera described the printing shops in Pressburg. The *Westungarische Volskzeitung* as well as other socialist booklets were printed at the printing shop *Lőwy and Alkalay* whose workers were adherents of the Social Democratic Party. The captain was well-informed about this printing shop since among the workers were two of his detectives. There was also a printing shop of Ján Brég which printed socialist press but recently came into disagreement with the functionaries of the Social Democratic Party and thus stopped printing for

them. The other printing shops did not print socialist press and would have definitely refused printing anarchist magazines. Lehotský, 1970, p. 269, footnote 6.

109 Ibid., p. 269.

110 Ibid., pp. 270–271.

111 MOL, K149-1880-1-193, report of the *főispán* to the minister of interior of 14.7.1880.

112 Hanzlíček, 1970, p. 47.

113 MOL, K149-1880-1-412, 427, 437.

114 MOL, K149-1880-1-4, letter of 11.8.1880.

115 MOL, K149-1880-1-698: "kifogástalan viseletű egyén."

116 Ibid.

117 This was the case with the socialist movement which turned into an organised mass-movement after the turn of the century, with clearer and better defined aims. It was also certainly the case with the nationalities' movements, especially the Slovak national movement. While the Slovak National Party (as the only Slovak political party) entered into political passivity in the 1880s, the growing pressure of Magyarisation as well as the emergence of a new generation of politicians around the turn of the century brought a crystallisation of different ideological streams within the Slovak national movement (the new civic-liberal, clerical and agrarian wings), clearer definition of aims and methods of work, better mobilisation of resources and increasingly successful spread of national ideas among the Slovak peasants who created the mass basis necessary for national ideas. Also persecution by the state authorities made the Slovak intelligentsia into martyrs. See Szarka, 1999.

118 Szarka, 1999, p. 219.

119 Glatz, 1995a, p. XVI.

120 In the area of education belonged the law XVIII/1879 on the teaching of Hungarian language, XXX/1883 on secondary schools, XV/1891 on kindergartens, and XXVII/1907 Lex Ápponyi (see Chapter two) which basically abolished all the positive features of the 1868 Nationalities Law in the areas of education, associational life and language usage. There was also a discriminatory law about land ownership which had an especially negative impact on Rumanians. In his circular of 1875 the Minister of Interior Kálmán Tisza restricted the founding of nationalities' associations. (Szarka, 1999, p. 176.) The XXIII/1898 law about cooperatives codified more discriminatory practices against the non-Magyar cooperatives. Copying its Prussian example this law strengthened centralisation. (Holec, 1999, p. 69.)

121 Szarka, 1999, p. 254.

122 Gellner, 1983, p. 34.

123 Sked, 1989, pp. 209–210. On the cultural supremacy of Magyars see the work of the extremely chauvinistic *alispán* of Zólyom county Béla Grünwald (*A felvidék. Politikai tanulmány.* Budapest, 1878) who considered Slovaks as well as other nationalities living in Hungary inferior beings who had to be "elevated" by Magyars to a higher cultural level. In Szarka, 1999, pp. 169, 221.

124 On this point see Breuilly, 1982, esp. pp. 92–99.

125 There were two great movements which worried the Hungarian government, although in reality not as powerful as imagined by the government, and these were the Pan-Slav and the Pan-German movements. The pan-German movement was not very relevant for Pressburg for it developed in other parts of Hungary inhabited by Saxon Germans and it never really found much echo among the Germans living on the later Slovak territory. The Magyar elite sometimes marked any efforts for German language use as Pan-Germanism. More relevant for Pressburg and its surrounding was Pan-Slavism which again when used by the Magyar elite or city elites marked any effort to organise cultural events in the Slovak language, or attempts to improve the status of it by bringing it into public administration and education. (This definition of Pan-Slavism was taken over from Béla Grünwald, *alispán* of Zólyom county, who described any expression of Slovak national feeling or its conscious development as Pan-Slavism. Grünwald's extreme opinions (see his study *A felvidék*) became the basis of the politics pursued towards Slovaks. 'Pan-Slavism' became almost equivalent to treason. Any sympathies towards Russia and other Slav nations were considered Pan-Slavism as well. The basis of this characterisation were the regular visits of the Slovak intelligentsia to Russia, as well as the financial support for *Národnie Noviny* coming from Russia, facts, which were however well known in Hungary and were not considered state-endangering. (Szarka, 1999, pp. 197, 227–229.) Part of the Slovak intelligentsia (the Martin wing) put all its hopes into the help of Russia as the great brotherly Slav state. The materials of the Ministry of Interior included rich material on Pan-Slavism, mainly in the central Slovakian counties. On Pan-Slavism in the context of European geopolitics see Heffernan, 1998, pp. 79–81. Heffernan claims that "Pan-Slavism was a crusade, led by Russian intellectuals, on behalf of all Orthodox and Slavic peoples, particularly those who lived under Ottoman and Austro-Hungarian 'oppression'." One of the Russian intellectuals Nikolai Danilevski had a vision of "a future Russian-dominated Pan-Slav Union stretching from Adriatic to the Pacific." Most of these ideas (as well as the German idea of eastern Lebensraum which was expressed in a similar way) were influenced by racial thinking.

126 Szarka, 1999, p. 161.

127 The county offices paid a lot of attention to 400–500 "Pan-Slavs" in the Turóc, Nyitra, Liptó counties and from time to time in the Trencsén county as well as in the

Pozsony county. Slovak politics were followed especially by lord lieutenants and border police. Szarka, 1999, p. 206.

128 By policing I mean the "combination of the accumulation of information and the exercise of direct supervision over a particular territory." In Ogborn, 1993, p. 506. I realise that surveillance is a combination of both policing and the effects it has on the behaviour of the individuals, and their internalising of certain models of behaviour. However, I have found it useful for the purposes of this chapter to separate these two aspects, although in reality they overlap and fuel each other.

129 MOL, K149–1882–2, 14.2.1882. According to this report in 1882 the Slovaks were more courageous than before but there was still no obvious activity thus the preventive measures were not necessary.

130 MOL, K149–1877–2–261.

131 MOL , K149–1899–2–52.

132 MOL, K149–1906–2–449.

133 SNA, UMV I, i. n. 58, 1904, c. 10, letter from the minister of justice to the minister of interior of 9.1.1904. The low number of lawsuits was caused by the less oppressive policies of the governments of Kálmán Széll (1902–June 1903) and Károly Khuen-Héderváry (June-November 1903) towards the nationalities and socialists.

134 E.g. SNA, UMV I, i. n. 83, 1912, c. 15, letter from the captaincy of the Hungarian border police to the minister of interior of 8.2.1912; i. n. 140, 1907, c. 6.

135 Az Ujság, 1.10.1907, p. 12, "Hírek rovat [News column]" in SNA, UMV I, i. n. 140, 1907, c. 6. See Chapter three.

136 SNA, UMV I, i. n. 84, 1913, c. 15, letter from the Pressburg's captain of the Hungarian border police to the minister of interior of 7.12.1912.

137 Ibid. The report of the captain included many details about Flórián Tománek since the captain claimed to have known him since 1908. Tománek was admittedly also the owner of a printing shop in Liptószentmiklós.

138 Kemény, G., 1966, pp. 636–637. In this letter the bishop Kolos Vaszary informed the *alispán* Bertalan Klempa that he could not move a priest of Slovak mother tongue to a purely Magyar environment as had been requested since there were not enough priests who understand Slovak and these were needed in Slovak church districts. See also Szarka, 1999, p. 264, Hrabovcová, 1999, p. 185.

139 SNA, UMV I, i. n. 11, 1890, c. 2, report from the *főispán* Count Zichy to the minister of interior of 20.10.1890.

140 MOL, K149–1895–6–29, 29.9.1895.

141 MOL, K149–1902–6–439, 6.5.1902.

142 SNA, UMV I, i. n. 14, 1893, c. 3, minutes of the municipal county assembly, meeting on 20.2.1893.

143 SNA, UMV I, i. n. 63, 1905, c. 10. The "Upper-Hungarian American action" was started by the Hungarian government at the beginning of the twentieth century because of the mass emigration of Slovaks. The state authorities were especially interested in the following topics: whether those returning back had strengthened their "anti-Hungarian" thinking, contacts between emigration and the Pan-Slav movement in Hungary, the financial support of the American Slovaks for the Slovak national movement in Hungary, and the distribution of American-Slovak publications in Hungary. In 1903 the Hungarian government even involved the monarchy's consul in the USA and sent out Slovak speaking priests to work among American Slovaks in order to counter-balance the activity of "anti-Hungarian" Slovak priests in the USA. However, Hungarian governments generally welcomed the emigration of non-Magyars and did not wish for their return while making an effort to bring back Magyar emigrants.(Szarka, 1999, pp. 250–253.) On the surveillance of the activities of the Roman Catholic priests in the USA see Hrabovcová, 1999, pp. 180–200. Diplomats often denied any real national conviction on the part of "agitators" and ascribed purely material reasons for their activities. (Ibid., p. 186.) Similarly, among socialists see Chapter three, footnote 59, the city captain's report on Niemczyk.

144 MOL, K149–1882–6, 2.4.1882. *Der Schulverein* was fighting for the retaining of the German language in schools as a language of instruction.

145 Foucault talks about "technologies of the self, which permit individuals to effect by their own means or with the help of others a certain number of operations on their own bodies and souls, thoughts, conduct and way of being, so as to transform themselves in order to attain a certain state of happiness, purity, wisdom, perfection, or immortality." In Foucault's account, "governmentality" is "the contact between the technologies of domination of others and those of the self." Foucault, 1988a, pp. 18–19. See also Foucault, 1979.

146 Definition of the "köztisztviselő" (civil/public servant) in Szabó, 1991, p. 22 as given in the law article V/1878. "*Officials generally*: As public servants (officials) are considered those who are fulfilling their duties in state public administration or jurisdiction, or any municipal or community authority's offices, are in their service or in a special assignment; also those who are employed in public institutions, hospitals, lunatic asylums managed by the state or the municipality as supervisors, doctors, clerks, or servants. The royal notaries are also considered public servants." The political identity of the civil/public servants and their solidarity was one-dimensional—the one of the state identity and this identification with the state policies was strengthened by the long rule of the same party, the Liberal party, from 1874 until 1905. Ibid., p. 26.

147 On this see articles in the *Nyugatmagyarországi Hiradó*, also MOL, P1747—

Notes to Chapter 5

Kálmán Thály, correspondence with Gábor Pávai Vajna.

148 Quoted in Boyer, 1994, p. 73.

149 Boyer, 1994, p. 343.

150 See also Uhl, 1999, pp. 138–139. Within the city itself there was a hierarchy of city spaces (which changed). This became evident especially in the case of elections when the voters of the governing party gathered on the main square or the streets leading to it while the voters of the opposition parties waited for the call of the election committee in small streets and more suburban areas. During the development of mass political parties in Hungary the established and traditional parties like the Liberal and Independent Parties had their gatherings in the best rooms of the city (hotels, casinos) or on squares while the newer parties like the Catholic People's Party, social democrats or nationalities' parties had meetings outside the city or in suburban pubs until they fought their way into more prestigious spaces. Lipták, 1999, pp. 120–121.

151 *Stadtverschönerungverein* developed a range of activities both within the city and in the close-by mountains and forest. It founded small parks, planted trees and alleys, set down benches, put memorial tablets on the houses where historical personalities once lived, took care of the up-keeping of the historic character of the new buildings, founded the "Blumenkultus" in 1904 which meant that the daily press appealed to the inhabitants to decorate their balconies and windows with flowers and once a year there was a competition for the most beautiful flower decoration. In the city surrounding (in *der Au*) the association put down benches in the Aupark, commissioned statues for the park, repaired the paths. In the mountain there were new roads made for walks, shelters made for the case of bad weather, a view-tower built as well as a Justi monument, and explanatory botanical tablets installed. In Győrik, 1918.

152 Ibid., pp. 39–43.

153 Ibid., p. 11: "Unter den vielen vornehmen und edlen Vereinen Pozsonys ist keiner, welcher für die Gesamtbevölkerung derart uneigennützig und segensvoll gewirkt hat, wirkt und hoffentlich auch weiterhin wirken wird, als der Pozsonyer Stadtverschönerungsverein."

154 On the *Ringstrasse* in Vienna as the embodiment of the values of liberal city fathers see Schorske, 1981, Chapter two. The whole street reflected the liberal values of the governing Viennese elite. The *Ringstrasse* was dominated by "centers of constitutional government and higher culture," where the bourgeois cultural ideal was expressed in "*Prachtbauten* [buildings of splendour]" built in different historic styles depending on what the building represented. (Ibid., p. 31.) A similar "ring" (even called the same as the Viennese one—*Körút*) was constructed in Budapest at the end of the nineteenth century, consisting mostly of large apartment buildings. (Hanák translates it as Grand Boulevard [*Nagykörút*]. Hanák, P., 1998, chapter one, esp. pp. 12–15). In the Josefov city district in Prague, the worst medieval areas were sanitised

in 1893 since the city elite considered such slums out of place in a modern city. In their place came buildings in neo-historicist styles and the streets were also widened. (Becker et al, 1999, p. 11.) On Hausmann's reconstruction of Paris, pulling down the medieval city centre so that the danger for the rich from the poor in the centre was removed and building wide boulevards instead see Edholm, 1993, pp. 139–168. In Hausmann's scheme, "buildings were described as historical monuments." (Woolf, 1988, p. 217.) "Buildings, bridges, roads and open spaces in the city conveyed a distinct sense of social order, and a confident belief in historical destiny." (Ibid., p. 216.) Sanitation of medieval, dark districts which were difficult to control was an attempt by the city elites to construct a 'good city' and destroy the 'bad city.'

155 Győrik, 1918, p. 19.

156 Ibid., p. 21. See Chapter four for descriptions of Pressburg as the "second capital of Hungary."

157 Ibid., pp. 16–17.

158 Boyer, 1994, p. 13.

159 Győrik, 1918, pp. 16–17. "Unsere Nation benötigt nicht nur grösseren Wohlstand, sondern namentlich auch ein höheres Niveau seiner Kultur...Die Zukunft unserer Nation sichern wir vor allem durch eine fortwährende Erhöhung seiner Kultur, welche zugleich die beste Gewähr der Hegemonie des Ungartums ist." It must be noted that Győrik's history of the association is influenced by the time in which it was written, towards the end of the First World War. In 1918 the hegemony of Hungarians was not very likely to turn into reality at that time, and even the Hungarian government was thinking about federalisation.

160 On museum-building in Leipzig see Penny III, Unpublished article, 1998. Also Green, A., Unpublished thesis, 1998.

161 Ortvay, *Pozsony város története, I-IV* (History of the city of Pressburg), Pozsony, 1892–1903. About the lost past and the need of its retrieval see Boyer, 1994, also Green, Unpublished thesis, 1998, especially Chapter four. See also Koshar, 1994, on the impulses leading to the turn of the century historic preservation in Germany. The collecting of artefacts and objects connected to folk-culture in order to instruct also the "lowest layers of nation" of the heritage of their ancestors was also typical for Slovaks. Such ethnographic collections started to be made in 1863. The *Slovenská muzeálna spoločnosť* (Slovak museum society) was founded in 1893 in Turócszentmárton. Profantová, 1999, pp. 253, 256.

162 There are examples of this, although not from Pressburg. However, one can assume that this was similar in the whole country. The main surgeon of the military hospital Nr. 23 in Agram during his holiday in Turócszentmárton in August 1909 took part in a banquet organised by the Slovak museum society. The report stated that Benovský was reminded by the leader of the hospital of this "improper conduct"

(*Unstatthäftigkeit*) and was advised not take part in any celebrations with a political tendency in future. (SNA, UMV I, i. n. 81, 1910, c. 14, report from the joint Ministry of War to the Hungarian Ministry of Interior of 18.2.1910.) Similarly in 1878, with regard to the political situation and the possibility of a war, the minister of interior in his letter to the ministers of finance, agriculture, industry and trade stressed that all the state employees had to be absolutely reliable and patriotic. Therefore he ordered that all employees working in custom houses, financial agencies, at the post and telegraph offices should be checked upon to make sure that they all were individuals with flawless political behaviour, patriots loyal to the Hungarian state. At the same time the minister wrote a letter to the minister of transport instructing him to check out the reliability of the railway employees. (MOL, K149-1878-2.) In 1908 the minister issued a decree which banned all the employees of the railways from being members either of the Social Democratic Party or any of its organs, including the trade unions. All employees had to confirm by their signatures that they were notified of this fact. If they trespassed this ban, they were to be dismissed from their work. SNA, SRH, i. n. 141, c. 6, decree of the minister of interior, 4.12.1908.

163 See Hanák, P., 1984b, on the clash between values of the state and national patriot in Hungary in 1898.

164 As Jonathan Steinberg points out, in the nineteenth century "The *questione della lingua* became a matter of imposing uniformity of speech in order to make what had been a patchwork of peoples into a national community." (Italics in original.) The appearance of the question of language always indicates re-organisation of cultural hegemony. Steinberg, 1987, pp. 204, 206.

165 *ST*, 14.4.1905, N. 16, p. 4, "Jako nažívame [How we live]."

166 *L'N*, 14.9.1906, N. 38, p. 5, "Prešporok."

167 *NH*, 1.7.1902, N. 148, p. 3, "Magyarosodunk [Magyarisation is progressing]."

168 *NH*, 6.2.1891, N. 29, p. 2, "Román tüntetés a kisdédóvó törvényjavaslat ellen [Romanian demonstration against the bill about kindergartens]."

169 Foucault, 1984, p. 252.

170 On sanitation of medieval districts as a way of getting rid of the 'bad city' see footnote 154. On difference between the "high" and "low" and keeping at distance those considered "low" by those in power see Pile, 1996, pp. 175–181.

171 Kearns, Unpublished article, 1997, Section "Governmentality and subjectivation."

172 Foucault, 1986, pp. 150–151.

173 For a review of the main developments in social politics, social legislature and public health in the Austro-Hungarian Empire see Benyóová-Dudeková, Unpublished thesis, 1991 and Dudeková, 1994.

174 Antolíková, 1998, p. 121.

175 Horváth, 1998, pp. 13–14; listed in *PW*, 1867–1914. As Nikolas Rose writes, "[n]ew forms of police organization, new mechanisms for recording crimes and the use of statistical devices to chart a kind of 'moral topography' of urban space appealed to reveal a breakdown in moral order at the heart of our great cities." Rose, 1990, p. 152.

176 These materials include reports also about agriculture and education. In 1903 the city captain asked for an increase of the police force to 120 men, detectives to 6 instead of 3 and also requested 8–10 policemen on horseback. From the report it is clear that the police was keeping records about the city associations (which was one of the city authorities' duties). See AMB, Mesto Bratislava, Inventár spisového materiálu IX, 13699, 1904, 2113. The city captain disposed of a staff of 99 officials, a physician, inspectors and watchmen. Horváth, 1998, p. 15.

177 Horváth, 1998, p. 14.

178 AMB, Mesto Bratislava, Inventár spisového materiálu IX, 13699, 1904, 2113.

179 On the workhouse in Pressburg see Duka, Unpublished thesis, 1967.

180 The president of the economic committee of the association was according to its statutes the Catholic city priest (*Stadtpfarrer*). However, after 1871 this happened by an election and in 1887 the position was taken by a prominent city personality like in 1887 by the mayor Gustav Dröxler and in 1907 by the parliament deputy and *Sparkasse* bank president Karl Neiszidler. The patrons for the association were women from aristocratic families, and the chairwomen were the prominent women of the city. The association initiated the building of a new children's hospital (there was one in the city since 1853) which was finished in 1894, aided much by the gift of 25.000 guldens from the *Sparkasse*. Kemény, L., 1930. At the beginning the association was called "Verein des guten und Nützlichen" (Association of Good and Useful). Ibid., p. 5.

181 Ibid., p. 5: "...einer wissenhaften Beaufsichtigung und Pflege der sich sonst ganz allein überlassenen Kinder vieler armen Leute, Verwahrung derselben von bösen Beispielen, Gewöhnung an Gehorsam, Sitte und religiöses Gefühl, endlich eine zweckmässige Vorbereitung für die Elementarschulen, und die dadurch zu erzielende Verhütung der Gasselbettelei."

182 Johann Heinrich Joh. Joach. Becher quoted in ibid., p. 3: "Dann wann es wahr ist / dass der grösste Schatz einer Gemeind in guten wackern Bürger und Unterthanen bestehet / solche aber / oder ihre Kinder ohne gute Aufferziehung nicht können gut werden / so folget ja / dass an solcher Aufferziehung alles gleichwie einem Bauersmann und Gärtner an Verrichtung *der ersten Saat.....*das meiste gelegen." (italics in original)

183 Johann Heinrich Joh. Joach. Becher quoted in ibid., p. 3.

184 Rose pays considerable attention to the normalisation of children in families. In the nineteenth century childhood began to be seen as a distinct period which influences the whole life of the individual and it was assumed that here lay the roots of criminality and bad morals. (Rose, 1991) Hence also the frequent separation of children within the working houses so as to prevent them from being infected by bad morals of their parents. See Driver, 1993.

185 Ibid., p. 5: "...der Kampf gegen den *Müssiggang, die Leerheit des Lebens, den ungeregelten Gang des menschlichen Geistes, die den Grund zu alle den Bahnen, welche in Kranken- und Irrenhäuser, Armen- und Zuchthäuser legen...*" (italics in original).

186 Jones, 1983, p. 191.

187 To these belonged die erste Pressburger Volksküche, die Neustädter Volksküche, israelitischer Volksküchenverein. See Stoličná, 1987.

188 For e.g. Evangelische Versorgungs-Anstalt (Evangelic nursing institute), Humanitas—association for the support of the poor, courageous and industrious pupils, Catholic and Evangelic associations for support of the ill (Krankenunterstützungs-Vereine), Jewish charitable institutions. Of all the associations in the city, charitable associations constituted almost a quarter in 1878. By the beginning of the twentieth century about one fifth of all associations was charitable. (Mannová, 1999b, p. 202.) Most charitable organisations in this period were still tied to a religious affiliation and religious rhetoric was prevalent. For example the Catholic associations supported the Catholic poor but often also promoted Hungarian patriotism and banned membership in any association "inimical to the church and fatherland, especially in a masonic one." Ibid., p. 206.

189 There were two basic strategies in the "civilising activity" of these charitable associations. "The first was to use legislation to create a physical and institutional environment in which undesirable working-class habits and attitudes would be deterred, while private philanthropy could undertake the active propagation of a new moral code. The material needs of the poor would then be used as a means towards their moral reformation."(Jones, 1983, p. 191.) Legislation involved such acts as common lodging house inspections, sanitary legislation clearing of slums and building model housing which was considered more appropriate by those with property. Little acts like insisting on regularity of rent payment as well as having rules for using such housing facilities also contributed towards building up habits of regularity and observation of rules. In London there was even created a Charity Organisation Society which investigated cases of all applicants and decided whether they deserved help. If they were found "deserving" ("showing signs of thrift and temperance") they were referred to a charity, if not ("drunken, improvident"), they were referred to the workhouse. Ibid., p. 192. See also Green, D., 1985. On the links between self control and cultural change in the "civilising process" see Elias, 1994.

190 Foucault, 1977, p. 212. In Germany also, associations served the middle class-

es for the moral and economic improvement of the "unterbürgerlichen" layers on the local level. See Tacke, 1995, p. 130.

191 *PT*, 27.4.1906, N. 3533, p. 2, "Die nazionalistiche Agitation [Nationalistic agitation]"; also workers' press regularly referred to this issue—to the fight for the souls of the poor who were becoming more open to socialist teachings.

192 Foucault, 1977, p. 212.

193 On the development of sport associations in Pressburg and Hungary see Grexa, 1997, pp. 259–264.

194 *PW*, 1867–1914; local daily press 1867–1914.

195 Gašparec, 1998, p. 42.

196 Although the city authorities were concerned about the 'bad city', the division of spaces within the city, the separation of the rich villa districts from the workers' and poor housing made the sources of badness spatially easily identifiable. "It is easier for society to tolerate minority groups and nonconforming activities if they are assigned their own separate spaces." Dennis, 2000, p. 224.

197 Even in housing and neighbourhoods of the poor and workers there is a certain culture concerned with "order, boundary and control" which is "rooted in the need to manage and bring meaning to the experience of poverty, endemic economic insecurity and ordered industrial production." Thus even when these neighbourhoods escape the state's surveillance (they hardly manage to do so completely), inhabitants develop a whole range of cultural practices which have "symbolic meaning, from the uses of space within the home to the employment of leisure time (in pubs and on weekends for instance) and the practices governing sexual conduct, for example." There is an effort to maintain a "public face" which is distinguished from private reality. Joyce, 1991, pp. 151–152.

198 Foucault, 1986, p. 149.

199 Georg Schulpe was born in 1867 in Nový Kneževac (in Vojvodina) in an aristocratic family. The family spoke at home German, Hungarian and understood Serb as well. The family moved to Pressburg in 1883, and here Schulpe studied law and state science. In years 1892–4 Schulpe left the career of a writer and threw himself into the study of social conditions. He travelled across almost all European countries, concentrating on the situation of workers. He used this knowledge in Hungary, in his many law proposals to the government aimed at enhancing workers' situation, and concrete reforms, carried out in Pressburg and other towns as well. Schulpe was an empirical sociologist whose aim was peace between the social classes and ethical social politics. He wrote a number of sociological works and over 600 articles. As a lawyer, he was a legal sociologist, and concentrated on changing the social legislature. He wrote a work about the city social politics, and his social model included all

areas of life, those areas in which the state intervened more and more in the nineteenth century (and Schulpe was convinced it should do so.) He did a lot to enhance the living conditions and raise the cultural level of the workers. One of his biggest successes was founding the Job agency (providing jobs for the unemployed) in 1905 in Pressburg, Temesvár and in 1907 in Brassó. The Pressburg agency gave night shelter for 3–4 thousand unemployed per year. He also represented Hungary on international congresses about different aspects of the workers' social situation. After 1918 Schulpe stayed in Pressburg but the new authorities did not treat him kindly. He died in 1936, and he left all his assets to the city of Bratislava. Dudeková, 1994.

200 Ibid., p. 12.

201 Ibid., p. 25. Also see *Magyarország vármegyei*, pp. 163–164.

202 Dudeková, 1994, pp. 29–30.

203 Schulpe was convinced that it was the state's obligation to provide conditions for bringing up good and responsible citizens: "Schulpe, 1893, p. 5: "Igy a jogállam—alkotó és fentartó minden eszköz,- mely a jogtársadalomban élő minden egyes egyénnek védését, nemesítését, tökéletesítését azaz boldogosítását célozza,—arra való, hogy az egyest öntudatának élredésére nevelve, önálló és szabad, jogaival élni és kötelességeit teljesíteni tudó honpolgárrá képezze, a ki ilyetén öntudatosan foglalja el az őt illető helyet az államban és ez által az emberiségben általában, a ki elismerve a törvény-teremtette rendet, önként, szabad elhatározásból hódol meg a törvény szentsége előtt." ("In this way the state of law—by creating and maintaining all means,—the aim of which in a legal society is to protect, ennoble, perfect and so make individuals happy,—exists in order to educate individuals towards awakening their self-awareness, to make them independent and free citizens capable of using their rights and fulfilling their duties, who in this way take up their proper place in the state and in humanity in general, and who by recognising the order created by law will of their own volition honour the sanctity of the law.")

204 Ibid., p. 3.

205 For the London poor "a concern to demonstrate self-respect was infinitely more important than any forms of savings based upon calculations of utility." Jones, 1983, p. 199.

206 Brenda Yeoh writes about everyday and ordinary forms of resistance, and in this context power is dealt with, re-negotiated, resisted in everyday life by creating alternative spaces to those defined by dominant groups. Yeoh, 2000, pp. 146–166.